Fifth Edition

AN INTRODUCTION TO THEORIES OF LEARNING

B. R. HERGENHAHN
Professor Emeritus
Hamline University

MATTHEW H. OLSON
Hamline University

PRENTICE HALL, Upper Saddle River, New Jersey 07458

Library of Congress Cataloging-in-Publication Data

Hergenhahn, B.R., (date)
  An introduction to theories of learning / B.R. Hergenhahn, Matthew
H. Olson. —5th ed.
     p.   cm.
  Includes bibliographical references (p.   ) and indexes.
  ISBN 0-13-241787-1 (case)
  1. Learning.   2. Learning, Psychology of.   I. Olson, Matthew H.
II. Title.
LB1060.H42   1997
370.15'23—dc20   96-21391
                                                                CIP

Editor in chief: Pete Janzow
Acquisitions editor: Nicole Signoretti
Editorial/production supervision
  and interior design: Mary Araneo
Cover design: Bruce Kenselaar
Cover photo: Photonica/IMA USA, Inc.
Buyer: Tricia Kenny

This book was set in 10/12 New Baskerville by A & A Publishing
Services, Inc., and was printed and bound by RR Donnelley
& Sons Company. The cover was printed by The Lehigh Press, Inc.

 © 1997, 1993, 1988, 1982, 1976 by Prentice-Hall, Inc.
Simon & Schuster/A Viacom Company
Upper Saddle River, New Jersey 07458

Printed in the United States of America

10 9 8 7 6 5 4 3 2 1

ISBN 0-13-241787-1

Prentice-Hall International (UK) Limited, *London*
Prentice-Hall of Australia Pty. Limited, *Sydney*
Prentice-Hall Canada Inc., *Toronto*
Prentice-Hall Hispanoamericana, S.A., *Mexico*
Prentice-Hall of India Private Limited, *New Delhi*
Prentice-Hall of Japan, Inc., *Tokyo*
Simon & Schuster Asia Pte. Ltd., *Singapore*
Editora Prentice-Hall do Brasil, Ltda., *Rio de Janeiro*

TO RUSTY AND CHET OLSON

CONTENTS

PART SIX   SOME FINAL THOUGHTS

PREFACE

As in previous editions, the four main goals of this textbook are to define learning and to show how the learning process is studied (Chapters 1 and 2); to place learning theory in historical perspective (Chapter 3); to present essential features of the major theories of learning (Chapters 4 through 15); and to examine some of the relationships that exist between learning theory and educational practices (Chapter 16).

We have attempted to retain the best features of earlier editions while making revisions that reflect current research and scholarship. The most significant revisions include the following:

Timberlake's development of the disequilibrium approach to reinforcement was included.

New material presenting Bouton's work with the reinstatement and renewal effects was added.

Ader's research involving classical conditioning and immune responses was included.

The discussion of biofeedback was expanded to include recent criticisms.

Estes' cognitive array model of classification and categorization was presented.

Each major theory includes an evaluation with significant contributions and criticisms.

We would like to express our gratitude to the individuals who's contributions helped shape this edition. They include Mark E. Bouton, University of Vermont, and William Timberlake, Indiana University, both of whom read and made suggestions for portions of the text. We are also grateful to Albert Bandura, Stanford University, and Doreen Kimura, University of Western Ontario, for providing photographs.

We are particularly indebted to Stanley Pliskoff, University of Maine; James Huntermark, Missouri Western State College; and Gail Peterson, University of Minnesota, who provided extensive formative reviews of the fourth edition and made significant recommendations for the fifth.

We would also like to thank the outstanding faculty of the Psychology Department at Hamline University, Professors Dorothee Dietrich, R. Kim Guenther, Chuck LaBounty, and Robin Parritz, who made it possible for Olson to devote time to this project. And we would like to thank departmental assistants Sarah Smith and Rachel Traver for making many trips to the library and for reading new sections of the text. In addition, Nicole Signoretti and Production/Copy Editor Mary Araneo provided outstanding assistance on behalf of Prentice Hall. Finally we would like to express our gratitude to Marce Soderman-Olson for her suggestions, support, and encouragement.

Any questions, suggestions, or comments about this text should be directed to Matthew Olson in the Psychology Department at Hamline University, St.Paul, MN 55104 or by e-mail: molson@piper.hamline.edu.

B. R. Hergenhahn
Matthew H. Olson

Chapter 1

WHAT IS LEARNING?

Learning is one of the most important topics in present-day psychology and yet it is an extremely difficult concept to define. The *American Heritage Dictionary* defines learning as follows: "To gain knowledge, comprehension, or mastery through experience or study." Most psychologists, however, would find this definition unacceptable because of the nebulous terms it contains, such as *knowledge, comprehension,* and *mastery.* Instead, the trend in recent years is to accept a definition of learning that refers to changes in observable behavior. One of the most popular of these definitions is the one suggested by Kimble (1961, p. 6), which defines learning *as a relatively permanent change in* **behavioral potentiality** *that occurs as a result of* **reinforced practice.** Although popular, this definition is far from universally accepted. Before reviewing sources of disagreement over Kimble's definition, let us look at it a bit more carefully.

First, learning is indexed by a change in *behavior;* in other words, the results of learning must always be translated into observable behavior. After learning, learners are capable of doing something that they could not do before learning took place. Second, this behavioral change is *relatively permanent;* that is, it is neither transitory nor fixed. Third, the change in behavior need not occur immediately following the learning experience. Although there may be a *potential* to act differently, this potential to act may not be translated into behavior immediately. Fourth, the change in behavior (or behavior potentiality) results from *experience* or practice. Fifth, the experience, or practice, must be reinforced; that is, only those responses that lead to reinforcement will be learned. Although the terms *reward* and *reinforcement* are often used synonymously, there are at least two reasons why they should not be. In Pavlov's work, for example, a reinforcer is defined as any unconditioned stimulus, that is, any stimulus that elicits a natural and automatic reaction from an organism. In Pavlovian research it is not uncommon for stimuli such as a mild acid or electric shock to be used as unconditioned stimuli. It is accurate to call such stimuli reinforcers but they can hardly be considered rewards, if rewards are thought of as desirable. The Skinnerians also oppose equating the terms *reinforcer* and *reward.* For them, a reinforcer strengthens any behavior that immediately precedes the *reinforcer's* occurrence. In contrast, a reward is usually thought of as something that is given or received only for a worthy accomplishment that required a considerable investment of time and energy or for an act deemed desirable by society. Furthermore, since such desirable behavior typically occurs long before it is acknowledged by reward, reward cannot be said to strengthen it. For the Skinnerians, then, reinforcers strengthen behavior but rewards do not. Skinner (1986) elaborated on these points:

> The strengthening effect [of reinforcement] is missed...when reinforcers are called *rewards.* People are rewarded, but behavior is reinforced. If, as you walk along the street, you look down and find some money, and if money is reinforcing, you will tend to look down again for some time, but we should not say that you were rewarded for looking down. As the history of the word shows, reward implies compensation, something that offsets a sacrifice or loss, if only the expenditure of effort. We give heroes medals, students degrees, and famous people prizes, but those rewards are not directly contingent on what they have done, and it is generally felt that rewards would not be deserved if they had not been worked for. (p. 569)

In this text we will acknowledge the above concerns and not equate the terms *reward* and *reinforcement*. Except where the term *reward* is appropriate as it is defined in Skinner's remarks in the preceding quotation, the terms *reinforcer* or *reinforcement* will be used exclusively.

Kimble's (1961) definition of learning provides a convenient frame of reference for discussing a number of important issues that must be confronted when attempting to define learning. We will review these issues in the following sections of this chapter.

MUST LEARNING RESULT IN A BEHAVIORAL CHANGE?

As we shall see in Chapter 3, psychology has become a *behavioral* science for good reason. A science requires an observable, measurable subject matter, and within the science of psychology, that subject matter is behavior. Thus, whatever we study in psychology must be expressed through behavior, but this does not mean that the behavior we are studying *is* learning. We study behavior so that we can make *inferences* concerning the process believed to be the cause of the behavioral changes we are observing. In this case, that process is learning. Most learning theorists covered in this text agree that the learning process cannot be studied directly; instead, its nature can only be inferred from changes in behavior. B. F. Skinner was the only theorist who took exception to this contention. For Skinner, behavioral changes are learning and no further process needs to be inferred. Other theorists say that behavioral changes *result from* learning. We will have more to say about Skinner's antitheoretical point of view in Chapter 5.

Except for the Skinnerians, then, most learning theorists look on learning as a process that mediates behavior. For them, learning is something that occurs as the result of certain experiences and precedes changes in behavior. In such a definition, learning is given the status of an intervening variable. An intervening variable is a theoretical process that is assumed to take place between the observed stimuli and responses. The independent variables cause a change in the intervening variable (learning), which in turn causes a change in the dependent variable (behavior). The situation can be diagrammed as follows:

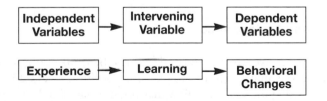

How Permanent Is Relatively Permanent?

Here we run into at least two problems. First, how long must a behavior change last before we say that learning has been demonstrated? This aspect was originally inserted into the definition to differentiate between learning and other events that may modify behavior, such as fatigue, illness, maturation, and drugs. Clearly, these events and their effects come and go quite rapidly, whereas learning lingers until forgetting takes place over time or until new learning displaces old learning. Thus temporary states as well as learning modify behavior, but with learning the modification is relatively more permanent. However, the duration of the modification that results from either learning or temporary body states cannot be given exactly.

A related problem is more serious. A number of psychologists have turned their attention to a phenomenon called **short-term memory** (see Chapters 14 and 15). They have found that if unfamiliar information, such as a nonsense syllable, is presented to human subjects who are prevented from rehearsing the information, they will retain the material almost perfectly for about three seconds. In the following fifteen seconds, however, their retention drops to almost zero (Murdock, 1961; Peterson & Peterson, 1959). Despite the fact that the information is lost over such a short period of time, we would hesitate to say that no learning had occurred.

Accepting the qualification of "relatively permanent" in a definition of learning will also determine whether the processes of **sensitization** and **habituation** are accepted as crude examples of learning. Both sensitization and habituation are examples of behavior modification that results from experience, but both are short-lived. Sensitization is the process whereby an organism is made more responsive to certain aspects of its environment. For example, an organism that may not ordinarily respond to a certain light or sound may do so after receiving a shock. The shock, therefore, sensitized the organism, making it more responsive to its environment. Feeling "touchy" or hypersensitive following an upsetting experience is a form of sensitization with which we are all familiar.

Habituation is the process whereby an organism becomes *less* responsive to its environment. For example, there is a tendency for an organism to attend to novel stimuli as they occur in its environment. This tendency is referred to as the orienting reflex, and it is exemplified when a dog turns in the direction of a sound that suddenly occurs. After attending to the sound, however, the dog will eventually ignore it (assuming that it poses no threat) and go about its business. We say, in this case, that the dog's response to the sound has habituated. Similarly, Sharpless and Jasper (1956) found that a tone, when first presented, will arouse a sleeping cat. With repeated presentations, however, the tone loses its ability to arouse the cat. Again, we say that habituation has occurred.

Learning and Performance

As mentioned above, what is learned may not be utilized immediately. Football players, for example, may learn how to play their position by watching films and listening to lectures during the week, but they may not translate that learning into behavior until game time. In fact, some players may be prevented from actually performing for a prolonged period of time because of an injury or an illness. We say, therefore, that the *potential* to act differently resulted from learning, even though behavior was not immediately affected.

This type of observation has led to the very important distinction between *learning* and *performance,* which will be considered in detail in Chapters 6, 12, 13, and 14.

Learning refers to a change in behavior potentiality, and *performance* refers to the translation of this potentiality into behavior.

Why Do We Refer to Practice or Experience?

Obviously not all behavior is learned. Much simple behavior is reflexive. A **reflex** can be defined as an unlearned response in reaction to a specific class of stimuli. Sneezing in response to a tickling in your nose, producing a sudden knee jerk when your knee is tapped sharply, or instantly withdrawing your hand when it touches a hot stove are examples of reflexive behavior. Clearly, reflexive behavior is unlearned; it is a genetically determined characteristic of the organism rather than a result of experience.

Complex behavior can also be unlearned. When complex behavior patterns are genetically determined, they are generally referred to as examples of **instinct.** Instinctive behavior includes such activities as nest building, migration, hibernation, and mating behavior.

For awhile psychologists explained complex behavior patterns by referring to them as instincts. Thus, we said, birds and fish migrate because they possess a migration instinct; birds build nests because of a nest-building instinct. Because the term *instinctive* was offered as an *explanation* of behavior, we now tend to use the term *species-specific behavior* (Hinde & Tinbergen, 1958) because it is more descriptive. Species-specific behavior refers to complex, unlearned, and relatively unmodifiable behavior patterns engaged in by a certain species of animal under certain circumstances.

Controversy continues, however, over whether species-specific behavior is completely determined by the makeup of the organism or whether some learning is involved. Do birds fly instinctively, or do they learn to fly? Some say that the young bird learns to fly through trial and error while falling to the ground from a tree. Others say that the birds respond reflexively to falling by flapping their wings and therefore fly without learning to do so.

A few examples, however, seem to demonstrate complex behavior that is clearly not influenced by learning. For example, many species of the cuckoo bird lay their eggs in other birds' nests, and the young cuckoo is raised by its foster parents. Since each adult cuckoo behaves in this way regardless of the foster parents' species, it is very difficult to imagine how such behavior could be learned.

Another example of what appears to be unlearned behavior is the nut-burying behavior of squirrels. Even when an infant squirrel is raised in isolation from other squirrels and sees a nut for the first time, it attempts to bury it. This nut-burying pattern of behavior occurs even if the nut is presented to the squirrel on a bare wooden floor. The squirrel makes scratching motions on the floor as if to dig a hole, tamps the nut with its nose in an apparent effort to push the nut into the floor, and then makes covering movements with its paws (Brown, 1965).

Other research supports the contention that some species-specific behavior is both learned and unlearned (Hess, 1958; Lorenz, 1952, 1965, 1970; Thorpe, 1963). Lorenz found, for example, that a newly hatched duckling would form an attachment to any kind of moving object and follow it as its mother, provided the object

Konrad Lorenz and a group of ducklings that have imprinted on him (Thomas McAvoy/ Time-Life Picture Agency, © 1973).

was presented at just the right moment in the duckling's life. Lorenz demonstrated attachments between ducklings and a wooden box on wheels, a human being, and a bird of a different species. The formation of an attachment between an organism and an environmental object is called **imprinting.** Imprinting was found to occur only during a **critical period,** after which it was difficult, if not impossible, to imprint the duckling on anything. With imprinting, we have a combination of learned and instinctive behavior. It appears that the animal's genetic endowment causes it to be maximally sensitive to a moving object for a short period of time, during which it can learn the strong habit of following a specific object. If the learning does not occur during that interval, however, it may never occur. Furthermore, the strong habit of following an object does not seem to be built up over time with practice. Rather, the habit seems to be learned at full strength in a single trial. We will have more to say about one-trial learning in Chapters 8 and 9.

Studies about imprinting raise a number of questions. The kind of learning, if any, involved in species-specific behavior and to what extent it is involved must be determined by future research. The main point to emphasize, however, is that to attribute a behavioral change to learning, the change must be relatively permanent and must result from *experience.* If an organism engages in a complex behavior pattern independent of experience, that behavior cannot be referred to as learned behavior.

Does Learning Result from a Specific Kind of Experience?

According to Kimble's (1961) definition, learning results from reinforced practice. In other words, only reinforced behavior will be learned. On this point, there is widespread disagreement among learning theorists. Theorists disagree not only over what constitutes reinforcement but also over whether it is a necessary prerequisite for learning to take place. In a sense, this book is an attempt to review various interpretations of the nature and importance of reinforcement. This is a subject, therefore, to which we will return often.

A Modified Definition of Learning

It is now possible to revise Kimble's (1961) definition of learning so that it would be neutral on the matter of reinforcement, thereby making it more widely accepted: *Learning is a relatively permanent change in behavior or in behavioral potentiality that results*

Gregory A. Kimble (Courtesy of Gregory A. Kimble.)

from experience and cannot be attributed to **temporary body states** *such as those induced by illness, fatigue, or drugs.*

Such a definition still stresses the importance of experience but leaves it to the theorist to specify the kind of experience he or she feels is necessary for learning to take place, for example, reinforced practice, contiguity between a stimulus and a response, or the acquisition of information. It also reminds us that experience can cause events other than learning that modify behavior. Fatigue is one such event.

ARE THERE DIFFERENT KINDS OF LEARNING?

Learning, as we have seen, is a general term that is used to describe changes in behavior potentiality resulting from experience. **Conditioning,** however, is a more specific term used to describe actual procedures that can modify behavior. Since there are two kinds of conditioning, **instrumental** and **classical,** many theorists conclude that there are at least two kinds of learning or that learning ultimately can be understood in terms of classical and/or instrumental conditioning. Although both conditioning procedures will be discussed in detail later on in this book, we will summarize both procedures briefly.

Classical Conditioning

We will look at classical conditioning in detail when we discuss Pavlov's views on learning in Chapter 7, but for now we can summarize classical conditioning as follows:

1. A stimulus, such as food, is presented to an organism and will cause a natural and automatic reaction, such as salivating. The stimulus causing this natural reaction is called the unconditioned stimulus (US). In this case, the food was the US. The natural, automatic reaction to the US is called the unconditioned response (UR). In this case, salivation was the UR.
2. A neutral stimulus (one that does not cause a UR), such as a tone or light, is presented to the organism just prior to the presentation of the US. This neutral stimulus is called the conditioned stimulus (CS).
3. After the CS and US are paired a number of times, with the CS always preceding the US, the CS alone can be presented, and the organism will salivate. This salivating response, similar to the organism's response to the US, now occurs in

response to the CS, the tone or the light. We now say that a conditioned response (CR) has been demonstrated.

In classical conditioning, the US is called reinforcement since the entire conditioning procedure depends on it. Note, however, that in classical conditioning, the organism has no control over reinforcement: It occurs when the experimenter wants it to occur. In other words, in classical conditioning, reinforcement is not contingent on any overt response made by the organism.

Instrumental Conditioning

The relationship between reinforcement and the organism's behavior is distinctively different in instrumental conditioning. With instrumental conditioning, the organism must act in a certain way *before* it is reinforced; that is, reinforcement is contingent on the organism's behavior. If the animal does not emit the desired behavior it is not reinforced. Thus in instrumental conditioning, the animal's behavior is "instrumental" in getting it something it wants, that is, a reinforcer.

A small experimental test chamber called the **Skinner box** is often used to demonstrate instrumental conditioning (or a closely allied form of conditioning called operant conditioning). Such a box is a Plexiglas cage with a grid floor that can be electrified and a lever that, when pressed, activates a feeder mechanism that delivers food pellets to the animal inside. The experimenter introduces a hungry rat (for example) into the Skinner box. As the rat explores the enclosure, it will eventually activate the lever and receive a pellet of food. Soon the rat will associate lever pressing with the appearance of food, and its rate of lever pressing will increase. In this case, the rat must engage in lever pressing in order to get food. The lever pressing is the conditioned behavior; the food is the reinforcement. If the Skinner box is programmed so that when a hungry animal presses the lever it is given a pellet of food, the rate at which it presses the lever will increase.

Escape and avoidance conditioning are special kinds of instrumental conditioning. For example, the rat is placed in the Skinner box and the electrified grid is activated, with the lever connected to an off-switch. As the rat leaps around from the shock, it will accidentally hit the lever and terminate the shock. The rat will associate the lever pressing with the termination of the shock. In this case the lever pressing is the conditioned behavior, and the termination of shock is the reinforcement. This is an example of **escape conditioning.**

To demonstrate avoidance conditioning, let the Skinner box grid be activated at intervals, with a signal, such as a light, set up to precede the onset of shock by, say, five seconds. The rat will soon learn to associate the light with the onset of shock, and it will press the lever in order to avoid the shock whenever it sees the light go on. The arrangement in which an organism can avoid an aversive stimulus by performing some appropriate response is referred to as **avoidance conditioning.**

Learning theorists have become increasingly aware that confining themselves to research involved with just classical and instrumental conditioning leaves out vast areas of human experience. For example, Gagné (1970) feels it is more realistic to assume that there are eight kinds of learning. Gagné believes that the eight kinds of learning are arranged in a hierarchy, with one sort being a prerequisite for the next. Thus, for Gagné, simple conditioning simply provides the basis for the more advanced kinds of learning. As we shall see in Chapter 12, Tolman took a similar position much earlier. Although many theorists believe that complex behavior ultimately can be understood in terms of classical or instrumental conditioning, other influential theorists oppose that contention.

LEARNING AND SURVIVAL

Through our long evolutionary past, our bodies have developed the capacity to respond automatically to certain needs. For example, we breathe automatically, and if our body temperature becomes too high or too low, mechanisms are triggered that cause sweating, which cools the body, or shivering, which raises body temperature. Likewise, if blood sugar is too low, the liver secretes sugar into the blood until the concentration of blood sugar is restored to a normal level. These automatic adjustment processes are called **homeostatic mechanisms** because their function is to maintain a physiological equilibrium, or *homeostasis*. In addition to the homeostatic mechanisms, we are also born with reflexes that facilitate survival. For example, most living organisms retreat reflexively from a painful stimulus.

Although both homeostatic mechanisms and reflexes are clearly conducive to survival, we would not survive long if we had to depend on them exclusively to meet our needs. For a species to *survive* it must satisfy its needs for such things as food, water, and sex, and to do so it must interact with the environment. No organism would survive long if it did not *learn* which environmental objects could be used to satisfy its basic needs. Nor could an organism survive long if it could not learn which environmental objects were safe and which were dangerous. It is the learning process that allows organisms to do commerce with the environment in a way that allows for the satisfaction of the basic needs that cannot be satisfied by homeostatic mechanisms or reflexes.

It is also the learning process that allows an organism to adjust to a changing environment. Sources of satisfaction and of danger often change, and therefore, if an organism's adjustments to the environment were not dynamic, it could not survive. The learning process provides an organism with the flexibility it needs to survive under a wide variety of environmental conditions. To survive, an organism must learn which environmental objects are positive (conducive to survival), which are negative (detrimental to survival), and which are neutral (irrelevant to survival). In addition to learning whether stimuli are positive, negative, or neutral, the organism must learn to behave in such a way as to obtain or avoid these various stimuli. For example, strawberries may be valued positively because of their ability to reduce the hunger drive, but one may need to get a job and perform specific functions in order to be able to go into a store and buy them. Likewise, a bear may value honey positively but may need to learn to climb trees in order to obtain it.

In general, it is through classical conditioning that we learn which environmental objects are conducive to survival and which are not; and it is through instrumental or operant conditioning that we learn how to acquire or avoid desirable and undesirable objects. The adaptive value of classical conditioning is further demonstrated by the fact that it typically takes several pairings between a CS and US before classical conditioning is established. Schwartz and Robbins (1995) elaborate on this adaptive feature of classical conditioning:

> Indeed, if we think of Pavlovian conditioning as a kind of predictive analysis, we can even see virtue in the fact that it usually takes numerous CS-US pairings before an association is formed. Suppose we learned after a single pairing of CS and US. If we did, then any stimulus that happened accidentally to precede, say, a shock, would produce conditioned fear. Since there is surely always some stimulus around when a shock (or some natural aversive event) occurs, we might end up walking around in fear of almost everything. But if conditioning requires multiple pairings, this possibility is largely eliminated. A tone might precede a shock once, or even twice, by accident. But if the tone precedes the shock 20 or 30 times, it can no longer be an accident. (p. 87)

Learning, then, should be looked on as a major tool in adapting to one's environment that supplements innate homeostatic mechanisms, reflexes, and at least in the case of nonhuman animals, unlearned adaptive behavior.

WHY STUDY LEARNING?

Because most human behavior is learned, investigating the principles of learning will help us understand why we behave as we do. An awareness of the learning process will allow greater understanding not only of normal and adaptive behavior but also of the circumstances that produce maladaptive and abnormal behavior. More effective psychotherapy might result from such an understanding.

Child-rearing practices can also utilize the principles of learning. Obviously, individuals differ from one another, and these individual differences may be explained in terms of differing learning experiences. One of the most important human attributes is language, and there is little doubt that specific language development results mainly from learning. No doubt many other human attributes are molded in a similar way by the interaction of the environment with the learning process. When parents know more about the learning experiences that create what they would call desirable traits, they may wish to organize the environment of their child so that it encourages these traits. Likewise, learning experiences that tend to produce socially maladaptive behavior can be avoided.

Moreover, there is a close relationship between the principles of learning and educational practices. In many cases, principles that have been uncovered while studying the learning process in the laboratory have eventually been utilized in the classroom. The widespread utilization of programmed learning, teaching machines, and computer-assisted instruction offer three examples of how research on learning influences teaching practices. The current trend in American education toward individualized instruction can also be considered a spinoff from research on the learning process. We may reasonably conclude that as our knowledge of the learning process increases, educational practices should become more efficient and effective.

DISCUSSION QUESTIONS

1. List the requirements that must be met before a change in behavior can be attributed to learning.
2. Describe the processes of sensitization and habituation as they have occurred in your life.
3. Differentiate between learning and performance.
4. Give a few examples of complex unlearned behavior. Do you feel that complex unlearned behavior exists on the human level? Explain.
5. Why was the term *instinct* replaced with the term *species-specific* behavior?
6. Differentiate between the terms learning and conditioning.
7. How many kinds of learning are there? Explain how you arrived at your answer.
8. What is meant by the statement "Imprinting seems to result from both learning and instinct"?
9. Describe the relationship between learning and survival.
10. Give a few reasons why it is important to study the learning process.

KEY TERMS

avoidance conditioning   The experimental arrangement whereby an organism can avoid experiencing an aversive stimulus by engaging in appropriate behavior.

behavioral potentiality   The ability to perform some act although the act is not being performed at the present time. Learning may result in a change in behavioral potentiality although the learning may not be translated into behavior until some time after the learning has taken place.

classical conditioning   An experimental arrangement whereby a stimulus is made to elicit a response that was not previously associated with that stimulus (i.e., the conditioned stimulus, CS, comes to elicit a response similar to the one elicited by the US).

conditioning   An experimental procedure used to modify behavior. Most learning theorists believe that there are two kinds of conditioning—classical and instrumental—and that all learning involves conditioning. To those holding such a belief, *learning* is a term used to summarize a large number of conditioned responses.

critical period   A period in an organism's life during which an important development occurs. If the development does not occur during that time, it may never occur. For example, if imprinting does not occur shortly after a duckling is hatched, it is difficult, if not impossible, to establish it. The period of time immediately following hatching, therefore, is the critical period for imprinting.

escape conditioning   The experimental arrangement whereby an organism can terminate an aversive stimulus by engaging in appropriate behavior.

habituation   The decreased tendency to respond to a stimulus that results from prolonged exposure to that stimulus.

homeostatic mechanisms   Automatic processes that function to keep the body operating within certain physiological limits, thus maintaining a physiological equilibrium, or homeostasis.

imprinting   The rapid formation, during a critical period, of a close attachment
between an organism and an environmental object.

instinct   The inborn capacity to perform a complex behavioral task. In recent years,
the term has been replaced by *species-specific behavior.*

instrumental conditioning   An experimental procedure whereby the rate or probability of a response is changed from one value before conditioning to another
value following conditioning. With instrumental conditioning, the organism
must perform an appropriate response in order to be reinforced.

learning   A relatively permanent change in behavior or behavioral potentiality that
comes from experience and cannot be attributed to temporary body states such
as illness, fatigue, or drugs.

performance   The translation of learning into behavior.

reflex   An unlearned response to a specific class of stimuli.

reinforced practice   Repeated performance under the conditions in which correct
response is followed by reinforcement. Reinforced practice is thought by many
learning theorists to be a necessary condition for learning to take place; other
theorists do not agree.

sensitization   The tendency to be more responsive to the environment following
an arousing experience.

short-term memory   The memory of an experience that lasts for only several seconds after the termination of the experience. This process is opposed to long-
term memory, which lasts considerably longer.

Skinner box   An experimental test chamber usually consisting of a grid floor, lever,
light, and food cup. Used to study instrumental or operant conditioning.

temporary body state   A temporary condition of the body such as fatigue, illness,
emotion, the presence of drugs, and sleep loss that causes a modification in
behavior. Such modifications in behavior are differentiated from those caused
by learning.

Chapter 2

APPROACHES TO THE STUDY OF LEARNING

We noted in Chapter 1 that most learning theorists contend that learning can be observed only indirectly through changes in behavior. Therefore when we study learning, we observe behavior, and based on these observables we infer that a particular type of learning has or has not occurred. The inaccessibility of learning is one reason why there are so many approaches to its study. Some feel, for example, that the best place to study learning is in the field rather than in the laboratory. This method of studying a phenomenon as it occurs naturally is called **naturalistic observation.** Using this technique, one would make detailed observations and recordings of what is being studied. Such research often results in a grouping or classification of the various elements of the phenomenon being investigated. For example, while using naturalistic observation to study learning in the classroom, one might classify learning to read or spell as verbal learning, the learning of athletic prowess as perceptual-motor skill learning, and the learning that requires complex mental processes as problem solving or concept formation.

Two major drawbacks of naturalistic observation become apparent. First, because the classroom situation is extremely complex it is very difficult to observe and record accurately. Second, there is a tendency to classify events into chunks that may be too comprehensive; for example, what is classified as concept formation may in reality consist of many different phenomena whose distinctions get lost in the classifying process. Classifications that seem rather straightforward at first may become extraordinarily complex under closer scrutiny.

Naturalistic observation can be an important first step for a study of learning, but eventually the psychologist must break up the recorded chunks of behavior for closer and more detailed analysis; that is, the psychologist must become more elementistic in order to discover the various laws operating in the learning situation, and discovering laws usually involves experimentation. In other words, naturalistic observation may be important in isolating groups of events for further study, but these must then be reduced into smaller components for further analysis. Such an approach is called **elementism.**

THE SYSTEMATIC STUDY OF LEARNING

In modern times, that portion of psychology concerned with the learning process has become more scientific. We will see in the next chapter that using the scientific method in the psychology of learning has been very productive. It is important, therefore, that we look at such a productive method in more detail.

What Is Science?

According to Stevens (1951), "**Science** seeks to generate **confirmable propositions** by fitting a formal system of symbols (language, mathematics, logic) to empirical observations" (p. 22). Stevens's statement points to a number of important characteristics of science. For example, science deals with confirmable propositions. The propositions of science must be capable of having their truth or falsity demonstrated publicly, so that any other interested researcher can replicate the experiment and, it is hoped, obtain the same results. This insistence on publicly verifiable propositions is what characterizes a science. Science is not concerned with private or unique events but only with statements that are empirically verifiable. The statement "I ate pickles last night and subsequently dreamt of elephants" is scientifically useless because it refers to a personal experience that is unique and undemonstrable. However, the statement "People who eat pickles tend to dream of elephants" can be thought of as scientific because it is in principle verifiable. If we feed pickles to a large number of people and they subsequently report dreaming of elephants, and if we repeat the procedure a number of times with the same outcome, we have discovered a **scientific law.** A scientific law can be defined as a consistently observed relationship between two or more classes of events. *All sciences seek to discover laws.* The lawful relationship we have discovered in the example above is between the eating of pickles and the *verbal report* of having dreamed of elephants. Again, if there is no way of publicly demonstrating whether a statement is true or false, it is scientifically useless.

Aspects of Theory

Scientific theories have two important aspects. First, a **theory** has a **formal aspect,** which includes the words and symbols the theory contains. Second, a theory has an **empirical aspect,** which consists of the physical events that the theory is attempting to explain. Although the relationship between the formal and empirical aspects of a theory is very complex, it should be noted that the formal part of a theory can make sense by itself even though it may make erroneous predictions about the physical world. The statement "All learning depends on drive reduction" makes sense formally but may not accurately explain learning. The point here is that a theory can sound valid, but it is devoid of scientific meaning unless it withstands the rigors of experimental tests. There is always the danger of being overly impressed by the wording of a theory and forgetting to check how accurately it predicts and describes empirical events. Most psychologists would agree that astrology is a highly developed formal system that has little or no relationship to actual empirical events. In other words, astrology sounds good but it adds virtually nothing to our understanding of human behavior.

It is important to remember that no matter how abstract and complex a theory becomes, it must ultimately make contact with observable physical events. All scientific theories, no matter how abstract their formal aspects become, begin and end with statements about observable events.

From Research to Theory

As a general example of the use of theory in psychology, we can refer to research examining the relationship between food deprivation and rate of learning, with food as the reinforcer. In this case, learning rate will be indexed by the number of trials it takes for an animal to learn to turn left on every trial in a T-maze. After many separate experiments, a researcher finds that as hours of food deprivation go up, learning occurs more rapidly. That is, animals deprived of food the longest learn to turn left in a T-maze most rapidly.

These results can be looked on as the demonstration of a law. Here the observed relationship is between degree of food deprivation and performance on a learning task. The researcher turns next to study water deprivation and again finds that as hours of water deprivation go up, learning time goes down. Now we have a second law: As hours of water deprivation go up, an animal learns to turn left faster in a T-maze when the water is used as a reinforcer.

Next, the researcher turns to the study of sexual behavior. This time the opportunity to copulate is used as a reinforcer for the rat to turn left in the T-maze. Again, it is found that increased hours of sexual deprivation result in faster learning.

Although the goal of science is to discover laws (observed relationships between events), it is seldom enough simply to observe and record hundreds or perhaps thousands of empirical relationships. Scientists usually attempt to make sense out of the laws they discover; that is, they attempt to group them in some coherent fashion. This grouping has at least two functions: (1) to synthesize a large number of observations and (2) to point the way to further research. The latter aspect of grouping or attempting to make sense out of data is called its **heuristic function.**

At this point, therefore, the researcher may wish to go beyond the data. He or she may make statements such as "Hungry animals tend to learn faster than food-satiated ones" or "Thirsty animals tend to learn faster than water-satiated ones." Both statements plunge the researcher into the realm of theory. Although the experiments involved specific situations (e.g., 2, 4, 6, and 8 hours of deprivation), the concept of hunger, which is an abstraction, covers all states of deprivation, even those not involved in the actual research (e.g., 26, 30, 37, 37½, and 50 hours of deprivation). Thus, by postulating the unobservable inner state of hunger, the researcher is at the same time attempting to tie together some of his or her observations and predicting the outcome of future research. The same is true when the concepts of thirst and sexual arousal are used.

The researcher can take an additional step and attempt to synthesize the three theoretical terms into still another theoretical term. He or she can conclude, for example, that deprivation increases drive, and animals with high drive learn faster. Note, in taking this step, the researcher is using the two functions of a theory: synthesizing and predicting avenues of future research. By stating that "animals with high drive learn faster than animals with low drive," he or she is suggesting research on oxygen deprivation, heat deprivation, or pain reduction. The relationship among the concepts of hunger, thirst, sexual arousal, and the empirical events from which they stem is shown in Figure 2–1.

The researcher could take still an additional step and postulate the even more general concept of motivation and include psychological factors as well as the physiological ones we have been considering (e.g., the need for achievement or for self-actualization).

Theories as Tools

Because a theory is merely a research tool it cannot be right or wrong; it is either useful or it is not useful. If a theory clarifies the various observations that have been made, and if it generates additional research, the theory is a good one. If it fails in either respect, the researcher is likely to search for a new theory.

If a hypothesis generated by a theory is confirmed, the theory gains strength. If a hypothesis generated by a theory is rejected, the theory is weakened and must either be revised or abandoned. Again we see how confirmation of a theory depends on

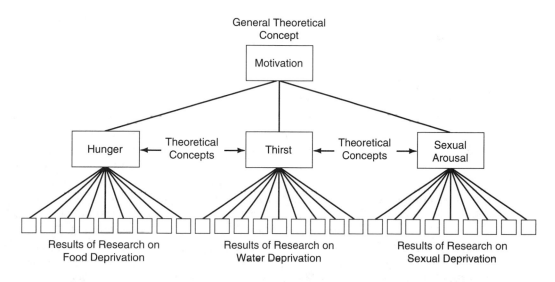

FIGURE 2–1 The relationship between theoretical concepts and the empirical events from which they stem.

empirical observation. Whether a theory is maintained, revised, or abandoned is determined by the outcome of the empirical research generated by the theory. Thus, we see that *theories must continually generate the very hypotheses that may prove they are ineffective.*

The Principle of Parsimony

We noted above that one characteristic of science is that it deals only with statements that are in principle empirically verifiable. Another characteristic of science is that it follows the **principle of parsimony** (sometimes called the principle of economy, Occam's razor, or Morgan's canon). This principle states that when two equally effective theories can explain the same phenomenon, but one explanation is simple and the other is complex, we must use the simpler explanation.

Summary of Characteristics of a Scientific Theory
1. A theory synthesizes a number of observations.
2. A good theory is heuristic; that is, it generates new research.
3. A theory must generate hypotheses that can be empirically verified. If such hypotheses are confirmed, the theory gains strength; if not, the theory is weakened and must be revised or abandoned.
4. A theory is a tool and as such cannot be right or wrong; it is either useful of it is not useful.
5. Theories are chosen in accordance with the law of parsimony: Of two equally effective theories, the simpler of the two must be chosen.
6. Theories contain abstractions, such as numbers or words, which constitute the formal aspect of a theory.
7. The formal aspect of a theory must be correlated with observable events, which constitute the empirical aspect of a theory.

8. All theories are attempts to explain empirical events and they must, therefore, start and end with empirical observations.

THE LEARNING EXPERIMENT

In the previous section we considered the course from research to theory; here we will look briefly at the course from theory to research. First, we must delineate a subject matter. This usually takes the form of a general definition of learning or a general description of the phenomenon to be studied. Next, we attempt to specify the conditions necessary for the phenomenon to occur. Lastly, we must convert our theoretical statements about the learning process in terms of identifiable and repeatable activities or experimental performances. This way of measurably defining a theoretical term is called an **operational definition.** In other words, an operational definition relates to what is being defined (in this case learning) to the operations used to measure it. For example, a common operational definition of learning rate is **trials to criterion,** which is the number of times an experimental subject needs to experience the material to be learned before being able to perform at some specified level, for instance, how many times the subject had to see a list of nonsense syllables before he or she could recite the entire list accurately. Once researchers have operationally defined their theoretical terms, they are ready to experiment.

Every experiment involves something whose changes are measured, the **dependent variable,** and something the experimenter manipulates to see its effect on the dependent variable, the **independent variable**. In the previously mentioned experiment concerning the relationship between the number of hours of food deprivation and rate of learning, rate of learning was measured and was, therefore, the dependent variable. Rate of learning was operationally defined as how many trials it took for the animal to learn to make a left turn in a T-maze a specified number of consecutive times. Thus, trials to criterion was used as the dependent variable. In learning experiments, the operational definition indicates the kind of behavior that will be used to index learning. Hours of food deprivation was systematically manipulated by the researcher and it, therefore, was the independent variable.

Arbitrary Decisions in Setting Up a Learning Experiment

Science is often thought of as a cold, highly objective means for arriving at the "truth." Scientists, however, are often highly emotional, very subjective, and the truth they disclose is dynamic and probabilistic. This characterization can be seen in the number of arbitrary decisions that go into the setting up of any learning experiment. A number of these arbitrary decisions are summarized below.

1. What Aspects of Learning Should Be Investigated?   What aspects should be investigated, of course, will be partially dictated by one's theory concerning learning. One can study learning in the laboratory, or one can observe learning as it occurs in a schoolroom via naturalistic observation. In addition, one can study instrumental conditioning, classical conditioning, concept formation, problem solving, or verbal or perceptual-motor learning. Although a theory of learning attempts to specify the conditions under which learning takes place, it is up to the experimenter to choose which of those conditions should be investigated.

2. Idiographic Versus Nomothetic Techniques   Should researchers intensely study the learning process of a single experimental subject under a wide variety of circumstances (**idiographic technique**), or should they use groups of experimental subjects and study their average performance (**nomothetic technique**)? Although quite different, both techniques are respectable and both yield useful information about the learning process. As we shall see later, Skinner used the idiographic technique, and Hull used the nomothetic technique. As we shall see in Chapter 9, the two techniques can result in entirely different conclusions about the nature of learning.

3. Humans Versus Nonhuman Animals as Subjects   If researchers choose to use humans as their experimental subjects, they are concerned about how their results generalize from the laboratory to the world outside. If, however, they use nonhuman subjects, such as rats, pigeons, or monkeys, they are concerned also about how the learning process generalizes from one species to another in addition to the first concern.

Why, then, use anything but human subjects? There are many reasons why researchers use nonhuman subjects instead of humans despite the difficulties involved.

1. Humans are often too sophisticated for certain learning experiments; that is, their previous experience interferes with a clear study of the learning process. The learning history of nonhuman subjects can be controlled with relative ease.
2. Often learning experiments are long and boring, and it would be difficult to find humans willing to run in them. Nonhuman subjects do not complain.
3. Some experiments are designed to test the effects of genetics on learning ability. By using nonhuman subjects, the genetic background of subjects can be systematically manipulated.
4. The relationship between certain drugs and learning can be investigated with nonhuman subjects, whereas using human subjects for such research would be difficult, if not impossible.
5. Various surgical techniques can be used on nonhuman subjects, but not on humans. The surgical removal of certain brain areas and direct brain stimulation by electrodes implanted in the brain are only two examples. Likewise, human subjects cannot be sacrificed after the experiment to check on such things as neuronal effects of the treatment condition.
6. Last, but not least, human subjects sometimes miss appointments to run in experiments, whereas nonhuman subjects almost always show up.

4. Correlation Versus Experimental Techniques   Some researchers may want to correlate learning (operationally defined as a score on an achievement test) with intelligence (operationally defined as a score on an IQ test). Because this step involves correlating one response (performance on the achievement test) with another response (performance on the IQ test), the resulting relationship is called an R-R law (response-response law). R-R laws are said to be **correlational** in that they describe how two classes of behavioral events vary together.

Other researchers may want to vary systematically one or more environmental events and note their effect on the dependent variables. Since the relationship examined here is between environmental events (stimuli) and responses (changes on the dependent variable), it is said to be an S-R, or stimulus-response, law.

Although one may argue about the relative merits of correlational or **experimental techniques,** the point here is that at least these two general approaches are available for doing research. Both approaches yield distinctly different information about learning. Which approach is taken depends on the preference of the individual researcher.

5. Which Independent Variables Should Be Studied?   Once learning has been operationally defined, the dependent variable in an experiment has been automatically set. If, for example, learning is operationally defined as "trials to criterion," this is what is measured in the experiment. Next, the researcher must ask, "What variable or variables are likely to have an effect on the behavior being measured?" The answer to that question could involve a long list of possible independent variables to choose from. A sample list follows.

Sex difference	Instructions
Age differences	Intelligence
Size of the stimulus materials used	Drugs
Rate of presentation	Intertrial interval
Meaningfulness of the material used	Interaction with other tasks

An additional function of a theory, by the way, is to give researchers some guidance in choosing their independent variable or variables.

6. What Levels of the Independent Variables Should Be Studied?   Once one or more independent variables have been chosen, the researcher must consider how many levels of it should be represented in the experiment. For example, if age is chosen as an experimental variable, how many ages and which ones should be studied are yet to be determined. There are some guidelines that could be used here to ensure that the levels of the independent variable chosen will have the greatest effect on the dependent variable (see Anderson, 1971), but this choice is basically arbitrary.

7. Choice of Dependent Variables   Common dependent variables in learning experiments include the following:

Scores on tests	Trials to criterion
Trials to extinction	Latency
Running speed	Probability of response
Rate of responding	Number of errors
Time to solution	Response amplitude

Because each results from an operational definition of learning, it should be clear that many acceptable operational definitions of learning are available to the researcher. Although which is chosen is arbitrary, the choice may have a profound effect on the conclusions one draws about the outcome of an experiment. In experiments having two dependent variables, it is common for one variable to show an effect due to the independent variable and for the other to show no effect. For example, when investigating the transfer of training from one hand to the other in our laboratory, we consistently find that practice with one hand increases the speed with which a task can be performed with the other hand (speed of responding being one dependent variable). Using speed as our dependent variable, we find evidence for positive transfer of training from one hand to the other. If, however, we use number of errors as our dependent variable, we discover that practice with one hand does not facilitate performance with the other hand. Thus we conclude that no transfer of training took place—two altogether dissimilar conclusions resulting from our choice of the dependent variable.

8. Data Analysis and Interpretation Once the data (scores on the dependent variable) have been gathered in an experiment, how does one analyze them? Although it is beyond the scope of this book to discuss them, the reader should be aware of the fact that many statistical techniques are available to the researcher for data analysis. Here again, the choice of a statistical test is somewhat arbitrary and yet may have a significant effect on one's conclusions.

Once the experiment has been designed, run, and analyzed, it must be interpreted. There are usually many interpretations of the data provided by an experiment, and there is really no way of knowing if the one finally decided on is the best. It is possible that even after following the most rigorous scientific procedures in the gathering of experimental data, the interpretation of those data could be totally inadequate. For example, there is the story of the researcher who trained a flea to jump every time he said "jump." After this preliminary training, the researcher began pulling legs off the flea, and after the removal of each leg, he said "jump" and the flea jumped. The experiment continued in this manner until the flea's last leg had been pulled off. Now when the experimenter said "jump," the flea did not move. The researcher jotted his conclusion in his notebook: "Fleas without legs are deaf." We exaggerate only to stress the point that there are any number of possible conclusions that could be drawn about the same experimental data.

It should be noted that although we refer to the decisions in this section as arbitrary, they are arbitrary only in the sense that there are a number of ways of arranging an experiment in a given area and any one of the ways might be scientifically correct. In a more practical sense, however, the choice of what to study, the kind of subject to use, independent and dependent variables, and the approach to data analysis and interpretation will be at least partially determined by such factors as cost, practicality, theoretical orientation, social and educational concerns, and availability of apparatus.

THE USE OF MODELS

The *Random House Dictionary of the English Language* defines **analogy** as "a partial similarity between like features of two things, on which a comparison may be based." In science, it is often useful to find that two things are analogous, especially when one thing is well known and the other is not. In such cases, we can use what is well known **as a model** in attempting to understand what is less known. At one time, noting the similarity between the functioning of mechanical pumps (about which a great deal was known) and the functioning of human hearts (about which less was known) provided a useful guide for heart research. Also, noting the similarities between lower animals and humans encouraged the intense study of lower animals in order to learn more about human processes.

In recent years, information-processing psychology has tended to use the computer as a model in the study of human intellectual processes. Many information-processing psychologists state that computers and humans are analogous because both receive information (input) from the environment, process that information in one or more ways, and then act on that information (output). These information-processing psychologists say that the software programs placed into computers determine how computers process the information fed into them. Likewise, humans are programmed by experience to process information in certain ways. Because of these similarities, many information-processing psychologists believe that much can be learned about how humans process information by assuming that computers and humans process information in similar ways. In Chapter 14, we will see that the computer has proved to be a useful model in the study of human cognitive processes. We will also see, however, that not all information-processing psychologists feel that the computer is a useful model for studying human cognitive processes.

Unlike a theory, a model is typically not used to explain a complicated process; rather, it is used to simplify the process and make it more understandable. The use of models involves showing how something is like something else. A theory, however, attempts to describe the processes underlying a complex phenomenon. Reinforcement theory, for example, is an attempt to explain why learning occurs. It is not an attempt to show what learning is *like*, as would be the case with a model. In the area of motivation one might say that an organism acts like a mule with a carrot dangling before it, or one might say that the physiological state of hunger is interacting with previously learned habits, causing the organism to run. In the former case, a model is being used to *describe* behavior; in the latter case, a theory is being used in an attempt to *explain* behavior.

LEARNING IN THE LABORATORY VERSUS NATURALISTIC OBSERVATION

Remember that science deals in statements that are verified through experimentation. Contrasted with naturalistic observation, where the researcher has no control over what is being observed, an experiment can be defined as controlled observation. Information is both gained and lost in laboratory experimentation. On the plus side, the experimenter controls the situation and therefore is able to examine systematically a number of different conditions and their effect on learning. On the negative side, the laboratory creates an artificial situation that is much different from the circumstances under which learning would ordinarily occur. This always brings into question how information gained in the laboratory is related to learning situations outside the laboratory. Some researchers feel that combining naturalistic observation and laboratory experimentation is best. That is, one could make initial observations in the field, examine them in greater detail in the laboratory, and then observe the phenomenon again in the field with the greater understanding that resulted from laboratory experimentation.

KUHN'S VIEWS OF HOW SCIENCES CHANGE

To picture science as an activity that gradually evolves toward an increasingly accurate understanding of nature, as we have done above, may be somewhat misleading. In his book *The Structure of Scientific Revolutions*, Thomas Kuhn (1973) portrays a much different view of science. According to Kuhn, scientists working in a given area usually accept a certain point of view about what they are studying. For example, at one time most physicists accepted the Newtonian point of view in their study of physics. Kuhn calls a point of view shared by a substantial number of scientists a **paradigm.** A paradigm provides a general framework for empirical research and, as such, is usually more than just a limited theory. A paradigm corresponds more closely to what is called a school of thought or an "ism," such as *behaviorism, associationism,* or *functionalism* (these terms will be explained in the next chapter).

The activities of scientists who accept a particular paradigm consist mainly of elaborating and verifying the implications of the framework it superimposes over the subject being studied. In other words, a paradigm is a way of looking at a subject that illuminates certain problems and suggests ways of solving those problems. Kuhn calls the problem-solving activities of scientists following a paradigm **normal science.** Normal science is what most of this chapter has been about.

The positive result of a community of scientists following a certain paradigm is that a certain range of phenomena, those on which the paradigm focuses, are explored thoroughly. The negative result is that following a particular paradigm blinds the scientists to other, perhaps more fruitful, ways of dealing with their subject matter. Thus, whereas research generated by a certain paradigm results in depth, it may inhibit breadth.

According to Kuhn (1973), scientists following a particular paradigm, that is, those engaged in normal science, are providing little more than a "mop-up operation." Kuhn puts the matter as follows:

> Mopping-up operations are what engage most scientists throughout their careers. They constitute what I am here calling normal science. Closely examined, whether historically or in the contemporary laboratory, that enterprise seems an attempt to force nature into the preformed and relatively inflexible box that the paradigm supplies. No part of the aim of normal science is to call forth new sorts of phenomena; indeed those that will not fit the box are often not seen at all. Nor do scientists normally aim to invent new theories, and they are often intolerant of those invented by others. Instead, normal-scientific research is directed to the articulation of those phenomena and theories that the paradigm already supplies. (p. 24)

How then do new paradigms emerge? According to Kuhn, innovations in science come when scientists following a particular paradigm are consistently confronted with events that are inconsistent with the point of view they are holding. Eventually, as the anomalies persist, an alternative paradigm will emerge that will be able to explain the anomalies as well as the events supporting the previous paradigm. The new paradigm will usually be associated with one individual or a small group of individuals who attempt to convince their colleagues that their paradigm is more effective than its predecessor. Typically, the new paradigm meets with great resistance and converts are won very slowly. Kuhn says that this resistance comes from the fact that a particular paradigm has implications for every aspect of one's scientific life, and therefore changing from one paradigm to another involves an enormous change in how one does science; for this reason, there is emotional involvement in the decision. Kuhn says, "Like the choice between competing political institutions, that between competing paradigms proves to be a choice between incompatible modes of community life" (p. 94). Because of this emotional involvement, scientists will usually do everything possible to make their accepted paradigm work before pondering a change. At some point, however, the older paradigm will be "overthrown" and the new one will replace it. The displacement of Newton's theory by Einstein's theory is one example, and the displacement of religious notions concerning the creation of human life by Darwin's theory of evolution is another.

According to Kuhn, then, a science changes (although it does not necessarily advance) through a series of **scientific revolutions,** which are similar to political revolutions, rather than through a continuous evolutionary process within a single theoretical framework. To Kuhn, the evolution of a science is at least as much a sociological phenomenon as it is a scientific phenomenon. We might add that because of the emotional involvement it also appears to be a psychological phenomenon.

As valid as Kuhn's argument appears to be, it seems most forceful when applied to the physical sciences rather than the behavioral sciences. Within the more mature physical sciences, it is the rule that most scientists accept some prevailing paradigm, and therefore a change in paradigm tends to be revolutionary. In the younger behavioral sciences, however, many paradigms exist simultaneously. The book you are now reading provides a good example since it offers various ways of looking at the learning process. Every theory in this book is accepted to some extent by a substantial number of researchers of the learning process. Although followers of one theory tend to form a camp, they still communicate and influence members of other camps. It would be difficult to find an area in physics for which this would be true. For example, one could not find a book on theories of gravity since there are not as many paradigms that exist simultaneously in that area.

Thus, it seems that under the conditions that exist in the behavioral sciences, the revolutionary change of paradigms is less possible and/or necessary. One possible exception to this contention would be the widespread acceptance of associationism, one of psychology's oldest and most widely accepted doctrines. In fact, most theories in this book assume some aspect of associationism. At the present time, there is growing dissatisfaction with the assumptions underlying associationism; thus we have the necessary condition for the kind of scientific revolution that Kuhn so eloquently describes in his book.

POPPER'S VIEW OF SCIENCE

As we have seen, science has traditionally been viewed as involving empirical observation, theory formation, theory testing, theory revision, and the search for lawful relationships. Like Kuhn, Karl Popper (1902–1994) was critical of this traditional view of science. According to Popper (1963), scientific activity does not start with empirical observation, as is so often claimed. Rather, it starts with the existence of a problem. For Popper, the idea that scientists wander around making empirical observations and then attempting to explain those observations was just plain silly:

> Twenty-five years ago I tried to bring home the same point to a group of physics students in Vienna by beginning a lecture with the following instruction: "Take pencil and paper: carefully observe, and write down what you have observed!" They asked, of course, *what* I wanted them to observe. Clearly the instruction, "Observe!" is absurd…observation is always selective. It needs a chosen object, a definite task, an interest, a point of view, a problem. (p. 46)

For Popper, then, problems determine which observations are made by scientists. The next step in scientific activity, according to Popper, is to propose a solution to the problem. A scientific theory is a proposed solution to a problem. What distinguishes a scientific theory from a nonscientific theory is the **principle of refutability** (sometimes called the principle of falsification). According to this principle, a scientific theory must make specific predictions about what will happen under certain circumstances. Furthermore, the predictions must be risky in the sense that there is a real possibility that the predictions will be erroneous and thus refute the theory on which they were based. Einstein's theory of relativity made the risky predictions that as objects approached the speed of light, they would diminish in size and increase in mass. If these predictions were found to be false, Einstein's theory would have needed to be revised or abandoned. It turns out, however, that his predictions were accurate.

Popper criticized a number of theories in psychology because they do not pass the test of refutability. Freud's theory, for example, makes no risky predictions. Everything that a person does can be "explained" by Freud's theory. If, for example, Freud's theory predicts that on the basis of early experience a man should hate women but is found to love them, the Freudian can say that he is displaying a "reaction formation." That is, he really does hate women on the unconscious level, and he is simply going overboard in the opposite direction to reduce the anxiety that his recognition of his true hatred of women would cause. Astrology suffers the same fate since there is no conceivable observation that could be made that would refute its claims. Contrary to common belief, if every conceivable observation agrees with a theory, the theory is weak, not strong.

Berkson and Wettersten (1984) suggest that there is a theory of learning contained within Popper's philosophy of science. We will discuss that theory and its implications for education in Chapter 16.

Kuhn Versus Popper

According to Popper, what Kuhn calls normal science is not science at all. For Popper, the subjective beliefs that Kuhn claims bind scientists to a paradigm inhibit effective problem solving. In his analysis of scientific activity, Kuhn stresses sociological and psychological factors, whereas Popper's analysis stressed the logical refutation of proposed solutions to problems. For Popper, either proposed solutions (theories) to problems pass the rigorous attempts to refute them or they do not; there is no room for subjectivity. Can the analyses of both Kuhn and Popper be correct? Robinson (1986) suggests that they can be, and we agree: "In a conciliatory spirit, we might suggest that the major disagreement between Kuhn and Popper vanishes when we picture Kuhn as describing what science has been historically, and Popper asserting what it ought to be" (p. 24).

DISCUSSION QUESTIONS

1. In what way(s) do you feel science differs from other fields of inquiry, such as philosophy and theology?
2. What is a *scientific law?* How does the scientific concept of law differ from how the term is used in a legal or a religious sense?
3. Discuss the strengths and weaknesses of naturalistic observation.
4. Briefly discuss the characteristics of a scientific theory.
5. Discuss the steps involved in going from experimentation to theory.
6. Discuss the steps involved in going from theory to experimentation.
7. What is a scientific model? Give an example of how a model has been used in psychology.
8. Differentiate between a theory and a model.
9. List and briefly describe the arbitrary decisions that are involved in setting up, running, and analyzing a learning experiment.
10. What does Kuhn mean when he says normal science is a "mop-up" operation?
11. Describe the process of scientific revolution as it is viewed by Kuhn.
12. Discuss Popper's criticisms of the traditional views of science.
13. How can the analyses of science offered by Kuhn and Popper be reconciled?

KEY TERMS

analogy   A partial correspondence or similarity between things otherwise dissimilar.

confirmable propositions   Propositions whose truth or falsity can be publicly demonstrated. Such propositions are also called verifiable.

correlational techniques   Research in which two response measures are related. Such research is usually interested in detecting how two kinds of behavior vary together. For example, how is performance on an IQ test related to performance on a creativity test? Correlational techniques generate R-R laws since two response measures are being related.

dependent variable   The variable that is measured in an experiment, usually some kind of behavior (e.g., trials to criterion).

elementism   The belief that the best way to study a complex phenomenon is to divide it up into smaller components.

empirical aspect of a theory   The empirical events that the theory purports to explain.

experimental techniques   Research in which one or more independent variables are systematically manipulated in order to detect their effects on one or more dependent variables. Since an experiment attempts to relate stimuli (independent variables) to responses (dependent variables) it is said to generate S-R laws. This process is contrasted with correlational techniques, which demonstrate R-R laws.

formal aspect of a theory   The signs, symbols, or words that a theory contains.

heuristic function of a theory   A theory's ability to generate research.

idiographic technique   The intense study of a single experimental subject.

independent variable   The variable that is systematically manipulated in an experiment. Typical independent variables would include hours of deprivation, sex of subject, age, rate of presentation, or degree of meaningfulness.

model   When a fairly well-known situation is used to describe a relatively less known situation. Models are used to show that the two situations are alike in some respects.

naturalistic observation   Studying a phenomenon as it occurs naturally in the environment.

nomothetic technique   The study of a group of experimental subjects, the interest being in the *average* performance of the group.

normal science   Those activities of scientists as they are guided by a particular paradigm.

operational definition of learning   A definition that states the procedures to be followed in determining whether, and to what extent, learning has taken place. Operational definitions of learning can range from grades on achievement tests to some behavioral measure in a learning experiment, such as trials to criterion or the number of errors in maze running.

paradigm   A point of view shared by a substantial number of scientists that provides a general framework for empirical research. A paradigm is usually more than just one theory and corresponds more closely to what is called a school of thought or an "ism."

principle of parsimony   When researchers have a choice between two equally effective theories, they are obliged to choose the simpler of the two.

principle of refutability (principle of falsification)   Popper's contention that in order for a theory to be scientific, it must make risky predictions that, if not confirmed, would refute the theory.

science   A method of inquiry that involves the use of experimentation to test theories about various aspects of nature.

scientific law   A consistently observed relationship between two or more classes of empirical events.

scientific revolution   According to Kuhn, the displacement of one paradigm with another. Such a displacement usually occurs over a fairly long period of time and after great resistance. A paradigm is associated with the scientist's total view of science—what counts as a good problem, what counts as a good answer, what a good experiment is like, and so on. Thus, a change in paradigm is a widespread change for scientists that invalidates almost every aspect of their previous scientific life. There is, therefore, emotional involvement in such a change.

theory   An attempted explanation that makes sense out of a large number of observations and indicates to the researcher where to look for additional information. Or, according to Popper, a proposed solution to a problem.

trials to criterion   The number of trials an experimental subject requires to reach the criterion that the experimenter sets as a definition of learning. For example, if perfect recall of a list of nonsense syllables is defined as learning the list, then trials to criterion is the number of times the subject had to go through the list before he or she could recall the items without error.

Chapter 3

EARLY NOTIONS ABOUT LEARNING

EPISTEMOLOGY AND LEARNING THEORY

Epistemology is a branch of philosophy that is concerned with the nature of knowledge. The epistemologist asks questions such as What is knowledge? What can we know? What are the limits of knowledge? What does it mean to know? What are the origins of knowledge? Questions of this kind go back at least as far as the early Greeks. In fact, the views of Plato and Aristotle concerning the nature of knowledge have set philosophical trends that have persisted until this day. Plato believed that knowledge was inherited and was, therefore, a natural component of the human mind. According to Plato, one gained knowledge by reflecting on the contents of one's mind. Aristotle, in contrast, believed that knowledge derived from sensory experience and was not inherited.

Although Plato believed that knowledge is inherited and Aristotle believed that it is derived from sensory experience, both exemplify **rationalism** because both believed that the mind is actively involved in the attainment of knowledge. For Plato, the mind must engage in active introspection to discover inherited knowledge. For Aristotle, the mind must actively ponder the information provided by the senses to discover the knowledge contained within that information. The term **nativism** can also be applied to Plato's position because he stressed that knowledge is innate. The position taken by Aristotle also exemplifies **empiricism** because he stressed the importance of sensory experience as the basis of all knowledge.

The philosophies of Plato and Aristotle show the difficulty in using such general philosophical terms as *rationalist, nativist,* and *empiricist.* A case can be made that all three labels accurately apply to any philosopher relevant to the history of learning theory. A rationalist maintains that the mind must be actively involved in the quest of knowledge (for example, by thinking, reasoning, or deducing). Certainly both Plato and Aristotle were rationalists. The nativist maintains that some important trait or attitude is inherited. For Plato, one such attribute is knowledge. Aristotle, however, did not totally reject nativism. For him the reasoning powers used to abstract knowledge from sensory experience are innate. The empiricist maintains that sensory information is the basis of all knowledge, and because Aristotle believed this he can be labeled an empiricist. This is not to say, however, that sensory information is unimportant in Plato's philosophy. For Plato, the search for, or the awareness of, innate knowledge is often triggered by sensory experience.

Because the type of overlap just described is common among philosophers, it is important to remember that labels such as rationalist, empiricist, or nativist are applied to a philosopher because of the *emphasis* of that philosopher's work. There are no pure rationalists, empiricists, or nativists. In their explanations of knowledge Plato can be called a nativist because he stressed inheritance, Aristotle can be called an empiricist because he stressed the importance of sensory information, and both Plato and Aristotle can be called rationalists because they stressed the importance of an active mind for the attainment of knowledge.

Because the views of Plato and Aristotle concerning the nature of knowledge have played such an important role in the history of learning theory, we will look at them in greater detail.

PLATO

Plato (ca. 427–347 B.C.) was Socrates's most famous student. In fact, Socrates never wrote a word about his philosophy—it was written by Plato. This is a most significant fact since the early Platonic dialogues were designed primarily to show the Socratic approach to knowledge and were memories of the great teacher at work. The later dialogues, however, represent Plato's own philosophy and have little to do with Socrates. Plato was so upset by the execution of Socrates for impiety that he went on a self-imposed exile to southern Italy, where he came under the influence of the **Pythagoreans.** This fact has important implications for Western people and is directly related to all approaches to epistemology, including learning theory, that have occurred since.

The Pythagoreans believed that the universe was governed by numerical relationships that influenced the physical world. In fact, numbers and their various combinations *caused* events in the physical world. And both events, the number and the empirical event that it caused, were real. Thus, to the Pythagoreans, the abstract had an independent existence and was capable of influencing physical objects. Furthermore, physical events were thought to be only manifestations of the abstract. Although number and matter interact, it is matter that we experience with our senses, not number. This results in a dualistic view of the universe, in which one aspect can be experienced through the senses and the other cannot. Following this notion, the Pythagoreans made great strides in mathematics, medicine, and music. Through time, however, they developed into a mystical cult, allowing only a few individuals to become members and share their wisdom. Plato was one such individual.

Plato's later dialogues reflect complete acceptance of the dualistic universe in which the Pythagoreans believed. He developed a theory of knowledge based on the Pythagorean notion that the abstract has an independent and influential existence.

Reminiscence Theory of Knowledge

According to Plato every object in the physical world has a corresponding abstract "idea" or "form" that causes it. For example, the abstract idea for *chair* interacts with matter to produce what we call a chair. The idea of *tree* interacts with matter to form what we see as a tree. All physical objects have such an origin. Thus, what we experience through our senses is a chair, a tree, or a house, but not chairness, treeness, or houseness. The pure idea or essence of these things exists independent of matter, and something is lost when the idea is translated into matter. Therefore, if we attempt to gain knowledge by examining things that we experience through the senses, we will be misled. Sensory information provides only opinion; the abstract ideas themselves are the only bases of true knowledge.

But how do we obtain information about the ideas if we cannot experience them through the senses? Plato said we experience them through the "mind's eye." We turn our thoughts inward and ponder what is innately available to us. All human beings have in their mind complete knowledge of all the ideas that make up the world; thus true knowledge comes from introspection or self-analysis. We must learn to divorce ourselves from sensory information that can only deceive or, at best, remind us of what we already know.

How does one come to have knowledge of the ideas? Here Plato becomes mystical. All humans possess a soul. Before being placed in the body at birth, the soul dwells in pure and complete knowledge. Thus, all human souls know everything before entering the body. Upon entering the body, the knowledge of the soul begins to be "contaminated" by sensory information. According to Plato if humans accept what they experience through the senses as truth, they are doomed to live a life of opinion or ignorance. Only by turning away from the physical impure world to the world of ideas, pondered by the mind's eye, can we hope to gain true knowledge. Thus, all knowledge is **reminiscence**, or recollection of the experience our soul had in the "heaven which is beyond the heavens." Plato advises the astronomer to "let the heavens alone" and use "the natural gift of reason" (*Republic* VII, p. 296).

As we have already seen, Plato was a nativist because he felt knowledge was inborn. He was also a rationalist because he felt this knowledge could only be made available through reasoning. As we shall see later, other rationalists were not as extreme as Plato in their negative attitude toward sensory information. However, it was Plato's philosophy that dominated Europe for the first 12 centuries of the Christian Era. It is largely through this early influence on Christianity, that we still have remnants of Platonism in Western culture today.

ARISTOTLE

Aristotle (384–322 B.C.), one of Plato's students, first followed Plato's teachings quite closely and later broke away from them almost completely. A basic difference between the two thinkers was in their attitude toward sensory information. To Plato, it was a hindrance and something to be distrusted, but to Aristotle sensory information was the basis of all knowledge. With his favorable attitude toward empirical observation, Aristotle compiled an extraordinarily large number of facts about physical and biological phenomena.

Reason, however, was in no way abandoned by Aristotle. He felt that sense impressions were only the beginning of knowledge—the mind must then ponder these impressions to discover the lawfulness that runs through them. The laws that govern the empirical world are not knowable through sensory information alone but must be discovered by active reason. Thus, Aristotle believed that knowledge was gained from sense experience *and* reasoning.

There are two major differences here between Aristotle's and Plato's theory of knowledge. First, the laws, forms, or universals that Aristotle was looking for did not have an existence independent of their empirical manifestation, as they did for Plato. They were simply observed relationships in nature. Second, for Aristotle, all knowledge is based on sensory experience. This, of course, was not the case with Plato. It is because Aristotle contended that the source of all knowledge is sensory experience that he is labeled an empiricist.

In elaborating his empiricistic view of knowledge, Aristotle formulated his **laws**

of association. He said that the experience or recall of one object will tend to elicit the recall of things similar to that object (law of similarity), recall of opposite things (law of contrast), or recall of things that were originally experienced along with that object (law of contiguity). Aristotle also noted that the more frequently two things are experienced together, the more likely it will be that the experience or recall of one will stimulate the recall of the second. Later in history, this came to be known as the law of frequency. Thus, according to Aristotle, sensory experience gives rise to ideas. The ideas stimulated by sensory experience will stimulate other ideas in accordance with the laws of similarity, contrast, contiguity, and frequency. Within philosophy, the contention that the relationships among ideas can be explained by the laws of association is called **associationism.** An example of how ideas become associated through contiguity is shown in Figure 3–1.

Besides making empirical investigation respectable, Aristotle made several other contributions to psychology. He wrote the first history of psychology, which was entitled *De Anima.* He wrote extensively on the human sensory apparatus, which he listed as consisting of sight, hearing, smell, taste, and touch. He contributed greatly to later conceptions of memory, thinking, and learning. As we saw above, his associative principles of similarity, contrast, contiguity, and frequency later became the bases for the doctrine of associationism, which is still very much part of modern learning theory. In view of his immense contributions, we can forgive him for locating the mind in the heart and treating the brain as a system for cooling the blood. About Aristotle's great influence on learning theory, Weimer (1973) said,

> A moment's recollection...shows that Aristotle's doctrines are at the heart of contemporary thought in epistemology and the psychology of learning. The centrality of associationism as the mechanism of the mind is so well known as to require only the observation that not one single learning theory propounded in this century has failed to base its account on associative principles. (p. 18)

With Aristotle's death died the hope for the development of empirical science. In the centuries following Aristotle there was no follow-up to the scientific study that Aristotelian thinking had promoted. The collapse of the Greek city-states, barbarian invasions throughout Europe, and the rapid spread of Christianity stunted the growth of scientific inquiry. Early medieval thinkers depended on the teachings of past authorities instead of seeking new information.

Plato's philosophy was an important influence on early Christianity. The conception of man that prevailed during these times is described by Marx and Cronan-Hillix (1987):

> Human beings were regarded as creatures with a soul possessed of a free will which set them apart from ordinary natural laws and subject only to their own willfulness and perhaps to the rule of God. Such a creature, being free-willed, could not be an object of scientific investigation.
>
> Even the human body was regarded as sacrosanct. Anatomists had to double as grave robbers, and that made anatomy a highly risky, or very expensive, occupation. The strictures against observation slowed the development of anatomy and medicine for centuries and allowed incredible misconceptions to persist for over a thousand years. A science of psychology could not flourish in such an atmosphere. (p. 28)

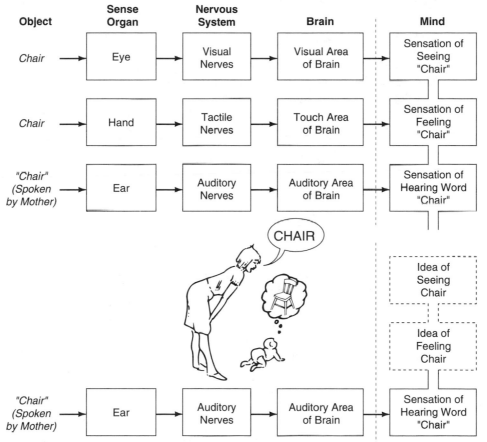

FIGURE 3–1 An example of how seeing and touching a chair and hearing the word chair become associated through contiguity. (From *Introduction to Modern Behaviorism*, 3rd ed., by Howard Rachlin. Copyright ©1991 W. H. Freeman and Company. Reprinted with permission.)

Religion has been defined as philosophy in the absence of dialogue; when Plato's views concerning the nature of knowledge were incorporated into Christian dogma, they could not be challenged. Some 1500 years elapsed before the rediscovery of Aristotle's writings challenged the antiempiricism of the Church. When inquiry into nature did begin again it spread like wildfire. For psychology, the writings of René Descartes represent one of the most important examples of this renaissance.

THE BEGINNING OF MODERN PSYCHOLOGY

René Descartes (1596–1650) tried to approach all philosophical inquiry with an attitude of complete doubt. "I can doubt everything," he argued, "except one thing, and that is the very fact that I doubt. But when I doubt I think; and when I think I must exist." He thus arrived at his celebrated conclusion, "I think; therefore I am." He went on from that point to prove the existence of God, and from there he inferred that our sensory experiences must be a reflection of an objective reality because God would not deceive us.

Descartes went on to postulate a separation between the mind and the body. He viewed the human body as a machine that moves in predictable ways; in this respect we were the same as any other animal. The mind, however, is a uniquely human attribute. The mind was free and could decide the actions of the body. Descartes believed the pineal gland to be the point of contact between the mind and the body. The mind could move the gland from side to side and could thus open or close the pores of the brain. Through these pores, the "animal spirits" flowed down tiny tubes to the muscles, filling and swelling them and making them become short and thick, thus moving the parts of the body to which they were connected. Although that physical action is what occurs when the mind causes behavior, sensory experience can also cause behavior. Motion outside the body exerts a pull on the "taut strings" that lead to the brain; the pull opens the pores of the brain, releasing the "animal spirits," which flow into the muscles and cause behavior. Therefore, the mind or the physical environment can initiate behavior. This description of *reflex action* was to have a long-lasting influence on psychology. Descartes can be considered a predecessor of the stimulus-response psychologists.

By comparing the human body to a machine, Descartes helped to make it accessible to scientific study. He urged physiologists to use the method of dissection to better understand the machinery of the body. Because Descartes believed that humans and animals were physiologically similar, the study of animals to learn about humans was given respectability. Descartes, therefore, did much to pave the way for physiological and comparative psychology.

The mind, however, was free and possessed by humans alone. In explaining the working of the mind, Descartes relied heavily on *innate ideas,* thus showing Plato's influence on his philosophy. Innate ideas were not derivable from experience but were integral to the mind. Examples of innate ideas included the concepts of God and the self; the axioms of geometry; and the ideas of space, time, and motion. The question of innate ideas caused much philosophical discussion following Descartes.

Thomas Hobbes (1588–1679) opposed the notion that innate ideas are a source of knowledge. He maintained that sense impressions are the source of all knowledge. With this belief, Hobbes reopened the philosophical school of empiricism and its related associationism.

Hobbes believed that stimuli either help or hinder the vital functions of the body. A stimulus that aids in the vital functioning of the body causes a feeling of pleasure; therefore, the person seeks to experience this pleasure again. Stimuli that hinder the vital functioning of the body cause an aversive feeling, and the person seeks to retreat from it. According to Hobbes, human behavior is controlled by these "appetites" and "aversions." Those events approached by a person are called "good," and those avoided are called "evil." Thus, the values of good and evil are individually determined; they are not abstract or absolute. Later, Jeremy Bentham (1748–1832) said that human behavior was governed by the "pleasure principle," an idea that was picked up by Freud and later by the reinforcement theorists.

Hobbes was mainly interested in the political and societal conditions under which humans live. He felt that humans were basically selfish and aggressive and if allowed to live in accordance with their nature, life would be characterized by self-satisfaction and war. Humans form political systems and societies because it is to our advantage to do so, not because we are by nature gregarious. Without agreed-upon rules and regulations concerning conduct, human existence would be characterized by "continual fear, and danger of violent death; and the life of man, solitary, poor, nasty, brutish, and short" (Hobbes, 1962 (1651), p. 100). In other words, Hobbes believed that forming human societies was the lesser of two evils since it reduced the likelihood of constant struggle with other humans. This view of the function of society comes very close to the one held by Freud many years later.

John Locke (1632–1704) also opposed the notion of innate ideas. For him, the mind is made up of ideas, and ideas come from experience. He indicated that if ideas were innate, people everywhere would possess them, but they do not. Rather, different cultural groups differ markedly in what they think and believe. Thus, the infant mind at birth is a *tabula rasa,* a blank tablet, and experience writes on it. The mind becomes what it experiences; *there is nothing in the mind that is not first in the senses.* Simple ideas come directly from sense experience; complex ideas come from combining simple ideas.

Clearly, then, Locke was an empiricist. Note, however, that his philosophy had a major rationalistic component. Although simple ideas come from experience they are combined by reflection, and reflection is a rational process. As Leibniz (1646–1716) said in summarizing Locke's philosophy, "There is nothing in the mind that is not first in the senses, *except the mind itself.*"

Like Galileo before him, Locke distinguished between primary and secondary qualities. Primary qualities are characteristics of the physical world powerful enough to cause accurate mental representations of themselves in the mind of a perceiver. Size, weight, quantity, solidity, shape, and mobility exemplify primary qualities. Secondary qualities are characteristics of the physical world too weak or minute to cause accurate mental representations of themselves in the mind of a perceiver. Electromagnetic energy, atoms and molecules, airwaves, and white corpuscles in the blood exemplify secondary qualities. Secondary qualities cause psychological experiences that have no counterparts in the physical world, for example, the experiences of colors, sounds, odors, tastes, and blood being entirely red.

Although it is not how Locke used the terms, it is often the case that *primary quality* is used to refer to physical objects and *secondary quality* to any psychological experience that has no exact counterpart in the physical world. In what follows we shall follow the latter convention. The distinction between primary and secondary qualities is often cited as the reason that psychology can never become a true science. It is claimed that since secondary qualities are purely cognitive, they cannot be objectively analyzed in the same way that primary qualities can be. For many it is this inaccessibility of secondary qualities to direct objective study that causes them to be beyond the reach of scientific scrutiny. Many years later, it was this very concern that caused many behaviorists to place the study of mental events off-limits in their analysis of human behavior.

George Berkeley (1685–1753) claimed that Locke did not go far enough. There was still a kind of dualism in Locke's view that physical objects cause ideas about them. Whereas Locke contended that there is an empirical world about which we have ideas, Berkeley claimed that we can experience only secondary qualities. Nothing exists unless it is perceived; *thus to be is to be perceived*. What we call primary qualities, such as shape and size, are really only secondary qualities or ideas. Ideas are the only things we experience directly and are therefore the only things we can be sure of. Despite such beliefs, however, Berkeley is still considered an empiricist because he believed the contents of the mind were derived from the experience of external reality. That external reality was not material or physical but rather God's perception: what we experience through our senses are God's ideas.

David Hume (1711–1776) carried the argument one step further. Although he agreed with Berkeley that we could know nothing for sure about the physical environment, he added that we could know nothing for sure about ideas. *We can be sure of nothing*. Mind, for Hume, was no more than a stream of ideas, memories, imaginings, associations, and feelings.

This is not to deny Hume's empiricist and associationist leanings. He believed strongly that human knowledge consists of ideas that somehow come from experience and come to be associated through the principles of association. Hume was saying, however, that we only experience the empirical world indirectly through our ideas. Even the laws of nature are constructs of the imagination; the "lawfulness" of nature is in our minds, not necessarily in nature. General concepts such as causation, for example, come from what Hume referred to as the "habitual order of ideas."

Needless to say, Hume upset everyone. To accept Hume was to question rational thought, science, psychology, and religion. All dogma, whether religious or scientific, now became suspect. Hergenhahn (1997) summarizes Hume's philosophy as follows:

> Hume had argued that all conclusions we reached about anything were based on subjective experience because that was the only thing we ever encountered directly. According to Hume, all statements about the nature of the physical world or about morality were derived from impressions and ideas and the feelings that they aroused, as well as from the way they were organized by the laws of association. Even causation, which was so important to many philosophers and scientists was reduced to a habit of the mind in Hume's philosophy. For example, even if B always follows A and the interval between the two is always the same we cannot ever conclude that A causes B, because there is no way for us to verify an actual, causal relationship between the two events. For Hume, rational philosophy, physical science, and moral philosophy were all reduced to sub-

jective psychology. Therefore, nothing could be known with certainty because all knowledge was based on the interpretation of subjective experience. (p. 169)

Immanuel Kant (1724–1804) claimed that Hume awoke him from his "dogmatic slumbers" and caused him to attempt to rescue philosophy from Hume's skepticism. Kant attempted to correct the impractical features of both rationalism and empiricism. Rationalism can involve only the manipulation of concepts, and empiricism confines knowledge to sensory experience and its derivatives. Kant attempted to reconcile both points of view.

Kant felt that careful analysis of our experience revealed certain categories of thought. For example, Kant indicated that we do have such ideas as causality, unity, and totality, but we never, as Hume had said, experience any of these things empirically. These categories of thought, or "faculties," are neither part of our sensory experience nor derived from it. If these thoughts are not the result of sensory experience, Kant reasoned, they must be **innate categories of thought.** These innate mental faculties are superimposed over our sensory experiences, thereby providing them with structure and meaning. Kant believed that there were twelve of these innate faculties that give meaning to our experiences of the physical world, including unity, totality, reality, existence, necessity, reciprocity, and causality.

What we consciously experience, according to Kant, is influenced by both sensory experience, caused by the empirical world, and the faculties of the mind, which are innate. The faculties of the mind transform sensory experience, thereby giving it greater organization and meaning. Any attempt to determine the nature of knowledge must, according to Kant, also take into consideration the active contribution of the mind. We will see a current example of this point of view when we review Gestalt psychology in Chapter 10 and Jean Piaget's theory in Chapter 11. Kant's philosophy can be viewed as the antecedent of modern information-processing psychology and cognitive science. Flanagan (1991, p. 181) says, "When cognitive scientists discuss their philosophical forebears one hears the name of Immanuel Kant more than any other." In this book cognitive science is represented by the work of Donald Norman (Chapter 14).

Thus, Kant kept rationalism alive by showing that the mind is the source of knowledge. In other words he kept alive an approach to explaining knowledge in terms other than its reduction to sensory experience. By taking a nativistic view—that much knowledge is inborn—Kant revived the Platonist view that had been losing ground since the time of Descartes.

John Stuart Mill (1806–1873) was disturbed by the contention of the early associationists, such as Hobbes and Locke, that complex ideas are nothing more than combinations of simple ideas. Although he remained an empiricist and an associationist, he made a very important revision in the position taken by other associationists. Accepting the notion that complex ideas are made up of simpler ideas, Mill added the notion that some simple ideas combine into a new totality that may bear little resemblance to its parts. For example, if we combine blue, red, and green lights, we get white. In other words, Mill believed that *the whole is different from the sum of its parts.* Thus, Mill modified the empiricist contention that all ideas reflect sensory stimulation. For him, when some ideas combine, they produce an idea that is unlike any of the elemental ideas that make up the emergent idea.

OTHER HISTORICAL INFLUENCES ON LEARNING THEORY

Thomas Reid (1710–1796) also opposed the elementism of the empiricists but his opposition took a different form than that of John Stuart Mill. Like Kant, Reid believed that the mind has powers of its own, which strongly influence how we perceive the world. He hypothesized twenty-seven faculties of the mind, most of which were thought to be innate. The belief in the existence of such faculties in the mind was later called **faculty psychology.** The faculty psychologist is a mixture of nativism, rationalism, and empiricism. Kant, for example, explored sensory experience (empiricism) in order to discover categories of thought (rationalism) that were innate (nativism).

Reid argued that Hume's contention that we cannot know anything directly about the physical world was ridiculous. Hergenhahn (1997) summarizes Reid's position:

> Reid argued that because all humans were convinced of the existence of physical reality, it must exist…. If Hume's logic caused him [Hume] to conclude that we could never know the physical world, then, said Reid, something was wrong with Hume's logic. We can trust our impressions of the physical world because it makes *common sense* to do so. We are naturally endowed with the abilities to deal with and make sense out of the world. (pp. 166–167)

Reid gives examples of what life would be like if we denied the fact that our senses accurately represent physical reality: "I resolve not to believe my senses. I break my nose against a post…. I step into a dirty kennel; and after twenty such wise and rational actions, I am taken up and clapped into a madhouse" (Beanblossom & Lehrer, 1983, p. 86). Reid's contention that reality is as we perceive it is called **naive realism** (Henle, 1986).

Franz Joseph Gall (1758–1828) carried faculty psychology several steps further. First, he assumed that the faculties were housed in specific locations in the brain. Second, he believed that the faculties of the mind did not exist to the same extent in every individual. Third, he believed that if a faculty was well developed, there would be a bump or protrusion on the part of the skull corresponding to the place in the brain that houses that faculty. Likewise, if a faculty was poorly developed, a hollow or depression would be found on the skull. Armed with these assumptions, Gall set out to examine the shape of people's skulls. He developed an elaborate chart showing what faculties the various parts of the skull correspond to. Using this chart and analyzing the bumps and hollows of a person's skull, Gall and his followers believed they could tell which of the person's faculties were the most highly developed and which were underdeveloped. This analysis of mental attributes by examining the characteristics of the skull is called **phrenology.** A typical phrenology chart is shown in Figure 3–2.

Phrenology had two lasting effects on psychology, one good and one questionable. First, it led to research designed to discover the function of various parts of

Affective Faculties   *Intellectual Faculties*

PROPENSITIES
? Desire to live
• Alimentiveness
1 Destructiveness
2 Amativeness
3 Philoprogenitiveness
4 Adhesiveness
5 Inhabitiveness
6 Combativeness
7 Secretiveness
8 Acquisitiveness
9 Constructiveness

SENTIMENTS
10 Cautiousness
11 Approbativeness
12 Self-Esteem
13 Benevolence
14 Reverence
15 Firmness
16 Conscientiousness
17 Hope
18 Marvelousness
19 Ideality
20 Mirthfulness
21 Imitation

PERCEPTIVE
22 Individuality
23 Configuration
24 Size
25 Weight and
   resistance
26 Coloring
27 Locality
28 Order
29 Calculation
30 Eventuality
31 Time
32 Tune
33 Language

REFLECTIVE
34 Comparison
35 Causality

FIGURE 3–2 A phrenology chart. (Suggested by G. Spurzheim, *Phrenology, or the Doctrine of Mental Phenomena.* Boston: Marsh, Capen & Lyon, 1834.)

the brain. It was this very research, however, that disproved the assumptions on which phrenology was based. Second, many faculty psychologists believed that the faculties became stronger with practice, just like the biceps become stronger with practice. For this reason the faculty psychologists were said to have taken a "mental muscle" approach to learning. Learning, to them, meant strengthening faculties by practicing those traits associated with them. One could improve one's reasoning abilities, for example, by formally studying such topics as mathematics or Latin. The belief that a particular course of training would strengthen certain faculties was called **formal discipline,** a concept that provides one answer to the question of how learning transfers from one situation to another. We will have more to say about the transfer of training when we discuss E. L. Thorndike in Chapter 4. It should be noted here, however, that the idea of formal discipline, based on faculty psychology, dominated school curricula for many years and was used to justify requiring students to study intensely the most difficult topics available, such as mathematics and Latin, regardless of their vocational aspirations. One suspects that many present-day educators still believe in the benefits of formal discipline. Indeed, there is some evidence that formal discipline is effective (see e.g., Lehman, Lempert, & Nisbett, 1988).

Charles Darwin (1809–1882) supported the notion of biological evolution with so much evidence that it finally had to be taken seriously. The Church bitterly opposed Darwin's notions. In fact, Darwin himself was so worried about the impact his findings would have on religious thought that he wished to have his research published only after his death.

The final acceptance of evolutionary theory by the scientific community marked a blow to the collective ego of humans equal only to the one dealt by Copernicus and the future one dealt by Freud. Evolution restored the continuity between humans and other animals that had been denied for centuries. No longer was there the clear-cut distinction between man and other animals that had been the cornerstone of so many philosophies, such as those of Plato, Aristotle, Descartes, and Kant. If we are biologically related to the "lower" animals, do they also have minds, souls, and innate categories of thought, and if so, to what extent? Obviously, animal research was now to take on a much greater respectability. Descartes's thinking tolerated animal research as a way of finding out how the human body works, but from his point of view, it could not disclose anything concerning the human mind. Until Darwin, humans' behavior commonly was thought to be rational and animal behavior to be instinctive. With Darwin, that handy dichotomy was lost. Many questions arose, such as "Can an animal's behavior also be rational, at least in part?" "Can humans' behavior be instinctive, at least in part?" A mind resulting from a long evolutionary process is looked at differently than a mind that is divinely implanted into the body by God.

Darwin changed all thoughts about human nature. Human beings were now looked on as a combination of their biological heritage and their life's experiences. The pure associationism of the empiricists was now coupled with physiology in a search for the underlying mechanisms of thought, and the function of behavior as a way of adjusting to the environment was studied intensely. Individuality was appreciated as never before and its study became popular. This new attitude was exemplified by Darwin's cousin, *Francis Galton* (1822–1911), who devised a number of methods, such as the questionnaire, free association, and the method of correlation, specifically designed to measure individual differences. Probably the most famous person directly influenced by Darwin was *Sigmund Freud* (1856–1939), who explored the problems of the human animal attempting to live in a civilized world.

Such philosophic questions as "How do humans think?" and "What can humans know?" changed to "How do humans adjust to their environment?" and "Given certain circumstances, what do humans *do*?" Thus, the mood was set for a science of behavior. If human behavior was now to be studied like any other aspect of nature, the experimental approach that had been so successful in the physical sciences could be applied to the study of the human being.

Hermann Ebbinghaus (1850–1909) is said to have emancipated psychology from philosophy by demonstrating that the "higher mental processes" of learning and memory could be studied experimentally. Rather than assuming that associa-

Hermann Ebbinghaus. (From *Great Experiments in Psychology,* p. 102a, by H. E. Garrett, 1930, New York: The Century Company.)

tions had already been formed, and studying them through reflection, as had been the case for many centuries, Ebbinghaus studied the associative process as it was taking place. Thus, he could systematically study the conditions that influenced the development of associations. He was an extremely careful researcher and repeated his experiments over a period of many years before he finally published his results in 1885. Many of his conclusions concerning the nature of learning and memory are still accepted.

An important principle of association was the law of frequency, which Ebbinghaus focused on in his research. The law of frequency stated that the more frequently an experience occurred, the more easily the experience was recalled. In other words, memory gains strength through repetition. To test this notion, Ebbinghaus needed material that was not contaminated by the subject's previous experience. To control for the effects of previous experience, he invented his now famous **nonsense material.** Nonsense material consists of syllables containing a vowel between two consonants (e.g., QAW, JIG, XUW, CEW, or TIB). Contrary to what is commonly believed, it was not the syllables in Ebbinghaus's research that were nonsense. The syllables he used often resembled words or actually were words. It was the relationships among the syllables that were meaningless. Thus we use the term *nonsense material* instead of *nonsense syllables.* The syllables were usually arranged in groups of twelve, although he varied group size to measure rate of learning as a function of the amount of material to be learned. He found that as the number of syllables to be learned became larger, it took a greater amount of time to learn them. Ebbinghaus was the first to demonstrate this fact that sounds so obvious to us today.

Using himself as a subject, Ebbinghaus looked at each syllable in the group for a fraction of a second and then paused fifteen seconds before starting through the group again. He continued in this manner until "complete mastery" had occurred, which meant he could recite each syllable in the group without making a mistake. At that point, he noted how many exposures to the group of syllables it took before mastery was reached. Also, he plotted the number of errors made as a function of successive exposures to the group of syllables, thus creating psychology's first learning curve.

At various intervals following original "mastery," Ebbinghaus went back and relearned a group of syllables. He noted the number of trials it took to relearn a group of syllables and subtracted that number from the number of exposures it took to learn the list originally. The difference was called **savings.** He plotted savings as a function of time elapsed since original learning, thus creating psychology's first retention curve. His graph indicated that the rate of forgetting is very fast for the first few hours following a learning experience and very slow thereafter. He also found that *overlearning* reduces the rate of forgetting considerably. That is, if he continued to expose himself attentively to a group of syllables even after they had been mastered, they would be retained much longer than if his learning stopped with only one perfect recitation of the syllables.

Ebbinghaus also studied the effects of what is now called meaningfulness on learning and retention. He found, for example, that it took nine readings to memorize eighty syllables of material from Byron's *Don Juan* but about nine times as many exposures to learn eighty of his syllables. Not only was the learning rate much faster for the more meaningful material but retention was far superior also.

Ebbinghaus's research revolutionized the study of the associative process. Instead of hypothesizing about the law of frequency, he demonstrated how it functioned. Ebbinghaus brought the "higher mental processes" into the laboratory, where they have been ever since.

PSYCHOLOGY'S EARLY SCHOOLS

Voluntarism

Psychology's first school was **voluntarism** and it was founded by **Wilhelm Maximilian Wundt** (1832–1920), who followed in the German rationalist tradition. Wundt's goals were to study consciousness as it was immediately experienced and to study the products of consciousness such as various cultural achievements. Wundt believed that

immediate consciousness could be studied scientifically, that is, as a systematic function of environmental stimulation. One of his experimental goals was to discover the elements of thought, those basic elements of which all thoughts consist. Wundt founded what is generally considered to be psychology's first experimental laboratory in 1879, and its major goals were to discover the elements of thought and the basic processes that govern conscious experience.

For Wundt, however, experimental psychology was of limited usefulness in studying the human mind. The most important aspects of the mind could be studied only indirectly by studying its products, such as religion, morals, myths, art, social customs, language, and law. These products of the mind could not be studied experimentally but only through naturalistic observation. That is, they could only be studied as they occurred historically or in the process of living.

Wilhelm Wundt. (Courtesy of Archives of the History of American Psychology, University of Akron, Ohio.)

Wundt spent the last 20 years of his life writing his ten-volume *Völkerpsychologie* (group or cultural psychology), in which he described his observations concerning the cultural behaviors mentioned previously.

In accordance with the German rationalistic tradition Wundt was primarily interested in the human will. He noted that humans could selectively attend to whatever elements of thought they wanted, causing those elements to be perceived clearly. Wundt referred to this selective attention as **apperception.** Also, the elements of thought could be willfully arranged in any number of combinations, a process Wundt referred to as **creative synthesis.** It was because of Wundt's emphasis on will that his school of psychology is called voluntarism.

Structuralism

When aspects of Wundt's voluntarism were transferred by his students to the United States, they were significantly modified and became the school of **structuralism. Edward Titchener** (1867–1927) created the school of structuralism at Cornell University. Structuralism, like the experimental aspect of Wundt's voluntarism, was concerned with the systematic study of human consciousness, and it too sought the elements of thought. In analyzing the elements of thought the major tool used by the voluntarists and the structuralists was **introspection.**

Experimental subjects had to be carefully trained not to misuse the introspective technique. They were trained to report their **immediate experience** as they perceived an object and not to report their interpretations of that object. In other words, Wundt and Titchener were interested in the subject's "raw" experiences but not in what they had learned about those experiences. In that sense, learning was looked on as more of a hindrance than a topic worthy of study for itself. When shown an apple, for example, the subject was supposed to report hues, brightnesses, and spatial characteristics rather than labeling the object as an apple. Naming the object of experience during an introspective report was called a **stimulus error,** for example, calling an apple an apple. In other words, the subject is reporting a compound idea rather than simple ones, and therefore the building blocks of the mind remain obscure. Clearly, the voluntarists and the structuralists were more interested in the contents of the mind than with the origins of those contents.

A search for the elements of thought was essentially all that voluntarism and structuralism had in common. In explaining how the elements combine to form complex thoughts, voluntarism stressed the will, apperception, and creative synthesis—following in the rationalistic tradition. In other words, voluntarists postulated an active mind. In their explanation of the formation of complex thoughts, structuralists stressed the laws of association—following in the empiricistic tradition. In other words they postulated a passive mind. Therefore, to equate voluntarism and structuralism, as is often done, is incorrect.

As a school of psychology, structuralism was short-lived and died within Titchener's own lifetime. There were many reasons for the death of structuralism, but the most important one was probably the rising popularity of functionalism, which we will consider below. The structuralists made a rather sterile attempt to use the methods of science to substantiate an ancient philosophical belief. That is, that simple ideas are combined into complex ones via the laws of association. It failed to take into consideration one of the most important developments in human history—the doctrine of evolution. As the importance of the evolutionary process became more apparent, increased attention was given to the organism's adaptation to its environment. Also, the doctrine of evolution made the study of "lower" animals a legitimate way of learning about people. Structuralism ignored both of these trends. It also ignored the growing evidence for the existence of unconscious processes that was being provided by researchers such as Freud. Finally, the structuralists opposed applied psychology, which was growing in popularity. They believed that knowledge concerning consciousness should be sought for its own sake without concern for its usefulness. For these and other reasons, structuralism came and went. It has been said that perhaps the most important thing about structuralism was that it appeared, it was tried, and it failed.

Functionalism

Functionalism also originated in the United States and initially coexisted with structuralism. Although functionalist beliefs diverged, their emphasis was always the same—*the utility of consciousness and behavior in adjusting to the environment.* Clearly, the functionalists were strongly influenced by Darwin's doctrine of evolution.

The founder of the functionalist movement is usually thought to be **William James** (1842–1910). In his highly influential book, *The Principles of Psychology* (1890),

William James. (Courtesy of Archives of the History of American Psychology, University of Akron, Ohio.)

James took the structuralists to task. Consciousness, he said, cannot be reduced into elements. Rather, consciousness functions as a unity whose purpose is to allow the organism to adjust to its environment. The "stream of consciousness" changes as total experience changes. Such a process cannot be reduced to elements because a person's conscious processes as a whole are involved with adaptation to his or her environment. The most important thing about consciousness, as far as James was concerned, was that it had a purpose. James also wrote about the importance of studying psychology scientifically. He emphasized that humans were both rational and irrational (emotional). He pointed out the importance of understanding the biological foundations of mental events and urged the study of lower animals to learn more about humans. Many of James's ideas are still current. It should be noted that James had a significant influence on psychology, both through his writings and through his ability as a teacher to inspire. Many consider James to be one of the greatest psychologists of all times.

In addition to James, two of the most influential members of the functionalist movement were John Dewey (1859–1952) and James R. Angell (1869–1949). In Dewey's (1896) famous article "The Reflex Arc Concept in Psychology," he attacked the growing tendency in psychology to isolate a stimulus-response relationship for study. He argued that isolating such a unit for study was a total waste of time since the purpose of behavior is overlooked. The goal for psychology should be to study the significance of behavior in adapting to the environment. The main contribution of Angell was that he built up a department of psychology at the University of Chicago around the functionalistic point of view.

The main contribution the functionalists made to learning theory is that they studied the relationship of consciousness to the environment rather than studying it as an isolated phenomenon. They opposed the introspective technique of the structuralists because it was elementistic, not because it studied consciousness. The functionalists were not opposed to studying mental processes but insisted that they should always be studied in relationship to survival. Unlike the structuralists, the functionalists were very interested in applied psychology. Most functionalists believed that one of their major goals should be to furnish information that could be used to improve the human condition.

Behaviorism

The founder of **behaviorism** was **John B. Watson** (1878–1958), who noted that consciousness could only be studied through the process of introspection, a notoriously unreliable research tool. Because consciousness could not be reliably studied, he said, it should not be studied at all. To be scientific, psychology needed a subject matter that was stable enough to be reliably measured, and that subject matter was behavior. Watson felt that the main concern for the psychologist should be with behavior and how it varies with experience. Leave the study of consciousness to the philosophers, he said. Thus, what was the focal point of epistemological inquiry for thousands of years was looked on by the behaviorist as only a hindrance in the study of human behavior.

No more introspection, no more talk of instinctive behavior, and no more attempts to study the human conscious or unconscious mind. Behavior is what we can see and therefore behavior is what we study. According to Watson (1913),

John Broadus Watson. (From *Psychologies of 1925,* 1926, Worchester, MA: Clark University Press.)

Psychology as the behaviorist views it is a purely objective experimental branch of natural science. Its theoretical goal is the prediction and control of behavior. Introspection forms no essential part of its methods, nor is the scientific value of its data dependent upon the readiness with which they lend themselves to interpretation in terms of consciousness. The behaviorist, in his efforts to get a unitary scheme of animal response, recognizes no dividing line between man and brute. The behavior of man, with all its refinement and complexity, forms only a part of the behaviorist's total scheme of investigation…. (p. 158)

Elsewhere Watson said (Watson & McDougall, 1929),

The behaviorist cannot find consciousness in the test tube of his science. He finds no evidence anywhere for a stream of consciousness, not even for one so convincing as that described by William James. He does, however, find convincing proof of an ever-widening stream of behavior. (p. 26)

Watson was enthusiastic about his work and its implications. He saw behaviorism as a means of stripping ignorance and superstition from human existence, thereby paving the way for more rational, meaningful living. Understanding the principles of behavior, he thought, was the first step toward that kind of life. Watson (1925) said,

I think behaviorism does lay a foundation for saner living. It ought to be a science that prepares men and women for understanding the first principles of their own behavior. It ought to make men and women eager to rearrange their own lives, and especially eager to prepare themselves to bring up their own children in a healthy way. I wish I had time more fully to describe this, to picture to you the kind of rich and wonderful individual we should make of every healthy child; if only we could let it shape itself properly and then provide for it a universe unshackled by legendary folk lore of happenings thousands of years ago; unhampered by disgraceful political history; free of foolish customs and conventions which have no significance in themselves; yet which hem the individual in like taut steel bands. (p. 248)

Clearly, Watson was a rebel. He took the various objective approaches to the study of psychology that were appearing here and there, and through his forceful writing and speaking, organized them into a new school of psychology. Unfortunately, Watson's career as a professional psychologist was cut short when he was asked to leave Johns Hopkins University because of marital troubles leading to divorce. The same year he left the university he married Rosalie Rayner, with whom he did the famous study with the infant named Albert (we will discuss this study in Chapter 7), and went into the advertising business. From that point on, instead of writing in professional journals, Watson published his ideas in *McCall's, Harper's,* and *Collier's* magazines.

Watson never wavered from his behaviorist outlook, and in 1936 he had the following to say about the position he took in 1912:

I still believe as firmly as ever in the general behavioristic position I took overtly in 1912. I think it has influenced psychology. Strangely enough, I think it has temporarily slowed down psychology because the older instructors would not accept it wholeheartedly, and consequently they failed to present it convincingly to their classes. The youngsters did not get a fair presentation, hence they are not embarking wholeheartedly upon a behavioristic career, and yet they will no longer accept the teachings of James, Titchener, and Angell. I honestly think that psychology has been sterile for several years. We need younger instructors who will teach objective psychology with no reference to the mythology most of us present-day psychologists have been brought up upon. When this day comes, psychology will have a renaissance greater than that which occurred in science in the Middle Ages. I believe as firmly as ever in the future of behaviorism—behaviorism as a companion of zoology, physiology, psychiatry, and physical chemistry. (p. 231)

Of course, the behaviorist's main point was that behavior should be studied because it could be dealt with directly. Mental events should be ignored because they could not be dealt with directly. Behaviorism had a profound effect on American learning theory. In fact, most of the theories of learning in this book can be thought of as behavioristic. It is possible, however, to make subdivisions within the behavioristic camp. Some theories concentrate on behavior related to an organism's survival. Such behavioristic theories can be called functional theories. Other behavioristic theories are less concerned with adaptive behavior and explain all learned behavior in terms of the laws of association. Such theories tend to treat functional and nonfunctional behavior in the same way. Thus, under the general heading of behaviorism we can list both functionalistic and associationistic theories. Whether a behavioristic theory is labeled as functionalistic or associationistic depends on the kind of behavior the theory concentrates on and how the theory explains the origins of that behavior. Watson had two lasting effects on psychology. First, he changed psychology's goal from attempting to understand consciousness to the prediction and control of behavior. Second, he made behavior psychology's subject matter. Ever since Watson, essentially all psychologists study behavior. Even cognitive psychologists use behavior to index postulated cognitive events. For this reason it can be said that all contemporary psychologists are behaviorists.

SUMMARY AND OVERVIEW

From the brief history presented in this chapter, it can be seen that learning theory has a rich and diverse heritage. As a result of this heritage, numerous viewpoints concerning the learning process exist today. In Chapter 2, we referred to a point of view shared by a substantial number of scientists as a paradigm. At least four such points of view can be identified among modern theories of learning.

One paradigm we will refer to as *functionalistic*. This paradigm reflects the influence of Darwinism in that it stresses the relationship between learning and adjustment to the environment. A second paradigm we will refer to as *associationistic* since it studies the learning process in terms of the laws of association. This paradigm originated with Aristotle and was perpetuated and elaborated on by Locke, Berkeley, and Hume. The third paradigm we shall label *cognitive* since it stresses the cognitive nature of learning. This paradigm originated with Plato and came to us through Descartes, Kant, and the faculty psychologists. The fourth paradigm is referred to as *neurophysiological* since it attempts to isolate the neurophysiological correlates of such things as learning, perception, thinking, and intelligence. This paradigm represents a current manifestation of a line of investigation that started with Descartes's separation of the mind and the body. The current goal of most neurophysiological psychologists, however, is to reunite mental and physiological processes.

These paradigms should be viewed as only very crude categories since it is difficult to find any theory of learning that fits unambiguously into any one of them. We will place a theory in a particular paradigm because of its major emphasis. However, within almost every theory, certain aspects of other paradigms can be identified. For example, even though Hull's theory is listed under the functionalistic paradigm below, it relies heavily on associationistic ideas. Similarly, Piaget's theory is listed under the cognitive paradigm only because of its major emphasis. Piaget's theory, as much influenced by Darwinism as any other, has a great deal in common with the theories listed under the functionalistic paradigm. Tolman's theory is also difficult to categorize since it has both functionalistic and cognitive elements. We list it as a cognitive theory only because the main emphasis of the theory is cognitive. Likewise, Hebb's theory, although its major emphasis is neurophysiological, also stresses cognitive events. In fact, Hebb's theory can be looked on as an effort to describe the neurophysiological correlates of cognitive experiences.

With these reservations in mind, the major theories of learning covered in this book are organized as follows:

Functionalistic Paradigm	**Cognitive Paradigm**
Thorndike	Gestalt theory
Skinner	Piaget
Hull	Tolman
Associationistic Paradigm	Bandura
Pavlov	Norman
Guthrie	**Neurophysiological Paradigm**
Estes	Hebb

Which paradigm is correct? Probably all of them. No doubt they all emphasize certain truths about the learning process and ignore others. At this point in history, it appears that to obtain the most accurate picture of the learning process, one must be willing to view it from a number of different angles. It is hoped that this book will allow the student to do just that.

DISCUSSION QUESTIONS

1. Compare Plato's theory of knowledge with that of Aristotle. Include a definition of the terms rationalism, nativism, and empiricism in your answer.
2. Summarize Descartes's influence on psychology.
3. Briefly describe what Kant meant by an "innate category of thought."
4. Summarize Reid's argument against Hume's skepticism.
5. Discuss phrenology and the theory of the mind on which it was based.
6. Discuss Darwin's influence on learning theory.

7. What was the significance of the work of Ebbinghaus as far as the history of learning theory is concerned?
8. Summarize the important features of the schools of voluntarism, structuralism, functionalism, and behaviorism.
9. What caused the downfall of structuralism?
10. What were the lasting effects of Watson's behaviorism on contemporary psychology?

KEY TERMS

apperception   According to Wundt, the clear perception that results from the willful force of one's attention.

Aristotle   (384–322 B.C.) Because he believed sensory experience to be the basis of all knowledge, he was the first major empiricist. He also proposed the laws of similarity, contrast, contiguity, and frequency to explain how ideas became associated with other ideas.

associationism   The philosophical belief that the relationships among ideas are explained by the laws of association.

behaviorism   A school of psychology, founded by J. B. Watson, that completely rejected the study of consciousness. To be scientific, psychology needed a subject matter that could be reliably measured, and according to the behaviorist, that subject matter was behavior.

Berkeley, George (1685–1753)   He said we can have no direct knowledge of the external world; we experience only the ideas that it causes us to have. His belief that nothing exists unless it is perceived led to his famous dictum "to be is to be perceived." What we call external reality is God's perception.

creative synthesis   According to Wundt, the ability to arrange willfully the elements of thought into any number of configurations.

Darwin, Charles (1809–1882)   He demonstrated the ability of behavior in adjusting to the environment and the fact that human development is biologically continuous with that of nonhuman animals. Both observations had a profound and lasting effect on psychology, especially on learning theory.

Descartes, René (1596–1650)   He postulated that the mind and the body were governed by different laws. The mind was free and possessed only by humans, whereas the body was mechanical and its functions were the same for both humans and other animals. He was responsible for creating the duality of mind and body, stimulating interest in physiological and comparative psychology, and reviving Plato's belief in innate ideas.

Ebbinghaus, Hermann (1850–1909)   He was the first to study learning and memory experimentally. Demonstrating how the law of frequency worked in the forming of new associations, he invented nonsense material to control for previous experience in a learning situation.

empiricism   The philosophical belief that sensory experience is the basis of all knowledge.

epistemology   The study of the nature of knowledge.

faculty psychology   The belief that the mind contains certain powers or faculties.

formal discipline   The belief held by some faculty psychologists that specific training can strengthen a specific faculty. For example, practicing being friendly would strengthen the friendliness faculty, thereby making the person more friendly.

functionalism   The primary goal of the functionalist was to discover how mental and behavioral processes are related to an organism's adaptation to its environment. Members of this school were strongly influenced by Darwin's writings.

Gall, Franz Joseph (1758–1828)   He believed that a person's strong and weak faculties could be detected by analyzing the bumps and depressions on the person's skull. This system of analysis was called phrenology.

Hobbes, Thomas (1588–1679)   He reasserted Aristotle's doctrine of associationism and also suggested that experiences of pleasure and pain influence how associations are formed.

Hume, David (1711–1776)   He said we can know nothing with certainty. All ideas are products of the mind and do not necessarily relate to a reality outside of the mind. Therefore, the so-called natural laws are more the result of "habits of thought" than of any lawfulness in nature.

immediate experience   The raw psychological experience that was the object of introspective analysis; experience that was not contaminated by interpretation of any kind.

innate category of thought   According to Kant, a genetically determined faculty of the mind that molds our cognitive experiences by giving them greater structure and meaning than they otherwise would have.

innate ideas   Ideas that are not derived from experience, but rather are thought to be inherited as part of the mind.

introspection   The reporting of one's own mental events while experiencing a certain object or situation; the technique employed by the structuralists to study the structure of the mind.

James, William (1842–1910)   The founder of the functionalist movement. He attacked the way that the structuralists used the introspective method to search for the elements of thought. Consciousness, he felt, could not be subdivided since it acted as a functional unit that was constantly changing. The most important thing about consciousness is that it aids human survival. He also encouraged psychology to embrace the scientific method, to search for the physiological correlates of mental processes, and to investigate human emotions as well as the intellect.

Kant, Immanuel (1724–1804)   He believed that the mind was active and not passive, as the empiricist-associationists had assumed. The mind has innate powers or faculties which act upon sense impressions and give them meaning.

laws of association   Principles such as similarity, contrast, contiguity, and frequency that are supposed to explain how one idea is related to another or how one experience elicits ideas related to it.

Locke, John (1632–1704)   He strongly opposed the notion of innate ideas and suggested that at birth the mind was a tabula rasa, or a blank tablet. He said "there is nothing in the mind that is not first in the senses." He distinguished between primary qualities, the physical characteristics of an object, and secondary qualities, the psychological experience caused by a physical object, such as the experience of color or taste.

Mill, John Stuart (1806–1873)   An associationist who disagreed with his fellow associationists' contention that complex ideas are nothing more than a compound of simpler ones. He felt that ideas could fuse together and the fusion could create an idea distinctly different from the simple ideas that made it up.

naive realism   The belief that physical reality is as we perceive it.

nativism   The philosophical belief that a mental attribute is inherited and therefore is independent of experience.

nonsense material   Material with little or no meaning invented by Ebbinghaus to control for previous experience in a learning situation.

phrenology   The study of the location of bumps and depressions on a person's skull in order to determine his or her strong and weak faculties.

Plato (427–347 B.C.)   He proposed a reminiscence theory of knowledge where knowing was explained as remembering the pure knowledge that the soul had experienced before entering the body. Plato was the first major rationalist and the first nativist.

Pythagoreans   Followers of Pythagoras who believed abstractions, such as numbers, were just as real as physical objects and that these abstractions could influence the physical world. Such beliefs had a strong influence on the development of Plato's theory of knowledge.

rationalism   The philosophical belief that the mind must become actively involved before knowledge can be attained.

Reid, Thomas (1710–1796)   He believed that any philosophical position that denied that we can reliably experience the physical world was ridiculous. Reid argued that we can believe that our sense impressions, and the ideas that they give rise to, accurately reflect the physical world because it makes common sense to do so.

reminiscence theory of knowledge   The belief held by Plato that all knowledge is present in the human soul at birth; thus to know is to remember the contents of the soul.

savings   The difference in the time it takes to relearn something as compared to the amount of time it took to learn it originally; a measure of retention used by Ebbinghaus.

stimulus error   The error of naming an object while introspecting about it instead of reporting one's immediate experience.

structuralism   Founded by Titchener, the goal of the school of structuralism was to discover the basic elements of thought by using the technique of introspection and to explain how those elements are held together by the laws of association.

Titchener, Edward (1867–1927)   Founder of the school of structuralism.

voluntarism   The school of psychology founded by Wilhelm Wundt that emphasized willful attention (apperception) and the willful arrangement of conscious elements (creative synthesis). Wundt believed that experimental psychology had only limited usefulness and that the higher mental processes could only be studied indirectly by the naturalistic observation of human cultural behavior.

Watson, John B. (1878–1958)   Founder of the school of behaviorism. According to Watson, the only reliable, observable, and measurable subject matter available to psychologists is behavior, and therefore behavior is all that psychologists should study.

Wundt, Wilhelm Maximilian (1832–1920)   Founder of the school of voluntarism; also founded psychology's first psychological laboratory in Leipzig, Germany, in 1879.

Chapter 4

EDWARD LEE THORNDIKE

It is fitting that we begin our discussion of the major learning theorists with Edward L. Thorndike (1874–1949), perhaps the greatest learning theorist of all time. He did pioneer work not only in learning theory but also in educational practices, verbal behavior, comparative psychology, intelligence testing, the nature-nurture problem, transfer of training, and the application of quantitative measures to sociopsychological problems (e.g., he developed scales with which to compare the quality of life in different cities). It may be of interest to note that Thorndike began this latter project, as well as many others, when he was more than 60 years old.

His research started with the study of mental telepathy in young children (which he explained as the unconscious detection on the part of the child of minute movements made by the experimenter). His later experiments involved chicks, cats, rats, dogs, fish, monkeys, and finally adult humans. He wanted to use apes also but could not afford to buy and maintain them.

Thorndike's scientific productivity was almost unbelievable. At his death in 1949 his bibliography comprised 507 books, monographs, and journal articles. Always attempting to measure everything, Thorndike reports in his autobiography that up to the age of 60 he had spent well over 20,000 hours reading and studying scientific books and journals—this in spite of the fact that he was primarily a researcher rather than a scholar.

Thorndike was born in Williamsburg, Massachusetts, in 1874, and was the second son of a Methodist minister. He claims never to have seen or heard the word *psychology* until he was a junior at Wesleyan University. At that time he read William James's *Principles of Psychology* (1890) and was deeply impressed. Later, when he went to Harvard and took a course from James, they became good friends. When Thorndike's landlady forbade him to continue hatching chicks in his bedroom, James tried to get him laboratory space on the Harvard campus. When this failed, James allowed Thorndike to continue his studies in the basement of his home—much to the dismay of James's wife and to the delight of his children.

After two years at Harvard, where Thorndike earned a living by tutoring students, he accepted a fellowship at Columbia, working under James McKeen Cattell. Although he carried two of his "most educated" chicks with him to New York, he soon switched from chicks to cats. His years of animal research was summarized in his doctoral dissertation, entitled, "Animal Intelligence: An Experimental Study of the Associative Process in Animals," which was published in 1898 and expanded and republished as *Animal Intelligence* (1911). The fundamental ideas put forth in these documents permeate all of Thorndike's writings and, in fact, most of

Edward L. Thorndike. (From *Psychologies of 1925,* 1926, Worcester, MA: Clark University Press.)

learning theory. The extent of Thorndike's influence is indicated by the following quotation from Tolman (1938):

> The psychology of animal learning—not to mention that of child learning—has been and still is primarily a matter of agreeing or disagreeing with Thorndike, or trying in minor ways to improve upon him. Gestalt psychologists, conditioned-reflex psychologists, sign-Gestalt psychologists—all of us here in America seem to have taken Thorndike, overtly or covertly, as our starting point. And we have felt very smart and pleased with ourselves if we could show that we have, even in some very minor way, developed new little wrinkles of our own. (p. 11)

ANIMAL RESEARCH BEFORE THORNDIKE

Descartes's contention that the bodies of both humans and nonhuman animals functioned according to the same mechanical principles did much to stimulate the anatomical investigations of nonhuman animals. It was Darwin, however, who suggested that humans and nonhumans were similar in all respects: anatomically, emotionally, and cognitively. Darwin's (1872) *The Expression of Emotions in Man and Animals* is generally considered the first text on comparative psychology. Not long after Darwin published the aforementioned book, his friend **George John Romanes** (1848–1894) published *Animal Intelligence* (1882), *Mental Evolution in Animals* (1884), and *Mental Evolution in Man* (1885). The evidence that Romanes offered to support the continuity of intelligent and emotional behavior from lower animals to humans was largely anecdotal and was often characterized by **anthropomorphizing,** or attributing human thought processes to nonhuman animals. For example, Romanes attributed the emotions of anger, fear, and jealousy to fish; affection, sympathy, and pride to birds; and slyness and reasoning to dogs. The following is one of Romanes's (1882, 1897) anecdotes:

> One day the cat and the parrot had a quarrel. I think the cat had upset Polly's food, or something of that kind; however, they seemed all right again. An hour or so later, Polly was standing on the edge of the table; she called out in a tone of extreme affection, "Puss, Puss, come then—come then, Pussy." Pussy went and looked up innocently enough. Polly with her beak seized a basin of milk standing by, and tipped the basin and all its contents over the cat; then chuckled diabolically, of course broke the basin, and half drowned the cat. (p. 277)

In an effort to describe animal behavior more objectively, **Conwy Lloyd Morgan** (1842–1936) gave the following advice to animal researchers in his book *An Introduction to Comparative Psychology* (1891). The advice became known as **Morgan's canon:** "In no case may we interpret an action as the outcome of the exercise of a higher psychical faculty, if it can be interpreted as the outcome of the exercise of one which stands lower in the psychological scale" (p. 53). As Hergenhahn (1997) points out, Morgan's canon is often misinterpreted as a warning against speculating about thoughts or feelings in nonhuman animals. In fact, Morgan did believe that nonhumans have cognitive processes. His canon tells us we cannot assume that human mental process are the same as those experienced by nonhumans and that we should

Margaret Floy Washburn. (Courtesy of Archives of the History of American Psychology, University of Akron, Ohio.)

not attribute a behavior to a complex cognitive process when it can be explained with one that is less complex.

Although Morgan's explanation of non-human animal behavior was much more parsimonious than that of Romanes, it still depended on naturalistic observation. That is, Morgan was still describing the behavior of animals as it occurred in the natural environment. For example, he described in great detail how his dog had learned to lift the latch of his garden gate, thereby escaping confinement. Morgan's research was an improvement over what had preceded it, but additional refinements were needed; animal behavior had to be studied systematically under controlled laboratory conditions. In other words, animal behavior had to be studied scientifically.

Margaret Floy Washburn (1871–1939), the first woman to earn the Ph.D. degree in psychology, took the study of nonhumans one step closer to the laboratory. Washburn's book, *The Animal Mind,* was first published in 1908 and new editions appeared regularly until 1936. In this text, Washburn reviewed and examined early sensory, perceptual, and learning experiments involving nonhumans and made inferences about consciousness based on the results of these studies, a strategy not unlike those used by many contemporary cognitive psychologists (Hergenhahn, 1997). Although Washburn drew her conclusions from experimental studies rather than from naturalistic observations, she did not identify, control, and manipulate the important variables related to learning. It was E. L. Thorndike who took this important next step.

MAJOR THEORETICAL NOTIONS

Connectionism

Thorndike called the association between sense impressions and impulses to action a bond or a connection. This marked the first formal attempt to link sensory events to behavior. Earlier brands of associationism attempted to show how *ideas* became linked together; thus Thorndike's approach is quite different and can be regarded as the first modern theory of learning. His emphasis on the functional aspects of behavior is due mainly to the influence of Darwin. In fact, Thorndike's theory can be understood as a combination of associationism, Darwinism, and the methods of science.

Thorndike's concern was not only for stimulus conditions and tendencies to action but also for what held the stimulus and response together. He believed they were connected by a neural bond. His theory is called **connectionism,** the connection referred to being the neural connection between stimuli (S) and responses (R).

Selecting and Connecting

To Thorndike the most basic form of learning was **trial-and-error learning,** or what he originally called **selecting and connecting.** He reached this basic notion through his early experimentation, which involved putting an animal in an apparatus that was arranged so that when the animal made a certain kind of response it escaped. The apparatus shown in Figure 4–1 was a small confining box with a pole sticking up in the middle or a chain hanging from its top. Pushing against the pole or pulling on the chain enabled the animal to escape. Some arrangements, however, required the animal to engage in a complex series of responses before it could escape. Different responses were called for at different times in Thorndike's experiments, but the idea was always the same—the animal had to perform in a certain way before it was allowed to leave the box. The following quotation from *Animal Intelligence* (1911) exemplifies his work with the puzzle box.

> The behavior of all but 11 and 13 was practically the same. When put into the box the cat would show evident signs of discomfort and of an impulse to escape from confinement. It tries to squeeze through any opening; it claws and bites at the bars or wire; it thrusts its paws out through any opening and claws at everything it reaches; it continues its efforts when it strikes anything loose and shaky; it may claw at things within the box. It

FIGURE 4–1   One kind of puzzle box that Thorndike used in his research on learning.

does not pay very much attention to the food outside, but seems simply to strive instinctively to escape from confinement. The vigor with which it struggles is extraordinary. For eight or ten minutes it will claw and bite and squeeze incessantly. With 13, an old cat, and 11, an uncommonly sluggish cat, the behavior was different. They did not struggle vigorously or continually. On some occasions they did not even struggle at all. It was therefore necessary to let them out of the box a few times, feeding them each time. After they thus associate climbing out of the box with getting food, they will try to get out whenever put in. They do not, even then, struggle so vigorously or get so excited as the rest. In either case, whether the impulse to struggle be due to instinctive reaction to confinement or to an association, it is likely to succeed in letting the cat out of the box. The cat that is clawing all over the box in her impulsive struggle will probably claw the string or loop or button so as to open the door. And gradually all the other non-successful impulses will be stamped out and the particular impulse leading to the successful act will be stamped in by the resulting pleasure, until after many trials, the cat will, when put in the box, immediately claw the button or loop in a definite way. (pp. 35–40)

Thus, whether working for a piece of fish or for release from confinement, all his animals learned to do whatever was necessary to escape from the box.

Thorndike plotted the time it took the animal to solve the problem as a function of the number of opportunities the animal had to solve the problem. Every opportunity was a trial, and the trial terminated when the animal hit on the correct solution. A typical graph generated under these circumstances is shown in Figure 4–2. In this basic experimental arrangement Thorndike consistently noted that the time it took to solve the problem (his dependent variable) systematically decreased as the number of trials increased; that is, the more opportunities the animal had, the faster it solved the problem.

Learning Is Incremental, Not Insightful

Noting the slow decrease in time to solution as a function of successive trials, Thorndike concluded that learning was **incremental** rather than **insightful.** In other words, learning occurs in very small systematic steps rather than in huge jumps. He noted that if learning was insightful, the graph would show that the time to solution would remain relatively stable and high while the animal was in the unlearned state. At the point where the animal would gain insight into the solution, the graph would drop very rapidly and would remain at that point for the duration of the experiment. Figure 4–2 also shows how the graph would look if the learning that took place was insightful.

Learning Is Not Mediated by Ideas

Based on his research, Thorndike (1898) also concluded that learning was direct and was not mediated by thinking or reasoning:

> The cat does not look over the situation, much less *think* it over, and then decide what to do. It bursts out at once into the activities which instinct and experience have settled on as suitable reactions to the situation *"confinement when hungry with food outside."* It does not ever in the course of its success realize that such an act brings food and there-

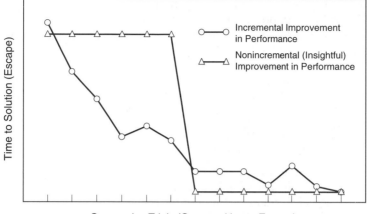

FIGURE 4–2   The figure exemplifies both the incremental improvement in performance observed by Thorndike and the nonincremental (insightful) improvement that Thorndike did not observe.

fore decide to do it and thenceforth do it immediately from decision instead of from impulse. (p. 45)

Elsewhere Thorndike (1911) made the same point with regard to monkeys:

> In discussing these facts we may first of all clear our way of one popular explanation, that this learning was due to "reasoning." If we used the word reasoning in its technical psychological meaning as the function of reaching conclusions by the perception of relations, comparison and inference, if we think of the mental content involved as feelings of relation, perceptions of similarity, general and abstract notions and judgments, we find no evidence of reasoning in the behavior of the monkeys toward the mechanisms used. And this fact nullifies the arguments for reasoning in their case as it did in the case of the dogs and cats. The argument that successful dealings with mechanical contrivances imply that the animal reasoned out the properties of the mechanisms, is destroyed when we find mere selection from their general instinctive activities sufficient to cause success with bars, hooks, loops, etc. There is also positive evidence of the absence of any general function of reasoning. (pp. 184–186)

Thus, following the principle of parsimony, Thorndike rejected reason in favor of direct selection and connection in learning. The demotion of reasoning and of the importance of ideas in learning was the beginning of what was to become the behavioristic movement in America.

All Mammals Learn in the Same Manner

Many were disturbed by Thorndike's insistence that all learning is direct and not mediated by ideas, especially because he also insisted that the learning of all mammals including humans followed the same laws. According to Thorndike, no special processes need to be postulated when one is attempting to explain human learning. The following quotation serves both to point out Thorndike's (1913b) belief that the laws of learning were the same for all animals and to introduce other aspects of his theory, to which we will turn next:

> These simple, semi-mechanical phenomena…which animal learning discloses, are the fundamentals of human learning also. They are, of course, much complicated in the more advanced states of human learning, such as the acquisition of skill with the violin, or of knowledge of the calculus, or of inventiveness in engineering. But it is impossible to understand the subtler and more planful learning of cultural men without clear ideas of the forces which make learning possible in its first form of directly connecting some gross bodily response with a situation immediately present to the senses. Moreover, no matter how subtle, complicated and advanced a form of learning one has to explain, these simple facts—the selection of connections by use and satisfaction and their elimination by disuse and annoyance, multiple reaction, the mind's set as a condition, piecemeal activity of a situation, with prepotency of certain elements in determining the response, response by analogy, and shifting of bonds—will as a matter of fact, still be the main, and perhaps the only, facts needed to explain it. (p. 16)

THORNDIKE BEFORE 1930

Thorndike's thinking about the learning process can be conveniently divided into two parts: one part consisting of his thoughts prior to 1930, and the second part consisting of his views after 1930, when some of his earlier views changed considerably.

The Law of Readiness

The **law of readiness,** proposed in his book *The Original Nature of Man* (Thorndike, 1913b), had three parts, abbreviated as follows:

1. When a conduction unit is ready to conduct, conduction by it is satisfying.
2. For a conduction unit ready to conduct, not to conduct is annoying.
3. When a conduction unit is not ready for conduction and is forced to conduct, conduction by it is annoying.

We notice some terms here whose subjectivity might worry the modern learning theorist. We must remember, however, that Thorndike was writing before the behavioristic movement and that many of the things he discussed had never been systematically analyzed before. It is also important to note that what appear to be subjective terms in Thorndike's writing may not be. For example, what he meant here by "a conduction unit ready to conduct" is merely a preparedness for action or goal directedness. Using current terminology we can restate Thorndike's law of readiness as follows:

1. When someone is ready to perform some act, to do so is satisfying.
2. When someone is ready to perform some act, not to do so is annoying.

3. When someone is not ready to perform some act and is forced to do so, it is annoying.

Generally, we can say that interfering with goal-directed behavior causes frustration and causing someone to do something they do not want to do is also frustrating.

Even terms such as *satisfying* and *annoying* were defined to be acceptable to most modern behaviorists (Thorndike, 1911): "By a satisfying state of affairs is meant one which the animal does nothing to avoid, often doing such things as attain and preserve it. By a discomforting or annoying state of affairs is meant one which the animal commonly avoids and abandons" (p. 245). These definitions of satisfiers and annoyers should be kept in mind throughout our discussion of Thorndike.

The Law of Exercise

Before 1930, Thorndike's theory included the **law of exercise,** which had two parts:

1. Connections between a stimulus and a response are strengthened as they are used. In other words, merely exercising the connection between a stimulating situation and a response strengthens the connection between the two. This is the part of the law of exercise called the **law of use.**
2. Connections between situations and responses are weakened when practice is discontinued or if the neural bond is not used. This is the portion of the law of exercise called the **law of disuse.**

What did Thorndike mean by the strengthening or weakening of a connection? Here again he was ahead of his time, and on this issue he could be speaking today. He defined strengthening as an increase in the probability that a response will be made when the stimulus recurs. If the bond between a stimulus and a response is strengthened, the next time the stimulus occurs there is an increased probability that the response will occur. If the bond is weakened, there is a decreased probability that the next time the stimulus occurs the response will occur. In brief, the law of exercise says we learn by doing and forget by not doing.

The Law of Effect

The **law of effect,** before 1930, refers to the strengthening or weakening of a connection between a stimulus and a response as a result of the consequences of the response. For example, if a response is followed by a **satisfying state of affairs,** the strength of the connection is increased. If a response is followed by an **annoying state of affairs,** the strength of the connection is decreased. In modern terminology, if a stimulus leads to a response, which in turn leads to reinforcement, the S-R connection is strengthened. If, on the other hand, a stimulus leads to a response that leads to punishment, the S-R connection is weakened.

The law of effect was a historical break from traditional associationistic theory that claimed frequency of occurrence or mere contiguity to be the determiners of the strength of an association. Although Thorndike accepted both the law of frequency and the law of contiguity, he went further by saying that the consequences of a response are important in determining the strength of association between the situation and the response to it. The importance of the consequences of an act in forming associations was only hinted at previously by philosophers such as Hobbes and Bentham. Here we see Thorndike's concern with the utility of behavior in helping the organism adjust to its environment, a concern that he shared with all the functionalists.

According to the law of effect, if a response results in a satisfying state of affairs, the S-R connection is strengthened. How can this happen, since the conduction unit has already fired before the satisfying state of affairs occurs? Thorndike attempted to answer this question by postulating the existence of a **confirming reaction,** which was triggered in the nervous system if a response resulted in a satisfying state of affairs. Thorndike felt that this confirming reaction was neurophysiological in nature and the organism was not conscious of it. Although Thorndike did not elaborate on the characteristics of this reaction, he did suspect that such a neurophysiological reaction was the true strengthener of neural bonds. We will have more to say about the confirming reaction when we consider Thorndike's concept of belongingness.

Some learning theorists have attempted to answer the question of how reinforcement can strengthen the response that produced it by postulating the existence of a neural trace that is still active when the satisfaction occurs. In other words, for these theorists, the conduction unit is still active at the time the organism experiences the satisfying state of affairs. Although the neural trace notion became a popular answer to the question, the problem of how reinforcement strengthens a response is still essentially unsolved.

SECONDARY CONCEPTS BEFORE 1930

Before 1930, Thorndike's theory included a number of ideas that were less important than the laws of readiness, effect, and exercise. These secondary concepts included multiple response, set or attitude, prepotency of elements, response by analogy, and associative shifting.

Multiple Response

Multiple response, or varied reaction, was for Thorndike the first step in all learning. It refers to the fact that if our first response does not solve the problem we try other responses. Trial-and-error learning, of course, depends on the animal trying first one response and then another until a response that works is found. When this happens the probability of that response being made again goes up. In other words, for Thorndike much learning depends on the fact that organisms tend to remain active until a response that solves an existing problem is made.

Set or Attitude

What Thorndike (1913a) called dispositions, preadjustments, or **sets (attitudes)** was his recognition of the importance of what the learner brings to the learning situation:

> It is a general law of behavior that the response to any external situation is dependent upon the condition of the man, as well as upon the nature of the situation; and that, if certain conditions in the man are rated as part of the situation, the response to it depends upon the remaining conditions in the man. Consequently, it is a general law of learning that the change made in a man by the action of any agent depends upon the condition of the man when the agent is acting. The condition of the man may be considered under the two heads of the more permanent or fixed and the more temporary or shifting, attitudes, or "sets." (p. 24)

Thus, individual differences in learning can be explained by the basic differences among people: their cultural and genetic heritage or by temporary states such as deprivation, fatigue, or various emotional conditions. What can act as a satisfier or an annoyer depends on both the organism's background and its temporary body state at the time of learning. For example, animals with considerable experience in a puzzle box will probably solve new puzzle box problems faster than animals with no prior puzzle box training. Furthermore, animals who have been deprived of food for a considerable length of time will probably find food more satisfying than food-satiated animals. It is with his concept of set or attitude that Thorndike recognized that an animal's drive state will, to a large extent, determine what is satisfying and/or annoying to it.

Prepotency of Elements

Prepotency of elements is what Thorndike (1913b) called "the partial or piecemeal activity of a situation." It refers to the fact that only some elements of any situation will govern behavior:

> One of the commonest ways in which conditions within the man determine variations in his responses to one same external situation is by letting one or another element of the situation be prepotent in effect. Such partial or piecemeal activity on the part of a situation is, in human learning, the rule. Only rarely does man form connections, as the lower animals so often do, with a situation as a gross total-unanalyzed, undefined, and, as it were, without relief. He does so occasionally, as when a baby, to show off his little trick, requires the same room, the same persons present, the same tone of voice and the like. Save in early infancy and amongst the feeble-minded, however, any situation will most probably act unevenly. Some of its elements will produce only the response of neglect; others will be bound to only a mild awareness of them; others will connect with some energetic response of thought, feeling or action, and become positive determiners of the man's future. (pp. 26–27)

With the notion of prepotency of elements, Thorndike recognized the complexity of the environment and concluded that we respond selectively to aspects of it.

In other words, we typically respond to some of the elements in a situation and not to others. Therefore, how we respond to a situation depends on both what we attend to and what responses are attached to what we attend to.

Response by Analogy

What determines how we respond to a situation we have never encountered before? Thorndike's answer, **response by analogy,** was that we respond to it as we would to a related situation that we had encountered before. The amount of **transfer of training** between the familiar situation and the unfamiliar one is determined by the number of elements that the two situations have in common. This is Thorndike's famous **identical elements theory of transfer** of training.

With his theory of transfer, Thorndike opposed the long-held view of transfer based on the doctrine of **formal discipline.** As we saw in Chapter 3, formal discipline was based on faculty psychology, which contended that the human mind was made up of several powers or faculties such as reasoning, attention, judgment, and memory. It was believed that these faculties could be strengthened with practice, for example, practicing reasoning made one a better reasoner. Thus, the study of mathematics and Latin were justified because they strengthened the reasoning and memory faculties. It should be obvious why this position was referred to as the "mental muscle" approach to education since it claims that faculties of the mind are strengthened with practice just as people would strengthen their biceps. This position also maintained that if students were forced to solve a number of difficult problems in school they would be able problem solvers outside of school. Thorndike (1906) felt that there was little evidence that education generalized so readily. In fact, he believed that education resulted in highly specific skills rather than general ones:

> A man may be a tip-top musician but in other respects an imbecile: he may be a gifted poet, but an ignoramus in music; he may have a wonderful memory for figures and only a mediocre memory for localities, poetry or human faces; school children may reason admirably in science and be below the average in grammar: those very good in drawing may be very poor in dancing. (p. 238)

Thorndike and Woodworth (1901) critically examined the formal discipline theory of transfer and found little support for it. Instead they found transfer from one situation to the next occurred only to the extent that both situations had elements in common. These elements, according to Thorndike, may be actual stimulus conditions or they may be procedures. For example, looking up words in a dictionary in school may transfer to a variety of situations outside of school that have nothing to do with the exact words you were looking up in the classroom, but the ability to look things up may transfer. This would be the transfer of procedure rather than of stimulus elements. Learning to pay attention for long periods and learning to be punctual would be further examples of the transfer of procedures rather than stimulus elements.

Why is it, then, that the more difficult courses seem to produce brighter students? Because, said Thorndike, the brighter students went into these courses to begin with. Thorndike (1924) summarized his elaborate study with Woodworth on the transfer of training involving 8,564 high school students as follows:

> By any reasonable interpretation of the results, the intellectual values of studies should be determined largely by the special information, habits, interests, attitudes, and ideals which they demonstrably produce. The expectation of any large differences in general improvement of the mind from one study rather than another seems doomed to disappointment. The chief reason why good thinkers seem superficially to have been made such by having taken certain school studies, is that good thinkers have taken such studies, becoming better by the inherent tendency of the good to gain more than the poor from any study. When the good thinkers studied Greek and Latin, these studies *seemed* to make good thinking. Now that the good thinkers study Physics and Trigonometry, these seem to make good thinkers. If the abler pupils should all study Physical Education and Dramatic Art, these subjects would seem to make good thinkers.... After positive correlation of gain with initial ability is allowed for, the balance in favor of any study is certainly not large. Disciplinary values may be real and deserve weight in the curriculum, but the weights should be reasonable. (p. 98)

Concerning the question of how many elements two situations must have in common before the same behavior occurs in both, Thorndike (1905) said, "The case may be likened roughly to that of the direction taken by a four horse team at a fork in the roads, when the team has never traveled either road *as a team* but some one horse or a pair *has*. Their previous habit of taking, say, the left turn, will cause the whole team to go that way" (pp. 212–213).

Because all schools are attempting to influence the way students behave outside of school, the problem of the transfer of training should be a central one for educators. Thorndike urged that the school curriculum be designed to include tasks that would be similar to those students will be asked to perform when they leave school. Thus, the study of mathematics should not be included because it strengthens the mind but because students will actually be using mathematics when they leave school. *For Thorndike, schools should emphasize the direct training of those skills thought to be important beyond the school.*

The transfer of identical elements theory was Thorndike's solution to the problem of how we respond to a novel situation and to the problem of the transfer of training in general. Thorndike (1913a) offered what some thought was a weakness in his theory, namely, the fact that we respond smoothly to new situations, as supportive evidence for his theory: "There is no arbitrary *hocus pocus* whereby man's nature acts in an unpredictable spasm when he is confronted with a new situation. His habits do not then retire to some convenient distance while some new and mysterious entities direct his behavior. On the contrary, nowhere are the bonds acquired with old situations more surely revealed in action than when a new situation appears" (pp. 28–29). When attempting to explain how what was learned transfers from one situation to another, it is Thorndike's theory of identical elements that many modern learning theorists still accept.

Associative Shifting

Associative shifting is closely related to Thorndike's identical elements theory of the transfer of training. The procedure for demonstrating associative shifting is to begin with a connection between a certain situation and a certain response. Then one gradually drops stimulus elements that were part of the original situation and adds stimulus elements that were not part of the original situation. According to Thorndike's identical elements theory, as long as there are enough elements from the original situation in the new situation, the same response will be given. In this way the same response can be carried through a number of stimulus changes and finally be made to stimulating conditions totally dissimilar to those associated with the original response. Thorndike (1913a) said,

> Starting with response X made to *abcde,* we may successively drop certain elements and add others, until the response is bound to *fghij,* to which perhaps it could never otherwise have become connected. Theoretically the formula of progress, from *abcde* to *abfgh* to *afghi* to *fghij,* might result in attaching any response whatever to any situation whatever, provided only that we arrange affairs so that at every step the response X was more satisfying in its consequences than balking or doing anything else that the person could do. (pp. 30–31)

An example of associative shifting is found in the work of Terrace (1963) on discrimination learning. Terrace first taught pigeons to make a red-green discrimination by reinforcing them with grain when they pecked at a red key but not when they pecked at a green key. Next Terrace superimposed a vertical bar over the red key and a horizontal bar over the green key. Gradually the red and green colors were faded out, leaving only the vertical and horizontal bars on the keys. It was found that the discrimination previously associated with red and green was transferred without error to the vertical and horizontal bar discrimination. Now the pigeons pecked at the vertical bar and ignored the horizontal bar. The shifting process is shown in Figure 4–3.

The association shifts from one stimulus (red) to another (vertical bar) because the procedure allows enough elements from the preceding situation to guarantee that the same response is made to the new stimulus. This, of course, demonstrates transfer of training according to Thorndike's identical elements theory.

In a more general way much advertising is based on the principle of associative shifting. The advertiser has only to find a stimulus object that elicits positive feelings, such as a picture of a beautiful female or handsome male, a respected personality, a medical doctor, a mother, or a romantic outdoor scene. Then the advertiser pairs this stimulus object with the product—a brand of cigarettes, an automobile, or a deodorant—as often as possible so that the product will elicit the same positive feelings elicited by the original stimulus object.

In reading Thorndike, we should note that associative shifting is really quite different from trial-and-error learning, which is governed by the law of effect. Unlike learning that depends on the law of effect, associative shifting depends only on contiguity. Associative shifting represents, therefore, a second kind of learning

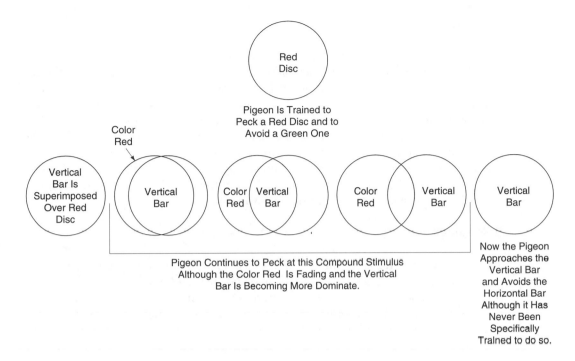

FIGURE 4–3 The process that Terrace used to shift a discriminatory response from one stimulus (the color red) to another stimulus (a vertical bar).

that is similar to the theories of Pavlov and Guthrie, which we consider in Chapters 7 and 8.

THORNDIKE AFTER 1930

In September 1929, Thorndike stood before the International Congress of Psychology in New Haven, Connecticut, and started his address by saying, "I was wrong." This admission points out an important aspect of good scientific practice: Scientists are obliged to change their conclusions if the data require it.

Revised Law of Exercise

Thorndike essentially renounced the entire law of exercise. The law of use, which stated that mere repetition strengthened a connection, was found to be inaccurate. By the same token, simple disuse did not weaken a connection to any large extent. Although Thorndike still maintained that practice led to minor improvement and that lack of practice led to slight forgetting, for all practical purposes he discarded the entire law of exercise after 1930.

Revised Law of Effect

After 1930, the earlier law of effect was found to be only half true. The salvaged half stated that a response followed by a satisfying state of affairs was strengthened. For the other half, Thorndike found that punishing a response had no effect on the strength of the connection. His revised law of effect states that *reinforcement increases the* **strength of a connection,** *whereas punishment does nothing to the strength of a connection.* This finding still has profound implications today. Thorndike's conclusion concerning the effectiveness of punishment is contrary to thousands of years of common sense and has numerous implications for education, child-rearing, and behavior modification in general. We will often return to the question of the effectiveness of punishment as a means of modifying behavior in the following chapters.

Belongingness

Thorndike observed that in the learning of associations a factor in addition to contiguity and the law of effect was often involved. If the elements of an association somehow belonged together, the association between them was learned and retained more readily than if the elements did not belong together. In one experiment designed to investigate this phenomenon Thorndike (1932) read his subjects the following sentences ten times:

> Alfred Dukes and his sister worked sadly. Edward Davis and his brother argued rarely. Francis Bragg and his cousin played hard. Barney Croft and his father watched earnestly. Lincoln Blake and his uncle listened gladly. Jackson Craig and his son struggle often. Charlotte Dean and her friend studied easily. Mary Borah and her companion complained dully. Norman Foster and his mother bought much. Alice Hanson and her teacher came yesterday. (p. 66)

Afterwards his subjects were asked the following questions:

1. What word came next after *rarely*?
2. What word came next after *Lincoln*?
3. What word came next after *gladly*?
4. What word came next after *dully*?
5. What word came next after *Mary*?
6. What word came next after *earnestly*?
7. What word came next after *Norman Foster and his mother*?
8. What word came next after *and his son struggle often*?

If contiguity was the only influential factor, all sequences of words should be learned and remembered equally well. This, however, was not the case. The average number of correct associations from the end of one sentence to the beginning of the next was 2.75, whereas the average number of correct associations between the first and second word combinations was 21.50. Clearly, something is operating here beyond mere contiguity, and that something is what Thorndike called **belonging-**

ness; that is, subjects and verbs belong together more than the last word in one sentence and the first in another.

Thorndike also related his notion of a confirming reaction, discussed earlier, to his concept of belongingness. He felt that if there was a natural relationship between the need state of the organism and the effect caused by a response, learning would be more effective than if the relationship was unnatural. We can say, for example, that a hungry animal would find food satisfying and a thirsty animal would find water satisfying. However, this is not to say that a hungry or thirsty animal would not find other things satisfying. Both would still find escape from confinement and freedom from pain satisfying, but the existence of a powerful drive creates a class of events that would be most satisfying at the moment. It was Thorndike's contention that an effect that belongs to the existing needs of the organism elicits a stronger confirming reaction than effects that do not belong to those needs, even though the latter effects may be powerful satisfiers under different circumstances.

We see, then, that Thorndike used the concept of belongingness in two ways. First, he used it to explain why, when learning verbal material, a person tends to organize what is learned into units that are perceived as belonging together. Second, he said that if the effects produced by a response are related to the needs of the organism, learning will be more effective than it would be if the effects produced by a response were not related to the organism's needs.

Many believed that with his concept of belongingness Thorndike was making concessions to the Gestalt psychologists who said organisms learn general principles and not specific S-R connections (see Chapter 10). Thorndike responded with his **principle of polarity,** which stated that a learned response is most easily given in the direction in which it was formed. For example, almost everyone can recite the alphabet forward but rarely can a person recite it backward. Likewise, most any schoolchild can recite the pledge of allegiance forward, but it would be uncommon to find a child able to recite it backward. Thorndike's point was that if general principles and/or understandings were learned instead of specific S-R connections, a person should be able to perform what had been learned in either direction with almost equal ease. Thus, even with his concept of belongingness, Thorndike maintained his mechanistic, nonmental view concerning the learning process.

Spread of Effect

After 1930, Thorndike added another major theoretical concept, which he called the **spread of effect.** During one of his experiments Thorndike accidentally found that a satisfying state of affairs not only increased the probability of recurrence of the response that led to the satisfying state of affairs but also increased the probability of recurrence of the responses surrounding the reinforced one.

One typical experiment demonstrating this effect involved presenting ten words, including *catnip, debate,* and *dazzle,* to subjects who were instructed to respond with a number from 1 to 10. If the subject responded to a word with a number that the experimenter had previously chosen to go with that word, the experimenter said "right." If the subject responded with any other number the experimenter said "wrong." The experiment proceeded in this fashion for several trials. Two important observations were made from this research. First, it was found that reinforcement (the experimenter saying "right") strongly increased the probability of the same number being repeated the next time the stimulus word was given, but punishment (the experimenter saying "wrong") did not reduce the probability of an incorrect number being repeated again. It was partially on the basis of this research that Thorndike revised his earlier law of effect. Second, it was found that the numbers that preceded and followed a reinforced number also increased in probability of recurring, even though they were not themselves reinforced and even if these surrounding numbers had themselves been punished. Thus, what Thorndike called a satisfying state of affairs apparently "spread" from the reinforced response to neighboring responses. He called this phenomenon the spread of effect. Thorndike also found that this effect diminishes with distance. In other words, the reinforced response has the greatest probability of recurring, then the responses next to the reinforced one, then the responses next to those, and so on.

In discovering the spread of effect, Thorndike felt that he had found additional confirmation for his revised law of effect since reinforcement not only increased the probability of a reinforced response but also increased the probability of neighboring responses, even though these may have been punished. He also felt that the spread of effect further demonstrated the automatic, direct nature of learning.

Thorndike on Education

Thorndike believed that educational practices should be studied scientifically. It was obvious to him that there should be a close relationship between the knowledge of the learning process and teaching practices. Thus, he expected that as more was discovered about the nature of learning, more could be applied to improve teaching practices. Thorndike (1906) said,

> Of course present knowledge of psychology is nearer to zero than to complete perfection, and its applications to teaching must therefore be often incomplete, indefinite and insecure. The application of psychology to teaching is more like that of botany and chemistry to farming than like that of physiology and pathology to medicine. Anyone of good sense can farm fairly well without science, and anyone of good sense can teach fairly well without knowing and applying psychology. Still, as the farmer with the knowledge of the applications of botany and chemistry to farming is, other things being equal, more successful than the farmer without it, so the teacher will, other things being equal, be the more successful who can apply psychology, the science of human nature, to the problems of the school. (pp. 9–10)

At many points Thorndike's thinking ran contrary to traditional notions about education; we saw one clear example in his identical elements theory of transfer. Thorndike (1912) also had a low opinion of the lecture technique of teaching that was so popular then (and now):

> The lecture and demonstration methods represent an approach to a limiting extreme in which the teacher lets the pupil find out nothing which he could possibly be told or

shown. They frankly present the student with conclusions, trusting that he will use them to learn more. They ask of him only that he attend to, and do his best to understand, questions which he did not himself frame and answers which he did not himself work out. They try to give him an educational fortune as one bequeaths property by will. (p. 188)

He also said,

The commonest error of the gifted scholar, inexperienced in teaching, is to expect pupils to know what they have been told. But telling is not teaching. The expression of the facts that are in one's mind is a natural impulse when one wishes others to know these facts, just as to cuddle and pat a sick child is a natural impulse. But telling a fact to a child may not cure his ignorance of it any more than patting him will cure his scarlet fever. (p. 61)

What then is good teaching? Good teaching involves first of all knowing what you want to teach. If you do not know exactly what it is you want to teach you will not know what material to present, what responses to look for, and when to apply satisfiers. This principle is not as obvious as it sounds. Only recently have we realized the importance of behaviorally defining educational objectives. Although Thorndike's (1922) seven rules that follow were formulated for the teaching of arithmetic, they represent his advice for teaching in general:

1. Consider the situation the pupil faces.
2. Consider the response you wish to connect with it.
3. Form the bond; do not expect it to come by a miracle.
4. Other things being equal, form no bond that will have to be broken.
5. Other things being equal, do not form two or three bonds when one will serve.
6. Other things being equal, form bonds in the way that they are required later to act.
7. Favor, therefore, the situations which life itself will offer, and the responses which life itself will demand. (p. 101)

One can see here the seeds of B. F. Skinner's attitude toward educational practices, which we will consider in Chapter 5.

Science and Human Values

Thorndike was criticized for assuming determinism in the study of human behavior. Reducing human behavior to automatic reactions to the environment destroys human values, the critics said. Thorndike (1940) answered that on the contrary, the human sciences offered people their greatest hope for the future:

The welfare of mankind now depends upon the sciences of man. The sciences of things will, unless civilization collapses, progress, extend man's control over nature, and guide technology, agriculture, medicine, and other arts effectively. They will protect man against dangers and disasters except such as he himself causes. He is now his own worst enemy. Knowledge of psychology and of its applications to welfare should prevent, or at least diminish, some of the errors and calamities for which the well-intentioned have been and are responsible. It should reduce greatly the harm done by the stupid and vicious. (p. v)

Elsewhere Thorndike (1949) said,

Thus, at last, man may become ruler of himself as well as of the rest of nature. For strange as it may sound man is free only in a world whose every event he can understand and foresee. Only so can he guide it. We are captains of our own souls only in so far as they act in perfect law so that we can understand and foresee every response which we will make to every situation. Only so can we control our own selves. It is only because our intellects and morals—the mind and spirit of man—are a part of nature, that we can be in any significant sense responsible for them, proud of their progress, or trustful of their future. (p. 362)

Obviously, Thorndike was a very colorful person who expressed opinions on a wide variety of topics. In this chapter we have concentrated on outlining his thoughts on the learning process and his views concerning the relationship between the learning process and educational practices. The student who is interested in knowing more about Thorndike is urged to read *The Sane Positivist: A Biography of Edward L. Thorndike* by Geraldine Joncich (1968).

EVALUATION OF THORNDIKE'S THEORY

Contributions

Thorndike's pioneering work provided a distinct alternative for conceptualizing learning and behavior and differed radically from earlier approaches. Prior to Thorndike's studies, there simply was no systematic, experimental treatment of learning. He not only accounted for and synthesized the data available to him, he also discovered and developed phenomena—trial-and-error learning and transfer of training, for example—that would define the domain of learning theory for years to come.

With his law of effect, Thorndike was the first to observe, under controlled conditions, that the consequences of behavior produced a backward acting effect on the strength of that behavior. Questions about the reasons for the effect, its limits, its duration, and problems associated with its definition and measurement would direct research efforts in the behavioral tradition for the next 50 years, and they are still the topics of research and debate today. Thorndike was among the first to investigate the nature of forgetting in his early law of exercise and the suppression of behavior in his treatment of punishment, and he was clearly willing to discard early treatments of both phenomena when data contradicted his hypotheses. In his treatment of transfer of training, Thorndike was the first to rigorously question common assumptions in educational practices (formal discipline). And although he can be considered an early behaviorist, his notions of prepotency of elements and response by analogy foreshadowed contemporary cognitive theories of learning.

Criticisms

While it has been demonstrated that some phenomena discovered by Thorndike, the spread of effect for example, are due to processes other than those he identified (Estes, 1969b; Zirkle, 1946), the important criticisms of Thorndike's theory focused on two major issues. The first concerns the definition of satisfiers in the law of effect. The second, also related to the law of effect, concerns the starkly mechanistic definition of learning in the theory. Critics of the law of effect said that Thorndike's argument was circular: If the response probability increased, it was said to be due to the presence of a satisfying state of affairs; if it did not increase, it was claimed that no satisfier was present. It was believed that such an explanation did not allow for a test of the theory because the same event (increased probability of a response) was used to detect both learning and a satisfying state of affairs. Later defenders of Thorndike argued that this criticism is invalid because once something has been shown to be a satisfier, it can be used to modify behavior in other situations (Meehl, 1950), but as we will see in Chapter 5, this defense has failed.

A second criticism of Thorndike's law of effect concerned the way that S-R connections were thought to be strengthened or weakened. As we have seen, Thorndike believed learning to be an automatic function of a satisfying state of affairs and not the result of any conscious mechanism such as thinking or reasoning. Clearly, Thorndike believed that an organism need not be aware of the relationship between a response and a satisfier in order for the satisfier to have an effect. Similarly, the intentions and strategies of the learner were considered nonessential for learning. Thorndike did not deny the existence of thoughts, plans, strategies, and intentions, although later radical behaviorists would deny the existence of all such cognitive events. However, Thorndike believed learning could be adequately explained without reference to such events. Contemporary students react negatively to this mechanical approach to the study of learning, as did many of Thorndike's contemporaries. William McDougall, for example, wrote in the 1920's that Thorndike's theory of selecting and connecting was a "theory of morons, by morons, and for morons" (Joncich, 1968). The debate concerning the nature of reinforcement and whether a learner must be aware of reinforcement contingencies before they can be effective continues today, and therefore we will return to it often throughout this book.

DISCUSSION QUESTIONS

1. Summarize the nature of animal research prior to Thorndike's efforts. In what way was Thorndike's research different from that which preceded it? Include in your answer a discussion of Morgan's canon.
2. Do you agree with Thorndike's contention that the same laws of learning apply to both human and nonhuman animals? Explain.
3. Assuming Thorndike's revised law of effect to be valid, do you feel classroom practice in this country is in accordance with it? Child-rearing practices? Explain.
4. Summarize the revisions that Thorndike made in his theory after 1930.

5. Discuss Thorndike's concept of the confirming reaction
6. Discuss the importance of sets or attitudes in Thorndike's theory.
7. According to Thorndike, what determines what will transfer from one learning situation to another?
8. Summarize Thorndike's criticisms of the formal discipline approach to education. How would you arrange schoolroom practices so that they take into consideration Thorndike's theory concerning the transfer of training?
9. Describe how you would reduce the probability of a child being fearful of a new situation, such as a new baby-sitter, using the procedure of associative shifting.
10. Discuss Thorndike's principles of belongingness and polarity.
11. Summarize what Thorndike learned from his research on the spread of effect.
12. What, according to Thorndike, provides humans with their greatest hope for the future?

KEY TERMS

annoying state of affairs   A condition that an organism actively avoids. If such a condition occurs the organism attempts to abandon it as soon as possible.

anthropomorphizing   Attributing human characteristics to nonhuman animals.

associative shifting   The process whereby a response is "carried" from one set of stimulating conditions to another by gradually adding new stimulus elements and subtracting old ones. The result is that a response that was originally given to one set of circumstances is now given to an entirely new set of circumstances. Associative shifting is based on the principle of contiguity.

belongingness   Material is learned more readily when it is structured in certain ways. Contiguity alone does not determine how well something will be learned. How the material "fits together" must also be taken into consideration. Also, Thorndike maintained that learning is most effective when there is a natural relationship between the needs of an organism and the effects produced by a response.

confirming reaction   A neurophysiological reaction which is stimulated when a response produces a satisfying state of affairs. The confirming reaction was thought by Thorndike to be the true strengthener of a neural bond.

connectionism   A term often used to describe Thorndike's explanation of learning since he assumed learning involved the strengthening of neural bonds (connections) between stimulating conditions and the responses to them.

formal discipline   See chapter highlights for Chapter 3.

identical elements theory of transfer   The theory which states that the likelihood of something which was learned in one situation being applied in a different situation is determined by the number of common elements in the two situations. As the number of common elements goes up the amount of transfer between the two situations goes up. The elements can be either stimuli or procedures.

incremental learning   Learning that occurs a little bit at a time rather than all at once.

insightful learning   Learning that occurs all at once rather than a little bit at a time (see also Key Terms for Chapter 10).

law of disuse   That portion of the law of exercise that states that the strength of a connection diminishes when the connection is not used. The law of disuse was discarded by Thorndike after 1930.

law of effect   The law that states that the strength of a connection is influenced by the consequences of a response. Before 1930, Thorndike believed that pleasurable consequences strengthened a connection and annoying consequences weakened a connection. After 1930, however, he believed that only pleasurable consequences had an effect on the strength of a connection.

law of exercise   The law that states that the strength of a connection is determined by how often the connection is used. The law of exercise has two components-the law of use and the law of disuse.

law of readiness   The law that states that when an organism is ready to act it is reinforcing for it to do so and annoying for it not to do so. Also, when an organism is not ready to act, forcing it to act will be annoying to it.

law of use   That portion of the law of exercise that states that the strength of a connection increases with its use. The law of use was discarded by Thorndike after 1930.

Morgan, Conwy Lloyd (1842–1936)   An early comparative psychologist who attempted to be objective in his descriptions of animal behavior by carefully avoiding anthropomorphizing.

Morgan's canon   Morgan's rule that animal researchers should never explain animal behavior as resulting from a higher mental process, such as reasoning or thinking, if that behavior could be explained by a lower process, such as instinct, habit, or association.

multiple response   Refers to the fact that if one response does not solve the problem the organism continues to try other responses until it hits on one that is effective in solving the problem; a prerequisite to trial-and-error learning.

prepotency of elements   Refers to the fact that different aspects of the environment evoke different responses; similar to what we now refer to as selective perception.

principle of polarity   The observation that learned material is most easily performed in the same direction in which it was originally learned.

response by analogy   Refers to the fact that our response to an unfamiliar situation is determined by its degree of similarity to a familiar situation. Insofar as two situations are similar they will tend to be similarly responded to. Thorndike describes similarity in terms of the number of elements that the two situations have in common. This observation is related to his identical elements theory of transfer of training.

Romanes, George John (1848–1894)   An early comparative psychologist whose evidence for the continuity between nonhuman and human mental processes was anecdotal and replete with anthropomorphizing.

satisfying state of affairs   A condition that an organism seeks out and attempts to preserve. Once such a condition exists, the organism does nothing to avoid it.

selecting and connecting   See **trial-and-error learning.**

sets (attitudes)   Temporary conditions, such as food deprivation, fatigue, or emotion, that determine what will be annoying or pleasurable to a given organism.

spread of effect   The observation that reinforcement not only strengthens the response that produced it but strengthens neighboring responses as well.

strength of a connection   Determined by how likely a certain response is in a given set of circumstances. In other words, the strength of a connection is equated with response probability.

transfer of training   When something learned in one situation is applied in another situation.

trial-and-error learning   The trying of different responses in a problem-solving situation until a response that is effective in solving the problem is found. Thorndike originally called this phenomenon selecting and connecting.

Chapter 5

BURRHUS FREDERIC SKINNER

Burrhus Frederic Skinner. (Courtesy of B.F. Skinner.)

Skinner (1904–1990) was born in Susquehanna, Pennsylvania and his ideas remain highly influential in contemporary psychology. He received his master's degree in 1930 and his Ph.D. in 1931 from Harvard University. His B.A. degree was obtained from Hamilton College in New York, where he majored in English. While at Hamilton, Skinner had lunch with Robert Frost, the great American poet, who encouraged Skinner to send him a sample of his writing. Frost reviewed favorably the three short stories that Skinner sent, and Skinner decided definitely to become a writer. This decision was a great disappointment to his father, who was a lawyer and wanted his son to become a lawyer.

Skinner's early efforts to write were so frustrating that he thought of seeing a psychiatrist. He eventually went to work for the coal industry summarizing legal documents. In fact, his first book, coauthored by his father, concerned those legal documents and was entitled *A Digest of Decisions of the Anthracite Board of Conciliation.* After finishing this book, Skinner moved to Greenwich Village in New York City, where he lived like a Bohemian for six months before going to Harvard to study psychology. By that time he had developed a distaste for most literary pursuits. In his autobiography (1967), he said, "I had failed as a writer because I had nothing important to say, but I could not accept that explanation. It was literature which must be at fault" (p. 395). When he failed in describing human behavior through literature, Skinner attempted to describe human behavior through science. Clearly, he was much more successful at the latter pursuit.

Skinner taught psychology at the University of Minnesota between 1936 and 1945, during which time he wrote his highly influential text, *The Behavior of Organisms* (1938). One of Skinner's students at the University of Minnesota was W. K. Estes, whose work has had a considerable impact on psychology (see Chapter 9). In 1945 Skinner went to the University of Indiana as chair of the psychology department, and in 1948 he returned to Harvard, to which he remained affiliated until his death in 1990.

As we shall see, Skinner's position was similar to Thorndike's position after 1930 in that it emphasized the effects of a response on the response itself. Moreover, like Thorndike, Skinner concluded that the effects of reinforcement and punishment are not symmetrical; that is, reinforcement changes the probability of a response's recurring, but punishment does not.

Through the years, Skinner was a highly prolific writer. One of his main concerns was to relate his laboratory findings to the solution of human problems. His work led to the development of programmed learning and teaching machines. Two representative articles in this area are "The Science of Learning and the Art of Teaching" (1954) and "Teaching Machines" (1958). Following his own ideas on this topic, he and his coauthor, Holland, produced a programmed text on his theoretical notions entitled *The Analysis of Behavior* (Holland & Skinner, 1961). In 1948 he wrote a Utopian novel called *Walden Two*. The title paid tribute to Thoreau's *Walden*. In *Walden Two,* which Skinner wrote in only seven weeks, he attempted to utilize his principles of learning in the building of a model society. More recently Skinner wrote *Beyond Freedom and Dignity* (1971), in which he showed how a technology of behavior could be used in designing a culture. In *Beyond Freedom and Dignity* he discussed why the idea of cultural engineering is met with so much opposition. Skinner's writings have been extended into the area of child development through the efforts of Bijou and Baer (1961, 1965). His thoughts have been related to the area of personality through the writings of Lundin (1974), who wrote *Personality: A Behavioral Analysis,* and to child-rearing by Hergenhahn (1972), who wrote *Shaping Your Child's Personality.*

Most students of psychology are well aware of the widespread utilization of Skinnerian notions in the area of psychotherapy. For example, Lovaas's early work with autistic children relied heavily on Skinner's ideas. Today the behavior modification approach, based on Skinner's ideas, has become the most widely used and most effective way of working with autistic or retarded children. Behavioral engineering, however, is by no means limited to children. The technique has been successfully applied to the alleviation of a number of adult problems such as stuttering, phobias, eating disorders, and psychotic behavior.

During World War II, while at the University of Minnesota, Skinner attempted to apply his theory to the problem of national defense. He trained pigeons to peck at discs on which moving pictures of enemy targets were being shown. The discs and the motion pictures were ultimately to be contained in a glider loaded with high explosives. The glider was called the *Pelican,* thus, the name of the article describing these events, "Pigeons in a Pelican" (1960). The pecking of the pigeons closed various electronic circuits and thereby kept the vehicle on target. This American version of kamikaze fighter planes would involve no loss of human lives. Although Skinner demonstrated to a group of America's top scientists that he and his co-workers had perfected a homing device that was almost immune to electronic jamming, was capable of reacting to a wide variety of enemy targets, and was simple to build, their proposed project was turned down. Skinner speculated that the whole idea was simply too fantastic for the committee to cope with.

MAJOR THEORETICAL NOTIONS

Respondent and Operant Behavior

Skinner distinguished two kinds of behavior: **respondent behavior,** which is elicited by a known stimulus, and **operant behavior,** which is not elicited by a known stimulus but is simply emitted by the organism. Unconditioned responses would be examples of respondent behavior since they are elicited by unconditioned stimuli. Examples of respondent behavior would include all reflexes, such as jerking one's hand when jabbed with a pin, the constriction of the pupil of the eye when it is exposed to bright light, and salivation in the presence of food. Because operant behavior is *not* initially correlated with known stimuli, it seems to appear spontaneously. Examples include beginning to whistle; standing up and walking about; a child abandoning one toy in favor of another; and moving one's hands, arms, or legs arbitrarily. Most of our everyday activities are operant behaviors. Note that Skinner did not say that operant behavior occurs independently of stimulation; rather, he said that the stimulus causing such behavior is unknown and that it is not important to know its cause. Unlike respondent behavior, which is dependent on the stimulus that preceded it, operant behavior is controlled by its consequences. We will say more about how consequences influence operant behavior.

Type S and Type R Conditioning

Along with the two kinds of behavior described above, there are two kinds of conditioning. Type S conditioning is also called **respondent conditioning** and is identical to classical conditioning. It is called Type S conditioning to emphasize the importance of the stimulus in eliciting the desired response. The type of conditioning that involves operant behavior is called Type R because of the emphasis on the response. Type R conditioning is also called **operant conditioning.**

It is important to note that in Type R conditioning the strength of conditioning is shown by *response rate,* whereas in Type S conditioning the strength of conditioning is usually determined by the *magnitude* of the conditioned response. We see, then, that Skinner's Type R conditioning very closely resembles Thorndike's instrumental conditioning, and Skinner's Type S conditioning is identical to Pavlov's classical conditioning. After making the distinction between Type S and Type R conditioning, Skinner's research was concerned almost entirely with Type R, or operant, conditioning.

Although Skinner and Thorndike were in close agreement on a number of important issues, there are still important differences between them. For example, the dependent variable in Thorndike's learning experiments (his measure of the extent to which learning took place) was *time to solution.* Thorndike was interested in measuring how long it took an animal to perform whatever task was necessary to release it from confinement. Skinner, in contrast, used *rate of responding* as his dependent variable. Although Skinner sometimes talked about how reinforcement affects the probability of a response's recurrence, his main concern was with how reinforcement affects the rate with which an operant response occurs. In other words, Thorndike was mainly interested in noting how long it took an animal to make a certain response, whereas Skinner was interested mainly in what variables affect rate or pattern of responding.

Operant Conditioning Principles

Two general principles are associated with Type R conditioning: (1) any response that is followed by a reinforcing stimulus tends to be repeated; and (2) a reinforcing stimulus is anything that increases the rate with which an operant response occurs.

Or as we saw above, we can say that a reinforcer is anything that increases the probability of a response's recurring.

Skinner (1953) did not provide a rule that one would follow in discovering what would be an effective reinforcer. Rather, he said that whether or not something is reinforcing can only be ascertained by its effect on behavior:

> In dealing with our fellow men in everyday life and in the clinic and laboratory, we may need to know just how reinforcing a specific event is. We often begin by noting the extent to which our own behavior is reinforced by the same event. This practice frequently miscarries; yet it is still commonly believed that reinforcers can be identified apart from their effects upon a particular organism. As the term is used here, however, the only defining characteristic of a reinforcing stimulus is that it reinforces. (p. 72)

In operant conditioning, the emphasis is on behavior and its consequences; with operant conditioning, the organism must respond in such a way as to produce the reinforcing stimulus. This process also exemplifies **contingent reinforcement,** because getting the reinforcer is contingent (dependent) on the organism's emitting a certain response. We will have more to say about contingent reinforcement in our discussion of superstitious behavior.

The principles of operant conditioning can apply to a variety of situations. To modify behavior, one merely has to find something that is reinforcing for the organism whose behavior one wishes to modify, wait until the desired behavior occurs, and then immediately reinforce the organism. When this is done, the rate with which the desired response occurs goes up. When the behavior next occurs, it is again reinforced, and the rate of responding goes up further. Any behavior that the organism is capable of performing can be manipulated in this manner.

The same principles are thought to apply to the development of human personality. According to Skinner, we are what we have been reinforced for being. What we call personality is nothing more than consistent behavior patterns that summarize our reinforcement history. We learn to speak English, for example, because we have been reinforced for approximating the sounds of the English language in our early home environment. If we happened to be brought up in a Japanese or Russian home, we would learn to speak Japanese or Russian because when we approximated sounds in that language, we would have been attended to or reinforced in some other way. Skinner (1971) said,

> The evidence for a crude environmentalism is clear enough. People are extraordinarily different in different places, and possibly just because of the places. The nomad on horseback in Outer Mongolia and the astronaut in outer space are different people, but, as far as we know, if they had been exchanged at birth, they would have taken each other's place. (The expression "change places" shows how closely we identify a person's behavior with the environment in which it occurs.) But we need to know a great deal more before that fact becomes useful. What is it about the environment that produces a Hottentot? And what would need to be changed to produce an English conservative instead? (p. 185)

Skinner defined culture as a set of reinforcement contingencies. His answers to the above questions were that a particular set of reinforcement contingencies produces a Hottentot and another set produces the English conservative. Different cultures reinforce different behavior patterns. This fact must be clearly understood before an adequate technology of behavior can be developed. Skinner said (1971),

> The environment is obviously important, but its role has remained obscure. It does not push or pull, it *selects,* and this function is difficult to discover and analyze. The role of natural selection in evolution was formulated only a little more than a hundred years ago, and the selective role of the environment in shaping and maintaining the behavior of the individual is only beginning to be recognized and studied. As the interaction between organism and environment has come to be understood, however, effects once assigned to states of mind, feelings, and traits are beginning to be traced to accessible conditions, and a technology of behavior may therefore become available. It will not solve our problems, however, until it replaces traditional prescientific views, and these are strongly entrenched. (p. 25)

If one controls reinforcement, one can also control behavior. However, this need not be looked on as a negative statement since behavior is constantly being influenced by reinforcement whether we are aware of that fact or not. It is never a question of *whether* behavior is going to be controlled but who or what is going to control it. Parents, for example, can decide to give direction to their child's emerging personality by reinforcing certain behavior, or they can let society rear their child by letting television, peers, school, books, and baby-sitters do the reinforcing. Giving direction to a child's life is difficult, however, and any parents wishing to do so must take at least the following steps (Hergenhahn, 1972):

1. Decide the major personality characteristics you want your child to possess as an adult. Let's say, for example, you want the child to grow up to be a creative adult.
2. Define these goals in behavioral terms. In this case you ask, "What is a child doing when he or she is being creative"?
3. Reward behavior that is in accordance with these goals. With this example, you would reward instances of creativity as they occurred.
4. Provide consistency by arranging the major aspects of the child's environment so that they too reward the behavior you have deemed important. (pp. 152–153)

Without knowledge of these principles, a parent could easily misapply them without knowing it. Skinner (1951) said,

> The mother may unwillingly promote the very behavior she does not want. For example, when she is busy she is likely not to respond to a call or request made in a quiet tone of voice. She may answer the child only when it raises its voice. The average intensity of the child's vocal behavior therefore moves up to another level....Eventually the mother gets used to this level and again reinforces only louder instances. This vicious circle brings about louder and louder behavior....The mother behaves, in fact, as if she has been given the assignment of teaching the child to be annoying. (p. 29)

According to Skinner, living organisms are constantly being conditioned by their environment. We can either allow the principles of learning to operate capriciously on our children, or by systematically applying those principles, we can give some direction to their development.

The Skinner Box

Most of Skinner's early animal work was done in a small test chamber that has come to be called the **Skinner box.** It is a direct descendant of the puzzle box used by Thorndike. The Skinner box usually has a grid floor, light, lever, and food cup. It is arranged so that when the animal depresses the lever, the feeder mechanism is activated and a small pellet of food is released into the food cup. A typical Skinner box is shown in Figure 5–1.

The Cumulative Recording

Skinner used a **cumulative recording** to keep track of an animal's behavior in the Skinner box. A cumulative recording is quite different from other ways of graphing data in learning experiments. Time is recorded on the x-axis and total number of responses is recorded on the y-axis. The cumulative recording never goes down—the line either climbs or remains parallel to the x-axis. Let's say we are interested in how often the animal presses the lever. When the cumulative recording shows a line parallel to the x-axis, it indicates no responding; that is, the animal is not pressing the lever. When the animal makes a lever-pressing response, the pen goes up a notch and remains at that level until the animal makes another response. If, for example, the animal presses the lever when it is first placed in the Skinner box, the pen will go up a notch and remain there until the animal responds again, at which time the pen will go up another notch, and so on. If the animal responds very rapidly, the line will rise very rapidly. The rate with which the line ascends indicates the rate of responding; a very steep line indicates very rapid responding, and a line parallel to the x-axis indicates no responding. If at any time you want to know the total number of responses made by the animal, you just measure the distance between the line of the graph

FIGURE 5–1 A typical Skinner box. (Courtesy of the Gerbrands Company, Inc.)

and the *x*-axis, and this can easily be transformed into the total number of responses. Sample cumulative recordings are shown in Figure 5–2.

Conditioning the Lever-Pressing Response

Typically, conditioning the lever-pressing response involves the following steps:

1. Deprivation   The experimental animal is put on a deprivation schedule. If food is to be used as the reinforcer, the animal is deprived of food for a 23-hour period for a number of days prior to the experiment, or it is maintained at 80 percent of its free-feeding body weight. If water is to be used as the reinforcer, the animal is deprived of water for a 23-hour period for a number of days prior to the experiment. (Some Skinner boxes are designed to deliver small pellets of food and others small drops of water.) Skinner does not say that these procedures "motivate" the animal; he even hesitates to say that they produce a drive state. Deprivation is simply a set of procedures that is related to how an organism performs on a certain task; nothing more needs to be said.

2. Magazine Training   After being on a deprivation schedule for a number of days, the animal is placed into the Skinner box. Using an external hand switch, the experimenter periodically triggers the feeder mechanism (also called the magazine), making sure the animal is not in the vicinity of the food cup when he or she does so (otherwise the animal would learn to remain near the food cup). When the feeder mechanism is activated by the hand switch, it produces a fairly loud clicking sound before delivering a pellet of food into the food cup. Gradually the animal associates

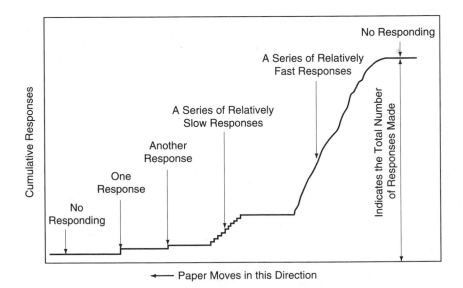

FIGURE 5–2   A cumulative recording. Note that the steeper the line, the faster the rate of responding. A line parallel to the baseline indicates no response.

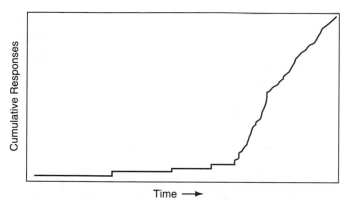

FIGURE 5–3 A typical cumulative recording that reflects the acquisition of a lever-pressing response.

the click of the magazine with the presence of a food pellet. At that point, the click has become a secondary reinforcer through its association with a primary reinforcement (food). (We will discuss secondary reinforcement in a later section.) The click also acts as a cue or signal indicating to the animal that if it responds by going to the food cup, it will be reinforced.

3. Lever Pressing Now the animal can be left in the Skinner box on its own. Eventually, it will press the lever, which will fire the food magazine, producing a click that reinforces the bar press and also signals the animal to go to the food cup, where it is reinforced by food. According to operant conditioning principles, the lever-pressing response, having been reinforced, will tend to be repeated, and when it is repeated it is again reinforced, which further increases the probability that the lever-pressing response will be repeated, and so on. A typical cumulative recording generated by an animal placed in a Skinner box after **magazine training** is shown in Figure 5–3.

Shaping

The process of operant conditioning we have described so far takes considerable time. As we saw above, one way to train the lever-pressing response is to place the deprived animal in the Skinner box and simply leave it there. The experimenter merely checks the cumulative recording periodically to see if the response has been learned. Under these conditions the animal either learns or dies.

There is another approach to operant conditioning that does not take as long as the procedure described above. Again, the animal is placed on a deprivation schedule and is magazine trained, and again the experimenter uses the hand switch to trigger the feeder mechanism externally. This time, however, the experimenter decides to fire the feeder mechanism only when the animal is in the half of the Skinner box containing the lever. When the animal is reinforced for being near the lever, it will tend to remain in that part of the test chamber. Now that the animal remains in the vicinity of the lever, the experimenter begins to reinforce it only when it is still closer to the lever. Next it is reinforced only when it touches the lever, then only when it is putting pressure on it, and finally only when it is pressing it by itself.

The process is similar to a childhood game called You're Hot, You're Cold, in which a child hides something and her or his playmates try to find it. As they get closer to the hidden object, the child who hid the object says, "You're getting warm, you're warmer, you're boiling hot, you're on fire." As they get farther from the object the child says, "You're getting cold, colder, very cold, you're freezing." When this game is played in the laboratory, it is called **shaping.** In the shaping procedure described above, the lever-pressing response was shaped rather than waited for.

Shaping has two components: **differential reinforcement,** which simply means some responses are reinforced and others are not; and **successive approximation,** which refers to the fact that only those responses that become increasingly similar to the one the experimenter wants are reinforced. In our example, only those responses that successively approximated the lever-pressing response were differentially reinforced.

Recently it has been found that under certain circumstances, pre-existing or even accidental contingencies between events in the environment and an animal's response automatically shape behavior. This phenomenon is called autoshaping, which we will have more to say about later in this chapter.

Extinction

As with classical conditioning, when we remove the reinforcer from the operant conditioning situation, we produce **extinction.** During acquisition, the animal gets a pellet of food whenever it presses the lever. Under these circumstances, the animal learns to press the lever and persists in doing so until it is satiated with food. If the feeder mechanism was suddenly disconnected, thus preventing a lever pressing from producing a pellet of food, we would note that the cumulative recording would gradually become shallower and would eventually become parallel to the x-axis, indicating that no lever-pressing responses are being made. At that point, we say that extinction has occurred.

We are being somewhat inaccurate when we say that after extinction a response is no longer made; it is more accurate to say that after extinction, the response rate goes back to where it was before reinforcement was introduced. This baseline rate is the frequency with which the response occurs naturally in the life of the animal without the introduction of reinforcement. This is called the **operant level** for that response. When we remove reinforcement from the experimental arrangement, as in extinction, the response tends to go back to its operant level.

Spontaneous Recovery

After extinction, if the animal is returned to its home cage for a period of time and then brought back into the experimental situation, it will again begin to press the lever for a short period of time without any additional training. This is referred to as **spontaneous recovery.** A cumulative recording showing both extinction and spontaneous recovery is shown in Figure 5–4.

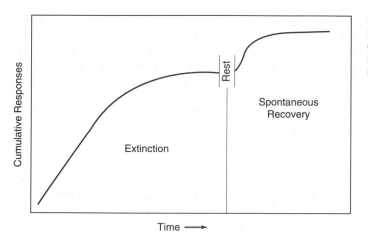

FIGURE 5–4 A cumulative recording that depicts the extinction and spontaneous recovery of a lever-pressing response.

Superstitious Behavior

In our earlier discussion of operant conditioning, we briefly mentioned contingent reinforcement. Reinforcement following the lever-pressing response is an example of contingent reinforcement since the reinforcer is dependent on the response. What would happen, however, if the situation was arranged so that the feeder mechanism would fire every now and then, independently of the animal's behavior? In other words, we are now going to arrange the situation so that the feeder mechanism delivers a pellet of food periodically *regardless of what the animal is doing.*

According to the principles of operant conditioning, we can predict that whatever the animal is doing when the feeder mechanism is activated will be reinforced, and the animal will tend to repeat the reinforced behavior. At some time the reinforced behavior will be repeated when the feeder mechanism randomly fires again, and the response will be strengthened. Thus the animal is apt to develop strange ritualistic responses; it may bob its head, turn in a circle, stand up on its back legs, or perform a series of actions according to what it was doing when the feeder mechanism fired. This ritualistic behavior is referred to as superstitious because the animal looks as if it believes that what it is doing is causing a pellet of food to appear. Because the reinforcer in this situation is independent of the animal's behavior, it is referred to as **noncontingent reinforcement.**

One can think of numerous examples of **superstitious behavior** on the part of humans. Organized sports, for instance, are filled with many examples. Imagine what happens to the baseball player who, after stepping to the plate, adjusts his hat in a certain way and hits the very next pitch out of the ball park. There will be a strong tendency on his part to adjust his hat in a similar way the next time he is at bat.

Discriminative Operant

Now we return to the Skinner box and discuss the light that we referred to earlier. After we have conditioned the animal to press the lever, we can make the situation more complex. We can arrange the situation so that the animal receives a pellet of food when the light in the Skinner box is on but not when the light is off. Under these conditions, we refer to the light as S^D, or a **discriminative stimulus.** The light being on defines the S^D condition, and the light being off defines the S^Δ condition (Δ=delta). With this arrangement, the animal learns to press the lever when the light is on and not to press when the light is off. The light, therefore, has become a signal (cue) for the lever-pressing response. We have developed a **discriminative operant,** which is an operant response given to one set of circumstances but not to another. The arrangement can be symbolized as follows: $S^D \rightarrow R \rightarrow S^R$ where R is the operant response and S^R is the reinforcing stimulus.

The concept of the discriminative stimulus allows for a more detailed statement about which stimulus-response relationship is of interest in operant conditioning. For Thorndike, the association of interest was between a general environmental situation and a response effective in solving a problem. For Skinner, the relationship of interest can be diagrammed as follows:

Discriminative stimulus $\rightarrow$ operant response $\rightarrow$ reinforcing stimulus
        (S^D) (R) (S^R)

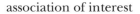

association of interest

Except for slight differences in terminology, Skinner's views of learning are quite similar to those of Thorndike after 1930. In fact, except for the way each researcher measured the dependent variable, which was pointed out earlier in this chapter, instrumental conditioning and operant conditioning can be considered the same procedure.

There is some slight similarity between the discriminative operant and respondent conditioning. You will recall that respondent behavior is elicited by a known stimulus. The behavior occurs because of its association with the stimulus. Such behavior, as we have seen, is not under the control of its consequences. In the case of the discriminative operant, the light becomes a signal associated with a certain response that the organism has learned will be followed by reinforcement.

Operant behavior is emitted behavior, but Skinner (1953) said,

Most operant behavior…acquires important connections with the surrounding world. We may show how it does so in our pigeon experiment by reinforcing neck- stretching when a signal light is on and allowing it to be extinguished when the light is off. Eventually stretching occurs only when the light is on. We can then demonstrate a stimulus-response connection which is roughly comparable to a conditioned or unconditioned reflex: the appearance of the light will be quickly followed by an upward movement of the head. But the relation is fundamentally quite different. It has a different history and different current properties. We describe the contingency by saying that a *stimulus* (the light) is the occasion upon which a *response* (stretching the neck) is followed by *reinforcement* (with food). We must specify all three terms. The effect upon the pigeon is that eventually the response is more likely to occur when the light is on. The process through which this comes about is called *discrimination*. Its importance in a theoretical analysis, as well as in the practical control of behavior, is obvious: when a discrimination has been estab-

> lished, we may alter the probability of a response instantly by presenting or removing the discriminative stimulus. (pp. 107–108)

Thus, the discriminative operant involves a signal that leads to a response, which in turn leads to reinforcement.

There are numerous examples of discriminative operants in everyday life. A certain time of the day (S^D) indicates that you must be in a certain place (R) to transact some business (S^R). As you're driving down the street, you encounter a red light (S^D), which causes you to stop (R), thereby avoiding a ticket or an accident (S^R). You see someone you don't care for (S^D), causing you to change the direction you are walking in (R), thereby avoiding the person (S^R).

Secondary Reinforcement

Any neutral stimulus paired with a primary reinforcer (e.g., food or water) takes on reinforcing properties of its own; this is the principle of secondary reinforcement. It follows then that every S^D must be a secondary reinforcer since it consistently precedes primary reinforcement.

One way to demonstrate the reinforcing properties of a previously neutral stimulus is to wire the Skinner box so that a light comes on before the animal receives food for making a lever-pressing response. According to the principle of secondary reinforcement, the pairing of the light with food should cause the light to take on reinforcing properties of its own. One way to test this notion is to extinguish the lever-pressing response so that the animal presses the lever and neither light nor food is produced. When the response rate decreases to its operant level, we arrange for the lever pressing to turn on the light but not deliver a pellet of food. We note that the response rate goes way up. Since the light alone has increased the response rate and thereby prolonged extinction, we say it has developed secondary reinforcing characteristics through its association with food during acquisition (training). A light not associated with a primary reinforcer will not produce a similar effect during extinction.

In addition to maintaining the lever-pressing response, we can now use the light to condition other responses. Once a previously neutral stimulus takes on reinforcing properties through its association with primary reinforcement, it can be used to reinforce any number of responses.

Keller and Schoenfeld (1950) provide an excellent summary of secondary reinforcement:

1. A stimulus that occasions or accompanies a reinforcement acquires thereby reinforcing value of its own, and may be called a conditioned, secondary, or derived reinforcement. A secondary reinforcement may be extinguished when repeatedly applied to a response for which there is no ultimate primary reinforcement.
2. A secondary reinforcement is positive when the reinforcement with which it is correlated is positive, and negative when the latter is negative.

3. Once established, a secondary reinforcement is independent and nonspecific; it will not only strengthen the same response which produced the original reinforcement, but it will also condition a new and unrelated response. Moreover, it will do so even in the presence of a different motive.

4. Through generalization, many stimuli besides the one correlated with reinforcement acquire reinforcing value—positive or negative. (p. 260)

Generalized Reinforcers

A **generalized reinforcer** is a secondary reinforcer that has been paired with more than one primary reinforcer. Money is a generalized reinforcer because it is ultimately associated with any number of primary reinforcers. The main advantage of the generalized reinforcer is that it does not depend on a certain condition of deprivation to be effective. Food, for example, is only reinforcing for an organism deprived of food, but money can be used as a reinforcer whether or not someone is deprived of food. Moreover, the very activities that once led to reinforcement may themselves become reinforcing. Skinner (1953) said,

> Eventually generalized reinforcers are effective even though the primary reinforcers upon which they are based no longer accompany them. We play games of skill for their own sake. We get attention or approval for its own sake. Affection is not always followed by a more explicit sexual reinforcement. The submissiveness of others is reinforcing even though we make no use of it. A miser may be so reinforced by money that he will starve rather than give it up. (p. 81)

With these comments, Skinner came very close to Gordon Allport's concept of **functional autonomy.** Allport (1961) maintained that although an activity may once have been engaged in because it led to reinforcement, after awhile the activity itself may become reinforcing. In other words, the activity may become independent of the reinforcer on which it was originally dependent. For example, a person might originally join the merchant marines in order to make a living but later in life go sailing because it is enjoyable to do so even though sailing no longer provides an income. In this case, we say that sailing has become functionally autonomous; that is, it continues in the absence of the original motive. Skinner said that such an activity must ultimately result in primary reinforcement or it would extinguish. Allport, however, would say that the activity no longer depends on primary reinforcement.

Chaining

One response can bring the organism into contact with stimuli that act as an S^D for another response, which in turn causes it to experience stimuli that cause a third response, and so on. This process is referred to as **chaining.** In fact, most behavior can be shown to involve some form of chaining. For example, even the lever pressing in the Skinner box is not an isolated response. The stimuli in the Skinner box act as S^Ds, causing the animal to turn toward the lever. The sight of the lever causes the animal to approach it and press it. The firing of the feeder mechanism acts as an

| S^D | $\rightarrow$ | R | $\rightarrow$ | S^D S^R | $\rightarrow$ | R | $\rightarrow$ | S^D S^R | $\rightarrow$ | R | $\rightarrow$ | S^R |

General Stimuli in the Test Chamber | Orient toward Lever | Sight of Lever Reinforces Response of Turning toward It and Acts as a Cue for the Next Response | Approach Lever | Contact with Lever Reinforces Approaching and Acts as Cue to Press | Press Lever | Food Pellet

FIGURE 5–5 An example of chained behavior.

additional S^D, which elicits the response of going to the food cup. Consuming the food pellet acts as an S^D, causing the animal to return to the lever and again press it. This sequence of events (chain) is held together by the food pellet, which of course is a primary positive reinforcer. It can be said that various elements of a behavioral chain are held together by secondary reinforcers but that the entire chain depends on a primary reinforcer.

To explain how chaining comes about from Skinner's point of view, one must utilize the concepts of secondary reinforcement and associative shifting. Because of their association with the primary reinforcer, the events prior to the delivery of the food pellet take on secondary reinforcing properties. Thus, the sight of the lever itself becomes a secondary reinforcer, and the response of looking at the lever is reinforced by the sight of the lever. Now, through a process similar to associative shifting (or higher-order conditioning, which we will discuss in Chapter 7), other stimuli more remote from the lever develop reinforcing properties. Thus, after considerable training, when the animal is placed in the Skinner box the initial stimuli it encounters will act as an S^D, causing the animal to orient toward the lever. The sight of the lever at this point acts both as a reinforcer and an S^D, eliciting the next response in the chain. The situation is diagrammed in Figure 5–5.

It is important to note that the development of a chained response always acts from the primary reinforcer backward. As more and more related stimuli take on reinforcing properties, the chain is extended. It is possible, for example, for the chain to extend gradually all the way back to the animal's home cage.

Occasionally rats have been trained to perform complex chained responses such as climbing a staircase, riding in a cart, crossing a bridge, playing a note on a toy piano, entering a small elevator, pulling a chain, riding the elevator down, and receiving a small pellet of food. This chain, too, is developed backward so that the events that precede the primary reinforcer gradually become secondary reinforcers. When they do, they reinforce the responses prior to them, and so on along the chain of behaviors.

Chained responses can also occur between two people. For example, seeing someone you know acts as an S^D to say "hello." Your hello acts as an S^D for your friend to say "hi." The response of "hi" acts not only as a reinforcer for your "hello" but also as an S^D for you to say "How are you?" This two-person chain can be diagrammed as follows:

Not only do the consequences of certain responses act as cues for other responses, but certain thoughts can act as S^Ds for other thoughts. Skinner (1953) said,

> A response may produce or alter some of the variables which control another response. The result is a "chain." It may have little or no organization. When we go for a walk, roaming the countryside or wandering idly through a museum or store, one episode in our behavior generates conditions responsible for another. We look to one side and are stimulated by an object which causes us to move in its direction. In the course of this movement, we receive aversive stimulation from which we beat a hasty retreat. This generates a condition of satiation or fatigue in which, once free of aversive stimulation, we sit down to rest. And so on. Chaining need not be the result of movement in space. We wander or roam verbally, for example, in a casual conversation or when we "speak our thoughts" in free association. (p. 224)

Positive and Negative Reinforcers

To summarize Skinner's position on reinforcement, we have first of all **primary positive reinforcement.** This is something that is naturally reinforcing to the organism and is related to survival, such as food or water. Any neutral stimulus associated with primary positive reinforcement takes on positive secondary reinforcing characteristics. A *positive reinforcer, either primary or secondary, is something that, when added to the situation by a certain response, increases the probability of that response's recurrence.*

A **primary negative reinforcer** is something naturally harmful to the organism, such as aversive high-pitched tone or an electric shock. Any neutral stimulus associated with a primary negative reinforcer takes on negative secondary reinforcing characteristics. A *negative reinforcer, either primary or secondary, is something that, when removed from the situation by a certain response, increases the probability of that response's recurrence.* For example, if a Skinner box is arranged so that an aversive tone is discontinued when the lever is pressed, the lever-pressing response will soon be learned. In this case, by pressing the lever, the animal avoids experiencing an aversive stimulus. Notice that positive reinforcement is not positive because responses produce pleasant or desirable outcomes. Similarly, negative reinforcement does not earn its name because a response produces nasty or unpleasant outcomes. In addition, negative reinforcement should not be confused with punishment (Skinner, 1953):

> Events which are found to be reinforcing are of two sorts. Some reinforcements consist of *presenting* stimuli, of adding something—for example, food, water, or sexual contact—to the situation. These we call *positive* reinforcers. Others consist of *removing* something—for example, a loud noise, a very bright light, extreme cold or heat, or electric shock—from the situation. These we call *negative* reinforcers. In both cases the effect

of reinforcement is the same—the probability of response is increased. We cannot avoid this distinction by arguing that what is reinforcing in the negative case is the *absence* of the bright light, loud noise, and so on; for it is absence after presence which is effective, and this is only another way of saying that the stimulus is removed. The difference between the two cases will be clearer when we consider the *presentation* of a *negative* reinforcer or the *removal* of a *positive.* These are the consequences which we call punishment. (p. 73)

Punishment

Punishment occurs when a response removes something positive from the situation or adds something negative. In everyday language we can say that punishment is either taking away something an organism wants, or giving it something it does not want. Skinner and Thorndike agreed on the effectiveness of punishment: It does not decrease the probability of a response. Although punishment suppresses a response as long as it is applied, it does not weaken the habit. Skinner (1971) said,

> Punishment is designed to remove awkward, dangerous, or otherwise unwanted behavior from a repertoire on the assumption that a person who has been punished is less likely to behave in the same way again. Unfortunately, the matter is not that simple. Reward and punishment do not differ merely in the direction of the changes they induce. A child who has been severely punished for sex play is not necessarily less inclined to continue; and a man who has been imprisoned for violent assault is not necessarily less inclined toward violence. Punished behavior is likely to reappear after the punitive contingencies are withdrawn. (pp. 61–62)

A typical experiment that led Skinner to this conclusion was done by one of his students, Estes (1944). Two groups of eight rats each were trained to press the lever in a Skinner box. After training, both groups were placed on extinction. One group was extinguished in the regular way; that is, food was withheld following lever pressing. Rats in the second group, in addition to not receiving food, received a shock when they pressed the lever. Rats in this group were shocked an average of nine times. There were three extinction sessions, and the rats were only shocked during the first of the three sessions. The second and third sessions were the same for both groups. The punished group made fewer responses during the first extinction session than did the nonpunished group. The number of responses made during the second extinction session was about the same for both groups, with the nonpunished group making slightly more responses. From the data of the first two sessions, one can conclude that punishment was effective since the number of responses to extinction was much lower for the punished group. During the third extinction session, however, the previously punished group made many more responses than did the nonpunished group. Thus, in the long run, the originally punished group caught up in the total number of responses to extinction to the nonpunished group. The conclusion was that simple nonreinforcement (extinction) is as effective in extinguishing a habit as nonreinforcement plus punishment. The results of the Estes study are summarized in Figure 5–6.

Skinner's main argument against the use of punishment is that it is ineffective in the long run. It appears that punishment simply suppresses behavior, and when the

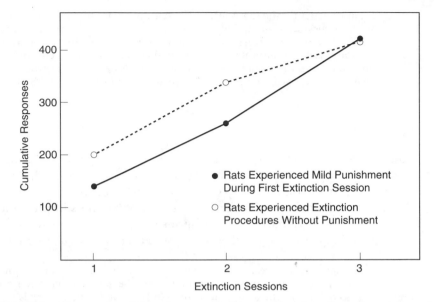

FIGURE 5–6 The results of Estes's research showing that the effect of punishment is to suppress the rate of responding only temporarily. (From W.K. Estes, An experimental study of punishment, *Psychological Monographs, 57,* Whole No. 263, 1944, 5.)

threat of punishment is removed, the rate with which the behavior occurs returns to its original level. Thus, punishment often appears to be very successful when, in fact, it has produced only a temporary effect. Other arguments against the use of punishment follow.

1. **It causes unfortunate emotional byproducts.** The punished organism becomes fearful and this fear generalizes to a number of stimuli related to those present as the punishment was occurring.
2. **It indicates what the organism should not do, not what it should do.** Compared to reinforcement, punishment conveys virtually no information to the organism. Reinforcement indicates that what was done is effective in the situation; therefore, no additional learning is required. Very often punishment informs the organism only that the punished response is one that will not work to bring reinforcement in a given situation, and additional learning is required to hit on a response that will work.
3. **It justifies inflicting pain on others.** This, of course, applies to the use of punishment in child-rearing. When children are spanked, the only thing they may be learning is that under some circumstances it is justifiable to inflict pain on others.
4. **Being in a situation where previously punished behavior could be engaged in without being punished may excuse a child to do so.** Thus, in the absence of a punishing agent, children may swear, break windows, be disrespectful to elderly people, push smaller children around, and so on. These children have learned to suppress these behaviors when they could lead to punishment, but in the absence of a punishing agent, there is no reason to avoid engaging in these activities.

5. **Punishment elicits aggression toward the punishing agent and others.** Punishment causes the punished organism to become aggressive, and this aggression may cause additional problems. For example, our penal institutions, which use punishment as their major means of control, are filled with highly aggressive individuals who will continue to be aggressive as long as punishment or the threat of punishment is used to control their behavior.

6. **Punishment often replaces one undesirable response with another undesirable response.** For example, a child who is spanked for making a mess may now cry instead, just as a person punished for stealing may now become aggressive and commit even more crimes when he or she has the opportunity.

In their study of how 379 New England suburban mothers brought up their children from birth to kindergarten age, Sears, Maccoby, and Levin (1957) concluded the following concerning the relative effects of emphasizing reinforcement as opposed to punishment in child rearing:

> In our discussion of the training process, we have contrasted punishment with reward. Both are techniques used for changing the child's habitual ways of acting. Do they work equally well? The answer is unequivocally "no"; but to be truly unequivocal, the answer must be understood as referring to the kind of punishment we were able to measure by our interview method. We could not, as one can with laboratory experiments on white rats or pigeons, examine the effects of punishment on isolated bits of behavior. Our measures of punishment, whether of the object-oriented or love-oriented variety, referred to *Levels of Punitiveness* in the mothers. Punitiveness, in contrast to rewardingness, was a quite ineffectual quality for a mother to inject into her child training.
>
> The evidence for this conclusion is overwhelming. The unhappy effects of punishment have run like a dismal thread through our findings. Mothers who punished toilet accidents severely ended up with bedwetting children. Mothers who punished dependency to get rid of it had more dependent children than mothers who did not punish. Mothers who punished aggressive behavior severely had more aggressive children than mothers who punished lightly. They also had more dependent children. Harsh physical punishment was associated with high childhood aggressiveness and with the development of feeding problems.
>
> Our evaluation of punishment is that *it is ineffectual over the long term as a technique for eliminating the kind of behavior toward which it is directed.* (p. 484)

Why, then, is punishment so widely used? Because, said Skinner (1953), it is reinforcing to the punisher:

> Severe punishment unquestionably has an immediate effect in reducing a tendency to act in a given way. This result is no doubt responsible for its widespread use. We "instinctively" attack anyone whose behavior displeases us—perhaps not in physical assault, but with criticism, disapproval, blame, or ridicule. Whether or not there is an inherited tendency to do this, the immediate effect of the practice is reinforcing enough to explain its currency. In the long run, however, punishment does not actually eliminate behavior from a repertoire, and its temporary achievement is obtained at tremendous cost in reducing the over-all efficiency and happiness of the group. (p. 190)

It is interesting to note that Skinner himself was never physically punished by his father and only once by his mother, who washed his mouth out with soap for swearing (Skinner, 1967, p. 390).

Alternatives to Punishment

Skinner lists a number of alternatives to the use of punishment. The circumstances causing the undesirable behavior can be changed, thereby changing the behavior. For example, removing fine china from the living room will eliminate the problem of a child's breaking fine china. The undesirable response can be satiated by letting the organism perform the undesired response until it is sick of it, such as letting a child continue to light matches or eat candy (advice similar to that given by Guthrie, as we shall see in Chapter 8). If the undesirable behavior is a function of the child's developmental stage, it can be eliminated by simply waiting for the child to outgrow it. Skinner (1953) said about the latter approach, "It is not always easy to put up with the behavior until this happens, especially under the conditions of the average household, but there is some consolation if we know that by carrying the child through a socially unacceptable stage we spare him the later complications arising from punishment" (p. 192).

Another method is simply to let time pass, but this approach may take too long. Habits are not soon forgotten. For example, in his "Pigeons in a Pelican" project, mentioned earlier, Skinner (1960) found that his trained animals "immediately and correctly" performed their task after six years of inactivity. Still another alternative to punishment is to reinforce behavior incompatible with the undesirable behavior (e.g., a child is reinforced for reading in the presence of matches rather than striking them). The best way to discourage an undesirable habit, however, is to ignore it (Skinner 1953):

> The most effective alternative process [to punishment] is probably *extinction*. This takes time but is much more rapid than allowing the response to be forgotten. The technique seems to be relatively free of objectionable by-products. We recommend it, for example, when we suggest that a parent "pay no attention" to objectionable behavior on the part of his child. If the child's behavior is strong only because it has been reinforced by "getting a rise out of" the parent, it will disappear when this consequence is no longer forthcoming. (p. 192)

Generally speaking, behavior persists because it is being reinforced; this is true of undesirable as well as desirable behavior. To eliminate objectionable behavior one needs to find the source of reinforcement and remove it. Behavior that does not lead to reinforcement extinguishes.

Schedules of Reinforcement

Although Pavlov (1927, pp. 384–386) had done some work with partial reinforcement, using classical conditioning, it was Skinner who thoroughly investigated the topic. Skinner had already published data on the effects of partial reinforcement when Humphreys (1939a, 1939b) startled the psychological world by showing that the extinction process was more rapid following 100 percent reinforcement than after partial reinforcement. That is, if an organism receives a reinforcer every time it makes an appropriate response during learning and then is placed on extinction, it will extinguish faster than an organism who had only a certain percentage of its correct responses reinforced during acquisition. In other words, partial reinforcement leads to greater resistance to extinction than continuous, or 100 percent, reinforcement, and this fact is called the **partial reinforcement effect (PRE).**

Skinner studied the partial reinforcement effect extensively and eventually wrote a book with Ferster called *Schedules of Reinforcement* (Ferster and Skinner, 1957). This book summarized years of research on various types of partial reinforcement. *Seven* schedules of reinforcement have become the most common and they are described below.

1. Continuous Reinforcement Schedule   Using a **continuous reinforcement schedule (CRF),** every correct response during acquisition is reinforced. Usually in a partial reinforcement study, the animal is first trained on a 100 percent reinforcement schedule and then switched to a partial reinforcement schedule. It is difficult to bring about the acquisition of any response when partial reinforcement is used during the initial training period.

2. Fixed Interval Reinforcement Schedule   Using a **fixed interval reinforcement schedule (FI),** the animal is reinforced for a response made only after a set interval of time. For example, only a response following a three-minute interval is reinforced. At the beginning of the fixed time interval the animal responds slowly or not at all. As the end of the time interval approaches, the animal gradually increases its speed of responding, apparently anticipating the moment of reinforcement. This kind of responding produces a pattern on the cumulative recording referred to as the *fixed-interval scallop*. Such a pattern is shown in Figure 5–7.

The behavior of an animal under this schedule is somewhat similar to the way a person behaves as a deadline approaches. After putting off a certain task as long as possible, the due date is rapidly approaching and activity increases accordingly. Often a student preparing a term paper will act in this manner.

3. Fixed Ratio Reinforcement Schedule   A **fixed ratio reinforcement schedule (FR)** occurs when every *n*th response that the animal makes is reinforced. FR5, for example, means that the animal will be reinforced at every fifth response. Here the important factor in determining when a response is reinforced is the number of responses made. Theoretically, an animal on a fixed interval schedule could make just one response at the end of the interval and be reinforced each time it responds. With a fixed ratio schedule, this is not possible; the animal *must* respond a fixed number of times before it is reinforced.

For both the FI and FR reinforcement schedules, a reinforced response is followed by a depression in the rate of responding. This is called the *postreinforcement pause*. There is considerable speculation about why such a pause exists. Perhaps the animal learns that the responses immediately following a reinforced response are never reinforced. However, the scallop on the cumulative recording of an FI schedule is usually not found on that of an FR schedule. The FR schedule usually generates a steplike cumulative recording, indicating that the animal temporarily stops responding after a reinforced response and then, at some point, resumes responding at a rapid rate. Such behavior has been characterized as "break and run." A cumulative recording generated by an animal under an FR schedule is shown in Figure 5–7.

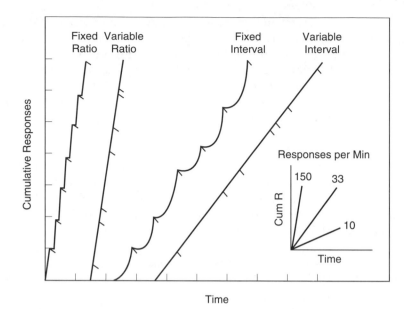

FIGURE 5–7 Typical cumulative recordings generated by fixed ratio, variable ratio, fixed interval, and variable interval reinforcement schedules. The slash marks in the recordings indicate a reinforced response.

4. Variable Interval Reinforcement Schedule   With the **variable interval reinforcement schedule (VI),** the animal is reinforced for responses made at the end of time intervals of variable durations. That is, rather than having a fixed time interval, as with FI schedules, the animal is reinforced on the *average* of, say, every three minutes, but it may be reinforced immediately after a prior reinforcement, or it may be reinforced after thirty seconds or after seven minutes. This schedule eliminates the scalloping effect found in FI schedules and produces a steady, moderately high response rate. A typical cumulative recording generated by an animal on a VI schedule is shown in Figure 5–7.

5. Variable Ratio Reinforcement Schedule   The **variable ratio reinforcement schedule (VR)** eliminates the steplike cumulative recording found with the FR schedule and produces the highest response rate of the five schedules considered thus far. With the FR schedule, an animal is reinforced after making a specific number of responses, say, five. With the VR5 schedule, the animal is reinforced on the *average* of every five responses; thus it might receive two reinforcers in a row or may make ten or fifteen responses without being reinforced. A cumulative recording produced by an animal under a VR schedule is shown in Figure 5–7.

The VR reinforcement schedule is the one governing the behavior of gamblers at a place like Las Vegas. The faster one pulls the handle of a slot machine, for example, the more frequently one is reinforced.

To summarize, continuous reinforcement yields the least resistance to extinction and the lowest response rate during training. All partial reinforcement schedules produce greater resistance to extinction and higher response rates during training than continuous reinforcement. Generally speaking, the VR schedule produces the highest response rate, FR produces the next highest rate, then VI, followed by FI, and finally CRF.

6. Concurrent Schedules and the Matching Law   Skinner (1950) trained pigeons to peck two operant keys that were available at the same time but that delivered reinforcements under different schedules. This procedure is referred to as a **concurrent reinforcement schedule.** He reported that the pigeons distributed their responses according to the schedules of reinforcement associated with each key and continued to do so during extinction. Ferster and Skinner (1957) also examined the effects of concurrent-schedule training, but in 1961, Richard Herrnstein (1930–1994) quantified the relationship between reinforcement and performance under concurrent schedules and provided direction for operant research for about the next 30 years. He refined Skinner's earlier observation by noting that under concurrent schedules, the relative frequency of behavior matches the relative frequency of reinforcement. This relationship is referred to as Herrnstein's **matching law.** The equation expressing matching is written as follows:

$$\frac{B_1}{B_1 + B_2} = \frac{R_1}{R_1 + R_2}$$

where B_1 is the frequency of pecking at key 1 and R_1 is the frequency of reinforcement for that behavior, and so on. Matching is illustrated in Figure 5–8.

In two subsequent papers, Herrnstein (1970, 1974) extended the implications of the matching law. First, he noted that even in a testing situation where there are

FIGURE 5–8
Results of two pigeons pecking on concurrent VI VI schedules. The pecking of key A is plotted relative to the pecking of key B. The total possible number of reinforcers from pecking both keys is 40 per hour; therefore, if pecking key A generated 10 percent of the reinforcers (4), pecking key B generated 90 percent (36). Notice that the relative rate of responding very nearly equaled the relative rate of reinforcement. (From R.J. Herrnstein, "Relative and Absolute Strength of Response as a Function of frequency of Reinforcement," *Journal of the Experimental Analysis of Behavior,* 1961, 4, 267–272. Copyright 1961 by the Society for the Experimental Analysis of Behavior, Inc.)

two keys for pigeons to peck, the pigeons engage in behaviors other than pecking. He included these extraneous behaviors (B_e) and the reinforcements that maintained them (R_e) in the matching equation:

$$\frac{B_1}{B_1 + B_2 + B_e} = \frac{R_1}{R_1 + R_2 + R_e}$$

Furthermore, he made the assumption that in any given testing situation, the sum of the rates of *all* behaviors taken together is a constant (k). That is, $B_1 + B_2 + B_e = k$. It is possible, then, to write an equation that expresses the response rate for any single behavior:

$$B_1 = \frac{(k)R_1}{\Sigma R}$$

where ΣR is the summation of the frequencies of reinforcement for all behaviors occurring under the circumstances.

This expression is called **Herrnstein's equation** or Herrnstein's hyperbola, in reference to the function it generates for different values of (k) and R_e. As shown in Figure 5–9, Herrnstein's hyperbola is a form of the learning curve—a mathematical statement of Thorndike's law of effect. Figure 5–9 also reveals the logic of the mathematical expression as it applies to a simple situation with one operant behavior (B_1), two different values of extraneous behaviors (B_e), and associated extraneous reinforcements $(R_e\text{s})$ but only one value of k. In the case illustrated on the left, there is little extraneous behavior and reinforcement $(R_e=5)$. In the case on the right, there are increased effects of extraneous reinforcement $(R_e=20)$.

Recall that the sum of rates of all possible behaviors is a constant (k). Therefore, the asymptote, or maximum rate, of the operant behavior in either case is k. In each instance, as the rate of reinforcement for B_1 increases, more and more of the total behavioral output is in the form of B_1, and B_e necessarily decreases toward zero (0). Notice that the effect of extraneous reinforcement is distraction from B_1. When values of extraneous reinforcement and the accompanying extraneous behavior are high, the learning curve for B_1 rises more slowly and asymptotic performance is delayed. Similarly, when more extraneous reinforcements are available, extraneous behavior (B_e) decreases more slowly despite increased reinforcement for B_1.

As an example of the effects of extraneous behavior and reinforcement on human perfor-

Richard J. Herrnstein. (Courtesy of Richard J. Herrnstein.)

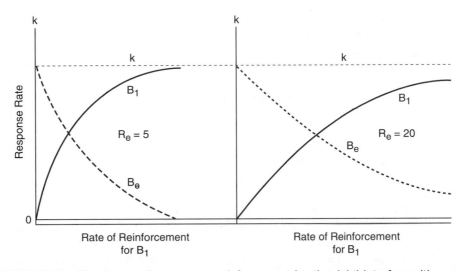

FIGURE 5–9 High levels of extraneous reinforcement (on the right) interfere with performance of a target operant behavior and prolong extraneous behaviors.

mance, imagine two piano students trying to master a difficult musical passage. One student is alone with the instructor. Contrary to the instructor's general policy, the other student has invited several friends to the lesson. The first student will be reinforced only by the instructor and will earn reinforcement only for correct musical performance. Therefore, extraneous behaviors and their reinforcements are minimized (as in Figure 5–9, where R_e=5). The second student has available more sources and potential types of reinforcement (as in Figure 5–9, where R_e=20) and can be reinforced for behaviors other than musical performance. He or she may engage in a number of nonmusical activities to earn approval, attention, and respect from the observing friends. Herrnstein's equation accounts for the observation that the first student will improve faster and master the musical passage sooner than the second.

Development of the matching law continues, and the current body of literature evolving from Herrnstein's early matching observation is extensive. The matching equation has been used to explain effects of delay, magnitude, quality, and duration of reinforcements, as well as those of punishment (see Davison & McCarthy, 1988). However, the mechanisms underlying matching phenomena continue to be debated (Herrnstein, 1990, 1991; Staddon 1991).

7. Concurrent Chain Reinforcement Schedule Whereas a concurrent schedule of reinforcement is used to investigate simple-choice behavior, a **concurrent chain reinforcement schedule** is used to investigate complex-choice behavior. With concurrent chain schedules an animal's behavior during the initial phase of the experiment determines what schedule of reinforcement it experiences during the second, or terminal, phase.

One interesting finding using concurrent chain schedules is in the area of self-control. Under ordinary circumstances, organisms will clearly prefer small, immediate reinforcers over large, delayed reinforcers. Using concurrent schedules, if response A is reinforced by small, immediate reinforcers and response B is reinforced by large reinforcers following a delay, response A will be overwhelmingly preferred. Likewise, using a concurrent chain schedule, if responding to alternative A switches in a schedule providing small, immediate reinforcers and responding to alternative B switches in a schedule producing large, delayed reinforcers, animals will show a strong preference for alternative A. Rachlin and Green (1972), however, showed that under certain circumstances, large, delayed reinforcers are preferred over small, immediate reinforcers. Rachlin and Green used a concurrent chain reinforcement schedule in which pigeons initially had a choice of pecking one of two white discs. Pecking the white disc on the left 15 times (FR 15) was followed by a ten second blackout and then a choice between a red and a green disc. Pecking the red disc produced two seconds of food (a relatively small reinforcer) immediately, and pecking the green disc produced four seconds of food (a relatively larger reinforcer) following a delay of four seconds. In the original choice phase of the experiment, if the white disc on the right was responded to 15 times (FR 15), there was also a ten-second blackout and then the opportunity to peck a green disc. Pecking the green disc produced a four-second delay followed by four seconds of food. Under these experimental conditions, it was found that pigeons chose the white disc on the right 65 percent of the time, thus reversing the preference for small, immediate reinforcers. The experimental arrangement used by Rachlin and Green is shown in Figure 5–10.

What is it that changed the preference for small, immediate reinforcers to large, delayed reinforcers? The answer seems to be time. It has been shown that reinforcers lose their reinforcement value over time. Thus, an organism may opt for a small reinforcer if it is immediately available but will not plan to have one sometime in the future. If a delay is involved, organisms tend to choose larger reinforcers over smaller ones. Schwartz and Robbins (1995) generalize these findings to humans:

> Consider, for example, the choice between going to the movies and studying on a particular evening. We could imagine that going to the movies involves a small but immediate reinforcement (an evening's entertainment) whereas studying involves a large delayed reinforcement (a good exam grade). Given the choice, at 7:45 P.M., between studying and an 8 P.M. movie, the student, like the pigeon, might choose the small immediate reinforcement. But if the choice were required at 9 A.M., so that now both reinforcers were going to be delayed, the student might choose to study. (p. 283)

Although it is beyond the scope of this text to explain how, it is interesting to note that the switchover in preference from small, immediate to large, delayed reinforcers found by Rachlin and Green (1972) is predicted by Herrnstein's matching law (see Rachlin, 1991, pp. 585–586, for an explanation).

Verbal Behavior

Skinner believed that verbal behavior (language) can be explained within the context of reinforcement theory. Talking and listening are responses that are influenced by reinforcement just as is any other response. Any utterance, therefore, will tend to be repeated if it is reinforced. Skinner classified verbal responses in terms of how they were related to reinforcement, that is, in terms of what was being done in order to be reinforced. These classifications are discussed briefly below.

FIGURE 5–10 The concurrent-chain reinforcement schedule used by Rachlin and Green. (From H. Rachlin, Behavior and Learning, p. 584. Copyright © 1976 W.H. Freeman and Company. Reprinted with permission.)

1. Mand   About the **mand**, Skinner (1957) said,

A mand is characterized by the unique relationship between the form of the response and the reinforcement characteristically received in a given verbal community. It is sometimes convenient to refer to this relation by saying that a mand "specifies" its reinforcement. *Listen!, Look!, Run!, Stop!,* and *Say yes!* specify the behavior of a listener; but when a hungry diner calls *Bread!,* or *More soup!,* he is specifying the ultimate reinforcement. Frequently both the behavior of the listener and the ultimate reinforcement are specified. The mand *pass the salt!* specifies an action (pass) and an ultimate reinforcement (the salt). (p. 37)

The word *mand* comes from the fact that a demand is being made. When the demand is met, the utterance (mand) is reinforced, and next time the need arises the person is likely to repeat the mand.

2. Tact   About **tact,** Skinner (1957) said,

This type of operant is exemplified when, in the presence of a doll, a child frequently achieves some sort of generalized reinforcement by saying *doll;* or when a teleost fish, or picture thereof, is the occasion upon which the student of zoology is reinforced when he says *teleost fish.* There is no suitable term for this type of operant. "Sign," "symbol," and more technical terms from logic and semantics commit us to special schemes of reference and stress the verbal response itself rather than the controlling relationship. The invented term "tact" will be used here. The term carries a mnemonic suggestion of behavior which "makes contact with" the physical world. A tact may be defined as a verbal operant in which a response of given form is evoked (or at least strengthened) by a particular object or event or property of an object or event. We account for the strength by showing that in the presence of the object or event, a response of that form is characteristically reinforced in a given verbal community. (pp. 81–82)

Generally speaking the tact involves naming objects or events in the environment appropriately, and its reinforcement comes from other people's reinforcement of the match between the environment and the verbal behavior.

3. Echoic Behavior   **Echoic behavior** is verbal behavior that is reinforced when someone else's verbal response is repeated verbatim. Echoic behavior is often a prerequisite to a more complicated verbal behavior; for example, first a child must imitate a word before he or she can learn how that word is related to other words or other events. Thus, repeating something someone else has said is reinforced, and when this response is learned, it permits the speaker to learn more complex verbal relationships.

4. Autoclitic Behavior   According to Skinner (1957), "The term 'autoclitic' is intended to suggest behavior which is based upon or depends upon other verbal behavior" (p. 315). The main function of **autoclitic behavior** is to qualify responses, express relations, and provide a grammatical framework for verbal behavior.

The most severe critic of Skinner's explanation of verbal behavior has been Noam Chomsky (1959). Chomsky contends that language is too complex for a child to have learned. Some process other than learning must explain all the verbal utterances that, say, a 3-year-old is capable of making. G. A. Miller (1965) in fact, points out that there are 10^{20} possible 20-word sentences in the English language, and it would take 1,000 times the estimated age of the earth just to listen to them all. Obviously, says Chomsky, operant conditioning just does not explain the complexity of our language capabilities. Chomsky's explanation of language development is that our brain is structured to generate language. The underlying grammatical structure of all human languages reflects an underlying brain structure. That is, we are "wired" to produce grammatical utterances, just as a computer can be wired to produce moves in a chess game. Chomsky and Skinner seem to be continuing the nature-nurture debate launched by Plato and Aristotle: Chomsky's deep brain structures theory of language acquisition represents the nature, or Platonic, side, and Skinner's view that verbal behavior is shaped by environment represents the nurture, or Aristotelian, side.

Programmed Learning

Skinner, like Thorndike, was very interested in applying his theory of learning to the process of education. To Skinner, learning proceeds most effectively if (1) the information to be learned is presented in small steps, (2) the learners are given rapid feedback concerning the accuracy of their learning (i.e., they are shown immediately after a learning experience whether they have learned the information correctly or incorrectly), and (3) the learners are able to learn at their own pace.

Skinner learned firsthand that these principles were not being used in the classroom. He reflected on a visit he made in 1953 to one of his daughter's classes (Skinner, 1967): "On November 11, as a visiting father, I was sitting in the back of the room in an arithmetic class. Suddenly the situation seemed perfectly absurd. Here were twenty extremely valuable organisms. Through no fault of her own, the teacher was violating almost everything we knew about the learning process" (p. 406).

It is interesting to note that the most common teaching technique is the lecture, and the lecture technique violates all three of the above principles. Skinner proposed an alternative teaching technique, **programmed learning,** which does incorporate all three principles. A device invented to present programmed material has been called a **teaching machine.** The advantages of using a teaching machine were outlined by Skinner (1958) as follows:

> The machine itself, of course, does not teach. It simply brings the student into contact with the person who composed the material it presents. It is a labor-saving device because it can bring one programmer into contact with an indefinite number of students. They may suggest mass production, but the effect upon each student is surprisingly like that of a private tutor. The comparison holds in several respects. (i) There is a constant interchange between program and student. Unlike lectures, textbooks, and the usual audio-visual aids, the machine induces sustained activity. The student is always alert and busy. (ii) Like a good tutor, the machine insists that a given point be thoroughly understood, either frame-by-frame or set-by-set, before the student moves on. Lectures, textbooks, and their mechanized equivalents, on the other hand, proceed without making sure that the student understands and easily leave him behind. (iii) Like a good tutor, the machine presents just that material for which the student is ready. It asks him to take only that step which he is at the moment best equipped and most likely to take. (iv) Like a skillful tutor, the machine helps the student to come up with the right answer. It does this in part through the orderly construction of the program and in part with techniques of hinting, prompting, suggesting, and so on, derived from an analysis of verbal behavior.... (v) Lastly, of course, the machine, like the private tutor, reinforces the student for every correct response, using this immediate feedback not only to shape his behavior most efficiently but to maintain it in strength in a manner which the laymen would describe as "holding the student's interest." (p. 971)

We will have more to say about programmed learning in Chapter 16.

Contingency Contracting

Contingency contracting is an extension of Skinnerian thinking. Briefly, it involves making arrangements so that a person gets something he or she wants when he or she acts in a certain way. Some arrangements can be simple and cover simple behavior, such as when a teacher says to a child, "If you sit quietly for five minutes, you can go out and play." Other arrangements can extend over a much longer period of time. For example, if a person has a weight problem and has difficulty losing weight on his own, he may wish to arrange the environment so that he is reinforced for losing weight. He may, for example, sign over to another person something personally important such as money, a record collection, a stamp collection, or favorite clothes. Taking money as an example, the person trying to lose weight may put up, say, 100 dollars and draw up an agreement whereby the other person gives back 10 dollars each week if 3 pounds are lost. Each week that he does not lose at least 3 pounds, he loses 10 dollars. The same kind of arrangement can be made by utilizing anything important to the person, and the behavior involved could as easily be smoking as losing weight.

The term *contingency contracting* comes from the fact that an agreement (contract) is made that certain activities will be reinforced that otherwise may not have been. In other words, the contract rearranges the reinforcement contingencies in the environment, causing them to be responsive to behavior patterns that one hopes to modify in some way.

Many behavior problems occur because our behavior is influenced more by immediate reinforcers than by distant ones. For example, for some the taste of food in the present is more reinforcing than the distant promise of a longer life if one eats in moderation. Likewise, the immediate effect of nicotine is more reinforcing than the promise of a longer life without smoking. Contingency contracting is a way of modifying behavior through current reinforcing contingencies rather than distant ones. It is hoped that as desirable behavior is shaped by using this procedure, the desirable behavior itself will be functional in obtaining reinforcers from the social environment. Not being overweight and not smoking both can be very reinforcing, but the problem is switching the overweight person and the smoker to another class of reinforcing experiences. Contingency contracting can be a very effective tool in accomplishing this switchover. Once the switch in reinforcement systems has been made, however, the desired behavior is usually sustained by the social environment, and therefore the artificial reinforcement contingencies are no longer needed.

Contingency contracting need not involve a second person; one can follow these procedures alone by giving oneself a "treat" of some kind each day one goes without smoking, drinking, or overeating. For a more detailed discussion of contingency contracting see Homme, Csanyi, Gonzales, and Rechs (1970).

Skinner's Attitude toward Learning Theory

Skinner believed that it is unnecessary to formulate complicated theories to study human behavior, and he believed it is unnecessary to know the physiological correlates of behavior. He believed that behavioral events must be described in terms of things that directly affect behavior and that it is logically inconsistent to attempt to explain behavior in terms of physiological events. For this reason, Skinner's method of research has been called "the empty organism approach."

Skinner also thought that complex theories of learning, such as Hull's (Chapter 6), are time-consuming and wasteful. Some day such theories may be useful in psychology, but not until we have collected much more basic data. Our main concern at this time should be, Skinner believed, to discover basic relationships between classes of stimuli and classes of responses. Therefore, the use of theory in studying the learning process cannot be justified (Skinner, 1950):

> Research designed with respect to theory is also likely to be wasteful. That a theory generates research does not prove its value unless the research is valuable. Much useless experimentation results from theories, and much energy and skill are absorbed by them. Most theories are eventually overthrown, and the greater part of the associated research is discarded. This could be justified if it were true that productive research requires a theory—as is, of course, often claimed. It is argued that research would be aimless and disorganized without a theory to guide it. The view is supported by psychological texts which take their cue from the logicians rather than empirical science and describe thinking as necessarily involving stages of hypothesis, deduction, experimental test, and confirmation. But this is not the way most scientists actually work. It is possible to design significant experiments for other reasons, and the possibility to be examined is that such research will lead more directly to the kind of information which a science usually accumulates. (pp. 194–195)

Skinner's (1953) approach to research was to do a **functional analysis** between stimulating events and measurable behavior:

> The external variables of which behavior is a function provide for what may be called a causal or functional analysis. We undertake to predict and control the behavior of the individual organism. This is our "dependent variable"—the effect for which we are to find the cause. Our "independent variables"—the causes of behavior—are the external conditions of which behavior is a function. Relations between the two—the "cause-and-effect relationships" in behavior—are the laws of a science. A synthesis of these laws expressed in quantitative terms yields a comprehensive picture of the organism as a behaving system. (p. 35)

Thus, Skinner manipulated hours of food or water deprivation and noted the effect on the rate with which the lever-pressing response was learned; or he observed the effect of schedules of reinforcement on response rate or resistance to extinction. In interpreting the results of his research, Skinner stayed very close to the data; that is, if partial reinforcement produces greater resistance to extinction than does 100 percent reinforcement, that is a fact and that is all that can be said. In other words, Skinner did not attempt to explain why this is the case.

Even in deciding *what* to investigate, Skinner claimed he was not guided by theoretical notions but rather used a hit-and-miss process. He tried first one thing and then another. If he saw that one line of research was not producing anything worthwhile, he would shift to something that looked more fruitful and he would continue in this trial-and-error fashion until he hit on something of value. This rather liberal attitude toward scientific investigation was summarized in Skinner's (1956) article "A Case History in Scientific Method."

The Need for a Technology of Behavior

Skinner felt very strongly that a carefully worked-out behavior technology could solve many human problems; yet many people would oppose such a technology because it seems to challenge a number of our cherished beliefs about ourselves, especially that human beings are rational, free, and dignified. Skinner (1971) believed that these beliefs were interfering with the solution of our major problems and also preventing the development of the very tool that could solve them:

> What we need is a technology of behavior. We could solve our problems quickly enough if we could adjust the growth of the world's population as precisely as we adjust the course of a spaceship, or improve agriculture and industry with some of the confidence with which we accelerate high-energy particles, or move toward a peaceful world with something like the steady progress with which physics has approached absolute zero (even though both remain presumably out of reach). But a behavioral technology comparable in power and precision to physical and biological technology is lacking, and those who do not find the very possibility ridiculous are more likely to be frightened by it than reassured. That is how far we are from "understanding human issues" in the sense in which physics and biology understand their fields, and how far we are from preventing the catastrophe toward which the world seems to be inexorably moving. (p. 5)

Elsewhere, Skinner (1953) said,

> The traditional view of human nature in Western culture is well known. The conception of a free, responsible individual is embedded in our language and pervades our practices, codes, and beliefs. Given an example of human behavior, most people can describe it immediately in terms of such a conception. The practice is so natural that it is seldom examined. A scientific formulation, on the other hand, is new and strange. Very few people have any notion of the extent to which a science of human behavior is indeed possible. In what way can the behavior of the individual or of groups of individuals be predicted and controlled? What are laws of behavior like? What over-all conception of the human organism as a behaving system emerges? It is only when we have answered these questions, at least in a preliminary fashion, that we may consider the implications of a science of human behavior with respect to either a theory of human nature or the management of human affairs. (pp. 9–10)

In an article entitled "What Is Wrong with Daily Life in the Western World?" Skinner (1986) renewed his plea for the utilization of behavior technology in solving human problems. In this article, Skinner argued that five cultural practices are eroding the strengthening effects of reinforcement contingencies. These cultural practices are: "(a) Alienating workers from the consequences of their work; (b) helping those who could help themselves; (c) guiding behavior with rules rather than supplying reinforcing consequences; (d) maintaining aversive sanctions of government and religions with long-deferred benefits for the individual; and (e) reinforcing looking, listening, reading, gambling, and so on, while strengthening few other behaviors" (p. 568).

According to Skinner, the many problems caused by these cultural practices could be solved by strengthening desirable behavior by using the principles derived from an experimental analysis of behavior, that is, by using the principles described in this chapter.

Skinner's theory of learning has had, and is having, a profound influence on psychology. No matter what area of psychology one studies, one is apt to find reference to some aspect of Skinner's work. As we noted in Chapter 2, a characteristic of any good theory is that it generates research, and Skinner's theory has certainly done that. We will now review the work of an important researcher who has been influenced by Skinner's work.

THE RELATIVITY OF REINFORCEMENT

David Premack

Traditionally, reinforcers have been thought of as stimuli. A primary reinforcer is usually thought of as being related to an organism's survival, and a secondary reinforcer is a stimulus that has been consistently paired with a primary reinforcer. Premack, however, has suggested that all *responses* should be thought of as potential reinforcers. Specifically, he suggests that any response that occurs with a fairly high frequency can be used to reinforce a response that occurs with a relatively lower frequency. Using Premack's notion of reinforcement, one would allow an organism to engage freely in whatever activities it wanted to and carefully record what activities were engaged in and with what frequency. Afterward, the various activities that the organism engaged in would be arranged in a hierarchy. The activity that was engaged in most frequently would be listed first, the next frequently engaged in activity would be listed next, and so on. By referring to this list, the experimenter would know exactly what could and could not be used to reinforce that particular organism. Say, for example, it was found that in a 24-hour period, the activity engaged in most frequently by a rat was eating, then drinking, then running in an activity wheel, then grooming, and finally gazing out of the cage. According to Premack, allowing the animal to eat could be used to reinforce any of the other activities. For example, if the animal was allowed to eat each time it groomed itself, grooming would increase in frequency. Likewise, allowing the animal to groom itself could be used to reinforce the animal for looking outside the cage. The opportunity to look outside the cage, however, could not be used to reinforce any of the other activities because they all occurred with a greater frequency than the response of looking outside the cage.

According to Premack, the way to find out what can be used as a reinforcer is to observe the organism's behavior while it has the opportunity to engage in any number of activities, and the activities that it engages in most often can be used to reinforce the activities that it engages in less often.

In summary we can say that if one activity occurs more often than another, it can be used to reinforce the activity that occurs less often. This is called the **Premack principle,** and it seems to hold for humans as well as for lower organisms.

To test his theory, Premack (1959) allowed 31 first-grade children either to play a pinball machine or to operate a candy dispenser as often as they wanted. Some of the children played mainly with the pinball machine, and they were

David Premack. (Courtesy of David Premack.)

called manipulators. The children who were primarily interested in the candy dispenser were called eaters. The first phase of the study merely determined the children's preferences for these two events.

In the second phase of the study, the groups of manipulators and eaters were each subdivided into two groups. One group was placed on manipulate-eat contingencies, in which the children had to play the pinball machine before they were allowed to operate the candy dispenser. The other group was placed on eat-manipulate contingencies, in which they had to operate the candy dispenser before they could play the pinball machine. It was found that for the manipulators the manipulate-eat arrangement made little difference in their behavior. They simply went right on playing the pinball machine as before. Under the eat-manipulate conditions, however, the frequency of eating went way up for the manipulators since they now had to eat in order to play the pinball machine. Likewise, for the eaters the eat-manipulate condition made little difference. They simply went on eating candy as before. But under the manipulate-eat conditions, their frequency of playing the pinball machine went way up. Thus, Premack found support for his contention that a less frequently engaged-in activity can be reinforced by the opportunity to engage in a more frequently engaged-in activity.

When preferences change, the reinforcers also change. For example, as long as an animal is hungry, it will eat frequently, and therefore the opportunity to eat can be used to reinforce any number of activities. When the animal is satiated, however, the frequency of its eating will decrease and the opportunity to eat will become ineffective as a reinforcer. Premack (1962) demonstrated the reversibility of reinforcement in a study involving a running response and a drinking response. It was found that if animals were deprived of water for a considerable length of time, they would turn an activity wheel in order to gain access to water. But they would not increase their drinking to run in the activity wheel. That is, drinking reinforced running, but running did not reinforce drinking. This is what one would predict from traditional reinforcement theory. Premack also found that if an animal was allowed to drink all the water it wanted but was prevented from running in the activity wheel, the situation was reversed. Under these circumstances, drinking activity increased if it resulted in having the opportunity to run, but running did not increase if it allowed the animal to drink. That is, now running could reinforce drinking but not vice versa.

The implications of Premack's research are far-reaching. For one thing, what can act as a reinforcer becomes a very personal and continuously changing thing. The teacher can apply this knowledge by noticing individual children's preferences in a free-choice situation and determining their reinforcers accordingly. For one child, the opportunity to run and play may be a reinforcer; for another child, playing with clay may be a reinforcer. The idea of recess as a way to improve the performance of the class as a whole will need to be looked at more carefully. For examples of how the Premack principle can be used to control the behavior of schoolchildren, see Homme, deBaca, Divine, Steinhorst, and Rickert (1963).

Revisions of the Premack Principle

You may remember from Chapter 4 that Thorndike's definition of a satisfier was criticized because it appeared to be circular. When Skinner defined a reinforcer as any event that increases the probability of a response, he neatly avoided the problems of describing physical, aesthetic, or chemical characteristics of reinforcers. Similarly, he avoided the difficulties associated with describing the biological aspects of reinforcement. Unfortunately, his definition has also been criticized as circular. Walker (1969) suggested that Skinner's operational definition has elusive and even "magical" qualities in that it suffices when a specific procedure produces reinforcing effects, but it cannot explain cases in which that same procedure has no effect or when it results in a decreased frequency of responding. Similarly, Gregory Kimble, from whom we borrowed our initial definition of learning (see Chapter 1), indicates that food is reinforcing at the beginning of a meal, is neutral mid-meal, and is punishing at the end (Kimble, 1993). He even suggests facetiously that the concept of reinforcement "suffers from terminal ambiguity and that it is a nominee for mercy killing." (p. 254).

The traditional defense when Thorndike or Skinner are attacked as circular is Meehl's (1950) "transituational" argument. According to this argument, a satisfier or reinforcer in one situation can be shown to modify behavior in another situation. It is argued that the transituational nature of reinforcers or satisfiers protects them from claims that their definitions are circular. One of the important findings derived from Premack's research is that the transituational argument is inadequate if not entirely incorrect. For example, if an animal prefers to spend 30 percent of its time eating, 20 percent drinking, and 10 percent in an activity wheel, the Premack principle tells us that we can use drinking to reinforce activity in the wheel. In a straightforward application of Premack's principle, we cannot use drinking to reinforce eating in that specific animal, and we may not be able to use drinking to reinforce wheel-running in an animal with different activity preferences. This demonstrates a first flaw in the transituational argument. Research conducted by William Timberlake and his associates (Timberlake, 1980; Timberlake & Allison, 1974; Timberlake & Farmer-Dougan, 1991) is instructive with respect to failure of the transituational argument, the limits of the Premack Principle, and the nature of reinforcement.

William Timberlake

Timberlake (Timberlake, 1980; Timberlake & Farmer-Dougan, 1991) distinguishes between the probability-differential hypothesis, the position taken by Premack, and the "disequilibrium hypothesis," a position that logically follows from Premack's (1962) drinking-activity wheel study described above. In contrast with Premack's suggestion that preferred activities can reinforce less preferred activities, the disequilibrium hypothesis states that any activity can be a reinforcer if a contingency schedule constrains an animal's access to that activity. Imagine that we watch a freely behaving rat for several days. Let us say that, as before, the rat spends 30 percent of its waking time eating, 20 percent of its time drinking, and 10 percent of its time running in an activity wheel. It distributes the remaining 40 percent of its time among a number of other activities. According to Timberlake, this proportional distribution of activities constitutes an equilibrium, a state of activity-balance freely maintained and preferred by the animal. If we establish a contingency schedule such that time devoted to eating is reduced below the baseline of 30 percent, we have created disequilibrium, a condition that will have motivational consequences. Under this condition of disequilibrium, eating can be used as a reinforcer for any other activity, and it will continue to have reinforcing properties until the animal has restored baseline equilibrium such that 30 percent of its time is allotted to eating.

On the other hand, the disequilibrium hypothesis predicts that wheel-running, the least probable of the activities above, can also be a reinforcer. For this to happen, however, a schedule must somehow be imposed in which wheel running is reduced below its 10 percent baseline, thus producing disequilibrium. As was the case with eating, wheel-running can be a reinforcer for any other behavior until wheel-running returns to 10 percent and equilibrium is restored.

The disequilibrium hypothesis also delineates conditions under which a specific activity can become punishing. To produce punishment, a schedule must be designed in which performance of one activity serves to increase another activity above its baseline. Imagine that the rat in our example is given food every time that it runs in the activity wheel. As long as eating takes less than 30 percent of the animal's time, food will reinforce wheel-running. However, if wheel-running produces conditions in which eating activity would exceed 30 percent of the animal's time, wheel-running will decrease under the wheel-food contingency. Eating has thus become a punisher.

Timberlake's position provides important new perspectives about reinforcement and reinforcement contingencies. Like Premack's, Timberlake's research shows clearly that the transituational argument concerning reinforcement is incorrect. Further, from this perspective, the role of a contingency schedule is to produce disequilibrium rather than to provide information relating a response to a reinforcer or to provide contiguity between a response and a reinforcer. And finally, from Timberlake's research we see that deprivation of food or water per se are not essential to make these substances reinforcers. Rather, it is restriction of access to them that serves to make them reinforcers.

While the positions taken by Premack and Timberlake are improvements on the older idea that "reinforcers are things that reinforce," we are still left with a number of unanswered questions. For example, neither position addresses the question of baseline preferences. Why should a rat spend more time eating than drinking? The answer can no longer be "Because it is more reinforcing to do so!"

There is no doubt that Skinnerian notions have had, and are having, far-reaching theoretical and practical implications. Recently, however, there has been a growing recognition of the limitations of operant principles in modifying behavior. In the next section we will examine why operant principles seem to have limited applicability.

THE MISBEHAVIOR OF ORGANISMS

We saw in the last chapter that Thorndike concluded that the same laws of learning apply to all mammals, including humans. Skinner, like many other learning theorists, agreed with Thorndike's conclusion. After observing how different species of animals performed under a certain schedule of reinforcement, Skinner (1956) commented, "Pigeon, rat, monkey, which is which? It doesn't matter. Of course, these species have behavioral repertoires which are as different as their anatomies. But once you have allowed for differences in the ways in which they make contact with the

Marian Bailey. (Courtesy of Marian Bailey.)

environment, and in the ways in which they act upon the environment, what remains of their behavior shows astonishingly similar properties" (pp. 230–231). Skinner went on to say that one can also add the performance of mice, cats, dogs, and human children and the curves would still have more or less the same characteristics.

The alternative to believing that the same laws of learning apply to all mammals seems to necessitate going back to the concept of instinct, which the behaviorists attempted to bury forever. Those believing in the existence of instincts say that different species have different inborn tendencies that interact with or even negate the laws of learning. In other words, because of their innate behavior tendencies, certain species can be conditioned to do some things but not others. According to this point of view, some responses should be easier to condition for some species than for others because the responses of interest may occur more naturally for some species than for others.

Current interest in how innate behavior tendencies interact with learning principles has been stimulated by two of Skinner's ex-associates, Marian Breland (now Marian Bailey) and Keller Breland. Armed with a knowledge of operant principles, the Brelands moved from Minnesota, where they had worked with Skinner, to Arkansas, where they started a business called Animal Behavior Enterprises. By using operant techniques the Brelands were able to train a wide variety of animals to perform many different tricks, and their trained animals were put on display at fairs, at conventions, at amusement parks, and on television. As of 1961, the Brelands reported having conditioned 38 species (totaling over 6,000 animals), including chickens, pigs, raccoons, reindeer, cockatoos, porpoises, and whales.

Everything seemed to be going fine for the Brelands until they began to experience breakdowns of conditioned behavior. Their problems became so pronounced that they were moved to report them in an article (Breland & Breland, 1961) whose title, "The Misbehavior of Organisms" (1961), was a parody of the title of Skinner's first major work, *The Behavior of Organisms* (1938).

The Brelands found that although their animals were initially highly conditionable, eventually instinctive behavior would appear and interfere with what had been learned. For example, an attempt was made to train raccoons to pick up coins and deposit them into a 5-inch metal box. Conditioning a raccoon to pick up a single coin was no problem. Next, the metal box was introduced, and that is when the problem began. The raccoon seemed to have trouble letting the coin fall into the box. The animal would rub the coin inside of the container, take it back out, and hold it firmly for several seconds. Eventually, however, the raccoon released the coin into the box and received its food reinforcement. The next phase in training required the raccoon to place *two* coins into the metal box before receiving reinforcement. It was found that the raccoon could not let go of the two coins. Instead, it would rub them together, dip them into the container, and then remove them. The rubbing behavior became more and more pronounced even though it delayed or even prevented reinforcement. The Brelands concluded that conditioning a raccoon to place two coins into a metal box was not feasible. It seemed that the innate behaviors associated with eating were too powerful to be overcome by operant conditioning principles. In other words, in this case, a raccoon's innate tendency to wash and manipulate its food competed successfully with the learned response of placing one or more coins into a container.

Another example of the **misbehavior of organisms** involved the training of pigs to pick up large wooden coins and deposit them in a large "piggy bank." The coins were placed several feet from the bank, and the pig had to transport them to the bank before receiving reinforcement. Early conditioning was very effective and the pigs seemed eager to perform the task. As time went on, however, the animals performed more slowly, and on their way to the "piggy bank" they would repeatedly drop the coin, root it (push it along the ground with their snouts), pick it up, drop it, root it, toss it in the air, and so on. The Brelands first believed that such behavior may have been the result of low drive, so they intensified the deprivation schedule that the animals were on, which only intensified the animal's misbehavior. Eventually it took the pigs about ten minutes to transport the coins a distance of about six feet, even when such delays postponed or eliminated reinforcement. Again, it appeared that the animal's instinctive behavior associated with eating became more powerful than the behavior it had learned.

From these and other similar observations, the Brelands (1961) concluded, "It seems obvious that these animals are trapped by strong instinctive behaviors, and clearly we have here a demonstration of the prepotency of such behavior patterns over those which have been conditioned" (p. 185). The Brelands called the tendency for innate behavior patterns gradually to displace learned behavior **instinctual drift,** which they describe as follows:

> The general principle seems to be that wherever an animal has strong instinctive behaviors in the area of the conditioned response, after continued running the organism will drift toward the instinctive behavior to the detriment of the conditioned behavior and even to the delay or preclusion of the reinforcement. In a very boiled-down, simplified form it might be stated as "Learned behavior drifts toward instinctive behavior." (p. 185)

The Brelands feel that their work challenges three assumptions made by the behaviorists, namely, (1) that animals come to the learning situation as a *tabula rasa* (blank tablet), (2) that differences among various species are unimportant, and (3) that any response can be conditioned to any stimulus. Rather than making these assumptions, the Brelands (1961) conclude, "After 14 years of continuous conditioning and observation of thousands of animals, it is our reluctant conclusion that the behavior of any species cannot be adequately understood, predicted, or controlled without knowledge of its instinctive patterns, evolutionary history, and ecological niche" (p. 126).

Thus, we are once again confronted with the age-old empiricism-nativism controversy; that is, is behavior learned or is it genetically determined? The phenomenon of instinctual drift seems to indicate that at least for some species, behavior can be nudged only a limited amount from its instinctual basis before instinctual tendencies override learned tendencies as the most powerful determiners of behavior. What about humans? Do we have within us the remnants of our evolutionary past toward which we periodically drift? Can culture, society, or circumstances push us only so far before we resort to more primitive forms of behavior? The answer depends on who is being asked. Many learning theorists such as Skinner would say no. Others such as Freud and the sociobiologists would say yes.

Autoshaping   Another phenomenon that seems to show the importance of instinctive behavior in a learning situation is **autoshaping.** We saw earlier in this chapter that the shaping process can be used to encourage an animal to make a response in a situation that it ordinarily would not make. To do so, the experimenter reinforces increasingly closer approximations to the desired behavior until the desired behavior is performed by the animal. In the case of autoshaping, however, the animal seems to shape its own behavior. For example, Brown and Jenkins (1968) found that if a pigeon was reinforced at certain intervals, regardless of what it was doing (noncontingent reinforcement), and if a disc was illuminated just prior to the presentation of the reinforcer (in this case, food), the pigeon learned to peck at the disc. The question is, why did the pigeon learn to peck at the disc when it had never been reinforced for doing so?

One attempt to account for autoshaping has likened it to superstitious behavior, saying that the pigeon may have been pecking at the disc just before food was delivered and therefore pecking the disc would be maintained as a superstitious response. One problem with this explanation is that almost all pigeons peck the disc under these circumstances. It seems that if superstitious behavior were involved, some pigeons would peck the disc, others would turn in circles, others would peck other parts of the test chamber, and so on. A second explanation of autoshaping has been based on classical conditioning principles. According to this explanation, the illuminated disc becomes a secondary reinforcer because of its proximity to food, a primary reinforcer. Under the circumstances described thus far, this explanation is reasonable, except that it does not explain why the pigeon would peck at the disc. Earlier in this chapter we saw that, indeed, discriminative stimuli (S^Ds) become secondary reinforcers and thus can be used to maintain behavior, but why the animal should respond overtly to the secondary reinforcer as if it were the primary reinforcer is not clear.

An experiment by Williams and Williams (1969) casts further doubt on explanations of autoshaping as either a superstitious or a classical conditioning phenomenon. In their experiment, Williams and Williams arranged the situation so that pecking at the lighted disc actually *prevented* reinforcement from occurring. Food was presented to the pigeons every 15 seconds, unless the pigeon pecked at the illuminated disc, in which case food was withheld on that trial. In this study, pecking at the illuminated disc was *never* followed by reinforcement. In fact, the more the pigeon pecked at the disc, the less food it received. According to the explanations of autoshaping in terms of both superstitious behavior and of classical conditioning, the experimental arrangement in this study should have eliminated or, at least, drastically reduced disc pecking. It did not, however. The pigeons went right on pecking at the disc at a high rate. In fact, for some pigeons disc pecking occurred so frequently that it virtually eliminated all reinforcement.

A study by Jenkins and Moore (1973) further complicates the situation. In their study it was found that if food was used as a reinforcer, pigeons responded to the disc with an eating posture, and if water was used as a reinforcer pigeons responded to the disc with a drinking posture. In other words, when food was used as a reinforcer the pigeons seemed to be eating the disc, and when water was used as a reinforcer they seemed to be drinking the disc.

By the process of elimination, one is forced to view the autoshaping phenomenon as involving instinctive behavior patterns. It can be assumed, for example, that a hungry organism in a situation in which eating is possible will most likely give responses related to eating. In the case of pigeons, pecking is such a response. Furthermore, it may be assumed that while in a high drive state, such behaviors can be easily elicited by any stimulus in the animal's environment that is vivid and on which an eating-related response could be easily released. A lighted disc in the environment of a hungry pigeon could be such a stimulus. According to this explanation, the lighted disc is simply eliciting instinctive behavior that has a high probability of occurring under the circumstances. Because disc pecking in autoshaping experiments is typically what the experimenter is looking for, it is not referred to as misbehavior as were certain instinctive responses in the Brelands' work.

If one accepts the instinctive explanation of autoshaping, one needs to conclude that no learning takes place at all. The animal simply becomes hypersensitive in the situation and releases innate responses that are appropriate under the circumstances to the most vivid stimuli in its environment. This is the position taken by Robert Bolles (see e.g., Bolles, 1979, pp. 179–184).

The work of the Brelands and the work on autoshaping are only two examples of a growing recognition in psychology that the innate response tendencies of an organism interact with the laws of learning. In other words, what may hold true for one type of organism may not hold true for another type of organism. Furthermore, what may hold true for a given organism at one developmental level may not hold true for that organism at another developmental level. For a more detailed elaboration of these points see Seligman and Hager (1972).

EVALUATION OF SKINNER'S THEORY

Contributions

B.F. Skinner's long and productive research program significantly influenced both applied and purely scientific psychology. Compared to many other learning researchers, Skinner's system was straightforward and could be easily applied to problems ranging from animal training to human behavior modification therapy. At another extreme, his work led to the matching law and had an indirect impact on current research in behavioral decision making.

Skinner's methodology was a departure from mainstream behaviorism. Verplanck (1954) noted that Skinner's approach "not only differs from the others in particulars of theoretical detail, but also represents a re-orientation toward the science" (p. 306). While other researchers tended to conduct research on groups of subjects, making nomothetic comparisons between different experimental conditions, Skinner utilized an ideographic approach in which single experimental subjects were observed for prolonged periods. This approach, along with almost exclusive use of the cumulative record of responding, provided an alternative to the dominant research method(s) in the field, and it resulted in the creation of a specialized journal, *Journal of Experimental Analysis of Behavior.* The method allowed for detailed study and analysis of reinforcement schedules and yielded a number of new behavioral laws. Throughout his life, Skinner was steadfast in his insistence that psychologists should avoid theorizing, especially about cognitive events, and be content with descriptive accounts of behavior.

Criticisms

Some criticisms of Skinner's theory are more warranted than others. For example, Staddon (1995), who traces his lineage to Skinner as a former student of Richard Herrnstein, finds Skinner's influence in a number of societal problems. Most responsible are Skinner's contentions that punishment is ineffective and that, because humans have no free will, they cannot be held responsible for their behavior. Staddon believes that these Skinnerian beliefs have resulted in faulty parenting and flawed legal practices, which in turn have led to increased crime rates, illegitimacy, and illiteracy. Although we would not go so far as to blame Skinnerian behaviorism for complex social and economic problems, there are aspects of his position that can be legitimately criticized.

Although the ideographic method developed by Skinner allowed the examination of an individual's operant behavior in detail, it was very difficult to compare results from his procedure with results obtained in laboratories using the nomothetic method. A second criticism follows from Skinner's refusal to develop formal theory. As we noted in Chapter 1, a primary function of a theory is explanation of existing data and phenomena. It is important to note, in the context of Skinner's position, that there is a great difference between describing a phenomenon and attempting to explain that phenomenon. In the first case, careful description is usually accurate, cannot be disputed, and tends to explain how and when behavior occurs. A theory, on the other hand, usually endeavors to explain why a behavior appears as well as the how's and when's. Theories, unlike descriptions, are often disputed, and such dispute may lead to scientific progress. Skinner's system did lead to progress, but it was a progress characterized by accumulation of behavioral phenomena rather than a deeper understanding of learning and motivation.

DISCUSSION QUESTIONS

1. Outline the procedure you would use while following Skinner's theory to increase the probability that a child would become a creative adult.

2. Would you use the same reinforcers to manipulate the behavior of both children and adults? If not, what would make the difference?

3. Are there some forms of adult human behavior for which you feel Skinner's theory is not applicable? Explain.

4. What would characterize the classroom procedures suggested by Skinner's theory of learning? List a few differences between these procedures and those now being followed in our schools.

5. Assuming the conclusions Skinner reached concerning the effectiveness of punishment are valid, what major change would they suggest in child-rearing? Criminal behavior? Education?

6. What is the partial reinforcement effect? Briefly describe the basic reinforcement schedules that Skinner studied.

7. Propose an explanation for the partial reinforcement effect.

8. Describe concurrent and concurrent chain schedules of reinforcement and give an example of each.

9. What is Herrnstein's matching law? What aspects of reinforcement has the law been found to hold true for? What are the implications of the law for dealing with human behavior problems?

10. What is contingency contracting? Give an example of how it could be used.

11. From Skinner's point of view, what are the advantages of programmed learning and teaching machines over the traditional lecture technique of teaching?

12. According to Skinner, why have we not developed a more adequate technology of behavior in this country? What would need to be done before we would be willing to utilize such a technology in solving our problems?

13. Give an example of how the Premack principle can be used to modify the behavior of a primary school child.

14. Discuss chaining from Skinner's point of view.

15. Explain language development from Skinner's point of view. Explain Chomsky's opposition to Skinner's explanation of language development.

16. Distinguish among positive reinforcement, negative reinforcement, and punishment.

17. Explain the difference between Premack's and Timberlake's views of reinforcers.

18. Describe the phenomenon of instinctual drift.

19. Describe autoshaping and attempt to account for it.

KEY TERMS

autoclitic behavior   Provides a grammatical framework for verbal behavior.

autoshaping   The observation that under certain circumstances the behavior of some organisms seems to be shaped automatically.

chaining   According to Skinner, chaining occurs when one response brings the organism into proximity with stimuli that both reinforce the last response and cause the next response. That response in turn causes the organism to experience stimuli that both reinforce the response and cause the next response, and so on.

concurrent chain reinforcement schedule   On such a schedule the responses made during an initial phase determine what response alternatives and what reinforcement schedules are available during the terminal phase.

concurrent reinforcement schedule   A schedule involving two alternative responses each of which is maintained by an independent schedule of reinforcement.

contingency contracting   Making arrangements, sometimes with another person, so that certain behavior will be reinforced. For example, each time the person goes a week without smoking he or she receives ten dollars.

contingent reinforcement   Reinforcement that only occurs if a specific response is made. If the response is not made, the organism is not reinforced.

continuous reinforcement schedule (CRF)   The condition in which the organism is reinforced each time it makes an appropriate response.

cumulative recording   A special kind of graphing technique used by Skinner. Each time a response is made, the cumulative recording rises one notch and remains at that level until another response is made. The steepness of the line, therefore, indicates rate of responding.

differential reinforcement   The condition in which some responses made by the organism are reinforced and others are not.

discriminative operant   An operant response that is made selectively to one set of circumstances but not to another set of circumstances.

discriminative stimulus (S^D)   A cue or signal indicating that if a certain operant response is made it will be reinforced.

disequilibrium hypothesis   Restricted access to a response makes access to that response reinforcing; excessive access to a response makes that response punishing.

echoic behavior   Repeating someone else's verbal utterances.

extinction of an operant response   In operant conditioning extinction involves the gradual decrease in the *frequency* with which a conditioned response occurs after it is no longer reinforced, whereas in classical conditioning the extinction of a conditioned response involves the gradual decrease in *amplitude* of the conditioned response following the removal of reinforcement. When the frequency of an operant response returns to its operant level, it is said to be extinguished.

fixed interval reinforcement schedule (FI)   The condition in which only the response made after a certain interval of time has passed is reinforced.

fixed ratio reinforcement schedule (FR)   The condition in which only the *n*th response made is reinforced.

functional analysis   The investigation of how certain stimuli and certain responses vary together. Skinner's approach to research was to avoid theorizing and to deal only with the manipulation of observable stimuli and note how their manipulation affected behavior; sometimes called the "empty organism" approach to research.

functional autonomy   A term introduced by Gordon Allport to explain behavior that apparently occurs independently of external reinforcement. Such behavior, according to Allport, was originally dependent on reinforcement but eventually becomes autonomous or self-reinforcing.

generalized reinforcers   Stimuli that derive their reinforcement properties from being paired with more than one primary reinforcer. Generalized reinforcers have wide application since their effectiveness does not depend on any particular need of the organism.

Herrnstein's equation   A mathematical expression derived from the **matching law** that describes the learning curve for a single operant behavior. It expresses response rate as a function of reinforcement rate.

instinctual drift   The tendency for the behavior of some organisms, after prolonged conditioning, to revert back to instinctual patterns of behavior.

magazine training   Training the animal to approach the food cup when it hears the feeder mechanism operate. Thus the click of the feeder mechanism is associated with food and thereby becomes a secondary reinforcer.

mand   A verbal command that is reinforced when the listener carries out the command. For example, the mand "pass the salt" is reinforced when the person receives the salt.

matching law   Herrnstein's observation that when two alternative responses are governed by two independent schedules of reinforcement, the relative rate of responding to the alternatives approximately matches the relative rate at which the alternatives are reinforced. The matching law holds not only for rate (frequency) of reinforcement but for amount and delay of reinforcement as well. All other things being equal, organisms will prefer schedules of reinforcement that produce frequent, large, and immediate reinforcers as compared to infrequent, small, and delayed reinforcers.

misbehavior of organisms   The term used by the Brelands to describe the tendency that some organisms have to behave instinctually instead of in a way that they had been conditioned to behave.

noncontingent reinforcement   Reinforcement that occurs independently of the organism's behavior.

operant behavior   Behavior that is simply emitted by the organism rather than elicited by a known stimulus. Operant behavior may come under the control of its consequences.

operant conditioning   Increasing the rate with which a response occurs or the probability of a response by arranging the situation so that the occurrence of that response is followed by reinforcement. Also called Type R conditioning.

operant level   The frequency with which an operant response occurs before it is systematically reinforced.

partial reinforcement effect (PRE)   The fact that a response that has been reinforced only sometimes takes longer to extinguish than a response that had been reinforced each time it occurred.

Premack principle   The opportunity to engage in a frequently occurring activity can be used to reinforce a less frequently occurring activity.

primary negative reinforcer   An aversive stimulus, which when removed from the situation following a response, increases the probability of the response's recurrence.

primary positive reinforcer   A stimulus related to an organism's survival, which when added to the situation following a response, increases the probability of the response's recurrence.

programmed learning A procedure that provides information to the learner in small steps, guarantees immediate feedback concerning whether or not the material was learned properly, and allows the learner to determine the pace with which he or she goes through the material.

punishment The arrangement whereby either a response produces an aversive stimulus or removes a positive one.

respondent behavior Behavior elicited by a known stimulus.

respondent conditioning The same as classical conditioning; also called Type S conditioning.

shaping The process whereby a desired response is encouraged through the use of differential reinforcement and successive approximation rather than simply waiting for it to occur.

Skinner box See key terms, Chapter 1.

spontaneous recovery of an operant response The increased frequency with which a conditioned operant response occurs following a delay after extinction and with no further training.

successive approximation Reinforcing only those responses that become increasingly similar to the response that is finally desired; a component of the process of shaping.

superstitious behavior Behavior that looks as if it is governed by the belief that it must be engaged in before reinforcement can be obtained, whereas in reality the behavior has nothing to do with the presence or absence of reinforcement. Superstitious behavior results from noncontingent reinforcement.

tact The verbal behavior of naming things. Such behavior results in reinforcement when objects or events are named correctly.

teaching machine A device used to present programmed material.

variable interval reinforcement schedule (VI) The condition in which only the response made after the passage of some *average* interval of time is reinforced.

variable ratio reinforcement schedule (VR) The condition in which a certain *average* number of responses needs to be made before the organism is reinforced.

Chapter 6

CLARK LEONARD HULL

Clark Leonard Hull. (From *A History of Psychology in Autobiography,* Vol. 4, p. x, by C.A. Murchison, ed., 1952, Worcester, MA: Clark University Press.)

Clark L. Hull (1884–1952) received his Ph.D. from the University of Wisconsin in 1918, where he also taught from 1916 to 1929. In 1929 he moved to Yale, where he stayed until his death.

Hull's career can be divided into three separate parts. His first major concern was with the testing of aptitudes. He gathered material on aptitude testing while teaching a course on the topic at the University of Wisconsin, and he published a book entitled *Aptitude Testing* in 1928. Hull's second major concern was with hypnosis, and after a long study of the hypnotic process, he wrote a book entitled *Hypnosis and Suggestibility* (1933b). His third concern, and the work for which he is most famous, was the study of the learning process. Hull's first major book on learning, *Principles of Behavior* (1943), radically changed the study of learning. It was the first attempt to apply comprehensive scientific theory to the study of a complex psychological phenomenon. We saw in Chapter 3 that Ebbinghaus was the first to use an experiment to investigate learning. But it was Hull who first utilized a rigorous theory to study and attempt to explain learning. Hull's theory, as presented in 1943, was extended in 1952 in *A Behavior System*. He intended to write a third book on learning but never did.

For his efforts, Hull received the Warren Medal in 1945 from the Society of Experimental Psychology. The award read,

> To Clark L. Hull: For his careful development of a systematic theory of behavior. This theory has stimulated much research and it has been developed in a precise and quantitative form so as to permit predictions which can be tested empirically. The theory thus contains within itself the seeds of its own ultimate verification and of its own possible final disproof. A truly unique achievement in the history of psychology to date.

Hull was physically disabled most of his life. He suffered partial paralysis from polio, which he had as a child. In 1948, he had a coronary attack, and four years later he died. In the last book he wrote (*A Behavior System*), he expressed regret that the third book that he had intended to write on learning would never be written.

Even though Hull felt that his theory was incomplete, it has had a profound influence on learning theory throughout the world. Kenneth Spence (1952), one of Hull's many famous students, indicated that 40 percent of all experiments in the *Journal of Experimental Psychology* and in the *Journal of Comparative and Physiological Psychology* between 1941 and 1950 refer to some aspect of Hull's work, and when one looks only at the areas of learning and motivation, this figure rises to 70 percent. Ruja (1956) reports that in the *Journal of Abnormal and Social Psychology* between 1949 and 1952 there are 105 references to Hull's *Principles of Behavior,* and the next most popular reference was listed only 25 times. In fact, it is still quite common for the student of learning to come across numerous references to Hull's work while going through the psychological journals. By any measure, Clark Hull was a major contributor to our knowledge of the learning process.

Hull, like most functionalistic learning theorists, was significantly influenced by Darwin's writings. The purpose of Hull's theory was to explain adaptive behavior and to understand the variables affecting it. In fact, it can be said that Hull was interested in developing a theory that explained how body needs, the environment, and behavior interact to increase the probability of the organism's survival.

HULL'S APPROACH TO THEORIZING

As a first step in developing his theory, Hull reviewed the research on learning up to that time. Next, he attempted to summarize those findings. Finally, he attempted to deduce testable consequences from those summary principles. We will look at this approach to theory construction in somewhat more detail.

Hull's approach to theory construction has been called **hypothetical deductive** (or **logical deductive**). His theory has a logical structure of postulates and theorems, much like Euclid's geometry. The postulates are general statements about behavior that cannot be directly verified. From the postulates, theorems are generated. The theorems follow logically—that is, they are *deduced*—from the postulates. Although the postulates are not testable, the theorems that they generate can be tested. An experiment is designed to test the theorem, and if the results of the experiment are as predicted the theorem is said to be correct and the postulate from which it is deduced gains in strength. If the experiment does not come out in the predicted direction, the theorem is said to be incorrect, and the postulate from which it is deduced must either be revised or abandoned.

It can be seen that this type of theorizing creates a dynamic, open-ended system. Hypotheses are constantly being generated; some of them are supported by experimental outcomes and some are not. When experiments come out in a predicted direction, the whole theory, including postulates and theorems, is strengthened. When the experiments do not come out as predicted, the theory is weakened and must be revised. A theory such as the one suggested by Hull must continually be updated in accordance with the outcome of empirical investigation. Hull (1943):

> Empirical observation, supplemented by shrewd conjecture, is the main source of the primary principles or postulates of a science. Such formulations, when taken in various combinations together with relevant antecedent conditions, yield inferences or theorems, of which some may agree with the empirical outcome of the conditions in question, and some may not. Primary propositions yielding logical deductions which consistently agree with the observed empirical outcome are retained, whereas those which disagree are rejected or modified. As the sifting of this trial-and-error process continues, there gradually emerges a limited series of primary principles whose joint implications are progressively more likely to agree with relevant observations. Deductions made from these surviving postulates, while never absolutely certain, do at length become highly trustworthy. This is in fact the present status of the primary principles of the major physical sciences. (p. 382)

As was mentioned in Chapter 2, any scientific theory is merely a tool that aids the researcher in synthesizing facts and in knowing where to look for new information. The ultimate value of a theory is determined by how well it agrees with observed facts or, in this case, with the outcome of experiments. The ultimate authority in science is the empirical world. Although a theory such as Hull's can become very abstract, still it must make statements concerning observable events. No matter how elaborate and abstract a theory becomes, it must ultimately generate propositions that are empirically verifiable; Hull's theory does exactly that.

MAJOR THEORETICAL CONCEPTS

Although Hull's 1952 version of his theory is highly complex, it is still an extension of his 1943 theory; therefore the best way to summarize Hull's thoughts on learning is to outline the 1943 version and then to point out the major changes that were made in 1952. Following that plan, we will first discuss Hull's sixteen major postulates as they appeared in 1943 and then, later in the chapter, we will turn to the major revisions Hull made in 1952.

Postulate 1: Sensing the External Environment and the Stimulus Trace External stimulation triggers an afferent (sensory) neural impulse, which outlasts the environmental stimulation. Thus, Hull postulates the existence of a **stimulus trace (s)** that continues for a few seconds after the stimulus event has terminated. Because this afferent neural impulse becomes associated with a response, Hull changes the traditional S-R formula to S-s-R, where s is the stimulus trace. For Hull, the association of interest is between s and R. The stimulus trace ultimately causes an efferent (motor) neural reaction (r) that results in an overt response. Thus we have S-s-r-R, where S is external stimulation, s is the stimulus trace, r is the firing of motor neurons, and R is an overt response.

Postulate 2: The Interaction of Sensory Impulses The **interaction of sensory impulses ($\bar{s}$)** indicates the complexity of stimulation and, therefore, the difficulties in predicting behavior. Behavior is seldom a function of only one stimulus. Rather, it is a function of many stimuli converging on the organism at any given time. These many stimuli and their related traces interact with one another and their synthesis determines behavior. We can now refine the S-R formula further as follows:

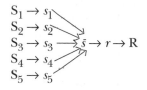

where $\bar{s}$ represents the combined effects of the five stimuli acting on the organism at the moment.

Postulate 3: Unlearned Behavior Hull believed that the organism is born with a hierarchy of responses, **unlearned behavior,** that is triggered when a need arises. For example, if a foreign object enters the eye, considerable blinking and tear secretion may follow automatically. If the temperature varies from that which is optimal for normal body functioning, the organism may sweat or shiver. Likewise, pain, hunger, or thirst will trigger certain innate response patterns that have a high probability of reducing the effects of those conditions.

The term *hierarchy* is used in reference to these responses because more than one reaction may occur. If the first innate response pattern does not alleviate a need, another pattern will occur. If the second response pattern does not reduce the need, still another will occur, and so on. If none of the innate behavior patterns is effective in reducing the need, the organism will have to *learn* new response patterns. Thus, according to Hull, learning is required only when innate neural mechanisms and their related responses fail to reduce an organism's need. Generally, as long as either innate responses or previously learned responses are effective in satisfying needs, there is no reason to learn new responses.

Postulate 4: Contiguity and Drive Reduction as Necessary Conditions for Learning
If a stimulus leads to a response and if the response results in the satisfaction of a biological need, the association between the stimulus and the response is strengthened. The more often the stimulus and the response that leads to need satisfaction are paired, the stronger the relationship between the stimulus and the response becomes. On this basic point, Hull is in complete agreement with Thorndike's revised law of effect. Hull, however, is more specific about what constitutes a "satisfying state of affairs." Primary **reinforcement,** according to Hull, must involve need satisfaction, or what Hull called **drive reduction.**

Postulate 4 also describes a secondary **reinforcer** as "a stimulus which has been closely and consistently associated with the diminution of a need" (Hull, 1943, p. 178). Secondary reinforcement following a response will also increase the strength of the association between that response and the stimulus with which it was contiguous. To summarize, we can say that if a stimulus is followed by a response, which in turn is followed by reinforcement (either primary or secondary), the association between that stimulus and that response is strengthened. It can also be said that the "habit" of giving that response to that stimulus gets stronger. Hull's term, **habit strength ($_sH_R$),** will be explained below.

Although Hull, like Thorndike and Skinner, was very much a reinforcement theorist, he was more specific about his definition of reinforcement. Skinner simply said that a reinforcer was anything that increased the rate with which a response occurred, and Thorndike talked about a nebulous "satisfying" or "annoying" state of affairs. For Hull, reinforcement was drive reduction, and reinforcers were stimuli that were capable of reducing a drive.

Habit Strength
Habit strength is one of Hull's most important concepts, and as stated above, it refers to the strength of the association between a stimulus and a response. As the number of reinforced pairings between a stimulus and a response goes up, the habit strength of that association goes up. The mathematical formula that

describes the relationship between $_sH_R$ and number of reinforced pairings between S and R is as follows:

$$_sH_R = 1 - 10^{-0.0305N}$$

N is the number of reinforced pairings between S and R. This formula generates a negatively accelerated learning curve, which means that early reinforced pairings have more of an effect on learning than do later ones. In fact, a point is reached where additional reinforced pairings have no effect on learning. Figure 6–1 shows that early reinforcements have more of an effect on learning than do later ones.

Postulate 5: Stimulus Generalization   Hull says that the ability of a stimulus (other than the one used during conditioning) to elicit a conditioned response is determined by its similarity to the stimulus used during training. Thus, $_sH_R$ will generalize from one stimulus to another to the extent that the two stimuli are similar. This postulate of **stimulus generalization** also indicates that prior experience will affect current learning; that is, learning that took place under similar conditions will transfer to the new learning situation. Hull called this process **generalized habit strength** ($_s\bar{H}_R$). This postulate essentially describes Thorndike's identical elements theory of the transfer of training.

Postulate 6: Stimuli Associated with Drives   Biological deficiency in the organism produces a **drive (D)** state and each drive is associated with specific stimuli. Hunger pangs which accompany the hunger drive, and dry mouth, lips, and throat which accompany the thirst drive, are examples. The existence of specific drive stimuli make it possible to teach an animal to behave in one way under one drive and

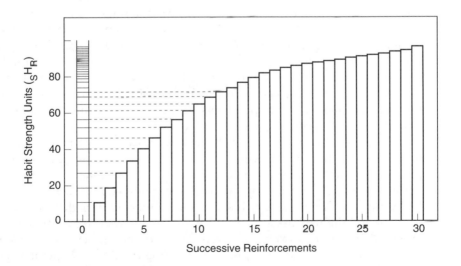

FIGURE 6–1 The relationship between gains in habit strength $_sH_R$ and successive reinforcements. (From *Principles of Behavior,* p. 116, by C.L. Hull, 1943, Englewood Cliffs, NJ: Prentice Hall.)

another way under another drive. For example, an animal can be taught to turn right in a T-maze when it is hungry and to turn left when it is thirsty. As we will see later in the chapter, the concept of drive stimuli became very important in Hull's 1952 revision of his theory.

Postulate 7: Reaction Potential as a Function of Drive and Habit Strength   The likelihood of a learned response being made at any given moment is called **reaction potential ($_SE_R$)**. Reaction potential is a function of both habit strength ($_SH_R$) and drive (D). For a learned response to occur, $_SH_R$ has to be activated by D. Drive does not direct behavior; it simply arouses it and intensifies it. Without drive, the animal would not emit a learned response even though there had been a large number of reinforced pairings between a stimulus and a response. Thus, if an animal has learned to press a bar in a Skinner box in order to obtain food, it would press the bar only when it was hungry, no matter how well it was trained. The basic components of Hull's theory that we have covered thus far can be combined into the following formula:

$$\text{Reaction potential} = {_SE_R} = {_SH_R} \times D$$

Thus, reaction potential is a function of how often the response was reinforced in that situation and the extent to which a drive is present. By looking at the above formula, it can be seen that if either $_SH_R$ or D were zero, $_SE_R$ would necessarily be zero. As we shall see in postulates 13 to 15, in addition to being related to response probability, $_SE_R$ is also related to resistance to extinction, latency, and amplitude of response.

Postulate 8: Responding Causes Fatigue, Which Operates Against the Elicitation of a Conditioned Response   Responding requires work, and work results in fatigue. Fatigue eventually acts to inhibit responding. **Reactive inhibition (I_R)** is caused by the fatigue associated with muscular activity and is related to the amount of work involved in performing a task. Since this form of inhibition is related to fatigue, it automatically dissipates when the organism stops performing. This concept has been used to explain the spontaneous recovery of a conditioned response after extinction. That is, the animal may stop responding because of the buildup of I_R. After a rest, the I_R dissipates and the animal commences to respond once again. For Hull, extinction not only is a function of nonreinforcement but is also influenced by the buildup of reactive inhibition.

Reactive inhibition has also been used to explain the **reminiscence effect,** which is the improvement of performance following the cessation of practice. For example, if experimental subjects are trained to track a rotating disc with a stylus, their performances will gradually improve until some asymptotic (maximal) level is reached. If the subjects are allowed to rest for a few minutes after this asymptotic level is reached and then are asked to track the disc again, their performances will tend to exceed their previous asymptotic levels. This is called the reminiscence effect, and it is explained by assuming that I_R builds up during training and operates against tracking performance. After a rest, I_R dissipates and performance improves. Figure 6–2 presents an example of the reminiscence effect.

Additional support for Hull's notion of I_R comes from research on the difference between **massed** and **distributed practice.** It is consistently found that when practice

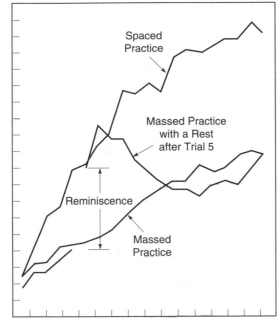

Mean Time on Target

Spaced Practice

Massed Practice with a Rest after Trial 5

Reminiscence

Massed Practice

Successive Trials

FIGURE 6–2 There were three groups of subjects in this experiment, which measured ability to track a rotating disc with a stylus. One group received distributed practice; another received massed practice; and a third group was first given massed practice, then a rest period, and then massed practice again. Clearly, the group receiving distributed practice performed much better than the other two groups. The vast improvement of the massed practice and rest group following the rest is an example of the reminiscence effect. (From *Principles of General Psychology,* 3rd ed., p. 290, by G.A. Kimble & N. Garmezy, 1968, New York: The Ronald Press Co. Copyright © 1968.)

trials are spaced far apart (distributed practice), performance is superior to what it is when practice trials are close together (massed practice). On a tracking task, for example, subjects resting between practice trials reach higher asymptotic levels of performance than subjects who go immediately from one practice trial to the next. Figure 6–2 shows the difference in performance under massed and distributed practice conditions.

    Postulate 9: The Learned Response of Not Responding   Fatigue being a negative drive state, it follows that not responding is reinforcing. Not responding allows I_R to dissipate, thereby reducing the negative drive of fatigue. The learned response of not responding is called **conditioned inhibition ($_sI_R$)**. Both I_R and $_sI_R$ operate *against* the elicitation of a learned response and are therefore subtracted from reaction potential ($_sE_R$). When I_R and $_sI_R$ are subtracted from $_sE_R$, **effective reaction potential ($_s\bar{E}_R$)** is the result.

$$\text{Effective reaction potential} = {}_s\bar{E}_R = {}_sH_R \times D - (I_R + {}_sI_R)$$

    Postulate 10: Factors Tending to Inhibit a Learned Response Change from Moment to Moment   According to Hull, there is an "inhibitory potentiality," which varies from moment to moment and operates against the elicitation of a learned response. This "inhibitory potentiality" is called the **oscillation effect ($_sO_R$)**.

    The oscillation effect is the "wild card" in Hull's theory—it is his way of taking into consideration the probabilistic nature of predictions concerning behavior. There is, he said, a factor operating against the elicitation of a learned response, whose effect varies from moment to moment but always operates within a certain range of values; that is, although the range of the inhibitory factor is set, the value that may be manifested at any time could vary within that range. The values of this inhibitory factor are assumed to be normally distributed, with middle values most likely to occur. If, by chance, a large inhibitory value does occur, it considerably reduces the chance that a learned response will be made. This oscillation effect explains why a learned response may be elicited on one trial but not on the next. Predictions concerning behavior based on the value of $_S\bar{E}_R$ will always be influenced by the fluctuating values of $_SO_R$ and will thus always be probabilistic in nature. The $_SO_R$ must be subtracted from effective reaction potential ($_S\bar{E}_R$), which creates **momentary effective reaction potential ($_S\dot{\bar{E}}_R$).** Thus we have

$$\begin{matrix} \text{Momentary effective} \\ \text{reaction potential} \end{matrix} = {}_S\dot{\bar{E}}_R = [\,_SH_R \times D - (I_R + \,_SI_R)\,] - \,_SO_R$$

Postulate 11: Momentary Effective Reaction Potential Must Exceed a Certain Value Before a Learned Response Can Occur   The value that $_S\dot{\bar{E}}_R$ must exceed before a conditioned response can occur is called the **reaction threshold ($_SL_R$).** Therefore, a learned response will be emitted only if $_S\dot{\bar{E}}_R$ is greater than $_SL_R$.

Postulate 12: The Probability that a Learned Response Will Be Made Is a Combined Function of $_S\bar{E}_R$, $_SO_R$, and $_SL_R$ In the early stages of training, that is, after only a few reinforced trials, $_S\bar{E}_R$ will be very close to $_SL_R$, and therefore because of the effects of $_SO_R$, a conditioned response will be elicited on some trials but not on others. The reason is that on some trials the value of $_SO_R$ subtracted from $_S\bar{E}_R$ will be large enough to reduce $_S\bar{E}_R$ to a value below $_SL_R$. As training continues, subtracting $_SO_R$ from $_S E_R$ will have less and less of an effect since the value of $_S\bar{E}_R$ will become much larger than the value of $_SL_R$. Even after considerable training, however, it is still possible for $_SO_R$ to assume a large value, thereby preventing the occurrence of a conditioned response.

Postulate 13: The Greater the Value of $_S\dot{\bar{E}}_R$ the Shorter Will Be the Latency Between S and R   Latency ($_St_R$) is the time between the presentation of a stimulus to the organism and its learned response. This postulate simply states that the reaction time between the onset of a stimulus and the elicitation of a learned response goes down as the value of $_S\dot{\bar{E}}_R$ goes up.

Postulate 14: The Value of $_S\dot{\bar{E}}_R$ Will Determine Resistance to Extinction   The value of $_S\dot{\bar{E}}_R$ at the end of training determines resistance to extinction, that is, how many nonreinforced responses will need to be made before extinction occurs. The greater the value of $_S\dot{\bar{E}}_R$ the greater the number of nonreinforced responses that have to be made before extinction takes place. Hull used n to symbolize the number of nonreinforced trials that occurred before extinction resulted.

Postulate 15: The Amplitude of a Conditioned Response Varies Directly with $_S\dot{\bar{E}}_R$ Some learned responses occur in degrees, for example, salivation or the galvanic skin response (GSR). When the conditioned response is one that can occur in degrees, its magnitude will be directly related to the size of $_S\dot{\bar{E}}_R$, the momentary effective reaction potential. Hull used A to symbolize response amplitude.

Postulate 16: When Two or More Incompatible Responses Tend to Be Elicited in the Same Situation, the One with the Greatest $_S\dot{\bar{E}}_R$ Will Occur   This postulate seems self-explanatory.

Summary of the Symbols Used in Hull's Theory

D = drive
$_SH_R$ = habit strength
$_SE_R$ = reaction potential = $_SH_R \times D$
I_R = reactive inhibition
$_SI_R$ = conditioned inhibition
$_S\bar{E}_R$ = effective reaction potential = $_SH_R \times D - (I_R + _SI_R)$
$_SO_R$ = oscillation effect
$_S\dot{\bar{E}}_R$ = momentary effective reaction potential = $_S E_R - _SO_R$
  = $[_SH_R \times D - (I_R + _SI_R)] - _SO_R$
$_SL_R$ = the value that $_S\bar{E}_R$ must exceed before a learned response can occur
$_St_R$ = reaction time
p = response probability
n = trials to extinction
A = response amplitude

MAJOR DIFFERENCES BETWEEN HULL'S 1943 AND 1952 THEORIES

Incentive Motivation (K)

In the 1943 version of his theory, Hull treated the magnitude of reinforcement as a learning variable: The greater the amount of reinforcement, the greater the amount of drive reduction, and thus the greater the increase in $_SH_R$. Research showed this notion to be unsatisfactory. Experiments indicated that performance was dramatically altered as the size of reinforcement was varied *after* learning was complete. For example, when an animal trained to run a straight runway for a small reinforcer was switched to a larger reinforcer, its running speed suddenly went up. When an animal trained on a large reinforcer was shifted to a smaller reinforcer, its running speed went down. Crespi (1942, 1944) and Zeaman (1949) were two early experimenters who found that performance changed radically when the magnitude of reinforcement was changed. The results of Crespi's (1942) experiment are shown in Figure 6–3.

The changes in performance following a change in magnitude of reinforcement could not be explained in terms of changes in $_SH_R$ since they were too rapid. Moreover, $_SH_R$ was thought to be fairly permanent. Unless one or more factors operated against $_SH_R$, it would not decrease in value. Results like those found by Crespi and Zeaman led Hull to reach the conclusion that organisms learn as rapidly for a small incentive as they do for a large one, but they *perform* differently as the size of the

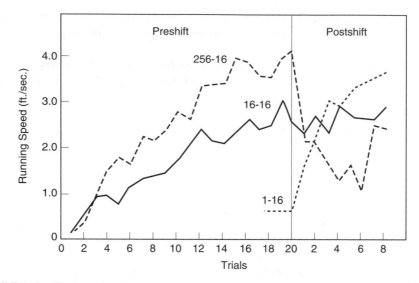

FIGURE 6–3   The results show that when animals are trained on a large reinforcer (256 pellets of food) and are then switched to a relatively small reinforcer (16 pellets of food), performance drops off repidly. Likewise, when animals are trained on a small reinforcer (1 pellet of food) and then are switched to a relatively large reinforcer (16 pellets of food), performance improves rapidly. (From *Theories of Motivation,* p. 293, after Crespi, 1942, by R.C. Bolles, 1975, New York: Harper & Row: Copyright © 1967, 1975 by R. C. Bolles. Reprinted by permission of Harper & Row, Publishers, Inc.)

incentive (K) varies. The rapid change in performance following a change in reinforcement size is referred to as the **Crespi effect,** after the man who first observed it.

Stimulus-Intensity Dynamism

According to Hull, **stimulus-intensity dynamism** (*V*) is an intervening variable that varies along with the intensity of the external stimulus (S). Stated simply, stimulus-intensity dynamism indicates that the greater the intensity of a stimulus, the greater the probability that a learned response will be elicited. Thus, we must revise Hull's earlier formula for momentary reaction potential as follows:

$$_{S}\dot{\bar{E}}_{R} = [_{S}H_{R} \times D \times V \times K - (I_{R} + _{S}I_{R})] - _{S}O_{R}.$$

It is interesting to note that since $_{S}H_{R}$, D, V, and K are multiplied together, if any one had a value of zero, reaction potential would be zero. For example, there could have been many reinforced pairings between S and R ($_{S}H_{R}$), but if drive is zero, reinforcement is absent, or the organism cannot detect the stimulus, a learned response will not occur.

Change from Drive Reduction to Drive Stimulus Reduction

Originally, Hull had a drive reduction theory of learning, but later he revised it to a **drive stimulus reduction** theory of learning. One reason for the change was the realization that if a thirsty animal is given water as a reinforcer for performing some act, it takes a considerable amount of time for the thirst drive to be satisfied by the water. The water goes into the mouth, the throat, the stomach, and eventually the blood. The effects of ingesting water must ultimately reach the brain, and finally the thirst drive will be reduced. Hull concluded that the drive reduction was too far removed from the presentation of the reinforcer to explain how learning could take place. What was needed to explain learning was something that occurred soon after the presentation of a reinforcer, and that something was the reduction of **drive stimuli** (S_D). As mentioned earlier in this chapter, drive stimuli for the thirst drive include dryness in the mouth and parched lips. Water almost immediately reduces such stimulation, and thus Hull had the mechanism he needed for explaining learning.

A second reason for changing from a drive reduction theory to a drive stimulus reduction theory was provided by Sheffield and Roby (1950), who found that hungry rats were reinforced by nonnutritive saccharine, which could not possibly have reduced the hunger drive. About this research Hull (1952) said,

> Sheffield and Roby appear to have presented a critical case in point....They showed that hungry albino rats are reinforced by water sweetened by saccharine which presumably is not at all nourishing (i.e., it does not reduce the need in the least). It may very well be that the ingestion of saccharine-sweetened water reduces hunger tension S_D for a brief period sufficient for a mild reinforcement, much as the tightening of the belt is said to do in hungry men, thus reinforcing that act. (p. 153)

Fractional Antedating Goal Response

You will recall that when a neutral stimulus is consistently paired with primary reinforcement, it takes on reinforcing properties of its own; that is, it becomes a secondary reinforcer. The concept of secondary reinforcement is vital in understanding the operations of the **fractional antedating goal response** (r_G), which is one of Hull's most important concepts.

Let us suppose we are training a rat to solve a multiple component maze. We place the animal in the start box and eventually it reaches the goal box, where it is reinforced with food, a primary reinforcer. All the stimuli in the goal box that were experienced just prior to primary reinforcement (food) will, therefore, through the process of classical conditioning, become secondary reinforcers. Moreover, following classical conditioning principles, the rat will develop a conditioned response that closely resembles the unconditioned response. In our present example, the unconditioned response would be that of salivation, chewing, and licking, caused by presenting food to a hungry animal. The conditioned response, also involving salivation, chewing, or licking, would be elicited by the various stimuli in the goal box as the rat approaches the food. It is the conditioned response to stimuli, experienced prior to the ingestion of food, that is called the fractional antedating goal response. The development of r_G is shown in Figure 6–4.

In the chapter on Pavlov we will learn that neutral stimuli paired with secondary reinforcers come to have reinforcing properties of their own through the process of higher-order conditioning (a process similar to associative shifting). When applied to maze learning, this process causes stimuli prior to those occurring in the goal box to

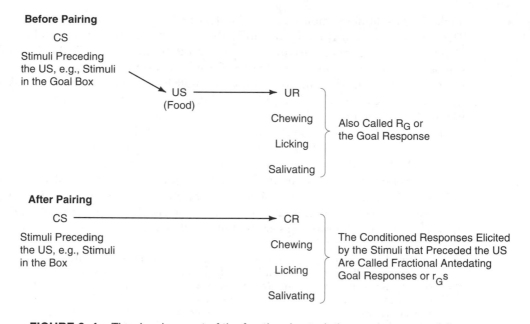

FIGURE 6–4   The development of the fractional antedating goal response (r_G).

also become reinforcers, and then the stimuli before them, and so on. Gradually the process works backward until even the stimuli in the start box come to have reinforcing properties. When these previously neutral stimuli become secondary reinforcers, they perform two very important functions: (1) They reinforce the overt responses that bring the organism into contact with them and (2) they elicit r_Gs.

Now as the animal leaves the start box, it comes into contact with a variety of stimuli, some with reinforcing properties, others without reinforcing properties. Those responses that bring the animal into close proximity to reinforcing stimuli will tend to be repeated and other responses will extinguish. In this manner the animal learns to make the correct turns in the maze. *Thus, maze learning is thought to involve both classical and instrumental conditioning.* Classical conditioning produces the secondary reinforcers and r_Gs; instrumental conditioning produces the appropriate motor responses that bring the animal into proximity with both the primary and secondary reinforcers. Thus far, the explanation for maze learning is essentially the same as Skinner's explanation of chaining (see Chapter 5); but as we shall see below, Hull assigned the r_G a prominent role in the learning of chained responses.

Two characteristics of the r_G must be noted. First, the r_G must always be some fraction of the goal response (R_G). If the goal response involves eating, the r_G will be minute chewing movements and perhaps salivation. Second, and more important, *the r_G produces stimulation.* Overt responding causes the kinesthetic receptors in the muscles, tendons, and joints to fire, causing what Guthrie (see Chapter 8) called movement-produced stimuli. More technically, the firing of these kinesthetic receptors causes **proprioceptive stimuli.** Like any other response, the r_G is associated with stimulation. The proprioceptive stimulation caused by the r_G is symbolized s_G. The r_G

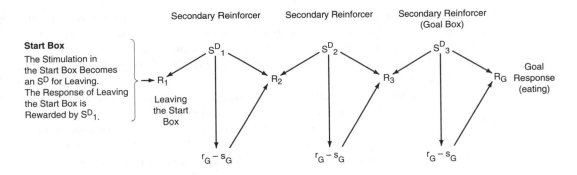

FIGURE 6–5 How S^Ds' overt responses (R), and the r_G–s_G mechanism combine to produce a chained response.

and s_G are inseparable since whenever r_G occurs, so does s_G. Perhaps the most important aspect of the r_G is the fact that it produces s_G.

After a considerable amount of maze learning has taken place, the situation that emerges is as follows: The stimuli in the start box will become signals, or S^Ds, for leaving the start box since leaving it brings the animal into proximity with secondary reinforcers. A secondary reinforcer in this situation does three things: It reinforces the response the animal just made; it acts as an S^D for the next overt response, and it elicits an r_G. When the r_G is elicited, it automatically produces an s_G. The main function of the s_G is to elicit the next overt response. Thus, both the secondary reinforcers, which are external, and the s_Gs, which are internal, tend to elicit overt responses. The response that exposes the animal to the next secondary reinforcer most rapidly will be the one that finally becomes associated with the s_G. When the next secondary reinforcer is experienced, it reinforces the overt response made prior to it, and it elicits the next r_G. When the r_G is elicited, it triggers the next s_G, which triggers the next overt response, and so on. The process continues in this manner all the way to the goal box. The chaining process, as Hull saw it, is diagrammed in Figure 6–5. An example of chaining on the human level is shown in Figure 6–6.

It should be clear that Hull really had two explanations for chaining that he used simultaneously. One explanation, which emphasized external stimuli, was very

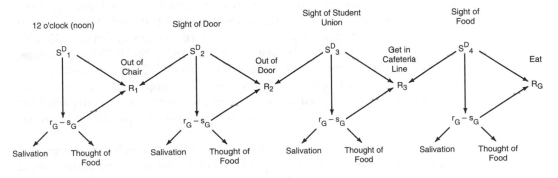

FIGURE 6–6 An example of chaining on the human level.

much like Skinner's explanation of chaining. The other, which emphasized internal events, was very much like Guthrie's explanation of chaining, as we shall see in Chapter 8. Hull, then, combined the notions of Skinner and Guthrie and said that chained behavior is a function of either internal or external cues or, more probably, of both internal and external cues.

One might ask why it is important to postulate the r_G-s_G mechanism if Skinner's explanation of chaining is adequate. The answer is that the r_G-s_G mechanism is thought to be important because of the other things that it may be related to. For example, the r_G-s_G mechanism can be thought of as the "mental" component of chaining. Generally speaking, the r_G-s_G concept provides an objective means of investigating thought processes. In the example in Figure 6–6, one can say that the time (noon) acted as an S^D, which triggered an r_G, which triggered the thought of food. Or one can say that the "expectation" of food was triggered, which keeps the person moving toward his or her goal of food. Clearly, at this point, the behavioristic point of view and the cognitive point of view come very close together. In fact, it can be said that the main value of the proposed r_G-s_G is opening up research in the area of cognition. In this regard Hull (1952) said,

> Further study of this major automatic device presumably will lead to the detailed behavioral understanding of thought and reasoning, which constitute the highest attainment of organic evolution. Indeed, the r_G-s_G mechanism leads in a strictly logical manner into what was formally regarded as the very heart of the psychic: interest, planning, foresight, foreknowledge, expectancy, purpose, and so on. (p. 350)

Thus Hull, in the tradition of Watson, Pavlov, and Guthrie, concluded that thinking consists of a minute internal representation of things that happen overtly. The "thought" of eating is nothing more than an s_G elicited by an r_G. We will review one of the many theoretical extensions of the r_G-s_G mechanism when we consider Abram Amsel's theory later on in this chapter. Also, we will see that Spence, who worked with Hull on the development of the r_G-s_G mechanism, later tied it closely to the concept of incentive motivation (K).

The Habit Family Hierarchy

Because there are any number of overt responses possible to any particular s_G, there are many alternative ways of reaching a goal. However, the route that is most likely is the one that brings the animal into proximity of reinforcement most rapidly. This fact was originally referred to as the "goal-gradient hypothesis" in Hull's early writings, but it appeared as a corollary to one of his postulates in 1952. The corollary concerned the delay of reinforcement (J) and read, "The greater the delay in reinforcement of a link within a given behavior chain, the weaker will be the resulting reaction potential of the link in question to the stimulus traces present at the time" (Hull, 1952, p. 126).

Here Hull is talking about a single link in a behavioral chain, but the same idea can be generalized to whole behavioral chains. Whether one is talking about a single response or a series of responses, delay of reinforcement has a deleterious effect on reaction potential. Likewise, either individual responses or chains of responses that are followed rapidly by reinforcement have relatively higher values of $_sE_R$ and are more likely to occur than those responses or behavioral chains with a longer delay between their occurrence and reinforcement.

The most direct route through a maze, whether a T-maze or a more complicated maze, has the greatest amount of $_sE_R$ because it results in less delay of reinforcement and also because there is less reactive and conditioned inhibition to be subtracted from $_sE_R$. But the shortest route through a maze is only one of many possible routes. The **habit family hierarchy** simply refers to the fact that in any learning situation, any number of responses are possible and the one that is most likely is the one that brings about reinforcement most rapidly and with the least amount of effort. If that particular way is blocked, the animal will prefer the next shortest route, and if that is blocked, it will go to the third route and so on.

There is a close relationship between the habit family hierarchy and how the fractional antedating goal response (r_G) and the stimulus it gives rise to (s_G) operate in chaining. We noted earlier that any number of overt responses can follow the occurrence of an s_G. Some of these responses will result immediately in exposure to a secondary reinforcer, and others will not. Eventually the responses that bring the animal into contact with the secondary reinforcers most rapidly will be the ones made since they will have the highest values of $_sE_R$. Remember, the greater the delay of reinforcement (J), the lower the value of $_sE_R$. Thus, there is a hierarchy of possible responses associated with every s_G, and therefore there is a large number of routes through a maze. If the route consisting of the responses with the highest value of $_sE_R$ is blocked, the next one in the hierarchy will be chosen, and so on. The situation can be diagrammed as follows:

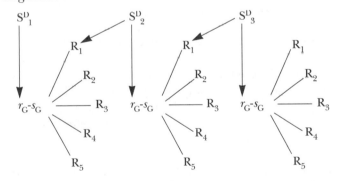

Hull's Final System Summarized

There are three kinds of variables in Hull's theory:

1. Independent variables, which are stimulus events systematically manipulated by the experimenter.
2. Intervening variables, which are processes thought to be taking place within

Independent Variables	Intervening Variables	Dependent Variables

W = Work
N = Number of Prior Reinforcements
T_D = Total Drive
w = Amount of Reinforcement
S = Stimulus Intensity
I_R = Reactive Inhibition
S^IR = Conditioned Inhibition
i_R = Combined Inhibitory Potential
S^HR = Habit Strength
S_D = Drive Stimulus
D = Drive
K = Incentive Motivation

V = Stimulus Strength
S^ER = Reaction Potential
$S^{\bar{E}}R$ = Effective Reaction Potential
S^OR = Behavioral Oscillation
S^LR = Response Threshold
$S^{\dot{\bar{E}}}R$ = Momentary Effective Reaction Potential
A = Response Amplitude
S^tR = Response Latency
n = Trials to Extinction
p = Probability of a Response

FIGURE 6–7 Summary of Hull's theory of learning after 1952.

the organism but are not directly observable. All the intervening variables in Hull's system are operationally defined (see Chapter 2).

3. Dependent variables, which are some aspect of behavior that is measured by the experimenter in order to determine whether the independent variables had any effect.

Figure 6–7 summarizes Hull's theory as it appeared in 1952. It should be noted that Hull's 1952 theory comprised 17 postulates and 133 theorems. Therefore the review of Hull in this chapter should be regarded as a brief introduction to a theory known for its thoroughness and complexity.

EVALUATION OF HULL'S THEORY

As mentioned earlier, Hull's learning theory had an enormous impact on psychology. Marx and Cronan-Hillix (1987) put the matter aptly:

Hull's most important contribution to psychology was his demonstration of the value of setting one's sights upon the ultimate goal of a thoroughly scientific and systematic behavior theory. He lived his own scientific life in pursuit of that goal, and thereby influenced even those who disagreed most vehemently with the details of his work. Few psychologists have had so great an effect on the professional motivation of so many researchers. He popularized the strictly objective behavioristic approach as it had never been popularized previously. (p. 326)

Contributions

As we indicated early in this chapter, Hull's influence on learning theory was demonstrated by the many publications that were dedicated to tests of different aspects of the theory itself or that cited Hull's work. It is probably safe to say that no theory of learning has been more thoroughly scrutinized, attacked, and dissembled than Hull's. Daniel Kahneman, a highly influential psychologist in the fields of human judgment and perception, began a keynote address at a 1993 Psychonomics meeting by criticizing Hull's theory. Thus, 41 years after his death, the theory still is cited in the context of current work.

One of the strengths in Hull's theory was the possibility of falsifying its various propositions. Hull was the first theorist that we encounter who was willing to take risks in theory construction. His insistence on precise definitions of concepts and exacting mathematical statements relating his concepts to behavior provided clear directions for testing the theory. For Hull, reinforcement hinged on the reduction of drive or drive stimuli produced by conditions of physiological need. This drive reduction hypothesis was the first attempt to break from the imprecise definitions of satisfiers/reinforcers that characterized both Thorndike's and Skinner's theories. Hull was also the first to make precise predictions about joint effects of learning and drive on behavior and about the effects of fatigue (via reactive and conditioned inhibition).

Criticisms

In spite of its overwhelming influence, Hull's theory did have its problems. It was criticized for being of little value in explaining behavior beyond the laboratory; for insisting too much that all concepts of interest be operationally defined; and most important, for making inconsistent predictions. In his review of the final version of Hull's theory (1952), Hill (1990) says,

> Suppose we want to know how many successive nonreinforced trials it would take to produce complete extinction. One approach would be to use Postulate 16, which translates excitatory potential directly into trials to extinction. A second approach would be to use Postulate 9 to calculate the amounts of reactive inhibition and subtract it from excitatory potential. A third would be to note (Postulate 7) that when the amount of reward is zero, the value of K is also zero, which makes excitatory potential zero regardless of the values of the other intervening variables. It turns out that these three approaches, to the extent that they give precise answers at all, give conflicting ones....When a theory makes incorrect predictions, it can be modified, as Hull intended that his theory should be. When a theory does not deal with a given issue at all, we can accept this limitation in its scope and hope that some day it may be expanded to include the neglected topic.

However, when a theory is internally inconsistent, so that it makes conflicting predictions about a given issue, its worth as a rigorous theory is seriously compromised. (pp. 63–64)

Despite his apparent willingness to subject his theory to critical tests, Koch (1954) suggested that Hull did not revise the theory enough in the face of problematic data and may have ignored many contradictory results. Contemporary critics echo that theme. Malone (1991), for example, portrays Hull as a researcher who used the power of his research facilities and talented students and his influence on journal editors to attack any opponents thus rendering "the self-correcting system more a self-perpetuating system!" (p. 165).

Even if such protective practices existed, subsequent research demonstrated that reinforcement occurred with or without reduction of drives or drive stimuli, and, as we will see, the mathematical form of the theory was challenged by Kenneth Spence. One interesting suggestion is that Hull approached theory building backwards. Shepard (1992) wrote

Rather than deducing empirically testable regularities from compelling first principles, Hull and Spence plotted empirically measured dependent variables....against experimentally manipulated independent variables....,searched for a mathematical function the shape of which seemed to approximate that of the plotted points, and then put forward the chosen function as a "postulate" of their theory. As George Miller once remarked..., Hull and his coworkers began by assuming what they should have ended up by deriving. (p. 419)

Yet, with all its faults, Hull's theory was among the most heuristic in psychology's history. In addition to stimulating an unprecedented number of experiments, Hull's explanations of reinforcement, drive, extinction, and generalization have become standard frames of reference in discussions of these concepts today.

After Hull's death the main spokesperson for the Hullian point of view was Kenneth W. Spence, who expanded and significantly modified Hull's theory (see Spence, 1956, 1960). We will encounter some of Spence's ideas later in this chapter. Other important followers of Hull include Neal E. Miller, who extended Hull's theory into the areas of personality, conflict, social behavior, and psychotherapy (e.g., Dollard & Miller, 1950; Miller & Dollard, 1941); Robert R. Sears, who translated a number of Freudian concepts into Hullian terms and who also worked extensively in experimental child psychology (e.g., Sears, 1944; and Sears, Whiting, Nowlis, & Sears, 1953); and O. Hobart Mowrer, who followed many of Hull's ideas while studying such areas as personality dynamics and the special characteristics of learning when fear or anxiety are involved. It is to Mowrer's work that we turn next.

O. HOBART MOWRER

O. Hobart Mowrer (1907–1982) was born in Unionville, Missouri, and received his Ph.D. from Johns Hopkins in 1932. During most of the 1930s, Mowrer was at Yale University, first as a postdoctoral fellow and then as an instructor of psychology. While at Yale, Mowrer was strongly influenced by Hull. In 1940, Mowrer joined the Harvard School of Education and remained there until 1948; he then moved to the University of Illinois (Urbana), where he stayed for the rest of his professional career.

The Problem of Avoidance Conditioning   Mowrer's career as a learning theorist began with his efforts to solve the problem that avoidance learning posed for Hullian theory. If an apparatus is arranged so that an organism receives an electric shock until it performs a specified response, it will quickly learn to make that response when it is shocked. Such a procedure is called **escape conditioning,** and it is diagrammed below:

$$\text{pain} \longrightarrow \text{R} \longrightarrow \text{escape from pain}$$
$$\text{(electric shock)} \quad \text{(response)} \quad \text{(reinforcement)}$$

Escape conditioning is easily handled by Hullian theory by assuming that the response is learned because it is followed by drive (pain) reduction. However, **avoidance conditioning** is not so easily explained by Hullian theory. With avoidance conditioning, a signal, such as a light, reliably precedes the onset of an aversive stimulus, such as an electric shock. Other than the presence of the signal that precedes the shock, the procedure is the same as for escape conditioning. The procedure used in avoidance conditioning is as follows:

$$\text{signal} \longrightarrow \text{pain} \longrightarrow \text{R} \longrightarrow \text{escape from pain}$$
$$\text{(light)} \quad \text{(electric shock)} \quad \text{(response)} \quad \text{(reinforcement)}$$

O. Hobart Mowrer. (Courtesy of Archives of the History of American Psychology, University of Akron, Ohio.)

With avoidance conditioning, the organism gradually learns to make the appropriate response when the signal light comes on, thus *avoiding* the shock. Furthermore, this avoidance response is maintained almost indefinitely even though the shock itself is no longer experienced. Avoidance conditioning posed a problem for the Hullians because it was not clear what was reinforcing the avoidance response. In other words, what drive does such a response reduce? In his effort to solve this problem, Mowrer proposed a two-factor theory of learning.

Mowrer's Two-Factor Theory of Learning
Mowrer noted that the early stages of avoidance conditioning were arranged so that Pavlovian or classical conditioning would occur. The signal acted as a conditioned stimulus (CS) and the electric shock acted as an unconditioned stimulus (US), which elicited, among other things, fear. Eventually, the CS, through its pairings with the US, would by itself elicit a response similar to the UR, that is, fear. Now when the light came

on, the organism would experience fear. Thus the first factor in Mowrer's **two-factor theory** is simply classical or Pavlovian conditioning. Mowrer called such conditioning **sign learning** because it explained how previously neutral stimuli, through their association with certain USs, could become signs of danger and thus elicit fear.

Mowrer called the second factor in this two-factor theory **solution learning,** and it is what Thorndike and Hull called instrumental conditioning or what Skinner called operant conditioning. Solution learning involves learning to perform those activities that will either terminate aversive stimuli or those negative emotions, such as fear, elicited by stimuli that have become signs of danger through classical conditioning.

Others, such as Skinner, had recognized two kinds of learning (respondent and operant conditioning), but Mowrer's contribution was in showing how the two are interrelated. Mowrer (1956) summarized his position as follows:

> Basically the two-factor, or two-process, hypothesis holds that *habits* are learned on the basis of the reinforcement provided by reward, or drive reduction, and that *fears* are learned (conditioned) on the basis of contiguous occurrence of a signal and punishment, in the sense of drive induction. Pavlov had held that *all* learning is a matter of conditioning or stimulus contiguity, while Thorndike and Hull had stressed habit formation on the basis of reward. Two-factor theorists, by contrast, have held that it is not here a matter of either-or but of *both:* both sign learning (conditioning) and solution learning (habit formation). (p. 114)

Thus Mowrer found the drive that the Hullians were looking for to explain avoidance conditioning, and that drive was conditioned fear. Mowrer believed that the onset of a CS that had been associated with pain motivated an avoidance response, which was reinforced by the termination of the CS.

Decremental and Incremental Reinforcement   In 1960, Mowrer extended his theory to show how emotions other than fear become associated with various CSs. Which emotion becomes associated with a CS depends on the kind of US that was involved and at what time the CS is presented. In his analysis, Mowrer first distinguished between USs that produce an increment in drive, for example, shock, and those that produce a decrement in drive, for example, food. The latter are called **decremental reinforcers** because they reduce a drive, in this case hunger. The former are called **incremental reinforcers** because they produce or increase drive. For each of the two kinds of USs, it is possible to present a CS at its onset or at its termination. If a CS is presented prior to the onset of shock, it will come to elicit the emotion of fear. If a CS is presented prior to the termination of shock, it will come to elicit the emotion of relief. If a CS is presented prior to the presentation of food, it will come to elicit the emotion of hope. If a CS is presented prior to the removal of food, it will come to elicit the emotion of disappointment. The two kinds of USs and the emotions conditioned by various CS-US relationships are shown in Figure 6–8.

By suggesting that important learning can occur as the result of both drive induction (onset) as well as drive reduction (termination), Mowrer moved away from the Hullian tradition, which stressed drive reduction. As we shall see in Mowrer's final position, he moved even farther away from Hullian theory.

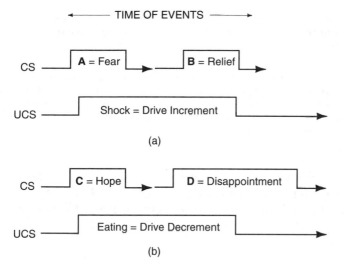

FIGURE 6–8 The emotion that becomes associated with a CS depends on which kind of US the CS is associated with and whether the CS is associated with the onset or termination of the US. Under the contingencies depicted, CS A will come to elicit fear, CS B will come to elicit relief, CS C will come to elicit hope, and CS D will come to elicit disappointment. (From G.H. Bower & E.R. Hilgard, *Theories of Learning,* 5th ed., p. 111, © 1981. Reprinted by permission of Prentice Hall, Englewood Cliffs, NJ.)

All Learning Is Sign Learning   In the final version of Mowrer's (1960) theory, all learning was considered sign learning. Mowrer had already shown that external stimuli associated with positive USs such as the termination of pain or the presentation of food come to elicit the emotions of relief and hope, respectively. Likewise, external stimuli associated with negative USs such as the onset of pain or the removal of food come to elicit the emotions of fear and disappointment, respectively. Why, Mowrer asked, should not the same principles hold true for internal stimuli?

Internal body reactions, for example proprioceptive stimuli caused by the firing of the kinesthetic receptors, always precede overt responses. When an organism is attempting to solve a problem, such as learning to escape from an aversive stimulus, learning to ride a bicycle, learning to speak a language, or learning to play tennis, certain overt responses will lead to success and others will lead to failure. The body sensations that precede successful overt responses will come to elicit hope for the same reasons that external stimuli come to elicit hope. The body sensations that precede unsuccessful or punished overt responses will come to elicit fear, again, for the same reasons that external stimuli come to elicit fear. In this way, body sensations provide an internal guidance system in the sense that certain sensations will signal impending failure, thus necessitating a behavioral correction, whereas other body sensations will provide information that things are being done correctly and success is imminent. Thus, in Mowrer's final position, even solution learning, previously thought to be learned through drive reduction, was seen as governed by signs learned because of their association with positive and negative outcomes. In other words, all learning was considered sign learning. Another way of phrasing Mowrer's final position is to say that organisms learn expectancies. That is, some signs, both external and internal, elicit the expectation of such things as pain or failure whereas others elicit the expectation of such things as pleasure or success.

In the final version of Mowrer's theory, emotions were of central importance. It was the emotions elicited by both internal and external stimuli that provided the primary guidance system for behavior. This emphasis on emotions was a major departure from traditional learning theory, but Mowrer (1960) felt no need to apologize for it:

> There has been a widespread tendency in Western civilization to look upon "the emotions" with a certain distrust and contempt and to elevate "the intellect" (reason, logic) high above them. If the present analysis is sound, the emotions are of quite extraordinary importance in the total economy of living organisms and do not at all deserve being put into opposition with "intelligence." The emotions are, it seems, themselves a high order of intelligence. (p. 308)

With his contention that all learning is sign learning, Mowrer created an essentially cognitive theory of learning. In particular, there is great similarity between Mowrer's final theory and Edward Tolman's cognitive theory, which we will review in Chapter 12.

KENNETH W. SPENCE

Although Hull had many ardent disciples, it was Kenneth W. Spence who became the major spokesperson for Hullian theory after Hull's death. For many years Hull and Spence had a reciprocal influence on each other. It is clear that Hull had a profound influence on Spence, but it is also clear that Spence influenced Hull's evolving theory in several important ways. The two worked so closely together that it is not uncommon for their combined efforts to be referred to as the Hull-Spence theory of learning. In the end, however, Spence made several radical changes in the traditional Hullian theory, and in so doing he created a learning theory that was essentially his own.

Kenneth W. Spence. (Reprinted by permission of University of Iowa, Office of Public Information.)

Spence was born in Chicago on May 6, 1907, and died in Austin, Texas, in 1967. At the age of four Spence moved to Montreal, Canada, where he remained until obtaining his B.A. degree in 1929 and his M.A. degree in 1930 from McGill University. Spence then moved to Yale, where he obtained his Ph.D. in 1933. After obtaining his doctorate, he remained at Yale as a research assistant and instructor until 1937. It was during his time at Yale that Spence came under the influence of Hull. Spence served on the faculty of the University of Virginia from 1937 to 1942, at which point he moved to the University of Iowa. He remained there for 26 years, until 1964, when he moved to the University of Texas (Austin), where he remained until his premature death in 1967.

Spence made several contributions to learning theory, but we can summarize only what seem to be his more important ones here.

Discrimination Learning In discrimination learning an animal is typically presented with two stimuli and is reinforced for responding to one and not reinforced for responding to the other. It was within the area of discrimination learning that Spence defended Hull's theory against an attack by a group of cognitively oriented psychologists. This group contended that during discrimination learning animals learn principles (subjective strategies) rather than S-R associations, as Hull had maintained. We will give more details of both the attack of the cognitive psychologists and Spence's reactions to it in Chapter 10, but in general here are the assumptions that Spence made about learning in a situation in which an organism must choose between two objects (Spence, 1936, 1937):

1. Habit strength ($_sH_R$) toward the stimulus that is reinforced increases with each reinforcement.
2. Inhibition (I_R and $_sI_R$) toward the stimulus that is not reinforced builds on each nonreinforced trial.
3. Both habit strength and inhibition generalize to stimuli that are similar to those that are reinforced and to those that are not reinforced.
4. The magnitude of generalized habit strength is greater than the magnitude of generalized inhibition.
5. Generalized habit strength and generalized inhibition combine algebraically.
6. Which stimulus is approached is determined by the algebraic summation of approach (habit strength) and avoidance (inhibition) tendencies.
7. When two stimuli are presented, the stimulus with the greatest net habit strength will be approached and responded to.

With these assumptions, Spence was able to use Hullian theory to explain phenomena that cognitive theorists were offering as evidence against it. Not only did Spence's assumptions and the research they generated prevail against the arguments of the cognitive theorists, but also they became the cornerstone of research on discrimination learning for many years.

Rejection of Reinforcement as a Necessary Condition for Instrumental Conditioning The Hullians were having difficulties accounting for the results of latent learning experiments, which seemed to be indicating that animals could learn without being reinforced. The term **latent learning** refers to learning that appears to take place in the absence of reinforcement. For example, Tolman and Honzik (1930) found that if rats were initially run through a maze without being reinforced in the goal box and were later reinforced for responding correctly, their performance rapidly matched (or exceeded) that of rats that had been reinforced on every trial (see Chapter 12 for the details of this experiment). Tolman and his followers argued that such results indicated that learning occurred independent of reinforcement.

Spence replicated a number of these so-called latent learning experiments and confirmed Tolman's findings. For example, Spence and Lippitt (1940) ran rats that were neither hungry nor thirsty through a Y-maze, where water was consistently found in one arm of the Y and food in the other. After reaching one of the two goals, the rat was removed from the apparatus. The rats were run for several trials while satiated with both food and water. During the second phase of the experiment, half of the original group was deprived of food and the other half was deprived of water. It was found that on the initial trial the hungry rat went directly to the arm of the Y-maze where they had previously experienced food, and the thirsty rats went directly to the arm of the Y-maze where they had previously experienced water. The rats had obviously learned where the reinforcer appropriate to their drive state was located during the first phase of the experiment, but such learning could not have involved drive reduction since the animals were satiated at the time. Hull's explanation of these findings was that removing the animal from the apparatus following a goal response provided enough of a reinforcer for the animal to learn under the circumstances. The reader will recall that Hull believed that learning occurred at the same rate whether the size of the reinforcer (K) was large or small. Thus, according to Hull, even though the reinforcer in this situation was small, it was sufficient to cause the animals to learn where things were in the maze.

Spence agonized over Hull's interpretation of the latent learning experiments and eventually came up with his own explanation. Spence was not comfortable with Hull's assumption that in learning there is no difference between a very small reinforcer and a very large reinforcer, but there is a very important difference between a very small reinforcer and no reinforcer at all. Remember, for Hull, reinforcement was a necessary condition for learning, but *how much* reinforcement occurred was irrelevant.

In one sense, Spence's solution to the problem placed him in essential agreement with Guthrie's theory of learning (see Chapter 8), and in another sense, in agreement with Tolman's theory (see Chapter 12). Spence concluded that *instrumental conditioning occurs independent of reinforcement.* The animal learns a response simply by making it. Thus, as far as instrumental conditioning was concerned, Spence was not a reinforcement theorist (as Hull was); rather, he was a contiguity theorist (as Guthrie was). The law of contiguity is one of Aristotle's laws of association, which states that events become associated simply because they occur together. Spence (1960) summarized his position on instrumental conditioning as follows:

> The habit strength (H) of the instrumental response, it is important to note, is assumed to be a function of the number of occurrences of the response (N_R) in the situation and to be quite independent of the occurrence or non-occurrence of a reinforcer. Thus, if the response occurs there will be an increment in H regardless of whether a reinforcer does or does not result. This assumption, it is apparent, makes this formulation a contiguity and not a reinforcement theory. (p. 96)

It should be clear that Spence also accepted Aristotle's **law of frequency,** which states that the more often two events are experienced together the stronger the association between them will become. We will see in Chapter 8 that although Guthrie accepted Aristotle's **law of contiguity,** he did not accept his law of frequency.

Incentive Motivation So, what function did reinforcement play in Spence's theory? According to Spence, reinforcement had an influence only through **incentive motivation (K).** Spence was largely responsible for Hull adding the concept of incentive motivation to his theory. In fact, it is widely believed that *K* was chosen as a symbol because it is the first letter in Spence's first name. It turns out, however, that Spence gave *K* a much more prominent role in his own theory than Hull gave it in his theory. In fact, Hull seemed to have problems with *K* because it was not clear to what physiological process it was related. Most of Hull's concepts were thought to have some physiological basis. For example, habit strength was tied directly to drive or drive stimulus reduction, and inhibition was tied directly to fatigue. However, it was not clear to Hull what physiological process *K* was related to, and that was troublesome.

Spence solved the problem by relating *K* direction to the r_G-s_G mechanism. As we saw earlier in the chapter, the r_G-s_G mechanism works back through a maze and eventually guides the animal's behavior from the start box to the goal box. Spence added the concept of incentive to this automatic guiding process. According to Spence, the strength of r_G-s_G is determined by *K,* and the stronger the r_G-s_G the greater the incentive to traverse the maze. Simply restated, the r_G-s_G mechanism creates in the animal the expectation of reinforcement, which motivates it to run, and the greater the expectation the faster the animal will run. By discussing the r_G-s_G mechanism as a means of providing the animal with expectations, Spence moved Hull's behavioristic theory closer to Tolman's cognitive theory. However, it should be noted that although Spence discussed expectations, he did so in mechanistic and not in mentalistic terms. In fact, Spence believed that the same laws that apply to overt S-R associations apply to the r_G-s_G mechanism.

For Spence, then, *K* was the energizer of learned behavior. The habit strength of an instrumental response develops in accordance with the laws of contiguity and frequency but independent of reinforcement. However, according to Spence, the r_G-s_G mechanism requires reinforcement for its development, and it is this mechanism that determines whether an organism will perform a learned response and, if so, with what degree of enthusiasm. Thus, Spence, like Mowrer before him, ended up with a two-factor theory. As we have seen, a two-factor theory postulates two different kinds of learning, each governed by a different set of principles. As far as instrumental conditioning was concerned, Spence was a contiguity theorist and not a reinforcement theorist. As far as classical conditioning was concerned (the process by which the r_G-s_G mechanism develops), he was a reinforcement theorist. In other words, Spence believed that instrumental behavior is learned without reinforcement, but reinforcement provides the incentive to perform what has been learned.

A Change in Hull's Basic Equation As the reader will remember, Hull combined the major components of his theory as follows:

$$_S\bar{E}_R = D \times K \times {}_SH_R - (I_R + {}_SI_R)$$

As we saw earlier in the chapter this equation means that if either D or K equals zero, a learned response will not be emitted no matter how high the value of $_SH_R$. In other words, for Hull, no matter how many times an animal has been reinforced for performing a response in a given situation, it will not perform the response if the animal is not in a drive state. Likewise, even if the animal is in a high drive state, it will not perform a learned response if there is no reinforcement for doing so. Again, Spence felt that Hull's assumptions were untenable and revised Hull's equation to read,

$$_S\bar{E}_R = (D + K) \times {_SH_R} - I_N$$

Note that Spence added D and K together rather than multiplying them as Hull did. The major implication of Spence's revision is that a learned response may be given in a situation even if no drive is present. For example, if one has eaten frequently at 6:00 P.M. in a certain location and one is in that location at 6:00 P.M., one may have the urge to eat even if one is not hungry. According to Spence's equation, as long as K and $_SH_R$ have a value greater than zero, a learned response will be emitted even if no drive is present. Thus, organisms sometimes eat when they are not hungry, drink when they are not thirsty, and perhaps even engage in sexual activities when they are not sexually aroused simply because they have developed strong tendencies to perform these acts under certain circumstances. Likewise, animals, including humans, may go on working for reinforcers that are no longer needed to satisfy basic drives, such as when a person continues to work to accumulate money even though he or she has more than enough to satisfy his or her basic needs.

Another implication of Spence's revised equation is that as long as D and $_SH_R$ have a value above zero, an organism should go on making a learned response even if K equals zero. In other words, an organism should go on making a learned response even if there is no reinforcement for doing so. How then does Spence explain extinction?

The Frustration-Competition Theory of Extinction   The astute reader may have noticed in the above equations that Hull's symbols for inhibition were I_R and $_SI_R$ and Spence's symbol was I_N. This apparently minor difference in symbols reflects a major theoretical difference between Hull and Spence concerning the nature of inhibition. For Hull, responding causes fatigue (I_R), which operates against the emission of a learned response. Likewise, when fatigue builds up it is reinforcing the animal not to respond. Therefore, there is a learned tendency not to respond ($_SI_R$), which also operates against the emission of a learned response. Hull explains extinction by saying that when reinforcement is removed from the situation ($K = 0$), I_R and $_SI_R$ become the dominant influences of behavior and the animal stops emitting the learned response.

Spence disagreed with Hull's explanation and proposed the **frustration-competition theory of extinction.** For Spence, nonreinforcement causes *frustration*, which elicits responses that are incompatible with the learned response and therefore compete with it. The frustration that occurs in the goal box when the animal finds the reinforcer missing is called **primary frustration (R_F).** With continued nonreinforced trials the animal learns to anticipate frustration, the **fractional anticipatory frustration reaction (r_F),** just as it has learned to anticipate reinforcement during acquisition (r_G). As nonreinforced trials continue, r_F generalizes (just as r_G did) and occurs earlier and earlier in the behavioral chain that previously led to reinforcement. Just as r_Gs give rise to s_Gs, which stimulate behavior compatible with reaching the goal box,

r_Fs give rise to s_Fs, which stimulate behavior that is incompatible with reaching the goal box. Eventually, the behavior stimulated by frustration and by the anticipation of frustration becomes dominant, and we say the learned response has extinguished.

Thus, Hull explained extinction in terms of the fatigue that results from responding in the absence of reinforcement, whereas Spence explained extinction as due to the active interference of learned behavior by the responses caused by frustration. Deductions from both of these positions have been tested experimentally, and Spence's explanation appears to fare best. For example, it has been found that during acquisition, using large reinforcers produces more rapid extinction than using small reinforcers (Hulse; 1958; Wagner, 1961). According to Spence's theory, removing a large reinforcer produces more frustration than removing a smaller reinforcer; thus, more competing behavior is stimulated. Since the magnitude of the competing behavior is greater than it would be if a smaller reinforcer was removed, it generalizes more rapidly through the chain of behavior that has been previously learned; therefore, extinction occurs more rapidly. According to Hull, magnitude of reinforcement during acquisition should have little or no effect on the speed with which extinction occurs.

Most, if not all, of Spence's modifications made Hullian theory much more capable of dealing with the higher mental processes with which the cognitive theorists are concerned. Spence has made it possible to deal effectively with concepts such as expectation and frustration without sacrificing scientific rigor. Spence's theory can be considered behavioristic, but it is a behavioristic theory that is much more compatible with cognitive theory than was Hull's.

Next we turn to the work of Abram Amsel, who was a student of Spence's at the University of Iowa. Amsel's relationship to Spence was much like Spence's relationship to Hull; that is, Amsel and Spence had a reciprocal influence on each other. Although Spence was equating inhibition and frustration as early as 1936, it was Amsel who worked out many of the details of Spence's frustration theory of extinction and who used the theory to explain the partial reinforcement effect.

ABRAM AMSEL

Amsel's work can be looked on as an elaboration of Spence's contention that extinction is caused by the competing responses caused by frustration. In general, Amsel (1958, 1962) assumes that after an organism is reinforced a number of times in a given situation, it learns to expect reinforcement in that situation. An organism experiences frustration when its expectation of reinforcement is unfulfilled. This frustration has motivational properties similar to those of punishment. For example, it has been found that animals will learn to perform a response that terminates a stimulus that was present when the animal experienced frustration (Daly, 1969; Wagner, 1963).

Further evidence for the motivational properties of frustration is provided by an experiment run by Amsel and Roussel (1952). In this experiment two straight alley runways were linked together. For the first 84 trials, the animals were reinforced at the end of each runway. After this preliminary training, however, the animals were run

Abram Amsel. (Courtesy of Abram Amsel.)

under conditions in which they were reinforced at the end of runway 1 on only 50 percent of the trials, whereas they continued to be reinforced at the end of runway 2 on each trial. It was found that running speed in runway 2 was significantly faster following nonreinforcement in runway 1 than it was following reinforcement in runway 1. This increased vigor following nonreinforcement is called the **frustration effect (FE).** This finding supports the contention that nonreinforcement causes frustration and that frustration is motivating, or drive inducing.

Further support for this contention was provided by a study by Bower (1962). Bower reasoned that the amount of frustration should be related to the amount of reinforcement reduction. To test his assumption, he used a two-runway apparatus similar to that used by Amsel and Roussel. In Bower's experiment, however, the rats were given four pellets of food at the end of each runway. The training phase of the experiment consisted of 6 trials a day for 24 days, or a total of 144 trials. After training, the conditions were changed so that the number of food pellets found at the end of the first runway was either four, three, two, one, or zero. The four food pellets found at the end of the second runway remained constant throughout the experiment. Bower found that running speed in runway 2 was inversely related to the number of food pellets present in runway 1 (fewer food pellets, faster running). That is, the animals ran fastest in runway 2 when they received no reinforcement in runway 1; next fastest when they received only one pellet, then two, then three, and slowest after receiving four food pellets in runway 1. This experiment supports Bower's hypothesis that the amount of frustration is related to the amount of reinforcement reduction, and this is in accordance with Spence's and Amsel's view of frustration.

Next we turn to the relationship between frustration and the Hull-Spence r_G-s_G mechanism. First, Amsel assumes, as Spence assumed, that when nonreinforcement occurs after a prolonged period of reinforcement, the organism experiences primary frustration (R_F). Thus, if an animal is reinforced a number of times for running down a straight alley and then is not reinforced after running down that same alley, it will experience primary frustration in the goal box where it had been previously reinforced.

We learned earlier in this chapter that when the animal experiences primary reinforcement in a goal box, the stimuli in the goal box take on secondary reinforcing properties; that is, they develop the capacity to elicit r_Gs, which in turn elicit s_Gs. We also saw that through stimulus generalization or higher-order conditioning, these r_Gs slowly develop associations all the way back to the start box. Then, when the animal leaves the start box, its behavior is guided to the goal box by these r_Gs and the s_Gs that they elicit. According to Amsel, the same process is associated with primary frustration. That is, stimuli associated with primary frustration will develop the capacity to elicit a fractional anticipatory frustration reaction, or r_F, which is associated with an s_F, just as an r_G necessarily is associated with an s_G. The r_G-s_G and the r_F-s_F mechanisms are associated with different behavior patterns, however. Whereas the r_G-s_G mechanism causes locomotion toward the goal box, r_F-s_F tends to cause avoidance of the goal box. In general, we can say that r_G is related to the expectancy of reinforcement, whereas r_F is related to the expectancy of frustration.

During extinction, the animal experiences nothing but frustration, which gradually generalizes backward to the start box through the r_F-s_F mechanism. When this happens, the animal experiences stimuli that elicit r_Fs either in the start box or shortly after leaving the start box, and they cause it to stop running. At that point we say that extinction has occurred.

Now we come to what is perhaps the most important aspect of Amsel's theory: its proposed explanation of the **partial reinforcement effect (PRE).** The PRE refers to the fact that it takes longer to extinguish a response that was intermittently reinforced during training than if it was continuously reinforced. In other words, PRE means that partial reinforcement yields greater resistance to extinction than does 100 percent reinforcement. A number of theories have been offered to explain the PRE, and Amsel's is one of the most widely accepted.

Amsel explains PRE as follows: First, the animal is trained to make a response, such as running down a straight alley. During this training, the animal usually experiences primary reinforcement (R_G) in the goal box on 100 percent of the trials. Under these circumstances, all the stimuli in the runway will eventually become associated with R_G through the r_G-s_G mechanism. Next, the animal is placed on a partial reinforcement schedule in which it is reinforced on, say, only 50 percent of the trials. Since the animal had developed a strong expectancy for reinforcement, it will experience primary frustration (R_F) on those trials when it does not receive reinforcement. As we saw above, the stimuli just prior to the experience of primary frustration will come to elicit r_Fs, which give rise to s_Fs. After several nonreinforced trials, a conflict develops because the same stimuli tend to elicit conflicting habits. When an r_G-s_G is elicited, the animal tends to run toward the goal box, but when an r_F-s_F is elicited, the animal tends to avoid the goal box. Since the animal had already developed a strong habit of running toward the goal during training prior to being switched to a partial reinforcement schedule, and perhaps because positive reinforcement is more influential than frustration, the animal continues to approach the goal box while under the partial reinforcement schedule. In other words, although there is an approach-avoidance conflict associated with the goal box, the approach tendency wins out.

Since the animal continues to approach the goal box even though it is not reinforced on some trials, eventually all the stimuli in the apparatus become associated with the running response, even those stimuli associated with frustration. Perhaps you have already anticipated Amsel's next step in his explanation of the PRE. When subjects trained on a continuous, or 100 percent reinforcement schedule are switched to extinction, they experience frustration for the first time. For them, the effects of this frustration associate backward to the start box, and normal extinction occurs. Subjects trained on a partial reinforcement schedule, however, have already experienced frustration during training and have learned to run in the presence of the stimuli associated with frustration. The partial reinforcement subjects will therefore take much longer to extinguish; thus the PRE.

One could deduce from Amsel's proposed explanation of the PRE that great variation in behavior would accompany the conflict stage of partial reinforcement training. That is, when the same stimuli in the apparatus are eliciting both approach and avoidance tendencies, the running speed should vary from trial to trial. At the same time, when the stimuli become associated with the running response later in training, the running response should stabilize. Amsel (1958) found support for both deductions. One could also deduce from Amsel's theory that the PRE will occur only when there are a substantial number of preliminary training trials because his explanation depends on frustration, and the animal will not experience frustration unless it has learned to expect a reinforcer. Evidence supporting this contention was also found by Amsel (1958). It was found that the PRE resulted if animals had 84 preliminary training trials before being switched to a partial reinforcement schedule but did not if they had only 24 preliminary training trials.

Amsel's theory of frustrative nonreinforcement is only one of the many creative extensions of the Hull-Spence r_G-s_G mechanism. The student of psychology or education will discover a number of others in advanced courses. In fact, a review of the many uses of the r_G-s_G mechanism to explain various psychological phenomena would make an excellent independent study project.

Finally, we turn to the contributions of Neal Miller, who studied with Hull and was strongly influenced by Hull's theory. Miller's work, which continues to make important contributions to contemporary psychology, was eclectic and was not limited to explorations of learning theory.

NEAL MILLER, VISCERAL CONDITIONING, AND BIOFEEDBACK

Among Hull's doctoral students at Yale was Neal Miller, a researcher who would extend Hullian influences into a variety of theoretical and applied areas. Miller was born in Milwaukee, Wisconsin in 1909. He completed his undergraduate work at the University of Washington where he studied with Edwin Guthrie, whose theory we introduce in Chapter 8. He earned his M.A. at Stanford University in 1932 and his Ph.D. at Yale University in 1935. Upon completion of his doctorate, Miller spent several months at the Vienna Psychoanalytic Institute studying Freudian psychoanalysis. When he returned to the United States, Miller joined the faculty at Yale, where he remained from 1936 until 1966. He then moved to Rockefeller University in New York where he attained the status of professor emeritus. He currently maintains his relationship with Rockefeller and is a research affiliate at Yale.

Neal E. Miller. (Courtesy of Neal Miller.)

While at Yale, Miller conducted research in both Hullian and Freudian psychology and began a fruitful collaboration with John Dollard. In 1941, Miller and Dollard wrote *Social Learning and Imitation,* a behavioristic, reinforcement theory of observational learning and imitation that we will discuss briefly in Chapter 13. In 1950, Dollard and Miller co-authored *Personality and Psychotherapy,* an influential synthesis of Hullian behaviorism and Freudian psychodynamics. Among Miller's many contributions were demonstrations that autonomic, internal responses could be conditioned using operant training procedures. These findings provided the groundwork for a therapeutic technique that is in use today and that remains the focus of research controversy.

Until the 1960s, it was believed that operant conditioning was possible only for responses that involve the skeletal or striped muscles and that responses involving the smooth muscles and glands could not be operantly conditioned. The smooth muscles and glands are controlled by the autonomic nervous system, and generally, it was believed that responses mediated by the autonomic nervous system could not be operantly conditioned.

There are now many experiments, a great number of them conducted by Neal Miller, demonstrating that both humans and nonhumans can control their own internal environment. For example, it has been found that individuals can control their own heart rate, blood pressure, and skin temperature.

To demonstrate that autonomic responses could be operantly conditioned, Miller and Carmona (1967) gave one group of thirsty dogs water whenever they salivated spontaneously. Another group of thirsty dogs was given water for going for long intervals of time without salivating. The rate of salivation went up for the former group and down for the latter group. Thus, it was demonstrated that salivation, which is governed by the autonomic nervous system, was modifiable through operant conditioning procedures. Other experiments demonstrated that conditioning of autonomic responses could be accomplished using secondary reinforcers. For example, Shapiro, Tursky, Gerson, and Stern (1969) taught 20 male college students to raise or lower their blood pressure by showing them a picture of a nude female from *Playboy* whenever their blood pressure was altered in the direction desired by the experimenter. At the conclusion of the experiment, the students, with only two exceptions, were unaware of the fact that their blood pressure had been systematically altered.

In other studies of autonomic conditioning, the practical applications are readily apparent. Researchers have reported that heart patients can learn to control their cardiac abnormalities, that epileptics can learn to suppress abnormal brain activity, and that individuals suffering from migraine headaches can learn to avoid them by controlling the dilation of blood vessels surrounding the brain. For more detailed reviews of this research see DiCara, 1970; Jonas, 1973; Kimmel, 1974; and N. E. Miller, 1969, 1983, 1984.

In cases such as those mentioned in the preceding paragraph, a device is used to display to the patients the changes in the internal events that they are trying to control, for example, high blood pressure or irregular heart activity. Such a display is called **biofeedback** because it provides the patient with information about some internal biological event. Reinforcers like food or water are typically not used in this procedure. The information provided by the feedback device is all that is needed for learning to occur. In a sense, the information itself serves as the reinforcer. Usually after monitoring the biofeedback for a period of time, the patients become aware of their internal state and can respond accordingly—either raise or lower their blood pressure—without the aid of biofeedback. Obviously, this whole area of research, sometimes called **visceral conditioning,** has vast implications for the practice of medicine.

Early research clearly demonstrated that we can learn to control many autonomic functions in the laboratory but there are serious questions about which autonomic functions are most readily controlled beyond the laboratory, and therefore about which kinds of disorders should be treated with the technique.

For example, it is now suggested that biofeedback may be of limited use for certain disorders. A research team led by Dr. David M. Eisenberg examined data from 1,264 patients who suffer from essential hypertension, a disorder characterized by unusually high blood pressure. These researchers found that in 26 well controlled studies, biofeedback techniques proved no more effective than two placebo techniques including a phoney biofeedback condition. The authors concluded that any type of relaxation technique, including biofeedback, was superior to leaving the condition untreated, but they did not recommend biofeedback as a replacement for medication (Eisenberg, Delbanco, Berkey, Kaptchuk, Kupelnick, Kuhl, & Chalmers, 1993).

Biofeedback has frequently been used to treat chronic headaches, although the therapeutic results, in some cases, have been attributed to nonspecific effects of positive expectations on the parts of both the patient and the practitioner (Roberts, 1994). Other studies seem to indicate that the efficacy of biofeedback for treatment of headache depends on the specific type of headache from which a patient suffers. Children who experience migraine headaches were taught to increase skin temperature with biofeedback and appeared to gain relief over a six-month period, compared to children who were on a headache clinic waiting list but were not treated (Labbe, 1995). Similarly, a meta-analysis (a mathematical analysis comparing experiments that test similar subjects and that use comparable procedures and controls) of studies using biofeedback for migraine headaches indicated that biofeedback treatment, coupled with progressive relaxation techniques, was more effective in treating migraine headaches than typically prescribed medications or drug placebos (Hermann, Kim, & Blanchard, 1995). In addition, patients who demonstrated greater skills in controlling either muscle tension or skin temperature using biofeedback tend to reduce their migraine headaches more than patients who were less able to control those responses (Shellick & Fitzsimmons, 1989). On the other hand, individuals suffering from headaches typically attributed to general tension seem to be more susceptible to placebo or nonspecific effects such as positive expectations (Blanchard, Kim, Hermann, & Steffek, 1994; Eisenberg, Kessler, Foster, & Norlock, 1993).

Biofeedback techniques are widely used today, but as the studies we have discussed indicate, we must be sure which disorders are most amenable to biofeedback treatment, particularly when biofeedback is offered as a cure for serious conditions ranging from alcoholism to neurological dysfunctions. In addition, further research will be required to determine which cures are best attributed to nonspecific placebo effects and which may actually result from patients learning to control autonomic functions.

DISCUSSION QUESTIONS

1. How would one overcome or minimize the negative contribution of work (I_R and $_sI_R$) in a learning situation?
2. According to Hull's theory, what effect would increasing the size of the reinforcer have on learning? Explain.
3. Describe a situation that would allow one to differentiate between learning and performance.
4. What would characterize classroom procedures designed in accordance with Hull's principles of learning? Give a few specific examples.
5. According to Hull's theory, who do you think would learn faster, high-anxious students or low-anxious students? Explain.
6. On what basic points would Skinner disagree with Hull? Where would the two most closely agree?
7. What do you think Hull means when he says "psychic phenomena" will someday be explained in terms of the r_G-s_G mechanism?
8. Explain chaining from Hull's point of view.
9. What is a habit family hierarchy?
10. Describe Hull's approach to theory construction. What is meant by the statement that Hull's theory is open-ended?
11. Diagram Hull's final version of his theory as it was presented in this chapter.
12. What kind of experiment could directly test Hull's contention that reinforcement depends on reduction of drives or drive stimuli?
13. You drive around a corner and see the house of the good friend you are about to visit and you begin to smile. How would Hull explain this smiling behavior?
14. Describe the procedure used in avoidance conditioning.
15. Describe the two-factor theory that Mowrer developed to explain avoidance conditioning. In your answer be sure to define sign learning and solution learning.
16. Discuss Mowrer's distinction between incremental and decremental reinforcement. Also discuss the ways that CSs can be made contingent on the two kinds of reinforcement and what emotions result from each contingency.

17. Summarize the final version of Mowrer's theory and explain why it is considered basically cognitive in nature.
18. Summarize the evidence that caused Spence to change from a reinforcement theorist to a contiguity theorist with regard to instrumental conditioning.
19. In what sense did Spence remain a reinforcement theorist?
20. Describe the implications of $D \times K \times {}_SH_R$ versus $(D + K) \times {}_SH_R$.
21. Summarize the Spence-Amsel frustration-competition theory of extinction.
22. Summarize Amsel's explanation of the partial reinforcement effect.
23. What experimental findings might make us cautious when reading about successful uses of biofeedback techniques?

KEY TERMS

avoidance conditioning   See Key Terms for Chapter 1.

biofeedback   The information provided to individuals by some mechanical device concerning the status of one or more of their internal biological events. For example, a flashing light can be set to reflect heart rate, or an auditory signal can be triggered when blood pressure rises beyond a certain level.

conditioned inhibition (${}_SI_R$)   A learned response of not responding. Since responding produces fatigue (I_R) and fatigue is a negative drive state, not responding is reinforcing; hence conditioned inhibition.

Crespi effect   The rapid change in performance level as the size of reinforcement is varied.

decremental reinforcer   According to Mowrer, an unconditioned stimulus that causes a reduction in drive, such as when food is given to a hungry animal.

distributed practice   Learning a skill under the conditions in which practice trials are separated by a considerable length of time.

drive (D)   The condition that exists when there is a biological deficiency in the body. For all practical purposes, the terms *drive* and *need* mean the same thing.

drive reduction   The satisfaction of a biological deficiency. Originally Hull thought it to be a necessary condition for learning. Hull later turned to a drive stimulus reduction theory of learning.

drive stimuli (${S_D}$)   The stimuli that characteristically accompany a certain drive, such as the dryness of the mouth, lips, and throat that accompany the thirst drive.

drive stimulus reduction   The reduction or removal of the stimuli that accompany a drive. This usually occurs before the drive itself is actually reduced; for example, the dryness of the mouth, lips, and throat are eliminated before the effects of drinking water can reach the brain and thereby reduce the thirst drive.

effective reaction potential (${}_S\bar{E}_R$)   Reaction potential (${}_SE_R$) minus the effects of I_R and ${}_SI_R$.

escape conditioning   See Key Terms for Chapter 1.

fractional antedating goal response (r_G)   A response that is conditioned to the stimuli present prior to the ingestion of a primary reinforcer. The conditioned response (r_G) is always some fraction of the goal response (R_G). For example, if the goal response is eating, r_G would consist of minute chewing responses. Each r_G automatically produces a stimulus, which is symbolized by s_G. The r_G-s_G mechanism plays an important role in Hull's explanation of chained behavior.

fractional anticipatory frustration reaction (r_F)   Stimuli that precede primary frustration will develop the capacity to elicit some portion of the primary frustration response. These fractions of the primary frustration response that occur prior to the goal are called fractional anticipatory frustration reactions, or r_Fs.

frustration-competition theory of extinction   Spence's and Amsel's contention that extinction is caused by responses stimulated by frustration, which interfere with the performance of a previously learned response.

frustration effect (FE)   The increased vigor of responses following nonreinforcement. For example, it has been found that rats will run faster following nonreinforcement than following reinforcement.

generalized habit strength ($_s\bar{H}_R$)   Habit strength from previous learning experiences that generalizes to a new learning experience because of the similarity between the new learning experience and older ones.

habit family hierarchy   A hierarchy of responses arranged according to their values of $_sE_R$. When a particular response is thwarted, the animal makes the next response available in its response repertory. Responses that result in the most rapid reinforcement have the greatest value of $_sE_R$ and are, therefore, most likely to occur. If a response with the highest value of $_sE_R$ is blocked, the response with the next highest value of $_sE_R$ will occur, and so on.

habit strength ($_sH_R$)   A measure of the strength of association between a stimulus and a response. The magnitude of the $_sH_R$ depends on the number of reinforced pairings between the stimulus and the response. In the final version of Hull's theory, $_sH_R$ was the only learning variable; the other factors were performance variables. In other words, Hull believed that the only thing that affected learning directly was the number of reinforced trials.

hypothetical deductive theory (logical deductive)   A theory consisting of postulates and theorems. Postulates are assumptions that cannot be verified directly; theorems are deduced from the postulates and they can be verified experimentally. If an experiment designed to test a theorem comes out in the predicted direction, its postulate is indirectly verified and the theory gains strength. If the experiment does not come out in the predicted direction, the theory loses strength. A hypothetical deductive theory is constantly changing in light of experimental evidence.

incentive motivation (K)   Size of reinforcement. Originally (1943), Hull felt that K affected learning, but he later (1952) concluded that it only affected performance. For Spence, incentive motivation was extremely important. It worked through the r_G-s_G mechanism and was the energizer of learned behavior.

incremental reinforcer   According to Mowrer, an unconditional stimulus that causes an increase in drive, such as electric shock.

interaction of sensory impulses ($\bar{s}$)   Behavior is usually the result of many stimuli impinging on sensory receptors at any given time. The afferent (sensory) neural impulses caused by these stimuli interact with one another, and it is their combined effect that causes an efferent (motor) neural impulse and finally an overt response (R).

latency ($_{S}t_{R}$)   The time between the presentation of a stimulus and the occurrence of a learned response.

latent learning   Learning that appears to take place independent of reinforcement and that remains dormant until the organism is given an incentive for translating what has been learned into behavior.

law of contiguity   When two or more events occur together they become associated with one another.

law of frequency   The more often two events or more occur together the stronger will be the association among them.

massed practice   Learning a skill under the conditions in which practice trials are separated by only a very short interval of time.

momentary effective reaction potential ($_{S}\dot{\bar{E}}_{R}$)   Effective reaction potential ($_{S}\bar{E}_{R}$) minus the effects of I_{R}, $_{S}I_{R}$, and $_{S}O_{R}$.

oscillation effect ($_{S}O_{R}$)   An "inhibitory potentiality" that opposes the emission of a conditioned response and whose value changes from moment to moment. The values of $_{S}O_{R}$ are normally distributed, and therefore the value that manifests itself at any given moment can be large or small but will most likely be a value that is neither very large nor very small.

partial reinforcement effect (PRE)   The fact that a response that had been reinforced only sometimes takes longer to extinguish than a response that had been reinforced each time it occurred.

primary frustration (R_{F})   The response that occurs when an organism experiences nonreinforcement after it had learned to expect reinforcement.

proprioceptive stimuli   The stimuli that result from the firing of the kinesthetic receptors in the muscles, joints, and tendons of the body. Also called movement-produced stimuli.

reaction potential ($_{S}E_{R}$)   Directly influences four response measures. As reaction potential goes up, the probability of a learned response being elicited by a stimulus goes up, resistance to extinction goes up, amplitude of a conditioned response goes up, and latency goes down.

reaction threshold ($_{S}L_{R}$)   The minimal value that the momentary effective reaction potential ($_{S}\dot{\bar{E}}_{R}$) must exceed before a learned response can occur.

reactive inhibition (I_{R})   The fatigue caused by responding that operates against the emission of a conditioned response.

reinforcement   Drive reduction or drive stimulus reduction.

reinforcer   Anything that causes either drive reduction or drive stimulus reduction.

reminiscence effect   The improvement of performance on a skill following a rest after cessation of practice.

sign learning   The kind of learning, in Mowrer's two-factor theory, whereby stimuli become signs of fear, hope, relief, or disappointment because of their proximity to various unconditioned stimuli.

solution learning   The kind of learning, in Mowrer's two-factor theory, whereby an organism learns the behavioral skills necessary to avoid aversive situations and to embrace positive ones.

stimulus generalization   See **Generalization** in Key Terms for Chapter 7.

stimulus-intensity dynamism (V)   The internal result of varying the magnitude of an external stimulus. A larger external stimulus will result in a larger stimulus trace, thereby increasing the probability that a learned response will be elicited.

stimulus trace (s)   The afferent (sensory) neural impulse that is caused by an external stimulus and continues for a short while after the external stimulus has ceased.

two-factor theory   A theory that postulates one set of principles to explain one kind of learning and a different set of principles to explain another kind of learning.

unlearned behavior   Associations between stimuli and responses that are genetically determined and therefore do not depend on experience for their development.

visceral conditioning   The conditioning of internal organs under the control of the autonomic nervous system, such as the stomach, intestines, heart, bladder, or arteries.

Chapter 7

IVAN PETROVICH PAVLOV

Pavlov was born in Russia in 1849 and died there in 1936. His father was a priest, and originally Pavlov himself studied to become a priest. He changed his mind, however, and spent most of his life studying physiology. In 1904 he won a Nobel Prize for his work on the physiology of digestion. He did not begin his study of the conditioned reflex until he was 50 years of age.

With Thorndike we saw that scientists are obliged to change their views when the data require it, an important characteristic of the scientific enterprise. With Pavlov, we see the importance of serendipity, or accidental discovery, in science. Pavlov's method of studying digestion involved a surgical arrangement on a dog that allowed gastric juices to flow through a fistula to the outside of the body, where it was collected. This arrangement is shown in Figure 7–1.

Pavlov was measuring stomach secretions as the dog's response to such things as meat powder when he noticed that the mere sight of the food caused the dog to salivate. In addition, the mere sight of the experimenter or the sound of his or her footsteps would cause salivation. Originally Pavlov called such responses "psychic" reflexes. Being an extremely objective scientist and at heart a physiologist, Pavlov originally resisted investigating the "psychic" reflex. After a long personal struggle, however, and contrary to the advice of some of his colleagues, he finally decided to delve into the issue. He decided to study it, however, as a purely physiological problem to guard against any subjective element entering into his research. In fact, Pavlov's co-workers were fined if they used subjective, nonphysiological language in describing their research (Watson, 1978, p. 441). An apparatus like the one used by Pavlov to study the psychic reflex is shown in Figure 7–2.

Just as Pavlov started a second career at age 50 when he turned to the study of the psychic reflex, he started a third career at age 80 when he turned to the application of his work on conditioning to mental illness. This work resulted in a book entitled *Conditioned Reflexes and Psychiatry* (1941), which many consider a significant contribution to psychiatry.

At the time Thorndike was developing his theory, American psychology was struggling to be objective. Structuralism, with its introspective method, was losing influence. In fact, consciousness per se was becoming a highly questionable subject matter. With his blending of associationism, Darwinism, and experimental science, Thorndike represented the best in American objective psychology. He was an important part of the functionalist movement, which as we have seen was one of the first

FIGURE 7–1 Dog with esophageal and gastric fistulae. Such an arrangement allowed the dog to be fed but prevented the food from reaching the stomach. Also, gastric juices flowing from the stomach could be measured. (From *Principles of General Psychology,* p. 208, by G.A. Kimble, N. Garmezy, & E. Zigler, 1974, New York: John Wiley & Sons, Inc.)

FIGURE 7–2
Dog with a tube entering its cheek. When the dog salivates, the saliva is gathered in the test tube and its quantity is recorded on the rotating drum to the left. (From *Great Experiments in Psychology,* p. 5, by H.E. Garrett, 1951, New York: Appleton-Century-Crofts.)

major psychological movements in America. Under the influence of Darwin, the functionalist's main concern was survival, which of course involved adapting to the environment. The functionalists tried to discover how human actions as well as thought processes contribute to adaptation and survival.

At the time Thorndike was doing his major research, Pavlov was also investigating the learning process. He, too, was impatient with subjective psychology and, in fact, had almost decided not to study the conditioned reflex because of its "psychic" nature. Although Pavlov (1928) did not have a high opinion of psychologists, he had considerable respect for Thorndike and acknowledged him as the first to do systematic research on the learning process in animals:

> Some years after the beginning of the work with our new method I learned that somewhat similar experiments on animals had been performed in America, and indeed not by physiologists but by psychologists. Thereupon I studied in more detail the American publications, and now I must acknowledge that the honour of having made the first steps along this path belongs to E. L. Thorndike. By two or three years his experiments preceded ours, and his book must be considered as a classic, both for its bold outlook on an immense task and for the accuracy of its results. (pp. 38–40)

Ivan Petrovich Pavlov. (From *Experimental Psychology and Other Essays,* p. 4, by I. P. Pavlov, 1957, New York: Philosophical Library.)

Thorndike and Pavlov, although traveling two different paths in many respects, shared an enthusiasm toward science and a belief in its ultimate ability to solve major human problems: "Only science, exact science about human nature itself, and the most sincere approach to it by the aid of the omnipotent scientific method, will deliver man from his present gloom, and will purge him from his contemporary shame in the sphere of interhuman relations" (Pavlov, 1928, p. 28). Pavlov never wavered from his scientific outlook, and in 1936 at the age of 87 he wrote the following letter to the young scientists of his country (Babkin, 1949):

> This is the message I would like to give to the youth of my country. First of all, be systematic. I repeat—be systematic. Train yourself to be strictly systematic in the acquisition of knowledge. First study the rudiments of science before attempting to reach its heights. Never pass on to the next stage until you have thoroughly mastered the one on hand. Never try to conceal the defects in your knowledge even by the most daring conjectures and hypotheses. Practice self-restraint and patience. Learn to do the drudgery of scientific work. Although a bird's wing is perfect, the bird could never soar if it did not lean upon the air. Facts are the air on which the scientist leans. Without them you will never fly upward. Without them your theories will be mere empty efforts. However, when studying, experimenting or observing, try not to remain on the surface of things. Do not become a mere collector of facts but try to penetrate into the mystery of their origin. Search persistently for the laws which govern them.
>
> The second important requisite is modesty. Never at any time imagine that you know everything. No matter how highly you are appreciated by others, have the courage to say to yourself, "I am ignorant." Do not let pride possess you.
>
> The third thing that is necessary is passion. Remember that science demands of a man his whole life. And even if you could have two lives, they would not be sufficient. Science calls for tremendous effort and great passion. Be passionate in your work and in your search for truth. (p. 110)

EMPIRICAL OBSERVATIONS

Development of a Conditioned Reflex

Exactly what is meant by a psychic or conditioned reflex is indicated by the following statement by Pavlov (1955):

> I shall mention two simple experiments that can be successfully performed by all. We introduce into the mouth of a dog a moderate solution of some acid; the acid produces a usual defensive reaction in the animal: by vigorous movements of the mouth it ejects the solution, and at the same time an abundant quantity of saliva begins to flow first into the mouth and then overflows, diluting the acid and cleaning the mucous membrane of the oral cavity. Now let us turn to the second experiment. Just prior to introducing the same solution into the dog's mouth we repeatedly act on the animal by a certain external agent, say, a definite sound. What happens then? It suffices simply to repeat the sound, and the same reaction is fully reproduced—the same movements of the mouth and the same secretion of saliva. (p. 247)

The ingredients necessary to bring about conditioning include (1) an **unconditioned stimulus (US),** which elicits a natural and automatic response from the organism; (2) an **unconditioned response (UR),** which is a natural and automatic response elicited by the US; (3) a **conditioned stimulus (CS),** which is a neutral stimulus in that it does not elicit a natural and automatic response from the organism. When these ingredients are mixed in a certain way, a **conditioned response (CR)** occurs.

To produce a CR, the CS and the US must be paired a number of times. First the CS is presented and then the US. The order of presentation is very important. Each time the US occurs, a UR occurs. Eventually the CS can be presented alone and it will elicit a response similar to the UR. When this happens, a CR has been demonstrated. The procedure can be diagrammed as follows:

$$\text{Training procedure: CS} \rightarrow \text{US} \rightarrow \text{UR}$$
$$\text{Demonstration of conditioning: CS} \rightarrow \text{CR}$$

In Pavlov's example above, the US was acid, the UR was salivation (caused by the acid), and the CS was a sound. The sound, of course, would not ordinarily cause the dog to salivate, but by being paired with the acid, the sound developed the capability to elicit salivation. Salivation as the result of hearing the sound was the CR.

Pavlov believed that the UR and the CR are always the same kind of response; if the UR is salivation, the CR must also be salivation. The magnitude of the CR, however, is always less than that of the UR. For example, Pavlov, who measured the magnitude of a response by counting drops of saliva, found that the US elicited more drops of saliva than did the CS. When we consider recent research on classical conditioning later in this chapter, we will see that Pavlov's contention that CRs are smaller versions of URs has been found, at least in some cases, to be incorrect.

Experimental Extinction

A CR depends on a US for its existence, and that is precisely why the US is referred to as a *reinforcer*. Obviously, without the US, a CS would never develop the capability of eliciting a CR. Likewise, if after a CR has been developed, the CS is continually presented without the US following the CS, the CR gradually disappears. When the CS no longer elicits a CR, experimental **extinction** is said to have occurred. Again, extinction results when the CS is presented to the organism and is not followed by reinforcement. In classical conditioning studies, reinforcement is the US. The terms *Pavlovian conditioning* and *classical conditioning* are synonymous.

Spontaneous Recovery

After a period of time following extinction, if the CS is again presented to the animal, the CR will temporarily reappear. The CR has "spontaneously recovered" even though there had been no further pairings between the CS and the US. Again, if there is a delay following extinction and the CS is presented to the organism, it will tend to elicit a CR. The extinction and **spontaneous recovery** of a CR are shown in Figure 7–3.

Higher-Order Conditioning

After a CS has been paired with a US a number of times, it can be used much like a US. That is, through its pairing with the US, the CS develops reinforcing properties of its own and it can be paired with a second CS to bring about a CR. Let us pair, for example, a blinking light (CS) with the presentation of food powder (US). Food powder will cause the animal to salivate, and after a number of pairings between the

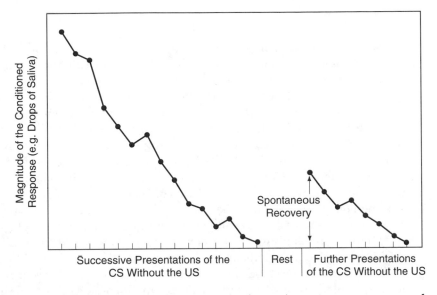

FIGURE 7–3 Typical curves showing the extinction and spontaneous recovery of a conditioned response.

CS and the US, the blinking light presented alone will cause the animal to salivate. That the animal salivates to the blinking light is, of course, a conditioned response.

Now that the blinking light can elicit salivation, it can be paired with a second CS, say, a buzzer. The direction of the pairing is the same as in the original conditioning: First the new CS (buzzer) is presented and then the old one (blinking light). Note that food is no longer involved. After a number of such pairings, the buzzer, when presented alone, causes the animal to salivate. In this example, the first CS was used much like a US is used to bring about a conditioned response. This is called *second-order conditioning.* We also say that the first CS developed *secondary reinforcing properties* since it was used to condition a response to a new stimulus. Therefore the CS is called a **secondary reinforcer.** Since secondary reinforcement cannot develop without the US, the US is called a **primary reinforcer.**

This procedure can be carried one more step. The second CS (buzzer) can be paired with one more CS, such as a 2,000-cps tone. The direction of the pairing is the same as before: first the tone, then the buzzer. Eventually, the tone presented alone will cause the animal to salivate. Thus, through its pairing with the blinking light, the buzzer also became a secondary reinforcer and therefore could be used to condition a response to another new stimulus, the 2,000-cps tone. This is *third-order conditioning.* Both second- and third-order conditioning come under the general heading of **higher-order conditioning.**

Since higher-order conditioning must be studied during the extinction process, it is very difficult, if not impossible, to go beyond third-order conditioning. In fact, such studies are quite rare. As one goes from first- to third-order conditioning, the magnitude of the CR becomes smaller and the CR lasts only for a few trials. In this example, the tone would only elicit a few drops of saliva and do so only the first few times it was presented to the animal.

Generalization

To illustrate **generalization,** we return to the basic conditioning procedure. We will use a 2,000-cps tone for our CS and meat powder for our US. After a number of pairings, the tone alone causes the animal to salivate; thus we have developed a CR. Once this has been accomplished, we enter the extinction phase of the experiment, only this time we will expose the animal to tones other than the one it was trained on. Some of the new tones will have a frequency higher than 2,000 cps, and some will have a lower frequency. Using the number of drops of saliva as our measure of the magnitude of the CR, we find that the CR has its greatest magnitude when the 2,000-cps tone is presented, but CRs are also given to other tones. The magnitude of the CR given to the other tones depends on their similarity to the tone the animal was actually trained on; in this case, the greater the similarity to the 2,000-cps tone, the greater the magnitude of the CR. An example of generalization is shown in Figure 7–4.

There is a relationship between Pavlov's concept of generalization and Thorndike's explanation of the transfer of training. With generalization, as the training and testing situations have more in common, there is a greater probability that the same response will be made to both. This statement could easily be subsumed under Thorndike's "identical elements" theory of transfer. Likewise, both generalization and transfer explain how we can have a learned reaction to a situation we have never encountered before; that is, we respond to a new situation as we would respond to a similar situation that we are familiar with.

It is important to note the distinction between Thorndike's spread of effect and Pavlov's generalization. The spread of effect refers to the influence of rein-

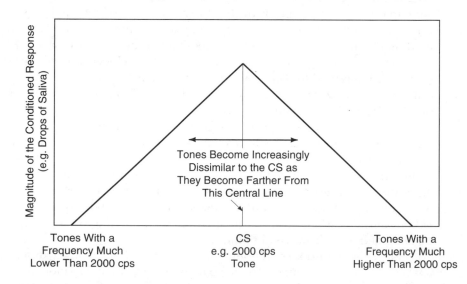

FIGURE 7–4   Idealized stimulus generalization curve showing that as stimuli become increasingly dissimilar to the one used as the CS during training, the magnitude of the CR goes down.

forcement on responses neighboring the reinforced response, regardless of their similarity to the reinforced response. With the spread of effect, proximity is the important thing. Generalization describes the increased capability of producing a CR by stimuli related to the stimulus that actually preceded reinforcement. With generalization, similarity and not proximity is the important thing.

Discrimination

The opposite of generalization is **discrimination.** As we saw above, generalization refers to the tendency to respond to a number of stimuli that are related to the one actually used during training. Discrimination, on the other hand, refers to the tendency to respond to a very restricted range of stimuli or to only the one used during training.

Discrimination can be brought about in two ways: prolonged training and differential reinforcement. First, if a CS is paired with a US many times, the tendency to respond to stimuli related to the CS, but not identical to it, goes down. In other words, if the minimum number of pairings between the CS and US necessary to develop a CR is used, there is a relatively strong tendency to respond to stimuli related to the CS during extinction; that is, there is considerable generalization. However, if training is prolonged, there is a reduced tendency to respond to stimuli related to the CS during extinction. Thus, it is possible to control generalization by controlling training level: The greater the amount of training, the less generalization.

The second way of bringing about discrimination is through differential reinforcement. This procedure involves, in the above example, presenting the 2,000-cps tone along with a number of other tones that will occur during extinction. Only the 2,000-cps tone is followed by reinforcement. After such training, when the animal is presented with tones other than the 2,000-cps tone during extinction, it tends not to respond to them. Thus, discrimination is demonstrated. Pavlov's attempt at providing a physiological explanation for generalization and discrimination will be considered later in this chapter.

Relationship between the CS and the US

Two general considerations about classical conditioning must be mentioned. First, there appears to be an optimal interval of presentation between the CS and US for conditioning to take place most rapidly. A number of investigators have found that if the CS comes on a half second before the US, conditioning proceeds most efficiently. The most common procedure is to have the CS come on and stay on until the US comes on. If the time between these two events is greater or less than 0.5 second, conditioning is relatively more difficult to establish. This explanation should be looked on as an oversimplification, however, since the optimal interval of time between the onset of the CS and the onset of the US for conditioning to occur depends on many factors, and it is the subject of a considerable amount of research. For example, when we consider research on taste aversion later in this chapter we will see that a phenomenon like classical conditioning occurs even when the delay between the CS and the US is several hours. Also, as we shall see below and again later in this chapter, there are circumstances in which a CS precedes a US at the optimal interval and yet no conditioning occurs.

The second matter is related to the first. Using traditional classical conditioning procedures, it was typically found that if the CS comes on *after* the US is presented, conditioning is extremely difficult, if not impossible, to establish. This is referred to as **backward conditioning.** One explanation for the apparent lack of backward conditioning is that a CS must be "informative" to the organism before conditioning will occur. Clearly, a CS that comes on after the US has already been presented cannot be used by the organism to predict the occurrence of the US. This would be true not only of the backward conditioning situation but also if CSs are redundant or unreliable. Evidence for this point of view is supplied by Egger and Miller (1962, 1963), who found that (1) if two CSs reliably predict a US, the first one presented will become conditioned, and the second one, which is redundant, will not; and (2) if two signals precede a US but one is always followed by the US and the other is only sometimes followed by the US, the more reliable signal becomes conditioned much more than the unreliable signal. It appears that stimuli that occurred after the US or stimuli that were either redundant or unreliably correlated with the US could not be used by the organism to predict the occurrence of primary reinforcements; that is, they had no **information value.** In general, Egger and Miller concluded that for classical conditioning to take place, the organism must be able to use the CS to predict whether or not reinforcement will occur. Egger and Miller's general conclusion is still widely accepted, but recent research on classical conditioning has necessitated a change in the beliefs about both backward conditioning and the circumstances under which a CS is informative. Later in this chapter we will discuss current research that shows that CSs presented *after* the US are as informative as CSs that are presented *before* the US, and therefore backward conditioning is not only possible but also under certain circumstances, as easy to establish as forward conditioning.

THEORETICAL EXPLANATIONS OF CONDITIONING PHENOMENA

Pavlov considered himself to be an experimental physiologist, and he therefore sought to explain his observations in physiological terms. Many of his physiological explanations were highly speculative and most have since been found erroneous, but correcting for the time and conditions under which they were made, they were quite remarkable. It was obvious to Pavlov that a CS and US became associated through the consistent pairings of the two. The question was, What is the physiological basis for this association? Pavlov answered this question as follows: The unconditional stimulus sets up a dominant activity in some area of the cerebral cortex. All other stimuli present at the time also cause cerebral activity, but this activity is weaker and is drawn toward the area of dominant activity caused by the US. The weaker activity is drawn toward the stronger activity, and a temporary connection is formed between these various centers in the brain. In this way, all the stimuli preceding the onset of the US become associated with it. Thus, when one of the stimuli that accompanied the US is presented to the organism, it causes activity in the area of the brain associated with it. If it is a visual stimulus, it will cause activity in the visual part of the brain. The activity in this area in turn causes activity in the area corresponding to the unconditioned stimulus because of the temporary connection between the two. The result is that the organism emits a response to the visual stimulus that is associated naturally with the US; that is, there is a conditioned response. To summarize, Pavlov simply said that brain centers that are repeatedly active together form temporary connections, and the arousal of one will cause the arousal of the others. Thus, if a tone is consistently presented to a dog just before it gets fed, the area of the brain aroused by the tone will form a temporary connection with the area of the brain that responds to food. When this connection is formed, the presentation of the tone will cause the animal to act as if food was present. At that point, we say a conditioned reflex has been developed.

Excitation and Inhibition

According to Pavlov, the two basic processes governing all central nervous system activity were **excitation** and **inhibition.** Babkin (1949) said,

> The fundamental theoretical conception of Pavlov concerning the functional properties of the nervous system, and of the cerebral cortex in particular, was that they were based on two equally important processes: the process of excitation and the process of inhibition. Very often he compared the nervous system with the ancient Greek god Janus, who had two faces looking in opposite directions. The excitation and the inhibition are only sides of one and the same process; they always exist simultaneously, but their proportion varies in each moment, at times the one prevailing, at times the other. Functionally the cerebral cortex is, according to Pavlov, a mosaic, consisting of continuously changing points of excitation and inhibition. (p. 313)

Pavlov believed that each environmental event corresponded to some point on the cortex and that as these events were experienced they tended either to excite or to inhibit cortical activity. Thus, the cortex is constantly being excited or inhibited, depending on what the organism is experiencing. This pattern of excitation and inhibition that characterizes the brain at any given moment is what Pavlov called the **cortical mosaic.** The momentary cortical mosaic determines how an organism will respond to its environment. As either the external environment or the internal environment changes, the cortical mosaic changes and behavior changes accordingly.

The Dynamic Stereotype

When events consistently occur in the environment, they come to have neurological representation and they become increasingly easy to respond to. Thus, responses to a familiar environment become rapid and automatic. When this happens, a **dynamic stereotype** is said to have been developed. Roughly, the dynamic stereotype is a cortical mosaic that has become stable because the organism has been in a highly predictable environment for a considerable length of time. As long as this cortical mapping accurately reflects the environment and produces appropriate responses, everything is fine. If, however, the environment is radically changed, the organism may find it difficult to change a dynamic stereotype. Pavlov (1955) put the matter as follows:

> The entire establishment and distribution in the cortex of excitatory and inhibitory states, taking place in a certain period under the action of external and internal stimuli, become more and more fixed under uniform, recurring conditions and are effected with ever-increasing ease and automatism. Thus, there appears a dynamic stereotype (systematization) in the cortex, the maintenance of which becomes an increasingly less difficult nervous task; but the stereotype becomes inert, little susceptible to change and resistant to new conditions and new stimulations. Any initial elaboration of a stereotype is, depending on the complexity of the system of stimuli, a difficult and often an extraordinary task. (p. 259)

To summarize, certain environmental events tend to be followed by certain other environmental events, and as long as this relationship continues to be true, the association between the two on the neural level continues to grow stronger. (Note the similarity here to Thorndike's early thinking concerning the effect of exercise on a neural bond.) If the environment abruptly changes, new neural paths must be formed, and that is no easy matter.

Irradiation and Concentration

Pavlov used the term *analyser* to describe the path from a sense receptor to a certain area of the brain. An analyser consists of sense receptors, the sensory tract in the spinal cord, and the area of the brain onto which the sensory activity is projected. Sensory information projected onto some area of the brain causes excitation in that area. Initially, this excitation spills over into neighboring brain areas; in other words, there is an **irradiation of excitation.** It is this process that Pavlov used to explain generalization. In our example of generalization described above, we noted that when an animal was conditioned to respond to a 2,000-cps tone, it responded not only to that tone but also to other related tones. The magnitude of the response was determined by the similarity between the tone being presented and the actual CS used during training. As the similarity increased, the CR's magnitude increased.

Pavlov's explanation for generalization was that neural impulses traveled from the sense receptors—in this case from the ears—to a specific area of the cortex that reacted to a 2,000-cps tone. The activity caused by the 2,000-cps tone irradiates from this location out into the neighboring regions. Pavlov assumed that tones closest to the 2,000-cps tone would be represented in brain regions close to the area corresponding to the one for the 2,000-cps tone. As tones become dissimilar, the brain regions representing them will be farther away from the area representing the 2,000-cps tone. In addition, Pavlov assumed that excitation diminished with distance: It was strongest at the point corresponding to the CS and weaker farther away. Therefore an association was made not only between the CS and the US but also with a number of stimuli related to the CS that had representation in neighboring brain regions. In addition to his hypothesis that excitation irradiated, or spread, to neighboring regions of the cortex, Pavlov found that inhibition also irradiated.

Pavlov also found that concentration, a process opposite to irradiation, can govern both excitation and inhibition. He found that under certain circumstances both excitation and inhibition can be concentrated at specific areas of the brain. As the process of irradiation is used to explain generalization, so is the process of concentration used to explain discrimination.

At first the organism has a generalized tendency to respond to a CS during conditioning. For example, if a signal is followed by a reinforcer, there is a learned tendency to respond to that and related signals. Likewise, if a signal is presented and is not followed by a reinforcer, there is a learned tendency not to respond to that and related signals. We say, therefore, that both excitation and inhibition have irradiated. With prolonged training, however, the tendencies to respond and not to respond become less general and increasingly specific to a narrow range of stimuli. In this case, we say the excitation and inhibition have been concentrated.

As we noted earlier in this chapter, discrimination, or the ability to respond differentially to related stimuli, can be brought about by prolonged training or differential reinforcement. If a large number of pairings are made between the CS and the US, the excitation begins to concentrate. After such training, one would find that the organism tends to respond only to the CS or to stimuli very similar to the CS. In other words, because excitation has been concentrated, very little generalization would take place.

Summary of Pavlov's Views on Brain Functioning

Pavlov saw the brain as a mosaic of points of excitation and inhibition. Each point on the brain corresponded to an environmental event. Depending on what was being experienced at the moment, a different pattern of excitation and inhibition would occur in the brain and that pattern would determine behavior. Some connections in the brain are between unconditioned stimuli and their associated responses, and some are between conditioned stimuli and their associated responses. The former are permanent, and the latter are temporary and change with varied environmental conditions.

When a temporary connection is first being formed in the brain, there is a tendency for a conditioned stimulus to have a very general effect in the brain. That is, the excitation caused by a conditioned stimulus irradiates over a relatively larger portion of the cortex. The same thing is true when an organism is learning not to respond to, or to avoid, a stimulus. The inhibitory effects of such a stimulus also irradiate over a fairly large portion of the brain in the early stages of learning. As learning proceeds, however, the excitation caused by a positive stimulus and the inhibition caused by a negative stimulus become concentrated in specific areas of the cortex. As the organism develops the connections between environmental events and brain processes that allow it to survive, a dynamic stereotype develops, which is a kind of neural mapping of the environment. The dynamic stereotype makes it easier to respond to a highly predictable environment but makes it difficult to adjust to a new environment.

Pavlov never explained how all of these processes interact to produce the smooth, coordinated behavior we see from organisms, but he did express amazement that systematic behavior did result from such a large number of influences. Pavlov (1955) put the matter as follows:

> Countless stimuli, different in nature and intensity, reach the cerebral hemispheres both from the external world and the internal medium of the organism itself. Whereas some of them are merely investigated (the orienting reflex), others evoke highly diverse conditioned and unconditioned effects. They all meet, come together, interact, and they must, finally, become systematized, equilibrated, and form, so to speak, a dynamic stereotype. What truly grandiose work! (p. 454)

The **orienting reflex** to which Pavlov referred is the tendency for organisms to attend to and explore novel stimuli that occur in their environment. The orienting reflex has been the topic of considerable research in recent years.

First and Second Signal Systems

Until Pavlov, most physiologists and psychologists concerned themselves with the importance of the present or the past for the behavior of organisms. That is, they focused on reflexive responses elicited by current stimulating conditions or on how the memory of past events influences behavior. Pavlov's work on conditioning provided a framework for understanding how organisms anticipate *future* events. Because CSs precede biologically significant events (URs), they become signals for those events that allow an organism to prepare for and to engage in behavior that is appropriate to their occurrence. Anoklin (1968) makes this point concerning the anticipatory nature of conditioned reflexes:

> Pavlov...rated very highly the ability of the conditioned reaction to act as a "signal" reaction or, as he expressed it many times, a reaction of "warning character." It is this "warning" character which accounts for the profound historical significance of the conditioned reflex. It enables the animal to adapt itself to events which are not taking place at that particular moment but which will follow in the future. (p. 140)

Pavlov referred to the stimuli that come to signal biologically significant events (CSs) as the **first signal system** or "the first signals of reality." In addition, however, humans also utilize language, which consists of *symbols* of reality. Thus, one may respond to the word *danger* as one would respond to an actual dangerous situation. Pavlov referred to the words that symbolize reality as the "signals of signals" or the **second signal system.** Once established these symbols can be organized into a complex system that guides much human behavior.

One example of how language complicates classical conditioning is found in the area of **semantic generalization** (sometimes called mediated generalization). Studies have shown that a response can be conditioned to the *meaning* of a stimulus rather than to the concrete stimulus itself. For example, if a response is conditioned to the number 4, human subjects will emit a conditioned response when they are confronted with such stimuli as $\sqrt{16}$, $2|8$, 2×2, $10|40$, and so forth. In other words, the number 4 elicits a conditioned response, but so will a variety of other stimuli that result in 4 after mental operations have been performed. The conclusion to be drawn is that for human subjects the true CS is the concept of "fourness." (See Razran, 1961, for additional examples of semantic conditioning.)

Semantic generalization also seems to vary as a function of age. In his work with children of different ages, Reiss (1946) found that after initial training, which involved visually presenting a word such as *right* as a CS, children generalized by giving conditioned responses according to their level of language development. He found that 8-year-olds generalized to visually presented homophones (e.g., *rite*); 11-year-olds generalized to antonyms (e.g., *wrong*); and 14-year-olds generalized to synonyms (e.g., *correct*).

Although the second signal system is clearly more complex than the first signal system, Pavlov felt that the same laws of conditioning govern both and therefore they both could be studied objectively. In other words, the process by which we develop a reaction to an environmental event is the same process by which we develop a reaction to a word or a thought.

A COMPARISON BETWEEN CLASSICAL AND INSTRUMENTAL CONDITIONING

The kind of conditioning that Thorndike studied is now called instrumental conditioning because the response being observed was instrumental in getting the animal something it wanted (reinforcement). In the case of the cat in the puzzle box, the cat had to learn to perform a certain response that released it from the box and was reinforced with a piece of fish. If the appropriate response did not occur, the animal was not reinforced. To summarize, we can say that in instrumental conditioning, any response that leads to reinforcement tends to be repeated, and a reinforcer is something the animal wants.

Classical conditioning elicits a response from the animal, and instrumental conditioning depends on the animal's emission of the response. The former can be said to be involuntary and automatic; the latter to be voluntary and under the animal's control.

The function of reinforcement is also quite different for classical and instrumental conditioning. With instrumental conditioning, reinforcement is presented to the animal *after* the response of interest has been made. With classical conditioning, however, the reinforcer (US) is presented in order to *elicit* the response of interest. The two situations can be diagrammed as follows:

Instrumental Conditioning

Environmental situation → Effective behavior → Reinforcement
(e.g., puzzle box)   (e.g., behavior which   (e.g., being released
                        releases the animal   from confinement
                        from confinement)   and/or receiving a
                                                  piece of fish)

Association of interest

Classical Conditioning

Conditioned Stimulus →   Reinforcement   → Unconditioned response
    (e.g., a tone)   (Unconditioned   (e.g., salivation)
       ↑   stimulus, e.g., food)

       └────────────────────────────→   Conditioned response
       Association of interest   (salivation)

Pavlov felt that he had discovered the physiological bases for the associations that philosophers and psychologists had been talking about for so many years. To him, conditioned reflexes could explain how the mind works. Pavlov (1955) placed himself squarely among the associationists with the following statement:

> Are there any grounds…for distinguishing between that which the physiologist calls the temporary connection and that which the psychologist terms association? They are fully identical; they merge and absorb each other. Psychologists themselves seem to recognize this, since they (at least, some of them) have stated that the experiments with conditioned reflexes provide a solid foundation for associative psychology, i.e., psychology which regards association as the base of psychical activity. (p. 251)

Both kinds of conditioning enhance an organism's survival: classical conditioning by creating a system of signs and symbols that allow the anticipation of significant events; instrumental conditioning through the development of appropriate behavior patterns in response to those significant events. Both kinds of conditioning are also dependent on reinforcement. In classical conditioning the US is the reinforcer, and if it is removed from the experimental arrangement extinction occurs. In instrumental conditioning the reinforcer is the "satisfying state of affairs" that *follows* an appropriate response. If reinforcement no longer follows a certain response, the probability of that response goes back to the point where it was before reinforcement was introduced. Classical and instrumental conditioning have in common not only the necessity of reinforcement (extinction follows when it is removed) but also the phenomena of spontaneous recovery, generalization, discrimination, and secondary reinforcement.

It should also be pointed out that it is impossible to separate instrumental and classical conditioning completely. For example, every instrumental conditioning study that utilizes a primary reinforcer (such as food or water) will necessarily produce classical conditioning. That is, all of the stimuli that consistently occur prior to the primary reinforcer will, through the process of classical conditioning, become secondary reinforcers.

RECENT RESEARCH ON CLASSICAL CONDITIONING

In his analysis of conditioning Pavlov emphasized contiguity. That is, if a CS precedes a US, eventually a CS will elicit a CR. We saw earlier that the work of Egger and Miller (1962, 1963) cast doubt on this analysis by showing that CSs that are unreliable or redundant do not become conditioned to a US. Recently several other researchers have also shown that factors other than simple contiguity are involved in classical conditioning. We will review the work of these researchers, but first we will discuss two possible inaccuracies in Pavlov's theory. The first is his view of CRs as smaller versions of URs. The second is his claim that extinction involved inhibition.

CRs Are Not Necessarily Little URs Pavlov believed that in the course of conditioning the CS comes to substitute for the US, which is why classical conditioning has sometimes been referred to as *stimulus substitute* learning. It was assumed that since the CS acts as a substitute for the US, CRs were smaller versions of URs. Indeed, there are times when the CR and UR have much in common, as when the UR caused by food (US) is, among other things, salivation and so is the CR. Also when the US is a puff of air to the eye, the UR is, among other things, an eye-blink, and a CS consistently paired with the US, will eventually, when presented alone, cause an eye-blink. Often a CR does look like a smaller version of the UR. However, careful study of the nature of CRs have shown them to often be quite different from URs. For example, Zener (1937) carefully photographed a classical conditioning experiment and made the following observations:

> Except for the component of salivary secretion the conditioned and unconditioned behavior is not identical. (a) During most of the time in which the bell is reinforced by the presence of food, chewing generally occurs with the head raised out of the food-pan but not directed either at the bell or into the food-pan, or at any definite environmental object. Yet this posture practically never, even chewing only occasionally, occurs to the conditioned stimulus alone. Despite Pavlov's assertions, the dog does not appear to be eating an imaginary food. (b) Nor is the behavior that does appear an arrested or partially unconditioned reaction consisting of those response elements not conflicting with other actions. It is a different reaction, anthropomorphically describable as a looking for, expecting, the fall of food with a readiness to perform the eating behavior which will occur when the food falls. The effector pattern is not identical with the unconditioned. (c) Movements frequently occur which do not appear as part of the unconditioned response to food: All the restless behavior of stamping, yawning, panting. (p. 393)

Not only has it been found that CRs and URs are often different in nature, but also some researchers have found them to be antagonistic. Obrist, Sutterer, and Howard (1972) verified the fact that the typical UR, when shock is used as the US, is heart rate acceleration. And as Pavlov would have predicted, with minimal pairings of the CS and US, the CR is heart rate acceleration. With prolonged training, however, the CR became heart rate *deceleration.*

Another example of CR and UR being antagonistic is found when drugs are used as USs. Shepard Siegel (1979) describes a series of experiments in which morphine was used as a US. One reaction to morphine is analgesia—or a reduction in the sensitivity to pain. Under the influence of morphine a rat will take significantly longer to remove its paw from a hot plate than a rat not under the influence of morphine. Since the injection itself precedes the experience of morphine (the US) it (the injection) can be viewed as a CS. Thus, after several injections of morphine, injecting the rat with plain water should reduce its sensitivity to pain. It turns out, however, that the opposite is true. Under the circumstances described above, rats become *more* sensitive to pain. That is, animals that were previously injected with morphine and are then injected with water remove their paw from a hot plate significantly *faster* than control animals that had never been injected with morphine. The CR (increased sensitivity to pain) appears to be opposite to the UR (decreased sensitivity to pain). Essentially the same results have been attained when lights or tones were used as CSs instead of the injection itself.

It has also been found (e.g., Holland, 1977) that even when the same US is used, CRs will take different forms when different CSs are paired with that US. Clearly the relationship between CRs and URs is much more complex than Pavlov had assumed. It turns out that sometimes CRs do mimic URs, sometimes CRs seem to prepare the organism for the US, and sometimes CRs are antagonistic to the UR. For a discussion of the different kinds of CR-UR relationships and the conditions that produce them, see Hilgard and Marquis (1940) and Hollis (1982).

Extinction Involves Interference   As we noted previously, Pavlov believed that during extinction, nonreinforced presentations of a CS result in learned inhibition that either suppressed or replaced previously learned excitatory associations between CS and US. Inhibition, rather than elimination of CS-US connections, was therefore seen as the mechanism underlying experimental extinction of a conditioned response. A modified approach proposed by Bouton (1993, 1994) suggests that during extinction, presentation of a CS without a US results in new learning, usually including inhibition of the CR, that interferes with a previously learned CS-US association. Original CS-US associations thus remain intact and coexist with newly learned CS-extinction associations. However, specific responses observed under subsequent test conditions will depend on experimental-contextual cues other than the CS itself.

This argument rests heavily on three reliable learning phenomena. The first, spontaneous recovery, has already been described. The second, called the renewal effect, is observed when a response that has been conditioned in one experimental context is extinguished in another. When the experimental subject is returned to the original setting and the CS is presented, the CR is readily elicited (Bouton, 1984, 1991; Bouton & Bolles, 1979a; Bouton & King, 1983, 1986). The third effect, reinstatement, is observed when a US is presented after experimental extinction seems to be complete. After a few unpaired presentations of the US, the original CS again elicits a CR, although not at levels observed prior to extinction (Bouton, 1988, 1991; Bouton & Bolles, 1979b; Rescorla & Heth, 1975).

Bouton (1993, 1994) proposes that contextual factors, comprised of temporal (time) and physical/spatial stimuli present during conditioning, serve as memory retrieval cues for CS-US associations. During extinction, those same context cues come to retrieve CS-extinction associations. After extinction, the CS is "ambiguous;" it evokes both the responses learned during CS-US pairing and the responses learned during extinction. Contextual cues determine which response occurs, depending on which association they elicit. If context cues most resemble those stimuli that existed during conditioning, the CS elicits the CR; if they are most like the cues that existed during extinction, the CS elicits extinction responses other than the CR. Experimental manipulations that reduce ambiguity emphasize these conclusions.

For example, reinstatement is not observed if the post-extinction US is presented in a context different than the one that existed during original conditioning

(Bouton, 1984; Bouton & Bolles, 1979b; Bouton & Peck, 1989). In addition, spontaneous recovery is significantly reduced if a distinctive (non-CS) cue that was present during extinction trials is reintroduced during tests for recovery (Brooks & Bouton, 1993). Although research in the area continues, Bouton's contextual interpretation may be the most parsimonious way to explain spontaneous recovery, renewal, and reinstatement.

Overshadowing and Blocking   Pavlov (1927) observed that if he used a compound stimulus as a CS and one component of the stimulus was more salient than the other, only the more salient component would be conditioned. This phenomenon is called **overshadowing.** If, for example, a compound CS consisted of a light and a loud noise (presented together), all the conditioning would occur to the loud noise because it was the stronger or more salient element of the compound. When a compound stimulus is used as a CS, overshadowing is demonstrated when conditioning occurs to the dominant component of the stimulus but not to the weaker component. The phenomenon of overshadowing is of theoretical interest because both elements of the compound stimulus are presented contiguously with the US, and yet conditioning occurs only in the case of one element. Much of the current research on classical conditioning has been designed to explain the phenomenon of overshadowing and the related phenomenon of blocking, which we will consider next.

In 1969, Leon Kamin reported an influential series of experiments on a phenomenon that he calls **blocking** (also called the blocking effect). Before discussing Kamin's work on blocking we need to describe the **conditioned emotional response** (**CER**), which he used to demonstrate the blocking phenomenon. The CER was first described by Estes and Skinner (1941) as a method of measuring the strength of a CS-US association. The procedure involves first placing a rat in a Skinner box and shaping it to press a lever for food reinforcement. The rat is then switched to a fixed interval schedule of reinforcement (e.g., an FI four-minute schedule) to produce a steady rate of responding. Next, the rat experiences one-hour experimental sessions during which a tone is sounded for three minutes at a time; on the termination of the tone, the rat receives a brief, unavoidable shock. Throughout the tone-shock sequences, the fixed interval reinforcement schedule remains in effect. After several sessions, the rats greatly reduced their rate of lever pressing each time the tone came on. The reduction in rate of responding when the CS (tone) was on is called **conditioned suppression.** It was found that the suppression lasted until the end of the shock that terminated each tone-shock sequence. After the shock was terminated, the response rate increased to its normal rate and continued at that rate until the tone came on again. During the time that the tone was on, Estes and Skinner noted emotional responses such as defecation, squealing, and freezing. It was these conditioned emotional responses that were thought responsible for suppressing the response rate. With this procedure, the extent of classical conditioning (tone-shock relationship) could be indexed by changes in the rate in which an operant response is made.

Kamin (1969) used a variation in the CER procedure to demonstrate blocking. First, rats were trained to press a lever for food reinforcement. Next, the rats were exposed to 16 trials in which a tone was followed by an electric shock. The result of this training was response suppression when the tone came on. The next phase of the study involved pairing the tone from the previous phase with a light, thus creating a compound stimulus. The light-tone compound stimulus was presented to the rat on 8 trials and was always followed by shock. The final phase of the study involved presenting only the light to the rat to see if it would produce response suppression, and it did not. A control group indicated that if both the light and the tone are paired with shock independently, both produce response suppression. If, however, the tone is first paired with shock and then is presented to the rat along with the light, little or no conditioning will occur to the light. Under these conditions, conditioning to the tone *blocked* conditioning to the light. The blocking effect is also found if the light is used first and is then paired with the tone, in which case no conditioning occurs to the tone. Kamin's procedure and results are summarized in Figure 7–5.

We will examine possible explanations for blocking shortly, but it should be noted here that blocking, like overshadowing, exemplifies a situation in which stimuli are paired in accordance with classical conditioning principles and yet no conditioning occurs. Once again it is suggested that something more than mere stimulus contiguity is involved in classical conditioning.

Overshadowing occurs when one component of a compound stimulus is intrinsically stronger than the other and therefore dominates the other, weaker component, thus preventing the weaker component from becoming conditioned. Blocking, in contrast, occurs because prior conditioning somehow prevents the formation of an association between a newly inserted stimulus and a US.

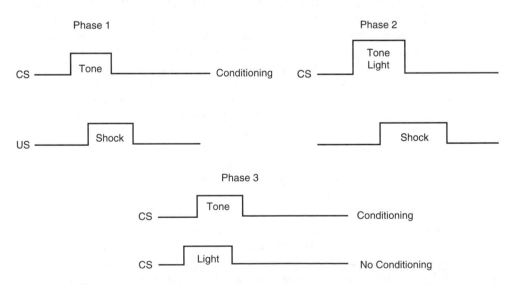

FIGURE 7–5 Kamin's blocking experiment. In Phase 1, a tone is paired with shock, and after several pairings, when presented alone, the tone causes response suppression. In Phase 2, the tone is paired with a light and both precede a shock. Phase 3 shows that the tone continues to cause response suppression, but the light does not. In spite of the fact that the light was reliably paired with the shock in Phase 2, such pairing did not result in conditioning.

The Rescorla-Wagner Theory of Classical Conditioning

Robert Rescorla and Allan Wagner have devised a theory that, in a sense, builds on the work of Egger and Miller (1962, 1963). The Rescorla-Wagner theory (see, e.g., Rescorla and Wagner, 1972; Wagner and Rescorla, 1972) provides an account of general classical conditioning phenomena, makes some unexpected predictions relevant to classical conditioning, and solves several critical problems associated with traditional classical conditioning theory. For example, it offers an explanation of blocking, which we will consider shortly.

The theory uses relatively simple mathematical and symbolic logic to summarize the dynamics of learning. First, as noted in Chapter 6, the learning curve increases gradually to a nearly level maximum, or asymptote. Rescorla and Wagner assume that the nature of the US determines the asymptotic, or maximum, level of conditioning that can be achieved. This maximum is symbolized by λ (lambda).

Next, associative learning acquired prior to a specific trial n is designated by V_{n-1}; and the *change* in learning due to conditioning on trial n is symbolized by ΔV_n. The symbol Δ (delta) indicates a change in V.

Finally, the Rescorla-Wagner theory includes two components that refer to the "conditionability" of a particular CS and US pair. The coefficient α (alpha) refers to the potential associative strength of a given CS. A loud tone, for example, will have a higher α value than a soft, inaudible tone. The coefficient β (beta) designates the potential associative strength of a specific US. A strong electric shock will elicit a more dramatic withdrawal reflex than a weak electric shock and therefore will have a greater value of β.

When we put all of these components together for a specified CS (CS_A) and US (US_A), we have

$$\Delta V_n = \alpha_A \beta_A (\lambda - V_{n-1})$$

This equation indicates that the change in strength of associative learning on any trial is a function of the *difference* between maximum possible learning and the amount already learned at the conclusion of the *preceding* trial.

Notice that because V_{n-1} grows with each trial and approaches λ, $(\lambda - V_{n-1})$ approaches zero, and ΔV_n is less on each successive trial. Thus, the function is asymptotic at the value of λ. It is not enough, however, for this expression to capture the dynamics of the learning curve; there are several mathematical expressions that can do the same (see, e.g., Chapter 6 or Chapter 9). The Rescorla-Wagner theory has the advantage of also accounting for anomalous findings in classical conditioning. Let us look, for example, at the way this theory explains blocking.

Recall that blocking occurs when a response is first conditioned to one CS_A (a light), then reinforced further with a compound CS_{AX}, made up of the initial CS_A (the light) and an additional CS_x (a tone). When the second element in the compound (the tone) is presented *alone*, it elicits little or no conditioned response. According to the theory, most of the conditioning possible for a particular US (e.g., a shock) is "used up" by the first CS.

In symbolic language, during initial conditioning, V_A approaches λ, and ΔV_A

approaches zero. When we begin *compound* stimulus training we have a condition in which

$$\Delta V_A = \alpha_A \beta \ (\lambda - V_{AX})$$

and

$$\Delta V_X = \alpha_X \beta (\lambda - V_{AX})$$

and according to the theory, $V_{AX} = V_A + V_X$. But remember that because of initial training with CS_A,

$$V_{AX} \cong V_A \cong \lambda$$

so V_X is functionally zero. If V_A has approached the value of λ, conditioning to CS_X is not possible because there is no conditioning left for the second CS. Essentially all the conditioning possible under the circumstances "belongs" to the first conditioned stimulus.

Contingency Not Contiguity

In his influential article "Pavlovian Conditioning: It's Not What You Think," Rescorla (1988) makes three observations about Pavlovian conditioning and delineates its importance in modern psychology.

First, like Egger and Miller (1962, 1963), he says it is essential that there be a correlation between US and CS that is more than mere coincidence or contiguity. Take, for example, a situation in which an animal experiences random USs and CSs over an extended period. There may be as many instances when the US and CS occur together (contiguity) as when they occur separately. Contrast this situation with one in which the US and CS are programmed so that they only occur together. These two conditions are represented in Figure 7–6, and it is important to notice that in both situations, CS and US occur together the *same* number of times.

Which CS-US relationship produces the best conditioning? It may seem intuitive, but it comes as a surprise to some psychologists that the latter situation produces the stronger classical conditioning, whereas the former produces weak conditioning, if any. Clearly, contiguity is not enough. Rescorla uses the term *contingency* to describe the relationship in which a CS provides a clear and informative marker for the US.

Second, like Zener (1937), Rescorla (1988) says that the common claim that a CR is a "miniature" or "abbreviated" UR is either an oversimplification or is entirely incorrect. A typical

Robert A. Rescorla. (Courtesy of Robert A. Rescorla.)

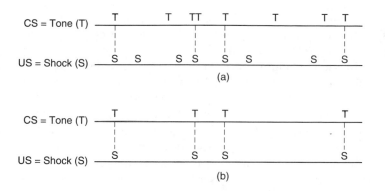

FIGURE 7–6
Although CS and US occur the same number of times in (a) and (b), the CS-US pairing in (a) produces little or no classical conditioning, but the CS-US pairing in (b) produces strong conditioning.

response to a US of electric shock in an open maze, for example, is increased activity or some version of a startle response. However, as seen in the conditioned suppression phenomenon described previously, if the CS used to signal shock is delivered during ongoing performance of a completely different response (lever pressing), the result is decreased activity. The CR can be several different responses, depending on the context in which the CS occurs.

These two points were clearly demonstrated when Rescorla (1966) trained dogs to jump over a hurdle in a shuttle box to avoid an electric shock that was delivered at regular intervals of 30 seconds. The situation was arranged so that the shock could be avoided if the dog jumped the hurdle before the end of the time interval. Each time the dog jumped over the hurdle, the clock was reset to zero and started running again. There was no external signal indicating when a shock would be delivered; the only signal was the animal's internal sense of the passage of time. All of the dogs in the experiment learned to jump often enough to avoid most of the shocks. The rate of jumping was then used as a frame of reference to judge the effects of other variables introduced into the experiment.

After the preliminary training described above, the dogs were removed from the hurdle-jumping apparatus and were subjected to tones followed by electric shock. The dogs were divided into three groups. Group 1 received standard conditioning in which a CS (a five-second tone) was always followed by a US (an electric shock). This procedure is generally referred to as **forward conditioning** and was called a positive contingency in Rescorla's study. Group 2 first experienced the US *and then* the CS. The situation for this group was arranged so that the CS was never paired with shock, nor was the CS ever followed within 30 seconds by the shock. The arrangement by which a CS *follows* a US, generally referred to as backward conditioning, was referred to as a negative contingency in Rescorla's study. This was an especially interesting experimental condition since it has been widely believed that when the CS follows the US, no conditioning occurs. Group 3 experienced the CS preceding the US and following it an equal number of times. By randomizing the occurrence of the CS relative to the US, a situation is created whereby there is no correlation between the two. That is, the US is as likely to occur following the presentation of the CS as it is when the CS does not occur. Therefore, for subjects in group 3, the CS had no predictive value.

In the final phase of the experiment, the dogs were placed back in the shuttle box and were again given avoidance training until the rate of their avoidance responses stabilized. At this point, the CS (tone) from the classical conditioning phase of the study was presented for five seconds a number of times. It was observed that when the CS was introduced to animals in group 1 (forward conditioning or positive contingency), they *increased* their rate of responding relative to what it was in the initial stage of the experiment. In fact, subjects in this group almost doubled their response rate when the tone came on. When the CS was introduced to animals in group 2 (backward conditioning or negative contingency), they *decreased* their rate of responding by about one-third. When the CS was introduced to animals in group 3 (no correlation), their rate of responding remained essentially the same as in the initial phase of the experiment.

One crucial point to remember while interpreting the results of this experiment is that all animals received the same number of shocks during the classical conditioning phase of the experiment. What was varied was the relationship between the CS and the US. As we have seen, Rescorla (1966, 1967) says that it is *contingencies* that determine whether conditioning takes place and, if so, what kind of conditioning. In group 1, there was a positive contingency between the CS and the US, and therefore the CS accurately predicted the occurrence of the US. This, according to Rescorla, is why the animals in this group jumped the hurdle more rapidly when the CS was presented. In group 2, there was a negative contingency between the CS and the US. That is, the CS was never paired with or followed by the US within thirty seconds. Thus, for subjects in this group, the CS became a signal for safety. Contrary to the common belief that no classical conditioning occurs under these conditions (backward conditioning), Rescorla found that the animals in this group indeed learned a contingency. They learned that the CS predicted the absence of the shock, and therefore when the CS was introduced to these animals, they inhibited their rate of jumping. Rescorla says that it is important to realize that the procedure followed in group 2 is the most common "control" condition in classical conditioning studies. It has been commonly believed that because no facilitative conditioning occurs under these circumstances, no conditioning of any kind occurs, but this is clearly not the case. Since inhibitory conditioning does take place, this procedure cannot be used as a control group in classical conditioning studies. It is only the procedures followed by group 3 that provide a **truly random control group** for classical conditioning studies. In this group the appearance of the CS and of the US were independent of each other, and therefore, animals in this group could not use the CS to predict either the subsequent presence or absence of the US. It is only under these conditions that there is no contingency between the CS and US, and this is why, according to Rescorla, no classical conditioning occurs.

Again, Rescorla's explanation of his results is similar to the one offered earlier by Egger and Miller (1962, 1963). Both claim that for conditioning to take place, a CS must be informative; that is, it must provide the organism with useful information about the US. Rescorla expanded on Egger and Miller's work, however, by showing that negative contingencies are as informative as positive ones. According to Rescorla, it is only the truly random control procedure that creates an uninformative relationship between the CS and US, and, thus, produces no conditioning.

Finally, Rescorla (1988) claims that Pavlovian conditioning is more than mere reflex learning and that it has a vital place in contemporary psychology. He insists that the emphasis he and his colleagues place on contingencies, rather than contiguity alone, reveals new and important information about the nature of associative learning. Therefore, he says, classical conditioning provides both a useful data base and a theoretical orientation for two topics of current interest and activity in modern psychology. These topics, the neuroscientific study of learning and computer simulation of neural networks, are discussed in Chapter 15.

LEARNED HELPLESSNESS

As we have just seen, Rescorla claimed that his truly random control group created a situation in which there was no predictive relationship between the CS and the US, and therefore, no conditioning should occur. Indeed, Rescorla and others have demonstrated that no conditioning does occur in the truly random control condition, but perhaps they are looking at the wrong kind of behavior.

Martin Seligman (1969, 1975) has provided convincing evidence that animals do indeed learn something very important under what Rescorla calls the truly random control condition. In his analysis, Seligman first points out that in a classical conditioning experiment, the organism is helpless, and it learns that it is helpless. To demonstrate that animals learn to be helpless as the result of classical conditioning, Seligman and his colleagues reversed the experimental procedures followed by Kamin and Rescorla and Wagner. Instead of first teaching animals an instrumental response and then exposing them to classical conditioning, Seligman gave his animals classical conditioning first and *then* attempted to teach them an instrumental response. It turns out that reversing the experimental procedures has a profound effect on the animals' behavior. Maier, Seligman, and Solomon (1969) report the results of a number of studies in which classical conditioning (using a shock as a US) preceded an attempt to teach animals an instrumental response. The consistent finding is that exposing animals to a series of brief, intense, and unavoidable electric shocks rendered animals unable to learn subsequently a simple instrumental response, like jumping a hurdle to escape from or avoid an electric shock. Furthermore, it did not matter how the CS was paired with the US. It was found that the animals were unable to learn a simple instrumental response in the second phase of the experiment, regardless of whether they had experienced what Rescorla referred to as a positive contingency, a negative contingency, or a truly random condition. Maier, Seligman, and Solomon contrast the ability of dogs that had received classical conditioning to learn a simple escape or avoidance response with that of naive animals that did not experience classical conditioning:

> In a dramatic contrast to a naive dog, a dog which has experienced inescapable shocks prior to avoidance training soon stops running and howling and remains silent until shock terminates. The dog does not cross the barrier and escape the shock. Rather it seems to give up and passively accept the shock. On succeeding trials, the dog continues to fail to make escape movements and will take as much shock as the experimenter chooses to give.

...Such dogs occasionally jump the barrier and escape or avoid, but then revert to taking the shock; they fail to profit from exposure to the barrier-jumping-shock-termination contingency. In naive dogs a successful escape response is a reliable predictor of future, short-latency escape responses. (pp. 311–312)

According to Seligman, an animal learns that it is helpless in a classical conditioning situation precisely because it *is* helpless. Furthermore, the helplessness that is learned has nothing to do with the shock that is experienced per se; rather, it has to do with the animal's inability to control the shock. To demonstrate the importance of control, or lack of it, Seligman and Maier (1967) performed a two-phase experiment using dogs as subjects. During phase 1 of the experiment, subjects in group 1 were shocked while constrained in a hammock. Subjects in this group could terminate the shock by pressing a panel with their snouts. Subjects in group 2 were shocked whenever subjects in group 1 were shocked, but subjects in group 2 could do nothing to terminate the shocks. A third control group was placed in the hammock but was given no shock. Seligman and Maier hypothesized that during phase 1 of the experiment, subjects in group 1 were learning that shock was potentially controllable through their behavior, whereas subjects in group 2 were learning that their behavior could have no influence on the shock. For them, shock was inescapable.

To test their hypothesis, Seligman and Maier (1967) employed escape-avoidance training using a shuttle box in phase 2 of their study. Prompt response to a tone by jumping the hurdle between compartments was followed by the termination of the tone and the shock. Subjects in group 1 (escapable shock) and group 3 (no shock) quickly learned to avoid shock by jumping the hurdle. In vivid contrast, subjects in group 2 (inescapable shock) learned neither to avoid nor to escape the shock. When the shock came on in the shuttle box, they just took the shock and whined. Even when a member of this group occasionally blundered over the hurdle, thus escaping the shock, the response was not repeated when the shock next occurred. According to Seligman and Maier, these animals had learned in phase 1 of the study that there was nothing that they could do to avoid shock, so in phase 2 of the study they tried nothing. When the belief that one can do nothing to terminate or avoid an aversive situation generalizes to other situations, it is called **learned helplessness.** Thus, learned helplessness is not caused by traumatic experience per se but by the inability, or perceived inability, to do anything about it. Animals who learned that they could not control an aversive situation became generally passive.

The phenomenon of learned helplessness has been found in many species of animals,

Martin Seligman. (Courtesy of Martin Seligman.)

including humans, using both appetitive and aversive USs. The symptoms of learned helplessness include a reluctance to initiate any action to attain reinforcement or to escape punishment, general passivity, withdrawal, fearfulness, depression, and general willingness to accept whatever happens. Seligman (1975) has suggested that learned helplessness in humans may be experienced as depression and may characterize individuals who have been so thwarted in their attempts in life that they become hopeless and withdrawn and finally just give up.

We see, then, that even in what Rescorla called a truly random control condition, organisms learn that they are helpless to avoid or escape an aversive situation so they no longer try to do so. This feeling of helplessness generalizes beyond the experimental situation and results in general passivity.

OTHER THEORETICAL ACCOUNTS OF CLASSICAL CONDITIONING

The Importance of Attention   Nicholas Mackintosh (1975) theorizes that organisms seek information that allows them to predict biologically significant events (e.g., USs). Once such relevant information is attained, the organism ignores other information. Thus, Mackintosh's position relies on the active processing of information. Attention is paid to stimuli in the environment until a cue that predicts a significant event is found, and at that point the search for predictive cues stops. A major difference between the position of Rescorla-Wagner and that of Mackintosh is that the former views the organism as passively receiving and recording information from the environment and Mackintosh does not. The Rescorla-Wagner position represents a modern example of the older view of learning, which sees the learning process as mechanical, automatic, and associative in nature. Schwartz and Robbins (1995) say of the Rescorla-Wagner theory:

> It provides a way of describing seemingly complex processes, involving the evaluation of probabilities and the selection of best predictors, in a mechanical, trial-by-trial fashion. The organism does not need to be able to consider its various experiences with CSs and USs over time and combine them in some complex fashion to be able to respond as though it were making these considerations. The Rescorla-Wagner theory gives the animal a simple solution to the complex problem of forming selective, informative associations. (p. 120)

Contrary to the Rescorla-Wagner position, Mackintosh emphasizes the active processing of information by the organism. Mackintosh's explanation of blocking is straightforward. When one CS (say a light) reliably predicts the occurrence of a biologically significant event (say a shock), the organism becomes aware of this predictive relationship. When the light is paired with a second predictive CS (say a tone), the second CS is not attended to because the first predictive relationship (light → shock) provides all the information that the organism requires. It may be remembered that the Rescorla-Wagner theory explained the lack of conditioning to the newly inserted CS by saying that all the conditioning that the US could support was "used up" by the first CS. So both the Rescorla-Wagner theory and Mackintosh's theory explain blocking, but they do so by making quite different assumptions about the nature of the learning process.

There is at least one phenomenon that Mackintosh's theory explains that presents a problem for the Rescorla-Wagner theory, and that is the effects of preexposure to the CS before conditioning. Many studies have shown that preexposing an organism to a CS before it is paired with a US retards conditioning when the CS and US are paired (e.g., Baker & Mackintosh, 1977; Best & Gemberling, 1977; Fenwick, Mikulka, & Klein, 1975). Adverse effects of preexposure are a problem for the Rescorla-Wagner theory because according to it, preexposure to the CS should have no effect on conditioning. According to the Rescorla-Wagner theory, only the salience and the intensity of the CS will influence its subsequent association with the US. Neither the salience nor the intensity of a CS is changed as the result of preexposure, and therefore, preexposure should not interfere with subsequent conditioning. Mackintosh explains the adverse effects of preexposure by saying that during the time that the CS is presented alone, the organism attends to it and learns that it is irrelevant, that is, that it is not correlated with any significant event. Once the CS is found to be irrelevant, it is ignored, and it continues to be ignored when it is first presented along with the US, thus retarding the formation of a predictive relationship between the two. Both blocking and the effects of preexposure to CSs are explained by Mackintosh as the learning by the organism to ignore irrelevant or redundant information.

Surprisingness In an effort to explain blocking, Kamin (1969) argued that when the US first comes on, the animal is surprised by it. If a CS reliably precedes the US, the animal gradually learns to expect the US shortly after the CS is presented. Eventually the animal is no longer surprised by the US, and no additional conditioning takes place. According to Kamin, when the CS elicits a memory of the US, the occurrence of the US is no longer surprising and there is no reason to learn anything else under the circumstances. Thus, for Kamin, the mechanism that explains classical conditioning is surprisingness. When the onset of the US is a complete surprise, the animal searches its memory for an event that anticipated the US. When such an event is found, surprisingness diminishes, and so does conditioning. If the CS was such an event, it will become associated with the US in the sense that when the CS comes on, it will elicit a memory of the US. The elicited memory of the US will at first be weak but will become stronger with increased pairings of the CS and US. As the memory of the US elicited by the CS becomes more vivid, surprisingness diminishes and so does conditioning.

Blocking is easily explained through the concept of surprisingness. Since stimulus A reliably predicts the US, the occurrence of the US is no longer surprising at the time stimulus B is introduced, and therefore no conditioning occurs to stimulus B. According to Kamin, no surprise means no conditioning. Wagner (1969, 1971, 1978) has elaborated on and substantiated Kamin's contention that surprisingness is reduced or eliminated to the extent that the CS elicits a memory of the US. Schwartz (1989) summarizes the Kamin-Wagner theory as follows.

1. We only learn about things to the extent that we process them actively.

2. We only process things actively to the extent that they are surprising, that is, to the extent that we do not yet understand them.
3. As conditioning proceeds, CS and US become less surprising. As a result they get processed less. And therefore we learn less about them. (p. 126)

It is possible to relate the positions of Rescorla-Wagner with that of Kamin-Wagner by assuming that the difference between the maximum amount of conditioning possible and the amount of conditioning that has already taken place reflects the extent to which an organism is surprised by the onset of the US. When the amount of possible conditioning matches the amount of conditioning that has taken place, there is no longer any surprise. Also, because the amount of conditioning possible is directly proportional to the amount of surprise, it should be clear how the Kamin-Wagner theory accounts for the negatively accelerated curve that typically characterizes the learning process.

Conditioning as the Formation of Expectancies Robert Bolles (1972, 1979) suggests that organisms do not learn any new responses during conditioning. Rather, they learn to execute species-specific reactions that are appropriate to the situation. According to Bolles, what organisms do learn are *expectancies* that guide their unlearned behavior. A *stimulus expectancy* is formed when a CS is correlated with an important outcome such as the presence or absence of a US. In other words, the typical classical conditioning experiment creates a stimulus expectancy. A stimulus expectancy involves predicting the presence of one stimulus (US) from the presence of another stimulus (CS). Organisms also learn *response expectancies*, which are predictive relationships between responses and outcomes. According to Bolles, reinforcement does not strengthen behavior; rather it strengthens the expectancy that a certain response will be followed by a reinforcer.

Bolles (1979) feels that recent findings call into question the traditional mechanistic-associationistic explanation of classical conditioning and proposes that his cognitive explanation be accepted instead:

> The unpredictability of the CR, the difficulty of not really knowing what kind of behavior to expect from a conditioned animal, suggests that what is learned in a Pavlovian situation is not a response at all. Perhaps what is learned is something else, perhaps something about the...CS-US relationship. Maybe what the animal learns then when the CS comes on is not to respond to it in some fixed manner but rather to expect the US. Whether or not we finally accept such a cognitive conclusion, it is clear that one of the oldest and most basic assumptions about the conditioning process is open to question. We can no longer take for granted that conditioning produces an automatic connection of some response to the CS. (p. 155)

In his explanation of conditioning, Bolles follows rather closely the theory of Edward Tolman. We will have more to say about Bolles's theory after our presentation of Tolman's theory in Chapter 12.

In the last few sections, we have learned that the principles governing classical conditioning are still being disputed. Basic questions such as "What is learned during classical conditioning?" and "Under what circumstances is it learned?" are the focus of much current research, theory, and discussion, and it looks like this will be true for some time. In any case, it is now clear that classical conditioning is much more complex than was realized before. Rather than attempting to determine which account of classical conditioning is the correct one, it seems that it would be more accurate to conclude that all accounts accurately explain some aspect of classical conditioning. It seems reasonable to conclude that when the entire story is told, aspects of classical conditioning will be found to depend on predictability of cues, memory processes, the formation of expectancies, attentional processes, and the automatic formation of associations when there is a contingent relationship between CSs and USs.

THE BIOLOGICAL BOUNDARIES OF LEARNING

Originally, it was believed that any stimulus that an organism could detect would become a CS if it was presented shortly before the onset of a US. As we have seen, this belief has been challenged by such individuals as Egger and Miller, Kamin, Rescorla, Mackintosh, Bolles, and Seligman. In this section, we will review evidence that casts further doubt on the contention that classical conditioning will occur automatically if any stimulus is paired with a US. As we saw in Chapter 5, there is growing recognition that the genetic endowment of an organism must be taken into consideration in any learning experiment. The Brelands' concept of instinctual drift demonstrated the importance of instinctive response tendencies in the operant conditioning situation. The importance of genetically determined tendencies has also been found in the classical conditioning situation. For example, Seligman (1970) maintains that some species learn associations more easily than other species do because they are biologically prepared to do so. Likewise, for some species an association may be difficult to learn because they are biologically contraprepared to learn them. Thus, where an association falls on the **prepared-contraprepared continuum** will determine how easily it will be learned.

A study by Wilcoxon, Dragoin, and Kral (1971) exemplifies Seligman's concept of preparedness. In their study, rats and quail were given blue, salty water that was treated to make them sick. After drinking the water and becoming ill, both species were offered a choice between blue water or salty water. The rats avoided the salty water whereas the quail avoided the blue water. This finding reflects the fact that rats rely on taste in an eating (or drinking) situation and quail rely on visual cues. Thus each species formed an association in accordance with its genetic makeup. In other words, although the US (treated, blue, salty water) and the UR (illness) were the same for both species, each species selected a CS in accordance with its genetic endowment. For the rats, the taste of salt became the CS, whereas for the quail, the color blue was the CS. In Seligman's terms, the rats were more biologically prepared to make the salt-illness association than were the quail, but the quail were more prepared to make the blue-illness association.

A series of experiments run by Garcia and his colleagues also give credence to the contention that genetic endowment influences what associations are made by an organism. Whereas the research of Wilcoxon, Dragoin, and Kral (1971) demonstrates that different associations will be optimal for different species, Garcia's research indicates that within a species certain associations will be easier to form than others because of the genetic endowment of that species. For example, Garcia and Koelling (1966) offered thirsty rats the opportunity to drink under four conditions. One group was offered bright, noisy water, and drinking it was immediately followed by an electric shock to the feet. The bright, noisy water was created by attaching an electrode to the drinking tube in a way that set off flashing lights and loud clicking sounds when the organism touched the water. A second group was offered the bright, noisy water, but instead of being shocked for drinking they were exposed to strong X-ray treatment to induce nausea. A third group was given water without the flashing lights and clicking sounds but with the taste of saccharin; these animals, like those in the first group, were shocked through the feet immediately after drinking the saccharin solution. A fourth group was given the saccharin solution and then was made ill by X-ray treatment.

Garcia and Koelling (1966) found that animals in group 1 developed an aversion to bright, noisy water, whereas animals in group 2 did not. In addition, animals in group 3 did not develop an aversion to saccharin-flavored water, whereas animals in group 4 did develop an aversion to the water. The experimental design and the results of the experiment can be summarized as follows:

Group 1: Bright, noisy water → shock: Developed an aversion to the water
Group 2: Bright, noisy water → nausea: No aversion to the water
Group 3: Saccharin solution → shock: No aversion to saccharin
Group 4: Saccharin solution → nausea: Developed an aversion to saccharin

It can be seen that bright, noisy water became an effective CS when paired with shock but not when paired with nausea. Likewise, the taste of saccharin was an effective CS when paired with nausea but not when paired with shock. Garcia and Koelling (1966) explained their results by saying that there was a natural relationship between external events and the pain that the animals experienced. In other words, the pain was coming from "out there," and therefore the animals searched for an external predictor of that pain, which in this case was the lights and noise associated with drinking. Nausea, however, is experienced internally rather than externally. Therefore, the animals associated the taste of saccharin (which is internal) and not the bright, noisy water (which is external) with nausea. To use Seligman's terminology, we can say that the rats were biologically prepared to form an association between bright, noisy water and pain but contraprepared to form an association between bright, noisy water and nausea. Likewise, the animals were biologically prepared to form an association between the taste of saccharin and nausea, but they were biologically contraprepared to form an association between the taste of saccharin and pain.

Although the Garcia and Koelling experiment seems to follow classical conditioning procedures, it presents a few problems when the results are interpreted as classical conditioning phenomena. First, the time delay between the CS (the taste of saccharin) and the US (nausea) greatly exceeds the time interval considered necessary for classical conditioning. The interval between the time an animal tastes a substance and then experiences illness can be several hours. Second, it is repeatedly found that a strong taste aversion can develop after only a few (sometimes only one) pairings of a substance and nausea. Ordinarily it takes many pairings between a CS and a US to produce a conditioned response (CR). Sometimes when strong punishment is used, conditioning has been found to take place in one trial, but never when the interval between the CS and the US is as long as it typically is in taste aversion studies. Third, although taste aversions develop after long time delays and, in some cases in just one trial, they are extremely resistant to extinction. Usually, resistance to extinction goes up as the number of pairings between the CS and the US goes up, but taste aversions seem to violate this principle. The effect observed by Garcia and Koelling was so unusual, relative to what was known about classical conditioning at the time, that their research report was initially rejected by a number of journals. Despite Garcia's 20 previous publications using X-ray technology in radiobiological research, one journal editor had the audacity to suggest that Garcia did not understand how X-rays worked (Garcia, 1981). Garcia and his colleagues persisted, however, and replicated the phenomenon, first replacing the X-ray treatment with injection of lithium chloride, a chemical that produces nausea (Garcia, Ervin & Koelling, 1966) and later demonstrating that rats learn aversions to taste cues but not to visual cues (size) of dry, laboratory food pellets (Garcia, McGowan, Ervin & Koelling, 1968).

Thus, taste aversions are formed rapidly and last a long time, and these facts seem directly related to an organism's survival. It seems that if an organism is biologically prepared to form any associations, they would be those conducive to survival, and that appears to be the case with the development of taste aversions. The formation of taste aversions has so many unique features that the phenomenon has been given a name (Bolles, 1979): "The remarkable facility with which rats (and a number of other animals) learn about the relationship between the taste of a particular food substance and a subsequent illness we shall call the 'Garcia effect' " (p. 167).

Does the **Garcia effect** have any practical implications? The answer seems to be yes. Recent interest in the Garcia effect stems from reports that cancer patients undergoing chemotherapy often acquire long lasting aversions to foods eaten prior to a treatment (Andresen, Birch, & Johnson, 1990; Bernstein, 1978)). There have also been reports that some chemotherapy patients exhibit anticipatory nausea, illness that is experienced prior to an upcoming chemotherapy session (Andrykowski & Redd, 1987; Andrykowski, Redd, & Hatfield, 1985). Drugs used in chemotherapy often produce strong nausea and may cause vomiting in some patients. From our knowledge of the Garcia effect, we would expect that flavor cues of foods eaten prior to treatment would become aversive, particularly if the subsequent chemotherapy treatment resulted in severe nausea. However, the effect may not be as widespread or as predictable as earlier reports indicated. Longitudinal studies (Jacobsen, Bovbjerg, Schwartz, Andrykowski, Futterman, Gilewski, Norton, & Redd, 1993) indicate that up to 50 percent of chemotherapy patients experience learned food aversions, but not all foods are likely to become aversive. Novel or unusual foods eaten prior to treatment tend to produce the effect more than familiar foods; and backward conditioning, aversion to foods eaten after treatments, is rare. In addition, taste aversions developed during the first few chemotherapy treatments are unstable and short-lived while those developed later in the course of therapy tend to last longer. Interestingly, the severity of nausea induced by chemotherapy is not a good predictor of learned food aversions.

In addition, the Garcia effect can be used to control predators. Wild coyotes have long been a problem in the western United States because they prey on lambs and other livestock. This problem has led to a debate between farmers and ranchers who often want to kill the coyotes and environmentalists who want to save the coyotes for ecological reasons. Gustavson, Garcia, Hankins, and Rusiniak (1974) have shown that the Garcia effect can be used to control the eating habits of coyotes. In their study, three coyotes were fed lamb flesh treated with lithium chloride and three were fed rabbit flesh treated with the same substance. After only one or two experiences with the treated flesh the coyotes avoided attacking the kind of animals whose flesh had made them ill but showed no avoidance of the other type of flesh. That is, those coyotes that ate treated lamb flesh avoided sheep but ate rabbits, and those coyotes that ate treated rabbit flesh avoided rabbits but ate sheep. Thus, it appears that we have a straightforward way of controlling the eating habits of predators that satisfies the wishes of both ranchers and farmers and the environmentalists.

The findings of instinctual drift, autoshaping, and the preparedness continuum are currently causing learning theorists to recognize that genetically determined response tendencies are powerful determinants of behavior and, therefore, must be taken into consideration when attempting to modify behavior by using either instrumental or classical conditioning principles. We will have more to say about how innate behavior patterns can influence the outcome of learning experiments when we discuss Bolles's theory of learning in Chapter 12.

JOHN B. WATSON'S EXPERIMENT WITH LITTLE ALBERT

Before discussing the clinical applications of classical conditioning in the next section, we will review **J. B. Watson's** famous experiment with an infant named Albert. We saw in Chapter 3 that Watson, the founder of the school of **behaviorism,** felt that psychology should be purged of all mentalistic concepts and explanations of human behavior based on instinct.

Personality was, to Watson, a collection of conditioned reflexes. Human emotion was a product of both heredity and experience. According to Watson, we inherit three emotions-fear, rage, and love. Through the conditioning process, these three basic emotions become attached to different things for different people. Speech is behavior that results from the movement of the muscles in the throat. Thinking is implicit or subvocal speech. During overt speech, the vocal apparatus responds with vigor; during thinking, the same apparatus is involved but its movements are minute. Speech can indeed be studied but it has to be studied as behavior and not as a tool used to investigate "inner experience."

Watson was a radical environmental determinist. He believed that all we come equipped with at birth are a few reflexes and a few basic emotions, and through classical conditioning these reflexes become paired with a variety of stimuli. He emphatically denied that we are born with any mental abilities or predispositions. The extreme to which Watson (1926) was willing to carry this position is exemplified by his following famous (or infamous) statement: "Give me a dozen healthy infants, well-formed, and my own specified world to bring them up in and I'll guarantee to take any one at random and train him to become any type of specialist I might select—doctor, lawyer, artist, merchant, chief, and yes, even beggarman and thief, regardless of his talents, penchants, tendencies, abilities, vocations, and race of his ancestors" (p. 10).

To demonstrate how inborn emotional reflexes become conditioned to neutral stimuli, Watson and Rosalie Rayner (1920) performed an experiment on an 11-month-old infant named Albert. In addition to Albert, the other ingredients in the experiment were a white rat, a steel bar, and a hammer. At the onset of the study, Albert showed no fear of the rat. In fact, he reached out and tried to touch it. During the initial part of the experiment, when Albert saw the rat and reached for it, the experimenter took the hammer and struck the steel bar behind the infant, making a loud noise. In response to the noise, Albert "jumped violently and fell forward." Again Albert saw the rat and reached for it, and again, just as his hand touched the rat, the bar was struck, making a loud noise. Again Albert jumped violently and began to whimper. Because of Albert's emotional state, the experiment was suspended for one week so Albert would not become too disturbed.

After a week, the rat was again presented to Albert. This time Albert was very cautious of the animal and watched it very carefully. At one point, when the rat came into contact with his hand, Albert withdrew his hand immediately. There were several more pairings between the rat and the sound, and eventually Albert developed a strong fear of the rat. Now when the rat was presented to Albert again, he began to cry and "almost instantly he turned sharply to the left, fell over, raised himself on all fours and began to crawl away…rapidly" (p. 5).

It was also shown that Albert's fear generalized to a variety of objects that were not feared at the onset of the experiment: a rabbit, dog, fur coat, cotton, and Santa Claus mask. Thus, Watson showed that our emotional reactions can be rearranged through classical conditioning. In this experiment, the loud noise was the US, fear produced by the noise was the UR, the rat was the CS, and the fear of the rat was the CR. Albert's fear of all white and furry objects showed that generalization also took place.

Bregman's Replication of Watson's Experiment   In 1934, E. O. Bregman replicated Watson's experiment and found that a child's fear could indeed be conditioned to a CS but that such conditioning took place only under certain circumstances. Bregman found that conditioning took place only if the CS was a live animal (as it was in Watson's experiment), but *no conditioning occurred if the CS was an inanimate object,* such as a block, a bottle, or even a wooden animal. Bregman's findings were inconsistent with Pavlov's and Watson's claim that the nature of a CS should be irrelevant to the conditioning process. However, her findings were consistent with Seligman's contention that some associations are easier to form than others because of the biological preparedness of the organism. In this case, Seligman (1972) says that since animals have the potential to do harm, humans are biologically prepared to suspect them and therefore learn with relative ease to fear or avoid them.

Eliminating Conditioned Fears   Watson had demonstrated that an innate emotion, such as fear, could be "transferred" to stimuli that did not originally elicit that emotion, and that the mechanism for the transfer was classical conditioning. This was an extremely important finding even if it would be demonstrated later that conditioning was easier with some stimuli than with others. If fears are learned, it should be possible to unlearn or extinguish them. Unfortunately, Watson and Rayner never removed Albert's fears because his mother removed him from the hospital where the experiment was being conducted shortly after fear was instilled (Harris, 1979, p. 152). Watson felt that his research had shown how learned fears develop and no further research of that kind was necessary. Instead, his strategy was to find a child who had already developed a fear and then attempt to eliminate it. Watson, now working with Mary Cover Jones (1896–1987), found such a child—a 3-year-old named Peter who was intensely frightened of, among other things, rats, rabbits, fur coats, frogs, and fish. Hergenhahn (1997) summarizes the efforts of Watson and Jones to eliminate Peter's fears:

> Watson and Jones first tried showing Peter other children playing fearlessly with objects of which he was frightened, and there was some improvement. (This is a technique called *modeling*, which Bandura and his colleagues employ today). [See Chapter 13 of this text.] At this point, Peter came down with scarlet fever and had to go to the hospital. Following recovery, he and his nurse were attacked by a dog on their way home from the hospital, and all of Peter's fears returned in magnified form. Watson and Jones decided to try counterconditioning on Peter. Peter ate lunch in a room 40 feet long. One day as Peter was eating lunch, a rabbit in a wire cage was displayed far enough away from him so that Peter was not disturbed. The researchers made a mark on the floor at that point. Each day they moved the rabbit a bit closer to Peter until one day it was sitting beside Peter as he ate. Finally, Peter was able to eat with one hand and play with the rabbit with the other. The results generalized, and most of Peter's other fears were also eliminated or reduced. This is one of the first examples of what we now call **behavior therapy**. In 1924, Jones published the results of the research with Peter, and in 1974 she published more of the details surrounding the research. (p. 361–362)

The procedure used by Watson and Jones to eliminate Peter's fear is quite similar to a procedure called systematic desensitization, which was developed much later. We will consider systematic desensitization in the next section.

Watson's Theory of Learning   It is interesting to note that although Watson did as much as anyone to introduce Pavlovian psychology to the United States, he never fully accepted Pavlovian principles. For example, he did not believe that conditioning depended on reinforcement. For Watson, learning occurred simply because events followed each other closely in time. Classical conditioning occurs, not because the US reinforces the CS, but because the CS and US follow each other in close succession. Also, the more often events occur together, the stronger will be the association between them. Watson, then, accepted *only* the ancient laws of contiguity and frequency. For him, other learning principles were either mentalistic, like Thorndike's law of effect, or unnecessary, like the notion of reinforcement. In the next chapter we will review Guthrie's theory of learning and see that it is very similar to Watson's theory.

FURTHER APPLICATIONS OF CLASSICAL CONDITIONING
TO CLINICAL PSYCHOLOGY

Extinction   Clinical practices based on classical conditioning assume that since behavior disorders or bad habits are learned, they can be unlearned or can be replaced by more positive behaviors. Let us assume that smoking and the excessive drinking of alcohol are behavior disorders, or at least bad habits. In such cases, the taste of alcohol or cigarettes can be considered CSs and the physiological effects of alcohol or nicotine are the USs. After many CS-US pairings, experiencing the CSs alone produces immediate pleasure (CR). One possible way to eliminate these habits is to present the CSs without presenting the USs, thus causing extinction. Schwartz and Robbins (1995) point out the problems with this procedure:

> First, it is impossible to recreate completely in a laboratory setting the complex and idiosyncratic set of event that serve as CSs in the real world....Second,...there is no evidence that extinction removes the underlying CS-US association. Instead, extinction blocks CRs temporarily until conditions such as passage of time (spontaneous recovery) or the reintroduction of either the US (reinstatement) or the context of training (renewal) act to reestablish responding....Finally, extinguished responses can always be retrained if drug use reoccurs. (p. 155)

Counterconditioning   A procedure more powerful than simple extinction is **counterconditioning.** In counterconditioning the CS is paired with a US other than the original one. For example, a person is allowed to smoke or drink and then is given a drug that produces nausea. With repeated pairings, the taste of cigarettes or alcohol will produce conditioned nausea, which in turn will create an aversion to smoking or drinking. For example, Mount, Payton, Ellis, and Barnes (1976) injected anectine into the arm of alcoholic clients immediately after they drank a glass of their favorite alcoholic beverage. Anectine produces a paralyzing effect on the respiratory system, which most people report as a frightening experience. After such treatment, only one of the nine individuals involved in this study started drinking again. Although counterconditioning has been found to be successful in a number of cases, the benefits from the procedure are often only temporary. Schwartz and Robbins (1995) say,

> Ultimately, counterconditioning suffers from the same difficulties that plague extinction training. For one, counterconditioning in the laboratory or clinic may not generalize well outside these settings. Addicts may only learn that their drug of choice is unpleasant *when taken in this artificial environment.*...Second, any tendency to reuse the drug outside the clinic setting will result in the rapid reestablishment of the original conditioned responses....Counterconditioning faces a further, unique difficulty. Even if the treatment were effective, convincing patients to undergo repeated exposures to shock or vomiting is no easy task. (p. 157)

Flooding   A major problem in treating phobias is the fact that individuals avoid or escape from frightening experiences. Since extinction is an active process (the CS must be presented and *not* followed by the US), avoiding fear-producing stimuli prevents extinction from occurring. If, for example, a person has a dog phobia, he or she is never with a dog long enough to learn whether it is safe or not. Any CS that elicits fear will cause the organism to escape or avoid it, and such behavior prevents the organism from learning that the CS may no longer be associated with an aversive US. So how can such a phobia be extinguished? In the natural environment it probably never would be. The only way of extinguishing a phobia is to force the organism to remain in the presence of the CS long enough to learn that nothing negative will follow. When such forced extinction is used to eliminate phobias, it is called **flooding.** Rimm and Masters (1979) report that flooding is a relatively fast way of eliminating phobias, but it produces results that are variable. With the flooding procedure, some individuals improve but some get worse. That some individuals become worse is not surprising in light of the fact that they are forced to experience something that they had spent a good deal of their lives fearing and thus avoiding. Also not surprising is the fact that client dropout rates are higher when flooding is used compared to the dropout rates for systematic desensitization, the therapeutic technique that we shall consider next.

Systematic Desensitization   One of the most thorough attempts to apply classical conditioning principles to psychotherapy was undertaken by Joseph Wolpe (1958), who developed a therapeutic technique referred to as **systematic desensitization.** Wolpe's technique, which is used primarily for treating clients with phobias, involves three phases. The first phase consists of developing an **anxiety hierarchy,** which is done by taking a sequence of related anxiety-provoking events and ordering them from those that produce the greatest amount of anxiety to those that produce the least amount. Let us say that a person has an extreme fear of flying in an airplane. Such a person's anxiety hierarchy may look something like this:

1. Flying in an airplane
2. Sitting in an airplane while it is on the ground with its engines running
3. Sitting in an airplane while it is on the ground with its engines turned off
4. Being in close proximity of an airplane
5. Seeing an airplane at a distance
6. Being in an airport
7. Hearing the sound of airplane engines
8. Talking about being on an airplane
9. Planning a trip without airplanes involved
10. Hearing others plan a trip without airplanes involved

In the second phase of his procedure, Wolpe teaches his clients to relax. He teaches them how to reduce muscle tension and, in general, how it feels when one is not experiencing anxiety. In the third phase, the client first experiences deep relaxation and then is asked to imagine the weakest item on the anxiety hierarchy. While experiencing this item the client is again asked to induce relaxation. When this is accomplished, the client is asked to ponder the next item on the list, and so forth through the entire list. It is assumed by Wolpe (1958) that if each time an item on the list is experienced along with relaxation (the absence of anxiety), a little bit of the phobic response associated with the terminal item on the list extinguishes. This procedure allows the client gradually to approximate the situation that he or she was too frightened to ponder previously. Such an anxiety-provoking experience must be approached gradually and with a great deal of care; otherwise the client will be unable to ponder the feared item, and therefore fear of it will never extinguish. As we have seen, one problem that a person with a phobia has is that he or she avoids the very experiences that will eliminate the phobia. In other words a person with a flying phobia typically avoids flying and all related experiences, the person with sex phobia avoids sexual and related experiences, and so on. If a phobia is ever going to extinguish, the feared item must be experienced in the absence of anxiety.

After this cognitive extinction has occurred, it is hoped that the person will be able to repeat the steps in the real world. After systematic desensitization, the client should be able to deal with his or her fear (or previous fear) more rationally and, in this case, fly in an airplane without experiencing disabling anxiety.

Whereas Wolpe had his clients move slowly closer to feared objects psychologically, Watson and Jones slowly moved a feared object physically closer to a child. Except for this difference the two approaches to extinguishing fears have much in common.

We will compare in Chapter 13 the effectiveness of Wolpe's technique of systematic desensitization with that of other techniques used to treat phobias.

APPLICATIONS OF CLASSICAL CONDITIONING IN MEDICINE

The many research programs stimulated by Pavlov included one by Metalnikov (Metalnikov, 1934; Metalnikov & Chorine, 1926), who performed a series of unique experiments in classical conditioning. Using guinea pigs as subjects, Metalnikov paired either heat or tactile (touch) stimuli (CSs) with injections of foreign proteins (US). Metalnikov reported that after repeated pairings of CS and US, presentation of the heat or touch stimuli alone resulted in a variety of nonspecific immune responses. These early studies were basically ignored by learning theorists in the United States, perhaps because they lacked rigorous experimental controls and accurate assessment of the immune-responses that were observed. Research by Robert Ader and his colleagues in the 1970s renewed interest in the topic and demonstrated clearly that the immune system could be conditioned. In doing so, these researchers effectively launched a new and exciting interdisciplinary area now called psychoneuroimmunology, an area concerned with interactions among psychological factors (learning, perception, emotion), the nervous system, and the immune system.

Ader (1974) was initially studying taste aversion by pairing a saccharin drinking solution (CS) with injection of a drug (US). The drug in this instance, cyclophosphamide, suppresses the immune system. After the initial taste aversion experiment, Ader noted an unusually high number of deaths in rats that continued to receive the saccharin solution (without the US). He suggested that conditioned suppression of the immune system, resulting in greater susceptibility to viral or bacterial infections, led to increased deaths. In a subsequent experiment, Ader and Cohen (1975) first paired the CS of saccharin-flavored water with the US of cyclophosphamide injection. Three days later, the rats were injected with a foreign protein (red blood cells of sheep), a procedure that produces long-term elevation of a highly specific antibody in healthy rats (Markovic, Dimitrijevic, & Jankovic, 1993). When aversion-conditioned animals were re-exposed to the saccharin CS, their blood levels of sheep cell antibodies were found to be lower than those of animals in control groups that were not re-exposed to either the CS or to the US. Ader and Cohen concluded that the saccharin CS had acquired the ability to suppress the immune system in a highly specific manner.

Since the publication of Ader's studies, over 50 experiments have demonstrated classical conditioning in the immune system. Although few of these studies have been done with humans, work with nonhuman animals has shown that both conditioned suppression as well as conditioned elevation of immune functions are possible (for reviews see Ader & Cohen, 1993, Markovic, Dimitrijevic, & Jankovic 1993). In the near future, psychoneuroimmunologists hope to use classical conditioning to assist patients with autoimmune disorders such as lupus or certain types of arthritis, to help prevent tissue rejections in patients who have undergone transplant surgeries, or perhaps to rally the immune system in cancer patients and patients with HIV or AIDS.

EVALUATION OF PAVLOV'S THEORY

Contributions

The questions that Pavlov formulated—and partly answered—concerning the dynamics of the CS-US relationship, the course of response acquisition, generalization and discrimination, and extinction and spontaneous recovery have continued to stimulate

Mark E. Bouton. (Courtesy of Mark E. Bouton.)

productive studies in contemporary psychology and in related medical research. By 1965, well over 5,000 experiments following Pavlov's experimental procedures had been conducted in both basic research areas as well as clinical applications (Razran, 1965). Thus, Pavlov rivals Skinner and Hull in terms of specific experimental-procedural contributions to the field. And in the preceding chapter, we saw that contemporary researchers such as Robert Rescorla and Mark Bouton continue to make discoveries in classical conditioning.

In the history of learning theory, Pavlov created the first theory concerned with anticipatory learning. His treatment of the CS as a signal event was unique compared to other learning theorists who treated stimuli either as causal events in S-R connections or as reinforcing events that follow responses. If we view habituation and sensitization as the most simple units of nonassociative learning, it is appropriate to consider the classically conditioned response as the fundamental unit of associative learning. Clearly, theorists other than Pavlov came to rely heavily on that fundamental, anticipatory unit.

Criticisms

Insofar as we can criticize Thorndike's, Watson's or other S-R theories for their simplistic, mechanistic views of learning, we can apply the same criticisms to Pavlov's theory. Pavlov avoided explanations of learning that involved complex mental processes and assumed that a learner's awareness of CS-US relationships was not needed for learning to occur.

We might wonder if Pavlov's influence might have been greater if he actually intended to study learning. Windholz (1992) points out that although the fundamental discovery of classical conditioning occurred in 1897, Pavlov considered his work pertinent to discovery of basic nervous system functions and was unaware that his work was relevant to the development of learning theory in the United states until the early 1930s. By that time, he was already in his 80s. During the last few years of his life, he speculated about both reflex learning and about trial and error learning and, as we noted earlier in this chapter, gave credit to E.L. Thorndike for developments in that area.

DISCUSSION QUESTIONS

1. Briefly describe the following: acquisition of a conditioned response, extinction, spontaneous recovery, generalization, discrimination, and higher-order conditioning.
2. Briefly describe Pavlov's physiological explanation of conditioning, generalization, and discrimination.
3. What observations did Egger and Miller make that were contrary to Pavlov's explanation of classical conditioning?
4. According to Pavlov, what determines how we respond to the environment at any given time?
5. Discuss the major differences and similarities between instrumental and classical conditioning.
6. Provide evidence that CRs are not necessarily small versions of URs.
7. First define overshadowing and blocking and then discuss how the phenomena are contrary to what the law of contiguity would predict.
8. Describe how conditioned emotional responses (CERs) are used to index the strength of CS-US associations.
9. Summarize the Rescorla-Wagner theory of classical conditioning.
10. How does the Rescorla-Wagner theory explain blocking?
11. Explain the distinction that Rescorla makes between contingency and contiguity as a necessary condition for classical conditioning to occur.
12. What experimental arrangement produces what Rescorla calls a truly random control condition? Why, according to Rescorla, is a truly random control group necessary in classical conditioning studies?

13. Describe what kind of conditioned behavior is produced by positive and negative contingencies.
14. What, according to Seligman, is learned helplessness? Describe the circumstances under which learned helplessness develops.
15. How, according to Seligman, can learned helplessness be avoided?
16. Discuss Mackintosh's theory of classical conditioning based on attention. Include in your answer Mackintosh's explanation of blocking.
17. Discuss Kamin and Wagner's theory of classical conditioning based on surprisingness. Include in your answer Kamin and Wagner's explanation of blocking.
18. Discuss Bolles's theory of classical conditioning based on expectancy formation. Why does Bolles feel that his theory is opposed to those theories of classical conditioning in the associationistic tradition?
19. What is the Garcia effect?
20. Summarize the problems involved in trying to explain the development of taste aversions as a classical conditioning phenomenon.
21. How can the Garcia effect be used to change the eating habits of predators?
22. If the Garcia effect exists on the human level, why do you suppose so many individuals continue to smoke or consume alcohol even though their initial experience with smoking or drinking alcohol made them extremely ill?
23. Explain Seligman's concepts of preparedness and contrapreparedness.
24. Explain emotional development from J. B. Watson's point of view.
25. Describe the procedure used by Watson and Jones to extinguish Peter's fear of rabbits.
26. Explain how extinction and counterconditioning are used as therapeutic techniques and explain why these techniques have limited usefulness.
27. Discuss flooding as a therapeutic technique. Include in your answer the problems associated with flooding.
28. Summarize Wolpe's therapeutic technique of systematic desensitization.

KEY TERMS

anxiety hierarchy   The initial stage of Wolpe's therapeutic technique of systematic desensitization, which involves taking a series of related anxiety experiences and ordering them from the experience that causes the greatest amount of anxiety to the experience that causes the least amount of anxiety.

backward conditioning   An experimental arrangement whereby the conditioned stimulus is presented to the organism after the unconditioned stimulus is presented.

behaviorism   The school of psychology founded by J. B. Watson. The behaviorist believes that the proper subject matter for psychology is behavior, not mental events.

behavior therapy   The utilization of learning principles in the treatment of behavior disorders.

blocking   (also called the blocking effect) When one CS (A) is paired with a US, it will become conditioned to that US. If, after initial conditioning, CS (A) is paired with a second CS (B) and presented to the organism as a compound stimulus CS (AB), it is found that little or no conditioning occurs to CS (B). It is as if the initial conditioning to CS (A) somehow blocked any conditioning to CS (B).

conditioned emotional response (CER)   A procedure used to determine the strength of a relationship between a CS and a US that combines operant or instrumental conditioning and classical conditioning. In phase 1, animals learn an instrumental or operant response to the point that it is emitted at a steady rate. In phase 2, the classical conditioning phase, a CS is paired with a US a number of times. In phase 3, as animals are again performing the instrumental or operant response, the CS from phase 2 is presented and its effect on the rate of responding is noted. Depending on how the CS and US were paired in phase 2, it is found that presenting the CS in phase 3 facilitates, inhibits, or has no effect on the rate with which the instrumental or operant behavior is emitted.

conditioned response (CR)   (also called conditioned reflex) A response that is made to a stimulus not originally associated with the response. For example, salivation to the sound of a tone is a conditioned response because an organism would not ordinarily salivate to the sound of a tone.

conditioned stimulus (CS)   A stimulus that before conditioning does not cause an organism to respond in any particular way. Before conditioning, the stimulus is a neutral stimulus. After conditioning, however, the conditioned stimulus elicits a conditioned response.

conditioned suppression   The inhibition of a conditioned response caused by conditioned emotional responses (CERs).

cortical mosaic   The pattern of excitation and inhibition that constitutes the activity of the cortex at any given moment.

counterconditioning   The technique used to eliminate undesirable behavior whereby a CS is paired with a US other than the one that originally reinforced the undesirable behavior. For example, if a CS was originally followed by shock, thus producing fear, the CS could be paired with food, thus producing a response incompatible with fear.

discrimination   Learning to respond to one stimulus but not to other stimuli although they may be related to the first. For example, through discrimination training a tone of 500 cps elicits a conditioned response, whereas a tone of 490 cps does not.

dynamic stereotype   A cortical mapping of events consistently occurring in the environment. A stable environment comes to have neurological representation on the cortex.

excitation   An increase in brain activity. A stimulus that causes excitation is called a positive stimulus.

extinction   The procedure whereby a conditioned stimulus is presented but is not followed by reinforcement. Under these circumstances, the magnitude of the conditioned response gradually becomes smaller. When a conditioned response is no longer elicited by a conditioned stimulus, the conditioned response is said to have been extinguished.

first signal system   Physical events in the environment and the responses that they produce.

flooding   Since organisms typically avoid experiencing those things that frighten them, it is unlikely that unjustified fears would ever extinguish naturally. Using the technique of flooding, the organism is forced to experience feared CSs long enough to learn that an aversive experience will not follow, thus creating the conditions necessary for extinction.

forward conditioning   An experimental arrangement whereby the conditioned stimulus is presented before the unconditioned stimulus.

Garcia effect   The name given to the observation that animals form strong taste aversions easily and in apparent contradiction to several principles of classical conditioning.

generalization   The tendency for an organism to respond not only to the specific stimulus it was trained on but also to other related stimuli. For example, if an organism was trained with a 500 cps tone as a conditioned stimulus, such tones as 600, 550, and 490 cps will also tend to elicit conditioned responses.

higher-order conditioning   After classical conditioning has taken place, a second conditioned stimulus is paired with the first conditioned stimulus. After a number of such pairings, the second conditioned stimulus can also elicit a conditioned response. This is called second-order conditioning. Once the second conditioned stimulus has the power to elicit a conditioned response, it can be paired with a third conditioned stimulus to produce third-order conditioning.

information value of a stimulus   The ability of a stimulus to act as a signal to an organism that a significant event is about to occur. For example, a stimulus that signals the occurrence of food for a hungry animal has information value.

inhibition   A decrease in brain activity. A stimulus that causes inhibition is called a negative stimulus.

irradiation of excitation   The tendency for excitation (or inhibition) in a specific area of the brain to spill over into neighboring brain regions.

learned helplessness   When organisms learn that their behavior is independent of outcomes, they sometimes give up trying. Such animals become passive and withdrawn and seem to accept whatever happens to them. With humans, learned helplessness is often associated with the emotional state of depression.

orienting reflex   The tendency for an organism to attend to and explore a novel stimulus as it occurs in its environment.

overshadowing   The observation that the most salient component of a compound stimulus will become conditioned to a US and the weaker component will not. It is as if a dominant component of a compound CS overshadows the weaker component.

preparedness-contrapreparedness continuum   Seligman's observation that each CS falls somewhere on a biologically determined continuum, and where it falls on that continuum determines how easily it can be conditioned to a US.

primary reinforcer   Something related to survival such as food, water, or sex. Pavlov believed that all conditioning ultimately depends on primary reinforcement. In classical conditioning, the primary reinforcer is the unconditioned stimulus.

secondary reinforcer   A previously neutral stimulus that takes on reinforcing properties through its close association with primary reinforcement. After conditioning has taken place, a conditioned stimulus must necessarily be a secondary reinforcer.

second signal system   Symbols that represent environmental events. These symbols, which Pavlov referred to as "signals of signals," constitute human language and are responsible for complex interactions with the environment.

semantic generalization   Generalization to symbols that have a meaning similar to the meaning of the conditioned stimulus used during training, although the physical characteristics of symbols may be totally dissimilar to those of the conditioned stimulus. For example, if human subjects are taught to salivate when they see the number 10, they will also salivate when they see $8\overline{|80}$ or $\sqrt{100}$. In semantic generalization, it is meaning that determines how much generalization occurs rather than the physical similarity between stimuli.

spontaneous recovery   When a conditioned response is no longer elicited by a conditioned stimulus, extinction is said to have taken place. Following a delay after extinction, the conditioned stimulus again elicits conditioned responses, although there were no further pairings between the conditioned stimulus and the unconditioned stimulus. The reappearance of the conditioned response after extinction has taken place is called spontaneous recovery.

systematic desensitization   A therapeutic technique developed by Wolpe whereby a phobia is extinguished by having a client approach the feared experience one small step at a time while relaxing after each step.

truly random control group   Rescorla has shown that the only true control condition for classical conditioning studies is one in which there is no predictive relationship between a CS and a US. In other words, in a truly random control condition, a US precedes and follows a CS an equal number of times. Rescorla says that in such a condition there is no contingency between the CS and the US.

unconditioned response (UR)   The natural and automatic response that is elicited when an unconditioned stimulus is presented to an organism. Withdrawing when stuck by a pin, salivating when food or acid is placed in the mouth, and the constriction of the pupil of the eye when light is shone into it are all examples of unconditioned responses.

unconditioned stimulus (US)   A stimulus that causes a natural and automatic response from the organism. An object that causes pain to a certain part of the body will cause the organism to withdraw automatically from the source of pain. Pain, therefore, is an unconditioned stimulus. Shining a light into the pupil of the eye will cause the pupil to constrict automatically; the light, therefore, is an unconditioned stimulus.

Watson, J. B.   The founder of the school of behaviorism. Watson relied heavily on Pavlov's theory of learning in his explanation of human behavior. Watson believed that except for a few basic emotions, human behavior was learned. Therefore, he believed that by controlling the learning process it is possible to control human personality. For this reason, Watson was considered a radical environmental determinist.

Chapter 8

EDWIN RAY GUTHRIE

Guthrie was born in 1886 and died in 1959. He was professor of psychology at the
University of Washington from 1914 until his retirement in 1956. His most basic work
was *The Psychology of Learning*, published in 1935 and revised in 1952. His style of writing is easy to follow, humorous, and involves many homespun anecdotes to exemplify his ideas. There are no technical terms or mathematical equations, and he firmly
believes that his theory—or any scientific theory for that matter—should be stated so
that it would be understandable to college freshmen. He placed a great emphasis
on practical application of his ideas and in this regard was very much like Thorndike
and Skinner. He was not really an experimentalist himself, although he certainly had
an experimental outlook and orientation. He, along with Horton, performed only one
experiment related to his theory of learning, and we will discuss that experiment
later on. He was, however, clearly a behaviorist. As a matter of fact, he felt theorists like
Thorndike, Skinner, Hull, Pavlov, and Watson were too subjective and that by carefully
applying the law of parsimony, it was possible to explain all learning phenomena by
using only one principle. As we shall see below, this one principle was one of Aristotle's laws of association. It is for this reason that we place Guthrie's behavioristic theory within the associationistic paradigm.

MAJOR THEORETICAL NOTIONS

The One Law of Learning

Most learning theories can be thought of as attempts to determine the rules by which
stimuli and responses become associated. Guthrie (1952) felt that the rules that had
been generated by theorists like Thorndike and Pavlov were unnecessarily complicated,
and in their place he proposed one law of learning, the **law of contiguity,** which he
stated as follows: "A combination of stimuli which has accompanied a movement will
on its recurrence tend to be followed by that movement. Note that nothing is here said
about 'confirmatory waves' or reinforcement or pleasant effects" (p. 23). Another
way of stating the law of contiguity is to say that if you did something in a given situation, the next time that you are in that situation, you will tend to do the same thing.
     Guthrie (1952) explained why, although the law of contiguity may be true, pre-
diction of behavior will always be probabilistic:

> Although the principle as it has just been stated is short and simple, it will not be clear
> without a considerable amount of elaboration. The word "tend" is used because behav-
> ior is at any time subject to a great variety of conditions. Conflicting "tendencies" or
> incompatible "tendencies" are always present. The outcome of any one stimulus or stim-
> ulus pattern cannot be predicted with certainty because there are other stimulus pat-
> terns present. We may express this by saying that the final behavior is caused by the total
> situation, but we may not, in making this statement, flatter ourselves that we have done
> more than offer an excuse for a failure to predict. No one has recorded and no one
> ever will record any stimulus situation in its totality, or observed any total situation, so that
> to speak of it as a "cause" or even as the occasion of a bit of behavior is misleading.
> (p. 23)

Edwin Ray Guthrie. (Courtesy of Peter M. Guthrie.)

In his last publication before he died, Guthrie (1959) revised his law of contiguity to read, "What is being noticed becomes a signal for what is being done" (p. 186). This was Guthrie's way of recognizing the enormous number of stimuli that confront an organism at any given time and the fact that the organism cannot possibly form associations with all of them. Rather, the organism responds selectively to only a small proportion of the stimuli confronting it, and it is that proportion that becomes associated with whatever response is being made. One can note the similarity between Guthrie's thinking and Thorndike's concept of "prepotency of elements," which also stated that organisms respond selectively to different aspects of the environment.

There is nothing new about the law of contiguity as a principle of learning. In fact, as we noted in Chapter 3, it goes all the way back to Aristotle's laws of association. Guthrie, however, made the law of contiguity the cornerstone of his unique theory of learning.

One-Trial Learning

Another of Aristotle's laws of association was the law of frequency, which stated that the strength of an association depends on the frequency with which it has occurred. If the law of frequency is modified to refer to the association between a response that leads to a "satisfying state of affairs" and the stimulating conditions preceding the response, Thorndike, Skinner, and Hull would accept it. The more often a response is reinforced in a given situation the greater the probability of that response being made when that situation recurs. If the association is between a CS and a US, Pavlov would accept the law of frequency. The greater the number of pairings between the CS and the US, the greater is the magnitude of the conditioned response elicited by the CS. Guthrie (1942) completely rejected the law of frequency as a learning principle.: *"A stimulus pattern gains its full associative strength on the occasion of its first pairing with a response"* (p. 30). Thus, to Guthrie learning was the result of contiguity between a pattern of stimulation and a response, and learning was complete (the association was at full strength) after only one pairing between the stimuli and the response.

The Recency Principle

The principles of contiguity and **one-trial learning** necessitate the **recency principle,** which states that that which was done last in the presence of a set of stimuli will be that which will tend to be done when that stimulus combination next recurs. In other words, whatever we did *last* under a given set of circumstances will be what we will tend to do again if those circumstances are reencountered.

Movement-Produced Stimuli

Although Guthrie reasserted his belief in the law of contiguity throughout his career, he felt it would be misleading to think of the learned association to be exclusively between environmental stimuli and overt behavior. For example, an environmental event and the response that it produces sometimes are separated by a fairly large interval of time, and it would be difficult, therefore, to think of the two as contiguous. Guthrie solved this problem by postulating the existence of **movement-produced stimuli,** which, as the name implies, are caused by the movements of the body. If we hear a sound and turn toward it, for example, the muscles, tendons, and joints produce stimuli that are distinctly different from the external stimulation that caused us to move. The important fact about movement-produced stimuli is that responses can be conditioned to them. That is, after a response has been initiated by an external stimulus, the body itself can produce the stimulus for the next response and that response can furnish the stimulus for the next one, and so on. Thus, the interval between the occurrence of an external stimulus and the response finally made to it is filled with movement-produced stimuli. Conditioning is still between contiguous events, but in some cases the contiguity is between movement-produced stimuli and behavior rather than between external stimuli and behavior. Guthrie (1935) gave the following example of how he believed movement-produced stimuli function:

> Such a movement as listening or looking is not over like a flash or an explosion. It takes time. The movement, once started, maintains itself by the stimuli it furnishes. When the telephone bell rings we rise and make our way to the instrument. Long before we have reached the telephone the sound has ceased to act as a stimulus. We are kept in action by the stimuli from our own movements toward the telephone. One movement starts another, then a third, the third a fourth, and so on. Our movements form series, very often stereotyped in the form of habit. *These movements and their movement-produced stimuli make possible a far-reaching extension of association or conditioning.* (p. 54)

A simplified version of the situation described in Guthrie's example could be diagrammed as follows:

External stimulation → Overt response → Movement-produced stimuli →
(telephone ringing) (e.g., turning
                      toward
                      telephone)

Overt response → Movement-produced stimuli → Overt response →
(e.g., rising   (e.g., walking
from chair)   toward telephone)

Movement-produced stimuli → Overt response
                            (e.g., picking up
                            telephone)

Guthrie's contention that a response can provide stimulation for the next response became very popular among learning theorists and is still usually involved in an explanation of **chaining.** As we have seen in Chapter 5, Skinner's explanation of chaining emphasized external stimuli and their secondary reinforcing properties. In this chapter we have seen that Guthrie's explanation of chaining emphasizes internal stimuli. Hull and Spence's explanation of chaining, covered in Chapter 6, can be looked on as a combination of Skinner's and Guthrie's views because it maintains that both internal and external stimulation are involved in chaining.

Why Does Practice Improve Performance?

To answer this question Guthrie differentiated between **acts** and **movements.** Movements are simple muscle contractions; acts are made up of a large number of movements. Acts are usually defined in terms of what they accomplish, that is, what change they make in the environment. As examples of acts, Guthrie listed such things as typing a letter, eating a meal, throwing a ball, reading a book, or selling a car. Guthrie and Horton (1946) explained improvement as the result of practice as follows:

> We have taken the position that acts are made up of movements that result from muscular contraction, and that *it is these muscular contractions that are directly predicted by the principle of association.* We are assuming that such movements are subject to conditioning or associative learning and that this conditioning is in itself an "all or none" affair, and its degree is not dependent on practice. One experience is sufficient to establish an association.
>
> But the learning of an act does take practice. We assume that the reason for this is that the act names an end result that is attained under varied circumstances and by movements varied to suit the circumstances. Learning an act as distinguished from a movement does require practice because it requires that the proper movement has been associated with its own cues. Even so simple an act as grasping a rattle requires different movements according to the distance and direction and position of the object. One successful experience is not sufficient to equip the infant with an act because the one movement acquired on that occasion might never again be successful. (pp. 7–8)

Just as an act is made up of many movements, a skill is made up of many acts. Thus, learning a skill such as playing golf or driving a car consists of learning thousands of associations between specific stimuli and specific movements. For example, learning to putt a golf ball into the cup from 10 feet away from a certain angle under specific conditions (wind coming from a certain direction at a certain velocity, temperature 85 degrees, and so on) is only one of thousands of responses that constitute the game of golf. Practice allows more and more of these specific associations to be made. The same is true of driving, typing, and all other skills. Guthrie (1942) said, "Learning occurs normally in one associative episode. The reason that long practice and many repetitions are required to establish certain skills is that these really require many specific movements to be attached to many different stimulus situations. A skill is not simple habit, but a large collection of habits that achieve a certain result in many and varied circumstances" (p. 59).

To summarize, a skill is made up of many acts, and acts are made up of many movements. The relationship between one set of stimuli and one movement is learned at full strength in one trial, but this learning does not bring about proficiency at a skill. For example, driving a car, typewriting, or playing baseball are all very complicated skills consisting of a large number of stimulus-response associations, and any one of these bonds or associations is learned at full strength in one trial. But it takes time and practice for all the necessary associations to be made. Learning to type the letter *A* while looking at an *A* on a written sheet of paper alongside the typewriter might be considered a specific stimulus-response (S-R) association. Looking at the letter *B* and typing the letter *B* is another specific association, as is looking at and typing the letter *C*. These specific associations must be built up for the entire alphabet and then for the numbers and then for the capital letters and finally for the various symbols that occur on the typewriter. Also, the typist must learn to make these responses under a wide variety of circumstances, such as varying lighting and temperature, different angles of seeing the material, and different kinds of paper. When all these responses have been learned, we say the person has become a proficient typist. Thus, a skill such as typing involves an enormously large number of specific S-R connections, each of which is learned in a single trial.

According to Guthrie, the reason Thorndike found systematic improvement through successive trials was that he was studying the learning of a skill, not the learning of individual movements. Guthrie and Horton (1946) said,

> We believe that when the puzzle-box situation varies indefinitely, as it did in the Thorndike box with the hanging loop, it is necessary for the cat to establish a large repertoire of specific escape movements adjusted to the specific differences in the situation. In other words, the cat establishes a skill, rather than a stereotyped habit. But the skill is made up of many specific habits. The gradual reduction of time reported by Thorndike is a consequence of the varied situation confronting the cat. (p. 41)

Whether or not learning occurs after one experience, as Guthrie believed, or in small increments, as Thorndike believed, is still a controversial issue and one that we will discuss in more detail in the next chapter.

Nature of Reinforcement

What is the place of reinforcement in Guthrie's theory? On this point Guthrie took issue with Thorndike, who, as you remember, made the revised law of effect the cornerstone of his theory. According to Thorndike, when a response led to a satisfying state of affairs, its probability of recurring increased. Guthrie felt the law of effect was completely unnecessary. For Guthrie, **reinforcement** was merely a mechanical arrangement, which he felt could be explained by his one law of learning. According to Guthrie, *reinforcement changes the stimulating conditions and thereby prevents unlearning.* For example, in a puzzle box, the last thing the animal does before receiving a reinforcer is to move a pole or pull on a ring, which allows it to escape from the box. Therefore, the response that allowed the animal to escape—moving the pole, in this case—changed the entire pattern of stimuli that the animal experienced. According to the recency principle, when the animal is placed back into the puzzle box, it will tend to move the pole again. In other words, being released from the puzzle box after moving the pole preserves the association between being in the puzzle box and moving the pole. In fact, the last response that was made in the puzzle box will be the response the animal makes when it is again placed into the box, *regardless of what that response was.* Guthrie and Horton (1946) said,

In our opinion the second occasion tends to repeat the behavior of the first, errors and all, except in so far as remaining in the puzzle box for a long time tends to establish new responses to the puzzle-box situation. *The reason for the remarkable preservation of the end action leading to escape is that this action removes the cat from the situation and hence allows no new responses to become attached to the puzzle-box situation.* Escape protects the end action from relearning. (p. 39)

Elsewhere Guthrie (1940) said,

The position taken in this paper is that the animal learns to escape with its first escape. This learning is protected from forgetting because the escape removes the animal from the situation which has then no chance to acquire new associations.

...What encountering the food does is not to intensify a previous item of behavior but to protect that item from being unlearned. The whole situation and action of the animal is so changed by the food that the pre-food situation is shielded from new associations. These new associations can not be established in the absence of the box interior, and in the absence of the behavior that preceded latch-opening. (pp. 144–145)

The Guthrie–Horton Experiment

Guthrie and Horton (1946) carefully observed approximately 800 escapes by cats from a puzzle box. Their observations were reported in a small book entitled *Cats in a Puzzle Box.* The puzzle box they used was very similar to the apparatus that Thorndike used in his selecting and connecting experiments. Guthrie and Horton used a large number of cats as subjects, but they noted that each cat learned to escape from the puzzle box in its own peculiar way. The particular response learned by a particular animal was the one the animal had hit on just prior to being released from the box. Since that exact response tended to be repeated the next time the animal was placed into the puzzle box, it was referred to as **stereotyped behavior.** For example, cat A would hit the pole by backing into it, cat B would push it with its head, or cat C would move it with its paw. Guthrie said that in each case the door's flying open was an abrupt change in the stimulating conditions. By changing the stimulating conditions, the response of backing into the pole, for example, is protected from unlearning. The last thing that the animal did before the chamber was opened was to back into that pole, and because it backed into the pole the stimulating conditions changed. Thus, applying the law of recency, the next time we put that animal into the puzzle box, it should respond by backing into the pole, and this is exactly what Guthrie and Horton observed. A pictorial record of a typical cat's performance is shown in Figure 8–1.

Guthrie and Horton (1946) observed that very often the animal, after escaping from the puzzle box, would ignore a piece of fish that was offered to it. Even though the animal ignored the so-called reinforcement, it was just as proficient at leaving the box the next time it was placed in it. This observation, according to Guthrie, added further support to his contention that reinforcement is merely a mechanical arrangement that prevents unlearning. Guthrie concluded that any event following the desired response from an animal would change the stimulating conditions and thereby preserve that response under the preceding stimulating conditions.

K-1   K-2   K-3   K-4   K-5   K-6   K-7   K-8   K-9

K-10   K-11   K-12   K-14   K-16   K-17   K-18   K-19   K-20

K-21   K-22   K-23   K-24   K-25   K-26   K-27   K-28   K-29

K-30   K-33   K-34   K-35   K-36   K-37   K-38   K-39   K-40   K-41

K-42   K-43   K-44   K-45   K-46   K-47   K-48   K-49   K-50   K-51

FIGURE 8–1   A pictorial record of a series of escape responses made by one of Guthrie's cats. The pictures were taken automatically when the cat moved the pole. Note that the cat tended to move the pole in the same way on each trial. (From *Cats in a Puzzle Box,* pp. 53-55, by E.R. Guthrie & G.P. Horton, 1946, New York: Hold, Rinehart & Winston. Reprinted by permission.)

Forgetting

Not only does learning occur in one trial but so does **forgetting.** All forgetting occurs, according to Guthrie, by causing an alternative response to occur in the presence of a stimulus pattern. After a stimulus pattern results in the alternative response, that stimulus pattern will thereafter tend to bring about the new response. Thus for Guthrie, *all forgetting must involve new learning.* This is an extreme form of **retroactive inhibition,** which refers to the fact that old learning is interfered with by new learning. To demonstrate retroactive inhibition, let us suppose someone learns task A and then learns task B and then is tested for retention on task A. Another person learns task A, does *not* learn task B, and is tested on task A. It is generally found that the first person remembers less of task A than does the second person. Thus, it is demonstrated that learning something new (task B) has interfered with the retention of what was learned previously (task A).

Guthrie (1942) accepted an extreme form of retroactive inhibition. His position was that whenever something new is learned it must completely "knock out" something old. In other words, all forgetting is due to interference. *No interference, no forgetting:*

> The child who has left school at the end of the seventh grade will recall many of the details of his last year for the rest of his life. The child who has continued on in school has these associations of the schoolroom and school life overlaid by others, and by the time he is in college may be very vague about the names and events of his seventh-grade experience.
>
> When we are somehow protected from established cues we are well aware that these may retain their connection with a response indefinitely. A university faculty member's wife recently visited Norway, the original home of her parents. She had not spoken Norwegian since the death of her grandmother when she was five and believed that she had forgotten the language. But during her stay in Norway, she astonished herself by joining in the conversation. The language and atmosphere of her childhood revived words and phrases she could not remember in her American home. But her conversation caused much amusement among her relatives because she was speaking with a facile Norwegian "baby talk." If her family in America had continued to use Norwegian, this "baby talk" would have been forgotten, its association with the language destroyed by other phrases.
>
> Forgetting is not a passive fading of stimulus-response associations contingent upon the lapse of time, but requires active unlearning, which consists in learning to do something else under the circumstances. (pp. 29–30)

Summary of Guthrie's Theory as Presented Thus Far

Associations between stimulating conditions and movements are constantly being made. An association between a stimulus and a response is made simply because the two occur together. The association can be between either external stimuli and overt responses or between movement-produced stimuli and overt responses. This association will continue until the same response occurs in the presence of other stimuli or until the same stimuli occur and the response is prevented from occurring. In a structured learning situation, such as a puzzle box, the environment is arranged so that there is an abrupt change in stimulation after a certain response is made. For example, if the cat hits the pole, the door opens and it is allowed to escape. Guthrie said that after the cat hit the pole the stimulus situation abruptly changed and whatever association existed before that time was preserved. The most recent association before the abrupt change was between the stimulation in the puzzle box and the response that allowed the animal to escape. According to the recency principle, when the animal is again placed in the puzzle box, it will tend to repeat that same response (it will tend to hit the pole again), and we say that the cat has learned how to escape from the box.

Unlike Thorndike, Skinner, Hull, and Pavlov, Guthrie was not a reinforcement theorist. Thorndike did, of course, discuss associative shifting, which he felt occurred independent of reinforcement. However, since Thorndike's main focus was on the kind of learning governed by the law of effect, he is generally considered a reinforcement theorist.

Of the theorists that we have covered thus far, Guthrie's theory is most similar to Watson's theory. Neither Watson nor Guthrie were reinforcement theorists. Watson believed that all learning could be explained by employing the laws of contiguity and frequency. The main difference between Watson's theory and Guthrie's is that Watson accepted the law of frequency whereas Guthrie did not.

HOW TO BREAK HABITS

A habit is a response that has become associated with a large number of stimuli. The more stimuli that elicit the response, the stronger the habit. Smoking, for example, can be a strong habit because the response of smoking has taken place in the presence of so many cues. Each cue present as a person smokes will tend to elicit smoking when next it is encountered. Guthrie (1952) indicated the complexities of a habit in the following quotation:

> The chief difficulty in the way of avoiding a bad habit is that the responsible cues are often hard to find, and that in many bad habit systems, they are extremely numerous. Each rehearsal is responsible for a possible addition of one or more new cues which tend to set off the undesired action. Drinking and smoking after years of practice are action systems which can be started by thousands of reminders, and which become imperative because the absence of the object of the habit, the drink or the smoke, results in a block to action and so in restlessness and tension. The desire, which includes tension in the muscles used in drinking or smoking, disrupts other action. The writer who "wants a smoke" is disturbed in his writing and the disturbed state will continue until the aroused action tendency is allowed to go through. The original wakening of the desire may be caused by any of the chance accompaniments of previous smoking—the smell of smoke, the sight of another person smoking, or of a cigar, the act of sitting back in the office chair, sitting down to a desk, finishing a meal, leaving the theater, and a thousand other stimulus patterns. Most smokers, while busily engaged in activities not associated with smoking, can go for long periods with no craving. Others find that the craving is strictly associated with such things as the end of a meal, if it has been their practice to smoke at that time. I once had a caller to whom I was explaining that the apple I had just finished was a splendid device for avoiding a smoke. The caller pointed out that I was smoking at that moment. The habit of lighting a cigarette was so attached to the finish of eating that smoking had been started automatically. (p. 116)

Threshold Method   To break a habit, the rule is always the same: Find the cues that initiate the bad habit and practice another response in the presence of those cues. Guthrie listed three ways in which an organism can be made to make a response, other than an undesirable one, to a certain pattern of stimuli. The first technique is referred to as the **threshold method.** According to Guthrie (1938), this method involves

> introducing the stimulus at such weak strengths that it will not cause the response and then gradually increasing the intensity of the stimulus, always taking care that it is below the "threshold" of the response. A gradual introduction to the motion of a ship which, unfortunately, cannot be controlled by human means, but depends on the gradualness of change in the weather, can bring about tolerance of a considerable storm. Most children

react to the taste of green olives by spitting them out. But if they begin with small nibbles, not enough to cause rejection, whole olives will eventually be taken with pleasure.

…Members of families learn to make use of this type of associative inhibition in dealing with their housemates. The proposal to send the daughter to an expensive school is "broken gently" to the father. Casual mention of the school's advantages without directly submitting the issue, criticism of the present school, at first so mild that it will not stir defense, prepare the father so that when the question is at last put squarely before him he does not make a scene over the expense. He is by this time used to the idea and there will be no violent reaction. (pp. 60–61)

The threshold method can also be exemplified by what is ordinarily done when a horse is being broken. If you walk up to a horse that has never worn a saddle and attempt to throw a saddle on its back, it will no doubt start kicking and run away. The horse will do whatever it can to prevent you from putting that saddle on its back. If, instead of the saddle, you put a very light blanket on its back, chances are that it will not react violently. If the horse remains calm, you can gradually increase the weight on its back by using heavier and heavier blankets. You can then go from blankets to a light saddle and finally to the regular saddle itself. There is a process akin to this in psychotherapy. If the therapist is trying to help a patient overcome a phobia of some kind, he or she may use the method of approximation described above. If the patient has a terrible fear of a relative, for example his or her mother, the therapist may first start out talking about people in general, then women, and then women who are related to the patient and, in this way, gradually build up to the point where they are talking about the mother without the patient being fearful. This method of treating a phobia is very much like Wolpe's technique of systematic desensitization, which was discussed in the last chapter.

Fatigue Method   The second method proposed by Guthrie is referred to as the **fatigue method.** Again, to take horse training as an example, the fatigue method would correspond to broncobusting, in which a saddle is thrown on the horse, the rider climbs on, and the horse is ridden until it gives up. That is, the horse is ridden until its fatigue causes it to do something other than buck while the saddle and the rider are on its back. Then, according to Guthrie, the response of riding calmly will replace the bucking response to the stimulus provided by the saddle and the rider. Once you get the animal to act calmly in the presence of the saddle and rider, then forevermore it will act calmly in their presence.

To break a dog of the habit of chasing chickens, all you have to do is to tie a chicken around the dog's neck and let it run around and try to get rid of it. When the dog eventually becomes fatigued it will be doing something other than chasing in the presence of the chicken. The chicken has then become a cue for doing something other than chasing.

Another example that Guthrie used in describing the fatigue method involved a little girl who upset her parents by lighting matches. Guthrie's advice was to allow the girl (or perhaps force her) to continue to light matches to the point where it is no longer fun. Under these conditions the sight of matches becomes a cue for avoidance rather than for lighting.

Incompatible Response Method   The third method of breaking a habit is called the **incompatible response method.** With this method, the stimuli for the undesired response are presented along with other stimuli that produce a response that is incompatible with the undesired response. For example, a young child receives a panda bear as a gift, and her first reaction is fear and avoidance. In contrast, the child's mother elicits a warm, relaxed feeling in the child. Using the incompatible response method, you would pair the mother and the panda bear; it is hoped that the mother will be the dominant stimulus. If she is the dominant stimulus, the child's reaction to the mother-panda bear combination will be one of relaxation. Once this reaction has been elicited in the presence of the bear, the bear can be presented alone, and it will produce relaxation in the child. With the incompatible response method, both stimuli are presented to the learner: the one that causes the undesired response and a stronger stimulus that causes a response incompatible with the undesired response. The learner then tends to make a response other than the undesired one in the presence of the stimuli that previously elicited the undesired response. Because of this pairing, the stimuli that used to elicit the undesired response will now elicit the response associated with the stronger stimulus.

All three of these methods for breaking a habit are effective for the same reason. Guthrie (1938) said, "All three of these methods are, of course, only one method. All of them consist in presenting the cues of an undesirable action and seeing to it that the action is not performed. Since there is always other behavior going on when we are awake, the cues we present become stimuli for this other behavior and are alienated from the obnoxious response" (p. 62).

The three examples we gave of breaking a habit can be summarized as follows:

Threshold Method
1. Regular saddle → kicking
2. Light blanket → calm
3. Heavier blanket → calm
4. A still heavier blanket → calm
5. Light saddle → calm
6. Regular saddle → calm

Fatigue Method
1. Saddle → kicking
2. Passage of time
3. Saddle → calm

Incompatible Response Method
1. Panda bear → fear
2. Mother → relaxation
3. Panda bear and mother → relaxation
4. Panda bear → relaxation

We noted in our discussion of Thorndike's theory (Chapter 4) that he believed associative shifting to be a second kind of learning, one based on contiguity alone and not governed by the law of effect. Since Guthrie believed learning is dependent on contiguity alone, one would expect to find a great deal of similarity between Thorndike's concept of associative shifting and Guthrie's views about learning. In fact, Guthrie's entire theory can be looked on as an effort to describe how a response that is associated with one stimulus shifts over and becomes associated with another stimulus.

The incompatible response method of breaking a habit seems to represent one kind of associative shifting. Stimulus 1, the mother, elicits relaxation. Stimulus 2, the panda bear, elicits fear. When stimulus 1 is presented along with stimulus 2, the response previously associated with stimulus 1 now is elicited by stimulus 2 simply because the two stimuli are contiguous. Now the panda bear elicits the response that was previously associated with the mother.

The threshold method of breaking a habit also appears to represent a kind of associative shifting. Using the threshold method to eliminate the child's fear of the panda bear would involve *gradually* associating the bear with the mother. To begin with, something only indirectly related to the bear, perhaps another of the child's toys, would be paired with the mother. Then the objects paired with the mother would become increasingly similar to the panda bear on successive pairings, and finally, the panda bear itself would be presented with the mother. Again, the end result is that the response once associated with mother "shifts over" to the panda bear.

Sidetracking a Habit

There is a difference between breaking a habit and sidetracking a habit. Sidetracking a habit can be accomplished by avoiding the cues that elicit the undesirable behavior. If you have accumulated a large number of behavior patterns that are not effective or for other reasons cause concern and anxiety, probably the best thing to do would be to leave the situation altogether. Guthrie advised going to an environment that would give you a fresh start since you would not have as many associations built up in a new environment. Going to a new environment would release you to develop new behavior patterns. This would be only a partial escape, however, since many of the stimuli causing your undesired behavior are internal and you would, therefore, be taking them with you to the new environment. Also, as we shall see, stimuli in the new environment identical or similar to stimuli in the old environment will tend to elicit the responses previously attached to them.

Punishment

Guthrie said the effectiveness of **punishment** is determined by what it causes the punished organism to do. Punishment works, not because of the pain experienced by the individual, but because it changes the way the individual responds to certain stimuli. Punishment is effective only when it results in a new response to the same stimuli. Punishment succeeds in changing the undesired habit because it elicits behavior incompatible with the punished behavior. Punishment fails because the behavior caused by the punishment is not incompatible with the punished behavior.

Let us say that you have a dog that chases cars and you want it to stop. Guthrie

(1952) said, get in your car and allow the dog to chase it. As it is running along the side of the car, reach down and slap its nose. This is likely to be effective. On the other hand, slapping its rear as it is chasing the car is not likely to be effective, although it can be assumed that a slap on the nose and a slap on the rear are equally painful to the dog. The difference is that the slap on the nose tends to make it stop and jump backward in the presence of the car, whereas the slap on the rear tends to make it continue forward, perhaps even a little more energetically. Thus one form of punishment causes incompatible behavior and is effective, and the other does not and is ineffective.

> What is learned will be what is done—and what is done in intense feeling is usually something different from what was being done. Sitting on tacks does not discourage learning. It encourages one in learning to do something else than sit. It is not the feeling caused by punishment, but the specific action caused by punishment that determines what will be learned. In training a dog to jump through a hoop, the effectiveness of punishment depends on where it is applied, front or rear. It is what the punishment makes the dog *do* that counts, or what it makes a man do, not what it makes him feel. The mistaken notion that it is the feeling that determines learning derives from the fact that often we do not care what is done as a result of punishment, just as long as what is done breaks up or inhibits the unwanted habit.
>
> …As the outcome of this discussion punishment and reward are not summarily to be ejected from the place they hold in public favor. No doubt whatever has been thrown on their general effectiveness. Children may still be spanked or caressed. But we shall have a much better insight into the uses of punishment and reward if we analyze their effects in terms of association and realize that punishment is effective only through its associations. Punishment achieves its effects not by taking away strength from the physiological basis of the connection…but by forcing the animal or the child to do something different and thus establishing inhibitory conditioning of unwanted habit. Punishment is effective *only in the presence of cues for the bad habit.*
>
> Furthermore, when the effect of punishment is only emotional excitement, punishment facilitates the stereotyping of the undesired habit. Punishment and reward are essentially moral terms, not psychological terms. They are defined not in terms of their effects on the recipient, but in terms of the purposes of the individual who administers them. Theory stated in their terms is bound to be ambiguous. (pp. 132–133)

Guthrie (1935, p. 21) talked about a 10-year-old girl who threw her hat and coat on the floor whenever she came home. Each time she did so, her mother scolded her and made her hang up her hat and coat. The situation continued until the mother guessed that her nagging had become the cue for the child to hang her clothes up. Realizing this, the next time the child threw her hat and coat on the floor, the mother made her pick them up and go back outside. Now as the girl came in the door, the mother insisted that she hang up her coat and hat immediately. This procedure was repeated a few times and soon the girl learned to hang up her hat and coat upon entering the house. Now the response of hanging up her clothes was attached to the stimuli present as she entered the house rather than to her mother's nagging. In this case, punishing the girl after her hat and coat were already on the floor could have no effect on the habit, except perhaps to strengthen it.

Guthrie and Powers (1950) also advise that a command should never be given if it could be disobeyed: "The skilled animal trainer never gives a command that he does not expect to be obeyed. In this he is like the army officer and the experienced teacher. If a teacher makes a request for silence in the room and it is disregarded, the request actually becomes a signal for disturbance" (p. 129).

Summary of Guthrie's Views on Punishment

Everything that Guthrie said about punishment is directly in accordance with his one law of learning—the law of contiguity. When stimuli and responses are paired, they become associated and remain associated unless the stimuli occur in the presence of another response, at which time they will become associated with the new response. While discussing ways of breaking a habit, we saw three mechanical arrangements that could be used to rearrange the associations between stimuli and responses. Punishment is another such arrangement. Punishment, when used effectively, causes stimuli that previously elicited an undesired response to elicit an acceptable response. Guthrie's views about punishment can be summarized as follows:

1. The important thing about punishment is not the pain it may cause but what it makes the organism do.
2. To be effective, punishment must cause behavior that is incompatible with the punished behavior.
3. To be effective, punishment must be applied in the presence of the stimuli that elicited the punished behavior.
4. If the conditions specified in 2 and 3 are not met, punishment will be ineffective or may even strengthen the undesired response.

Thus, when punishment is effective, it causes the organism to do something other than what it was punished for doing while the stimuli that elicited the punished behavior are still present. This response, of course, causes a new association to be formed, and the next time those stimuli appear, they will tend to elicit a favorable response instead of an unfavorable one.

Is there anything other than the anecdotal evidence that Guthrie offers to support his views on punishment? The answer is yes. Fowler and Miller (1963) trained rats to traverse a runway for food reinforcement. Subjects in the control group simply ran the runway and obtained food. Subjects in one experimental group were given a mild electric shock to the *front paws* just as they reached the food cup. Subjects in a second experimental group received a mild electric shock to the *hind paws* just as they reached the food cup. Relative to the running speed of the control subjects, subjects that had their front paws shocked as they reached the food cup ran slower on subsequent trials, whereas the subjects that had their hind paws shocked ran *faster.* Just as Guthrie predicted, shocking the rats on their hind paws actually facilitated running rather than inhibiting it. Since members of both experimental groups received the same intensity of shock, it was not the shock itself that facilitated or inhibited running speed. Rather, it was what the shock caused the animals to do. Shocking the front paws caused behavior incompatible with running whereas shocking the hind paws caused faster running.

Not all research on punishment has been supportive of Guthrie's theory, and it is now realized that Guthrie's account was at best incomplete. For a review of the complex topic of punishment see, for example, Walters and Grusec (1977).

Drives

Physiological **drives** provide what Guthrie called **maintaining stimuli** that keep the organism active until a goal is reached. For example, being hungry produces internal stimulation that continues until food is consumed. When food is obtained, the maintaining stimuli are terminated and therefore the stimulating conditions have changed, thus preserving the response that led to the food. It should be emphasized, however, that physiological drives are only one source of maintaining stimuli. Any persistent source of stimulation, whether it be internal or external, can provide maintaining stimuli. Guthrie (1938) said,

> To explain this requires that we first understand what a problem is. What makes the puzzle box or an unyielding parent a problem? The answer to this is that problems are persistent stimulus situations of such a nature that they keep the animal or the person disturbed and excited until some act is hit upon which removes the "maintaining stimuli" and allows the excitement to subside.
>
> Such persistent and disturbing stimuli are sometimes called "drives." In a hungry animal, the recurring spasms of the stomach serve to make the animal disturbed and to produce excitement....
>
> The same behavior could be produced by some artificial and external stimulation. A paper bag fastened to the cat's foot with a rubber band will similarly activate the cat, and it will become disturbed and excited and this state will continue until some one of its movements eventually removes the bag. (p. 96)

He went on to say,

> And here is a point very apt to be overlooked. The next time that the disturbers are present, they will tend to call out, by virtue of their last association, the act that removed them. Other acts associated with them have been dissociated or unconditioned each by the next act. But after successful removal of the disturber, it is no longer there to be associated with a new act. The drive remains faithful to the act that removed it because that was its last association. After that no new associations could be established because the drive is gone. (p. 98)

Guthrie explained the habitual use of alcohol and other drugs in a similar way. Let us say, for example, that a person feels tense or anxious. In this case, tension or anxiety provides maintaining stimuli. If under these circumstances, the person takes a drink or two, his or her tension may be reduced. According to Guthrie, this result assures the relationship between tension and drinking. Therefore, the next time the person feels tense, he or she will tend to have a drink. Gradually tension will tend to elicit drinking (or drug taking) under a wider range of circumstances, with the result that the person becomes a habitual drinker or a drug addict.

Intentions

Responses that are conditioned to maintaining stimuli are called **intentions.** They are called intentions because maintaining stimulation from a drive usually lasts for a period of time (until the drive is reduced). Thus the *sequence of behavior* preceding the drive-reducing response is repeated next time the drive, with its related stimuli, occurs. The sequence of behavior associated with maintaining stimuli seems to be interrelated and logical and is, therefore, referred to as intentional. If an animal is hungry and is allowed to eat, it will do so. If, however, the direct satisfaction of the hunger drive is not possible, the animal will tend to perform whatever behaviors led to food the last time it was hungry: It may turn in a certain direction in a maze, press a lever, or move a pole. If a person is hungry and has a sandwich in her office, she will eat it; if, however, she forgot her lunch, she will get up, put on her coat, get into her car, find a restaurant, enter the restaurant, place an order, and so on. Different reaction patterns have been associated with the maintaining stimuli from hunger plus the stimuli from environmental circumstances, that is, having one's lunch or not. Behavior triggered by maintaining stimuli may look purposive or intentional, but Guthrie felt it too could be explained by the law of contiguity.

Transfer of Training

It should be clear that Guthrie expected very little transfer of training. He said that if a child learns to add 2 and 2 at the blackboard, there is no guarantee that that child is going to know how to add 2 and 2 when he returns to his seat. The stimulating conditions under which that association was made are much different than those prevailing at his seat. So the child really must learn the response of adding 2 and 2 at the blackboard, at his seat, at home, and wherever he hopes to practice that response.

Guthrie would say to the college student, if you want to get the most from your studies, you should practice in exactly the same situation in which you are going to be tested. The best place to study, according to Guthrie, is in the room where you are going to be tested because all the stimuli in that room will be associated with the information you are studying. If you learn something in your dorm room, there is no guarantee that this knowledge will transfer into the classroom. This is how Guthrie explained why a student may say after taking a test, "I don't know what happened to me; I went over that material a hundred times; I knew it quite well, and yet, it didn't come to me during the test." Guthrie said that there simply was not enough similarity between the conditions under which the student studied and the conditions under which he or she was tested.

Guthrie's advice is always to practice the exact behaviors that are going to be demanded of us; in addition we should practice them in the exact conditions under which we are going to be tested or evaluated. If we want to utilize this information beyond the testing situation, we must go beyond the classroom and associate other stimuli with the behavior that the book or the class or the lecture caused us to do. Guthrie's advice to the student preparing for an essay examination is the same: In preparing for an essay test, write essay questions. Guess what the questions will be and answer them. Force yourself to respond to the questions under the time conditions that you are going to be exposed to during the test. Guthrie would give the same advice to the automobile mechanic or the electrician. If you want to learn how to fix engines, work on engines, and work on them under conditions similar to those that will prevail in real-life situations. This practice will maximize transfer.

Essentially, Guthrie accepted Thorndike's identical elements theory concerning the transfer of training. The probability of making the same response to two different situations is determined by the similarity between the two situations. Like Thorndike, Guthrie rejected the formal discipline theory of transfer and felt that acceptance of such a position generated unfortunate classroom practices. Guthrie and Powers (1950) said,

> The teacher's acceptance or rejection of the formal discipline theory of transfer, the identical elements or generalization explanation, will be reflected in numerous day-to-day teaching practices. *The subject-matter* teacher no doubt would give evidence of an actual, if not verbal, acceptance of the formal discipline doctrine. Exposure to the content of certain courses becomes in itself, then, the objective of education; methods of teaching and the attempt to link content and the needs of the learner are of relatively secondary importance. The student must conform to subject matter requirements and must develop a docile, submissive role.
>
> A challenging or questioning attitude on the part of the teacher as regards the validity of the formal discipline doctrine paves the way for educational experimentation. The teacher will ask what values, direct and indirect, are being served by pupil participation in given curricular areas. He will be willing to revise content and method as facts regarding transfer are uncovered. The child will be viewed as a growing and developing organism constantly organizing and reorganizing experience into more or less efficient patterns of behavior. The discovery of the child's interests and wise use of effective incentives in order to motivate participation become primary tasks of instruction. (p. 256)

Elsewhere Guthrie (1942) said, "It is essential that the student be led to do what is to be learned…a student does not learn what was in a lecture or in a book. He learns only what the lecture or book caused him to do" (p. 55). According to Guthrie, *we learn what we do*. The notions of insight, understanding, and thinking had little or no meaning to Guthrie. The only law of learning is the law of contiguity, which states that when two events occur together, they are learned. All learning, whether it be subhuman or human, simple or abstract, is subsumed under the law of contiguity and its related principles. There is no reference to conscious events in Guthrie's theory, nor is there any special interest in the survival value of learned behavior. According to Guthrie, incorrect responses are learned just as readily as correct ones, and the acquisition of both is explained by the same law of learning.

VOEKS'S FORMALIZATION OF GUTHRIE'S THEORY

As mentioned earlier, Guthrie did little research to test the validity of his own theory. Three explanations for Guthrie's lack of experimentation have been offered. First, Bolles (1979) suggests that it was because Guthrie's theory minimized the roles of motivation and reinforcement. These two components of most other learning theories in the 1930s and 1940s stimulated most of the research associated with them. Second, Carlson (1980) suggests that because psychology, at the time that Guthrie was at the University of Washington, was offered only on the undergraduate level, and the theses and dissertations of graduate students, which were often used to test other theories experimentally, were not available to Guthrie. Third, as Guthrie himself realized, his principles of learning were stated in terms that were too general to be tested easily.

Virginia W. Voeks (1921–1989), who was a student at the University of Washington when Guthrie was influential there, attempted to restate Guthrie's theory in terms that were precise enough to be empirically verifiable. Voeks obtained her B.A. in 1943 from the University of Washington, where she was influenced by Guthrie, and her Ph.D. in 1947 from Yale, where she was apparently influenced by Hull. In fact, the outcome of Voeks's work was a theory whose structure was Hullian but whose content was Guthrian. After obtaining her doctorate, Voeks returned to the University of Washington, where she worked until 1949. In 1949, she moved to San Diego State College, where she remained until her retirement in 1971.

In Voeks's restatement of Guthrie's theory there are four basic postulates, eight definitions, and eight theorems. The postulates attempt to summarize many of Guthrie's general principles of learning, the definitions attempt to clarify several Guthrian concepts (such as stimulus, cue, response, and learning), and the theorems are deductions from the postulates and definitions that are experimentally testable. Voeks tested a number of her deductions and found considerable support for Guthrie's theory.

Most of Voeks's formalization of Guthrie's theory, and the research that it stimulated, is too complex to be presented here. Voeks's four postulates, however, act both as a convenient summary and as a sample of her thoughtful formalization of Guthrie's theory.

Postulate I: Principle of Association   *(a)* Any stimulus-pattern which once accompanies a response, and/or immediately precedes it by one-half second or less, becomes a full-strength direct cue for that response. *(b)* This is the only way in which stimulus-patterns not now cues for a particular response can become direct cues for that response (Voeks, 1950, p. 342).

Postulate II: Principle of Postremity   *(a)* A stimulus which has accompanied or immediately preceded two or more incompatible responses is a conditioned stimulus for only the last response made while that stimulus was present. *(b)* This is the only way in which a stimulus now a cue for a particular response can cease being a cue for that response (Voeks, 1950, p. 344).

Postulate III: Principle of Response Probability   The probability of any particular response's occurring…at some specified time is a…function…of the proportion…of the stimuli present which are at the time cues for that response…. (Voeks, 1950, p. 348).

Postulate IV: Principle of Dynamic Situations   The stimulus-pattern of a situation is not static but from time to time is modified, due to such changes as result from the subject's making a response, accumulation of fatigue products, visceral changes and other internal processes of the subject, introduction of controlled or uncontrolled variations in the stimuli present (Voeks, 1950, p. 350).

The reader should not conclude that Guthrie's theory of learning is of historical interest only. As we shall see in the next chapter when we consider the work of

William K. Estes, one trend in modern learning theory is toward the greater use of mathematical models in explaining the learning process. It was Guthrie's theory of learning that formed the bases for the early mathematical models of learning and continues to be at the heart of most of them.

EVALUATION OF GUTHRIE'S THEORY

Contributions

Guthrie was unique in his insistence that learning resulted from contiguity between stimuli and responses and from contiguity alone. Even early reviewers of learning theory (Mueller and Schoenfeld, 1954) pointed out that Guthrie's simple contiguity approach could account for all of basic phenomena addressed in Skinner's or Hull's analyses. The great appeal to scientists was the fact that Guthrie could explain learning, extinction, and generalization with a simple analysis while other theories approached these problems in more complex ways. In addition, extensions of this theory to practical application were straightforward generalizations of his single, simple learning principle and were revealed by Guthrie in pleasant anecdotal fashion rather than in stark therapeutic prescription.

Although Guthrie's theory did not generate research and controversy comparable to that instigated by Hull or Skinner, it provided an important alternative explanation of learning. In addition, it served as a constant reminder that a theory need not be extraordinarily complex to explain seemingly complex behaviors. As we will see in the next chapter, William K. Estes was able to develop a diverse body of theory and research that extends into the 1990s using the basic ingredients of Guthrie's position.

Criticisms

There is substantial appeal in a position that can explain escape learning, reward learning, extinction, and forgetting with the same principle. It is this ease of universal explanation, however, that makes many psychologists uneasy about Guthrie's position. Recalling Popper's concern with theories that seem to be able to explain everything, we note that there are circumstances in which Guthrie's position becomes ambiguous and is too easily invoked to explain too many phenomena (Mueller & Schoenfeld, 1954).

Mueller and Schoenfeld (1954) also pointed out that while Guthrie was a strict critic of poor experimental methodology and of ambiguous language in other theories, he did not hold his own theory to the same standards. The Guthrie and Horton (1946) experiment, which was presented as an important demonstration of the theory, exemplifies Mueller and Schoenfeld's criticism. Moore and Studdard (1979) suggest that, like most members of the cat family, including domestic cats, the cats in the Guthrie and Horton experiment were engaging in an instinctive nuzzling or rubbing behavior that is typically exhibited when a cat "greets" another (friendly) cat or a familiar human. These researchers observed that cats displayed the same consistent, stereotyped behavior reported by Horton and Guthrie (1946) even when rubbing against a vertical pole produced no reinforcement or change in stimulus conditions whatsoever.

DISCUSSION QUESTIONS

1. What law of association did Guthrie build his theory around? Describe this law and explain how the recency principle is deduced from it.
2. Given Guthrie's belief in one-trial learning, how did he explain the improvement in performance that results from practice? Include in your answer a distinction among movements, acts, and skills.
3. Is Guthrie's theory a reinforcement theory or not? Justify your answer.
4. How did Guthrie explain forgetting?
5. For Guthrie, what was the relationship between drives and "intentions"?
6. Explain how, according to Guthrie, the transfer of skills from where they are learned to where they are applied could be facilitated.
7. What suggestions did Guthrie offer for breaking a bad habit? Choose one of the suggestions and show how it could be used to break the smoking habit.
8. How would Guthrie explain the phenomenon of regression, for example, the tendency to act as you did at a younger age under certain conditions, such as when you visit the house or room you grew up in?
9. How would Guthrie explain the tendency for someone to act like a "different person" under various conditions?
10. How would you revise your study habits so that they are in accordance with Guthrie's theory?
11. How would Guthrie explain the development of drug addiction?
12. Describe Guthrie's use of the term *reinforcement*.
13. According to Guthrie, under what circumstances would punishment be an effective technique in modifying behavior? Do you feel punishment is usually used as Guthrie said it should be? Explain.
14. What was Guthrie's purpose in introducing the notion of movement-produced stimuli?
15. Design an experiment to test Guthrie's contention that anything that disrupts a stimulus pattern will preserve the last response made to that stimulus pattern.
16. Discuss the key points of Voeks's restatement of Guthrie's theory.

KEY TERMS

acts Complicated behavior patterns usually involving some goal accomplishment. Acts are made up of many individual movements.

chaining The process whereby the stimulation caused by one response acts as a stimulus for another response and that response in turn triggers another and so on. Chaining, according to Guthrie, depends on movement-produced stimuli.

drives   Maintaining stimuli usually caused by some physiological need, such as hunger or thirst.

fatigue method of breaking a habit   Forcing an organism to continue to respond to a source of stimulation until it is fatigued. When it is fatigued it will respond to the source of stimulation in a way different from the way it originally responded to it.

forgetting   All forgetting, according to Guthrie, involves the blocking out of old associations by the formation of new ones. This is an extreme form of retroactive inhibition.

incompatible response method of breaking a habit   The stimulus for an undesired response is presented along with another stimulus that will cause a response incompatible with the undesired one. Because of this pairing, the stimulus that originally elicited the undesired response will no longer do so.

intentions   Behavior patterns that are conditioned to maintaining stimuli.

law of contiguity   Guthrie's one law of learning, which states that when a pattern of stimuli is experienced along with a response, the two will become associated so that when that pattern of stimuli next recurs, it will tend to elicit that response. In 1959, Guthrie revised the law of contiguity to read, "What is being noticed becomes a signal for what is being done."

maintaining stimuli   Any source of stimulation that persists until some specific act is performed. For example, putting a rubber band around an animal's nose provides maintaining stimuli until it is removed, and the hunger drive provides maintaining stimuli until the animal eats.

movement-produced stimuli   Stimulation caused by the receptors found in the muscles, tendons, and joints of the body. As the body moves, these receptors fire, thereby providing a source of stimulation, or what Guthrie called movement-produced stimuli.

movements   Specific responses to specific stimuli. Acts are made up of many specific movements.

one-trial learning   The contention that the association between a pattern of stimuli and a response develops at full strength as a result of just one pairing between the two.

principle of association   Voeks's first postulate, which states that when a stimulus and response occur together they become associated and that it is only through such contiguity that S-R associations are formed.

principle of dynamic situations   Voeks's fourth postulate, which states that stimulus patterns are dynamic since they can be changed by such things as an organism's response, fatigue, or by the systematic control of an experimenter.

principle of postremity   Voeks's second postulate, which states that only the last response made in a situation is the response that will be made when the situation recurs and that other responses previously made in the situation will no longer be associated with it.

principle of response probability   Voeks's third postulate, which states that the probability of a response being made in a given situation is a function of the number of cues in that situation associated with the response.

punishment   The presentation of an aversive stimulus in order to modify behavior. According to Guthrie, two conditions must be met before punishment will be effective: (1) The punishment must produce behavior that is incompatible with the undesired response; and (2) the punishment must be applied in the presence of the stimuli that elicit the undesired response.

recency principle   The principle that the response that was last made in a situation is the response that will be made when that situation next recurs.

reinforcement   According to Guthrie, one of many events that can change a stimulus pattern, thus allowing the association between the previous stimulus pattern and the last response made to it to remain intact. Reinforcement, to Guthrie, was nothing more than a mechanical arrangement that prevents unlearning.

retroactive inhibition   The interference of old learning by new learning.

stereotyped behavior   The tendency to repeat exactly the behavior patterns that were previously made in a situation.

threshold method of breaking a habit   A change in stimulating conditions is introduced so slowly that the organism does not notice it. Finally, the organism is reacting to the changed conditions in a manner other than it would have if the change had not occurred so slowly.

Chapter 9

WILLIAM KAYE ESTES

One current trend in learning theory is to move away from the broad, comprehensive theory and toward miniature systems. Researchers are marking off an area of interest and exploring it thoroughly. Breadth is sacrificed for depth. Exemplifying this trend are the so-called statistical learning theorists, who attempt to build a rigorous mini-system from which a restricted range of learning phenomena can be deduced. The most influential of these, and one of the earliest, was developed by Estes (1950). Estes, born in 1919, began his professional career at the University of Indiana. He moved first to Stanford University and then to Rockefeller University and is now at Harvard. In Chapter 5, we encountered some of the research on punishment that Estes performed while he was a student of Skinner at the University of Minnesota. It is for his development of statistical learning theory, however, that Estes is best known. His theory can be thought of as an attempt to quantify Guthrie's theory of learning. Guthrie's theory appears deceptively simple, but when one asks about the nature of a stimulus in more detail, for example, one soon realizes that his theory is much more complex than it appeared to be at first. Estes investigates this complexity and offers a model that effectively deals with it.

ESTES'S STIMULUS SAMPLING THEORY

Before giving an example of how Estes's **stimulus sampling theory (SST)** works, we will look at the assumptions made by Estes:

Assumption I   The learning situation comprises a large but finite number of stimulus elements. These elements consist of the many things that the learner experiences at the onset of a learning trial. They include the experimental conditions themselves, such as a light, a buzzer, verbal material presented in a memory drum, the sight of a bar in a Skinner box, or the runway in a T-maze. They also include the experimenter, the room, the temperature, extraneous noises inside and outside the room, and conditions within the experimental subject such as fatigue or headache. All these stimulus elements taken collectively are symbolized by S. Again, S is the total number of stimuli that accompany a trial in any learning situation.

William Kaye Estes. (Courtesy of W.K. Estes.)

Assumption II   All responses made in the experimental situation fall into one of two categories. If the response is one that the experimenter is looking for (such as salivation, an eye-blink, bar-pressing, turning right in a T-maze, or reciting a nonsense syllable correctly), it is called an A_1 response. If the response is anything other than that which the experimenter wants, it is wrong and is labeled A_2. Thus, Estes divides all responses that may occur in a learning experiment into two classes: correct (A_1) or incorrect (A_2). There are no gradations in between: Either an animal makes a conditioned response or it does not; either students recite a nonsense syllable correctly or they do not.

Assumption III   All elements in S are attached to either A_1 or A_2. Again, this is an all-or-nothing situation: All stimulus elements in S are either conditioned to the correct response (A_1) or to an incorrect response (A_2). Elements conditioned to A_1 tend to elicit A_1 responses, and elements conditioned to A_2 tend to elicit A_2 responses. At the beginning of an experiment, almost all of the stimuli will be conditioned to A_2 and will tend to elicit A_2 responses. Therefore, in the early stages of an operant bar-pressing experiment, the animal will tend not to press the bar.

Assumption IV   The learner is limited in its ability to experience S. The learner experiences or samples only a small proportion of the stimuli available on any learning trial, and the size of the sample is assumed to remain constant throughout the experiment. *The constant proportion of S experienced at the beginning of each learning trial is designated by θ* **(theta).** After each trial, the sample of elements in θ is returned to S.

Assumption V   A learning trial ends when a response occurs; if an A_1 response terminates a trial, a proportion of S equal to θ becomes conditioned to the A_1 response. Following Guthrie, Estes accepts a contiguity explanation of learning. When an A_1 response occurs, an association is formed between that response and the stimuli that preceded it. In other words, since θ proportion of the stimulus elements in S were sampled at the beginning of the trial, those elements become conditioned to A_1 through the principles of contiguity whenever an A_1 response terminates a trial. As the number of elements in S that are conditioned to A_1 goes up, the tendency for an A_1 response to be elicited at the beginning of a learning trial increases. In this manner, the number of stimulus elements attached to A_1 relative to the number of elements attached to A_2 gradually changes, and this is what Estes calls learning. The **state of the system** at any given moment is the proportion of elements attached to A_1 and A_2 responses.

Assumption VI   Because θ is returned to S at the conclusion of a trial, and because θ sampled at the beginning of a learning trial is essentially random, the proportion of elements conditioned to A_1 in S will be reflected in the elements in θ at the beginning of every new trial. If none of the elements in S are conditioned to A_1, θ will not contain any elements conditioned to the correct response. If 50 percent of the elements in S are conditioned to A_1, 50 percent of the elements in a random sample θ from S can be expected to be conditioned to A_1.

What determines whether an A_1 or an A_2 response occurs on a learning trial? How can Estes's theory reconcile his claim of all-or-none learning with the fact that performance is probabilistic—that the A_1 response will sometimes not occur even after several successful learning trials? The answer to these questions indicates why Estes's theory is called a statistical learning theory. The theory states that the probability of an A_1 response is equal to the proportion of stimulus elements in θ conditioned to A_1 at the beginning of a learning trial, and each θ is a *random* sample from S. If all elements in θ are conditioned to A_1, the response has a 100 percent chance of occurring. If, however, only 75 percent of the elements in θ are conditioned to A_1, we expect an A_1 response about 75 percent of the time and an A_2 response 25 percent of the time. In other words, the probability of observing an A_1 response depends on the **state of the system.**

Using the above assumptions, we can derive a mathematical expression that summarizes the learning process as seen by Estes:

1. The probability of response A_1 on any trial n (P_n) is equal to the proportion of elements conditioned to A_1 on that trial (p_n).

$$P_n = p_n$$

2. From assumption II, all elements are either A_1 elements (with probability p) or A_2 elements (with probability q). And these constitute 100 percent of the elements in the situation.

$$p + q = 1.00$$

so

$$p = 1.00 - q$$

3. From assumption V, elements *not* conditioned to A_1 on any trial n (reflected in q) must be elements that were not conditioned to A_1 prior to the first trial *and* that were not conditioned to A_1 on any previous trial. On any trial n, the probability that an element was not preconditioned on trial 1 is $(1 - P_1)$; and the probability that an element was not conditioned to A_1 on a *previous* trial is $(1 - \theta)^{n-1}$. The joint probability of two events occurring together (i.e., the probability that an element is not preconditioned *and* has not yet been conditioned) is the mathematical product of their individual probabilities. Therefore,

$$q = (1 - P_1)(1 - \theta)^{n-1}$$

4. Substituting from 3, we get

$$P_n = 1 - (1 - P_1)(1 - \theta)^{n-1}$$

How does Estes's theory relate performance and training? The following example might be helpful: Assume that we have two learners. One begins with $P_1 = 0$ and $\theta = .05$. The second also begins with $P_1 = 0$ but is able to sample a larger number of stimuli in the learning environment. For the second learner, $\theta = .20$.

For the first learner,

on trial 1, $P_1 = 1 - (1)(1 - .05)^0 = 0$
on trial 2, $P_2 = 1 - (1)(1 - .05)^1 = .05$
on trial 3, $P_3 = 1 - (1)(1 - .05)^2 = .10$

and performance approaches 100 percent $(P_n = 1.00)$ at about 105 trials, assuming each of these trials terminates in an A_1 response.

For the second learner,

on trial 1, $P_1 = 1 - (1)(1 - .20)^0 = 0$
on trial 2, $P_2 = 1 - (1)(1 - .20)^1 = .20$
on trial 3, $P_3 = 1 - (1)(1 - .20)^2 = .36$

and performance approaches 100 percent ($P_n = 1.00$) at about 23–25 trials, again assuming each of the trials ends in an A_1 response.

The formula generates a negatively accelerated learning curve with an asymptote of 1 that can vary from case to case, as we see in the above example, depending on the size of θ and the value of P_1. The learning curve produced by Estes's formula is essentially the same as the one generated by Hull's formula, described in Chapter 6 (see Figure 6–1). Both Estes and Hull assume that more learning takes place in the early stages of a learning experiment than in the later stages.

The **negatively accelerated learning curve** occurs, according to Estes, because trials in a learning experiment usually end with an A_1 response, and as a result, an increasing number of elements become conditioned to A_1. But there are diminishing returns. Taking as an example the situation in which, at the onset of an experiment, an A_1 response is highly unlikely (e.g., with eye-blinking conditioning), we see that almost all elements in S would be conditioned to A_2 (not blinking when a light is presented). Suppose, however, that blinking occurs at the end of trial 1. In this case, all the elements sampled on that trial (θ) switch from A_2 to A_1 since they were all conditioned to A_2 to begin with. On the next trial, a few elements will be conditioned to A_1, but most will still be conditioned to A_2. Therefore, it is now possible that some elements conditioned to A_1 will be sampled along with those conditioned to A_2. Thus the rate of changeover (from A_2 to A_1) will not be as great on trial 2 as it was on trial 1 since only those elements conditioned to A_2 can be transferred to A_1. As we saw earlier, this changeover from A_2 to A_1 is what constitutes learning. In the later trials, more and more elements are already conditioned to A_1, and therefore the number of elements conditioned to A_2 responses contained in θ on any given trial is small. It can be seen then that as learning trials progress, the rate of learning goes down. When all the elements in S are conditioned to A_1, no further learning can occur and the probability that an A_1 response will occur is 1. Thus, we have a negatively accelerated learning curve, which again simply indicates that learning progresses more rapidly in the early stages than it does in the later stages. This negatively accelerated rate of changeover of the stimulus elements is diagrammed in Figure 9–1.

Generalization

Generalization from the original learning situation to other situations is easily taken care of by stimulus sampling theory. Estes takes the same position on transfer as did Thorndike and Guthrie. That is, transfer takes place to the extent that two situations have stimulus elements in common. If many of the elements previously conditioned to an A_1 response are present in a new learning situation, the probability is high that an A_1 response will be elicited in the new situation. If no elements are conditioned to A_1 at the onset of new learning situations, the probability of an A_1 response is zero. In a new situation, as with original learning, the probability of an A_1 response is equal to the proportion of stimulus elements in S conditioned to it.

Stimulus Element Conditioned to an A_2 Response

Stimulus Element Conditioned to an A_1 Response

FIGURE 9–1 Estes's model of how stimulus elements change from the unconditioned state to the conditioned state.

Extinction

Estes handles the problem of extinction in essentially the same way as Guthrie did. Since in extinction, a trial usually ends with the subject doing something other than A_1, the stimulus elements previously conditioned to A_1 gradually switch back to A_2. The laws for acquisition and for extinction are the same. In fact, in Estes's system, it does not make sense to speak of extinction. What is called extinction results whenever conditions are arranged so that stimulus elements are switched from an A_1 response to an A_2 response.

Spontaneous Recovery

As you may remember from Chapter 7, spontaneous recovery refers to the reappearance of a conditioned response after that response has undergone extinction. To explain spontaneous recovery, Estes expands slightly on his notion of *S*. Earlier in this chapter, S was defined as the total number of stimulus elements present at the beginning of a trial in a learning experiment. We also noted that these stimulus elements include transitory events such as extraneous noises from the outside (e.g., a car backfiring, thunder, and loud voices) and temporary body states of the experimental subject (e.g., indigestion, headache, and anxiety). Since these and many other events are transitory, they may be part of S on one occasion but not on others. Likewise, when they are part of S, they are available to be sampled by the subject; when they are not part of S, they cannot be sampled. In other words, only those elements present in S can be sampled as part of θ.

Under the above conditions, it is possible that during training, A_1 responses become conditioned to many of these transitory elements. If it turns out that these elements are not available during extinction, the A_1 response conditioned to them cannot be switched to A_2 responses. Switching can occur only for stimulus elements actually sampled; thus if certain elements had been conditioned to A_1 responses during training and are subsequently not available during extinction, their status remains the same, that is, attached to A_1.

Now the importance of these transitory elements for spontaneous recovery becomes evident. It is entirely possible that many elements that were conditioned to A_1 during acquisition are not available during extinction but may reappear some time after extinction has taken place. Thus, if the subject is placed back into the experimental situation some time after extinction, a portion of these elements may now be present and would therefore tend to elicit an A_1 response. Spontaneous recovery is explained then by assuming that the extinction process (switching elements from A_1 to A_2) was never complete in the first place.

Probability Matching

For years, behaviorists puzzled over the phenomenon of **probability matching.** The traditional probability matching experiment involves a signal light that is followed by one of two other lights. When the signal light comes on, the subject is to guess which of the other two lights will come on. The experimenter arranges the situation so that the lights come on in any pattern he or she wishes, such as left light 75 percent of the time, right light 25 percent of the time; or left light 100 percent of the time, right light zero percent of the time. The results of such an arrangement are usually that the subject ends up guessing the frequencies at which the lights come on almost exactly as the experimenter had arranged them; for example, if the right light comes on 80 percent of the time, the subject will predict that that light will come on about 80 percent of the trials. This is referred to as probability matching.

To handle these results, we need to add symbols for the two new stimulus events to Estes's theory:

$$E_1 = \text{left light going on}$$
$$E_2 = \text{right light going on}$$

In this case, an A_1 response is predicting E_1, and A_2 is predicting E_2. In Estes's analysis of probability matching, the subject's actual guess is irrelevant. It is assumed that when E_1 occurs, it evokes in the subject an implicit A_1 response, and when E_2 occurs, it evokes an implicit A_2 response. Thus, for Estes, the event itself acts as a "reinforcer" (see Estes & Straughan, 1954, for greater detail). The experimental situation can be diagrammed as follows:

$$\text{Signal Light} \rightarrow \begin{array}{|c|} \hline \text{Guess} \\ A_1 \\ A_2 \\ \hline \end{array} \rightarrow \begin{array}{|c|} \hline \text{Event} \\ E_1 \\ E_2 \\ \hline \end{array} \rightarrow \text{Implicit behavior terminates trial}$$

Two additional symbols are necessary for Estes's analysis of probability matching:

$$\pi = \text{the probability of } E_1 \text{ occurring}$$
$$1 - \pi = \text{the probability of } E_2 \text{ occurring}$$

On a trial in which E_1 occurs, all elements sampled from S on that trial become conditioned to A_1, and on a trial on which E_2 occurs, the sample of elements will become conditioned to A_2.

As before, the probability of an A_1 response on any given trial (P_n) is equal to the proportion of elements in S that are conditioned to A_1 and the probability of an A_2 response is equal to the proportion of those elements not conditioned to A_1 or $(1 - P_n)$. As before, θ equals the proportion of elements sampled on each trial, and again, this value remains the same throughout the experiment.

The probability of an A_1 response after n trials is given by the following formula:

$$P_n = \pi - (\pi - P_1)(1 - \theta)^{n-1}$$

Because $(1 - \theta)$ is less than 1, with n getting larger, this equation yields a negatively accelerated curve with an asymptote of π. Thus, whatever the value of π, this formula predicts that the proportion of A_1 responses made by the subject will eventually match the proportion of E_1 occurrences set by the experimenter. In other words, Estes predicts probability matching by the subject, and this is what occurs. For more detail concerning the application of Estes's theory to probability matching, see Estes and Straughan (1954) or Estes (1964b).

ESTES'S MARKOV MODEL OF LEARNING

All statistical learning theories are probabilistic; that is, the dependent variable that they study is response probability. There is, however, a difference in opinion over what these changing response probabilities tell us about the nature of learning. The classic argument is over whether learning is gradual or complete in one trial. Thorndike concluded that learning was gradual, that it increased in small increments from trial to trial. Hull and Skinner went along with Thorndike on this matter. Guthrie differed by saying that learning occurred in an all-or-none fashion and only looked gradual because of the complexity of the task being learned. We shall see in Chapter 10 that Gestalt theorists, with their insight studies, also felt they demonstrated that the learner went from the unlearned state to the learned state very rapidly and not bit by bit.

Estes's early stimulus sampling theory accepted both an incremental (gradual) and an all-or-none point of view concerning the learning process. You will remember that only a small proportion of the total number of stimulus elements present during an experiment is sampled on any given trial. The sampled elements were conditioned in an all-or-none fashion to whatever response terminated the trial. However, since only a small portion of elements is conditioned on any given trial, learning proceeds bit by bit, and this is how the characteristic negatively accelerated learning curve is generated. To repeat, Estes's early position was that those stimulus elements that were sampled on a given trial were conditioned in an all-or-none manner; but since only a small number of them were sampled on a trial, learning proceeded in an incremental or gradual fashion. The probability of making an A_1 response changed gradually from one trial to the next, and if the total number of stimulus elements present in the experiment was large enough, the all-or-none nature of learning could not be detected. That is, with a large number of stimulus elements present in an experiment, there would be very small changes in response probabilities from one learning trial to the next, and when those probabilities were plotted, it would look *as if* learning was incremental rather than all-or-none in nature.

Later, Estes designed a number of studies that allowed the learning process to be observed in more detail (e.g., Estes, 1960, 1964a; Estes, Hopkins, & Crothers, 1960). These studies showed that when the number of elements to be sampled is very small, learning clearly occurs in an all-or-none fashion; in fact, it can be said that learning occurs completely on one trial or it does not occur at all—there appears to be no in-between. This rapid change from the unlearned state to the learned state is said to correspond to a **Markov process,** which is characterized by an abrupt, stepwise change in response probabilities rather than a relatively slow, gradual change from trial to trial.

In one study, Estes (1964a) used *paired associates* to show the stepwise nature of learning. In **paired associate learning,** subjects learn pairs of items so that when they are shown the first member of the pair, they can respond with the other. Estes used a variation of paired associate learning in which subjects were shown the first member of the pair, and had four responses to choose from, only one of which was correct. Thus, after subjects see the first member of the pair, the probability of their choosing the correct response by chance alone was .25 (1 in 4). Estes found that if a subject guessed correctly on one trial, the probability of guessing correctly on the next trial went to 1 and stayed there. In other words, after guessing correctly, the subject would be correct on 100 percent of the subsequent trials. Subjects who did not guess correctly went on guessing at chance level until they guessed correctly, at which time their subsequent probability of being correct jumped to 1. The most important fact here is that different subjects learned the correct response at different points in the experiment; that is, when subjects learned, they learned completely, but this learning occurred on different trials for different subjects, as shown in Figure 9–2.

What happens when the individual instances of going from the unlearned to the learned state are overlooked and the data from all subjects are pooled together? Under these circumstances, the probabilities of making a correct response for the subjects in the unlearned state would be combined with those in the learned state and *average* probabilities would be plotted. For example, if there were five subjects in an experiment and three were in the unlearned state (probability of making a correct

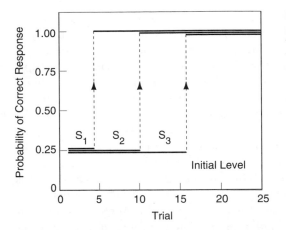

FIGURE 9–2 Subjects go from chance-level performance to perfect performance in just one trial, but this process occurs at different times for different subjects. (From "All-or-None Processes in Learning and Retention," by W.K. Estes, 1964, *American Psychologist, 19,* pp. 16–25. Copyright by the American Psychological Association. Reprinted by permission of the publisher and author.)

response = .25) and two were in the learned state (probability of making a correct response = 1), the average probability of making a correct response for the group would be .55. As more learning trials occur, more subjects will enter the learned state, and the average probability for the group would increase. This process is demonstrated in Figure 9–3 $P(C_{n+1}|N_n)$ is read, "the probability that subjects will be correct on trial $n+1$, given that they were incorrect on trial n." $P(C_n)$ is the probability that subjects will be correct on trial n.

It is important to note that because the data were combined, one gets the impression that learning is gradual and improves slightly from trial to trial. When one looks at individual performance, however, the illusion of gradual learning disappears.

In an earlier study, Estes (1960) used another paired associate situation involving a nonsense syllable and a number. He ran 48 subjects on an eight-item paired associate list; that is, there were eight pairs of nonsense syllables and numbers. Each subject was presented with each of the eight syllable-number pairs once and then tested by seeing the syllable alone and guessing the number that was associated with it. This time there was not a multiple choice, as there was in the other paired associate study mentioned above.

FIGURE 9–3 Even though individual subjects learned completely in one trial, when the data from a number of individual subjects are pooled, a negatively accelerated learning curve is generated. This curve gives the erroneous impression that learning is continuous and does not occur in an all-or-none fashion. (From "All-or-None Processes in Learning and Retention,: by W.K. Estes, 1964, American Psychologist, 19, pp. 16–25. Copyright by the American Psychological Association. Reprinted by permission of the publisher and author.)

To differentiate between the point of view that says learning is gradual and the one that says it is all or none, Estes hypothesizes four subjects who start the experiment with zero probability of being correct. These four hypothetical subjects see a syllable and a number paired once. When tested, one of the four anticipates the number correctly after seeing the nonsense syllable. Estes supposes that the probability of being correct on subsequent tests is raised from zero to .25 for the group. But this increase in the probability of being correct can occur in two ways: (1) Those who believe in the gradual nature of learning would say that the "associative strength" is increased in all four subjects, and therefore on subsequent tests all members of the group have a probability of being correct of .25 and a probability of being wrong of .75; (2) one member of the group formed the correct association whereas the other three did not. According to the principle of all-or-none learning, one person will always be correct on subsequent tests and the other three will always be wrong. The difference between the associative strength point of view and the all-or-none point of view is diagrammed in Figure 9–4.

Now we return to the real experiment involving forty-eight subjects. Estes indicates that according to the associative strength point of view, how subjects perform on a second test, in the situation described above, should have little to do with whether or not they were correct on the first test. In other words, if the performance of subjects who were wrong on the first test is compared with the performance of subjects who were correct on the first test, it should show that they do about as well on the second test. The all-or-none point of view, however, says that all or most of the subjects who were correct on the first test should also be correct on the second test, and the subjects who were wrong on the first test should also be wrong on the second test. Estes ran such a test and the results are summarized in Figure 9–5.

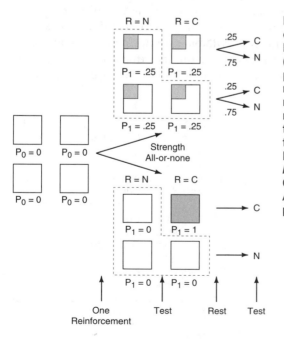

FIGURE 9–4 The diagram shows what the effects of a single reinforcement are thought to be according to the "associative strength" (upper part of diagram) and all-or-none (lower part of diagram) points of view. N = an incorrect response; C = a correct response; R = the response made on a test trial following one reinforcement. For example, $R = N$ means that the subject made an incorrect response on the test trial. (From "Learning Theory and the 'New Mental Chemistry'," by W.K. Estes, 1960, *Psychological Review, 67,* pp. 207–223. Copyright 1960 by the American Psychological Association. Reprinted by permission of the publisher and author.)

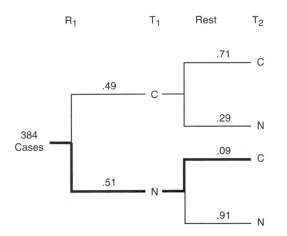

R$_1$ T$_1$ Rest   T$_2$

FIGURE 9–5 Results of paired associated learning experiment. See text for explanation. (From "Learning Theory and the 'New Mental Chemistry',", by W.K. Estes, 1960, *Psychological Review, 67,* pp. 207–223. Copyright 1960 by the American Psychological Association. Reprinted by permission of the publisher and author.)

It can be seen in Figure 9–5 that of the 384 possibilities of being correct (48 subjects × 8 paired associates), 49 percent of the responses on test 1 were correct and 51 percent were incorrect. Seventy-one percent of the items that were responded to correctly on test 1 were also responded to correctly on test 2, whereas only 9 percent of the items that were responded to incorrectly on test 1 were responded to correctly on test 2. This result lends support to the notion that when something is learned, it is learned completely; if it is not learned completely, it is not learned at all. Estes ran some trials with control groups that showed that the 51 percent of the items missed were just as difficult as the 49 percent not missed and that the subjects missing the 51 percent had the same average learning ability as the other subjects.

As with most notions in learning theory today, Estes's work has not gone uncriticized. Underwood and Keppel (1962), for example, find fault with many aspects of the experiment we have just discussed. Among other things, they wonder, if the all-or-none point of view is correct, why were *all* the items that were correct on the first test not also correct on the second test instead of only 71 percent of them? Underwood and Keppel feel that Hull's incremental learning theory is better able to handle the data than Estes's all-or-none theory:

> it could be said that if an item were incorrect on the first test trial then it was below the performance threshold; there is no reason why it should be correct on the second test with no intervening study. Likewise, an item above threshold on the first test trial has a high probability of being correct on the second. Items which were correct on the first test trial but not on the second, and those which were not correct on the first but correct on the second, would be handled by some incremental theories via the notion of *oscillation.* (pp. 3–4)

As you will recall, the oscillation effect ($_sO_R$) was part of Hull's theory of learning (see Chapter 6). According to Hull, the oscillation effect operated against a learned response in varying amounts from trial to trial and in a random fashion. When the value of $_sO_R$ happened to be high, the probability of a learned response on that particular trial was low. When the value of $_sO_R$ was low, it had little effect on the elicitation of a learned response. Hull used the oscillation effect to explain why a learned response may occur on one trial but not on a subsequent trial.

ESTES AND COGNITIVE PSYCHOLOGY

Although Estes remains a contiguity theorist, in more recent years, he has been emphasizing cognitive mechanisms in his analysis of learning (see, e.g., Estes 1969a, 1969b, 1971, 1972, 1973, 1978). As we have seen, his earlier analysis followed Guthrie by assuming that whatever stimuli were present at the termination of a learning trial became associated with whatever response terminated the trial. Both Guthrie and Estes viewed learning as the mechanical, automatic association of contiguous events. Essentially, organisms, including humans, were viewed as machines that could sense, record, and respond. Although still mechanistic, Estes's current analysis of learning is much more complex because it considers the influence of cognitive events.

The Importance of Memory Earlier, Estes maintained that stimuli and responses become associated by contiguity, and once associated, when the stimuli recur, they will elicit the responses associated with them. Later, Estes added a third element to his analysis, namely, memory (see, e.g., Estes, 1969a, 1972, 1973, 1978). In Estes's more recent analysis, rather than stimuli leading directly to responses, stimuli elicit memories of previous experiences, and it is the interaction of current stimulation with memories of previous experiences that produces behavior.

Estes (1976) describes what he believes occurs in a decision-making situation in which different responses are associated with different outcomes. For example, making an $A1$ response will yield five points and making an $A2$ response will yield three points. First, according to Estes, the subject learns the value of each response, and this information is stored in memory. Subsequently, when given the opportunity to respond, the subject will scan the situation to determine what responses are possible and recall what their outcomes are. Given this information, the subject will choose to make the response that yields the most valuable outcome. Estes (1976) calls this the **scanning model of decision making.** In general, the model claims that in any decision-making situation, an organism will utilize whatever information it has stored in memory concerning response-outcome relationships and will respond in such a way as to produce the most beneficial outcome. It is this scanning model that Estes now uses to explain probability matching (see Estes, 1976).

Memory also plays a prominent role in Estes's analysis of higher-order cognitive operations such as those involving language. Following in the tradition of the British empiricists, Estes assumes that simple memories are combined to form complex memories. In learning a language, for example, first individual letters of the alphabet are learned and retained, then words, then sentences, and then other principles of organization. Language utilization, then, requires memories arranged in a hierarchy ranging from the memory of simple elements (e.g., letters) to the memory of complex grammatical rules and principles. Estes (1971) says that complex human behavior such as that involving language "is better understood in terms of the operation of rules, principles, strategies, and the like than in terms of successions of responses to particular stimuli" (p. 23). According to Estes, it is the interaction of such complex cognitive processes with sensory stimulation that determines how a situation is responded to.

The Cognitive Array Model: Classifying and Categorizing

Estes sees SST as a mathematical extension of Thorndike's identical elements theory of transfer. That is, it was developed to make precise predictions about transfer of learning from one situation to another, based on stimulus elements common to both. In his most recent work Estes (1994) expands on a problem first explored by Medin and Shaffer (1978) and continues to develop Thorndike's identical elements approach. But this time the model is applied specifically to the behaviors of classification and categorization. Examining a creature, noting that it has feathers, that it flies, and that it lays eggs, and then calling it "bird" is one example of this kind of behavior. Physicians who gather data and diagnose a common cold, rather than pneumonia, and market analysts who declare a company to be a good investment, rather than a risky venture, are classifying or categorizing. Although Estes' approach to classification is strictly cognitive, we will see that there are similarities between the kinds of behaviors predicted by SST and by his model of classification. Furthermore, some of Estes' important assumptions about learning, made in his cognitive approach, are similar to those he made in the earlier development of SST.

Recall that in SST, learning occurs in an all-or-none, one-trial manner and that it only requires contiguity between stimuli and a particular response. On subsequent learning trials, subjects sample a limited number of stimulus elements from the stimulus set, and the resulting response depends on the proportion of stimuli in the sample that are attached to that response. If the sample contains no conditioned elements, either because of the random nature of sampling or because the environment has changed, the response is not elicited.

In Estes' cognitive model of classification, subjects are assumed to examine a complex stimulus and attend to (sample) its important or salient features. As in SST, those stimulus features, along with information about their category or class membership, are learned all-or-none, in one trial. It is at this point where Estes' cognitive approach, called the array model, differs from SST. In the case of the array model, the stimulus characteristics and category designation are stored in memory as a set—an array—that keeps the important features or attributes distinct and ready for comparison with attributes of other stimuli. When a new stimulus is encountered, salient features of the new stimulus are compared with previously learned and stored sets of features. Classification of a new stimulus is then based on the similarity of its attributes to stimulus attributes stored in memory arrays. There is an additional difference between SST and the array model that deserves mention. The focus of SST is on stimulus-response associations formed in the past and the way in which those associations were accumulated. The focus of the array model is on the classification of events that are encountered in the present or that will be encountered in the future. In noting that we do not acquire an exact, perfectly detailed memory record of situations previously encountered, Estes (1994) says

> Situations never recur exactly, and therefore the record alone would be of no help to us in dealing with present problems or anticipating the future. Memory is essential to adaptive behavior because it is organized in ways that make information gained from past

experience applicable to present situations. And the essence of memory is classifica-tion....Suffice it to say that classification is basic to all of our intellectual activities. (p. 4)

SST Assumes Additive Stimulus Relationships   Although both SST and the array model reflect Thorndike's identical elements theory of transfer, they do so in dif-ferent ways. A simple example can help to illustrate these differences. Let us look first at a problem in which subjects learn to discriminate between two stimuli called "A" and "B" and the way that sampling theory deals with the problem of generaliza-tion of the "A" response. In our example, the stimuli will have three distinct features or sampling elements: They are size, color, and shape. The "A" stimulus is large, it is red, and it is a circle. Subjects learn to say "B" to a distinct second stimulus that is a small, blue, square. After discrimination training with these initial stimuli, subjects are tested on two new stimuli. These are a large, red, square and a large, blue, square. The problem is displayed in Table 9–1.

As indicated on the lower right, we want to know how subjects will respond to the test stimuli, 2A and 2B, after discrimination has been learned with the training stim-uli. Notice that the large, red square shares two elements with the training stimulus that the subject learned to call "A" but has only one element in common with the training stimulus called "B." Similarly, the large, blue square shares two elements with training stimulus "B" but only one element with "A." A basic prediction from SST, based on this straightforward *additive* combination of stimulus elements, is that subjects will call the large, red square an "A" about 66 percent of the time because this stimulus shares two-thirds of the properties of the training stimulus that have been attached to response "A." They should also call the large, blue square an "A" about 33 percent of the time because one-third of its elements are attached to Response "A" during initial discrimination training. This is a fairly straightforward demon-stration of how Thorndike's idea of identical elements is used in SST to predict gen-eralization, and the predictions for a very simple learning problem like this one are, in fact, quite accurate (cited in Atkinson & Estes, 1963, p. 193).

A significant problem with SST is that, in situations more complex than the one just described, the theory cannot account for the large detrimental effects that are observed when either human or nonhuman learners are tested in contexts or

TABLE 9–1

Training Stimuli:		1A	1B	Test Stimuli:	2A	2B
	1	*large*	small		*large*	*large*
Sampling Elements	2	*red*	blue		*red*	blue
	3	circle	square		square	square
RESPONSE		"A"	"B"		"??"	"??"
				Predicted:	(66% "A")	(33% "A")

with stimuli that are very different from those that existed during training. In his book *Cognition and Classification*, Estes (1994) indicates that the critical flaw is the assumption of additive stimulus effects—the conceptual and mathematical idea, demonstrated in our example above, that stimulus elements combine in an additive manner in order to elicit learned responses. As an alternative, the array model assumes that elements combine multiplicatively to elicit responses.

The Array Model Assumes Multiplicative Stimulus Relationships.   According to the array model, we judge the similarity of stimuli in a new context relative to the stimuli in the training situation by comparing stimulus attributes or elements. In each case of comparison, a factor called s, the similarity coefficient, describes the degree of similarity between pairs of stimulus attributes. Estes writes "We compare the two situations....feature by feature, applying a similarity coefficient of unity if the features match and a coefficient with some smaller value s, if they differ. The measure of similarity is the *product* [italics added] of these coefficients."(p. 19). Therefore, the probability of response transfer from a training situation to a test situation is a function of the product of the similarity coefficients. Clearly, if all stimulus element comparisons yield perfect matches, all similarity coefficients are equal to 1.00, and the measure of similarity will be (1 x 1 x 1 x 1...) or 1. The probability of response transfer is then 1.00 or certainty. Response probability decreases from certainty whenever there is a mismatch between the compared stimuli. In the example above, the similarity coefficients for comparisons of size and color are both 1.00 because both stimuli are large and red. However, the similarity coefficient for comparison of shape is s, some number less than 1.00, because the shapes do not match perfectly. Thus, the measure of similarity between stimuli 1A and 2A is (1 x 1 x s) or s, and because the similarity measure for 1A and 2A is less than 1.00, we would not expect perfect response transfer between the two stimuli. Note that with an appropriate value of s, the array model can be applied to the generalization problem in Table 9–1 and make a prediction similar to that made by SST.

However, the array model is intended to describe and predict how people judge stimuli to be members of specific categories, not how a conditioned response is generalized or transferred to a new situation, and we can use the stimuli from our generalization problem to demonstrate the basics of the array model. In our example, the three stimulus attributes or elements are restricted so that they can each have only one of two values. With respect to size, a stimulus can be large (designated with a "+") or it can be small (designated with a "-"). It can be either red (+) or blue (-); and it can be either a square (+) or a circle (-). And in our basic, general description, s is assigned a single value for all attribute comparisons. The categorization rule that we arbitrarily determine for this experiment is that all large, red things belong in category A; all small, blue things belong in category B. The stimuli will be presented one at a time, the subject will respond by categorizing the stimulus as "A" or "B," and the experimenter will indicate whether or not the categorical response is correct.

Items within a Category Are Similar to Each Other.   The first step in developing the array model for the problem developed above is to determine similarity of items

TABLE 9–2 Elements in Category A

	SIZE	COLOR	SHAPE
STIMULUS 1A	+	+	+
STIMULUS 2A	+	+	-
coefficient	1	1	*s*
PRODUCT: (1 x 1 x *s*) = *s*			

within categories. We can see that two of our stimuli actually belong in category A. In Table 9–2 we show their coefficients of similarity and the product of those coefficients as a measure of the similarity of those items to each other. Keep in mind that the coefficient of similarity is 1 when the values of an element match (both + or both -) and is *s*, some value less than 1 when the values are different.

There are also two members of category B, and we show their similarity coefficients and the product for those stimuli in Table 9–3.

The measure of similarity of any stimulus with itself is, of course, 1.00 because all features match. In both categories A and B, the measure of similarity of the two stimuli within the category, indicated by the product of the similarity coefficients, is *s* and is less than 1.00 because, in each case, two features match perfectly but there is a mismatch with respect to shape. Note, however, that the measures of similarity between stimuli from different categories are even smaller than *s*. If two stimuli have one matching element and two mismatches, the product is (1 x *s* x *s*) or s^2. If two stimuli mismatch on all three features, the product is (*s* x *s* x *s*) or s^3. If we set *s* = .7 in this example (this setting is arbitrary and is used for illustration only), we see

two matches; one mismatch = (1 x 1 x .7) = .7
one match; two mismatches = (1 x .7 x .7) = $(.7)^2$ = .49
no matches; three mismatches = (.7 x .7 x .7) = $(.7)^3$ = .34

Stimulus Items Represent a Whole Category. The next step in applying the array model is to determine the degree to which a particular stimulus is representative of its category as a whole. To do this, we construct a similarity coefficient matrix comparing elements within a category to other elements in that category, including com-

TABLE 9–3 Elements in Category B

	SIZE	COLOR	SHAPE
STIMULUS 1B	-	-	-
STIMULUS 2B	-	-	+
coefficient	1	1	*s*
PRODUCT: (1 x 1 x *s*) = *s*			

TABLE 9–4

	STIMULUS 1A	STIMULUS 2A	(SIMILARITY TO A)
STIMULUS 1A	1	s	$(1 + s)$
STIMULUS 2A	s	1	$(1 + s)$

parison of a single stimulus with itself. The matrix for stimuli in category A appears in Table 9–4. In the far right column we see that the similarity of stimulus 1A to all the items in category A is $(1 + s)$, the similarity of that item to itself plus the similarity of that item to the other member of the category. The similarity of 2A to all items in A is also $(1 + s)$.

Next, we can construct a matrix representing the similarity of items in A with items in B, thereby representing the similarity of each item in A to category B as a whole. The summed similarity of an item in A to each of the items in B is indicated in the column to the right in Table 9–5.

Finally, we can make a probabilistic prediction about the correct categorization of a stimulus. This prediction is based on the similarity of a stimulus to its own (correct) category relative to the sum of its similarities to all possible categories. Thus, the probability of correctly categorizing stimulus 2A is calculated by dividing the similarity of stimulus 2A to category A by the similarity of stimulus 2A to categories A and B. That is, the probability of correctly recognizing stimulus 2A as a member of A is

$$\frac{(1 + s)}{(1 + s) + (s^2 + s^3)}$$

To see how the model might work with a concrete example, let's say that we train subjects on items 1A and 1B, and, as above, $s = .7$. The array model predicts that, when stimulus 2A appears, the probability that it will be categorized as an "A" is

$$\frac{(1 + .7)}{(1 + .7) + (.49 + .34)}$$

$$= 1.7/2.53$$

$$= .67$$

It might be a useful exercise for the reader to use the model to predict the probability of correct categorization of 2B under the same conditions. Note, however, that these mathematical manipulations are not just exercises so that experimenters can predict performance in categorical learning tasks. The theory assumes that subjects engage in cognitive processes that are captured in the mathematics of the theory. Estes (1994) writes:

TABLE 9–5

	STIMULUS 1B	STIMULUS 2B	(SIMILARITY TO B)
STIMULUS 1A	s^3	s^2	$(s^3 + s^2)$
STIMULUS 2A	s^2	s^3	$(s^2 + s^3)$

At the beginning of each trial after the first, the subject *computes* [italics added] the similarity of the exemplar presented to each member of the current memory array, *sums* [italics added] its similarity to all of the members associated with each category, *computes* [italics added] the probability of each category, and *generates* [italics added] a response based on these probabilities. It is not, of course, assumed that the individual carries out these calculations as a computer would do, only that the processing system accomplishes in some manner a set of computations leading to the same response probabilities as those produced by a computer programmed to simulate the model. (p. 46)

Clearly, with his more recent analyses, Estes has embraced cognitive psychology in general and information-processing psychology in particular. Information-processing psychology will be discussed in Chapter 14.

Estes's View of the Role of Reinforcement   Estes's current view of reinforcement is also cognitive in nature. Estes has never been a reinforcement theorist, and he is not one now. His earlier position rejected the law of effect, which stated that reinforcement strengthened the bond or connection between a stimulus and a response. Following Guthrie, Estes believed that reinforcement prevented the unlearning of an association by preserving the association between certain stimuli and certain responses. Estes's more recent view of the role of reinforcement stresses the *information* that it provides to the organism (see, e.g., Estes, 1969b, 1971, 1978).

According to Estes, organisms learn not only S-R relationships but R-O (response-outcome) relationships as well. That is, organisms learn, and remember, which responses lead to which consequences. In a given situation, some responses lead to reinforcement, some lead to punishment, and others lead to neither. Reinforcement and punishment do not strengthen or weaken behavior since R-O relationships leading to neither reinforcement nor punishment are learned as readily as those that do (Estes, 1969b). The organism simply learns what leads to what, and this information determines which response is preferred over others that are possible.

In his analysis of reinforcement, Estes makes the important distinction between learning and performance. For him, reinforcement and punishment are not learning variables since learning occurs in their absence. Rather, reinforcement and punishment are performance variables since they determine how material already learned will manifest itself in behavior.

Although Estes's position emphasizes cognitive mechanisms (e.g., memory) and views reinforcement and punishment as providing information to the organism, his position still views humans as machinelike. In this regard the major difference between his earlier position and recent one is that the machine has become much more complex. Hulse, Egeth, and Deese (1980) nicely summarize Estes's views on how reinforcement and punishment automatically guide behavior:

The function of reinforcement, in Estes's theory, is not to strengthen directly the formation of new associations; simple contiguity suffices for that. In this regard he is in close harmony with Guthrie. Instead, reinforcing events have their effects on *performance,* which, in Guthrie's terms, means the tendency for a given sequence of learned responses to run to some final conclusion. The function of reinforcement is to provide feedback based on the anticipation...of impending reward or punishment which *summates* with current stimuli (or stimuli recalled from memory) in the learning situation and so *guides* behavior preferentially along one path as opposed to another. In essence, in other words, Estes's theory emphasizes a cybernetic model for the influence of reinforcement upon performance: behavior is guided toward goals and away from aversive situations through positive or negative feedback from the reinforcing event. (pp. 73–74)

The term *cybernetic* in this quotation refers to a system that is automatically guided by feedback from the environment. Examples of cybernetic systems include the automatic pilot on an aircraft or a thermostat that regulates the temperature of a home. We will have more to say about cybernetic models in Chapter 14.

With his informational interpretation of reinforcement and distinction between learning and performance, Estes aligns himself with the theories of Edward Tolman (see Chapter 12) and Albert Bandura (see Chapter 13). Estes, Tolman, and Bandura all believe that we learn what we observe and that how this information is translated into behavior depends on the goals of the organism. There is also a kinship between Estes's recent position and the information-processing approach to psychology. Information-processing psychology maintains that input from the environment (stimuli) interacts with one or more mental processes before it results in output (behavior). Like Estes, many information-processing psychologists accept a cybernetic model in explaining human behavior.

LEARNING TO LEARN

The controversy over the incremental versus the all-or-none position of learning (sometimes called the **continuity-noncontinuity controversy**) is still very much alive and promises to be for some time to come. As with most extreme positions, however, the truth will probably be found somewhere between the two. An example that seems to be satisfactory to both sides of the debate is Estes's earlier position that, with a complex learning environment, learning proceeds in an all-or-none fashion, only it does so a little bit at a time. In fact, logically, all incremental theories of learning can be reduced to all-or-none theories. What the theorists are really arguing over is the size of the chunk of material that is learned on any given trial.

Harry F. Harlow. (Courtesy of Harry F. Harlow, University of Wisconsin Primate Laboratory.)

Indeed, there is considerable evidence showing that the incremental and all-or-none positions are both correct. One example comes from the famous work of Harry Harlow. Harlow (1905–1981) received both his undergraduate and graduate education at Stanford University and then went to the University of Wisconsin, where he remained until his death. He was pres-

FIGURE 9–6 The Wisconsin General Test Apparatus. (From "The Formation of Learning Sets," by H.F. Harlow, 1949, *Psychological Review, 56,* p. 52. Copyright 1949 by the American Psychological Association. Reprinted by permission.)

ident of the American Psychological Association (APA) in 1957 and was given the Distinguished Scientific Contribution Award by the APA in 1960. Through the years, Harlow has used his creative research on monkeys to shed light on a variety of topics relevant to human behavior. It is his work on the learning process that concerns us here.

Using the Wisconsin General Test Apparatus shown in Figure 9–6, Harlow (1949) confronted monkeys with a total of 344 discrimination problems, including 32 practice problems. On each problem, they were to pick the one of two objects that had a reinforcer placed underneath it. Each of the 344 problems involved a different set of objects. Harlow's remarkable finding was that the more discrimination problems the monkeys solved, the better they became at solving them. It appeared that the animals were **learning to learn,** or forming what Harlow called a **learning set.** In the early discrimination problems, the monkeys tended to make a large number of errors, and improvement from problem to problem was fairly slow. The later problems, however, tended to be solved either with only one error or with none. On the last block of 56 problems, the monkeys chose the correct object 95 percent of the time by the second trial. It was as if they had developed the strategy of "win-stay, lose-shift." That is, if they picked the correct object on the first trial, they stayed with it on the next; if their first choice was incorrect, however, they switched to the other object on the next trial. The percentage of correct responses for the first six trials of each of the discrimination problems is shown in Figure 9–7.

The gains from the early learning trials were slow and incremental in nature. Later learning, however, was very rapid and more like the all-or-none variety. Har-

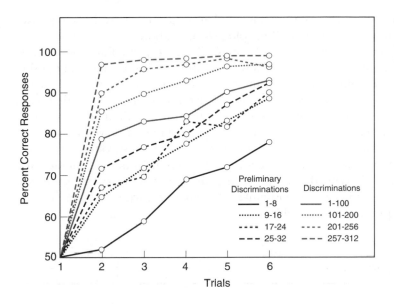

FIGURE 9–7
Harlow found a gradual
improvement in the ability to
solve discrimination
problems. Although
performance is relatively
poor on early discrimination
problems, later problems
tend to be solved in just one
trial. (From "The Formation
of Learning Sets," by H.F.
Harlow, 1949, *Psychological
Review, 56,* pp. 51–65.
Copyright 1949 by the
American Psychological
Association. Reprinted by
permission.)

low (1949) said, "Before the formation of a discrimination learning set, a single training trial produces negligible gain; after the formation of a discrimination learning set, *a single training trial constitutes problem solution.* These data clearly show that *animals can gradually learn insight*" (p. 56).

To explain his results, Harlow (1950, 1959) used the concept of **error factors.** Error factors are erroneous strategies that have to be extinguished before a discrimination problem can be solved. In other words, error factors are response tendencies that lead to incorrect responses. One error factor could be the tendency always to choose the object on the left (position preference); another might be the tendency to continue to choose the same object although it is incorrect (stimulus preservation). For Harlow, learning was a matter more of eliminating incorrect strategies (error factors) than of strengthening a correct response. Thus, early learning is slow since it involves the elimination of error factors; later learning is rapid since it is based on a strategy that can be effectively applied to all two-choice discrimination problems.

Another theorist who accepts both the slow incremental and rapid all-or-none interpretations of learning is Donald Hebb. According to Hebb, learning that occurs very early in life is of the incremental variety, whereas later learning is cognitive, insightful, and more all-or-none in nature. We will have more to say about Hebb's views of learning in Chapter 15.

THE CURRENT STATUS OF MATHEMATICAL MODELS OF LEARNING

Although we have minimized the mathematics in our coverage of Estes in this chapter, his approach is often referred to as a mathematical model of learning because he attempts to show how the learning process can be described in terms of various mathematical formulations. Mathematical models of learning are relatively new in psychology, and their newness is evident. Psychologists have always wanted to be scientific, and the language of science is mathematics. Therefore, when an opportunity came along to use mathematics in a new way in psychology, it was met with considerable enthusiasm and optimism. One of the main contributions of the mathematical study of learning has been to allow a precise description of phenomena that have been studied for years without being described in terms of mathematical models. Outside of this cleanup operation, however, mathematical models have provided little new information concerning the nature of the learning process. Currently, there is a large number of mathematical formulations, without any unifying theme running through them, to describe different learning phenomena. To say that there is a lack of synthesis is not a criticism of mathematical models of learning; rather, it characterizes any new approach to the field.

EVALUATION OF ESTES' THEORY

Contributions

Shepard (1992) sees Estes as the primary influence in changing the directions of learning theory, moving it toward a new, more cognitively oriented field characterized by "formal elegance and conceptual precision... combined with a secure grounding in observation." (p. 210).

If we compare the mathematics of SST with Hull's extended formula, we see that Estes' approach is really quite simple, using only two factors that combine through the logical principles of probability theory. Like Guthrie, his learning theory requires only contiguity, and, like Guthrie, he posits interference as the vehicle for extinction and forgetting.

In SST, however, it is the logic of probability and sampling that generates the predictions of the theory, including the familiarly shaped learning curve or the extinction curve. Similarly, it is the logic of probability theory that leads to explanation of categorical judgments in the more recent array model. Thus, we see Estes' approach as "Top-Down," beginning with a few fundamental principles and generating a variety of precise predictions about behavior.

Estes is credited by Shepard (1992) with a more important departure from the mainstream behaviorists of the 1950s. His theory was readily extended to learning in human subjects and was expanded into more and more complex kinds of learning, such as classification and concept learning (Estes, 1957, 1960 ; Estes & Burke, 1955), thus laying a groundwork for contemporary cognitive science. In addition, Bower (1994) writes

> Therefore, in a broad historical perspective, although the specific assumptions and experimental paradigms of SST have been superseded and modified over the years, the current enthusiasm for parallel distributed, connectionist models of learning and cognition [Chapter 15] may be viewed as a partial outgrowth and legacy of the SST framework. It should come as no surprise that in the current scene one of the more creative

and vigorous investigators of adaptive network models is that inimitable and indefatigable theorist, William K. Estes. (p. 298)

Criticisms

There are a number of criticisms that have been raised against Estes' theory. The first, and the one most often noted by students of learning theory, concerns the restricted scope of the theory. Earlier theories were far more ambitious than Estes' theory, building grand structures that might account for all sorts of learning phenomena. Thorndike's theory began with the mechanisms underlying learning and extended into educational practices. Even Pavlov's theory stretches beyond the learning of simple reflexive responses and into such complex phenomena as language. Estes' theory represents a trade-off between scope and precision of predictions characteristic of many mathematical-psychological theories. Even in their restricted problem areas, there are occasions where such precisely formulated theories make extreme, and sometimes incorrect, predictions (Estes, 1994; Estes & Hopkins, 1961).

Shepard (1992) raises two additional criticisms of Estes' approach. First, Estes' theory, like Guthrie's, assumes no mechanism other than stimulus-response contiguity for strengthening learning connections, although both do assume that stimulus conditions must change when a correct response is emitted. Estes, however, does not make the important distinction between contiguity and contingency identified by Rescorla.

Second, Shepard (1992) makes the observation that Estes and his colleagues allow the mathematical abstractions in the theory to severely constrain experimental conditions. If an experiment is so constrained as to become artificial, thus failing to reflect a real-world learning environment, then the results of that experiment may lack validity, and the theory itself is undermined.

DISCUSSION QUESTIONS

1. Categorize each of the following theorists as accepting either an incremental explanation of learning or an all-or-none explanation: Thorndike, Pavlov, Watson, Guthrie, Skinner, and Hull. Briefly explain your reason(s) for categorizing each theorist as you did.
2. Design an experiment that would allow one to determine clearly whether learning is incremental or all-or-none.
3. Discuss the importance of memory in the revised version of Estes's learning theory.
4. Describe Estes's scanning model of decision making.
5. Why is Estes's explanation of behavior referred to as a cybernetic model?
6. List some advantages and disadvantages of statistical learning theory.
7. From your everyday experience do you feel that learning is incremental or all-or-none? What place do personal feelings of this kind have in science? Explain.
8. Do you feel that a process similar to "learning to learn" occurs in the life of the student? Explain becoming "testwise" in terms of learning to learn.

9. How does Harlow's error factor theory of learning compare to most of the other theories of learning you have read about in this book? For example, does his theory emphasize the "stamping in" of correct responses?

10. Regarding the learning process, briefly describe the incremental (continuity) position, the all-or-none (noncontinuity) position, and the compromise position that would accent both continuity and noncontinuity at different times or for different reasons.

11. How does the size of θ influence the learning process as Estes views it? List some factors you feel might influence the size of θ.

12. What stimulus features might be used in an array model to explain how we classify leaves as "oak" or "maple?"

KEY TERMS

array model   Estes' cognitive model of classification/categorization. Stimulus features are assumed to be stored and compared in a memory array.

continuity-noncontinuity controversy   Another label for the debate over whether learning occurs gradually and in small increments or in large steps in an all-or-none fashion.

error factors   False strategies that operate against the solution of a problem. According to Harlow, learning is a matter more of eliminating error factors than of strengthening correct responses.

learning to learn   The tendency to become increasingly effective at solving problems as more problems are solved. Also called learning set.

learning set   See **learning to learn.**

Markov process   The situation whereby the probability of a response increases and decreases in a stepwise fashion rather than in small, steady amounts.

negatively accelerated learning curve   A learning curve that shows the rate of learning to be more rapid during the early trials in a learning situation than in the later trials. In other words, as the number of successive learning trials increases, the rate of learning decreases.

paired associate learning   Learning pairs of stimuli so that when subjects see the first member of the pair, they can respond by reporting the second member.

probability matching   In a situation in which subjects are asked to guess whether or not an event will occur, the proportion of the trials in which they predict the event will occur comes approximately to match the proportion of the trials that it does actually occur. For example, if a light is illuminated on 60 percent of the trials, subjects will come to predict that it will be illuminated on about 60 percent of the trials.

scanning model of decision making   Estes's description of the decision-making process as involving first learning which responses lead to which outcomes. Given this knowledge of response-outcome relationships, when the person is in a choice situation, he or she will scan the response possibilities and then choose the response that will result in the most valuable outcome.

state of the system   The proportion of stimulus elements in S that are conditioned to A_1 and A_2 responses at any given point in a learning experiment.

stimulus sampling theory (SST)   A theory such as the one developed by Estes that attempts to show how stimuli are sampled and attached to responses.

theta (θ)   The proportion of stimulus elements sampled from S at the onset of a trial in a learning experiment.

Chapter 10

GESTALT THEORY

After J. B. Watson, behaviorism became the rage among American psychologists, and since his time most eminent learning theorists, such as Guthrie, Skinner, and Hull, have been behaviorists. The behavioristic attack on the introspective method of Wundt and Titchener resulted in the almost complete abandonment of introspectionism. At about the same time the behaviorists were attacking introspection in America, a group of psychologists began attacking its use in Germany. This small group of German psychologists called themselves Gestalt psychologists. As the behavioristic movement is thought to have been launched by Watson's article "Psychology as the Behaviorist Views It," which appeared in 1913, the Gestalt movement is thought to have been launched by Max Wertheimer's article on apparent motion, which appeared in 1912.

Although Max Wertheimer (1880–1943) is considered the founder of Gestalt psychology, from its very inception he worked closely with two men who can be considered cofounders of the movement, Wolfgang Köhler (1887–1967) and Kurt Koffka (1886–1941). Köhler and Koffka acted as subjects in the first experiments performed by Wertheimer. Although all three men made significant and unique contributions to Gestalt psychology, their ideas were always in close agreement.

Apparently, the entire Gestalt movement started as the result of an insight Wertheimer had while riding a train heading for the Rhineland. It occurred to him that if two lights blink on and off at a certain rate, they give the observer the impression that one light is moving back and forth. He left the train and bought a toy stroboscope (a device that is used to present visual stimuli at various rates) with which he conducted numerous simple experiments in his hotel room. He substantiated the notion he had on the train that if the eye sees stimuli in a certain way, they give the illusion of motion, which Wertheimer called the **phi phenomenon.** His discovery was to have a profound influence on the history of psychology.

The importance of the phi phenomenon is that it is different from the elements that cause it. The sensation of motion could not be explained by analyzing each of the two lights flashing on and off; somehow the experience of motion emerged from the combination of the elements. For this reason, the members of the Gestalt school believed that although psychological experiences result from sensory elements, they are different from the sensory elements themselves. In other words, they believed that phenomenological experience (e.g., apparent motion) results from sensory experience (e.g., flashing lights) but cannot be understood by analyzing the phenomenal experience into its components. That is, *the phenomenological experience is different from the parts that make it up.*

Max Wertheimer. (From "Max Wertheimer," by W. Köhler, 1944, *Psychological Review, 51,* pp. 142–145.)

Thus, the Gestaltists, following in the Kantian tradition, believed that the organism adds something to experience that is not contained in sensory data, and that something is organization. **Gestalt** is the German word for *configuration* or *organization*. The members of this school believed that we experience the world in meaningful wholes. We do not see isolated stimuli but stimuli gathered together into meaningful configurations, or *Gestalten* (plural of *Gestalt*). We see people, chairs, cars, trees, and flowers. We do not see lines and patches of color. Our perceptual field is broken up into organized wholes, or Gestalten, and these should be the basic subject matter of psychology.

The battle cry of the Gestaltists became "the whole is different than the sum of its parts" or "to dissect is to distort." You cannot really get the full impact of the "Mona Lisa" by looking at first one arm and then another, then the nose, then the mouth, and then trying to put all these experiences together. You cannot understand the experience of listening to a symphony orchestra by analyzing the separate contributions of each of the musicians. The music emanating from the orchestra is different than the sum of the various notes being played by the various musicians. The melody has an *emergent quality*, which is something different from the sum of the parts.

OPPOSITION TO VOLUNTARISM, STRUCTURALISM, AND BEHAVIORISM

The structuralists had used the introspective method in order to discover the elements of thought. Influenced by the success of physical chemistry, they attempted to isolate the elements of thought that they believed were combined to produce our complex mental experiences. The structuralists, for example, were interested in studying the mental analog to sensation; thus, they instructed their experimental subjects to avoid naming things and otherwise reading things into their experience. Instead, they were instructed to describe their raw experiences. The structuralists were associationists in that they believed that complex ideas were made up of simpler ideas that were combined in accordance with the laws of association. Their main concern was to discover these simpler ideas that supposedly were the building blocks of more complicated thoughts.

The functionalist movement, under the influence of Darwinian thought, was gaining momentum in America and began to challenge structuralism. The functionalists were primarily concerned with how human behavior or thought processes were related to survival, and they attacked the structuralists for the irrelevance of that approach. Thus, the structuralists were being criticized even before the behaviorists came along.

The behaviorists attempted to make psychology completely scientific, and being scientific necessarily involved measurement. They concluded that the only psychological subject matter that could be reliably and publicly measured was overt behavior. The description of conscious elements, as in voluntarism and structuralism, was unreliable because it was influenced by, among other factors, the verbal ability of the reporter. Because it can be studied only indirectly, the behaviorists found consciousness a dubious subject matter for a science.

The Gestalt psychologists maintained that the voluntarists, the structuralists, and the behaviorists were all making the same basic error in using an elementistic approach. They attempted to divide up their subject matter into elements in order to understand it; the voluntarists and the structuralists sought the elemental ideas that combine to form complex thoughts, and the behaviorists attempted to understand complex behavior in terms of habits, conditioned responses, or stimulus–response combinations.

The Gestaltists saw nothing wrong with the introspective method in general, but they felt the voluntarists and the structuralists had misused it. Rather than using the introspective method to divide experiences, it should be used to investigate whole, meaningful experiences. It should be used to investigate how people perceive the world. When the technique is used in this way, it is found that a person's perceptual field consists of events that are organized and meaningful. It is these organized and meaningful events that the Gestaltists believed should be the subject matter of psychology. When these Gestalten are divided up in any way, they lose their meaning. Therefore, perceptual phenomena are to be studied directly and without further analysis. Because of this approach of studying perceptual phenomena directly, Gestalt psychology has sometimes been called **phenomenology.** A phenomenologist studies meaningful, intact mental events without dividing them up for further analysis. The term *phenomenon* means "that which is given." Following is a list of terms that have been used to describe both the Gestalt and the behavioristic approaches:

Gestalt	Behavioristic
holistic	atomistic, elementistic
molar	molecular
subjective	objective
nativistic	empiricistic
cognitive, phenomenological	behavioral

The only terms on the list whose meaning may not be obvious are *molar* and *molecular*. In general, *molar* means "large" and *molecular* means "small"; when describing behavior, however, **molar behavior** refers to a large segment of behavior that is goal-directed and purposive, and **molecular behavior** refers to a small segment of behavior, such as a conditioned reflex, that is isolated for analysis. Obviously, the former would be of more interest to the Gestalt psychologist than the latter. We will have more to say about molar behavior in our discussion of Tolman in Chapter 12.

MAJOR THEORETICAL CONCEPTS

Field Theory

Gestalt psychology can be thought of as an attempt to apply **field theory** from physics to the problems of psychology. Roughly speaking, a *field* can be defined as a dynamic interrelated system, any part of which influences every other part. The important thing about a field is that nothing in it exists in isolation. Gestalt psychologists utilized the concept of field on many levels. Gestalten themselves, for instance, can be thought of as a small field; the perceived environment can be looked on as a field; and peo-

Kurt Lewin. (From "Kurt Lewin," by E.C. Tolman, 1948, *Psychological Review,* 55, pp. 1–4.)

ple themselves can be thought of as a dynamic, interrelated system. Gestalt psychologists believed that whatever happens to a person influences everything else about him or her; for example, the world simply does not look the same if one has a sore toe or an upset stomach. For the Gestalt psychologist, the emphasis was always on a totality or whole and not on individual parts.

Kurt Lewin (1890–1947), another early Gestalt psychologist, developed a theory of human motivation around field theory. He said that human behavior at any given time is determined by the total number of psychological facts being experienced at that time. A psychological fact, according to Lewin, is anything of which a person is conscious, including being hungry, a memory of a past event, being in a certain physical location, the presence of certain other people, or having a certain amount of money. All of these psychological facts make up the person's **life space.** Some of these facts will exert a positive influence on the person's behavior and some a negative influence. It is the totality of these events that determines behavior at any given time. For Lewin, only those things consciously experienced can influence behavior; therefore, before anything experienced in the past can influence current behavior, the person must be conscious of it. A change in any psychological fact rearranges the entire life space. Thus, the causes of behavior are continually changing; they are dynamic. The person exists in a continually changing field of influences, and a change in any one of them affects all the others. This is what is meant by a psychological field theory.

Nature versus Nurture

The behaviorists tended to look on the brain as the passive receiver of sensations that, in turn, produce responses. The brain to them is a complex switchboard. Human nature, said the behaviorists, is determined by what we experience. The content of the "mind" is therefore looked on as the synthesis of our experiences, and little else. The Gestaltists assigned a more active role to the brain. The brain, to them, is not a passive receiver and storer of information from the environment. The brain acts on incoming sensory information in such a way as to make it more meaningful and organized. This is not a learned function but is the result of the brain's structure.

Being a physical system the brain creates a field that influences information entering it, much like a magnetic field influences metal particles. It is this field of forces that organizes conscious experience. What we experience consciously is sensory information *after* it has been acted on by the force fields in the brain. It is tempting to call the Gestaltists nativists because the brain's ability to organize experiences is not derived from experience. However, the Gestaltists pointed out that the brain's organizational abilities were not inherited; rather, such abilities characterized any physical system, the brain being but one example. In any case, the behaviorists postulated a passive brain that responded to and stored sensory information, and the Gestaltists postulated an active brain that transformed sensory information. With this distinction the behaviorists followed in the tradition of the British empiricists and the Gestaltists followed in the Kantian tradition.

Law of Prägnanz

The Gestalt psychologists' main concern was always with perceptual phenomena. Through the years, well over one hundred perceptual principles have been studied by Gestalt theorists. However, one overriding principle applies to all mental events, including the principles of perception, and that is the **law of Prägnanz** (*Prägnanz* is the German word for "essence"). Koffka (1963 [1935]) defined the law of Prägnanz as follows: "Psychological organization will always be as good as the controlling circumstances allow" (p. 110). By "good," Koffka meant such qualities as simple, concise, symmetrical, or harmonious. In other words, there is a tendency for every psychological event to be meaningful, complete, and simple. A good figure, a good perception, or a good memory cannot be made simpler or more orderly through any kind of perceptual shift; that is, there is nothing more we can do mentally that would make the conscious experience any more organized. The law of Prägnanz was used by the Gestaltists as their guiding principle while studying perception, learning, and memory. Later it was also applied to personality and psychotherapy.

Of the many principles of perception studied by the Gestalt theorists we will discuss only the **principle of closure** because it relates directly to the topics of learning and memory. The principle of closure states that we have a tendency to complete incomplete experiences. For example, if a person looks at a line that is almost circular except for a small gap, the person will tend to fill in the gap perceptually and respond to the figure as if it were a complete circle (see Figure 10–1). This principle, like all the others, follows the general law of Prägnanz, which says that we respond to the world so as to make it maximally meaningful under existing conditions.

FIGURE 10–1 Examples of how imcomplete figures are perceived as complete ones, thus exemplifying the principle of closure. (The cat example is from *Psychology: Understanding Human Behavior,* 4th ed., p. 229, by Q.A. Sartain, J.A. North, R.J. Strange, & M.H. Chapman, 1973, New York: McGraw-Hill. Reprinted by permission.

It is the field forces in the brain that provide for these organized, meaningful experiences. Remember that it is sensory information after it has been transformed by field forces in the brain that we experience consciously. Thus, an incomplete circle may be what we experience sensorially, but it is a complete circle that we experience consciously.

THE BRAIN AND CONSCIOUS EXPERIENCE

Every major psychological theory must in some way deal with the mind-body problem. The problem can be stated in many ways, for example, "How can something purely physical cause something purely mental?" or "What is the relationship between the body (brain) and consciousness?" No matter how elementistic one's answer becomes— even studying how individual brain cells respond to various forms of stimulation—the question concerning how the external world or patterns of neural activity are translated into conscious experience still remains.

The behaviorists solved the mind-body problem by ignoring it. In fact, they concentrated their investigations on behavior in order to avoid the mind-body problem. The voluntarists believed that the mind could willfully arrange the elements of thought into any number of configurations and that behavior was instigated by the resultant configurations. Thus, for the voluntarists an active mind profoundly influenced behavior. Following in the tradition of British empiricism, the structuralists believed that body sensations passively gave rise to, or caused, mental images. These mental images were thought to vary as a function of sensory experience and have no causal relationship to behavior. The belief that the contents of the mind vary passively as a function of sensory experience is referred to as **epiphenomenalism.** Thus, for the structuralists, there is a direct relationship between the body (sensation) and the mind (the ideas caused by sensations).

The Gestaltists took a different approach to the mind-body problem. They assumed an **isomorphism** between psychological experience and the processes that exist in the brain. External stimulation causes reactions in the brain, and we experience those reactions *as they occur in the brain.* The main difference between this point of view and the one held by the structuralists is that the Gestaltists believed that *the brain actively transformed sensory stimulation.* The brain, they thought, organized, simplified, and made meaningful incoming sensory information. We experience the information only after it has been transformed by the brain in accordance with the law of Prägnanz. Köhler (1947) said, "Experienced order in space is always structurally identical with a functional order in the distribution of underlying brain processes" (p. 61). Koffka (1963 [1935]) said, "Thus, isomorphism, a term implying equality of form, makes the bold assumption that the 'motion of the atoms and molecules of the brain' are not 'fundamentally different from thoughts and feelings' but in their molar aspects, considered as processes in extension, identical" (p. 62). Over and over, the Gestalt psychologists stated their belief that the phenomenal world (consciousness) is an accurate expression of the circumstances, that is, field forces, that exist in the brain.

With their concept of psychophysical isomorphism, the Gestaltists felt they had solved a major problem that the more mechanistic theories had not solved, that is, "How does the *mind* organize sensory information and make it meaningful?" The Gestalt psychologists answered this question by saying that the content of thought (consciousness) comes to us already organized; it is organized by the brain before we experience it or as we are experiencing it. Therefore, to the Gestaltists, *the activities of the brain correspond dynamically with the content of thought.* It should be made clear that from this point of view, the brain is much more than a complex switchboard. According to the Gestaltists, the brain actively transforms incoming sensory information according to the law of Prägnanz, and it is transformed information of which we are "conscious." The relationship among external stimulation, the brain, and conscious experience can be diagrammed as follows:

Because of their strong belief in an "active mind," the Gestaltists are clearly rationalists, and because they believe the "powers of the mind" are genetically determined, they are clearly nativists. These beliefs place them in the tradition of Plato, Descartes, and Kant.

SUBJECTIVE AND OBJECTIVE REALITY

Since we can experience impulses from the physical world only after they have been transformed by the brain, what is it that determines behavior? It cannot be the physical environment because, in a sense, we never experience the physical environment directly. For the Gestalt theorists, it is consciousness or subjective reality that determines behavior, and that fact has important implications. According to the Gestalt theorists, the law of Prägnanz is not the only thing that transforms and gives meaning to what we experience physically. Things such as beliefs, values, needs, and attitudes also embellish what we experience consciously. This means, of course, that people in exactly the same physical environment will vary in their interpretation of that environment and, therefore, in how they react to it. To make this point, Koffka distinguished between the **geographical environment** (objective or physical reality) and the **behavioral environment** (psychological or subjective reality). Koffka believed that to understand why people act as they do, it is more important to know their behavioral environments than it is to know their geographical environment. Koffka (1963 [1935]) used an old German legend to show the importance of subjective reality in determining behavior:

> On a winter evening amidst a driving snowstorm a man on horseback arrived at an inn, happy to have reached a shelter after hours of riding over the windswept plain on which the blanket of snow had covered all paths and landmarks. The landlord who came to the

door viewed the stranger with surprise and asked him whence he came. The man pointed in the direction straight away from the inn, whereupon the landlord, in a tone of awe and wonder, said: "Do you know that you have ridden across the Lake of Constance?" At which the rider dropped stone dead at his feet.

In what environment, then, did the behavior of the stranger take place? The Lake of Constance? Certainly, because it is a true proposition that he rode across it. And yet, this is not the whole truth, for the fact that there was a frozen lake and not ordinary solid ground did not affect his behavior in the slightest. It is interesting for the geographer that this behavior took place in this particular locality, but not for the psychologist as the student of behavior; because the behavior would have been just the same had the man ridden across a barren plain. But the psychologist knows something more: since the man died from sheer fright after having learned what he had "really" done, the psychologist must conclude that had the stranger known before, his riding behavior would have been very different from what it actually was. Therefore the psychologist will have to say: There is a second sense to the word environment according to which our horseman did not ride across the lake at all, but across an ordinary snow-swept plain. His behavior was a riding-over-a-plain, but not a riding-over-a-lake.

What is true of the man who rode across the Lake of Constance is true of every behavior. Does the rat run in the maze *the experimenter* has set up? According to the meaning of the word "in," yes and no. Let us therefore distinguish between a *geographical* and a *behavioral* environment. Do we all live in the same town? Yes, when we mean the geographical, no, when we mean the behavioral "in." (pp. 27–28)

Thus, according to Koffka, beliefs are powerful determinants of behavior. In this regard, he was in close agreement with the theories of Tolman and Bandura, which will be covered in Chapters 12 and 13.

GESTALT PRINCIPLES OF LEARNING

The most significant work on learning by a member of the Gestalt school was done by Köhler between 1913 and 1917 at the University of Berlin Anthropoid Station on Tenerife, one of the Canary Islands. Köhler (1925) summarized his findings in *The Mentality of Apes*. While on Tenerife, he also studied the problem-solving ability of chickens, although this work is seldom mentioned.

Since Gestalt psychologists were primarily field theorists interested in perceptual phenomena, it is no surprise to find them looking at learning as a special problem in perception. They assumed that when an organism is confronted with a problem, a state of cognitive disequilibrium is set up and continues until the problem is solved. Therefore, to the Gestalt psychologist, cognitive disequilibrium has motivational properties that cause the organism to attempt to regain the balance in its mental system. According to the law of Prägnanz, cognitive balance is more satisfying than cognitive disbalance. On this point the Gestaltists are in close agreement with both Guthrie and Hull. It can be said that problems provide maintaining stimuli (or drive, to use Hull's term), which persist until the problems are solved, at which point the maintaining stimuli terminate (the drive is reduced). Support for this point of view was provided by the work of Bluma Zeigarnik, who found that uncompleted tasks were remembered longer and in greater detail than completed ones. She explained this phenomenon in terms of the motivational properties of a problem that persist until

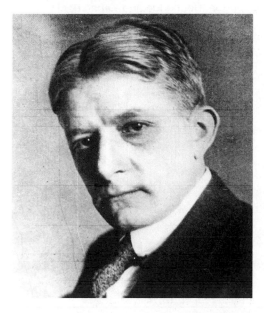

Wolfgang Köhler. (From *Psychologies of 1925*, p. 144, by C. Murchison, ed., 1926, Worcester, MA: Clark University Press.)

the problem is solved. The tendency to remember uncompleted tasks better than completed ones has come to be called the **Zeigarnik effect.**

Learning, to the Gestaltist, is a cognitive phenomenon. The organism "comes to see" the solution after pondering a problem. The learner thinks about all of the ingredients necessary to solve a problem and puts them together (cognitively) first one way and then another until the problem is solved. When the solution comes, it comes suddenly; that is, the organism gains an *insight* into the solution of a problem. The problem can exist in only two states: (1) unsolved and (2) solved; there is no state of partial solution in between. As we saw in Chapter 4, Thorndike believed that learning was continuous in that it increased systematically in small amounts as a function of reinforced trials. The Gestaltists believed that either a solution is reached or it is not; learning to them was discontinuous.

To test his notions about learning, Köhler used a number of creative experimental arrangements. One arrangement involved detour problems in which the animal can clearly see its goal but is unable to reach it directly. The animal must turn away from the sight of the object it wants and take an indirect route to reach it. A typical detour problem is diagrammed in Figure 10–2. With this type of problem, Köhler found that chickens had great difficulty in reaching a solution, but apes did so with relative ease.

A second kind of arrangement utilized by Köhler necessitated the use of an implement of some kind in reaching a goal. For example, a banana was placed just out of the reach of an ape so that the ape must either use a stick to reach it or put two sticks together so that they are long enough to reach it. In either case, the animal had all the ingredients necessary to solve the problem; it was just a matter of putting them together in an appropriate manner.

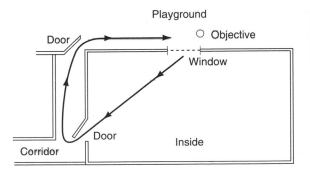

FIGURE 10–2　A typical detour problem. (From *The Mentality of Apes*, p. 21, by W. Köhler, 1925, London: Routledge and Kegan Paul Ltd.)

FIGURE 10–3 An ape named Chica using a pole to obtain food. (From *The Mentality of Apes,* p. 72a, by W. Köhler, 1925, London: Routledge and Kegan Paul Ltd.)

FIGURE 10–4 An ape named Grande using a stack of boxes to obtain food as Sultan watches. (From *The Mentality of Apes,* p. 138a, by W. Köhler, 1925, London: Routledge and Kegan Paul Ltd.)

FIGURE 10–5   Grande creating an even more elaborate structure. (From *The Mentality of Apes,* p. 152a, by W. Köhler, 1925, London: Routledge and Kegan Paul Ltd.)

Figure 10–3 shows the ape named Chica using a pole to obtain fruit. Figure 10–4 shows the ape named Grande using a stack of boxes that it arranged to reach some bananas. Figure 10–5 shows Grande putting together an even more complex structure. Figure 10–6 shows Chica using both boxes and a pole to obtain the fruit. Figure 10–7 shows Sultan, Köhler's most intelligent ape, putting together two sticks to reach fruit that otherwise would be inaccessible.

The Presolution Period

Usually a rather lengthy period of time elapses before an insightful solution to a problem is reached. Describing what happens during this period, the Gestalt psychologists came close to the concept of trial-and-error learning, but the trial-and-error learning they referred to is cognitive rather than behavioral. The organism, they said, runs through a number of "hypotheses" concerning an effective way to solve the problem. The animal *thinks* about different possible solutions until it hits on one that works, and then it acts on that solution behaviorally. When the correct strategy is discovered, insight is said to have occurred. Of course, for insightful learning to occur, the organism must be exposed to all elements of the problem; if it is not, its behavior will seem to be blind and groping. This, said the Gestaltists, was the problem with Thorndike's research. Thorndike found what appeared to be incremental learning because important elements of the problem were hidden from the animal, thus preventing insightful learning. The reader can experience the "Aha" experience that usually accompanies insightful learning by trying to find the hidden bear in Figure 10–8. Typically one searches through a good portion of the picture before the hidden shape is found. The problem creates a cognitive disequilibrium from which tension lasts until the problem is solved. In this case, discovering the bear restores cognitive equilibrium, relaxes the tension, and may make one feel like saying, "Aha."

Insightful Learning Summarized

Insightful learning is usually regarded as having four characteristics: (1) the transition from presolution to solution is sudden and complete: (2) performance based on a solution gained by insight is usually smooth and free of errors; (3) a solution to a problem gained by insight is retained for a considerable length of time; (4) a principle gained by insight is easily applied to other problems. We shall see an example of this

FIGURE 10–6 Chica beating down her objective with a pole. (From *The Mentality of Apes*, p. 146a, by W. Köhler, 1925, London: Routledge and Kegan Paul Ltd.)

FIGURE 10–7 Sultan putting two sticks together.(From *The Mentality of Apes,* p. 128a, by W. Köhler, 1925, London: Routledge and Kegan Paul Ltd.)

FIGURE 10–8   Can you find the hidden bear? (From Introduction to Psychology, p. 164, by N.L. Munn, D.L. Fernald, Jr., & P.S. Fernald, 1972, Boston: Houghton Mifflin.)

gained by insight is easily applied to other problems. We shall see an example of this last characteristic in our discussion of transposition.

Transposition

When a principle learned in one problem-solving situation is applied to the solution of another problem, the process is referred to as **transposition.** Köhler's early work on transposition was done with chickens and apes. The typical experiment involved training an animal to approach one of two shades of gray paper; for example, chickens were fed on a dark shade of gray paper but not on a lighter shade. After such training, when the animal was given a choice between the two shades of gray, it approached the darker one. If the experiment was to end at this point, the behaviorists would be pleased since that is exactly how the animal should react according to their point of view. It is the second part of the experiment, however, that the Gestaltists felt was most revealing.

After the preliminary training, the animal was given a choice between the dark paper on which it was trained and a still darker sheet of gray paper. The situation is diagrammed in Figure 10–9. How will the animal respond to the new situation? The answer to that question depends on how one views the learning process. The Gestaltists felt that the behaviorists would have to predict that the animal would approach the lighter of the two shades of gray in the new situation since it is the exact one that had been reinforced in the first phase of the experiment. The Gestaltists, however, did not view learning as the development of specific habits or S-R connections. To them what was learned in this kind of a situation was a relational principle; that is, they

Stimuli: Used During Preliminary Training

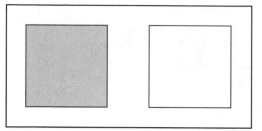

FIGURE 10–9 First the animal is taught to approach a dark gray stimulus and then is offered a choice between the dark gray stimulus and a still darker gray stimulus. If the animal chooses the darker of the two, transposition is said to have been demonstrated.

Stimuli: Used During the Transposition Test

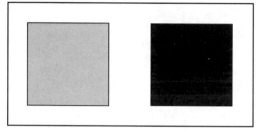

felt that the animal learned the principle of approaching *the darker of the two objects* in the first phase of the experiment and that that same principle would be applied in the second phase of the experiment. The Gestaltists predicted, therefore, that the animal would choose the darker of the two objects in phase 2, although they had been reinforced for choosing the other object in phase 1. Generally speaking, the prediction made by the Gestalt psychologists in this situation is accurate.

The Behaviorists' Explanation of Transposition

In the kind of learning situation described above, the behaviorists tend to talk about the learning of specific S-R connections. As a result, their views on learning have been referred to as an **absolute theory.** In contrast, since the Gestalt view of learning emphasizes the comparison between the two stimuli, it has been referred to as a **relational theory.** Köhler's research created some problems for the absolute position until Spence came up with his explanation of the transposition phenomenon based on S-R concepts (Spence, 1937).

Suppose, said Spence, that an animal is reinforced for approaching a box whose lid measures 160 square centimeters, and not reinforced for approaching a box whose lid measures 100 square centimeters. Soon the animal will learn to approach the larger box exclusively. In phase 2 of this experiment, the animal chooses between the 160 square centimeter box and a box whose lid is 256 square centimeters. The animal will usually choose the larger box (256 square centimeters) even though the animal had been reinforced specifically for choosing the other one (160 square centimeters) during phase 1. This finding seems to support the relational learning point of view.

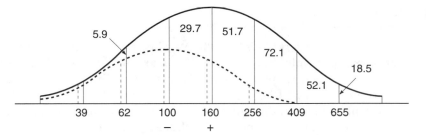

FIGURE 10–10 According to Spence's explanation of transposition, the tendency to avoid a stimulus (dashed curve) must be subtracted from the tendency to approach a stimulus (solid curve). It is the net value that results when these positive and negative influences are added algebraically that determines which of the two stimuli will be approached. (From "The Basis of Solution by Chimpanzees of the Intermediate Size Problem," by K.W. Spence, 1942, *Journal of Experimental Psychology, 31,* p. 259.)

Spence's behavioristic explanation of transposition is based on generalization. As was mentioned in Chapter 6, Spence assumed that the tendency to approach the positive stimulus (160 square centimeters) generalizes to other related stimuli. Second, he assumed that the tendency to approach the positive stimulus (and the generalization of this tendency) is stronger than the tendency to avoid the negative stimulus (and the generalization of this tendency). What behavior occurs will be determined by the algebraic summation of the positive and negative tendencies. Spence's explanation is diagrammed in Figure 10–10.

Whenever there is a choice between two stimuli, the one eliciting the greatest net approach tendency will be chosen. In the first phase of Spence's experiment, the animal chose the 160-square-centimeter box over the 100-square-centimeter box because the net positive tendency was 51.7 for the former and 29.7 for the latter. In phase 2, the 256-square-centimeter box was chosen over the 160-square-centimeter box because the net positive tendency was 72.1 for the former and still 51.7 for the latter.

Spence's explanation has the advantage of making some unexpected predictions of transpositional phenomena. For example, his theory would predict that transposition should break down at some point, and in the example above, the animal would choose the smaller object in a pair of test stimuli. This choice would occur if the animal were presented with a 256-square-centimeter box and any box larger than 409 square centimeters. In all choices involving a 256-square-centimeter box and a box 409 square centimeters or larger, the animal will choose the *smaller of the two,* thereby reversing the principle the animal was supposed to have learned. Likewise, if the animal is given a choice between a 160 square-centimeter box and one slightly larger than 409 square centimeters, the choices will be about equally divided since the net positive tendency for each box is about the same.

Since Spence's theory could predict both the successes and failures of the transposition phenomenon, his point of view was more widely accepted than the Gestalt point of view. Research on various aspects of transposition, however, has demonstrated that both S-R and Gestalt predictions fail under certain circumstances, and the matter is still unsettled.

PRODUCTIVE THINKING

During the later years of his life, Max Wertheimer was especially interested in applying Gestalt principles to education. His book *Productive Thinking*, which addressed educational issues, was published in 1945, two years after his death, and was expanded and republished in 1959 under the editorship of his son Michael. In his book, Wertheimer explored the nature of problem solving and the techniques that could be used to teach it, that is, **productive thinking.** The conclusions reached were based on personal experience, experimentation, and personal interviews with individuals such as Albert Einstein. For example, Chapter 10 in his book is entitled "Einstein: The Thinking That Led to the Theory of Relativity."

Wertheimer contrasted rote memorization with problem solving based on Gestalt principles. With the former, the learner learns facts or rules without truly understanding them. Such learning is rigid, forgotten easily, and can be applied only to limited circumstances. Learning in accordance with Gestalt principles, however, is based on an understanding of the underlying nature of the problem. Such learning comes from within the individual and is not imposed by someone else; it is easily generalizable and remembered for a long time.

When one acts on memorized facts or rules without understanding them one can often make stupid mistakes, such as when a nurse, while making her rounds on the night shift, wakes up patients to give them their sleeping pills (Michael Wertheimer, 1980). As a further example of what can result if basic principles are not understood, Wertheimer (1959 [1945], pp. 269–270) gave the example of a school inspector who was impressed by the children he had observed but wanted to ask one more question before departing. "How many hairs does a horse have?" he asked. Much to the amazement of both the inspector and the teacher, a 9-year-old boy raised his hand and answered, "3,571,962." "How do you know that your answer is correct?" asked the inspector. "If you do not believe me," answered the boy, "count them yourself." The inspector broke into laughter and vowed to tell the story to his colleagues when he returned to Vienna. When the inspector returned the following year for his annual visit, the teacher asked him how his colleagues responded to the story. Disappointedly, the inspector said, "I wanted very much to tell the story but I couldn't. For the life of me, I couldn't remember how many hairs the boy had said the horse had." Although the story was admittedly hypothetical, Wertheimer used it to demonstrate what can happen if a person depends on memorized facts instead of on the understanding of principles.

Wertheimer insisted that two traditional approaches to teaching actually inhibit the development of understanding. The first is teaching that emphasizes the importance of logic. Both inductive and deductive logic prescribe rules that must be followed in arriving at conclusions. Although such rules may have relevance for a narrow range of problems, they do not, according to Wertheimer (1959 [1945]), facilitate problem-solving ability. "Traditional logic is concerned with the criteria that guarantee exactness, validity, consistency of general concepts, propositions, inferences and syllogisms. The main chapters of classical logic refer to these topics. To be sure, sometimes the rules of traditional logic remind one of an efficient police manual for regulating traffic" (p. 6).

According to Wertheimer, reaching an understanding involves many aspects of learners, such as their emotions, attitudes, and perceptions, as well as their intellects. In gaining insight into the solution to a problem, a student need not—in fact should not—be logical. Rather, the student should cognitively arrange and rearrange the components of the problem until a solution based on understanding is reached. Exactly how this process is done will vary from student to student.

The second teaching strategy believed by Wertheimer to inhibit understanding is based on the doctrine of associationism. This approach to teaching typically emphasizes the learning of correct S-R connections through drill, memorization, and external reinforcement. Although Wertheimer believed that learning does occur under these circumstances, he believed it to be trivial compared to insightful learning. Wertheimer (1959 [1945]) made the following comment about teaching based on associationism: "Basically the items are connected in the way in which my friend's telephone number is connected with his name, in which nonsense syllables become reproducible when learned in a series of such syllables, or in which a dog is conditioned to respond with salivation to a certain musical sound" (p. 8).

Wertheimer believed that any teaching strategy based either on associationism or on logic could do little to enhance understanding but could do a great deal to inhibit it.

As an example of the difference between rote memorization of facts or rules and understanding based on insight, Wertheimer gave the example of students learning to determine the area of a parallelogram. The standard way of teaching children to find the area of a parallelogram is as follows:

1. First students are taught how to find the area of a rectangle by multiplying its altitude by its base.
2. Next a parallelogram is introduced and the teacher demonstrates how it is converted into a rectangle by drawing three lines as follows:

3. Once converted into a rectangle the area can be found by multiplying altitude times base.

Wertheimer discovered that following such training, students could find the areas of parallelograms presented in a standard way but many were confused when figures were presented in a nonstandard way or when they were asked to find the areas of geometric forms other than parallelograms. An example of a figure that caused confusion in some students is shown in Figure 10–11. Other students, however, seemed to

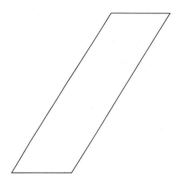

FIGURE 10–11 An example of a figure that caused confusion in students who attempted to find its area by dropping perpendicular lines from the two upper corners to the baseline. (From *Productive Thinking,* p. 15, by M. Wertheimer, 1959, New York: Harper & Row. Copyright © 1945, 1959 by Valentin Wertheimer. Reprinted by permission of Harper & Row, Publishers, Inc.)

grasp the principle behind the formula. They saw that a rectangle was a balanced figure that could be subdivided into columns and rows of small squares which when multiplied together gave the number of squares in the entire rectangle, or its area. For example,

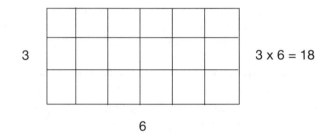

It was this conceptualization that was behind the formula altitude x base. Students with this insight knew that the manipulations done on the parallelogram merely rearranged the configuration so that the squares could be easily counted. Students understanding the "squares solution" were able to solve a wide variety of problems that the other students without such an understanding were unable to solve. The students who had gained insight into the nature of the problem knew that their task was to take whatever form was presented to them and rearrange it so that its area was represented as a rectangle.

Figure 10–12 shows three figures presented to students and how the students with an understanding of the principle involved found their areas as compared to the students who blindly attempted to apply the rule they had been taught to reach their solutions. Note that when students attempted to apply the formula that they had memorized in finding the areas of these figures, their results were incorrect.

When the insight of rearranging a geometric form so that its area is represented as a rectangle is reached, students know which kinds of problems can be solved by using this principle and which cannot. Students with this insight know that the "excesses" in the forms on the left in Figure 10–13 equal the indentations, and therefore they can be solved by using this principle; the figures on the right cannot.

The students solving the problems with understanding seem to see the various

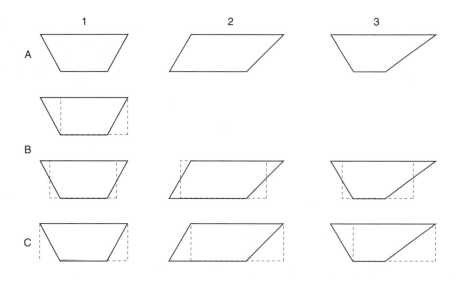

FIGURE 10–12 The portion of the figure labeled A indicates the forms presented to students. The portion of the figure labeled B shows how students with an understanding of the problem found the areas of the forms. The portion of the figure labeled C indicates how students without an understanding of the problem attempted to find the areas of the forms. (From *Productive Thinking,* p. 18, by M. Wertheimer, 1959, New York: Harper & Row. Copyright © 1945, 1959 by Valentin Wertheimer. Reprinted by permission of Harper & Row, Publishers, Inc.)

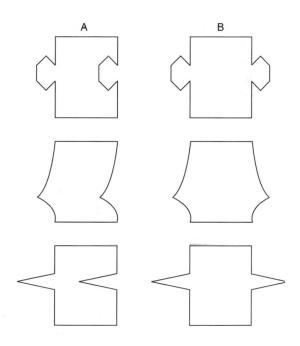

FIGURE 10–13 The areas of the forms in Column A can be found using the strategy of balancing excesses and discrepancies, whereas the areas of the forms in Column B cannot be. (From *Productive Thinking,* p. 19, by M. Wertheimer, 1959, New York: Harper & Row. Copyright © 1945, 1959 by Valentin Wertheimer. Reprinted by permission of Harper & Row, Publishers, Inc.)

Cut

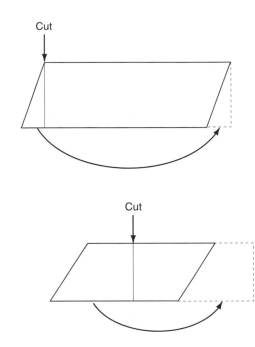

Cut

FIGURE 10–14 Two methods used by students to convert a parallelogram into a rectangle. (From *Productive Thinking*, p. 48, by M. Wertheimer, 1959, New York: Harper & Row. Copyright © 1945, 1959 by Valentin Wertheimer. Reprinted by permission of Harper & Row, Publishers, Inc.)

figures as having "too much here" and "not enough there." Their goal, then, becomes one of balancing the figures so that the part that is "too much" is placed in the part of the figure where there is "not enough." In this way the "strange" figures are converted into ones they are familiar with and therefore can be dealt with. This rearrangement can be cognitive or physical. For example, one of the students that Wertheimer worked with asked for a scissors and cut one end of the parallelogram and placed it on the other end, thus creating a rectangle. Another student asked for a scissors and cut the parallelogram in the middle and fastened the two pieces together, creating a rectangle. These operations are shown in Figure 10–14.

Wertheimer emphasized the same point over and over. That is, learning based on understanding is deeper and more generalizable than learning involving rote memorization. To truly learn, students must come to see the nature or the structure of the problem and this they must do themselves. It is true that a teacher can guide students to such insights, but ultimately they must occur within the students themselves.

In closing this section, one additional example of the difference between rote memorization and understanding will be offered. Michael Wertheimer (1980) describes an experiment performed by Katona in 1940. In this experiment, a slip with the following fifteen digits was handed to a group of subjects with the instruction that they study the digits for fifteen seconds:

1 4 9 1 6 2 5 3 6 4 9 6 4 8 1

After the subjects observed the list of digits, they were asked to reproduce the sequence of numbers in the order that they appeared. Most subjects were able to reproduce only a few of the numbers. After a week most of the subjects remembered none of the digits. Another group of subjects was asked, prior to seeing the series of digits, to look for a pattern among the digits. Upon seeing the series some of these subjects declared, "Those are the squares of the digits from 1 to 9." The subjects who saw the pattern were able to reproduce the series perfectly not only during the experiment but also weeks and months afterward. Thus we see again that learning based on an understanding of the principles involved in a problem-solving situation is very thorough and is retained almost perfectly for long periods of time. Also note that no external reinforcement was involved in this experiment. The only reinforcement was intrinsic and came when the learner gained an insight into the solution of the problem. The emphasis on intrinsic reinforcement as opposed to extrinsic reinforcement has characterized most of the cognitive theories since the early work of the Gestalt psychologists.

THE MEMORY TRACE

We mentioned earlier that Gestalt psychologists emphasized the fact that the brain is a physical system that generates field forces. These forces, in turn, transform the sensory information entering them and thus determine conscious experience. This analysis gives the impression that the Gestaltists ignored or minimized the influence of past experience, but this impression is incorrect. Koffka (1963 [1935]) attempted to link the past with the present through his concept of the **memory trace.** His treatment of the memory trace is long and complicated, and only a rudimentary sketch of it can be presented here.

Koffka assumed that a current experience gives rise to what he called a **memory process.** The process is the activity in the brain caused by an environmental experience. This process could be simple or complex, depending on the experience it is based on. When a process is terminated, a trace of its effect remains in the brain. This trace, in turn, will influence all similar processes that occur in the future. According to this point of view, a process, which is caused by an experience, can occur only once in "pure" form; thereafter similar experiences result from the interaction between the process and the memory trace. Thus, each time a process is aroused, it modifies the organism and that modification influences future experiences. In fact, Koffka said, if one defines learning as a modification in behavior potential that results from experience, each elicitation of a process can be looked on as a learning experience.

Kurt Koffka. (From *Psychologies of 1925,* by C. Murchison, ed., 1926, Worcester, MA: Clark University Press.)

What is the nature of the influence of the trace on the process? Koffka (1963 [1935]) answered that a trace "exerts an influence on the process in the direction of *making it similar to the process which originally produced the trace*" (p. 553). The stronger the memory trace, the stronger will be its influence on the process; therefore, one's conscious experience will tend to be more in accordance with the trace than with the process.

According to this point of view, if the last thing one did in a problem-solving situation was to solve the problem, the solution becomes "etched" in one's mind. The next time one is in a similar problem-solving situation, a process will occur that will "communicate" with the trace from the previous problem-solving situation. The trace then will influence the ongoing process in the direction stated above, making the problem easier to solve. With repetition the trace becomes more and more influential over the process. In other words, as the animal solves more problems that are similar, it becomes a better problem solver. Koffka explained improvement in a skill as the result of the increasing influence of the trace on the process.

At this point in Gestalt theorizing, we see considerable agreement with Guthrie. It seems, for example, that Koffka accepted the recency principle, which states that what an organism did last in a situation is what it will do if the situation recurs. Likewise, as we shall see below, the Gestaltists are in essential agreement with Guthrie's explanation of how repetition results in improvement of a skill.

Individual Trace versus Trace System

Solving an individual problem is only a specific occurrence of problem-solving behavior, and learning to type the letters *A, B,* and *C* are only specific occurrences of the more general behavior we call typing. Every complex skill can be looked on as consisting of many processes and their corresponding traces, and yet each **individual memory trace** is related to the same skill. Numerous interrelated individual traces are referred to as a **trace system.** Koffka (1963 [1935]) assumed that through repetition the trace system becomes more important than the individual traces that make it up. The "wholeness" quality of the skill comes to dominate the individual traces, thereby causing them to lose their individuality. This phenomenon may at first seem paradoxical; that is, repetition can help in learning although it tends to destroy the traces of individual experiences:

> There is loss of consolidation of the *single individual* traces which we are apt to overlook because it is accompanied by a gain in the stability *trace system*. When we learn to type, the individual lessons will soon be forgotten, and the clumsy movements which we originally executed will at a later stage be impossible; i.e., the traces of the first lessons have become changed by the aggregate of traces which has been produced by the many repetitions and is responsible for the improvement of the skill. Similarly, when we stay in a room for any length of time, we get a great number of impressions of it by moving about or merely letting our eyes roam. But only a few of them can be recalled. (p. 545)

Just as the individual trace exerts a greater influence on future processes as it becomes more fixed, so does the trace system exert greater influence on related processes as it becomes more fixed. This contention has very interesting implications. For example, it is assumed that through the years we develop trace systems that correspond to similar experiences. Thus we develop trace systems that correspond to chairs, dogs, trees, males, females, or pencils. These trace systems will be a kind of neurological summation of all our experiences with objects in a certain class, such as cows or clowns. Since these trace systems become firmly established, they will have a profound effect on any individual experience we may have. For example, if we look at an individual elephant, the process aroused by that elephant will be influenced by the trace system that resulted from all of our other experiences with elephants. The resulting experience will be a combination of the two influences, with the trace system being the most important. Our memory of that event, then, will be one of "elephantness" that has little to do with any particular elephant but has more to do with what they have in common. This theory also serves to explain the phenomenon of closure. The individual experience of a partial circle is dominated by the trace system of "circleness," and the resulting experience is one of a complete circle.

Memory, like perception and learning, follows the law of Prägnanz. Memories tend to be complete and meaningful, even when the original experience was not. Irregular experiences tend to be remembered as regular, unique events are remembered in terms of something familiar (e.g., a catlike object will be remembered as a cat), and minor flaws or discrepancies in a figure will tend to be forgotten. It is the enduring features of past experience, rather than uncommon occurrences, that guide our behavior. Again, the emphasis is on the pattern, the Gestalt, the wholeness of experience and the recollection of experience. This theory is contrasted with the association theory of memory that is accepted by the behaviorists. The associationists accept the "bundle hypothesis," which states that complex thoughts are made up of simple ideas bound together by contiguity, similarity, or contrast. Memory occurs when one element in the bundle causes the recall of the other elements. The Gestaltists rejected association theory in favor of the law of Prägnanz in explaining all aspects of human experience, including perception, learning, and memory.

Behaviorism had nothing to say about perception, and early Gestalt theory had little or nothing to say about learning. But when the Gestaltists fled to America from Nazi Germany, they began to address the problem of learning because it was a major interest of American psychologists. Gestalt theory was clearly better able to handle problems in perception, mostly because behaviorism, in excluding mental events from its domain of study, ignored the topic of perception. So on the one hand we had the Gestalt theorists attempting to expand their perceptual theory to cover learning, and on the other hand, we had the behaviorists ignoring perceptual learning. As usual, accepting a paradigm as an ideology blinded both the Gestaltists and the behaviorists to important aspects of the learning process. Fortunately, later thinkers have attempted to utilize the best of both paradigms. A good example of an effort to combine the two paradigms is Tolman's theory of learning, to which we turn in Chapter 12.

The healthy debate between the Gestalt psychologists and the behaviorists resulted in the modification of each point of view because of criticism from the other. Both positions were extreme and both have left an indelible mark on psychology. Thanks, to a large extent, to the Gestalt psychologists the study of cognitive processes is no longer taboo. However, cognitive processes currently are being studied under rigorous laboratory conditions under such headings as risk taking, problem solving, and concept formation. For the insistence on operationally defining these concepts and indexing them behaviorally, we can thank the behavioristic influence.

EVALUATION OF GESTALT THEORY

Contributions

An important contribution of Gestalt psychology was its criticism of the molecular or atomistic approaches of S-R behaviorism. Crucial to this criticism were demonstrations that both perception and learning were characterized by cognitive processes that organized psychological experience. Like Kant, the Gestalt psychologists posited that the brain automatically transformed and organized experiences, adding qualities that were not inherent in the sensory experience. The organizational processes identified by Wertheimer and his colleagues have had enormous impact on the fields of learning, perception, and psychotherapy, and they continue to influence contemporary cognitive sciences.

Gestalt psychology provided challenges that were productive even for behavioristic researchers. Spence's (1942) brilliant research on transposition, for example, was made necessary by Köhler's cognitive explanation of transposition. The Gestalt psychologists' focus on insightful learning also provided an alternative way of conceptualizing reinforcement. By drawing attention to the satisfaction that comes from discovery or from solving problems, Gestalt psychology turned our attention from extrinsic to intrinsic reinforcement.

Criticisms

Although Gestalt psychology did offer important challenges to behaviorism, it never attained mainstream status in learning theory. Behavioristic psychologists were interested in reducing the problem of learning to the most simple models possible, accumulating a vast store of data concerning the smallest problems in learning, and then building more global theories from tested elementary principles. When Gestalt psychologists joined the quest, they described learning in terms of "understanding," "meaning," and "organization," concepts that were themselves all but meaningless in the context of behavioristic research. Estes (1954) reflected the attitude of the dominant behavioristic school toward Gestalt learning theory:

> Typically the [Gestalt] theorists have developed their systems in other areas, then have attempted to collect the psychology of learning as an extra dividend without much additional investment....From the writings of Köhler, Koffka, Hartmann, and Lewin one would gather that field interpretations of learning are demonstrably superior to all others. From the experimental literature on learning, on the other hand, one would conclude that if this view is correct, then the most superior theories of learning have had the least influence upon research. (p. 341)

DISCUSSION QUESTIONS

1. What was it about the approaches to the study of psychology used by the structuralists, and the behaviorists that the Gestalt theorists disagreed with?
2. What is meant by the statement "The law of *Prägnanz* was used by the Gestalt psychologists as an overriding principle in their explanation of perception, learning, memory, personality, and psychotherapy"?
3. Discuss the term *isomorphism* as it was used in Gestalt theory.
4. Distinguish between geographical and behavioral environments. Which of the two did the Gestalt theorists believe was the more important determinant of behavior? Explain why you do or do not agree with the Gestalt theorists on this matter.
5. Discuss the topic of memory from the point of view of a Gestalt psychologist. Include in your answer the concepts of memory process, individual memory trace, and trace system.
6. Explain transposition from both a Gestalt and a behavioristic point of view.
7. Summarize the characteristics of insightful learning.
8. What is meant by the statement "For the Gestalt psychologist, learning is basically a perceptual phenomenon"?
9. List some differences between classroom procedures developed according to Gestalt principles and those developed according to S-R principles. In general, do you feel American public schools are based on a Gestalt model or a behavioristic model? Explain.
10. Summarize Wertheimer's thoughts on productive thinking. Include in your answer some of the differences between solutions to problems that are based on rote memorization and those based on an understanding of the principles involved in the problem.

KEY TERMS

absolute theory   The contention of the behaviorists that what an organism learns are specific responses to specific stimuli.

behavioral environment   According to Koffka, the environment as it is consciously experienced. Also referred to as subjective reality.

epiphenomenalism   The belief that body sensations cause mental images. In other words, mental images are seen as the byproducts of body experiences.

field theory   The belief that the environment consists of interdependent events. In psychology, field theory assumes that behavior or cognitive processes are a function of many variables that exist simultaneously, and a change in any one of them changes the effect of all the others.

geographical environment   According to Koffka, the physical or objective environment. Also referred to as objective reality.

Gestalt   A German word meaning "pattern" or "configuration."

individual memory trace   The memory trace left by a specific experience.

insightful learning   Learning that occurs very rapidly, is remembered for a considerable length of time, and transfers readily to situations related to the one in which the insightful learning took place.

isomorphism   As the term was used by the Gestalt psychologists, it means the relationship that exists between brain activity and consciousness.

law of Prägnanz   The overriding principle in Gestalt psychology, which states that all mental events tend toward completeness, simplicity, and meaningfulness.

life space   A concept employed by Kurt Lewin to describe the simultaneous influences on a person at a given time. Anything that can affect behavior was called a "psychological fact," and the total number of "psychological facts" influencing a person at any given moment was his or her life space.

memory process   The brain activity that is caused by environmental stimulation.

memory trace   The remnants of an environmental experience after the experience is terminated.

molar behavior   A large segment of behavior that is goal—directed and therefore purposive.

molecular behavior   A small segment of behavior, such as a conditioned reflex, that is isolated for detailed study.

phenomenology   The study of intact, meaningful mental events. These intact, meaningful mental events are called phenomenological experiences, which structuralists wanted their subjects to avoid actively and Gestalt psychologists felt were the basic subject matter of psychology.

phi phenomenon   The experience of apparent motion that is caused by lights flashing on and off at a certain frequency. Wertheimer's discovery of apparent motion launched the Gestalt school of psychology.

principle of closure   Tendency to complete incomplete experiences, thereby making them more meaningful.

productive thinking   Wertheimer's term for thinking that is based on the understanding of the principles involved in a problem rather than on logic or the rote memorization of facts or rules.

relational theory   The contention of the Gestalt psychologists that organisms should learn principles or relationships and not specific responses to specific stimuli.

trace system   A number of interrelated individual memory traces.

transposition   The Gestalt version of transfer of training, which states that a principle that works in solving a problem will tend to be applied to the solution of similar problems.

Zeigarnik effect   The tendency to remember uncompleted tasks longer than completed ones.

Chapter 11

JEAN PIAGET

Jean Piaget was born on August 9, 1896, in Neuchâtel, Switzerland. His father was a historian whose specialty was medieval literature. Piaget showed early interest in biology and when only 11 years old he published a one-page article on a partially albino sparrow he had seen in a park. Between 15 and 18, he published a number of articles on mollusks. Piaget noted that because of his many publications, he was accidentally offered the position of curator of the mollusk collection in the Geneva Museum while he was still a secondary school student.

As an adolescent, Piaget vacationed with his godfather, who was a Swiss scholar. It was through this visit with his godfather that Piaget developed an interest in philosophy in general and in **epistemology** in particular. (Epistemology is a branch of philosophy that is concerned with the nature of knowledge.) Piaget's interests in biology and epistemology continued throughout his life and were clearly evident almost everywhere in his theoretical writings.

Piaget received his Ph.D. in biology at the age of 21, and by the time he was 30 he had published over 20 papers, mainly on mollusks but on other topics as well. For example, at the age of 23, he published an article on the relationship between psychoanalysis and child psychology. After receiving his doctorate, Piaget held a variety of jobs, among them a position with the Binet Testing Laboratory in Paris, where he helped to standardize intelligence tests. The Binet Laboratory's approach to testing was to develop a number of test questions, which were then presented to children of different ages. It was found that older children could answer more questions correctly than younger children and that some children could answer more questions correctly than other children of the same age. The former children were considered to be more intelligent than the latter children. Thus, the child's intelligence quotient was derived from the number of questions a child of a certain age could answer correctly. It was during his employment at the Binet Laboratory that Piaget developed his interest in the intellectual abilities of children. This interest, as well as his interests in biology and epistemology, permeated all of Piaget's work.

While working on the standardization of intelligence tests, Piaget noted something that was to have a major influence on his later theory of intellectual development. He discovered that a child's *incorrect* answers to test questions were more informative than the correct answers. He observed that the same kind of mistakes were made by children of approximately the same age and that the kind of mistakes generally made by children of one age was *qualitatively* different from the kinds of mistakes made by children of different ages. Piaget observed further that the nature of these mistakes could not be explored adequately in a highly structured testing situa-

Jean Piaget. (Courtesy of the Université de Genève.)

tion, in which children either answered questions correctly or they did not. Instead, Piaget employed the **clinical method,** which was an open-ended form of questioning. Using the clinical method, Piaget's questions were determined by the child's answers. If the child would say something of interest, Piaget would formulate a number of questions designed to explore that item further.

During his employment at the Binet Laboratory Piaget began to realize that "intelligence" could not be equated with the number of test items that a child answered correctly. To Piaget, the more basic question was *why* some children were able to answer some questions correctly and other children were not, or why a child could answer some items correctly but miss other items. Piaget began his search for the variables influencing the test performance of children. His search was to result in a view of intelligence that some consider to be as revolutionary as Freud's view of human motivation.

Piaget left Binet's laboratory to become director of research at the Jean-Jacques Rousseau Institute in Geneva, Switzerland, where he was able to pursue his own interests, using his own methods. Soon after his affiliation with the institute, his first major works on developmental psychology began to appear. Piaget, who never had a course in psychology, soon became an internationally known authority on child psychology. He continued his work, using his own three children as subjects. He and his wife (a former student of his at the Rousseau Institute) made careful observations about their children over a long period of time and summarized their findings in several books. That Piaget's own children were used as sources of information in the development of his theory has often been criticized. The fact that more elaborate observations, involving large numbers of other children, have been in agreement with Piaget's earlier observations has tended, however, to still this criticism.

Piaget published about 30 books and over 200 articles and continued doing productive research at the University of Geneva until his death in 1980. His theory of intellectual development in the child was extensive and complicated, and in this chapter we merely will summarize its essential features. It will also become apparent that Piaget's explanation of the learning process is different from all the other explanations in this text.

The information in this chapter was compiled from several sources. The secondary sources were Beard, 1969; Flavell, 1963; Furth, 1969; Ginsburg and Opper, 1979; and Phillips, 1975, 1981. The primary sources were Inhelder and Piaget, 1958; Piaget, 1966, 1970a, 1970b; and Piaget and Inhelder, 1969.

MAJOR THEORETICAL NOTIONS

Intelligence

We noted earlier that Piaget was opposed to defining **intelligence** in terms of the number of items answered correctly on a so-called intelligence test. To Piaget, an intelligent act is one that causes an approximation to the conditions optimal for an organism's survival. In other words, intelligence allows an organism to deal effectively with its environment. Since both the environment and the organism are changing constantly, an "intelligent" interaction between the two must also change constantly.

An intelligent act always tends to create optimal conditions for the organism's survival *under the existing circumstances.* Thus, for Piaget, intelligence is a dynamic trait since what is available as an intelligent act will change as the organism matures biologically and as it gains experience. Intelligence, according to Piaget, is an integral part of any living organism since all living organisms seek those conditions conducive to their survival, but how intelligence manifests itself at any given time will necessarily vary as conditions vary. Piaget's theory has often been referred to as **genetic epistemology** since it attempts to trace the development of intellectual capabilities. It should be clear that here the term *genetic* refers to developmental growth rather than biological inheritance. Piaget's views on how intellectual potential develops will be summarized in the remainder of this chapter.

Schemata

A child is born with a few highly organized reflexes such as sucking, looking, reaching, and grasping. Rather than discussing individual occurrences of any one of these reflexes, Piaget chose to talk about the general potential to do such things as suck, look, reach, or grasp. The potential to act in a certain way was labeled **schema** (plural: *schemata*). For example, the grasping schema refers to the general ability to grasp things. The schema is more than a single manifestation of the grasping reflex. The grasping schema can be thought of as the cognitive structure that makes all acts of grasping possible.

When any particular instance of grasping is being observed or described, one must talk in terms of a specific response to specific stimuli. These aspects of any particular manifestation of a schema are called **content.** Again, *schema* refers to a general potential to perform a class of behaviors, and *content* describes the conditions that prevail during any particular manifestation of that general potential.

Schema was an extremely important term in Piaget's theory. A schema can be thought of as an element in the organism's cognitive structure. The schemata available to an organism will determine how it can respond to the physical environment. Schemata can manifest themselves in overt behavior, as in the case of the grasping reflex, or they can manifest themselves covertly. Covert manifestations of a schema can be equated roughly with thinking. We will have more to say about covert manifestations of a schema later in this chapter. In both overt behavior and in thinking, the term *content* refers to the specifics of a particular manifestation of a schema.

Obviously, the way a child is able to deal with its environment changes as he or she grows older. For new organism-environment interactions to occur, the schemata available to the child must change. We will examine next the circumstances under which schemata change.

Assimilation and Accommodation

As we saw above, the number of schemata available to an organism at any given time constitutes that organism's **cognitive structure.** How an organism interacts with its environment will depend on the kind of cognitive structure it has available. In fact, how much of the environment can be understood, or even responded to, is determined by the various schemata available to the organism. In other words, the cognitive structure determines what aspects of the physical environment can even "exist" for the organism.

The process of responding to the environment in accordance with one's cognitive structure is called **assimilation,** which refers to a kind of matching between the cognitive structures and the physical environment. The cognitive structure that exists at any given moment sets bounds on what can be assimilated by the organism. For example, if only the sucking, looking, reaching, and grasping schemata are available to a child, everything she or he experiences will be assimilated into those schemata. As the cognitive structure changes it becomes possible for the child to assimilate different aspects of the physical environment.

Clearly, if assimilation were the only cognitive process, there would be no intellectual growth since an organism would simply go on assimilating its experiences into its existing cognitive structure. However, a second, equally important process provides a mechanism for intellectual growth: **accommodation,** the process by which the cognitive structure is modified.

Every experience a person has involves both assimilation and accommodation. Events for which the organism has corresponding schemata are readily assimilated, but events for which the organism has no existing schemata necessitate accommodation. Thus, all experiences involve two equally important processes: recognition, or knowing, which corresponds to the process of assimilation, and accommodation, which results in the modification of the cognitive structure. Such modification can be roughly equated with learning. To put the matter still another way, we respond to the world according to our previous experience (assimilation), but each experience contains aspects unlike anything we had experienced before. These unique aspects of experience cause changes in our cognitive structures (accommodation). Accommodation, then, provides a major vehicle for intellectual development. Ginsburg and Opper (1979) give an example of how assimilation and accommodation are related:

> Suppose an infant of 4 months is presented with a rattle. He has never before had the opportunity to play with rattles or similar toys. The rattle, then, is a feature of the environment to which he needs to adapt. His subsequent behavior reveals the tendencies of assimilation and accommodation. The infant tries to grasp the rattle. In order to do this successfully he must accommodate in more ways than are immediately apparent. First, he must accommodate his visual activities to perceive the rattle correctly, for example by locating it in space. Then he must reach out, adjusting his arm movements to the distance between himself and the rattle. In grasping the rattle, he must mold his fingers to its shape; in lifting the rattle he must accommodate his muscular exertion to its weight. In sum, the grasping of the rattle involves a series of acts of accommodation, or modifications of the infant's behavioral structures to suit the demands of the environment.
>
> At the same time, grasping the rattle also involves assimilation. In the past the infant has already grasped things; for him, grasping is a well-formed structure of behavior. When he sees the rattle for the first time he tries to deal with the novel object by incorporating it into a habitual pattern of behavior. In a sense he tries to transform the novel object to something that he is familiar with—namely, a thing to be grasped. We can say, therefore, that he is assimilates the objects into his framework and thereby assigns the object a "meaning." (p. 19)

Assimilation and accommodation are referred to as **functional invariants** because they occur at all levels of intellectual development. It should be clear, however, that early experiences tend to involve more accommodation than later experiences because more and more of what is experienced will correspond to existing cognitive structures, making substantial accommodation less necessary as the individual matures.

Equilibration

One might ask what the driving force behind intellectual growth is. For Piaget, the answer would be found in his concept of **equilibration.** Piaget assumed that all organisms have an innate tendency to create a harmonious relationship between themselves and their environment. In other words, all aspects of the organism are geared toward optimal adaptation. Equilibration is this innate tendency to organize one's experiences to assure maximal adaptation. Roughly, equilibration can be defined as the continuous drive toward equilibrium or balance.

The concept of equilibration is for Piaget what the concept of hedonism was for Freud or self-actualization was for Maslow and Jung. It is his major motivational concept, which along with assimilation and accommodation, is used to explain the steady intellectual growth observed in children. We will now describe how these three processes interact.

As we have seen, assimilation permits the organism to respond to a present situation in accordance with previous knowledge. Because the unique aspects of the situation cannot be responded to on the basis of previous knowledge, these novel or unique aspects of an experience cause a slight cognitive disbalance. Since there is an innate need for harmony (equilibrium), the organism's mental structures change in order to incorporate these unique aspects of the experience, thus causing the sought-after cognitive balance. As with the Gestalt psychologists, lack of cognitive balance has motivational properties that keep the organism active until a balance is attained. In addition to restoring the balance, however, this adjustment paves the way for new and different interactions with the environment. The accommodation described causes a change in mental structures, so that if those previously unique aspects of the environment were again encountered they would not cause a disbalance; that is, they would be readily assimilated into the organism's existing cognitive structure. In addition, this new cognitive arrangement forms the basis for new accommodations since accommodation always results from a disbalance, and what causes a disbalance must always be related to the organism's current cognitive structure. Gradually, through this adaptive process, information that could not at one time be assimilated eventually can be. The dual mechanisms of assimilation and accommodation, along with the driving force of equilibration, provide for slow but steady intellectual growth. The process can be diagrammed as follows:

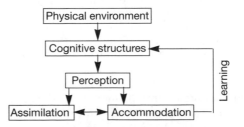

Interiorization

Children's early interactions with the environment are strictly sensorimotor; that is, they respond directly to environmental stimuli with reflex motor reactions. Children's early experiences, then, involve the use and elaboration of their innate schemata such as grasping, sucking, looking, and reaching. The results of these early experiences are registered in the cognitive structures and gradually transform them. With increasing experience, children expand their cognitive structures, thereby making it possible for them to adapt more readily to an ever-increasing number of situations.

As a more elaborate cognitive structure develops, children are capable of responding to more complex situations. Also, they are less dependent on the here and now. For example, they are capable of "thinking" of objects that are not before them. Now, what children experience are functions of both physical environment and their cognitive structures, which reflect their cumulative prior experiences. This gradual decreasing dependence on the physical environment and the increased utilization of cognitive structures is called **interiorization.**

As the cognitive structures develop, they become increasingly important in the adaptive process. For example, elaborate cognitive structures make more complex problem solving possible. As more experiences are interiorized, thinking becomes a tool in adapting to the environment. Early in development a child's adaptive responses are direct and simple and without thought. The child's early adaptive responses are mainly overt. As the process of interiorization continues, however, the child's adaptive responses become more covert; they involve internal actions rather than external ones. Piaget called these internal covert actions **operations,** and the term *operation* can be roughly equated with "thinking." Now, rather than manipulating the environment directly, the child can do so mentally through the use of operations.

The most important characteristic of any operation is that it is reversible. **Reversibility** means that once something is thought, it can be "unthought"; that is, an operation, once performed, can be mentally undone. For example, one can first mentally add 3 and 5, making a total of 8, and then mentally subtract 3 from 8, making a total of 5.

As we have seen, first the child's adjustment to the environment is direct and involves no thinking (operations). Next, as the child develops a more complex cognitive structure, thinking becomes more important. The early use of operations depends on those events the child can experience directly; that is, the child can think about those things that he or she can see. Piaget called these **concrete operations** since they are applied to concrete environmental events. Later operations, however, are completely independent of physical experience, and they therefore allow the child to solve purely hypothetical questions. Piaget called the latter **formal operations.** Unlike the concrete operation, the formal operation is not bound to the environment.

Interiorization, then, is the process by which adaptive actions become increasingly covert rather than overt. In fact, operations can be thought of as interiorized actions. Adaptive behavior, which first involves only sensorimotor schemata and overt behavior, evolves to the point where formal operations are utilized in the adaptive process. The use of formal operations characterizes the highest form of intellectual development.

Although intellectual growth is continuous, Piaget found that certain mental abilities tend to appear at certain stages of development. It is important to note the word *tend*. Piaget and his colleagues found that although mental abilities appear around a certain age level, some children will show the ability earlier and some later than other children. Although the actual age at which an ability appears may vary from child to child or from culture to culture, the order in which mental abilities appears does not vary since mental development is always an extension of what has already preceded. Thus, although children of the same age may have different mental abilities, the order with which the abilities emerge is constant. We will summarize the various stages of intellectual development suggested by Piaget.

STAGES OF DEVELOPMENT

1. Sensorimotor Stage (Birth to About 2 Years)   The **sensorimotor stage** is characterized by the absence of language. Because the children have no words for things, objects cease to exist when children are not dealing directly with them. Interactions with the environment are strictly sensorimotor and deal only with the here and now. Children at this stage are egocentric. Everything is seen with themselves as a frame of reference, and their psychological world is the only one that exists. Toward the end of this stage, children develop the concept of object permanence. In other words, they come to realize that objects go on existing even when they are not experiencing them.

2. Preoperational Thinking (About 2 to 7 Years)   The **preoperational thinking** stage has two subdivisions:

1. *Preconceptual thinking (about 2 to 4 years)*. During this part of preoperational thinking, children begin rudimentary concept formation. They begin to classify things in certain classes because of their similarity, but they make a number of mistakes because of their concepts; thus, all men are "Daddy," all women are "Mommy," and all toys they see are "mine." Rather than being either inductive or deductive, their logic is *transductive*. An example of transductive reasoning would be "Cows are big animals with four legs. That animal is big and has four legs; therefore, it is a cow."

2. *Period of intuitive thought (about 4 to 7 years)*. During this part of preoperational thinking, the child solves problems intuitively instead of in accordance with some logical rule. The most striking characteristic of the child's thinking during this stage is his or her failure to develop **conservation.** Conservation is defined as the ability to realize that number, length, substance, or area remains constant even though they may be presented to the child in a number of different ways. For example, a child is shown two containers filled to some level with some liquid.

Next, the contents of one container are poured into a taller, thinner container.

At this stage of development, the child, who observed that the first containers contained an equal amount of liquid, will now tend to say that the taller container has more liquid because the liquid is higher in the container. The child at this stage cannot mentally reverse cognitive operations, which means that he or she cannot mentally pour the liquid from the tall container back into the shorter one and see that the amount of liquid is the same in both.

For Piaget, conservation is an ability that occurs as a result of the child's cumulative experiences with the environment, and it is not an ability that can be taught until the child has had these preliminary experiences. As with all stage theories, teachability is a central issue. Do various capabilities come about because of certain experiences (e.g., learning), or do they unfold as a function of maturation along some genetically determined path? For Piaget it was both. Maturation provides the necessary sensory apparatus and brain structures, but it takes experience to develop the ability. The question of whether conservation can be taught before "its time has come" is still open; some say yes (e.g., LeFrançois, 1968), and some say no, thus agreeing with Piaget (e.g., Smedslund, 1961).

3. Concrete Operations (About 7 to 11 or 12 Years)   Children now develop the ability to conserve, along with the abilities to deal adequately with classes, with seriation (i.e., they can arrange things from smallest to largest and vice versa), and with number concepts. During this stage, however, the thought processes are directed to real events observed by the child. The child can perform rather complex operations on problems as long as the problems are concrete and not abstract.

The following diagram represents a typical problem given to children who are about 11 years old to study their thought processes. Their task is to determine what letter should go into the empty section of the circle. Perhaps you would like to try to solve the problem yourself.

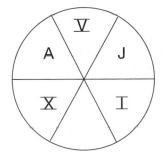

To solve the problem, one must realize that the letter of the alphabet opposite the Roman numeral *I* is *A,* the first letter of the alphabet. Also, the letter across from Roman numeral *X* is *J,* the tenth letter of the alphabet. Thus, the letter across from Roman numeral *V* must be the fifth letter of the alphabet, or *E.* At least two concepts must be utilized in solving such a problem: "one-to-one correspondence" and "opposite to." That is, it must be realized that Roman numerals and letters of the alphabet can be placed so that they correspond, and it must also be realized that the corresponding numerals and letters are placed opposite one another. If children do not have these concepts available, they cannot solve the problem. Likewise, if they can solve the problem, they must have the concepts available.

   4. Formal Operations (About 11 or 12 to 14 or 15 Years)   Children can now deal with hypothetical situations and their thought processes are not tied down exclusively to what is immediate and real. Thinking at this stage is as logical as it will ever become. Thus the mental apparatus that a person has is as sophisticated as it ever will be, but this apparatus can be directed toward the solution of a never-ending array of problems throughout one's life.

OPTIMAL CONDITIONS FOR LEARNING

It should be clear that if something cannot be at least partially assimilated into an organism's cognitive structure, it cannot act as a biological stimulus. It is in this sense that the cognitive structures create the physical environment. As the cognitive structures become more elaborate, the physical environment becomes better articulated. Likewise, if something is so far from an organism's cognitive structure that it cannot be accommodated, no learning will take place. For optimal learning to take place, information must be presented that can be assimilated into the present cognitive structure but at the same time be different enough to necessitate a change in that structure. If the information cannot be assimilated, it simply cannot be understood. If it is completely understood, however, no learning is necessary. In fact, in Piaget's theory, assimilation and understanding mean about the same thing. This is what Dollard and Miller meant by their term **learning dilemma,** which points out that all learning depends on failure. According to Piaget, failure of previous knowledge to allow for assimilation of an experience causes accommodation, or new learning. Experiences should be moderately challenging in order to stimulate cognitive growth. Again, no such growth will occur if only assimilation occurs.
   One must determine for each individual learner what kind of cognitive structures are available and slowly change these structures one small step at a time. It is for this reason that Piaget would favor a one-to-one relationship between teacher and pupil. It should be obvious, however, that he would favor such a relationship for much different reasons than a theorist like Skinner, who also favors such a relationship.
   Often Piaget is thought of as a nativist who believed intellectual development occurs as the result of biological maturation, but this was not entirely true. Piaget believed that maturation provides only the framework for intellectual development, but in addition to this framework, both physical and social experience are indis-

pensable for mental development. Inhelder and Piaget (1958) put the matter as follows: "The maturation of the nervous system can do no more than determine the totality of possibilities and impossibilities at a given stage. A particular social environment remains indispensable for the realization of these possibilities. It follows that their realization can be accelerated or retarded as a function of cultural and educational conditions" (p. 337). Elsewhere Piaget (1966) said,

> The human being is immersed right from birth in a social environment which affects him just as much as his physical environment. Society, even more, in a sense, than the physical environment, changes the very structure of the individual, because it not only compels him to recognize facts, but also provides him with a ready-made system of signs, which modify his thought; it presents him with new values and it imposes on him an infinite series of obligations. (p. 156)

Ginsburg and Opper (1979) summarize the ways in which Piaget felt that heredity influenced cognitive development: "(a) Inherited physical structures [e.g., the nervous system] set broad limits on intellectual functioning; (b) Inherited behavioral reactions [e.g., reflexes] have an influence during the first few days of human life but afterward are extensively modified as the infant interacts with his environment; and (c) The maturation of physical structures may have psychological correlates [e.g., when the brain matures to the point where language development is possible]" (p. 17). And as we have seen, equilibration, or the tendency to seek a harmony between one's self and the physical environment, is also inherited.

INTO WHAT CAMP DOES PIAGET'S THEORY FALL?

Clearly, Piaget is not an S-R theorist. As we have seen, S-R theorists attempt to determine the relationship between environmental events (S) and responses to those events (R). Most S-R theorists assume a passive organism that builds up response capabilities by accumulating habits. Complex habits, according to this point of view, are merely combinations of simpler habits. Certain S-R relationships are "stamped in" either by reinforcement or by contiguity. Knowledge, according to such a point of view, represents a "copy" of conditions that exist in the physical world. In other words, through learning, relationships that exist in the physical world come to be represented in the organism's brain. Piaget referred to this epistemological position as a copy theory of knowledge.

Piaget's theory is diametrically opposed to the S-R conception of knowledge. As we have seen, Piaget equated knowledge with cognitive structures that provide the potential to deal with the environment in certain ways. The cognitive structures provide a framework for experience; that is, they determine what can be responded to and how it can be responded to. In this sense, the cognitive structures are projected onto the physical environment and thus create it. In this way the environment is constructed by the cognitive structure. But it also is correct to say that the environment plays a large part in creating the cognitive structures. As we have seen, the interaction between the environment and the cognitive structures through the processes of assimilation and accommodation is of primary importance in Piaget's theory. Piaget (1970b) differentiated his views of intelligence and knowledge from those of empiricists as follows:

> In the common view, the external world is entirely separate from the subject, although it encloses the subject's own body. Any objective knowledge, then, appears to be simply the result of a set of perceptive recordings, motor associations, verbal descriptions, and the like, which all participate in producing a sort of figurative copy or "functional copy" (in Hull's terminology) of objects and the connections between them. The only function of intelligence is systematically to file, correct, etc., these various sets of information; in this process, the more faithful the critical copies, the more consistent the final system will be. In such an empiricist prospect, the content of intelligence comes from outside, and the coordinations that organize it are only the consequences of language and symbolic instruments.
>
> But this passive interpretation of the act of knowledge is in fact contradicted at all levels of development and, particularly, at the sensorimotor and prelinguistic levels of cognitive adaptation and intelligence. Actually, in order to know objects, the subject must act upon them, and therefore transform them: he must displace, connect, combine, take apart, and reassemble them.
>
> From the most elementary sensorimotor actions (such as pushing and pulling) to the most sophisticated intellectual operations, which are interiorized actions, carried out mentally (e.g., joining together, putting in order, putting into one-to-one correspondence), knowledge is constantly linked with actions or operations, that is, with *transformations*. (pp. 703–704)

There is both agreement and disagreement between Piaget's theory and Gestalt's theory. Both agree that experiences are organized. Both believe that there is an innate need for a psychological balance and that a disbalance has motivational properties. Both believe that prior experience influences present experience. As we noted in the last chapter, the Gestalt theorists contended that as the memory trace becomes more fully established, it has an increased influence on conscious experience. Thus, when the memory trace of "circleness" is firmly established, an incomplete circle is experienced as a complete circle. The memory trace therefore "constructed" an experience that was not in accordance with physical reality. In a way, we can say that experiences are assimilated into existing memory traces, just as they are assimilated into existing cognitive structures. Just as cognitive structures are slowly changed by cumulative experiences, so are memory traces.

The major source of disagreement between the Gestalt theorists and Piaget is over the developmental nature of one's organizational ability. The Gestalt theorists believed that humans are born with a brain that organizes experiences according to the law of Prägnanz (see previous chapter). They believe that sensory data are experienced in an organized fashion at all stages of development. Piaget, in contrast, believed that the organizational abilities of the brain develop as the cognitive structures develop. To him, experience is always organized in terms of the cognitive structures, but the cognitive structures are always changing as a function of both biological maturation and sensory experience. Thus, Piaget used the term **progressive equilibrium** to describe the fact that the balance or organization that is sought is optimal under existing circumstances and that those circumstances are constantly changing.

The difference between Piaget and the Gestalt theorists on the matter of innate organizational abilities would result in a difference in educational practices. On the one hand, teachers attempting to utilize Gestalt principles in their teaching practices would tend to emphasize the "Gestalt" at all levels of education; seeing the total picture would be all-important. Such teachers would accept group discussions or even the lecture system. On the other hand, Piagetian teachers would be concerned about the individual student. These teachers would first attempt to determine what stage of development a particular student was at before deciding what information to present. They would realize that knowing something about the student's cognitive structure would enable them to present the student with information that he or she would be ready to assimilate. There is considerable difference, then, in assuming that the brain is constantly organizing experiences and in assuming that organizational ability varies at different stages of development.

One can see that Piaget's theory is hard to classify in the traditional categories. It is empirical in the sense that knowledge depends on experience, but clearly it is not empirical in the same way that an S-R theory is. One is tempted to compare Piaget's theory of knowledge with that of Kant (see Chapter 3), but Kant's categories of the mind were innate whereas Piaget's were the result of maturation and cumulative experience. Piaget's theory is not entirely empirical, however. The concept of equilibration provides a nativistic component to his theory. It is this innate drive toward harmony between the internal and external environment that provides the basis of all intellectual growth. We see in Piaget's theory, then, a creative mixture of many points of view; for that reason his theory is similar to that of Tolman, to which we turn in the next chapter.

SUMMARY OF PIAGET'S THEORY

According to Piaget, children are born with a few sensorimotor schemata, which provide the framework for their initial interactions with the environment. The child's early experiences are determined by these sensorimotor schemata. In other words, only those events that can be assimilated into these schemata can be responded to by children, and they therefore set limits on their experience. Through experience, however, these initial schemata are modified. Each experience contains unique elements that the child's cognitive structure must accommodate. Through this interaction with the environment, the child's cognitive structure changes, allowing for an ever-growing number of experiences. This is a slow process, however, since new schemata always evolve from those that existed previously. In this way, intellectual growth that starts out with the child's reflexive response to the environment develops to the point where the child is able to ponder potential events and to explore mentally probable outcomes.

Interiorization results in the development of operations that free children from needing to deal directly with the environment by allowing them to deal with symbolic manipulations. The development of operations (interiorized actions) provides children with a highly complex means of dealing with the environment, and they are therefore capable of more complex intellectual actions. Since their cognitive structures are more articulated, so are their physical environments; in fact, their cognitive structures can be said to construct the physical environment. It should be remembered that the term *intelligent* is used by Piaget to describe all adaptive activity. Thus, the behavior of a child grasping a rattle is as intelligent as an older child solving a complex problem. The difference is in the cognitive structures available to each child. According to Piaget, an intelligent act always tends to create a balance between the organism and its environment under the existing circumstances. The ever-present drive toward this balanced state is called equilibration.

Although intellectual development is continuous during childhood, Piaget chose to refer to stages of intellectual development. He described four major stages: (1) sensorimotor, in which children deal directly with the environment by utilizing their innate reflexes; (2) preoperational, in which children begin rudimentary concept formation; (3) concrete operations, in which children use interiorized actions or thought to solve problems in their immediate experience; and (4) formal operations, in which children can ponder completely hypothetical situations.

Piaget's theory had a significant effect on educational practice. Many educators have attempted to formulate specific policies based on his theory (e.g., Athey & Rubadeau, 1970; Furth, 1970; Ginsburg & Opper, 1979). Others have attempted to develop an intelligence test in accordance with his theory (e.g., Goldschmid & Bentler, 1968). Clearly Piaget's theory opened new avenues of research that were either unnoticed or ignored by those accepting an associationistic point of view. As we noted in Chapter 2, one characteristic of a good scientific theory is that it is heuristic, and Piaget's theory is certainly that. In 1980, the year Piaget died, Jerome Kagan paid him the following tribute:

> Piaget uncovered a host of fascinating, handy phenomena which were under everyone's noses but which few were talented enough to see. The reliability of those discoveries (the eight-month old who is suddenly able to retrieve a hidden toy...and the shift at age 7 from a nonconserving to a conserving reply to the beakers of water) was so consistent across cultures that they resembled demonstrations in a chemistry lecture hall...few would question the conclusion that Piaget's writings have been a primary basis for the centrality of the cognitive sciences in contemporary psychology....With Freud, Piaget has been a seminal figure in the sciences of human development. (pp. 245–246)

EVALUATION OF PIAGET'S THEORY

Contributions

Unlike many of the learning theorists we have studied, Piaget is not easily categorized as a reinforcement theorist, a contingency theorist, or a contiguity theorist. Like many researchers in what is loosely labeled the "cognitive" school, he assumes that learning happens more or less continuously and that it involves both acquisition of information and cognitive representation of that information. Piaget's unique contribution within this general perspective is his identification of the qualitative aspects of learning. Specifically, the concepts of assimilation and accommodation identify two different types of learning experience. Both are learning; both entail the acquisition and storage of information. Assimilation, however, is a static kind of learning, limited by the current cognitive structure, while accommodation is a progressive growth of the cognitive structure that changes the character of all subsequent learning.

Criticisms

Many contemporary psychologists point out problems inherent in Piaget's research methodology. His clinical method can provide information that is not readily recorded in rigorously controlled laboratory experiments. It can be an ideal method to discover directions for further research under more carefully defined conditions, but one must be cautious when drawing inferences from observations made with the clinical method precisely because it lacks rigorous experimental controls. A related criticism concerns the extent to which Piaget's observations can be generalized, given that he did not observe children or adults from cultures that differed significantly from his own. For example, Egan (1983), writes

> If we find, for example, that most Australian Aborigine adults fail Piagetian tests of the conservation of continuous quantity, are we to believe that aborigine adults will store water in tall thin cans in order to "have more water"; do they think they lose water when they pour it from a bucket into a barrel? That these confusions are not evident in their culture suggest that the classic Piagetian task, in such a context, is yielding obscure data that possibly have nothing much to do with general intellectual capacity. (pp. 65–66)

Although Piaget's notion of development through increasingly complex stages seems to be generally correct, there are indications that very young children are not as limited as was initially believed. Infants may well have a fundamental understanding of object permanence (Baillargeon, 1987, 1992; Bowers, 1989), and preschool children may exhibit conservation of number skills usually associated with older children. Perhaps more worrisome, adults may not attain formal operations even when faced with the kinds of experience that Piaget believed would lead to those structures. For example, Piaget and Inhelder (1956) devised a now well-studied water-level task. In this task, subjects are asked to indicate the orientation of liquid in a tilted container. Children tend not to realize that the liquid will remain horizontal with respect to the ground. Contrary to Piaget's expectations, nearly 40 percent of adults also fail to understand this (Kalichman, 1988). To make matters worse, 20 professional female waitresses (working for breweries at the Oktoberfest in Munich) and 20 professional bartenders (employed at bars in Munich), all of whom would be expected to have substantial experience with liquids in tipped containers, perform more poorly at the water-level task than groups of students and other professionals (Hecht & Proffitt, 1995).

DISCUSSION QUESTIONS

1. How did Piaget's method of studying intelligence differ from the one used at the Binet Laboratory?
2. Explain why Piaget's view of intelligence is called genetic epistemology.

3. Give an example of an experience that involves both assimilation and accommodation.
4. What did Piaget mean by interiorization?
5. Explain how, according to Piaget, heredity and experience both contribute to intellectual growth.
6. Explain what Piaget meant when he said that the cognitive structures "construct" the physical environment.
7. Discuss the nature of knowledge from both the empiricist's point of view and Piaget's point of view.
8. Discuss Piaget's concept of progressive equilibrium.
9. Describe the educational implications of Piaget's theory.
10. Compare and contrast Piaget's theory of learning with any one of the associationistic theories covered in this text.
11. What do you suppose Piaget's views on the transfer of training would have been? In other words, according to Piaget, what would make it possible to utilize what was learned in one situation in other situations?
12. Outline the major stages of intellectual development as they were viewed by Piaget.

KEY TERMS

accommodation   The modification of cognitive structures as the result of an experience that could not be assimilated into existing cognitive structures. Accommodation can be roughly equated with learning.

assimilation   Responding to the physical environment in accordance with existing cognitive structures. Assimilation refers to a kind of matching between the cognitive structures and the physical environment. Assimilation can be roughly equated with recognition or knowing.

clinical method   An open-ended form of questioning in which the researcher's questions are guided by the child's answers to previous questions.

cognitive structure   The schemata that an organism has available at any given time to interact with the physical environment. Cognitive structure results from both biological maturation and cumulative experience. The cognitive structure not only is affected by experience but also determines what can be experienced. If a physical event cannot be at least partially assimilated into the organism's cognitive structure, that physical event cannot constitute a biological stimulus. The dual processes of assimilation and accommodation must always occur with the existing cognitive structure as a point of departure.

concrete operations   The stage of intellectual development in which children can deal logically with only those events that they can experience directly.

conservation   The realization that number, length, substance, or area has not changed although it may be presented in a number of different ways. The ability to conserve requires the use of reversible operations.

content   The ingredients that accompany a specific manifestation of a schema.

epistemology   The study of knowledge.

equilibration   Piaget's major motivational concept; the innate need for balance between the organism and its environment and within the organism itself. Disbalance has motivational properties that cause the organism to do whatever is necessary to regain balance. Equilibration is an invariant because it is present at all stages of intellectual development. In fact, it is responsible for continuous intellectual development.

formal operations   The stage of intellectual development in which children can deal logically with hypothetical events in addition to those events that they can experience directly.

functional invariants   Processes that are not stage-specific but are present at all stages of development. Examples would include assimilation, accommodation, and equilibration.

genetic epistemology   A term often used to describe Piaget's theory. The term *genetic* means *developmental* rather than having anything to do with inheritance. Epistemology refers to the study of knowledge; thus the term *genetic epistemology* is used to describe the study of knowledge as a function of maturation and experience.

intelligence   Intelligence is a complex term in Piaget's theory, but in general it can be said that an intelligent act always tends to create optimal conditions for an organism's survival under existing circumstances. Intelligence is always related to an organism's adaptation to its environment.

interiorization   The increased tendency to rely more and more on mental operations in adjusting to the environment as the cognitive structure becomes more articulated. An operation is referred to as an "interiorized" action since it is an adaptive response that occurs mentally rather than overtly.

learning dilemma   Dollard and Miller's contention that for learning to occur, previously learned behavior and innate behavior patterns must be ineffective in solving a problem. In this sense failure is a prerequisite for learning.

operation   Cognitive action. As a sensorimotor schema manifests itself in overt behavior, an operation manifests itself in covert behavior or thinking. An operation can be thought of as interiorized action.

preoperational thinking   The stage of intellectual development in which children begin to classify objects and events into rudimentary categories.

progressive equilibrium   Living organisms constantly seek a balance between themselves and their environment. But according to Piaget, the cognitive structures of an organism are always changing as the result of maturation and experience. Therefore, a balance can never be absolute but must rather be a progressive equilibrium, which is a balance that is the best under the prevailing circumstances. As circumstances change, what an optimal balance would consist of must change accordingly.

reversibility   An important characteristic of mental operations that refers to the process of reversing a thought. For example, one can mentally pour liquid from one container into another and then reverse the process by mentally pouring the liquid back into the original container. Reversibility of mental operations is a necessary condition for **conservation** to occur.

schema   The general potential to engage in a class of overt or covert actions. A schema can also be thought of as an element in an organism's cognitive structure.

sensorimotor stage   The initial stage of intellectual development in which children respond directly to events as they occur in the environment. During this stage of development, children adjust to the environment in terms of their schemata such as grasping, looking, sucking, and reaching.

Chapter 12

EDWARD CHACE TOLMAN

Tolman (1886–1959) was born in Newton, Massachusetts, and received his B.S. degree from the Massachusetts Institute of Technology in electrochemistry in 1911. His M.A. (1912) and Ph.D. (1915) degrees were earned at Harvard University in psychology. He taught at Northwestern University from 1915 to 1918, at which time he was released for "lack of teaching success"; but more likely it was because of his pacifism during wartime. From Northwestern, he went to the University of California, where he remained until his retirement. His stay at the University of California was interrupted, however, when he was dismissed for refusing to sign a loyalty oath. He led a fight against the loyalty oath as an infringement on academic freedom and was reinstated when the professors won their case.

Tolman was raised in a Quaker home, and his pacifism was a constant theme in his career. In 1942, he wrote *Drives Toward War,* in which he suggested several changes in our political, educational, and economic systems that would increase the probability of world peace. In the preface, he stated his reasons for writing the book: "As an American, a college professor, and one brought up in the pacifist tradition, I am intensely biased against war. It is for me stupid, interrupting, unnecessary, and unimaginably horrible. I write this essay within that frame of reference. In short, I am driven to discuss the psychology of war and its possible abolition because I want intensely to get rid of it" (p. xi).

Edward Chace Tolman. (From *A History of Psychology in Autobiography,* Vol. 4, p. xii, by C. Murchison, ed., 1952, Worcester, MA: Clark University Press.)

Tolman spent much of his life being a rebel. He opposed war when war was a popular cause, and we shall see that he opposed Watsonian behaviorism when behaviorism was a popular school of psychology.

As we mentioned at the conclusion of Chapter 10, Tolman's theory of learning can be looked on as a blend of Gestalt theory and behaviorism. While still a graduate student at Harvard, Tolman traveled to Germany and worked for a short time with Koffka. The influence of Gestalt theory on his own theorizing had a significant and lasting effect. His favorable attitude toward Gestalt theory did not, however, preclude a favorable attitude toward behaviorism. Like the behaviorists, Tolman saw little value in the introspective approach, and he felt psychology had to become completely objective. His main disagreement with the behaviorists was over the unit of behavior to be studied. Behaviorists such as Pavlov, Guthrie, Hull, Watson, and Skinner represented, according to Tolman, the psychology of "twitchism," because they felt that large segments of behavior could be divided into smaller segments, such as reflexes, for further analysis. Tolman felt that by being elementistic, the behaviorists were throwing away the baby with the bathwater. He believed that it was possible to be objective while studying molar behavior (large, intact, meaningful behavior patterns). Unlike the other behaviorists, Tolman chose to study molar behavior systematically. It can be said that Tolman was methodologically a behaviorist but metaphysically a cognitive theorist. In other words, he studied behavior in order to discover cognitive processes.

MOLAR BEHAVIOR

The chief characteristic of **molar behavior** is that it is purposive; that is, it is always directed toward some goal. Perhaps now the reader can better understand the title of Tolman's major work, *Purposive Behavior in Animals and Men* (1932). Tolman never contended that behavior could not be divided into smaller units for the purposes of study; rather, he felt that whole behavior patterns had a meaning that would be lost if studied from an elementistic viewpoint. Thus, for Tolman, molar behavior constituted a Gestalt that was different from the individual "twitches" that made it up. In other words, purposive behavior patterns can be looked on as behavioral Gestalten:

> It will be contended by us (if not by Watson) that "behavior-acts," though no doubt in complete one-to-one correspondence with the underlying molecular facts of physics and physiology, have, as "molar" wholes, certain emergent properties of their own. And it is these, the molar properties of behavior-acts, which are of prime interest to us as psychologists. Further, these molar properties of behavior-acts cannot in the present state of our knowledge, i.e., prior to the working-out of many empirical correlations between behavior and its physiological correlates, be known even inferentially from a mere knowledge of the underlying molecular facts of physics and physiology. For, just as the properties of a beaker of water are not, prior to experience, in any way envisageable from the properties of individual water molecules, so neither are the properties of a "behavior-act" deducible directly from the properties of the underlying physical and physiological processes which make it up. Behavior as such cannot, at any rate at present, be deduced from a mere enumeration of the muscle twitches, the mere motions *qua* motions, which make it up. It must as yet be studied first hand and for its own sake. (pp. 7–8)

The type of behavior that Tolman (1932) labels as molar is exemplified in the following passage:

> A rat running a maze; a cat getting out of a puzzle box; a man driving home to dinner; a child hiding from a stranger; a woman doing her washing or gossiping over the telephone; a pupil marking a mental-test sheet; a psychologist reciting a list of nonsense syllables; my friend and I telling one another our thoughts and feelings—*these are behaviors (qua molar)*. And it must be noted that in mentioning no one of them have we referred to, or, we blush to confess it, for the most part even known, what were the exact muscles and glands, sensory nerves, and motor nerves involved. For these responses somehow had other sufficiently identifying properties of their own. (p. 8)

PURPOSIVE BEHAVIORISM

Tolman's theory has been referred to as a **purposive behaviorism** because it attempts to explain goal-directed behavior, or **purposive behavior.** It must be emphasized that

Tolman used the term *purpose* as purely descriptive. He noted, for example, that the searching behavior of a rat in a maze will persist until food is found; therefore it looks "as if" its behavior is goal-directed or purposive. For Tolman, the term *purposive* was used to describe behavior, just as the terms *slow, fast, correct, incorrect,* or *right turn* might be used to describe behavior. There is some similarity between Guthrie and Tolman on this point. For Guthrie, behavior persists as long as maintaining stimuli are being provided by some need state. For Tolman, behavior will look "as if" it is goal-directed as long as the organism is seeking something in the environment. In both cases, the behavior will look purposive. Tolman (1932) said,

> It must…be emphasized that purposes and cognition which are thus immediately, imminently, in behavior are wholly objective as to definition. They are defined by characters and relationships which we observe out there in the behavior. We, the observers, watch the behavior of the rat, the cat, or the man, and note its character as a getting to such and such by means of such and such a selected pattern of commerces-with. It is we, the independent neutral observers, who note these perfectly objective characters as imminent in the behavior and have happened to choose the terms *purpose* and *cognition* as generic terms for such characters. (pp. 12–13)

Although Tolman was freer with the terms he was willing to employ in his theory than most behaviorists, he remained a behaviorist, and an objective one. As we shall see below, Tolman developed a cognitive theory of learning, but in the final analysis, he was dealing with what every other behaviorist deals with—observable stimuli and overt responses. Tolman (1932) said, "For a Purposive Behaviorism, behavior, as we have seen, is purposive, cognitive, and molar, i.e., "Gestalted." Purposive Behaviorism is a molar, not a molecular, behaviorism, but it is none the less a behaviorism. Stimuli and responses and the behavior-determinants of responses are all that it finds to study" (p. 418).

THE USE OF RATS

Some may think it strange for a cognitive theorist to use rats as experimental subjects, but Tolman had a special fondness for them. He stimulated the use of rats in psychological experiments at the University of California, and he dedicated his 1932 book to the white rat. Throughout Tolman's writings, one finds humor and wit, as exemplified by his following thoughts on the use of rats as experimental subjects: "Let it be noted that rats live in cages; they do not go on binges the night before one has planned an experiment; they do not kill each other off in wars; they do not invent engines of destruction, and if they did, they would not be so inept about controlling such engines; they do not go in for either class conflicts or race conflicts; they avoid politics, economics, and papers on psychology. They are marvelous, pure, and delightful" (1945, p. 166).

Elsewhere Tolman (1938) said, "I believe that everything important in psychology (except perhaps such matters as the building up of a super-ego, that is, everything save such matters as involve society and words) can be investigated in essence through the continued experimental and theoretical analysis of the determiners of rat behavior at a choice-point in a maze. Herein I believe I agree with Professor Hull and also with Professor Thorndike" (p. 34).

MAJOR THEORETICAL CONCEPTS

Tolman introduced the use of intervening variables into psychological research and Hull borrowed the idea from Tolman. Both Hull and Tolman used intervening variables in a similar way in their work. Hull, however, developed a much more comprehensive and elaborate theory of learning than did Tolman. We will consider the formal aspects of Tolman's theory later in this chapter, but first we will turn to a few of his general assumptions about the learning process.

What Is Learned?

The behaviorists, such as Pavlov, Watson, Guthrie, and Hull said that stimulus-response associations are learned and that complex learning involves complex S-R relationships. Tolman, however, taking his lead from the Gestalt theorists, said that learning is essentially a process of discovering what leads to what in the environment. The organism, through exploration, discovers that certain events lead to certain other events or that one sign leads to another sign. For example, we learn that when it's 5:00 P.M. (S_1), dinner (S_2) will soon follow. For that reason, Tolman was called an S-S rather than an S-R theorist. Learning, for Tolman, was an ongoing process that required no motivation. On this matter Tolman was in agreement with Guthrie and in opposition to Thorndike, Skinner, and Hull.

It should be pointed out, however, that motivation was important in Tolman's theory because it determined which aspects of the environment would be attended to by the organism. For example, the hungry organism would attend to food-related events in the environment, and the sexually deprived organism would attend to sex-related events. In general, an organism's drive state determines which aspects of the environment will be emphasized in its perceptual field. Thus, for Tolman, motivation acted as a perceptual **emphasizer.**

According to Tolman, what is learned is "the lay of the land"; the organism learns what is there. It learns that if it turns to the left, it will find one thing, and if it turns to the right, it will find another thing. Gradually it develops a picture of the environment that can be used to get around in it. Tolman called this picture a **cognitive map.** On this point, Tolman was diametrically opposed to the other behaviorists. According to him, it is futile to look at individual responses or even individual routes to a goal. Once the organism has developed a cognitive map, it can reach a particular goal from any number of directions. If one commonly used route is blocked, the animal simply takes an alternate route, just as the human takes a detour on the way home from work if the route usually taken is not available. The organism will, however, choose the shortest route or the one requiring the least amount of work. This is referred to as the **principle of least effort.**

There is a great deal of similarity between Tolman's principle of least effort and Hull's notion of the habit family hierarchy. Both theorists concluded that after training, an organism can reach a goal through alternate routes. Tolman said that the organism's first choice is the route requiring the least amount of effort. Hull said that the organism prefers the shortest route because it has the shortest delay of reinforcement (J) and therefore the greatest amount of $_sE_R$. Furthermore, the response that has the greatest amount of $_sE_R$ will tend to occur in any given situation. Later in this chapter, we shall see some of Tolman's ingenious experimentation designed to show that animals respond according to cognitive maps rather than to simple S-R processes.

Confirmation versus Reinforcement

As with Guthrie, the concept of reinforcement was unimportant to Tolman as a learning variable, but there is some similarity between what Tolman called confirmation and what the other behaviorists called reinforcement. During the development of a cognitive map, expectations are utilized by the organism. Expectations are hunches about what leads to what. Early tentative expectations are called **hypotheses,** and they are either confirmed by experience or not. Hypotheses that are confirmed are retained, and those that are not are abandoned. Through this process, the cognitive map develops.

An **expectancy** that is consistently confirmed develops into what Tolman referred to as a **means-end readiness,** or what is commonly referred to as a belief. When an expectation is consistently confirmed, the organism ends up "believing" that if it acts in a certain way, a certain result will follow, or if it sees a certain sign (stimulus), another sign will follow. Thus, the **confirmation of an expectancy** in the development of a cognitive map is similar to the notion of reinforcement, as other behaviorists may have used the term. It should be noted, however, that the production, acceptance, or rejection of hypotheses is a cognitive process that need not involve overt behavior. Also, the hypotheses-testing process, so important to the development of a cognitive map, does not depend on any physiological need state of the organism. As mentioned above, learning is taking place constantly and does not depend on any motivational state of the organism.

Vicarious Trial and Error

Tolman noted a characteristic of rats in a maze that he took as support for his cognitive interpretation of learning. Often a rat would pause at a choice point and look around as if it were thinking about the various alternatives available to it. This pausing and looking around at the choice point Tolman called **vicarious trial and error.** Instead of behavioral trial and error, in which first one response is tried and then another until a solution to the problem is reached, with vicarious trial and error the testing of different approaches is done cognitively rather than behaviorally.

Learning versus Performance

We saw in Chapter 6 that Hull distinguished between learning and performance. In Hull's final theory, the number of reinforced trials was the only learning variable;

the other variables in his system were performance variables. Performance can be thought of as the translation of learning into behavior. Although the distinction between learning and performance was important for Hull, it was even more important for Tolman.

According to Tolman, we know many things about our environment but only act on this information when we need to do so. As mentioned above, this knowledge, which comes about through reality testing, lies dormant until a need arises. In a state of need, the organism utilizes what it has learned through reality testing to bring it into proximity to those things that will alleviate the need. For example, there may be two drinking fountains in your building and you may have passed them both many times without having paused for a drink; but if you became thirsty, you would merely walk over to one of them and take a drink. You knew for some time how to find a drinking fountain, but you did not need to translate that knowledge into behavior until you became thirsty. We will discuss the learning-performance distinction in more detail when we consider latent learning.

The points that we have made so far can be summarized as follows:

1. The organism brings to a problem-solving situation various hypotheses that it may utilize in attempting to solve the problem. These hypotheses are based largely on prior experience, but as we shall see later, Tolman believed that some problem-solving strategies may be innate.
2. The hypotheses that survive are those that correspond best with reality, that is, those that result in goal achievement.
3. After awhile a clearly established cognitive map develops, which can be used under altered conditions. For instance, when an organism's preferred path is blocked, it simply chooses, in accordance with the principle of least effort, an alternative path from its cognitive map.
4. When there is some sort of demand or motive to be satisfied, the organism will make use of the information in its cognitive map. The fact that information can exist but only be utilized under certain conditions is the basis for the very important distinction between learning and performance.

Latent Learning

Latent learning is learning that is not translated into performance. In other words, it is possible for learning to remain dormant for a considerable length of time before it is manifested in behavior. The concept of latent learning was very important to Tolman and he felt he succeeded in demonstrating its existence. The now famous experiment that Tolman and Honzik (1930) ran involved three groups of rats learning to solve a maze. One group was never reinforced for correctly traversing the maze, one group was always reinforced, and one group was not reinforced until the eleventh day of the experiment. It was the last group that was of greatest interest to Tolman. His theory of latent learning predicted that this group would be learning the maze just as much as the group that was being regularly reinforced and that when reinforcement was introduced on the eleventh day, this group should soon

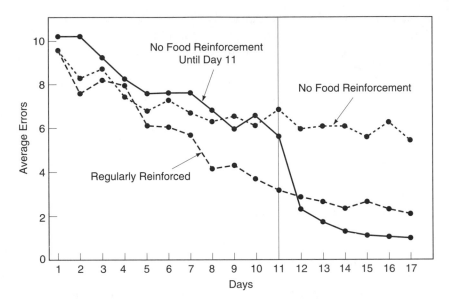

FIGURE 12–1   The results of the Tolman and Honzik experiment showing that when animals are reinforced after a period of nonreinforcement, their performance very rapidly equals or exceeds that of animals that had been reinforced from the onset of the experiment. (From "Introduction and Removal of Reward, and Maze Performance in Rats," by E.C. Tolman & C.H. Honzik, 1930, *University of California Publications in Psychology, 4,* pp. 257–275.)

perform as well as the group that had been continually reinforced. The results of the experiment are shown in Figure 12–1.

By examining Figure 12–1, three things became apparent: (1) There is slight improvement in performance even in the group never receiving reinforcement; (2) the reinforced group showed steady improvement throughout the seventeen days of the experiment; and (3) when reinforcement was introduced on the eleventh day to the group not previously receiving reinforcement, their performance vastly improved. In fact, the last group performed even better than the group that was reinforced throughout the experiment. Tolman took the results to support his contention that reinforcement was a performance variable and not a learning variable.

The S-R theorists insisted that reinforcement was, in fact, not removed from the situation; why, they asked, would the group never receiving food show slight improvement? They pointed out that simply being removed from the apparatus after reaching the goal box could act as a reinforcer for reaching the goal box. Another S-R interpretation of latent learning, one based on the concept of incentive motivation, will be presented after our discussion of latent extinction.

Latent Extinction   It may be remembered that reinforcement theorists such as Pavlov, Hull, and Skinner viewed extinction as an active process. For them, in order for extinction to occur, a previously reinforced response must be made but not reinforced. Under these circumstances, the rate or magnitude of the previously reinforced response will go back to the level that it was at before reinforcement was introduced. But what does Tolman say? According to Tolman, learning occurs through observation and is independent of reinforcement. What an animal learns is to expect reinforcement if a certain response is made because it is this expectation that is confirmed during the acquisition phase of a learning experiment. Tolman's theory predicts that if an animal who has learned an R-S expectancy (e.g., that a certain response will lead to the presence of food) is given the opportunity to *observe* that that response will no longer lead to food, such observation will itself produce extinction. For example, if a rat that had previously learned to traverse a maze or a runway to obtain food is placed directly into a now-empty goal box, it will stop traversing the maze or runway on subsequent trials. Extinction that occurs under these circumstances is called **latent extinction** because it does not involve the nonreinforced performance of the previously reinforced response. Evidence for latent extinction has been found by many researchers, for example, Deese, 1951; Moltz, 1957; and Seward and Levy, 1949. Bower and Hilgard (1981) summarize these findings:

> These…results…imply that the strength of an instrumental response sequence can be altered without *that response* occurring and receiving the altered conditions of reinforcement,….Such results create difficulties for an S-R reinforcement theory which supposes that responses can have their habit strengths altered only when they occur and are then explicitly punished or nonrewarded. The results seem to call for two assumptions; that at the start of a behavior sequence, organisms have available some representation of what goal they expect to achieve at the end of the response sequence; and that that goal expectation can be altered by direct experience with the goal situation without execution of the prior response sequence leading up to it. These, of course, are exactly the assumptions made in Tolman's theory. (pp. 340–341)

S-R theorists, such as Spence, explain latent extinction in terms of motivational factors. We saw in Chapter 6 that Spence believed that response learning occurred because of contiguity. That is, a goal response is learned simply because it is made. What reinforcement does, according to Spence, is provide an incentive for performing a response that had been learned independent of reinforcement. Furthermore, stimuli that occur prior to primary reinforcement take on secondary reinforcing properties, and it is these secondary reinforcers that provide the incentive for the animal to traverse a maze or runway. According to Spence, what happens in the latent extinction situation is that the animal experiences these stimuli without primary reinforcement, and therefore their secondary reinforcing properties extinguish. Thereafter, when the animal is placed in the experimental apparatus, it has less incentive to perform the learned response. This is essentially the same explanation Spence would offer for latent learning. That is, animals learn a variety of responses in a maze or a runway simply by making those responses. When at some point reinforcement is introduced, it gives the animal the incentive to perform a response that it had previously learned through the law of contiguity. The question of whether latent learning and latent extinction are explained best in terms of expectancies or in terms of incentive motivation is yet unanswered.

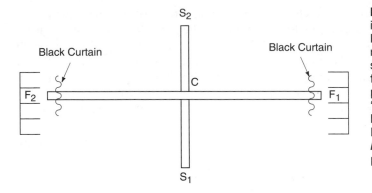

FIGURE 12–2 Apparatus used in the Tolman, Ritchie, and Kalish experiment on place vs. response learning. S_1 and S_2 are starting points, F_1 and F_2 are food boxes, and C is the center point of the maze. (From "Studies in Spatial Learning II," by E.C. Tolman, B.F. Ritchie, & D. Kalish, 1946, *Journal of Experimental Psychology, 36,* p. 223.)

Place Learning versus Response Learning

Tolman maintained that animals learn where things are, whereas the S-R theorists maintained that specific responses are learned to specific stimuli. Tolman and his collaborators performed a series of experiments designed to determine whether animals were place learners, as Tolman suggested, or response learners as S-R theory suggested. A typical experiment in this area was done by Tolman, Ritchie, and Kalish (1946b). The apparatus they used is diagrammed in Figure 12–2.

Two groups of rats were utilized. Members of one group were sometimes started at S_1 and sometimes at S_2, but no matter where they started from, they always had to turn in the same direction to be reinforced. For example, if the group was learning to turn right, it was fed at F_1 if they started at S_1 and were fed at F_2 if they started at S_2. This was the **response learning** group. Members of the other groups were always fed at the same place (e.g., F_2). If a member of this group started at S_1, it had to turn left to be reinforced. If it started at S_2, it had to turn right. This was the **place learning** group.

The animals were given six trials a day for twelve days, or seventy-two trials. The criterion for learning was ten successive errorless trials. At the end of the experiment, only three of the eight rats in the response learning group had reached criterion, whereas all eight rats in the place learning group reached criterion. In fact, the mean trials to criterion for the latter group was only 3.5, whereas it was 17.33 for the three response learners that reached criterion. The place learners solved their problem much faster than the response learners solved theirs. It appeared, therefore, that it was more "natural" for animals to learn places than specific responses, and this result was taken as support for Tolman's theory. The results of the experiment are shown in Figure 12–3.

In another study by Tolman, Ritchie and Kalish (1946a), animals were first trained in the apparatus shown in Figure 12–4. The animals had to learn to follow the route A, B, C, D, E, F, and G. H indicates the place where a 5-watt bulb was located, the only illumination in the room during the experiment. After preliminary training, the apparatus shown in Figure 12–4 was removed and replaced with the apparatus shown in Figure 12–5 (see p. 308).

The path the animals were trained to take in the first phase of the experiment was now blocked, but the animals could choose among eighteen alternative paths. On

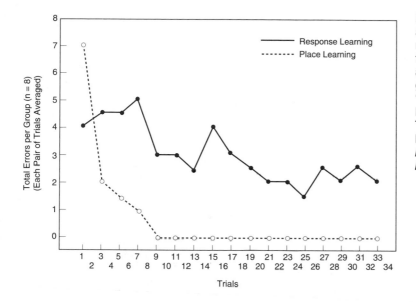

FIGURE 12–3 The average number of errors made on successive trials by place learning and response learning groups of rats. (From "Studies in Spatial Learning II," by E.C. Tolman, B.F. Ritchie, & D. Kalish, 1946, *Journal of Experimental Psychology, 36,* p. 226.)

the basis of S-R theory, one might expect that when the original path was blocked, the animals would choose the unblocked path closest to the original. This, however, was not the case. The most frequently picked was alley number 6, the one pointing directly to where the goal was during the first phase of the experiment. In fact, the alleys closest to the original alley were only infrequently chosen (alley 9 by 2 percent of the rats and alley 10 by 7.5 percent). Tolman, Ritchie, and Kalish (1946a) reported that the first pathway, the one chosen with the second greatest frequency, was the alley pointing to the place in the room where the animals had been fed in their home cages. The results of the experiment are shown in Figure 12–6 (see p. 309).

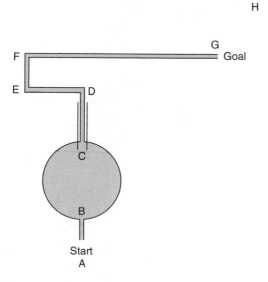

FIGURE 12–4 Apparatus used for preliminary training in the experiment by Tolman, Ritchie, and Kalish on place vs. response learning (From "Studies in Spatial Learning II," by E.C. Tolman, B.F. Ritchie, & D. Kalish, 1946, *Journal of Experimental Psychology, 36.*)

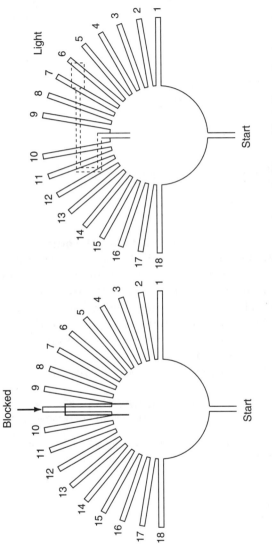

FIGURE 12-5 After preliminary training on the apparatus shown in Figure 12–4, the animals were allowed to choose one of the eighteen alleys shown in the figure to the left. The figure to the right shows the apparatus used for preliminary training superimposed over the test apparatus so that the relationship between the two can be seen. (From "Studies in Spatial Learning I" by E.C. Tolman, B.F. Ritchie, & D. Kalish, 1946, *Journal of Experimental Psychology, 36*.)

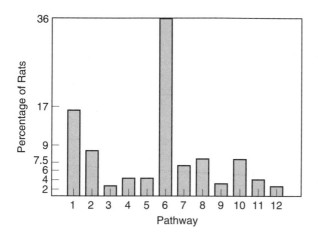

FIGURE 12–6 The results of the experiment diagrammed in Figures 12–4 and 12–5. It can be seen that the most frequently chosen path on the test trial was the one pointing directly to the goal. Tolman, Ritchie, and Kalish also pointed out that the second most frequently chosen path was the one that pointed to the animals' home cages, where they were fed. (From "Studies in Spatial Learning I" by E.C. Tolman, B.F. Ritchie, & D. Kalish, 1946, *Journal of Experimental Psychology, 36.*)

Once again it looked as if the animals were responding in terms of where something was rather than in terms of specific responses. The S-R theorists felt that such experiments did not support place learning since it was entirely possible that the animals simply learned the response of running toward the light. The cognitive theorists refuted this interpretation by saying that if that were true, the animals would have chosen alleys 5 and 7 at least as often as alley 6, and this of course was not the case.

Reinforcement Expectancy

According to Tolman, when we learn, we come to know the "lay of the land." The term *understanding* was not foreign to him as it was to other behaviorists. In a problem-solving situation, we learn where the goal is and we get to it by following the shortest possible route. We learn to expect certain events to follow other events. The animal expects that if it goes to a certain place, it will find a certain reinforcer. The S-R theorist would expect that changing reinforcers in a learning situation would not disrupt behavior as long as the quantity of reinforcement was not changed drastically. Tolman, however, predicted that if reinforcers were changed, behavior will be disrupted since in **reinforcement expectancy** a particular reinforcer becomes a part of what is expected.

Tolman (1932, p. 44) reported an experiment by Elliott, who trained one group of rats to run a maze for bran mush and another to run a maze for sunflower seeds. On the tenth day of training, the group that had been trained on bran mush was switched to sunflower seeds. The results of Elliott's experiment are shown in Figure 12–7. We see that switching reinforcement considerably disrupted performance, thus supporting Tolman's prediction. It should be noted, however, that the group trained on bran mush performed consistently better than the group trained on sunflower seeds before the switch. The Hullians said that because the bran mush had a larger incentive value (K) than did the sunflower seeds, reaction potential would be greater. After the switch to sunflower seeds, K would go down accordingly. The Hullian explanation can only partially account for the results, however, since the group that switched

FIGURE 12–7 The results of an experiment by Elliott (reported by E.C. Tolman, *The Fundamentals of Learning,* New York: Teachers College Press, 1932, p. 44) showing the disruption in behavior that occurs when a reinforcer other than the one that is expected is experienced. (Reprinted by permission.)

to sunflower seeds performed much worse than the group consistently trained on sunflower seeds. Even correcting for the differences in incentive value, there still seems to be considerable disruption of performance that can be explained by the departure from what was expected.

The reader can certainly recall situations in which there has been a discrepancy between what was expected and what was experienced. Examples might include a good friend or relative acting "totally unlike himself," a familiar house torn down while you have been on vacation, or receiving a raise in pay either larger or smaller than that which you expected. In each case, the expected events were not the ones that actually occurred. If a person has important expectations, their failure in being realized could be traumatic. Leon Festinger (1957) constructed a theory of personality around this notion. According to Festinger, when a person's beliefs do not conform to what actually occurs, the person experiences a psychological state called **cognitive dissonance.** Cognitive dissonance is a negative drive state and the person experiencing it seeks ways to reduce it, just as the person experiencing hunger seeks to reduce the hunger drive.

THE FORMAL ASPECTS OF TOLMAN'S THEORY

As an example of Tolman's (1938) more abstract theorizing, we will summarize his article "The Determiners of Behavior at a Choice Point." In this example, the choice point is where the rat decides to turn either right or left in a T-maze. Some of the symbols we will be using are seen in the diagram of the T-maze shown in Figure 12–8.

In an experiment in which a rat was being trained to turn left in a T-maze, Tolman's dependent variable was a behavior ratio defined as follows:

$$\frac{B_L}{B_L+B_R}$$

This formula gives the percentage tendency to turn left at any stage of learning. If, for example, an animal turned left six times out of ten times, we would have

$$\frac{6}{6+4} = 60\%$$

Tolman felt that the behavior ratio was determined by the collective experiences that come from having turned both ways at the choice point on various trials. This experience allows the animal to learn what leads to what. The cumulative nature of these experiences was diagrammed by Tolman as follows:

Rather than repeating this cumbersome diagram, Tolman abbreviated it ΣOBO, which stands for the accumulated knowledge that comes from making both B_L and B_R responses and seeing what they lead to. The events involved in T-maze learning are diagrammed in Figure 12–8.

FIGURE 12–8
A diagram of a T-maze. (From "The Determiners of Behavior at a Choice Point," by E.C. Tolman, 1938. *Psychological Review, 45,* p. 1. Copyright © 1938 by the American Psychological Association. Reprinted by permission.)

Environmental Variables

Unfortunately, the situation is not so simple as suggested above. Tolman thought of ΣOBO as an independent variable since it directly influenced the dependent variable (i.e., the behavior ratio), and it was under the control of the experimenter who determined the number of training trials. In addition to ΣOBO a number of other independent variables could have an effect on performance. Tolman suggested the following list:

M = maintenance schedule. This symbol refers to the animal's deprivation schedule, for example, the number of hours since it has eaten.

G = appropriateness of goal object. The reinforcer must be related to the animal's current drive state. For example, one does not reinforce a thirsty animal with food.

S = types and modes of stimuli provided. This symbol refers to the vividness of the cues or signals available to the animal in the learning situation.

R = types of motor responses required in the learning situation, for example, running, sharp turns, and so on.

P = pattern of succeeding and preceding maze units; the pattern of turns that needs to be made to solve a maze as determined by the experimenter.

ΣOBO = the number of trials and their cumulative nature (see above).

It should be clear that Tolman was no longer talking only about the learning of T-mazes but the learning of more complex mazes as well.

Individual Difference Variables

In addition to the independent variables described above, there are the variables that the individual subjects bring into the experiment with them. The list of individual difference variables suggested by Tolman is as follows (note that their initials create the acronym HATE, a somewhat strange word for Tolman to use):

H = heredity
A = age
T = previous training
E = special endocrine, drug, or vitamin conditions.

Each of the individual difference variables interacts with each of the independent variables, and a combination of all these variables working together is what produces behavior (seen in Figure 12–9).

Intervening Variables

Up to this point, we have been discussing the effects of observed stimulus variables (independent variables) on observed behavior (dependent variables). It would be possible, as Skinner suggested, to conduct thousands of experiments showing how

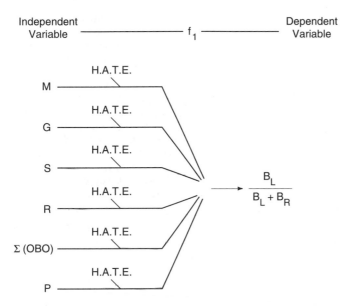

Independent Variable ——————— f_1 ——————— Dependent Variable

M ——————— H.A.T.E.

G ——————— H.A.T.E.

S ——————— H.A.T.E.

R ——————— H.A.T.E.

Σ (OBO) ——————— H.A.T.E.

P ——————— H.A.T.E.

$$\dfrac{B_L}{B_L + B_R}$$

FIGURE 12–9 Illustration of the relationship among the independent variables, the individual difference variables, and behavior. (From "The Determiners of Behavior at a Choice Point," by E.C. Tolman, 1938, *Psychological Review, 45,* p. 8. Copyright © 1938 by the American Psychological Association. Reprinted by permission.)

those variables are related to each other in various combinations. The functional analysis suggested by Skinner, however, was not appealing to Tolman (1938), who wanted to move beyond the facts:

> But why, you may ask, can we not be satisfied with just experiments and the "facts" resulting from them? I find that there are two reasons. In the first place, an entirely factual empirical establishment of the complete functional relation, f_1, to cover the effects on (B_L/B_L+B_R) of all the permutations and combinations of M, G. S, etc., etc., would be a humanly endless task. We have time in this brief mortal span to test only a relatively limited number of such permutations and combinations. So, in the first place, we are forced to propose theories in order to use such theories to extrapolate for all these combinations for which we have not time to test.
>
> But I suspect that there is another reason for theories. Some of us, psychologically, just demand theories. Even if we had all the million and one concrete facts, we would still want theories to, as we would say, "explain" those facts. Theories just seem to be necessary to some of us to relieve our inner tensions. (pp. 8–9)

Tolman defined a theory as a set of intervening variables. An intervening variable is a construct created by the theorist to aid in explaining the relationship between an independent variable and a dependent variable. The example given in Chapter 2 was hunger. It has been found that performance on a learning task varies with hours of food deprivation, and that is an empirical relationship. If one says, however, that *hunger* varies with hours of deprivation and in turn influences learning, the concept of hunger is being used as an intervening variable. As Tolman said, such a concept is used to fill in the blanks in a research program.

For similar reasons, Tolman created an intervening variable to go along with each of his independent variables. In each case, the intervening variable was systematically tied to both an independent variable and a dependent variable. In other words, each of Tolman's intervening variables was operationally defined. **Mainte-**

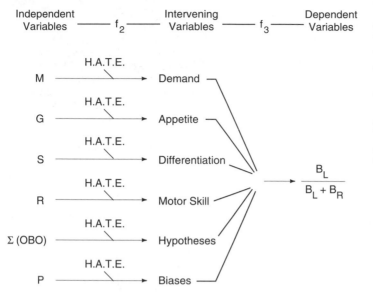

FIGURE 12–10 The relationship suggested by Tolman among independent variables, individual difference variables, intervening variables, and the dependent variable. (From "The Determiners of Behavior at a Choice Point," by E.C. Tolman, 1938, *Psychological Review, 45,* p. 16. Copyright © 1938 by the American Psychological Association. Reprinted by permission.)

nance schedule, for example, creates a **demand,** which in turn is related to performance. Appropriateness of the goal object is related to *appetite,* which in turn is related to performance. Types of stimuli provided are related to the animal's capability for *differentiation,* and so on. A summary of Tolman's system, showing his use of intervening variables, is shown in Figure 12–10.

One can now see the similarity between Tolman and Hull in the use of intervening variables. Hull, as we have mentioned, borrowed the approach from Tolman, who introduced the use of intervening variables into psychology. The part of the system shown in Figure 12–10 that relates most closely to the main theme in Tolman's theory is the intervening variable of "hypotheses." As the result of previous experience (ΣOBO) hypotheses are developed that affect behavior ($B_L / B_L + B_R$). As these hypotheses are confirmed by experience, they become means-end readinesses, or beliefs. The function of an intervening variable is seen clearly at this point. It is an empirical fact that performance improves as a function of the number of learning trials, but the intervening variables are created in an effort to explain why this is the case. According to those who use intervening variables, the facts would be the same without their use, but our understanding of the facts would be severely limited.

MacCORQUODALE AND MEEHL'S FORMALIZATION OF TOLMAN'S THEORY

MacCorquodale and Meehl (1953) attempted to do for Tolman's theory what Voeks attempted to do for Guthrie's. That is, they attempted to make Tolman's terms more precise and his concepts more easily tested. Most of MacCorquodale and Meehl's restatement of Tolman's theory is beyond the scope of this book, but the brief sample of their work offered below nicely summarizes a few of Tolman's more important concepts.

MacCorquodale and Meehl (1953) describe Tolman's theory as an S_1-R_1-S_2 theory, where S_1 elicits an expectancy of some kind, R_1 indicates the manner in which the expectancy is acted on, and S_2 indicates what the organism thinks will happen as a result of its actions under the circumstances. In other words, the organism seems to think, "under these circumstances (S_1), if I do this (R_1), I will have a certain experience (S_2)." An example would be seeing a friend (S_1) and believing that saying "hello" (R_1) will result in a warm greeting from the friend (S_2). Or, seeing a certain intersection (S_1) and believing that turning to the right (R_1) will result in finding a service station (S_2). The more often the S_1-R_1-S_2 sequence occurs, the stronger the expectation will become. Likewise, if S_1 and R_1 occur and S_2 does not follow, the expectation becomes weaker. MacCorquodale and Meehl handle the concept of stimulus generalization within Tolman's theory by saying that if an expectancy is elicited by S_1, it will also be elicited by stimuli similar to S_1.

SIX KINDS OF LEARNING

In his 1949 article, "There Is More Than One Kind of Learning," Tolman proposed six kinds of learning. Each is briefly summarized below.

Cathexes

Cathexis (plural, cathexes) refers to the learned tendency to associate certain objects with certain drive states. For example, certain foods might be available to satisfy the hunger drive of individuals who live in a particular country. Persons who live in a country where fish is usually eaten will tend to seek fish to satisfy their hunger. The same individuals may avoid beef or spaghetti because, for them, those foods have not been associated with the satisfaction of the hunger drive. Since certain stimuli have been associated with the satisfaction of a certain drive those stimuli will tend to be sought out when the drive recurs: "When a type of goal has been positively cathected it means that when the given drive is in force the organism will tend to apprehend, to approach, and to perform the consummatory reaction upon any instance of this type of goal which is presented by the immediate environment" (p. 146). When the organism has learned to avoid certain objects while in a certain drive state, a negative cathexis is said to have occurred. There is little difference between Tolman and the S-R theorists concerning this kind of learning.

Equivalence Beliefs

When a "subgoal" has the same effect as the goal itself, the subgoal is said to constitute an **equivalence belief.** Although this is close to what the S-R theorists call secondary reinforcement, Tolman (1949) felt that this kind of learning more typically involved the "social drives" rather than the physiological drives. He gave the following example: "Insofar as it can be demonstrated that with the reception of the high grades there is some temporary reduction in this student's need for love and approbation even without his going on to tell others about his grade, then we would have evidence for an equivalence belief. The A's would then be accepted by him as equivalent to the love or approbation to which they were originally a mere means" (p. 148).

Here again, there is little difference between Tolman and the S-R theorists, except for the fact that Tolman talked about "love reduction" as the reinforcement, and the S-R theorists would prefer to remain with the reduction of drives such as hunger or thirst.

Field Expectancies

Field expectancies are developed in the same way a cognitive map is developed: The organism learns what leads to what. Upon seeing a certain sign, for instance, it expects that a certain other sign will follow. This general knowledge of the environment is used to explain latent learning, latent extinction, place learning, and the use of shortcuts. This is not S-R learning but rather S-S, or sign-sign, learning; that is, when the animal sees one sign, it learns to expect another to follow. The only "reinforcement" necessary for this kind of learning to take place is the confirmation of an hypothesis.

Field-Cognition Modes

The kind of learning about which Tolman was least confident, a **field-cognition mode** is a strategy, a way of approaching a problem-solving situation. It is a tendency to arrange the perceptual field in certain configurations. Tolman suspected that these tendencies were innate but could be modified by experience. In fact, the most important thing about a strategy that works in solving a problem is that it will be tried in similar situations in the future. Thus, effective field-cognition modes, or problem-solving strategies, transfer to related problems. In that way they are similar to means-end readinesses (beliefs), which also transfer to similar situations. Tolman (1949) summarized his thinking about this kind of learning as follows: "In a word, I am trying to summarize under this fourth category all those principles as to the structure of environmental fields which are relevant to all environmental fields, and which (whether innate or learned) are carried around by the individual and applied to each new field with which he is presented" (p. 153).

Drive Discriminations

Drive discrimination simply refers to the fact that organisms can determine their own drive state and therefore can respond appropriately. It has been found, for example, that animals can be trained to turn one way in a T-maze when they are hungry and the other way when they are thirsty (Hull, 1933a; Leeper, 1935). Since Tolman believed in social as well as physiological drives, **drive discrimination** was an important concept to him. Unless an organism can clearly determine its own drive state, it will not know how to read its cognitive map. If an organism's needs are not clear, its goals are not clear and therefore its behavior may be inappropriate. How people will act when they need love, for example, will be different from how they will act when they need water.

Motor Patterns

Tolman pointed out that his theory is mainly concerned with the association of ideas and is not overly concerned with the manner in which those ideas become associated with behavior. **Motor pattern** learning is an attempt to resolve this difficulty. Of all people, Tolman (1949) accepted Guthrie's interpretation of how responses become associated with stimuli. He did accept Guthrie reluctantly, however, which is exemplified by the following quotation: "In default of other experimental theories about the learning of motor patterns I am willing to take a chance and to agree with Guthrie that the conditions under which a motor pattern gets acquired may well be those in which the given movement gets the animal away from the stimuli which were present when the movement was initiated" (p. 153).

Tolman was truly an eclectic. Somewhere among the six kinds of learning he described, there is agreement with almost every other major theory of learning. Combining the ideas of Hull, Gestalt theory, and Guthrie in one system would have confused a lesser mind. As for his reason for postulating many kinds of learning rather than one or two kinds, Tolman (1949) said the following:

> Why did I want thus to complicate things; why do I not want one simple set of laws for all learning? I do not know. But I suppose it must be due to some funny erroneous equivalence belief on my part to the effect that being sweeping and comprehensive though vague, is equivalent to more love from others than being narrow and precise. No doubt, any good clinician would be able to trace this back to some sort of nasty traumatic experience in my early childhood. (p. 155)

Tolman's Attitude Toward His Own Theory

Tolman presented the final version of his theory in *Psychology: A Study of a Science,* edited by Sigmund Koch, which appeared in 1959, the year Tolman died. There is probably no better indication of how Tolman felt toward his own theory and toward science in general than the first and last paragraphs of his chapter in that volume. First, Tolman's (1959) opening statement:

> I would like to begin by letting off steam. If in what follows I have not done a very clear or useful job, I would plead some half-dozen reasons. First, I think the days of such grandiose, all-covering systems in psychology as mine attempted to be are, at least for the present, pretty much passé. I feel therefore, that it might have been more decent and more dignified to let such an instance of the relatively immediate dead past bury its dead. Secondly, I don't enjoy trying to use my mind in too analytical a way. Hence, I have found it frustrating and difficult to try to subject my system to the required sorts of analyses. Thirdly, I suppose I am personally antipathetic to the notion that science progresses through intense, self-conscious analysis of where one has got and where one is going. Such analyses are obviously a proper function for the philosopher of science and they may be valuable for many individual scientists. But I myself become frightened and restricted when I begin to worry too much as to what particular logical and methodological canons I should or should not obey. It seems to me that very often major new scientific insights have come when the scientist, like the ape, has been shaken out of his up-until-then approved scientific rules such as that food can be reached only by the

hand and discovers "out of the blue," and perhaps purely by analogy...the new rule of using a stick (or a sign-Gestalt). Fourthly, I have an inveterate tendency to make my ideas too complicated and too high-flown so that they become less and less susceptible to empirical tests. Fifthly, because of increasing laziness, I have not of late kept up, as I should have, with the more recent theoretical and empirical discussions which bear upon my argument. If I had, the argument would have been different and better and also I would have given more credit to those to whom credit is due. Finally, to talk about one's own ideas and to resort frequently to the use of the first person singular, as one tends to do in such an analysis, brings about a conflict, at least in me, between enjoying my exhibitionism and being made to feel guilty by my superego. (pp. 93–94)

And Tolman's (1959) last statement about his theory was as follows:

I started out, as I indicated in the introduction, with considerable uneasiness. I felt that my so-called system was outdated and that it was a waste of time to try to rehash it and that it would be pretentious now to seek to make it fit any accepted set of prescriptions laid down by the philosophy of science. I have to confess, however, that as I have gone along I have become again more and more involved in it, though I still realize its many weak points. The system may well not stand up to any final canons of scientific procedure. But I do not much care. I have liked to think about psychology in ways that have proved congenial to me. Since all the sciences, and especially psychology, are still immersed in such tremendous realms of the uncertain and the unknown, the best that any individual scientist, especially any psychologist, can do seems to be to follow his own gleam and his own bent, however inadequate they may be. In fact, I suppose that actually this is what we all do. In the end, the only sure criterion is to have fun. And I have had fun. (p. 152)

BOLLES'S THEORY OF LEARNING

We have already seen in Chapter 7 that Bolles explains classical conditioning as the development of expectancies. That is, upon seeing one stimulus (CS), the organism expects that another stimulus will follow. In everyday life, seeing lightning and expecting thunder would exemplify an S-S expectancy. Whereas classical conditioning involves the development of S-S expectancies, operant and instrumental conditioning involve the development of R-S expectancies (Bolles, 1972). For example, the rat learns to expect that if it presses the bar in a Skinner box, food will follow. In everyday life, expecting to hear the sound of a bell when a doorbell is pressed exemplifies an R-S expectancy. In discussing R-S expectancies, it helps to think of the S as an *outcome* produced by the response.

Whereas Tolman concentrated almost exclusively on *learned* S-S and R-S expectancies, Bolles emphasizes *innate* S-S and R-S expectancies in his analysis of behavior. An example of an innate S-S relationship is when a young infant displays fear of a loud noise, suggesting that the infant expects a dangerous event to follow. Innate R-S expectancies are exemplified by the stereotyped behavior that many species of animals engage in in the presence of food, water, danger, and other biologically significant objects or situations.

As evidence for the importance of innate R-S expectancies, Bolles (1970, 1972)

Robert C. Bolles. (Courtesy of Robert C.
Bolles.)

notes how animals typically respond to pain with a series of **species-specific defensive reactions (SSDRs).** For the rat, such reactions include freezing, fleeing, screaming, leaping up, and aggressing toward some object. In the natural environment, one or more of these innate reactions may lead to safety, and if so, the problem is solved. Also, in a laboratory, if one of these innate reactions to pain allows the animal to escape pain, the escape response will be learned rapidly. In fact, under the circumstances just described, the animal really learned nothing; the aversive stimulation simply caused the animal to engage in SSDRs. Avoidance conditioning is a bit more complicated. According to Bolles, avoidance conditioning involves both S-S and R-S expectancies. Since in avoidance conditioning a signal precedes an aversive event (e.g., shock), the animal learns to expect pain when, say, a tone is sounded. Since the tone signals danger, it comes to elicit the same SSDRs that are elicited by the aversive stimulus itself. Thus, according to Bolles, either warnings of pain or pain itself evoke SSDRs.

An obvious prediction from Bolles's analysis is that the closer the response required of an animal in an experiment is to what that animal would do naturally in that situation, the more readily the response will be learned. If the required response is not part of the animal's innate response repertoire, it will be learned with great difficulty or perhaps not at all. An example is the fact that pigeons can easily be taught to fly from one perch to another to avoid shock, but it is almost impossible to teach pigeons to peck a key to avoid shock (Bolles, 1979, p. 185). Thus, the choice of the response required of an animal in a learning experiment is a major factor in determining the results of the experiment.

> Even a casual look at rats in different avoidance learning situations reveals that what response we require of them is a tremendously important consideration; it can make the difference between some learning in one trial and no learning in 1000 trials. It is vastly more important than the reinforcement contingencies, various experimental parameters, the animal's prior experience, or different kinds of physiological interventions that might be made. The choice of what the response shall be is clearly not an arbitrary matter, or just a question of convenience, it is the governing factor in whether or how rapidly learning will occur. It is a serious indictment of our classical learning theories that they provide no hint that the choice of the response is so important. (p. 185)

Just as Bolles believes that innate responses play a major role in escape and avoidance learning, so too does he believe that innate responses play a major role in appetitive learning. Not only are there innate reactions to pain, there are also innate reactions to food and water. For example, many species have stereotyped ways of taking and eating food, such as grasping, tearing, chewing, washing, or rooting. According to Bolles, the extent to which such responses are called for in an experiment in which food is a reinforcer will determine how easily learning will occur. As with the case of learning to escape or avoid an aversive stimulus, the more unnatural is the response that the animal is required to make, the more difficult it will be for the animal to learn it.

By noting the importance of innate R-S expectancies, Bolles is essentially in agreement with Seligman's contention that how easily an association is learned depends on where that association falls on the preparedness-contrapreparedness continuum. Associations for which an animal is biologically prepared are learned easiest. Also, Bolles agrees with the explanation of instinctual drift offered by the Brelands (see Chapter 5). That is, the natural responses associated with eating are more powerful than the responses that the animals had learned in order to obtain food. Therefore, the unnatural learned responses were gradually displaced by the stronger natural responses. Finally, as we saw in Chapter 5, Bolles said that autoshaping could be explained as the triggering of innate responses that are appropriate to the situation. Therefore, for Bolles, autoshaping is not shaping at all. Because of the importance that he places on innate behavioral tendencies, he joins the growing number of modern psychologists who find it necessary to consider the biological boundaries of learning.

EVALUATION OF TOLMAN'S THEORY

Contributions

When we look for the contributions that Tolman made to the study of learning, it is tempting to seize a single finding or important study and explore its importance. The demonstration of latent learning by Tolman and Honzik (1930) is one such example. Another, the radial-maze experiment by Tolman, Ritchie, and Kalish (1946b), in which it was demonstrated that rats learn spatial relations rather than simple responses, has been identified as the predecessor of current studies in comparative cognition (Olton, 1992). Tolman's greatest contributions, however, lie less in specific research findings and more in his role as an antagonist against the dominance of Hullian neobehaviorism. While Hull and others were able to dismiss challenges by Gestalt psychologists or by Piaget, pointing to differences in both the experimental subjects and methodologies, they were not able to ignore the well designed and controlled experiments conducted in Tolman's laboratories.

Tolman may have lost many skirmishes with the S-R behaviorists, but with the current emphasis in psychology on the study of cognitive processes, his theory may end up winning the war. The many current theories that emphasize the learning of expectancies and claim that the function of reinforcement is to provide information rather than to strengthen behavior owe a great debt to Tolman's theory. As we have seen, Bolles's is one such theory. In the next chapter we shall see that the theory proposed by Albert Bandura is another.

Criticisms

Scientific criticisms of Tolman's theory are certainly valid. The theory is not easily subjected to empirical scrutiny. It involves such a large number of independent, individual, and intervening variables that it is extremely difficult to account for all of them. Unfortunately for scientific critics, Tolman anticipated such criticisms and, as reflected in his (1959) statement on the preceding pages, did not seem to care. And he did have fun.

Malone (1991) raises the serious criticism that, with his extensive introduction of intervening variables, Tolman actually caused regression of psychology back into the mentalistic orientations of the nineteenth century rather than progression of psychology through the twentieth century. As evidence of this claim, Malone (1991) pointed to the lack of practical applications generated by Tolman's theory. Although lack of applicability may be a valid issue, the claim that Tolman's theory is regressive may not be. As we will see in upcoming chapters, information-processing approaches and neural networks may not have immediate applicability to practical problems, and they are often encumbered by intervening constructs. It would be incorrect, however, to categorize them as regressive.

DISCUSSION QUESTIONS

1. Why can Tolman's theory be considered a combination of Gestalt psychology and behaviorism?
2. What is purposive behaviorism?
3. Why is Tolman's theory called an S-S theory rather than an S-R theory?
4. Describe a situation that would allow you to determine whether or not an animal is utilizing a cognitive map to solve a problem. Do not use any of the specific studies discussed in this chapter.
5. For Tolman, is reinforcement a learning or a performance variable? Explain.
6. Describe briefly the six kinds of learning proposed by Tolman.
7. Summarize the study performed by Tolman and Honzik on latent learning. What conclusions can be drawn from their results?
8. Describe a typical latent extinction experiment and explain why the phenomenon of latent extinction was thought to support Tolman's theory.
9. Describe, according to Tolman, what events take place as an animal is learning to solve a maze. Incorporate as many of Tolman's theoretical terms into your answer as possible.
10. What would characterize classroom procedures designed in accordance with Tolman's theory?
11. Give instances from your own personal life that would either support or refute Tolman's theory of learning.
12. Explain the importance of species-specific defensive reactions (SSDRs) in Bolles's analysis of escape and avoidance learning.
13. According to Bolles, what determines the ease with which a response required in a learning experiment is learned?

KEY TERMS

cathexis   The formation of an association between a certain drive state, such as hunger, and certain stimuli, such as the foods one is accustomed to eating. When a drive occurs, one actively seeks out the stimuli that have been previously associated with its satisfaction. Cathexis is one of Tolman's six proposed kinds of learning.

cognitive dissonance   A psychological state experienced when there is a discrepancy between what is expected and what actually occurs.

cognitive map   A mental picture of the environment.

confirmation of an expectancy   When the prediction made about some future event is found to be accurate.

demand   The intervening variable that corresponds to maintenance schedule. As the number of hours without eating goes up, for example, demand is thought to increase.

drive discriminations   The fact that organisms can discriminate between various drive states and can therefore adjust their behavior so that appropriate goal objects can be experienced. Drive discrimination is one of Tolman's six proposed kinds of learning.

emphasizer   A role that motivation plays in Tolman's theory. The motivational state of an organism determines which environmental events will be emphasized in that organism's perceptual field.

equivalence beliefs   Similar to the notion of secondary reinforcement, in that a previously neutral event develops the capability of satisfying a need. One of Tolman's six proposed kinds of learning.

expectancy   A belief or hypothesis about the occurrence of a future event.

field-cognition modes   Learned or inherited strategies that are utilized while attempting to solve problems. Field-cognition modes are one of Tolman's six proposed kinds of learning.

field expectancies   Similar to a cognitive map, in that the organism comes to know which events in a given environment lead to other events. Field expectancies is one of Tolman's six proposed kinds of learning.

hypotheses   Expectancies that occur in the early stages of learning.

latent extinction   Extinction that occurs simply because an animal is allowed to observe that a reinforcer is no longer available. Such extinction does not depend on the performance of nonreinforced responses.

latent learning   Learning that occurs but is not translated immediately into performance. Rather, it is learning that remains dormant until there is some reason for utilizing it, at which time it is translated into behavior.

maintenance schedule   The feeding schedule arranged by the experimenter for an organism during a learning experiment.

means-end readiness   An expectancy that is consistently confirmed; sometimes referred to as a belief.

molar behavior   See Key Terms for Chapter 10.

motor patterns   The learning of the overt behavior that the organism must utilize in reaching a desired goal. Motor patterns is one of Tolman's six proposed kinds of learning.

place learning   Learning where an object is located. According to Tolman, once the location of an object is known, it can be reached by any number of alternate routes.

principle of least effort   The contention that a task will always be done in a manner that requires the least amount of effort or work.

purposive behavior   Behavior directed toward some goal, such as going to the store, cooking a meal, or solving a maze.

purposive behaviorism   A behavioristic approach that studies purposive behavior as such and does not attempt to reduce such behavior into smaller elements for further analysis.

reinforcement expectancy   The fact that an organism learns to expect a certain reinforcer if it engages in certain behaviors. It has been found that performance is disrupted when the original reinforcer used in a learning situation is replaced with a different reinforcer.

response learning   The learning of specific responses that are effective in solving a problem and thereby providing reinforcement.

species-specific defensive reactions (SSDRs)   According to Bolles, the innate responses that are triggered by an aversive situation and that under ordinary circumstances would allow the animal to escape or avoid the aversive situation.

vicarious trial and error   The hesitation at a choice point in a learning situation, where it looks "as if" the animal is weighing the alternatives before it decides what to do.

Chapter 13

ALBERT BANDURA

Albert Bandura. (Courtesy of Albert Bandura.)

Albert Bandura was born on December 4, 1925, in Mundare, a small town in Alberta, Canada. He obtained his B.A. from the University of British Columbia and his M.A. in 1951 and his Ph.D. in 1952, both from the University of Iowa. He did a postdoctoral internship at the Wichita Guidance Center in 1953 and then joined the faculty at Stanford University, where he has been ever since, except for the 1969–1970 year when he was a fellow at the Center for the Advanced Study in the Behavioral Sciences. Bandura is currently the David Starr Jordan Professor of Social Science in Psychology at Stanford University.

Among Bandura's many honors are a Guggenheim Fellowship, 1972; a Distinguished Scientist Award from Division 12 of the American Psychological Association, 1972; a Distinguished Scientific Achievement Award from the California Psychological Association, 1973; Presidency of the American Psychological Association, 1974; and the James McKeen Cattell Award, 1977. In addition, Bandura holds office in several scientific societies and is a member of the editorial boards of seventeen scholarly journals.

While at the University of Iowa, Bandura was influenced by Kenneth Spence, a prominent Hullian learning theorist, but Bandura's major interest was in clinical psychology. At this time, Bandura was interested in clarifying the notions thought to be involved in effective psychotherapy and then empirically testing and refining them. It was also during this time that Bandura read Miller and Dollard's (1941) book *Social Learning and Imitation,* which greatly influenced him. Miller and Dollard used Hullian learning theory (see Chapter 6) as the basis of their explanation of social and imitative behavior. As we shall see later in this chapter, Miller and Dollard's explanation of imitative learning dominated the psychological literature for over two decades. It was not until the early 1960s that Bandura began a series of articles and books that were to challenge the older explanations of imitative learning and expand the topic into what is now referred to as observational learning. There is little doubt that Bandura is now looked on as the leading researcher and theorist in the area of observational learning, a topic that is currently very popular.

EARLIER EXPLANATIONS OF OBSERVATIONAL LEARNING

The belief that humans learn by observing other humans goes back at least to such early Greeks as Plato and Aristotle. For them education was, to a large extent, selecting the best models for presentation to students so that the model's qualities may be observed and emulated. Through the centuries **observational learning** was taken for granted and was usually explained by postulating a natural tendency for humans to imitate what they see others do. As long as this nativistic explanation prevailed, little was done either to verify the fact that the tendency to learn by observation was innate or, indeed, to determine whether observational learning occurred at all.

It was Edward L. Thorndike who first attempted to study observational learning experimentally. In 1898, he placed one cat in a puzzle box and another cat in an adjoining cage. The cat in the puzzle box had already learned how to escape, so the second cat had only to observe the first cat to learn the escape response. However, when Thorndike placed the second cat in the puzzle box it did not perform the escape response. The second cat had to go through the same trial-and-error process that the first cat went through before it also learned the escape response. Thorndike ran the same type of experiment with chicks and dogs, with the same results. No matter how long a naive animal watched a sophisticated one, the naive animal seemed to learn nothing. In 1901, Thorndike ran similar experiments with monkeys, but contrary to the popular belief that "monkey see, monkey do," no observational learning took place. Thorndike (1901) concluded, "Nothing in my experience with these animals...favors the hypothesis that they have any general ability to learn to do things from seeing others do them" (p. 42).

In 1908, J. B. Watson replicated Thorndike's research with monkeys; he too found no evidence for observational learning. Both Thorndike and Watson concluded that learning can result only from **direct experience** and not from indirect or **vicarious experience.** In other words, they felt that learning occurred as a result of one's personal interactions with the environment and not as a result of observing another's interactions.

With only a few exceptions, the work of Thorndike and Watson discouraged further research on observational learning. It was not until the publication of Miller and Dollard's book *Social Learning and Imitation* (1941) that interest in observational learning was again stimulated.

Miller and Dollard's Explanation of Observational Learning

Like Thorndike and Watson, Miller and Dollard sought to challenge the nativistic explanation of observational learning. However, unlike Thorndike and Watson, Miller and Dollard did not deny the fact that an organism could learn by observing the activities of another organism. They felt that such learning was rather widespread but that it could be explained objectively within the framework of Hullian learning theory. That is, if **imitative behavior** is reinforced, it will be strengthened like any other kind of behavior. Thus, according to Miller and Dollard, imitative learning is simply a special case of instrumental conditioning.

Miller and Dollard (1941) divided imitative behavior into three categories: (1) **Same behavior** occurs when two or more individuals respond to the same situation in the same way. For example, most people stop at a red light, applaud when a play or concert is over, and laugh when others laugh. With same behavior, all the individuals involved have learned independently to respond in a particular way to a particular stimulus, and their behavior is triggered simultaneously when that stimulus, or one like it, occurs in the environment; (2) **Copying behavior** involves the guiding of one person's behavior by another person, such as when an art instructor gives guidance and corrective feedback to an art student who is attempting to draw a picture. With copying behavior, the final "copied" response is reinforced and thereby strengthened; (3) **Matched-dependent behavior,** an observer is reinforced for blindly repeating the actions of a model. As an example, Miller and Dollard describe a situation in which an older child had learned to run to the front door upon hearing his father's footsteps as the father approached the house and the father reinforced the child's efforts with candy. A younger child found that if he happened to be running behind his brother when he ran to the door, he (the younger child) would also receive candy from the father. Soon the younger child learned to run to the door whenever he saw his older brother doing so. At this point the behavior of both children was being maintained by reinforcement, but each boy associated reinforcement with different cues. For the older child, the sound of the father's approaching footsteps triggered the running response, which was reinforced by candy. For the younger child, the sight of his brother running toward the door triggered running on his part, which was also reinforced by candy.

Matched-dependent behavior also seems to characterize the behavior of adults who are in an unfamiliar situation. When one is in a foreign country, for example, one may avoid many problems by observing how the natives respond to various situations and then responding as they do, even if the rationale for the behavior is not clearly understood. Perhaps this is the rationale behind the old saying, "When in Rome, do as the Romans do."

Miller and Dollard (1941) also pointed out that imitation itself could become a habit. In the situation described previously, the younger child could have learned that imitating the behavior of his older brother had often led to reinforcement, and therefore the probability of his acting like his older brother in a wide variety of situations would have increased. Miller and Dollard referred to this learned tendency to imitate the behavior of one or more individuals as **generalized imitation.**

Miller and Dollard (1941) saw nothing unusual or special about imitative learning. For them the role of the model was to guide the observer's responses until the appropriate one had been made or to demonstrate to an observer which response would be reinforced in a given situation. According to Miller and Dollard, if imitative responses were not made and reinforced, no learning would take place. For them, imitative learning was the result of observation, overt responding, and reinforcement. There is nothing in these conclusions that disagrees with the conclusions reached by Thorndike and Watson. Like their predecessors, Miller and Dollard found that organisms do not learn from observation alone. Perhaps, Miller and Dollard might say that the only mistake that Thorndike and Watson made was not placing the naive animal *inside* the puzzle box with the sophisticated animal. This placement would have allowed the naive animal to observe, to respond, and to be reinforced, and therefore imitative learning probably would have occurred.

Unlike the nativistic explanations of imitative learning that prevailed for many centuries, Miller and Dollard's explanation offered the first empirical explanation of the phenomenon. Their explanation was in accordance with a widely accepted theory of learning and was firmly supported by rigorous experimental research.

As we saw earlier, the work of Thorndike and Watson had laid interest in imitative learning to rest for over three decades. Miller and Dollard's work had the same effect for over two decades. It was not until the early 1960s that the topic was again scrutinized. It was at this time that Bandura challenged earlier explanations of imitative learning and began to formulate his own theory, which broke away from the behavioristic mold of the preceding theories. As we shall see, Bandura views observational learning as primarily a cognitive process, which involves a number of attributes thought of as distinctly human, such as language, morality, thinking, and the self-regulation of one's behavior.

BANDURA'S ACCOUNT OF OBSERVATIONAL LEARNING

Up to this point we have been using the terms *imitation* and *observational learning* interchangeably; however, for Bandura a distinction must be made between the two concepts. According to Bandura, observational **learning** may or may not involve imitation. For example, while driving down the street you may see the car in front of you hit a pothole, and based on this observation you may swerve in order to miss the hole and avoid damage to your car. In this case, you learned from your observation, but you did not imitate what you had observed. What you learned, according to Bandura, was *information,* which was processed cognitively and acted on in a way that was advantageous. Observational learning, therefore, is much more complex than simple imitation, which usually involves mimicking another person's actions.

If one had to choose a theory of learning that is closest to Bandura's, it would be Tolman's theory. Although Tolman was a behaviorist, he used mentalistic concepts to explain behavioral phenomena (see Chapter 12), and Bandura does the same thing. Also, Tolman believed learning to be a constant process that does not require reinforcement, and Bandura believes the same thing. Both Tolman's theory and Bandura's theory are cognitive in nature, and neither are **reinforcement theories.** A final point of agreement between Tolman and Bandura concerns the concept of motivation. Although Tolman believed that learning was constant, he believed further that the information gained through learning was only acted on when there was reason for doing so, such as when a need arose. For example, one may know full well where a drinking fountain is but will act on that information only when one is thirsty. For Tolman, this distinction between learning and performance was extremely important, and it is also important in Bandura's theory.

The learning-performance distinction is nicely demonstrated in a study performed by Bandura (1965). In this experiment, children observed a film in which a **model** was shown hitting and kicking a large doll. In Bandura's theory a model can be anything that conveys information, such as a person, film, television, demonstration, picture, or instructions. In this case, a film showed an adult modeling aggressiveness. One group of children saw the model reinforced for his aggressiveness. A second group of children saw the model punished for his aggressiveness. For a third group the consequences of the model's aggressiveness were neutral; that is, the model was neither reinforced nor punished. Later, children in all three groups were exposed to the doll, and their aggressiveness toward it was measured. As might be expected, the children who saw the model reinforced for aggressiveness were most aggressive; the children who saw the model punished for aggressiveness were least aggressive; and the children who saw the model experience neutral consequences were between the two other groups in their aggressiveness. This much of the study is interesting because it demonstrates that the children's behavior was influenced by indirect or vicarious experience. In other words, what they observed another person experiencing had an impact on their own behavior. The children in the first group observed **vicarious reinforcement**, and it facilitated their aggressiveness; children in the second group observed **vicarious punishment,** and it inhibited their aggressiveness. Although the children did not experience reinforcement or punishment directly, it modified their behavior just the same. This is contrary to Miller and Dollard's contention that observational learning will occur only if the organism's *overt* behavior is followed by reinforcement.

The second phase of the study described above was designed to shed light on the learning-performance distinction. In this phase, *all* the children were offered an attractive incentive for reproducing the behavior of the model, *and they all did so.* In other words, all the children had *learned* the model's aggressive responses but they had *performed* differentially, depending on whether they had observed the model being reinforced, punished, or experiencing neutral consequences. The results of this study are summarized in Figure 13–1.

Note the similarity between the Bandura (1965) experiment and the one run by Tolman and Honzik (1930). In the latter study it was found that if a rat that had run a maze without **reinforcement** was suddenly given reinforcement for making the correct goal response, its **performance** rapidly equaled that of a rat that had been reinforced on every trial. Tolman's explanation was that even the nonreinforced rats were learning the maze, and inserting reinforcement into the situation merely caused them to demonstrate the information that they had been accumulating all along. Thus, the purpose of Bandura's experiment was similar to that of Tolman and Honzik's, and the findings and conclusions about the distinction between learning and performance were also similar. The major finding from both experiments was that reinforcement is a performance variable and not a learning variable. This, of course, is exactly opposite to the conclusion Hull reached about reinforcement. For him, reinforcement was a learning variable, not a performance variable.

Thus, Bandura disagrees sharply with Miller and Dollard's account of observational learning. For Bandura, observational learning occurs all the time. "After the capacity for observational learning has fully developed, one cannot keep people from learning what they have seen" (1977, p. 38). Also for Bandura, contrary to Miller and Dollard's contention, observational learning requires neither overt responding nor reinforcement.

The Skinnerian Analysis of Observational Learning

The Skinnerian explanation of observational learning is very similar to that of Miller and Dollard's. First, a model's behavior is observed, next the observer matches the response of the model, and finally the matching response is reinforced. Furthermore, once learning has occurred in this fashion, it is maintained by some kind of

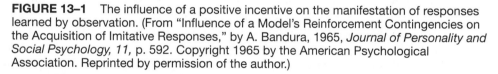

FIGURE 13–1 The influence of a positive incentive on the manifestation of responses learned by observation. (From "Influence of a Model's Reinforcement Contingencies on the Acquisition of Imitative Responses," by A. Bandura, 1965, *Journal of Personality and Social Psychology, 11,* p. 592. Copyright 1965 by the American Psychological Association. Reprinted by permission of the author.)

schedule of reinforcement in the natural environment. Thus, according to the operant analysis of observational learning, the model's behavior acts as a discriminative stimulus indicating which actions will result in reinforcement. Imitation, then, is nothing more than a discriminative operant (see Chapter 5).

Bandura finds several things incorrect about Skinner's and Miller and Dollard's explanation of observational learning. First, they do not explain how learning can occur when neither the models nor the observers are reinforced for their actions, which research has indicated is the case. Second, they do not explain **delayed modeling,** in which an observer exhibits learning that occurred from observations made at a much earlier time. Furthermore, it has been found that the observer need not be reinforced for exhibiting this prior learning. Third, unlike Miller and Dollard and Skinner, who believe that reinforcement serves automatically and mechanically to strengthen behavior, Bandura (1977) believes that an observer must be aware of the reinforcement contingencies before they can have any effect: "Because learning by response consequences is largely a cognitive process, consequences generally produce little change in complex behavior when there is no awareness of what is being reinforced" (p. 18).

In short, Bandura maintains that all of the ingredients essential for an operant analysis of observational learning are missing. That is, there is often no discriminative stimulus, no overt responding, and no reinforcement.

NONHUMANS CAN LEARN BY OBSERVING

A series of recent studies provides an unusual source of support for Bandura's contentions about observational learning. These studies are surprising because the data suggest that, despite claims to the contrary by Thorndike and Watson, nonhumans can acquire fairly complex learning by observing other members of their species. In a study conducted by Nicol and Pope (1993), observer chickens were first paired with "demonstrator" chickens. Each observer watched as her demonstrator learned to peck one of two operant keys for food. When the observers were tested in the operant chamber, they showed a significant tendency to pick the key that had been reinforced for their demonstrators. In a series of studies with laboratory rats, a team of British researchers (Heyes & Dawson, 1990; Heyes, Dawson & Nokes, 1992) trained a group of demonstrator rats to push a lever to either the right or the left to earn food. Observer rats tested with the joystick-lever tended to press the lever in the same direction that their demonstrators did, even though presses in either direction were reinforced. In an interesting extension of this research, Heyes, Jaldow and Dawson (1993) first trained rats to press the joystick either to the left or to the right. Observers then watched as demonstrator rats experienced extinction. One group of rats, trained to press to the right, watched as similarly trained demonstrators experienced extinction of the right-pressing response. Another group of right-pressing observers watched left-pressing demonstrators during extinction. (Left-trained rats also watched as their demonstrators extinguished either the same-directional or different-directional pressing responses.) The animals that watched same-directional extinction produced fewer responses during extinction than did those animals that watched different-directional extinction, and both of the observation groups extinguished faster than rats that did not observe extinction in demonstrators. Clearly, the observer rats in this study acquired more than simple motor behaviors when they observed extinction.

VARIABLES AFFECTING OBSERVATIONAL LEARNING

To say that observational learning occurs independent of reinforcement is not to say that other variables do not affect it. Bandura (1986) lists four processes that influence observational learning, and they are summarized below.

Attentional Processes

Before something can be learned from a model, the model must be attended to. As was noted above, Bandura thought learning to be an ongoing process, but he points out that only what is observed can be learned. Craighead, Kazdin, and Mahoney (1976) make this point in a rather humorous way:

Suppose that you are holding a 4-year-old child on your lap while two other 4-year-olds play on separate areas of your living room floor and that, as Child A gently pets your English sheepdog, child B inserts a butter knife into an electrical outlet. Everyone would learn something from this incident. Because it was directly associated with severe, unexpected pain and accompanying autonomic arousal, child B would learn to avoid using wall sockets as knife holders, and possibly, to stay away from electrical outlets altogether. Child A might learn, or at least begin to learn, to avoid the sheepdog, or dogs in general. When child B suddenly screamed and cried, it startled child A, and since the occurrence of any strong, sudden, unexpected, and novel stimulus produces autonomic arousal, the harmless dog was associated with a strong, unconditioned response to a stressful stimulus. Depending upon the focus of his or her attention at the time, the child on your lap might later display avoidance of wall sockets (if he/she was watching child B), of dogs (if he/she was watching child A), or of you. Incidentally, since many of the principles of learning apply to both humans and animals, it is also possible that this sheepdog may subsequently try to avoid children. (p. 188)

So the question arises, what determines what is noticed? First, a person's sensory capacities will influence the **attentional processes.** Obviously, the modeling stimuli used to teach a blind or deaf person will need to be different from those used to teach a person with normal sight or hearing.

An observer's selective attention can be influenced by past reinforcements. For example, if prior activities learned through observation have proved functional in obtaining reinforcement, similar behaviors will be attended to in subsequent modeling situations. In other words, prior reinforcement can create a perceptual set in the observer that will influence future observations.

Various characteristics of models will also affect the extent to which they are attended to. Research has demonstrated that models will be attended to more often if they are similar to the observer (i.e., same sex, age, etc.), are respected, have high status, have demonstrated high competence, are thought of as powerful, and are attractive. In general, Bandura (1986) says, "[People] pay attention to models reputed to be effective and ignore those who, by appearance or reputation, are presumed to be ineffectual....Given the choice, people are more likely to select models who are proficient at producing good outcomes than those who repeatedly get punished" (p. 54).

Retentional Processes

For information gained from observation to be useful, it must be retained. It is Bandura's contention that there are **retentional processes** in which information is stored symbolically in two ways, imaginally and verbally. The imaginally stored symbols are actual stored pictures of the modeled experience, which can be retrieved and acted on long after the observational learning has taken place. Here we have another point of agreement between Bandura's theory and Tolman's theory. Bandura says that behavior is at least partially determined by mental images of past experiences; Tolman said that much behavior is governed by a cognitive map, which consists of the mental representation of prior experiences in a given situation. The second, and for Bandura the more important, kind of symbolization is verbal:

Most of the cognitive processes that regulate behavior are primarily conceptual rather than imaginal. Because of the extraordinary flexibility of verbal symbols, the intricacies and complexities of behavior can be conveniently captured in words. To take a simple example, the details of a route traveled by a model can be acquired, retained, and later performed more accurately by converting the visual information into a verbal code describing a series of right and left turns (e.g., RLRRL) than by reliance on visual imagery of the circuitous route, with its many irrelevant details. (1986, p. 58)

Although it is possible to discuss imaginal and verbal symbols separately, they are often inseparable when events are represented in memory. Bandura (1986) says, "Although verbal symbols embody a major share of knowledge acquired by modeling, it is often difficult to separate representation modes. Representational activities usually involve both systems to some degree....Words tend to evoke corresponding imagery, and images of events are often verbally cognized as well. When visual and verbal stimuli convey similar meanings, people integrate the information presented by these different modalities into a common conceptual representation" (p. 58).

Once information is stored cognitively, it can be retrieved covertly, rehearsed, and strengthened long after the observational learning has taken place. According to Bandura (1977), "It is the advanced capacity for symbolization that enables humans to learn much of their behavior by observation" (p. 25). These stored symbols make delayed modeling possible—that is, the ability to utilize information long after it has been observed.

Behavioral Production Processes

Behavioral production processes determine the extent to which that which has been learned is translated into performance. It is clear that one may learn, by observing monkeys, how to swing from tree to tree by a tail, but one would be at a loss to replicate those behaviors if one does not possess a tail. In other words, one may learn a great deal cognitively but be unable to translate that information into behavior for a variety of reasons; for example, the motor apparatus necessary to make certain responses may not be available because of one's maturational level, injury, or illness.

Bandura maintains that even if one is equipped with all the physical apparatus to make appropriate responses, a period of cognitive rehearsal is necessary before an observer's behavior can match that of a model. According to Bandura, the symbols retained from a modeling experience act as a template with which one's actions are compared. During this rehearsal process individuals observe their own behavior and compare it to their cognitive representation of the modeled experience. Any observed discrepancies between one's own behavior and the memory of the model's behavior trigger corrective action. This process continues until there is an acceptable match between the observer's and the model's behavior. Thus, the symbolic retention of a modeling experience creates a "feedback" loop, which can be used gradually to match one's behavior with that of a model by utilizing self-observation and self-correction.

Motivational Processes

In Bandura's theory, reinforcement has two major functions. First, it creates an *expectation* in observers that if they act like a model who has been seen being reinforced for certain activities, they will be reinforced also. Second, it acts as an *incentive* for translating learning into performance. As we have seen, what has been learned observationally remains dormant until the observer has a reason to use the information. Both functions of reinforcement are *informational.* One function creates an expectancy in observers that if they act in a certain way in a certain situation, they are likely to be reinforced. The other function, the **motivational processes,** provides a motive for utilizing what has been learned.

This is a major departure from traditional reinforcement theories, which claim that only those responses that are overtly made and reinforced in a given situation are strengthened. According to Bandura, not only is reinforcement not necessary for learning to take place but neither is direct experience. An observer can learn simply by observing the consequences of the behavior of others, storing that information symbolically and utilizing it when it is advantageous to do so. Thus, for Bandura, *vicarious* reinforcement or punishment is as informative as direct reinforcement or punishment. In Bandura's theory then, reinforcement and punishment are important but for much different reasons than they are for most reinforcement theorists. Most reinforcement theorists assume that reinforcement or punishment operate gradually, automatically, and usually without the awareness of the organism to strengthen or weaken an association between a stimulus and a response. For Bandura, however, learners gain information by observing either the consequences of their own behavior or of the behavior of others. The information gained by these observations can then be utilized in a variety of situations when a need to use it arises. Since actions, either one's own or someone else's, that bring about reinforcement or avoid punishment are especially functional, it is those actions that individuals will tend to observe and encode into memory for future use. Armed with information gained by prior observations, individuals anticipate that if they act in certain ways in certain situations certain consequences will follow. In this way, anticipated consequences at least partially determine behavior in any given situation. It is important to note, however, that anticipated *environmental* consequences are not the only determiners of behavior. Behavior is also partially influenced by anticipated *self-reactions,* which are determined by one's internalized standards of performance and conduct and by one's perceived self-efficacy. We will have more to say about self-regulated behavior later in this chapter.

To summarize, we can say that observational learning involves attention, retention, behavioral abilities, and incentives. Therefore, if observational learning fails to occur, it could be that the observer did not observe the relevant activities of the model, did not retain them, was physically incapable of performing them, or did not have the proper incentive to perform them. Figure 13–2 summarizes the variables that Bandura feels influence observational learning.

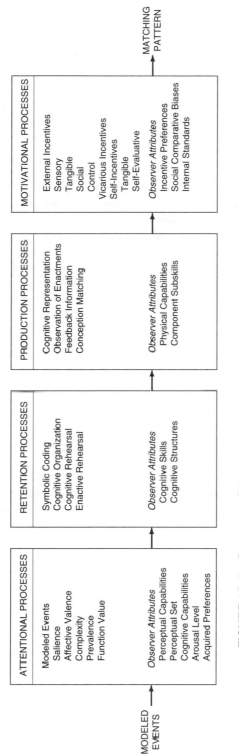

FIGURE 13-2 Summary of the various processes thought by Bandura to influence observational learning. (From *Social Foundations of Thought & Action*, p. 52, by A. Bandura, © 1986. Reprinted by permission of Prentice Hall, Upper Saddle River, New Jersey.)

RECIPROCAL DETERMINISM

Perhaps the most basic question in all of psychology is "Why do people act as they do?" and depending on one's answer to this question, one can be classified as an environmentalist (empiricist), nativist, existentialist, or something else. Environmentalists (e.g., Skinner) said that behavior is a function of reinforcement contingencies in the environment, and therefore if you change reinforcement contingencies you change behavior. Nativists would emphasize inherited dispositions, traits, or even ideas. Existentialists would emphasize free choice, that is, people do more or less what they choose to do. Thus most of the traditional answers to this question claim that behavior is a function of the environment, of certain traits or dispositions, or of the freedom that humans possess.

Bandura's answer to the question falls into the "something else" category. His answer is that the person, the environment, and the person's behavior itself all interact to produce the person's subsequent behavior. In other words, none of the three components can be understood in isolation of the others as a determiner of human behavior. Bandura (1986, p. 24) summarizes this three-way interaction as follows:

where P is the person, E is the environment, and B is the person's behavior. This position is referred to as **reciprocal determinism.** One deduction from this concept is that it is as valid to say that behavior influences the person and the environment as it is to say that the environment or the person influences behavior.

As an example of behavior influencing the environment, Bandura (1977, p. 196) describes an experiment in which a shock is scheduled to be delivered to a rat every minute unless it presses a bar, in which case the shock is delayed for 30 seconds. Those rats learning to press the bar with a certain frequency can avoid shock completely; those rats who fail to learn the response must go on experiencing periodic shocks. Bandura (1977) concludes, "Though the **potential environment** is identical for all animals, the **actual environment** depends upon their behavior. Is the animal controlling the environment or is the environment controlling the animal? What we have here is a two-way regulatory system in which the organism appears either as an object or an agent of control, depending upon which side of the reciprocal process one chooses to examine" (p. 196).

Bandura maintains that reinforcements, like punishments, exist only potentially in the environment and are only actualized by certain behavior patterns. Therefore, which aspects of an environment influence us are determined by how we act on that environment. Bandura (1977) goes further by saying that behavior can also *create* environments: "We are all acquainted with problem-prone individuals who, through their obnoxious conduct, predictably breed negative social climates wherever they go. Others are equally skilled at bringing out the best in those with whom they interact" (p. 197).

Thus, according to Bandura, people can influence the environment by acting in certain ways and the changed environment will, in turn, influence their subsequent behavior. But Bandura points out that even though there is an interaction among people, the environment, and behavior, any of these components may be more influential than the others at any given time. For example, a loud noise in the environment may momentarily have more of an effect on a person's behavior than anything else. At other times, one's beliefs may be the most influential determiner of one's actions. In fact, many studies have shown that the behavior of humans is governed more by what they believe is going on than by what really is going on. For example, Kaufman, Baron, and Kopp (1966) ran a study in which all subjects were reinforced about once every minute (variable-interval schedule) for performing a manual response. Although all the subjects were *actually* on the *same* schedule of reinforcement, some were misled about the schedule that they were on. One group was told the truth about the schedule, another group was told that their behavior would be reinforced every minute (fixed-interval schedule), and a third group was told they would be reinforced after they had made on the average of 150 responses (variable-ratio schedule). It was found that those subjects who believed they were on a fixed-interval schedule responded very slowly, those believing they were on a variable-ratio schedule responded very rapidly, and those that were told the truth about being on a variable-interval schedule responded with a rate in between the other two groups. On the basis of this and similar studies Bandura (1977) concludes, "Beliefs about the prevailing conditions of reinforcement outweighed the influence of experienced consequences" (p. 166).

Undoubtedly it is best to have one's beliefs correspond to reality. In the experiment just summarized the participants were misinformed, and they believed and acted on the misinformation. Many factors in everyday life can create nonadaptive beliefs in individuals, which can lead to ineffective or even bizarre actions. We will consider these factors when we consider faulty cognitive processes later in the chapter.

To summarize, Bandura's concept of reciprocal determinism states that behavior, the environment, and people (and their beliefs) all interact and that this three-way interaction must be understood before an understanding of human psychological functioning and behavior can occur.

SELF-REGULATION OF BEHAVIOR

According to Bandura (1977), "If actions were determined solely by external rewards and punishments, people would behave like weathervanes, constantly shifting in different directions to conform to the momentary influences impinging upon them. They would act corruptly with unprincipled individuals and honorably with righteous ones, and liberally with libertarians and dogmatically with authoritarians" (p. 128). The situation described in this quotation is obviously not the case, but if external reinforcers and punishers do not control behavior, what does? Bandura's answer is that human behavior is largely **self-regulated behavior.** Among the things that humans learn from direct or vicarious experience are **performance standards,** and once these standards are learned, they become the basis of self-evaluation. If a person's performance in a given situation meets or exceeds one's standards, it is evaluated positively; if it falls short of one's standards it is evaluated negatively.

One's standards can arise from one's direct experience with reinforcement by placing a high value on behaviors that have been effective in bringing praise from the relevant individuals in one's life, such as one's parents. Personal standards can also develop vicariously by observing those behaviors for which others have been reinforced. For example, Bandura and Kupers (1964) found that children who were exposed to models who set high performance standards reinforced themselves only for superior performance, and children who were exposed to models who reinforced themselves for minimal performances also reinforced themselves for minimal performances.

Bandura (1977, p. 107) believes that the intrinsic reinforcement that comes from self-evaluation is much more influential than the extrinsic reinforcement dispensed by others. In fact, he gives several examples of cases in which extrinsic reinforcement for engaging in activities has *reduced* the motivation to engage in them. After reviewing a great deal of research on the relative effectiveness of extrinsic (externally administered) versus intrinsic (self-administered) reinforcement Bandura concludes, "...self-rewarded behavior tends to be maintained more effectively than if it has been externally reinforced" (p. 144).

Unfortunately, if one's standards of performance are too high, they can be a source of personal distress. Bandura (1977) says, "In its more extreme forms, harsh standards for self-evaluation give rise to depressive reactions, chronic discouragement, feelings of worthlessness, and lack of purposefulness" (p. 141). According to Bandura, working at goals that are too distant or too difficult can be disappointing: "Subgoals of moderate difficulty are therefore likely to be most motivating and satisfying" (p. 162).

Like internalized performance standards, **perceived self-efficacy** plays a major role in self-regulated behavior. Perceived self-efficacy refers to one's beliefs concerning what one is capable of doing, and it arises from a variety of sources including personal accomplishments and failures, seeing others who are seen as similar to oneself succeed or fail at various tasks, and verbal persuasion. Verbal persuasion may temporarily convince people that they should try or avoid some task, but in the final analysis it is one's direct or vicarious experience with success and failure that will most strongly influence one's perceived self-efficacy. For example, a football coach may "fire up" his team before a game by telling its members how great they are, but the enthusiasm will be short-lived if the opposing team is clearly superior.

Persons with high perceived self-efficacy try more, accomplish more, and persist longer at a task than persons with low perceived self-efficacy. The former also tend to experience less fear than the latter. Bandura (1980b) speculates that because people with high perceived self-efficacy tend to have more control over the events in their environment, they therefore experience less uncertainty. Since individuals tend to fear events over which they have no control and therefore are uncertain of, those individuals with high perceived self-efficacy tend to experience less fear.

One's *perceived* self-efficacy may or may not correspond to one's **real self-efficacy.** People may believe their self-efficacy is low when in reality it is high, and vice versa. The situation is best when one's aspirations are in line with one's capabilities.

On the one hand, people who continually attempt to do things beyond their capabilities experience frustration and despair and may eventually give up on almost everything. On the other hand, if people with high self-efficacy do not adequately challenge themselves, their personal growth may be inhibited. The development of perceived self-efficacy and its impact on self-regulated behavior are topics about which Bandura is writing extensively (see, e.g., Bandura 1980a and 1980b).

Moral Conduct

Like one's performance standards and one's perceived self-efficacy, one's **moral code** develops through interactions with models. In the case of morality, the parents usually model the moral rules and regulations that are ultimately internalized by the child. Once internalized, one's moral code determines which behaviors (or thoughts) are sanctioned and which are not. Departure from one's moral code brings **self-contempt,** which is not a pleasant experience, and thus one typically acts in accordance with one's moral code. Bandura (1977) says, "The anticipation of self-reproach for conduct that violates one's standards provides a source of motivation to keep behavior in line with standards in the face of opposing inducements. There is no more devastating punishment than self-contempt" (p. 154).

Bandura states his opposition to stage theories (e.g., Piaget and Kohlberg) and trait theories (e.g., Allport) rather forcefully. His primary reason for this opposition is that such theories predict a stability in human behavior that Bandura feels does not exist. Stage theories, for example, predict that a person's intellectual or moral capabilities are set by maturation, and therefore those intellectual or moral judgments one can make are set by one's age. The same is true for type or trait theories, which say that people will act consistently in a wide range of situations because they are certain types of people or because they possess certain traits. Bandura maintains that human behavior is not all that consistent. Rather, he says, it is more circumstantial. In other words, Bandura believes that human behavior is determined more by the situation one is in and by one's interpretation of that situation than it is by one's stage of development, by one's traits, or by the type of person one is.

There is no better example of the situational nature of behavior than the topic of morality. Even though one has firm moral principles, there are several mechanisms that can be used to dissociate reprehensible acts from self-sanctions. These mechanisms make it possible for people to depart radically from their moral principles without experiencing self-contempt (Bandura, 1986, pp. 375-385):

1. Moral Justification   In **moral justification,** one's otherwise reprehensible behavior becomes a means to a higher purpose and therefore is justifiable. "I committed the crime so that I could provide food for my family." Bandura gives another example:

> Radical shifts in destructive behavior through moral justification are most strikingly revealed in military training. People who have been taught to deplore killing as morally condemnable can be transformed rapidly into skilled combatants, who feel little compunction and even a sense of pride in taking human life....In justifying warfare, one sees oneself fighting ruthless oppressors who have an unquenchable appetite for conquest,

protecting one's way of life, preserving world peace, saving humanity from being sub-jugated to an evil ideology, and honoring the country's international commitments. Such restructuring of circumstances is designed to get even considerate people to regard violent means as morally justifiable to achieve humane ends. (p. 376)

2. Euphemistic Labeling By calling an otherwise reprehensible act something other than what it really is, one can engage in an act without self-contempt. For exam-ple, nonaggressive individuals are far more likely to be aggressive toward another person when doing so is called a game. Bandura gives other examples of how **euphemistic labeling** is used to make the reprehensible respectable: "Through the power of hygienic words, even killing a human being loses much of its repugnancy. Soldiers 'waste' people rather than kill them....When mercenaries speak of 'fulfilling a contract,' murder is transformed by admirable words into the honorable discharge of duty" (p. 378).

3. Advantageous Comparison By comparing one's self-deplored acts with even more heinous acts, it makes one's own reprehensible acts look trifling by **advanta-geous comparison:** "Sure I did that, but look at what he did." Bandura offers examples:

> Promoters of the Vietnamese War and their supporters...minimized the slaying of count-less people as a way of checking massive communist enslavement. Given the trifling comparison, perpetrators of warfare remained unperturbed by the fact that the intended beneficiaries were being killed at an alarming rate. Domestic protesters, on the other hand, characterized their own violence against educational and political institutions as trifling, or even laudable, by comparing it with the carnage perpetuated by their coun-try's military forces in foreign lands. (p. 379)

4. Displacement of Responsibility Through **displacement of responsibility,** some people can readily depart from their moral principles if they feel a recognized author-ity sanctions their behavior and takes responsibility for it: "I did it, because I was ordered to do so." Bandura says, "Nazi prison commandants and their staffs felt lit-tle personal responsibility for their unprecedented inhumanities. They were simply carrying out orders. Impersonal obedience to horrific orders was similarly evident in military atrocities, such as the My Lai massacre" (p. 379).

5. Diffusion of Responsibility A decision to act in a reprehensible manner that is made by a group is easier to live with than an individual decision. Where every-one is responsible, that is, when there is **diffusion of responsibility,** no single individual feels responsible.

6. Disregard or Distortion of Consequences In **disregard or distortion of conse-quences,** people ignore or distort the harm caused by their conduct, and therefore there is no need to experience self-contempt. The farther people remove themselves from the ill effects of their immoral behavior, the less pressure there is to censure it. "I just let the bombs go and they disappeared in the clouds."

7. Dehumanization If some individuals are looked on as subhuman, they can be treated inhumanly without experiencing self-contempt. Once a person or a group has been **dehumanized,** the members no longer possess feelings, hopes, and concerns, and they can be mistreated without risking self-condemnation: "Why not take their land, they are nothing but savages without souls."

　　8. Attribution of Blame　　One can always choose something that a victim said or did and claim that it caused one to act in a reprehensible way. Bandura gives an example of the **attribution of blame:** "Rapists and males who acknowledge a proclivity to rape subscribe to myths about rape embodying the various mechanisms by which moral self-censure can be disengaged....These beliefs hold rape victims responsible for their own victimization because they have supposedly invited rape by sexually provocative appearance and behavior and by resisting sexual assault weakly" (pp. 384–385).

　　Bandura (1977) attributes most misconduct to these dissociative mechanisms rather than to faulty moral codes: "Because internalized controls are subject to dissociative operations, marked changes in people's moral conduct can be achieved without altering their personality structures, moral principles, or self-evaluative systems. It is self-exonerative processes rather than character flaws that account for most inhumanities" (p. 158).

Determinism versus Freedom

Does the fact that much behavior is self-regulated mean that humans are free to do whatever they choose? Bandura (1986, p. 42) defines **freedom** in terms of the number of options available to people and their opportunities to exercise them. According to Bandura, constraints to personal freedom include incompetence, unwarranted fears, excessive self-censure, and social inhibitors such as discrimination and prejudice.

　　Thus, in the same physical environment some individuals are freer than others. As we shall see, another constraint on personal freedom could be faulty cognitive processes, which may prevent people from interacting effectively with their environments.

FAULTY COGNITIVE PROCESSES

Bandura places great importance on cognitive processes in the determination of human behavior. We have seen how one's internalized performance standards, perceived self-efficacy, and moral codes play a major role in the self-regulation of behavior. Further evidence for the influence of cognitive processes comes from the fact that we can *imagine* ourselves into almost any emotional state we wish to. We can make ourselves nauseated, angry, peaceful, or sexually aroused simply by conjuring up appropriate thoughts. Thus, according to Bandura, behavior can be strongly influenced by one's own imagination.

　　Since one's behavior is at least partially determined by one's cognitive processes, it follows that if these processes do not accurately reflect reality, maladaptive behavior can result. Bandura gives several reasons for the development of **faulty cognitive processes.** First, children may develop false beliefs because they tend to evaluate things on the basis of appearance; thus, they conclude that a tall, narrow beaker contains more water than a short, wider beaker because for them "taller" means "bigger." Piaget would say that a child reaching this conclusion has not learned the principle of conservation. Second, errors in thought can occur when information is derived from insufficient evidence. Bandura (1977) gives the following example: "Learning from the images conveyed by the mass media is a good case in point. People partly form impressions of the social realities with which they have little or no contact from televised representations of society. Because the world of television is heavily populated with villainous and unscrupulous characters it can distort knowledge about the real world" (p. 184). According to Bandura (1973), this distorted view of reality can sometimes result in criminal behavior: "Children have been apprehended for writing bad checks to obtain money for candy, for sniping at strangers with BB guns, for sending threatening letters to teachers and for injurious switchblade fights after witnessing similar performances on television…" (pp. 101–102).

Bandura (1977) says that once false beliefs are established, they become self-perpetuating because those holding them seek out individuals or groups who share the same false beliefs. "The various cults and messianic groups that emerge from time to time typify this process" (p. 185). Furthermore, once false beliefs are established, they can be self-fulfilling prophecies. For example, if people believe that they are stupid, they will seek experiences and engage in activities that support their belief.

Third, fallacies in thinking can arise from the faulty processing of information. For example, if people believe that all farmers lack intelligence, they would necessarily conclude that any particular farmer lacks intelligence. This deduction is false because the premise (belief) is false, but Bandura points out that one can also make erroneous deductions from correct information. In other words, even if people possess accurate information, their deductions may be faulty. An example would be correctly observing that unemployment is higher among black individuals than it is among white individuals but erroneously concluding from this fact that black individuals are less motivated than white individuals.

In some cases, faulty beliefs can cause bizarre behavior, such as when one's life is directed by the belief that one is "God." Also phobias can trigger extreme defensive behaviors, such as when people refuse to leave their houses because they are too frightened of dogs. In this case, the fact that most dogs do not bite can never be realized because the people never encounter dogs. What these phobics need, according to Bandura, are "powerful disconfirming experiences," which will force them to change their expectations of how dogs behave. How observational learning is used to treat phobics will be covered in the next section.

PRACTICAL APPLICATIONS OF OBSERVATIONAL LEARNING

What Modeling Can Accomplish

Modeling has been found to have several kinds of effects on observers. New responses may be acquired by watching a model being reinforced for certain actions. Thus, the **acquisition** of behavior results from vicarious reinforcement. A response that otherwise might be readily made in a situation is inhibited when a model is seen being punished for making that response. Thus response **inhibition** results from vicarious punishment. Also seeing a model engage in a feared activity without experiencing any ill effects can reduce inhibitions in the observer. The reduction of fear that results from observing a model's unpunished participation in the feared activity is called **disinhibition.** A model may also elicit from an observer a response that has already been learned and for which there is no inhibition. In this case, by performing a response, the model simply increases the likelihood that the observer will make a similar response. This is called **facilitation.** Modeling can also stimulate **creativity,** which can be accomplished by exposing observers to a variety of models that causes the observer to adopt combinations of characteristics or styles. Bandura (1977) says,

> The progression of creative careers through distinct periods provides notable examples of this process. In his earlier works, Beethoven adopted the classical forms of Haydn and Mozart....Wagner fused Beethoven's symphonic mode with Weber's naturalistic enchantment and Meyerbeer's dramatic virtuosity to evolve a new operatic form. Innovators in other endeavors in the same manner initially draw upon the contributions of others and build from their experiences something new. (p. 48)

Innovation can also be stimulated more directly by modeling unconventional responses to common situations. In this case, observers may already possess strategies that are effective in solving a problem, but the model teaches bolder, more unconventional problem-solving strategies.

With the possible exception of modeled creativity, the use of modeling to convey information has been criticized for stimulating only a response mimicry or imitation. That this is not the case is clearly demonstrated by **abstract modeling,** in which people observe models performing various responses that have a common rule or principle. For example, the models could solve problems by using a certain strategy or generate sentences that embody a certain grammatical style. It is found, under these circumstances, that observers typically learn whatever rule or principle is being exemplified in the diverse modeling experiences. Furthermore it is found that after the rule or principle is learned by the observer, it can be applied to situations unlike any involved during the modeling. For example, once a problem-solving strategy is extracted from a number of modeling experiences, it can be used effectively to solve problems that are unlike any experienced before. Thus abstract modeling has three components: (1) observing a wide variety of situations that have a rule or principle in common; (2) extracting the rule or principle from the diverse experiences; and (3) utilizing the rule or principle in new situations.

Since humans constantly encounter a wide variety of modeling experiences, it seems safe to conclude that most of the principles and rules that govern human behavior are derived from something like abstract modeling. Bandura (1977) says, "On the basis of observationally derived rules, people learn, among other things, judgmental orientations, linguistic styles, conceptual schemes, information-processing strategies, cognitive operations, and standards of conduct" (p. 42).

It should be noted that inhibition, disinhibition, and facilitation all increase or decrease the probability of making a response that has already been learned.

Acquisition, creativity, and rule or principle extraction involve the development of new learning through modeling.

In addition to acquisition, inhibition, disinhibition, facilitation, rule or principle extraction, and creativity, modeling has also been used to influence observers' moral judgments and their emotional responses. In fact, according to Bandura (1977, p. 12), *anything that can be learned from direct experience can also be learned by indirect or vicarious experience.* Furthermore, it can be learned more efficiently through modeling since much of the trial-and-error process involved in learning by direct experience is eliminated: "Observational learning is vital for both development and survival. Because mistakes can produce costly, or even fatal consequences, the prospects for survival would be slim indeed if one could learn only by suffering the consequences of trial and error....The more costly and hazardous the possible mistakes, the heavier is the reliance on observational learning from competent examples" (p. 12).

Modeling in the Clinical Setting

According to Bandura, psychopathology results from dysfunctional learning, which causes incorrect anticipations about the world. The job of the psychotherapist is to provide experiences that will disconfirm erroneous expectations and replace them with more accurate and less disabling ones. Bandura has little patience with those psychotherapists who look for "insights" or "unconscious motivations" in their clients. In fact, Bandura (1977) feels that the clients of these therapists are used to confirm the therapists' own belief systems.

> Advocates of different theoretical orientations repeatedly discover their chosen motivators at work but rarely find evidence for the motivators emphasized by the proponents of competing views. In fact, if one wanted to predict the types of insights and unconscious motivators that persons are apt to discover in themselves in the course of such analyses, it would be more helpful to know the therapists' conceptual belief system than the clients' actual psychological status. (p. 5)

Bandura and his colleagues have run a number of studies to test the effectiveness of modeling in treating several psychological disorders. For example, Bandura, Grusec, and Menlove (1967) showed children who had a strong fear of dogs a peer interacting fearlessly with a dog. The fear-provoking character of the model's behavior was gradually increased from session to session by relaxing the physical constraints on the dog and by varying the directness of the model's interactions with it. A control group also consisting of phobic children did not have the modeling experience. The approach behavior of all the children was measured for both the dog actually involved in the experiment and for an unfamiliar dog. Measures were taken immediately after treatment and one month later. Approach scores were determined by a graded sequence of interactions with the dogs; that is, children were asked to approach and pet the dogs, release them from their pen, take their leashes off, and finally spend time with the dogs in their pen. It was found that the children who had seen a peer model interact fearlessly with a dog were capable of significantly more approach responses than children in the control group. In fact, two-thirds of the children in the treatment group were able to remain alone with the dog in its pen, whereas none of the children in the control group could do so. It was also found that the effects of treatment generalized to the unfamiliar dog and the effects were still present one month after the experiment.

It can be seen from this study that not only can new responses be learned by observing the consequences of the behavior of models but also responses can be extinguished in the same way. Thus, **vicarious extinction** is as important as vicarious reinforcement in Bandura's theory. In this study, vicarious extinction was used to reduce or eliminate the avoidance response to dogs and thereby disinhibit the approach response to dogs.

In another study, Bandura and Menlove (1968) had three groups of children with dog phobias watch a series of films under three different conditions: **single modeling,** in which children saw a model interact with a single dog with increased intimacy; **multiple modeling,** in which children saw a variety of models interacting fearlessly with a number of dogs; and a *control condition,* in which children saw movies involving no dogs. Again, as in the 1967 study, the willingness of the children to approach the dog was measured. It was found that both single and multiple modeling significantly reduced the children's fear of dogs, as compared to children in the control group, but only the children in the multiple-modeling group had their fear reduced to the point where they were able to be left alone with the dog in its pen. Again it was found that the effects of treatment generalized to other dogs and endured one month after the experiment. Comparing the results of this study with those of the 1967 study described above, Bandura concluded that although both **direct modeling** (seeing a live model) and **symbolic modeling** (seeing a model in a film) are both effective in reducing fears, direct modeling appeared to be more effective. However, the apparent reduced effectiveness of symbolic modeling was overcome by showing a variety of models instead of just one.

In the final study to be considered, Bandura, Blanchard, and Ritter (1969) compared the effectiveness of symbolic modeling, modeling with participation, and desensitization as techniques in treating a phobia. In this study, adults and adolescents with a snake phobia were divided into four groups. Group 1 (*symbolic modeling*) was exposed to a film showing children, adolescents, and adults interacting with a large snake. The scenes were graduated, showing increased interaction with the snake. Subjects in this group were trained in relaxation techniques and could stop the film whenever they became too anxious. When relaxed enough, they started the film again. Each subject continued in this manner until he or she could watch the film without anxiety. Group 2 (**modeling-participation**) watched a model handle a snake and then were helped by the model to actually come in contact with the snake. The model would first touch the snake and help the observer to do so also; then the model would stroke the snake and encourage the observer to do likewise. This process continued until the observer could hold the snake in his or her lap without assistance. Group 3 received **desensitization therapy,** which consisted of asking subjects to imagine anxiety-provoking scenes with snakes, starting with imaginary scenes that caused little anxiety and slowly progressing to imaginary scenes that caused great anxiety. Subjects were asked to continue imagining each scene until it no longer made them anxious. Group 4 received no treatment of any kind. The results of the study indicated that all three treatment conditions were effec-

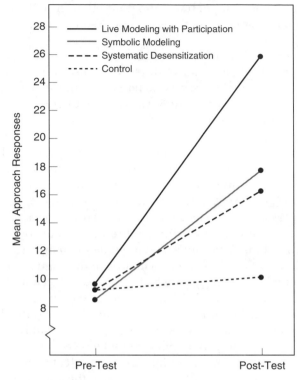

FIGURE 13–3   The tendency to approach a snake before and after various kinds of therapeutic treatments. (From "Relative Efficacy of Modeling Therapeutic Changes," by A. Bandura, E.B. Blanchard, & B.J. Ritter, 1969, *Journal of Personality and Social Psychology, 13,* p. 183. Copyright 1969 by the American Psychological Association. Reprinted by permission of the publisher and author.)

tive in reducing the fear of snakes but that the modeling-participation method was by far the most effective (see Figure 13–3).

In fact, Bandura, Blanchard, and Ritter isolated all of the subjects who were unable to achieve the ability to hold the snake in their lap (including the control subjects) and used the modeling-participation method. In just a few sessions each subject was able to hold the snake in his or her lap. Follow-up research indicated that not only did the effects of treatment endure but they also generalized to other areas in which fear had existed prior to the experiment. Bandura and his associates used a questionnaire to measure the magnitude of various fears before and after the experiment. The change in the magnitude of these fears as a function of the various treatment conditions is shown in Figure 13–4.

THE INFLUENCE OF THE NEWS AND ENTERTAINMENT MEDIA

As we have seen, Bandura believes that we can learn as much from vicarious experiences as from observing the consequences of our behavior. We have also seen that Bandura defines a model as anything that conveys information. It follows, then, that newspapers, television, and motion pictures act as models from which we can learn a great deal. Of course, not everything learned from the news and entertainment media is negative, but sometimes it can be. We have already seen that television can

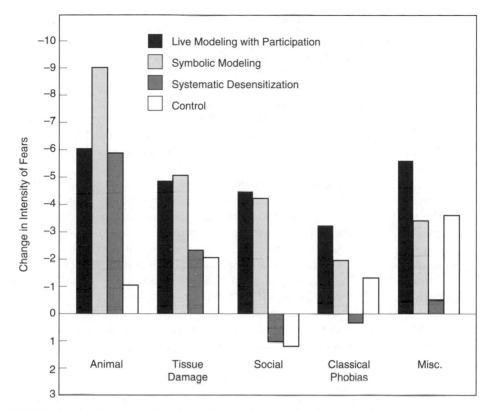

FIGURE 13–4 The generalized effects of various kinds of therapeutic treatments on the inttensity of fears other than the one specifically treated. The higher the minus score, the greater the difference in the intensity of fear before and after treatment. (From "Relative Efficacy of Modeling Therapeutic Changes," by A. Bandura, E.B. Blanchard, & B.J. Ritter, 1969, *Journal of Personality and Social Psychology,* 13, p. 186. Copyright 1969 by the American Psychological Association. Reprinted by permission of the publisher and author.

cause the development of faulty cognitive processes which in turn can lead to criminal behavior. Bandura (1986) gives another example of how television programming can stimulate antisocial behavior:

> Sometimes it is the fictional media that furnishes the salient example for the spread of an aggressive style of conduct. The television program *Doomsday Flight* provides an excellent illustration because of its novel modeled strategy. In this plot, an extortionist threatens airline officials that an altitude-sensitive bomb will be exploded on a transcontinental airliner in flight as it descends below 5,000 feet for its landing. In the end, the pilot outwits the extortionist by selecting an airport located at an elevation above the critical altitude. Extortion attempts using the same barometric-bomb plot rose sharply for two months following the telecast....Moreover, a day or two after the program was rerun in different cities in the United States and abroad, airlines were subjected to further extortion demands of money to get the extortionists to reveal the placement of altitude-sensitive bombs allegedly planted in airliners in flight. Planes were rerouted to airports at high elevations, and some extortion demands were paid by airline officials, only to learn

that the airliner contained no bomb. A rebroadcast of the program in Anchorage made an Alaskan viewer $25,000 richer, and a rerun in Sydney made an Australian instantly wealthy, after collecting $560,000 from Qantas. He added considerable force to his threat by directing Qantas officials to an airport locker where he had placed a sample barometric bomb he had built. (p. 173)

Bandura dismisses the suggestion that all of the above episodes were mere coincidence and, therefore, had nothing to do with the television program "Doomsday Flight." According to Bandura, the novelty of the strategy used for extortion and the fact that the episodes followed so closely after the program seem to preclude chance as an explanation.

In general, Bandura (1986) reaches the following conclusion concerning violence in fictional television: "Analyses of televised programs reveal that violent conduct is portrayed, for the most part, as permissible, successful, and relatively clean....Witnesses to the violence in the dramatic presentations are more likely to approve of such behavior or to join in the assaults rather than to seek alternative solutions. Violence not only is shown to pay off but is readily used by superheroes, who dispose of their adversaries in a quick, perfunctory way as though slaying human beings was of no great concern" (p. 292).

As we have just seen, violence portrayed on fictional television can encourage violence in some viewers, but what about nonfictional television? According to Bandura (1986) nonfictional television, too, can encourage violence:

> There are several ways in which newscasts of violence can serve as an instrument of influence....If televised reports convey detailed information about acts and strategies of aggression, they can contribute to the spread of the very methods they report through the instruction they provide. In addition, media reports of violent episodes can influence restraints over aggression by how the consequences are portrayed. Because each point in audience ratings means millions of dollars in advertising revenue, the visual displays accompanying news reports are selected to attract and hold viewers, as well as to inform. The outcomes of aggression, especially collective actions, are easily misrepresented when dramatic pictorials are favored over less interesting but important consequences. Thus, showing people running off with appliances and liquor from looted stores during an urban riot is more likely to promote aggression in viewers living under similar circumstances than showing the terror and suffering caused by the massive destruction of one's neighborhood. (p. 292)

Pornographic Movies Clearly not everyone exposed to violence on television or in the newspapers becomes violent. Similarly, not everyone exposed to sexually explicit literature or movies becomes a sexual deviant. In fact, erotic material has been used successfully to treat individuals with sexual problems. Bandura (1986) says, "Sexual modeling has been shown to have long-term effects when used for therapeutic purposes with persons suffering from sexual anxieties and dysfunctions...modeling of mutual pleasure alleviates sex anxieties, creates more favorable attitudes toward sex, and sparks inactive sex lives" (p. 294).

In the case of pornography, however, sexual aggression toward women is often modeled, and such modeling can stimulate similar behavior in some viewers. Bandura (1986) explains,

> Content analyses reveal an increase in abusive behavior toward women in pornographic depictions....Research has added to our understanding of how violent erotica affects viewers. Males exposed to modeled sexual assault behave more punitively toward women than if exposed to modeled sexual intimacy devoid of aggression....Violent erotica often depicts women initially resisting but eventually relishing being raped. Such portrayals reinforce rape myths and weaken restraints over harshness toward women by indicating they enjoy being manhandled. Depictions of rape as pleasurable to women heighten punitiveness toward women regardless of whether males are angry or not. (pp. 294–295)

Although "humane living requires reducing social influences that promote cruelty and destructiveness" and "society has the right to regulate obscene materials that can cause harm" (Bandura, 1986, p. 296), the recognition and control of such influences and materials are complex matters. First, there is widespread disagreement over what is harmful and what is not. Second, there is concern that suppression of one form of expression (e.g., sexual expression) may threaten other forms of expression. Obviously, this is not a matter that will be resolved soon.

SOCIAL COGNITIVE THEORY

Although Tolman's and Bandura's theories are both cognitive in nature, Tolman concentrated almost exclusively on explaining the learning process; Bandura's cognitive theory is much more comprehensive. Dollard and Miller's theory focused on social behavior and incorporated Hullian learning theory. Bandura also concentrates on social behavior, but his theoretical orientation is not Hullian. Thus, to describe both Dollard and Miller's and Bandura's theories as *social learning theory,* as is often the case, is misleading. To differentiate his theory from those such as Tolman's and Dollard and Miller's, Bandura prefers the label **social cognitive theory.** In the preface of his book, *Social Foundations of Thought and Action: A Social Cognitive Theory,* Bandura (1986) explains his choice of this label:

> The theoretical approach presented in this volume is usually designated as social learning theory. However, the scope of this approach has always been much broader than its descriptive label, which is becoming increasingly ill-fitting as various aspects of the theory are further developed. From the outset it encompassed psychosocial phenomena, such as motivational and self-regulatory mechanisms, that extend beyond issues of learning. Moreover, many readers construe learning theory as a conditioning model of response acquisition, whereas within this theoretical framework learning is conceptualized mainly as knowledge acquisition through cognitive processing of information. The labeling problem is further compounded because several theories with dissimilar postulates [such as] Dollard and Miller's drive theory...bear the social learning label. In the interests of more fitting and separable labeling, the theoretical approach of this book is designated as *social cognitive theory.* The social portion of the terminology acknowledges the social origins of much human thought and action; the cognitive portion recognizes the influential causal contribution of thought processes to human motivation, affect, and action. (p. xii)

The current popularity of Bandura's theory can be partially explained by its recognition of the uniqueness of humans. It describes humans as dynamic; information processing; problem solving; and above all, social organisms. Whether we learn from direct experience or from vicarious experience, most of our learning usually involves other people in a social setting. It is on the basis of our observations and interactions with other people that our cognitions, including our standards for performance and for moral judgment, are developed. In addition, Bandura's research typically reflects real-life situations and problems. His subjects are humans interacting with other humans, not humans learning lists of nonsense syllables or rats running mazes or pressing a lever in a Skinner box. According to Bandura (1977), it is the human capacity to symbolize that "enables them to represent events, to analyze their conscious experience, to communicate with others at any distance in time and space, to plan, to create, to imagine, and to engage in foresightful action" (p. vii).

SUMMARY

The long avoidance of studies into observational learning was ended by Bandura's research, which first appeared in the literature in the early 1960s. Bandura disagreed with Miller and Dollard's earlier account of observational learning, which described it as a special case of instrumental conditioning. Bandura's explanation of learning is close to Tolman's, in that learning is assumed to be continuous and not dependent on reinforcement. For Bandura, as for Tolman, reinforcement is a performance variable, not a learning variable. Either direct or vicarious reinforcement provides information about what behaviors lead to reinforcement in various situations; when a need arises, this information is translated into behavior. Thus, reinforcement provides information that allows observers to anticipate reinforcement if they behave in certain ways. Reinforcement, according to Bandura, does not act directly to strengthen the responses that produce it. In fact, much, if not most, human learning occurs in the absence of direct reinforcement. Rather, human learning typically occurs by observing the consequences of the behavior of models. Such vicarious learning is made possible by the human capacity to symbolize and store information and then to act on that information at a later time.

Four major processes are thought to influence the course of observational learning: attentional processes, which determine which aspects of a modeling situation are attended to; retentional processes, which involve the imaginal and verbal coding of information so that it may be stored and utilized in the future; behavioral production processes, which involve the ability to make the responses necessary to translate that which has been learned from observation into behavior; and motivational processes, which, since learning occurs continuously, determine which aspects of previously learned responses are translated into action. Reinforcement is the major motivational process since it not only causes an observer to focus on the functional aspects of a model's behavior but also provides an incentive for acting on the information gained by such observation. The information gained by observing reinforcement contingencies can come from either one's direct experience with reinforcement or by vicariously observing the consequences of a model's behavior.

One of Bandura's major concepts is reciprocal determinism, which states that there is a constant interaction among the environment, the behavior, and the person. According to Bandura, it makes as much sense to say that behavior influences the environment as it does to say that the environment influences behavior. In addition, the person influences both behavior and the environment.

Unlike traditional learning theorists, Bandura believes that much human behavior is self-regulated. Through direct and observational learning, performance standards develop that act as guides in evaluating one's own behavior. If one's behavior meets or exceeds one's performance standards, it is evaluated positively; if it falls short of one's standards, it is evaluated negatively. Likewise, one's perceived self-efficacy develops from one's direct and vicarious experiences with success and failure. Perceived self-efficacy influences self-regulated behavior in several ways: It determines what is attempted, how long one persists at a task, and what is hoped for. Intrinsic reinforcement (self-reinforcement) has been found to influence one's behavior more than extrinsic, or externally administered, reinforcement. One's moral behavior is governed by internalized moral codes. If one acts contrary to one's moral code, one experiences self-contempt, which acts as a severe punishment. However, Bandura describes a number of mechanisms that allow people to disengage themselves from their moral principles and thereby escape self-contempt for immoral behavior. These disengagement mechanisms include moral justification, euphemistic labeling, advantageous comparison, displacement of responsibility, diffusion of responsibility, disregard or distortion of consequences, dehumanization, and attribution of blame.

Faulty cognitive processes can develop from inaccurate perceptions, overgeneralization, or incomplete or erroneous information. Most phobias probably result from the overgeneralization from one or more direct or vicarious painful experiences. One way to correct faulty cognitive processes, including phobias, is to provide powerful disconfirming experiences, which eventually reduce or eliminate one's inhibitions or fears. In addition to reducing or eliminating inhibitions, modeling can also be used to teach new skills, inhibit responses, facilitate responses, teach creativity, and teach general rules and principles.

Symbolic, live, and participant modeling in the clinical setting have been found effective in treating phobias. However, of all the methods tried, participant-modeling has been found to be the most effective. The process of reducing one's fears by observing another person interacting fearlessly with a feared object is called vicarious extinction. Bandura provides evidence that news and entertainment media act as powerful models and can sometimes encourage aggressive, violent, and criminal behavior.

Bandura's theory is called a social cognitive theory because it emphasizes the fact that most of the information we gain comes from our interactions with other people. Because of its emphasis on such cognitive processes as language and memory, its effectiveness as a guide in psychotherapeutic practices, its implications for child-rearing and educational practices, and its ability to stimulate new lines of research, Bandura's theory is very popular today and promises to become even more popular in the future.

EVALUATION OF BANDURA'S THEORY

Albert Bandura's work has had widespread influence among learning theorists, social psychologists, and cognitive psychologists. Like Estes, his work combines behaviorism and cognitive theory and continues to generate research. Even before Bandura's (1986) influential *Social Foundations of Thought and Action,* Bower and Hilgard (1981) recognized his approach as "the best integrative summary of what modern learning theory has to contribute to the solution of practical problems...a compatible framework within which to place information-processing theories of language comprehension, memory, imagery, and problem-solving" (p. 472).

Contributions

When Bandura's contributions are pointed out to contemporary readers, they often treat his theory as common sense observations that we have all made at some time in the past. We must remember, however that the foundations of Bandura's theory were developed at a time when most, if not all, learning theorists insisted that learning had its foundations in direct experience with the environment. As we noted at the beginning of this chapter, both Thorndike and Watson disregarded observational learning, and for Miller and Dollard, imitative learning was tied inevitably to reinforcement of actual imitated behavior. Even Piaget (1973) denied completely the role of observational learning in young children:

> It is absolutely necessary that learners have at their disposal concrete material experiences (and not merely pictures), and that they form their own hypotheses and verify them (or not verify them) themselves through their own active manipulations. *The observed activities of others, including those of the teacher, are not formative of new organizations in the child.* [italics added] (pp. ix)

Thus, Bandura's demonstrations that we learn by watching others and that such learning occurs with or without imitation and with or without reinforcement was a significant contribution to learning theory. A second major contribution is the three-way interaction represented in his notion of reciprocal determinism. Bandura (1978, 1983, 1986) points out that earlier, behavioristic theories tended to view behavior as an end product of person and environment or of person-environment interactions. Reciprocal determinism views behavior both as a product of person and environment and as an influence on person and environment, thereby shifting our perspective from a focus on behavior per se to the dynamic interplay of person, environment, and behavior.

Criticisms

Phillips and Orton (1983) have criticized the principle of reciprocal determinism on several grounds. They point out that systemic interaction is not new and may be traced back to philosophical, as well as scientific, writings in the nineteenth century.

Secondly, they argue that, while Bandura claims to be a determinist, the principle of reciprocal determinism defies standard causal analysis. That is, if behavior causes changes in the person while the person causes changes in the behavior while the environment causes changes in behavior and the person and so on, the task of discovering what causes what becomes practically impossible.

A second criticism of Bandura's position falls in the category of "too much of a good thing." While most theories of learning and cognition have become more narrow in scope and more precise in their formulations over the last 30 years, Bandura's theory is similar to the broad, encompassing theories formulated by Skinner and Tolman. As we have seen, Bandura's cognitive social learning theory addresses problems in learning, memory, language, motivation, personality, moral conduct, psychological dysfunctions, and societal issues such as media influences on behavior. Whether or not such a theory can survive the many trends toward specialization will remain to be seen.

DISCUSSION QUESTIONS

1. What conclusions did Thorndike and Watson reach about observational learning and why did they reach them?
2. Describe Miller and Dollard's research on observational learning and their explanation for what they found.
3. Defend the statement "Bandura's theory of learning is not a reinforcement theory."
4. Describe the role of reinforcement in Bandura's theory. Include in your answer the ways in which Bandura's view of reinforcement differs from the views of traditional reinforcement theorists.
5. Define the terms *vicarious reinforcement* and *vicarious punishment* and explain their importance to Bandura's theory.
6. Compare Bandura's theory to Tolman's theory.
7. Briefly describe attentional, retentional, behavioral production, and motivational processes and describe their influence on observational learning.
8. Define and give examples of Bandura's concept of reciprocal determinism.
9. How, according to Bandura, is behavior self-regulated?
10. List several mechanisms that allow a person to act immorally without experiencing self-contempt.
11. Describe several ways in which faulty cognitive processes can develop. Give examples of the kinds of behavior that faulty cognitive processes can generate.
12. Describe how modeling can be used to produce each of the following: acquisition, inhibition, disinhibition, facilitation, creativity, and rule-governed behavior. Begin your answer by defining each of the terms.
13. Define each of the following terms: *symbolic modeling, live modeling, multiple modeling, participant-modeling, desensitization therapy,* and *vicarious extinction.*
14. Describe how modeling is used to reduce or eliminate a phobia. Which procedure did Bandura find most effective in treating phobias?

15. Explain why someone who accepts Bandura's theory would be very concerned about the content of children's TV programs.
16. Give a few examples of how Bandura's theory might be used in education and in child-rearing.
17. Summarize Bandura's opposition to stage, type, and trait theories.
18. Based on Bandura's theory, do you feel a person would be more likely to respond to the cries of help from an acquaintance or from a stranger? Explain.
19. Attempt to account for those occasions in which a person does not learn from observation. For example, if you watched a brain surgeon performing an operation, would you be capable of performing such an operation? Why or why not?
20. Answer the following question from Bandura's point of view: "Why do children imitate some behaviors that they observe and not others?"
21. According to Bandura, what is probably learned by a child who is spanked by a parent for misbehaving?
22. In attempting to explain why people learn vicariously, it has been suggested that answering the question "What makes a horror movie horrifying to the observer" would shed some light on the matter. Attempt to answer the question about horror movies and then generalize your answer to the area of observational learning.

KEY TERMS

abstract modeling   The situation in which observers are presented with a variety of modeling experiences from which they extract a common rule or principle. Once extracted, the rule or principle can be applied to new situations.

acquisition   The gaining of new information from one's observations.

actual environment   That proportion of a potential environment that is actualized by an organism's behavior.

advantageous comparison   An attempt to escape from self-contempt by comparing one's immoral actions to another person's even more immoral actions.

attentional processes   Those variables that determine what is attended to during **observational learning.**

attribution of blame   An attempt to escape self-contempt by saying the victim of one's immoral actions caused one to act as one did.

behavioral production processes   Those variables that determine which aspects of what has been learned and retained cognitively can be produced behaviorally.

copying behavior   A kind of imitative behavior studied by Miller and Dollard in which a sophisticated individual guides the behavior of a naive individual until an appropriate response is made.

creativity   The innovation that results from either synthesizing the influences of several models or from observing a single **model** demonstrate unconventional problem-solving strategies.

dehumanize   Make the victim of one's immoral actions appear to be less human in an attempt to escape self-contempt.

delayed modeling   The case in which an observer does not display what has been learned from a modeling experience until sometime after the modeling experience has been terminated.

desensitization therapy   The procedure whereby clients are asked to imagine an anxiety-provoking thought until they are able to ponder the thought without experiencing anxiety.

diffusion of responsibility   An attempt to escape self-contempt by saying that the decision to engage in an immoral act has been made by a group.

direct experience   The events that one experiences as a result of one's own personal interactions with the environment.

direct modeling   The observation of a live model.

disinhibition   The removal or reduction of an inhibition to perform a certain response that results from either performing the response without experiencing negative consequences or from seeing a model perform the response without experiencing negative consequences.

displacement of responsibility   An attempt to escape self-contempt by claiming that a person in a position of authority caused one to act immorally.

disregard or distortion of consequences   An attempt to escape self-contempt by minimizing the harm caused by one's immoral actions.

euphemistic labeling   An attempt to escape from self-contempt by calling an immoral act something other than what it really is.

facilitation   The increased probability of making a previously learned response that results from observing another person making the response.

faulty cognitive processes   Those cognitive processes that prevent or inhibit effective and efficient interactions with the social or physical environment.

freedom   According to Bandura, the number of options available to a person and her or his opportunity to exercise them.

generalized imitation   The learned tendency to imitate the behavior of others in order to be reinforced.

imitative behavior   The learned tendency to mimic the behavior of a model whose behavior has been seen being reinforced. According to Bandura, imitative behavior is only one of many possible results of observational learning.

inhibition   The reduced probability of performing a previously learned response that results from either direct or **vicarious punishment** of that response.

learning   According to Bandura the acquisition of information that results from observation.

matched-dependent behavior   A kind of imitative behavior studied by Miller and Dollard in which the behavior of one person acts as a cue for another person to behave in a similar way. In operant terms the first person's behavior acts as a discriminative stimulus for the second person that triggers a response that leads to reinforcement. According to the operant analysis, matched-dependent behavior is a kind of discriminative operant.

model   Anything that conveys information to an observer. In Bandura's theory, a model can be a person, film, picture, instructions, description, animal, television, or newspaper.

modeling-participation   The situation in which a live model guides the behavior of an observer until an appropriate response is made. This is much like the copying behavior studied by Miller and Dollard.

moral codes   The internalized criteria that come from direct or vicarious experience used to monitor and evaluate one's own ethical behavior. If one's behavior violates an internalized moral code he or she experiences **self-contempt.**

moral justification   An attempt to escape from self-contempt by attributing one's immoral behavior to a higher cause.

motivational processes   Those variables that provide incentives for translating what has been learned and stored cognitively into behavior.

multiple modeling   The observation of two or more models.

observational learning   The process whereby information is acquired by attending to events in the environment.

perceived self-efficacy   What a person believes he or she is capable of doing; often contrasts with **real self-efficacy.**

performance   The translation of what has been learned into behavior.

performance standards   The internalized criteria that come from either direct or vicarious experiences used to monitor, evaluate, and reinforce or punish one's own behavior.

potential environment   The environmental events available to an organism if it acts in ways that actualize them.

real self-efficacy   What a person is actually capable of accomplishing; may or may not correspond to **perceived self-efficacy.**

reciprocal determinism   Bandura's contention that the environment, the person, and the person's behavior all interact to produce behavior.

reinforcement   According to Bandura, reinforcement gives the observer information concerning what leads to what in the environment, so that she or he can anticipate certain outcomes from certain behaviors. Because reinforcement creates expectations, it is said (by Bandura) to work forward in time rather than backward to strengthen the response that produced it, as the traditional reinforcement theorists had assumed.

reinforcement theory   Any theory that claims learning cannot occur without reinforcement. Bandura's is not a reinforcement theory.

retentional processes   The variables involved in encoding certain observations for memory. Bandura believes that observations are stored in memory through imaginal and verbal symbols.

same behavior   A kind of imitative behavior studied by Miller and Dollard in which two or more individuals respond in the same way to the same stimulus.

self-contempt   The self-imposed punishment that is administered when an individual's internalized moral code is violated.

self-regulated behavior   Behavior that is regulated by one's own performance standards, moral codes, or imagination.

single modeling   The observation of a single model.

social cognitive theory   A term Bandura used to describe his theory.

symbolic modeling   The observation of something other than a live model, such as a film or television.

vicarious experience   The impact on one's own learning or behavior that comes from observing the consequences of another person's behavior.

vicarious extinction   The extinction of a response that comes from observing the fact that a model's performance of that response is not reinforced.

vicarious punishment   The process by which observing another person's behavior being punished decreases the probability of the observer acting in a similar way.

vicarious reinforcement   The process by which observing another person's behavior being reinforced increases the probability of the observer acting in a similar way.

Chapter 14

DONALD A. NORMAN

In this chapter we will review the information-processing approach to psychology. In general, this approach views humans as receiving information from the environment, processing that information in one or more ways, and then acting on that information. Before discussing Donald Norman's contributions to the information-processing approach, we will first discuss some antecedents to it.

ANTECEDENTS TO THE INFORMATION-PROCESSING APPROACH TO PSYCHOLOGY

S-R Psychology

Associationistic theorists such as Pavlov, Watson, and Guthrie viewed living organisms as automatons whose responses to environmental stimuli are governed by the organism's sensory system, response system, and central nervous system consisting of innate circuitry and memories of prior experiences. In other words, Pavlov, Watson, and Guthrie explained the behavior of organisms in terms of environmental stimuli, innate and acquired neural circuitry, and response capabilities.

With slight changes in terminology we see a great deal of similarity between the approach taken by the associationistic theorists and that taken by psychologists who stress information processing. All that needs to be done is to replace the term *stimuli* with **input,** replace *response* with **output,** and replace the *neural mechanisms* that mediate the relationship between the S and the R with *information-processing mechanisms.* Some information-processing psychologists view their approach as very much in this associationistic tradition.

Cognitive Psychology

Most information-processing psychologists equate input with information. That is, what comes into the system from the environment is information. Through experience, we learn what events have in common, how some events are related to other events, what events are to be approached, what events are to be avoided, what activities work in solving problems, and in general what to expect in a given situation. According to the information-processing psychologist, the output (behavior) in a given situation is determined by the input provided by the situation and by the evaluation of the situation, based in part on the memories of what had resulted in similar situations.

Again with slight changes in terminology we can see a great deal of similarity between the information-processing approach and cognitive theories such as those of Tolman, Piaget, and Bandura. For Tolman, information was learned and stored by the organism, and expectancies, or the anticipation of what leads to what, were learned and utilized by the organism. These learned expectancies were ultimately reflected in the organism's cognitive map. In Tolman's approach to learning theory, independent variables can be equated with what the information-processing psychologist calls input, his intervening variables can be equated with information-processing mechanisms, and his dependent variables can be equated with output. Bandura's theory also stresses the learning of information, which takes the form of expectancies. We concluded Chapter 13 by noting the similarity between Bandura's theory and the information-processing approach.

Even though there may be conceptual similarities between the kinds of cognitive psychology just described and information-processing psychology, Norman insists that there is an important difference between the two:

> The important point about information-processing psychology is that it attempts to understand and specify the internal mechanism....It is not simply a matter of "expectancies." It is not simply a matter of "processing." The whole point is that one tries to be very specific about the exact stages of processing that take place and to spell out the properties of the internal mechanisms. This is the major difference between information-processing approaches to psychology and other approaches....Hence, the detailed analysis and specification of the operation of such things as short-term memory. (personal communication, September 19, 1986)

Of all the approaches to cognitive psychology, Piaget's approach seems to have most influenced **information-processing psychology.** His concept of schema has been widely adapted by information-processing psychologists and is viewed as an information-processing mechanism. Norman, for example, whose work we will feature in this chapter, relies very heavily on Piaget in his discussion of learning in his influential book *Human Information Processing: An Introduction to Psychology* (Lindsay & Norman, 1977). Both Piaget and those following the information-processing approach assume that information from the environment is acted on (organized, simplified, transformed, selected for further analysis, or ignored) by one's cognitive structure before it is translated into behavior. In other words, both stress the importance of schemata in processing information.

Cybernetics

In 1948, Norbert Wiener (1894–1964) defined **cybernetics** as the study of the structure and function of information-processing systems. Wiener was concerned with how various mechanical and biological systems record, process, and transmit information. Of particular interest to Wiener were the automatic control systems called *servomechanisms*. A servomechanism is a system that compares input with some standard or desired state and, if there is a discrepancy between the two, activates mechanisms that attempt to alleviate the discrepancy. The results of corrective action are fed back into the system, and another comparison is made. If there is still a mismatch between the input and the desired state, further corrective action is triggered. The process continues until there is an acceptable match between input and the desirable state. The automatic pilot of an airplane and a thermostat are examples of servomechanisms. Another example is shown in Figure 14–1.

In the language of cybernetics, humans can be described as servomechanisms that compare information coming from the environment with what is optimal under the circumstances. If there is a discrepancy humans act on their environments to make

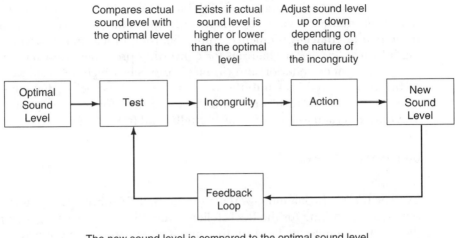

Compares actual sound level with the optimal level

Exists if actual sound level is higher or lower than the optimal level

Adjust sound level up or down depending on the nature of the incongruity

Optimal Sound Level → Test → Incongruity → Action → New Sound Level

Feedback Loop

The new sound level is compared to the optimal sound level. If there is an acceptable match, the adjustive process stops. If there is a mismatch, the corrective process continues.

FIGURE 14–1   A person adjusting the sound level of a radio exemplifies a servomechanism.

input match what is considered optimal (or at least acceptable). The results of various activities provide **feedback** about the effectiveness of those activities in reducing or eliminating the discrepancy between input and what is considered optimal.

A great deal of what is now called information-processing psychology came directly from Wiener's (1948) notion of cybernetics.

Robotology

Robotology consists of designing a machine that is capable of performing some human function. In 1952, W. R. Ashby created the *Homeostat,* which was a machine capable of regulating its own internal environment. In 1953, W. G. Walter designed a machine that mimicked the behavior of an organism in search of food or shelter. In 1954, J. A. Deutsch developed a machine that imitated maze learning in rats, and in 1962, H. S. Hoffman devised a machine that displayed a number of classical conditioning phenomena. Why is it important to build such machines and what do they say about human behavior? According to Bower and Hilgard (1981), building such devices allows us to test theories of human behavior.

> The prevailing consensus is that a machine which accurately simulates relevant aspects of some organism's behavior indeed constitutes a genuine explanation of that behavior. The idea is that the abstract principles involved in designing the machine—its functional components and their organization—could in fact be the same as those describing the design and functioning of the living organism...it is claimed that we have a fairly complete understanding of a piece of behavior when we know how to build a machine that would behave in just that way. (p. 354)

Robots and living organisms both have (1)mechanisms for receiving information from their external environments; (2) mechanisms for receiving information from their internal environments; (3) mechanisms for learning, processing, and storing information; (4) mechanisms for converting processed information into some form of output or behavior; and (5) mechanisms by which the results of the output or behavior are fed back into the systems. We shall see below that computers also have all of these characteristics, and therefore they, too, can be considered robots that mimic certain aspects of human intellectual functioning.

Information Theory

In 1949, Claude E. Shannon, working for the Bell Telephone Laboratories, and Warren Weaver, working for the Rockefeller Foundation, were seeking ways to improve the purity of a message between the time it is sent to the time it is received. Their work is seen as the beginning of **information theory** (Shannon & Weaver, 1949). The steps involved in sending and receiving a message are referred to as a *communication system*, which involves the following:

1. The information source, which selects the message to be sent out of many possible messages
2. The transmitter, which encodes the message into a signal that is sent out over the communication channel from the transmitter to the receiver
3. The receiver, which reconstructs (decodes) the signal into the original message

To determine whether or not various procedures enhance communication, Shannon and Weaver (1949) needed a precise way of measuring information. The unit of measure that they utilized was the *binary digit* or *bit*. A bit is defined as the amount of information that distinguishes between two likely alternatives. To determine whether the number that I jotted down was a 1 or a 2, you would need 1 bit of information. You could ask if the number was either 1 or 2, and regardless of the answer you would learn which number I wrote down. That is, if you asked if the number was 1, and I said yes, you would know that the number was 1. Likewise, if you asked if the number was 2, and I said no, you would know that it was 1. Now suppose that I jotted down a number from 1 through 4. How many bits would you need to discover the correct number? The answer is 2. You could ask, for example, whether the number was 3 or higher (first bit), and if so your next question could be "Is the number 3?" (second bit). Again, no matter what the answer is you have all the information you need to discover the correct number. Three bits of information would allow you to decide among eight equally likely alternatives, 4 among sixteen, and 5 among thirty-two. The general rule is that every time the number of possible alternatives is increased by a factor of two, we need an additional bit of information to make the correct decision. This general rule can be summarized as follows:

Alternatives	Bits Needed
2	1
4	2
8	3
16	4
32	5
64	6 etc.

Not only did information theory provide an objective way of measuring information, it also demonstrated the many ways that information could be recoded. For example, a telephone transmitter transforms (recodes) the sound of the human voice into electrical signals, which are then reconstructed into the human voice by the receiver. Both computers and humans can be viewed as information systems that recode input in a variety of ways and then translate that recoded input into a desired outcome (output). Most information-processing psychologists believe that humans process information on several levels. For example, information is processed on the sensory level, then on the perceptual level, and then in terms of the memories of prior experience. At each level, information is recoded, and in the process, some information is lost or distorted. Information-processing psychology, like information theory, attempts to discover those processes, structures, and mechanisms that determine what happens to information from the time that it is sent to the time that it is received and acted on. It is believed that as the operation of these processes, structures, and mechanisms become known, information processing can be enhanced and communication facilitated.

Computers

For most psychologists using the information-processing approach, the computer provides an analogy for how humans process information. Loftus and Loftus (1976) describe this analogy:

> Both computers and humans take in information from the environment. Computers do this using card readers, tape drives, etc., whereas humans do it using their sense organs. Inside a computer, the information from the environment is manipulated, recoded, and combined with other information already there. This is done via activation of electronic registers. Inside a person, information is manipulated, recoded, and combined with other information already there. This is done via activation of neurons. Finally, a computer outputs information to the environment via output devices, such as teletypes and line printers. Likewise, humans output information to the environment via such output devices as mouths and hands. (pp. 5–6)

Loftus and Loftus extend the analogy by noting that both computers and humans have **hardware.** For the computer, hardware consists of such items as a metal frame, transistors, resistors, and electronic circuitry. For the human, hardware consists of such items as muscles, bones, skin, and neural circuitry. Also, both computers and humans possess **software.** For a computer, software consists of programs that allow it to perform various operations. A computer program is a set of instructions that tells the computer what operations to perform on the information presented to it. For humans, software consists of operations typically learned from experience, for example, how to add and subtract, how to speak and write, how to drive a car, how to recognize and classify objects, how to read, and so on. These learned programs allow humans to perform the actions that are appropriate in various situations. When a human performs apparently complex operations while processing information, we refer to such operations as intelligence. When a computer engages in such operations, it is said to exemplify **artificial intelligence.** For example a computer programmed to play chess demonstrates artificial intelligence.

Extending the analogy between humans and computers still further, Loftus and Loftus (1976) say that the behavior of both may only appear to be too complicated to understand.

> To extend and use the analogy as a basis for theorizing about human behavior, we note that computers (as do humans) exhibit, on the face of things, very complicated behavior. However, we know that the complicated behavior exhibited by computers is interpretable in terms of relatively simple, understandable computer programs. Now we speculate that the complicated behavior of humans may also be generated by relatively simple, understandable programs. The task of the information-processing oriented psychologist then becomes one of deducing (from experimental data) what these programs may look like. (p. 7)

The similarity between computers and humans as processors of information is depicted in Figure 14–2.

It is widely believed that computers provide an excellent way of testing our theories concerning various human processes. Bower and Hilgard (1981) say, "Any theory that is sufficiently well specified can be realized as a computer program" (p. 355). A computer then, can be used to test the accuracy of theories of learning, intelligence, memory, concept formation, and problem solving. Once programmed, we can put the theories into action via the computer. Hill (1990) says,

> What do computer programs tell us about the actual processes of learning and thinking in living organisms? Nothing directly…the fact that a computer can be programmed to learn or think by certain processes does not demonstrate that either humans or rats learn or think by the same processes. What these programs can show are the implications of certain assumptions about how organisms learn. A theorist can write a computer program to follow the laws of learning that he thinks organisms follow, then run the program to see what happens. If what happens is similar to the outcome of human or animal learning, this finding makes it more plausible that humans or animals do in fact follow those hypothetical processes when they learn. If what happens is quite different from the outcome of "real" learning, the theorist's assumptions are probably false. Thus the computers provide a more precise way of doing what Hull wanted to do; if he had made use of computers he might have avoided some of the contradictions in his system. The role of the computer program is much like that of mathematical analysis—not to change the logic of theory construction, but to carry out that logic more precisely and more thoroughly. (pp. 166–167)

Although the computer is used by a number of information-processing psy-

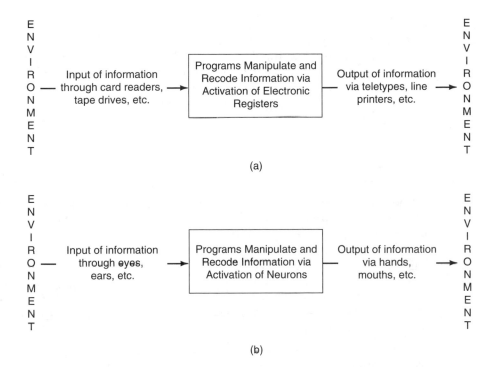

FIGURE 14–2 Similarity of computers and humans as processors of information. (From G.R. Loftus & E.F. Loftus *Human Memory: The Processing of Information,* Hillsdale, NJ: Erlbaum, 1976, p. 6.)

chologists as a model for how humans process information, there are some who warn that the analogy can be carried too far. In fact, Donald Norman, whose work will be featured next, insists that humans often process and act on information in ways that are quite different from the ways in which computers process and act on information. Norman (1981) gives the following example:

> An important aspect of everyday behavior is that we do several different activities at the same time, oftentimes for simultaneous (and possibly conflicting) purposes. Even when we do not attempt simultaneous actions, we still might be planning or reviewing one set of things while performing or accomplishing another. We delay and defer goals or actions as needed, waiting for appropriate times for them to be accomplished. This occurs for several reasons. Some biological goals do not need to be satisfied at any particular instant, but within reason, can be executed at convenience (e.g., such things as eating, sleeping, or toilet activities). Some daily tasks have similar characteristics (e.g., going to the bank or post office, purchasing some needed item). Some tasks have to be deferred because there is not sufficient time or information to complete them during one session of work (e.g., writing a scientific paper, reading a book, learning a complex task). Finally, even for tasks that are continually active from start to completion, they may span such a long duration that other things are also done along the way, and the individual components of the major task may have to wait for minutes or even hours before being executed. (p. 1)

Because of observations such as these, Norman says, "I argue that analyses of human performance imply a class of processing structures quite different than is commonly envisioned within Artificial Intelligence...the human is a special kind of biological processor, and I suspect that surprisingly little of what we know of...computers applies to the human" (p. 1).

We next turn to Donald Norman's specific contributions to information-processing psychology.

DONALD A. NORMAN

We chose Donald Norman as the representative of information-processing psychology because of his special interest in learning and because his concerns have been much more comprehensive than most others working in the area.

Donald A. Norman (b. 1935) is professor of psychology at the University of California, San Diego, where he is director of the Institute for Cognitive Science and chair of the Interdisciplinary Ph.D. Program in Cognitive Science. Norman received his B.S. degree from the Massachusetts Institute of Technology in electrical engineering in 1957. He received his M.A. from the University of Pennsylvania in electrical engineering in 1959 and his Ph.D. from the same institution in mathematical psychology in 1962. He was lecturer and research fellow at Harvard University from 1963 until he joined the faculty at the University of California, San Diego, where he has been ever since.

Donald A. Norman. (Courtesy of Donald A. Norman.)

Norman has written many articles and several influential books, including *Human Information Processing: An Introduction to Psychology* (1977), which he coauthored with Peter H. Lindsay. Norman is as much interested in application as he is in theory. His applied work focuses on what he calls "cognitive engineering," which can be used to develop human-machine interactive systems that will reduce the incidence of human error. He also wrote *The Psychology of Everyday Things* (1988), showing how the proper design of machines and equipment can significantly reduce errors and accidents. Norman's research includes topics ranging from memory, attention, and learning to the role of conscious and subconscious mechanisms in the control of human behavior. His emphasis is always on how all cognitive and body systems *interact* and never on isolated systems.

THE DEFINITION AND THE LAWS OF LEARNING

For Norman, learning and remembering are closely related, but learning is more than simply remembering: It involves the ability to perform a task with skill. In his book *Learning and Memory,* Norman (1982) says, "I use the term 'learning' to refer to the act of deliberate study of a specific body of material, so that the material can be retrieved at will and used with skill. Learning involves purposeful remembering and skillful performance" (p. 3).

With this definition, Norman disagrees with those theorists who view learning as an automatic process. For example, Thorndike's law of effect states that learning will occur automatically when a response is followed by a desirable outcome, to which Lindsay and Norman (1977) reply:

> For our purposes, the law of effect is not a sufficient explanation of learning. In our opinion, it suffers the problem of attempting to describe the phenomena of learning by simple description of the events and responses of the organism, without any consideration of the internal information processing that must also be taking place. As a result, the law gets into serious difficulties in attempting to explain the real behavior of complex organisms. The problems result from several sources. First, the law of effect is vague about the temporal conditions that are involved. Second, it ignores the necessity for causal relationships between the actions and the outcome. Finally, the law of effect emphasizes the desirability of the outcome, known as its *reinforcing* value. We believe that the important part of an outcome is its *information.* The outcome serves as a signal to the organism about the result of its acts. (p. 501)

By emphasizing the importance of the information gained from experience, Norman aligns himself with the theories of Tolman and Bandura. In further elaborating what is learned, however, Norman closely follows Piaget.

> In the language of one of the foremost investigators of cognitive development, Jean Piaget, the organism learns by constructing sensorimotor schemas [in our chapter on Piaget we chose schemata as the plural of schema]. It extracts the relationship between the information picked up by its sensory system and its actions (motor activities). A *sensorimotor schema* is a plan (a scheme) for performing an organized sequence of actions to perform some specific act, coordinating the information picked up by the sensory system with the necessary motor (muscle) movements. The acts of eating, walking, or riding a bicycle require their own well-developed sensorimotor schemas. In order to construct these schemas the organism must be particularly sensitive to certain kinds of consequences, such as those associated with a desirable and necessary outcome, like food. (Lindsay & Norman, 1977, p. 500)

Norman continues to follow Piaget closely by assuming that when something is learned or remembered it is added to what has already been learned or remembered: "Our view of learning is the same as our view of memory: when new information is learned, it is added to preexisting meaning structures within the memory system. The problem facing the learner is to determine the conditions that are relevant to the situation, to determine what the appropriate actions are, and to record that information properly" (p. 500).

The Laws of Learning

Norman summarizes his thoughts on learning in three laws, all of which emphasize the *causal* relationship between actions and outcomes.

1. The Law of Causal Relationship   For an organism to learn the relationship between a specific action and an outcome, there must be an apparent causal relation between them. This is the **law of causal relationship.**

2. The Law of Causal Learning   The **law of causal learning** has two parts: First, for desirable outcomes, the organism attempts to repeat those particular actions that have an apparent causal relationship to the desired outcome. Second, for undesirable outcomes, the organism attempts to avoid those actions that have an apparent causal relation to the undesirable outcome.

3. The Law of Information Feedback   In the **law of information feedback,** the outcome of an event serves as information about that event.

Norman (Lindsay & Norman, 1977) uses the term *apparent* causal relationship because humans typically are not in a position to know if there is a true causal relationship between their actions and various outcomes.

> The apparent causality may not reflect the real causality that operates in the world. Sometimes real and apparent causality will be the same. Sometimes humans will infer causal relations where there are none. Sometimes, they will not notice causal relations that actually do exist. Unless humans are capable of performing scientific experiments that can reveal the actual causal relationships, they must deal with inferred or apparent causal relationships between their actions and the outcomes. (p. 502)

It may be remembered that in Chapter 5 on Skinner's theory, we noted that superstitious behavior resulted from noncontingent reinforcement. Under such reinforcement, the organism acts "as if" there is a causal relationship between its actions and a reinforcing outcome, but in reality there is no such relationship. That is, the causal relationship is apparent but not real.

In his book *Social Foundations of Thought and Action,* Bandura (1986) points out that apparent but not real relationships are often dysfunctional; that is, they produce undesirable or inappropriate behavior. In a section of this book entitled "On Misreading Events," Bandura describes three ways in which dysfunctional beliefs can develop. One way is through **coincidental association.** Outcomes are typically preceded by numerous events, and therefore it is always possible to select as a predictor of an outcome the wrong events. Bandura gives as an example a woman who had a negative relationship with a man who wore a bow tie. Afterward, all her experiences with men who wore bow ties were negative, and she reached the conclusion that all men who wore bow ties were undesirable. According to Bandura, this woman's belief became a self-fulfilling prophecy:

Misbeliefs would not last long were it not for the fact that they influence selection and production of experiences. Coincidental association is often converted through misbeliefs into a genuine correlation. To the extent that anticipatory distrust evokes negative counterreactions from bow-tied men, defensive behavior is perpetuated by the unpleasant experiences it creates. In this process, the inappropriate belief and its accompanying defensiveness are maintained by self-produced reality, rather than by conditions that have existed in the past but are no longer in effect. (p. 219)

A second way in which faulty beliefs can develop is through **inappropriate generalization;** for example, an attack by one dog generalizes into the erroneous belief that all dogs are dangerous, or the crash of one airplane generalizes into the belief that all airplanes are dangerous. Bandura's (1986) third kind of dysfunctional belief is **perceived self-inefficacy**.

Persons who judge themselves as lacking coping capabilities, whether the self-appraisal is objectively warranted or not, will perceive all kinds of dangers in situations and exaggerate their potential harmfulness....When a few mishaps are read as signs of basic coping inefficacy, all kinds of situations become fraught with danger. To understand people's judgments of external threats it is, therefore, necessary to analyze their judgments of their own coping capabilities which, in large part, determine the subjective perilousness of environmental events. (p. 220)

Learned Helplessness   As we saw in Chapter 7, if a person believes that there is nothing that he or she can do to terminate an unpleasant situation, the phenomenon called **learned helplessness** can result. It may be that the person in fact was in an unpleasant situation in which no action would terminate it, and if so, it would make sense to give up and to develop the belief that "Nothing that I can do will make a difference." This belief becomes faulty, however, if conditions change, so that a behavioral solution is now possible, or if it generalizes into the belief that "I am just not capable of dealing with life's problems." If the person does generalize and concludes that he or she does not possess the skills necessary for solving life's problems, *depression* may result. Believing that one is helpless, when in fact one is not, exemplifies what Norman calls an apparent but not real relationship and what Bandura calls perceived self-inefficacy.

SKILLED PERFORMANCE

Throughout his writings, Norman emphasizes the interrelatedness of learning, memory, and performance. The study of memory attempts to determine how information is stored and retrieved. The study of performance attempts to determine how information is utilized. The study of learning attempts to determine how an organism acquires new information, that is, how it profits from experience. In Norman's (1982) view, learning is closely related to understanding.

You have learned to play chess when you understand the moves, the purpose and the basic strategy of the game. When you learn to drive or to sail, you learn something of the mechanics of the situation, something of the rules of the road, and most important, something of the relationship between your actions and the response of the car or boat. From the outsider's point of view, learning is closely related to performance. You may think you understand chess, but if you cannot play a challenging game, I would say you have not really learned it. (p. 66)

But what is **skilled performance?** Norman is interested in understanding the difference between the skilled performance of experts such as tennis champions and veteran airplane pilots and that of less skilled individuals or amateurs. He lists five variables that differentiate between the two.

1. **Smoothness.** Professionals do their job with ease, grace, smoothness, and less effort than amateurs.
2. **Automaticity.** Most experts perform their task without an awareness of exactly what they are doing. "Ask skilled typists how they type a space. Do they always use the same thumb or do they alternate thumbs according to the particular words they are typing? Many typists do not know what they do" (Norman, 1982, p. 72).
3. **Mental effort.** "As skill increases, mental effort decreases. The task appears easier, there is less mental fatigue, less need to monitor each action with care. Skilled performers can hold conversations with others, even while performing intricate tasks with their bodies" (pp. 72–73).
4. **Stress.** The performance of amateurs tends to deteriorate under stress, whereas the performance of experts tends not to.
5. **Point of view.** When first learning a skill, one must attend to a wide variety of activities. In learning to drive a car, one needs to learn how to steer, back up, apply the brakes, park, accelerate, decelerate, and so on. As an amateur driver, all of these things are attended to. As an expert driver, however, one just drives. Norman (1980a) put it as follows:

Consider what happens when you first learn to drive an automobile. The instructions you receive emphasize the actions and mechanics: hold the steering wheel this way, synchronize foot (for clutch) and hand (for gearshift) that way. As you progress, the point of view changes. Now you are turning the wheel, not moving your hands clockwise. Then you are turning the car, later you are entering that driveway. Eventually, when a truly expert driver, you drive to the bank, go shopping. The differences in the qualitative feeling of the performance are great. At the expert level, you may no longer be aware of all the subsidiary operations that you perform: you look at the driveway, form the intention to enter, and the car obediently follows suit. Driving the car becomes as natural as walking, the car becoming as much a part of the body's controlled appendages as the limbs. (p. 25)

Missionaries and Cannibals   In his book *Learning and Memory* (1982), Norman beckons his readers to experience what it feels like to go from being an amateur to being a skilled performer. As a vehicle for this transition he uses the missionaries and cannibals problem. The problem, as presented by Norman, is found in Figure 14–3.

The Missionaries and Cannibals Problem

Three missionaries were lost, exploring the jungles of the planet Aurilion. Separated from their companions, without food or radio, they knew only that their destination was ahead. They stood at a river that blocked their path, wondering what to do. All at once, three cannibals appeared, carrying with them a boat. They too were about to cross the river. Groups of cannibals and missionaries had met before. Each was respectful of the other, but not fully trusting; missionaries took advantage of cannibals whenever they outnumbered them, and the unwitting cannibals were baptized before they could escape.

   The three cannibals were willing to help the missionaries cross the river, but their boat could hold only two people at a time, and the cannibals would not let themselves even be outnumbered by the missionaries. How can the problem be solved?

The Task

   Your task is to manipulate the paper clips back and forth across the river: let large clips represent missionaries and small ones cannibals. You must imagine the boat. Remember that the boat holds a maximum of two people at a time. If on one side of the river there are ever more missionaries than cannibals, you have failed and must start over. Remember to count whoever is in the boat, so that one missionary and one cannibal on the river bank plus one or two missionaries in the boat at the same side of the river spells trouble.

   Try it. Move the paper clips back and forth. Expect to take as long as 10 minutes to solve it the first time.

   Time each attack on the problem. If you err in any maner (dropping a paper clip, moving the wrong clip by mistake, or finding a baptized cannibal), you must start the problem over but without stopping the timing. The time for the task must include all your actions from the start to a successful completion.

   Write down the time for each trial on a piece of paper. Keep at the task until you can do it twice in a row in less than 10 seconds each time.

FIGURE 14–3   The missionaries and cannibals problem. (From *Learning and Memory,* pp. 76–77, by D.A. Norman, 1982, New York; W.H. Freeman and Company. Copyright © 1982 W.H. Freeman and Company. Reprinted with permission.)

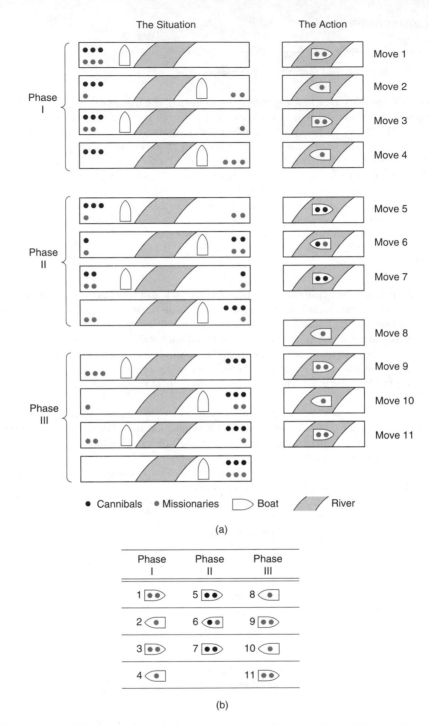

The Situation   The Action

Phase I

Move 1

Move 2

Move 3

Move 4

Phase II

Move 5

Move 6

Move 7

Move 8

Phase III

Move 9

Move 10

Move 11

● Cannibals   ● Missionaries   ▷ Boat   ▨ River

(a)

Phase I	Phase II	Phase III
1 ●●	5 ●●	8 ●
2 ●	6 ●●	9 ●●
3 ●●	7 ●●	10 ●
4 ●		11 ●●

(b)

FIGURE 14–4 Solution to the missionaries and cannibals problem. (a) shows how the amateur typically solves the problem; (b) shows how the expert solves it. (From *Learning and Memory,* pp. 79, by D.A. Norman, 1982, New York: W.H. Freeman and Company. Copyright © 1982 W.H. Freeman and Company. Reprinted with permission.)

During the early attempts to solve the problem, one is an amateur and performance is slow, deliberate, and often incorrect. As one continues, however, performance becomes smooth and automatic and requires less mental effort. Although the early stages of solving this problem involve learning the correct strategy, Norman maintains that the conversion from amateur to expert is not so much a matter of learning how to solve the problem as it is learning how to *perform*, or how to effectively translate what has been learned into behavior. The typical solution to the problem is diagrammed in Figure 14–4(a). After presenting this problem to his classes for many years, Norman himself has reached the point where he can leave out many of the steps typically involved in the solution. Norman's expert method of solution is shown in Figure 14–4(b).

Norman follows Woodworth (1938) in his description of the sequence of experiences that characterize the learning of a complex task such as the solution to the missionaries and cannibals problem. That sequence is chaos, analysis, synthesis, and automatization.

> The sequence proceeds from whole to part and back to whole again. At first the task is chaotic-unorganized. Not enough is known even to perceive the situation easily. Then, with more experience, some of the units emerge. Systematic analysis reveals the component parts, which can then be learned separately, interrelated, and combined. Larger organizational units emerge; the topic takes on some structure and finally seems to be manageable. With further experience, the use of the knowledge becomes automatic, the skilled performance becomes subconscious. (Norman, 1982, pp. 78, 80)

MODES OF LEARNING

In their discussion of the modes of learning, Rumelhart and Norman (1981) display the close relationship between their information-processing approach and Piaget's view of developmental knowledge.

Accretion

According to Rumelhart and Norman (1981), **accretion** is the most common mode of learning and involves the encoding of new information in terms of preexisting memory schemata. Thus, new information is processed in terms of old information. The very act of processing the information changes the existing schemata, however, and the resultant schemata are used to interpret similar future experiences, for example, learning to drive a car that you have not driven before. Norman (1982) writes, "Presumably you already have a good framework of knowledge for the structure of automobiles and for the mechanics of driving. Still, you must learn the specific details of a new car—where the horn and the emergency brake are located, how much free play the steering wheel has, and how tight the brakes are. Basically, as you come across each new aspect of the car, you are able to tuck it away in memory in some well-established manner" (p. 82).

In Piaget's terminology, when an experience can be effectively recognized, understood, and dealt with by a schema, assimilation occurs. When a schema must change in order to deal effectively with an experience, accommodation occurs. Norman's concept of accretion involves a large amount of assimilation and only a relatively small amount of accommodation.

Structuring

When existing schemata do not allow effective negotiations with the environment, new ones must be formed. Norman refers to the learning of new schemata as **structuring,** the most difficult kind of learning. Using the above example, when one first learned how to drive one had to learn a driving schema; once this difficult task was accomplished, it could be applied to almost any automobile with relative ease. Norman's discussion of schema development parallels Piaget's quite closely.

Tuning

It is **tuning** that transforms an amateur into a skilled performer. According to Norman (1982),

> Tuning is the fine adjustment of knowledge to a task. The proper schemas exist and appropriate knowledge is within them. But they are inefficient for the purpose, either because they are too general or because they are mismatched to the particular use that is required of them, so the knowledge must be tuned, continually adjusted to the task. Practice is one way of accomplishing tuning. It may take thousands of hours of practice to reach the stage of tuning that characterizes an expert. Tuning is perhaps the slowest of the modes of learning, but it is what changes mere knowledge of a topic into expert performance. (pp. 81–82)

Tuning, then, consists of a long series of accretions. That is, tuning involves the large number of slight accommodations that are required when adjusting to the unique aspects of experiences that otherwise would not be completely assimilated into a schema.

Learning by Analogy

Norman equates accretion with memory since with both an experience is interpreted and acted on in terms of existing schemata. Since each experience is unique, such learning does not result in slight modifications of existing schemata (i.e., it results in slight accommodation), but it is mainly a matter of what Piaget called assimilation. As mentioned above, tuning involves a series of slight modifications and eventually allows for expertise or skilled performance.

If all learning involved only accretion or tuning, no new schemata would ever be required and, therefore, would not develop. Since new schemata (programs for interpreting and acting on environmental experience) do develop, the question is by what mechanism are new schemata acquired? Norman's answer is that they develop by analogy to existing schemata.

> We have proposed that complex new procedures can be readily created by modeling them on existing schemas and modifying them slightly. We believe that the typical course

of such a learning process consists of an initial creation of a new schema by modeling it on an existing schema. This new schema, however, is not perfect. It may occasionally mispredict events and otherwise be inadequate. We then believe that the newly acquired schema undergoes a process of refinement that we have dubbed *tuning*...we believe that this modeling process is properly called learning by analogy. (Rumelhart & Norman, 1981, p. 357)

Complex learning, then, involves finding the most relevant existing schema and applying it to the new situation. This process of **learning by analogy** according to Norman, will allow at least a partial understanding of the new situation.

Consider, for example, how we teach children the concept of a fraction. Most curricula use the pie analogy. One-half corresponds to one piece of a pie that has been cut down the middle. One-fourth corresponds to one piece of a pie cut into four equal pieces, etc. Here, the teacher is taking advantage of the child's spatial intuitions to teach the abstract notions of a fraction. This analogy is very useful: upon learning it, the reasoning and problem-solving strategies implicit in his knowledge of pies, operations that can be performed on them, etc., can be carried over into this abstract domain. The child can see that two-quarters make a half, that if you have a whole and take away one-quarter, you have three-quarters remaining, etc. The child needn't know *how* he knows this. These inferences are simply implicit in the analogy. (Rumelhart & Norman, 1981, p. 340)

It is seldom the case, however, that an existing schema is a perfect analogy for another. In other words, learning by analogy is almost always less than perfect.

Sometimes operations are required in the target domain (in this case with learning fractions) that are difficult or unnatural within the domain of the analogical source. Thus, whereas addition and subtraction of fractions is natural within the pie analogy, multiplication and division of fractions is unnatural and difficult to conceptualize. How do you take one piece of pie times another or, worse yet, how do you divide one piece of pie *into* another? (Rumelhart & Norman, 1981, p. 340)

To remedy the shortcomings of a particular analogy, Norman suggests that several analogies might be necessary to teach a complex topic. If the schemata for multiplication and division have been learned, they could be applied to the above situation to alleviate the inadequacies of the pie analogy.

What Goes on in the Mind of the Learner?   In his article, "What Goes on in the Mind of the Learner," Norman (1980b) reflects on some of the mistakes that he has made as a teacher and what he has done to correct them. Originally Norman assumed,

In order to teach, one must have knowledge of the topic that is to be taught, plus an understanding of the knowledge that the student already possesses. Then, one simply teaches the differences between them.,.,.Learning is really very simple, according to this point of view. Teaching is relatively simple, also. All one has to worry about is a proper understanding of the knowledge and of the student, and proper selection of the order of presentation.
    Unfortunately, it does not work that way. (p. 39)

Norman's problem was in accepting the epistemology of the associationists:

What was wrong was the simple theory of learning. Essentially, I had assumed that students were passive receptacles and that an ideal teaching situation would be one where the students would come into the classroom, unscrew the top of their skulls, and the instructor could walk around the class, peer intently into the brain of each student, and say something like, "Hmmm, you seem to have this connection missing," and then proceed to add the necessary connections. What a lovely vision!

But students are not passive receptors of knowledge. (p. 42)

Instead, Norman discovered that students will always respond to what is presented to them in terms of their preexisting ideas, or schemata. Students always interpret and understand new material in terms of material that they have already learned:

The student comes to the learning situation with a large set of preexisting ideas, and the material that is presented is interpreted according to these ideas. You cannot prevent it: I have tried. I have tried to present material in a neutral fashion. I have tried methods of discovery learning, in which the student interacts with the task, discovering the important principles of the day. I have carefully worked to set up the task so that the "discovery" leaps out and waves itself in the student's face. Well, sure the student will interact, and sure the student will discover things. But what is discovered and how it is interpreted is up to the student, and sometimes I feel I have remarkably little control over the process. (p. 42)

So, in answer to the question "What Goes on in the Mind of the Learner?" Norman (1980b) says, a lot! Although humans have a strong desire to understand new experiences, they always do so in terms of what they already understand. Norman likens learning to theory building, which is both good and bad. As a theorist, the learner will attempt to explain his or her experiences, to give them meaning. That's the good part. "But, like a theorist, a learner builds on incomplete evidence, tends to ignore information that does not fit, and will grasp at any evidence that can serve as confirmation" (p. 42).

Norman is saying what Piaget had said: If an experience cannot be at least partially assimilated into existing schemata, it cannot exist for the learner. It is inevitable, then, that much of what is presented to students will not register. What, if anything, does register will always depend on how the learner's previous experiences were encoded into memory in the form of schemata. Norman refers to this as the **iceberg model of learning.** From the point of view of the learner, the small visible part of the iceberg represents the facts being presented by the teacher. Based on these facts, the learner must determine the larger structure of knowledge they represent. From the point of view of the teacher, the tip of the iceberg is the behavior of the student. To be effective the teacher must realize that this behavior reflects the much larger, submerged part of the iceberg, which consists of the schemata in terms of which the facts are understood (or misunderstood) by the learner. Norman (1980b) says, "The student has erected a huge structure, and if the teacher is to understand the difficulties eventually faced by the student, this structure must somehow be uncovered" (p. 44).

We see that according to Norman, all important learning is learning by analogy. On the basis of preexisting models (ideas, structures, schemata), new experiences are evaluated, interpreted, understood, misunderstood, learned, or not learned.

MEMORY

If an experience can be assimilated to a large extent into an existing schema, memory can adequately deal with it. According to Norman (1982), "To remember is to have managed three things successfully: the acquisition, retention, and retrieval of information" (p. 2). Recall that in Chapter 10 we discussed the Gestalt view of memory. According to the Gestalt theorists, each experience we have leaves a memory trace, which as one has more and more related experiences, becomes increasingly strong. Each new experience changes the trace slightly, and in turn the experience is changed by the trace. Thus, according to the Gestalt theorists, memory is an active process that is transformed by experience and, in turn, modifies subsequent experiences. Since each new experience slightly changes a trace, it can be viewed as a learning experience. This is essentially what Norman means when he discusses accretion as both a form of learning and a model of memory.

However, accretion is the simplest kind of learning. How does memory relate to the kind of learning Norman calls "structuring"? In other words, how does memory come into play when we learn by analogy? To answer this question we must trace what happens to information from the time it enters the organism through various sense receptors, is transformed by various information-processing mechanisms, and is finally translated into some form of behavior.

Sensory Memory

When environmental stimuli impinge on a sense receptor, they are converted into neural impulses, and the information contained in the stimuli remains available for about one second after the stimuli are terminated. The fact that receptor systems retain environmental information for a brief period of time is called **sensory memory,** or *sensory store,* and it is with sensory store that Norman begins his analysis of learning and memory. Sensory store is the first stage of information processing, and it is the stage on which all higher, more complex stages of processing depend. Although each sensory system has the ability to store information for a short time, the visual and auditory systems have been given the most attention because they are the sense modalities through which we get most of our knowledge of the environment. The sensory memory corresponding to the visual sense is called **iconic store.** The sensory memory corresponding to the auditory sense is called **echoic store.** Norman (1982) gives the following examples of sensory memory:

> Wave your hand in front of your face. The faint trace that remains after your hand is gone, a remnant of the event just past, is visible evidence of a sensory memory system. Close your hand into a fist, rapidly extend two fingers, then as quickly as possible form a fist again. If you watch closely, you will see a trace of your fingers that lasts long enough for you to count them. Move your hands parallel to each other but in opposite directions. Quickly wave them once before your eyes. Notice the subtle, indescribable feeling of motion associated with each faint trace. The feeling is real. Suppose there is flashed before you a complex image consisting of many objects, some moving clockwise in small circles, others moving counterclockwise. The image vanishes and an arrow points somewhere within the former area of the image. You will be able to report the direction in

which the object in that particular place moved. The trace lasts for a few hundred milliseconds after the physical image is gone. (p. 5)

Although there is a vast amount of information in sensory store at any given moment, only a fraction of it is attended to and thus made available for the next stage of information processing.

Short-Term Memory

Sensory memory has a large capacity. For example, if you were to look up an address in a telephone book, essentially all of the names and addresses on a page will be in sensory memory for about one second. Only the address of interest will be attended to, however, and thus will enter **short-term memory** (also called short-term store and primary memory), which lasts about 15 seconds, long enough to get a piece of paper and a pencil and jot it down. Unless information in short-term memory is selected for further processing, it, too, will be forgotten in a very short period of time.

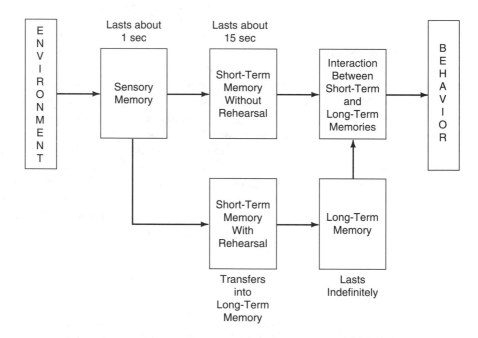

FIGURE 14–5 The relationships among environmental information, sensory memory, short-term memory, and long-term memory. Depending on the needs of the organism, certain information from sensory memory is selected for further processing in short-term memory. Depending on the organism's needs, certain information is selected from short-term memory to be rehearsed and thereby transferred into long-term memory. At any given moment, then, an organism's behavior is determined by the interaction between stimulating conditions and the long-term memories that those conditions elicit.

Long-Term Memory

Let us say that you wanted to remember the address that you just looked up for a long time. In that case, you would rehearse it over and over, enough times to record it in **long-term memory** (also called long-term store and secondary memory). Most significant, recurring events in our lives are transferred into long-term memory and thus can be used to interpret, categorize, and respond to our everyday experiences. It is in long-term memory that the schemata that have been learned are stored. As we have seen, Norman believes that the most significant kind of learning occurs by analogy, and analogy (comparison) would be impossible if previously learned schemata were not stored in long-term memory. Loftus and Loftus (1976) stress the importance of long-term memory: "We are all aware that humans are able to store vast amounts of information—words, names, faces, places—permanently or semipermanently in long-term store. Without long-term store there would be nothing: no books, no television, no learning, no communication—for it is our ability to recall the past that allows us to interact with our environment in a dynamic way" (p. 56).

Once long-term memories are established, new experiences are processed and acted on in accordance with them. Again, the schemata (programs) that we have learned are stored in long-term memory, and it is from long-term memory that information appropriate to a situation is retrieved and utilized.

The relationships among the environment, sensory memory, short-term memory, long-term memory, and behavior are depicted in Figure 14–5.

TWELVE ISSUES FOR COGNITIVE SCIENCE

There is a tendency on the part of those using the computer as a model for studying human thought processes to view the human as a rational, logical information-processing system. That is, there is information from the environment (input), the processing of that information by various programs (e.g., memory and schemata), and output in the form of behavior. This view of humans can be seen as a variation of the old S-R conception of humans offered by associationists such as Pavlov, Watson, and Guthrie. In other words, this view of information-processing psychology is still a brand of S-R psychology. The only difference is that between the S and the R, there are mechanisms that encode, transform, modify, store, retrieve, and translate information from the environment. It is believed that the way humans process information is not unlike what happens to a telephone message between the time it is sent and the time it is received. Both human and telephone systems are viewed as complex but automatic and machine-like, and the computer is accepted as an accurate analogy for how humans process information. As we have seen, Norman does not adhere to this conception. According to Norman, the modern view of human information-processing has added several more processing mechanisms, and this is a step in the right direction, but the view still omits several important facts. Norman (1980a) summarizes in his article "Twelve Issues for Cognitive Science" the present view of the human information-processing system (Figure 14–6) and then goes on to point out its weaknesses:

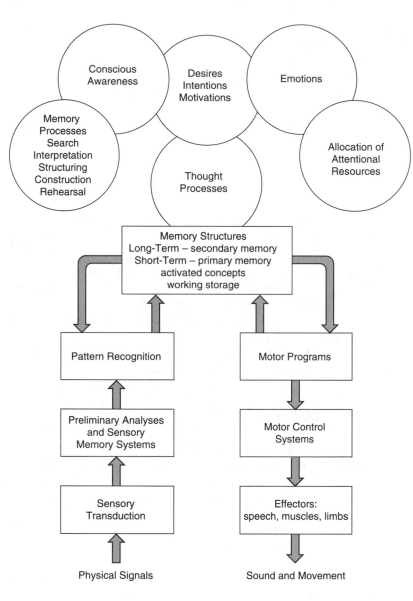

FIGURE 14–6
Norman's summary of the modern view of the human information-processing system. (From "Twelve Issues for Cognitive Science," by D.A. Norman, 1980a, *Cognitive Science, 4.*) Norman feels that such a view is inadequate for reasons found in the text.

The human is a physical symbol system, yes…But the human is more: The human is an animate organism with a biological basis and an evolutionary and cultural history. More-over, the human is a social animal, interacting with others, with the environment, and with itself. The core disciplines of cognitive science have tended to ignore these aspects of behavior. The results have been considerable progress on some fronts, but sterility over-all, for the organism we are analyzing is conceived as pure intellect, communicating with one another in logical dialogue, perceiving, remembering, thinking where appro-priate, reasoning its way through the well-formed problems that are encountered in the day. Alas, that description does not fit actual behavior.…I conclude that there is more to human intelligence than the pure cognitive system, and that a science of Cognition can-not afford to ignore these other aspects. (pp. 2–4)

Following are the 12 issues that Norman believes cognitive science should address.

1. Belief Systems   According to Norman, what we believe to be true about the world and ourselves (whether those beliefs are correct or not) influences memory, perception, problem solving, and the interpretation of experience in general. It is essential, then, that we know how belief systems are formed, how they operate and how they change. Norman (1980a) has personally experienced the importance of belief systems: "My brief excursions into this area have left me impressed with how much my own hidden belief structures influence my 'pure' logical inference, memory processes, and social interactions. I suspect that we will find that more of our behavior is thus determined, not less" (p. 16).

Insofar as beliefs can be equated with expectancies, researchers such as Bandura have already made substantial gains in determining the importance of beliefs in the living of one's life, but as Norman suggests, much remains to be done.

2. Consciousness   According to Norman (1980a),

> Consciousness, under which I include the issues of conscious and subconscious thought, the problem of self-awareness, attention, the control structures of cognition, the formation of intentions. Here too are such issues as the phenomenological states of awareness, states of consciousness. Hypnosis: a powerful force, potentially a powerful tool for the investigation of consciousness, but little understood, not sufficiently well explored. (p. 16)

Even attention, the aspect of consciousness that has been studied the most, is still little understood. In 1890, William James described attention as follows: "It is the taking possession of the mind, in clear and vivid form, of one out of what seems several simultaneously possible objects or trains of thought. Focalization, concentration of consciousness are of its essence. It implies withdrawal from some things in order to deal effectively with others" (Vol. 1, pp. 403–404).

But, says Norman (1980a),

> It is exactly the description given in the quote from James that we do not understand, cannot understand until we come to a better appreciation of the working of the mind, of the several simultaneous trains of thought that can occur, of the differences between conscious and subconscious processing, and of what it means to focus upon one train of thought to the exclusion of others. What—who—does the focussing, what happens to those other trains of thought as they are excluded? (Some, I am certain continue silently, unheeded, as subconscious processes that may later interrupt to again force conscious attention to themselves.) And what does it mean to have *conscious attention?* Can there be attention that is not conscious? What—who—experiences the result of conscious attentional processes? (pp. 16–17)

3. Development   Like Piaget, Norman (1980a) believes that children and adults process information differently because different schemata are available to them. Unfortunately, many researchers overlook this fact.

> In the study of adult cognition there seems to be the implicit assumption that once we come to understand adults, children will simply be seen to be at various stages along

the pathway toward the adult. Perhaps. But perhaps also that the complexity and experience of the adult will forever mask some properties. Automatic behavior masks the underlying structure, pushing things beneath the conscious surface to the inaccessibility of subconscious processes. Well established belief and knowledge systems mask their content.

Much of cognitive behavior could be studied best through the developmental cycle, with the history of the development leading to better understanding of the adult. Animate organisms take very long times to reach adulthood: the human is learning new concepts throughout the entire life span. Language learning goes on through the late teenage years, and vocabulary learning never ceases. We are fundamentally organisms that learn, that develop over time. By ignoring this aspect of behavior and concentrating on the static phases we may miss the keys to understanding. (p. 18)

4. Emotion   Many believe that human emotions are an evolutionary carryover from an earlier time, when emotional behavior was related to survival, and that for modern humans, emotions are irrelevant or even a nuisance. Norman, however, believes that emotions play an important part in our commerce with the environment and he places them between the regulatory system and the cognitive system (Figure 14-7). This model would explain why, when we have experiences or thoughts conducive to survival, we experience positive emotions such as joy, happiness, pleasure, or love. When we have experiences or thoughts that are not conducive to survival, we experience negative emotions such as anger, anxiety, depression, or hate.

For Norman (1980a), it is essential to learn how our cognitive experiences are painted by the brush of emotions: "And what is the role of emotion in the study of cognition? We leave it to the poet, the playwright, the novelist. As people, we delight in art and in music. We fight, get angered, have joy, grief, happiness. But as students of mental events, we are ignorant of why, how" (p. 18).

5. Interaction   Humans are social organisms, and yet,

Much of the study of cognitive processes has been the study of the isolated person. Much of the study of interactive groups has been of the dynamics of the situation, or of the behavioral aspects of the group. To my knowledge, little has been done to combine these efforts, to examine the individual cognitive processes as they are used within

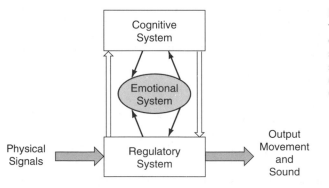

FIGURE 14–7   Norman's contention that emotions intercede between an organism's regulatory system (the system related to the organism's survival) and its cognitive system. (Adapted from "Twelve Issues for Cognitive Science," by D.A. Norman, 1980a, *Cognitive Science, 4,* 1–32.)

interactive settings. But, because the normal mode for the human is to interact, the studies of memory and language and problem solving and decision making in isolation address only one part of the mechanisms of human cognition. (Norman, 1980a, p. 19)

6 and 7. Language and Perception   The problem, according to Norman, is that language and perception receive too much attention. In fact, there is a tendency to equate cognitive science with the study of these two topics. Norman feels that this is a mistake because a complete understanding of human cognition will come only when the nature and influence of such factors as beliefs, consciousness, social interactions, culture, emotions, learning, and memory are understood. These and other factors all interact as the human processes information, and to overemphasize a few at the expense of the others is a mistake.

8. Learning   Norman (1980a) does not think kindly of most of the other theories of learning covered in this text. "Psychologists developed global theories of human and animal behavior, often built around such fundamental learning principles as 'the law of effect' or 'associative properties of learning and memory.' It all has come to nought" (p. 20).

Earlier in this chapter we reviewed Norman's views of the learning process, especially his emphasis of the importance of learning by analogy. He believes his efforts are just a first step toward understanding the nature of learning, however. In the meantime, little has been done and is being done to understand the nature of complex learning. Norman (1980a) says,

> There has been remarkably little study of learning—real learning, the learning of complex topics, the learning that takes months, even years to accomplish. Elsewhere I have estimated that experts at a task may spend 5,000 hours acquiring their skills: that is not such a long time; it is 2 ½ years of full-time study, 40 hours a week, 50 weeks a year. Not much time to become a professional tennis player, or computer programmer, or linguist. What goes on during that time? Whatever it is, it is slow, continuous. No magic dose of knowledge in the form of pill or lecture. Just a lot of slow, continual exposure to the topic, probably accompanied by several bouts of restructuring of the underlying mental representations, reconceptualizations of the concepts, plus many hours of accumulation of large quantities of facts. (p. 20)

9. Memory   Norman (1980a) warns us about memory:

> Do not be impressed by all that is presumably known about the psychology of memory. Less is known than you might think....How does one find the information required to answer a question when the form of the question was not anticipated at the time of acquiring the information? Not possible with artificial systems today, a commonplace occurrence with people. And how is the desired information recognized once it is found if it wasn't known in the first place? If I seek the name of a long-lost colleague and retrieve the name Isaac Newton, how do I reject that as the name I seek when I do not know the sought-for name?...How do we remember stories, events, experiences? More to the point, how do we retrieve them when least we expect them?
> Memory has some other puzzles. We recognize the meanings of words in tenths of sec-

onds (as in reading), yet may take hours or days to retrieve one of those words when we seek it for use in a sentence. And what is it that keeps the memory search going for those hours or days, while conscious thought proceeds in other directions, when the need for the word may have long passed? Current events bring to mind previous experiences, not always in any obvious fashion. It is a well accepted statement that memory is associative, that memory structures are organized into some form: networks, concepts, prototypes, basic levels, schemas, frames, units, scripts. How? We need to understand the representation of knowledge, including the process that operates upon the representation. (pp. 21–22)

10. *Performance*   Norman (1980a) marvels at the motor performance of, say, expert typists and indicates that such performance is little understood.

The problems of performance are real, they require understanding of computational issues of considerable sophistication, and they interact with perceptual and thought processes in fundamental ways. It is possible to argue that much of our knowledge of the world resides in our knowledge of the procedures that interact with the world, that the perceptual-cognitive-motor schemas are unitary memory constructs, and the separation of one from the others destroys the whole. (p. 24)

11. *Skill*   As we have seen earlier in this chapter, Norman believes that there is both a quantitative and a qualitative difference between someone who is merely competent at a task and someone who is an expert. The expert performs with ease, automatically and without awareness of the many activities involved in performance of the task. The major differences between skilled and unskilled individuals are just now being noted and studied.

12. *Thought*   Norman believes that too much time and energy has been spent studying pure, abstract thought processes. For example, some information-processing psychologists view humans as general-purpose computational devices. This view stresses general problem-solving skills and minimizes the problem-solving strategies that come from specific environmental experiences. Norman (1980a) says, "I believe that too much emphasis has been given to possible formal properties of human reasoning, not enough to informal, experiential based models of reasoning" (p. 25).

Norman's list of 12 issues for cognitive science suggests that such a science is in its infancy. Although it is true there is much remaining to be understood, Norman (1980a) is pleased that we at least know enough to raise the issues: "The fact that I can write such a paper, ask such questions, complain with some reasonable specificity, is a positive sign about the emergence of a new discipline. It is a sign of progress that things are sufficiently well understood that the list of non-understood topics can be prepared" (p. 28).

It should now be clear that Norman argues that no aspect of cognition can be, nor should be, studied in isolation. Norman (1980a) concludes his article by saying, "I wish Cognitive Science to be recognized as a complex interaction among different issues of concern, an interaction that will not be properly understood until all the parts are understood, with no part independent of the others, the whole requiring the parts, and the parts the whole" (p. 29).

COGNITIVE ENGINEERING

For many years, Norman has studied human errors ranging from turning off an automobile engine while attempting to turn off the windshield wipers to accidents in nuclear power plants and airplane disasters. In almost all cases, Norman (1982) finds fault not with the persons involved but in the design of the equipment they were operating. "I claim that such errors are not the fault of the operators; they are system induced errors" (p. 114).

> It is surprising how badly technology matches human capabilities. People are flexible, amazingly so. The range of our abilities is immense. We manage and cope with a wide variety of circumstances. Those who design and construct the tools of modern society, however, seem to have little understanding of our capabilities. As a result, we are slaves to technology. We make errors [and] we assume it is natural and proper to do so. If we get upset about the errors, we are upset at ourselves for being so stupid or forgetful. Nonsense. (p. 113)

To solve the problem, we need **cognitive engineering,** that is, everything that we know about cognition must be utilized in designing the machines with which we interact.

> The human is a system of interacting components. Within each of us there are many cognitive mechanisms interacting with one another, interacting with emotions and motivations, with intentions and goals, and with the biological systems and physical parts of the body. Each person also interacts with a complex sociocultural setting. Anyone who attempts to design devices that take into account human functioning must consider all aspects, from the details of short-term memory and attentional limitations to the interactions of human, machine, and society. It will not suffice simply to design a knob to match human requirements; the whole system must be designed to take into account the whole human being....Once I argued that it was time for a new discipline: cognitive engineering. At that time I was thinking of education, of the problems of teaching and tutoring, of automated instructional systems. Now, with a wider perception of the need to make technology our friend and ally, not our enemy, I think the time for such a discipline has more than come. (pp. 116–117)

Norman's interest in cognitive engineering is pursued in his book *The Psychology of Everyday Things* (1988).

SUMMARY

Antecedents to information-processing psychology include (1) S-R psychology, which viewed humans as interacting with the environment in an automatic, machinelike way; (2) the kinds of cognitive psychology suggested by Tolman, Bandura, and Piaget, which stressed the importance of information, expectancies, beliefs, and schemata; (3) cybernetics, which viewed humans as constantly testing sensory input against some standard and then, if there is a discrepancy between the two, engaging in appropriate behavior until the discrepancy is eliminated; (4) robotology, which was successful at creating a variety of machines and devices that successfully mimicked certain activities of living organisms; (5) information theory, which conceptualized the bit as an objective way of measuring information and showed how information is lost as it is encoded and decoded within a communication system; and (6) the computer, which acted as a powerful model with which to study human cognitive processes.

For Norman, the concepts of learning and understanding are closely linked. To learn a task is to come to understand the task well enough so that it can be performed with skill. Norman criticizes the law of effect mainly because it ignores the fact that for learning to occur, there must be an apparent relationship between an action and an outcome. Sometimes organisms will reach erroneous conclusions about the causal relationships between actions and outcomes, and these faulty conclusions can be dysfunctional. If individuals develop the belief that nothing they can do will produce a favorable outcome or eliminate a negative one, the phenomenon of learned helplessness may result. Since learned helplessness results in a feeling that one is totally ineffective in dealing with life's problems, it often ends in depression. Norman is very interested in skilled performance and lists five facts that differentiate skilled from amateur performance: smoothness, automaticity, mental effort, effects of stress, and point of view.

Norman discusses three modes of learning. Accretion, the most common mode, involves the application of an existing schema to a new situation, which results in a slight modification of the schema. Structuring, the most difficult kind of learning, involves the formation of new schemata. Tuning, the slowest kind of learning, involves the application of a schema to a large number and wide variety of related experiences. In his explanation of how new schemata are formed, Norman stresses learning by analogy. New schemata always result from extensions, generalizations, or modifications of existing schemata. Effective teaching, then, must always use a student's existing schemata as a frame of reference in deciding what can be taught and how it can be taught. All humans interact with the world and interpret their experiences in terms of their schemata.

There are three kinds of memory. Sensory memory has enormous capacity but lasts only about one second. Short-term memory consists of those events from sensory memory selected for further processing, and it lasts for about 15 seconds. The information from short-term memory that is attended to and rehearsed becomes part of long-term memory, which lasts indefinitely. The schemata that we have learned from past experience are stored in long-term memory. The interactions between present stimulating conditions and the retrieval of relevant information from long-term memory determines how we respond to a situation.

Norman lists 12 issues that he feels must be addressed to improve cognitive science. He says cognitive scientists must recognize the importance of belief systems; understand more fully the nature of conscious and subconscious thought, including selective attention; study the ways children process information to understand better how adults do; recognize the influence of emotions on human information-processing; learn how all of the influences on humans interact among themselves; stop equating science with the study of language and perception;

study in more depth the nature of complex learning; continue their efforts to unravel the mysteries of memory; put forth greater effort to understand the nature of skilled performance; and determine how our reasoning abilities are derived from experience.

Norman believes that if what is now known in cognitive science were applied to the design of the tools of modern society, errors could be greatly reduced. He calls the marriage between cognitive science and technology cognitive engineering.

EVALUATION OF NORMAN'S THEORY

Contributions

The information-processing approach provides a framework within which complex cognitive processes can be studied systematically and objectively. For years it was believed that cognitive processes were too mysterious or inaccessible to be studied scientifically. The information-processing approach suggests that this belief is false.

The information-processing approach, especially as presented by Norman, encourages the synthesis of many human attributes. For example, Norman stresses the fact that human behavior results from the interaction of current stimulating conditions, memories of past experiences, emotions, beliefs, attitudes, cultural and societal influences, and the presence of fellow humans. According to Norman, to truly understand why humans act as they do, we must understand how these and other variables interact with one another. This approach discourages the study of isolated human attributes such as intelligence, memory, concept formation, or problem solving. Thus the richness and complexity of humans are recognized.

The information-processing approach is compatible with computer technology, at least in more simple sequential applications. As we have seen, many information-processing psychologists view humans and computers as functionally very similar. Even if the analogy between computers and humans is not accepted entirely, the information-processing psychologist, like no other psychologist, is in a position to utilize computers to test his or her assumptions about how humans process information. The computer is both a powerful research tool and an intriguing model of human cognitive functioning, and many information-processing psychologists use the computer in both ways.

Because information-processing psychologists often use computers to simulate processes that they study, this approach has caused psychologists to be more precise with their concepts and theories. As we have noted, before a theory can be converted into a computer program, it must be stated clearly and precisely, and it must be logically consistent. If an unclear program is fed into a computer, the computer will either not work or produce meaningless results. Thus the information-processing approach to psychology provides the same service as did mathematical models of learning. That is, they both cause researchers to clarify the definition of their terms and to be precise in the formulation of their theories.

Criticisms

Other than providing a cleaning-up operation for some concepts and theories, information-processing psychology does not really add anything new. We have seen in this chapter, for example, that Norman's views on learning are, to a large extent, a refinement of Piaget's views. It is not clear, in fact, that Norman's views improve substantially on those of Thorndike. Response by analogy (Thorndike) and learning by analogy (Norman), are obvious parallels. Insisting that an outcome provides information does not necessarily supersede or improve on the claim that an outcome is either reinforcing, punishing or neutral. Similar criticisms have been made about the treatment of intelligence, memory, and perception. Even the information-processing approach itself has been found to be nothing new. Leahey (1980) says, for example, "The most modern psychology, information processing cognitive psychology, is remarkably similar to Aristotle's account of mind. Both view the acquisition of knowledge as the internalization and processing of information about the environment which is then stored in some form of memory" (p. 385).

The information-processing approach, particularly as espoused by Norman, exhibits disdain for the rich history of experimental psychology as it pertains to learning, and it ignores or minimizes important areas of psychology, most obviously, abnormal behavior and psychotherapy. Even though Lindsay and Norman's book *Human Information Processing: An Introduction to Psychology* (1977) is billed as an introduction to psychology, it excludes the sections on abnormal behavior and psychotherapy typically found in introductory texts. An effort to explain individual differences, which is typically included in a section on theories of personality, is also missing. Norman and others working within information-processing psychology recognize these weaknesses and are beginning to correct them. Norman's emphasis on the importance of emotions in human behavior exemplifies his understanding of the shortcomings of the information-processing approach.

Although the computer is a useful analogy for several human attributes, humans are not computers. Although both humans and computers perform complex operations and retain information, only humans struggle to survive, interact with other humans, and have feelings. Computers programmed to simulate the sequences of cognitive processes defined in information-processing psychology repeatedly fail to do many of the simple things that humans do every day-learning, for example. The computer, then, has only limited value as a model for studying humans.

Radical behaviorists in the Skinnerian tradition maintain that information-processing psychologists make the same mistake that the mental philosophers made, which was believing that cognitive events are causally related to behavior. Since these behaviorists believe that the causes of behavior are found in the environment, everything between the environment and behavior can be, and should be, ignored. For these behaviorists, information-processing psychology is just one more example of the kind of mentalistic psychology that has done nothing to enhance our understanding of human behavior and may have retarded it.

Finally, the information-processing psychology of the 1970s and 1980s exhibited remarkably little interest in research in neuroscience as it related to learning and cognition. They were, perhaps, more interested in the capabilities of sophisticated computers as models for cognitive processes than they were in discovering how the brain actually mediated those processes. Connectionist models, which we discuss in the next chapter, do not make this error.

DISCUSSION QUESTIONS

1. In what way(s) is information-processing psychology compatible with the associationistic views of such individuals as Pavlov, Watson, and Guthrie?
2. Discuss the similarity between information-processing psychology and the views of Tolman, Bandura, and Piaget.
3. First define cybernetics and then describe how it influenced information-processing psychology.
4. First define robotology and then describe how it influenced information-processing psychology.
5. Summarize the accomplishments of information theory and show how they influenced information-processing psychology.
6. In what ways are humans and computers similar? In what ways are they dissimilar?
7. Discuss the various ways in which information-processing psychologists use computers.
8. Summarize Norman's criticisms of Thorndike's law of effect.
9. What does Norman mean by his contention that for learning to occur there must be an apparent causal relationship between action and outcome?
10. Describe the negative consequences that can result when apparent causes of outcomes are not real causes.
11. What kinds of experiences result in the phenomenon of learned helplessness?
12. What, according to Norman, distinguishes skilled performance from unskilled, or amateur, performance?
13. Discuss and give an example of accretion, structuring, and tuning.
14. What does Norman mean when he says that most complex learning occurs by analogy? Give an example.
15. Define sensory, short-term, and long-term memories and describe how they interact.
16. List and briefly describe the 12 issues that Norman feels cognitive science should address.
17. What is cognitive engineering and why does Norman feel that there is a need for it?

KEY TERMS

accretion   The addition of knowledge to existing schemata, without changing their structure in any fundamental way. Accretion is the most common kind of learning.

artificial intelligence   A scientific discipline usually part of a computer science or cognitive science department. A person who studies artificial intelligence attempts to build machines that exhibit the same intelligence as humans. Although most work on artificial intelligence is done on the digital computer, it is not necessary for a computer to be utilized.

cognitive engineering   The field that would take the facts from cognitive science and apply them to modern technology.

coincidental association   According to Bandura, a process by which an event that is present but not causally related to an outcome erroneously becomes associated with that outcome.

cybernetics   Studies systems that act on feedback from the environment in such a way as to optimize the relationship between their external and internal environments.

echoic store   Sensory memory corresponding to the auditory sense modality.

feedback   Information provided by the outcome of actions that becomes the basis for further actions.

hardware   The physical properties of an information-processing system.

iceberg model of learning   From the learner's point of view the facts being presented by the teacher are the tip of the iceberg, and the structure of knowledge that those facts represent is the larger, submerged part of the iceberg. From the teacher's point of view the student's behavior is the tip of the iceberg, and the student's structure of knowledge is the larger, submerged part of the iceberg.

iconic store   Sensory memory corresponding to the visual sense modality.

inappropriate generalization   According to Bandura, the process by which outcomes that are causally related to one event become expected when similar events are encountered.

information-processing psychology   The kind of psychology that views humans as receiving input from the environment in the form of information; encoding, transforming, and modifying that information; and then responding to that information in some way. The emphasis is on the determination of the properties of the internal mechanisms that encode, transform, and store information.

information theory   Devised the bit to measure information objectively. The goal of information theory was to increase the accuracy with which a message is transmitted from its source over a transmitting channel to a receiver.

input   The information entering an information-processing system.

law of causal learning   An organism learns to repeat those actions that have an apparent causal relationship to desirable outcomes and to avoid those actions that have an apparent causal relationship to undesirable outcomes.

law of causal relationship   For an organism to learn, there must be an apparent causal relationship between its actions and the outcomes of those actions.

law of information feedback   The outcomes of various actions provide information about the effectiveness of those actions.

learned helplessness   The general feeling of helplessness that results when it seems that there is nothing that one can do to terminate an unpleasant situation. In extreme cases, learned helplessness causes a person to give up trying and to become depressed.

learning by analogy   Norman's contention that the learning of new schemata is always relative to existing schemata.

long-term memory (also called long-term store and secondary memory)   If material in short-term memory is rehearsed long enough, it becomes part of long-term memory. It is in long-term memory that schemata are stored. Such memory lasts indefinitely.

output   The response made by an information-processing system after information has been processed.

perceived self-inefficacy   According to Bandura, the belief that one is incapable of performing certain actions even if, in reality, one is capable of performing them.

robotology   The building of machines or devices that mimic certain aspects of the behavior of living organisms.

sensory memory (also called sensory store)   Begins when sense receptors are activated and lasts for about a second. Such memory stores a great deal of information, but that information is available for only a very short period of time.

short-term memory (also called short-term store and primary memory)   Memory of material selected from sensory memory for further processing. Such memory lasts for about 15 seconds.

skilled performance   Performance that is differentiated from amateur performance by its smoothness, automaticity, small amount of mental effort required, resistance to deteriorization under stress, and the point of view that one has while performing.

software   The programs that allow information-processing systems to process information.

structuring   The creation of new schemata. Structuring is the most difficult kind of learning.

tuning   The adjustment of a schema to a wide variety of related situations. Tuning is what converts amateur into skilled performance and represents the slowest kind of learning.

Chapter 15

DONALD OLDING HEBB

Donald Olding Hebb was born on July 22, 1904, in Chester, Nova Scotia. Both his parents were medical doctors. His mother obtained her medical degree from Dalhousie University in Halifax, Nova Scotia, in 1896, making her only the third female to become a physician in the province of Nova Scotia at that time.

In 1925 Hebb received his B.A. from Dalhousie University with the lowest course average a person could have without actually failing. Since Hebb was one of psychology's most creative researchers and theorists, undergraduate grade point average, in his case, had no predictive value. After graduation, Hebb taught school in the village where he grew up. At the age of 23 he read Freud and decided that psychology had a lot of room for improvement. Since the chair of the Psychology Department at McGill University in Montreal was a friend of his mother, he was admitted as a part-time graduate psychology student in spite of his poor undergraduate record. Hebb continued to teach elementary school while he was a graduate student, however, and had a compulsion to reform educational practices. He tried several experiments with various degrees of success. In one experiment he decided that extra schoolwork should not be used as a punishment because doing so would create a negative attitude toward schoolwork. Since he felt some form of punishment was necessary to maintain order, he reverted to slapping mildly the student's hand with a strap for a wrongdoing. Hebb (1980) described an occasion when this disciplinary technique backfired: "One day I set out to strap a boy who flinched so that the end of the strap went by his hand and hit my trousers at the level of the glans penis. It hurt like the devil, and I said to the boy, 'This hurts me more than it does you.' But I don't think he understood the joke" (p. 282).

In addition to wanting to become an educational reformer, another of Hebb's early passions was to write novels for a living, but like Skinner's, his efforts failed.

During his years at McGill, Hebb was trained in the Pavlovian tradition, and after writing a thesis compatible with this tradition, he obtained his M.A. in 1932. In spite of his training Hebb saw restrictions in Pavlovian theory and doubted its importance. While at McGill, Hebb read Köhler's *Gestalt Psychology* and Lashley's work on brain physiology (which we will consider briefly below) and found them both to his liking. In 1934, Hebb decided to continue his education at the University of Chicago, where he worked with Lashley and took a seminar from Köhler. Lashley's work cast doubt on the prevailing belief that the brain is a complex switchboard. This **switchboard** (or relay station) **conception of the brain** was held mainly by the behaviorists, for example, Thorndike, Hull, and Watson, and by the associationists, for example, Pavlov and Guthrie. It was assumed by those holding this view that certain sensory events stimulate certain areas of the brain, causing specific reactions. Learning causes a change in neural

Donald O. Hebb (Photograph by Chris Payne.)

circuitry so that sensory events come to stimulate responses other than those they originally stimulated. Lashley's research, which used rats as subjects, raised serious questions about this conception of the brain. The most startling outcome of his research was his finding that the *location* of the destroyed portion of the brain was not as important as the *amount* of destruction. This consistent finding became Lashley's principle of **mass action,** which stated that the disruption of learning and retention goes up as the amount of cortical destruction goes up, regardless of the location of the destruction. Lashley concluded that the cortex functioned as a whole during learning, and if one part of the cortex was destroyed, other parts of the cortex could take over the destroyed portion's function. This ability of one portion of the cortex to take over the function of another was referred to by Lashley as **equipotentiality.** Thus, mass action indicated that the amount of learning and memory disruption is a function of the amount of the cortical area destroyed, and equipotentiality indicated that the location of the cortical ablation was unimportant.

Clearly, these findings were not in accordance with Hebb's early training at McGill University, and his opposition to Pavlov, which was at first tenuous, now became outright disagreement. "I had all the fervor of the reformed drunk at a temperance meeting; having been a fully convinced Pavlovian, I was now a fully convinced Gestalter-*cum*-Lashleyan" (Hebb, 1959, p. 625). Once again, we are reminded of an important characteristic of good scientists; they are willing to change their minds.

In 1935, Lashley accepted a professorship at Harvard, and he invited Hebb to go with him. In 1936, Hebb obtained his Ph.D. from Harvard and remained there an additional year as a teaching and research assistant.

In 1937, Hebb went to the Montreal Neurological Institute to work with the famous brain surgeon Wilder Penfield. Hebb's job was to study the psychological status of Penfield's patients after brain surgery. Much to Hebb's amazement, he found that even after substantial loss of tissue from the frontal lobes of the brain, there was no loss in intelligence, and in some cases, he even detected a gain in intelligence. In some cases, the tissue loss was as much as 20 percent. These observations cast further doubt on the switchboard concept of the brain and supported the contention that somehow the brain functioned as a whole. According to Hebb (1980), the questions raised by these observations acted as a stimulus for his subsequent work: "I could find no sign of loss after large amounts of brain tissue were removed from the frontal lobe....It was this problem that set the main course for all my subsequent work..." (p. 290).

After studying Penfield's patients for five years (1937–1942), Hebb (1980) reached a conclusion about intelligence that was later to become an important part of his theory: "Experience in childhood normally develops concepts, modes of thought, and ways of perceiving that constitute intelligence. Injury to the infant brain interferes with that process, but the same injury at maturity does not reverse it" (p. 292).

By now Hebb had made three observations that his later theory would attempt to explain: (1) The brain does not act as a simple switchboard, as the behaviorists and associationists had assumed. If it did, destroying large amounts of brain tissue from the frontal lobes would have been more disruptive. (2) Intelligence comes from experience, and therefore, is not genetically determined. (3) Childhood experiences

Karl Lashley. (From *Great Experiments in Psychology,* p. 22, by H. E. Garrett, 1951, New York:Appleton-Century-Crofts.)

are more important in determining intelligence than adult experiences.

In 1942, Lashley accepted an appointment as director of the Yerkes Laboratories of Primate Biology in Orange Park, Florida, and again, asked Hebb to join him. While at the Yerkes Laboratories (1942–1947), Hebb (1980) studied the emotions and personalities of chimpanzees and made several observations that further stimulated his own neurophysiological theory of learning and perception: "[Chimpanzees] were frightened—or better perhaps, horrified—at the sight of a clay model of a chimpanzee head or...any recognizable part of either a chimpanzee or a human body (e.g., a head or a hand from a display mannequin)" (p. 294). Based on these and other observations, Hebb developed his own unique explanation of fear, which we will review in a later section of this chapter.

In 1948, after five years at the Yerkes Laboratories, Hebb accepted an appointment as professor of psychology at McGill University, where he remained until his retirement. At the time of this appointment, physiological psychology was not very popular and Hebb felt very fortunate to get the job. He believed that there were two major reasons why neurophysiological explanations of learning were avoided at this time. First, as the philosophy of science developed and as more was learned about the logic of science, many researchers felt that explaining observable behavior in terms of physiological events was like mixing apples and oranges. Using physiological mechanisms to explain overt behavior involved a change in the level of discourse, and drawing conclusions from one level to the other violated the canons of scientific logic. In other words, it was believed that physiological events, like overt behavior, constitute a self-contained system, and the relationship between the two systems remained indeterminate.

Second, the very nature of the behavioristic movement was mainly a reaction against introspection. To the behaviorist, the only legitimate subject matter for psychology was something tangible that everyone could see and investigate. This was not true for the experiences reported on introspectively, and it was not true for physiological events. In concentrating on overt, measurable behavior the behaviorists excluded neurophysiology.

To a large extent it was Hebb who made neurophysiological explanations of learning respectable. Hebb (1949) suggested that the behavioristic movement was only the first stage of a revolution within psychology, a revolution against the older subjective, philosophic schools. According to Hebb, behaviorism insisted on the objective study of overt behavior, and that was good, but by insisting on *only* the study of behavior, the behaviorists threw out the baby with the bathwater. Now, said Hebb, we were ready for the second phase of the revolution—that is, to study cognitive processes objectively. Hebb, as we shall see, has taken the neurophysiological approach to studying cognitive processes, but his was only one approach. The important thing, to Hebb (1959) was that the study of cognitive processes should no longer be avoided.

> How are we to learn more about these ideational or mediating processes, and the limits of their role in behavior, except by forming hypotheses (as explicit as we can reasonably make them) and then seeing what implications they have for behavior, and whether these implications are borne out in experiment? By all means, if you will, call these central events mediating processes instead of ideas or cell assemblies, but let us get busy and investigate them. (p. 630)

It is fortunate for psychology that many investigators followed Hebb's suggestion. The Gestalt psychologists, Piaget, Tolman, Bandura, and the information-processing psychologists exemplify theorists emphasizing the study of cognitive processes, but unlike Hebb's approach, they do not emphasize neurophysiological concepts.

Among Hebb's many honors were eight honorary doctorates, the presidency of the Canadian Psychological Association (1952), the presidency of the American Psychological Association (1959), winner of the Warren Medal (1958), and recipient of the distinguished scientific contribution award of the American Psychological Association (1961).

Once converted from the kind of behaviorism derived from Pavlov's theory, Hebb launched an attack on behaviorism that continued all his life. His first major book was *The Organization of Behavior* (1949). The initials of that book, OOB, bore a strange resemblance to the initials of Skinner's major book, *The Behavior of Organisms* (1938), which was affectionately known as BOO. A later publication, "Drives and the C.N.S. (Conceptual Nervous System)" showed Hebb's (1955) willingness to "physiologize" about psychological processes. His very readable *Textbook of Psychology* (1972) provides an excellent overview of his theory. A more technical account of Hebb's theory appears in *Psychology: A Study of a Science* (1959). Hebb's approach is diametrically opposed to Skinner's method of functional analysis, in which relationships between stimuli and responses are determined without any reference to internal events.

After his retirement from McGill University in 1974, Hebb moved back to a small farm near Chester, Nova Scotia, where he was born. He remained psychologically and physically active until he died on August 20, 1985, while in the hospital for what was thought to be routine hip surgery (Beach, 1987, p. 187). Some of Hebb's more important theoretical concepts are reviewed below.

CELL ASSEMBLIES AND PHASE SEQUENCES

We have seen that while working with Penfield, Hebb had reached the conclusion that childhood experience was more important for intellectual development than adult experience. Several other sources also confirmed the importance of early experience. The German ophthalmologist von Senden (1932) had studied adults who had been blind since birth and then were suddenly able to see after an operation such as the removal of cataracts. It was found that these individuals could immediately detect the presence of an object but they could not tell what the object was. These findings suggested that some kind of figure-ground perception is innate, but visual experience with various objects is necessary before objects can be differentiated from one another. Gradually, these previously blind individuals learned to identify objects in the environment and their perceptions approached normality.

Austin Riesen (1947) reared infant chimpanzees in total darkness until they were about 2 years old. When they were finally taken from the darkness they acted as if they were completely blind. Within a few weeks, however, they began to see, and eventually they behaved like other chimpanzees that had been reared normally. Hebb concluded that the adults that von Senden studied and the chimpanzees that Riesen studied had to *learn* to see.

Numerous other studies supported the conclusion that by restricting early experience, one interferes with normal intellectual and perceptual development. In a study run in Hebb's laboratory (Melzack & Thompson, 1956), it was even shown that Scottish terriers reared in partial isolation were oblivious to pain, in addition to being less aggressive than their normally reared littermates.

All these observations strengthened Hebb's empiricistic position. Intelligence, perception, and even emotions are learned from experience and therefore are not inherited, as the nativist claims. Hebb developed a theory that assumed that infants are born with a neural network with random interconnections. According to Hebb, sensory experience causes this neural network to become organized and to provide a means of interacting effectively with the environment. The two key concepts in Hebb's theory are cell assembly and phase sequence.

Cell Assemblies

According to Hebb, each environmental object we experience fires a complex package of neurons called a **cell assembly.** For example, as we look at a pencil, we will shift our attention from the point to the eraser to the wooden shaft. As our attention shifts, different neurons are stimulated. However, the entire package of neurons stimulated at the time corresponds to one environmental object—a pencil. All aspects of this complex neural package will, at first, be independent. For example, as we look at the point of a pencil, a certain group of neurons will fire. They will not, however, initially influence the neurons that fire while we are looking at the eraser or the wooden shaft. Eventually, however, because of the closeness in time between the firing of the neurons corresponding to the point and those corresponding to other parts of the pencil, the various parts of the neurological package become interrelated. Hebb's (1949) "neurophysiological postulate" suggested the mechanism by which initially independent neurons become linked into stable cell assemblies:

> When an axon of cell A is near enough to excite a cell B and repeatedly or persistently takes part in firing it, some growth process or metabolic change takes place in one or both cells such that A's efficiency, as one of the cells firing B, is increased. (p. 62)

Hebb (1949) saw cell assemblies as dynamic, rather than fixed or static, systems of neurons. He provided mechanisms by which neurons could either leave or join cell assemblies, thus allowing assemblies to be refined through learning or development:

> In the integration which has been hypothesized…there would necessarily be a gradual change of the frequency characteristics of the system. The consequence would be a sort of fractionation and recruitment, and some change in the neurons making up the system. That is, some units, capable at first of synchronizing with others in the system would drop out: "fractionation." Others, at first incompatible, would be recruited. *With perceptual development there would thus be a slow growth in the assembly,* understanding by "growth" not necessarily an increase in the number of constituent cells, but a change. (pp. 76–77)

A cell assembly can be large or small, depending on the environmental object or event it represents. For example, the cell assembly associated with *doorknob* would consist of a relatively small number of neurons, but the cell assembly for *house* would consist of a relatively large number of neurons. The entire cell assembly is an interrelated neurological package that can be fired by either external stimulation, internal stimulation, or a combination of the two. When a cell assembly fires, we experience the thought of the event the assembly represents. To Hebb, the cell assembly is the neurological basis of an idea or thought. In this way, Hebb explains why houses, cows, or loved ones need not be present for us to think of them.

Phase Sequences

Just as different aspects of the same object become neurologically interrelated to form cell assemblies, so do cell assemblies become neurologically interrelated to form phase sequences. A **phase sequence** is "a temporally integrated series of assembly activities; it amounts to one current in the stream of thought" (Hebb, 1959, p. 629). Once developed, a phase sequence, like a cell assembly, can be fired internally, externally, or by a combination of internal and external stimulation. When any single cell assembly or combination of assemblies in a phase sequence is fired, the entire phase sequence tends to fire. When a phase sequence fires, we experience a stream of thought, that is, a series of ideas arranged in some logical order. This process explains how a whiff of perfume or a few strains from a favorite song may trigger memories of a loved one. Hebb (1972) said the following about the development of phase sequences:

> Cell-assemblies that are active at the same time become interconnected. Common events in the child's environment establish assemblies, and then when these events occur together the assemblies become connected (because they are active together). When the baby hears footsteps, let us say, an assembly is excited; while this is still active he sees a face and feels hands picking him up, which excites other assemblies—so the "footsteps assembly" becomes connected with the "face assembly" and the "being-picked-up assembly." After this has happened, when the baby hears footsteps only, *all three* assemblies are excited; the baby then has something like a perception of the mother's face and the contact of her hands before she has come in sight—but since the sensory stimulations have not yet taken place, this is ideation or imagery, not perception. (p. 67)

For Hebb, there were two kinds of learning. One involves the slow buildup of cell assemblies early in life and can probably be explained by one of the S-R theories of learning, such as Guthrie's. This kind of learning is straight associationism. Likewise, the development of phase sequences can be explained with associationistic terminology. That is, objects and events that are related in the environment come to be related on the neurological level. After cell assemblies and phase sequences are developed, however, subsequent learning is more cognitive. Adult learning, for example, often characterized by insight and creativity, probably involves the rearrangement of phase sequences. Thus, Hebb maintained that the variables influencing childhood learning and those influencing adult learning are not the same. Childhood learning provides the framework for later learning. For example, learning a language is a slow, cumbersome process, which probably involves the building up of millions of cell assemblies and phase sequences. However, once a language has been learned, an individual can rearrange it in any number of creative ways, perhaps in the form of a poem or a novel. However, said Hebb, first come the building blocks and then come the insight and creativity that characterize adult learning.

SENSORY DEPRIVATION

We have already seen that restricting the early sensory experience of an organism severely retards its perceptual, intellectual, and emotional development. Hebb's explanation was that curtailed sensory experience limits the organism's capacity to develop cell assemblies and phase sequences, which are the building blocks of all cognitive activity.

It has been well established that restricted sensory experience inhibits the development of neurophysiological networks that represent objects and events in the environment. But what happens if sensory experience is restricted *after* normal neurophysiological development has already taken place? A series of experiments were run at McGill University under Hebb's supervision to answer this question. In one of these experiments (Heron, 1957) a group of college students were paid twenty dollars a day *to do nothing*. They had only to lie on a comfortable bed with their eyes covered by translucent plastic, which permitted them to see diffuse light but not to recognize objects. A constant buzzing sound was transmitted to the subjects through earphones. To inhibit auditory perception further, air-conditioning equipment hummed monotonously in the background. The subjects wore cotton gloves and cardboard cuffs, which extended over their fingertips, to minimize tactile stimulation. These conditions prevailed for almost twenty-four hours a day and were interrupted only when the subject ate or needed to go to the washroom. This experimental arrangement is shown in Figure 15–1.

Most subjects could stand the conditions for only two or three days (the longest was six). The subjects typically became irritable and almost childlike in their limited interactions with the experimenter. Much to the surprise of Hebb and his co-workers, **sensory deprivation** produced an effect far beyond simple boredom. Hebb and Donderi (1987) summarize the results of the Heron experiment as follows:

> The experiment showed that humans can be bored, which we knew, but it showed too that boredom is too mild a word for some of the effects of sensory deprivation. The

FIGURE 15–1   An experimental participant in Heron's sensory deprivation experiment. (From "The Pathology of Boredom," by W. Heron, 1957, January, *Scientific American,* p. 53. Copyright © 1957 by Scientific American, Inc. All rights reserved.)

need for the normal stimulation of a varied environment is fundamental. Without it, mental functioning and personality deteriorate. The subjects in isolation complained of being unable to think coherently, they became less able to solve simple problems, and they began to have hallucinations. Some of them saw such things as rows of little men wearing black caps, squirrels marching with sacks over their shoulders, or prehistoric animals in the jungle. These scenes were described as being like animated cartoons. More fundamentally disturbing were somesthetic hallucinations, when a subject perceived two bodies somesthetically or felt as if his head were detached from his body....The subjects' very identity had begun to disintegrate. (p. 255)

Later studies have shown that when the conditions of sensory deprivation are made even more severe, subjects can stand them for only a very short period of time. For example, when subjects are immersed in water (breathing through a snorkle tube) in complete darkness, they typically can last no more than a few hours before terminating their involvement in the experiment (see Zubek, 1969).

Hebb concluded from this research that not only is sensory experience necessary for proper neurophysiological development but it is also necessary for the maintenance of normal functioning. In other words, once the consistent events in a person's life are represented neurophysiologically in the form of cell assemblies and phase sequences, they must go on being coordinated with environmental events. If the sensory events that ordinarily occur in someone's life do not occur, the person experiences stress, fear, or disorientation. So, not only do consistent environmental events give rise to certain neurological circuits, but also those same events must go on supporting those circuits. Thus, to the various needs that organisms have, such as the need for food, water, sex, and oxygen, Hebb added the need for stimulation. Even if all of one's other needs are satisfied, if one does not experience normal stimulation, severe cognitive disorientation results.

ENRICHED ENVIRONMENTS

If sensory deprivation causes a disruption either in development or in normal functioning, is it possible that a rich sensory environment could enhance development? The answer to this question seems to be yes. Hebb (1949, pp. 298–299) ran what was probably the first experiment designed to investigate the effects of different kinds of rearing conditions on intellectual development. Two groups of rats were involved: One was reared in cages in Hebb's laboratory; the other was reared in Hebb's home by his two daughters. Rats in the latter group spent considerable time roaming around the house, presumably playing with Hebb's children. After several weeks, the "pet" rats were returned to the laboratory and compared to the cage-reared rats. It was found that the performance of the pet rats on a series of detour and maze problems was consistently superior to that of the rats reared in the laboratory.

Numerous studies have supported Hebb's early research. For example, a series of experiments run at the University of California by Bennett, Diamond, Krech, and Rosenzweig (1964) have confirmed the fact that rats reared in an **enriched environment** are faster learners than their littermates raised in relative isolation. In this research, the enriched environment consisted of a large cage containing other rats and numerous toylike objects (see Figure 15–2). Control animals were reared alone in cages that contained no objects.

Hebb's explanation of these findings is straightforward. The greater sensory

FIGURE 15–2   Animals being reared in an enriched environment. (From "Chemical and Anatomical Plasticity of the Brain," by E.L. Bennett, M.C. Diamond, D. Kreoh, & M.R. Rosenzweig, 1964, *Science, 146,* p. 611. Copyright © 1964 by the American Association for the Advancement of Science.)

diversity provided by the enriched environment allowed the animals to build up a larger number of cell assemblies and more complex phase sequences. Once developed, these neural circuits could be utilized in new learning. Because of their more austere sensory experiences, control animals had less complex neural circuitry and were therefore inferior problem solvers. The implications of this research for education and child-rearing seem rather clear; the more complex the early sensory environment, the better are the later problem-solving skills.

Are the effects of an impoverished early environment permanent? According to the research of Rosenzweig and his colleagues, apparently not. It was found that the effects of an impoverished sensory environment could be reversed with relative ease by merely placing the animals in an enriched environment for only a few hours a day. Thus, the damage done by a restricted early environment can be undone if conditions change for the better. In other words, there does not appear to be a critical developmental stage beyond which the damage caused by a restricted sensory environment early in life cannot be remedied.

THE NATURE OF FEAR

While at the Yerkes Laboratories of Primate Biology, Hebb investigated the sources of **fear** in chimpanzees. He exposed his subjects to a wide variety of test objects, for example, a plaster cast of a chimpanzee's head; a doll representing a human infant; a lifelike, full-sized human head from a window-display dummy; and an anesthetized infant chimpanzee.

Hebb observed that chimpanzees showed no sign of fear until they were about 4 months old. After that age, his subjects showed no fear of objects that were completely familiar or completely unfamiliar to them. *It was only when familiar objects were shown in unfamiliar ways that fear was expressed.* For example, whole chimpanzee or human bodies elicited no fear, whereas models of parts of chimpanzee or human bodies did. Two examples of fear-producing objects are shown in Figure 15–3.

Hebb felt that the spontaneity of the fear ruled out an explanation in terms of conditioned responses. Such an explanation would stress repeated pairings of neutral objects (e.g., a model of a chimpanzee's head) with an aversive stimulus. Fear developed in this way would develop slowly from experience. This was not the case in the fear that Hebb observed. Rather, the fear response was exhibited at full strength the first time an object was shown to a subject. Hebb's explanation involved cell assemblies and phase sequences. If a completely unfamiliar object is shown to an organism, no cell assembly would have been developed corresponding to that object. With repeated exposures such an assembly would gradually develop, and no fear is involved. Likewise, if a familiar object is shown to an organism, the neural circuits that developed from prior experience with that object would be activated and there would be no disruption in behavior. It is only when an object triggers an existing cell assembly or phase sequence and is subsequently not followed by the events that normally accompany the object that fear is elicited. An anesthetized chimpanzee, for example, will trigger the phase sequence associated with the sight of a chimpanzee, but the events that ordinarily follow such a perception do not follow. Instead of the

FIGURE 15–3   Objects that were found to cause fear in chimpanzees. (From *Textbook of Psychology,* 4th ed., p. 246, by D.O. Hebb & D.C. Donderi, 1987, Philadelphia: W.B. Saunders. Copyright © 1958, 1966, 1972 by W.B. Saunders Company. Reprinted by permission of Holt, Rinehart & Winston.)

typical responses and sounds made by a chimpanzee, there is no movement and there is silence. Thus, a phase sequence was triggered but was not supported by the sensory events that caused the development of the phase sequence to begin with. This lack of sensory support, according to Hebb, causes fear. Hebb explained the human reaction to dead or mutilated bodies in the same way. Thus Hebb (1946) reached the following conclusion about fear: "Fear occurs when an object is seen which is like familiar objects in enough respects to arouse habitual processes of perception, but in other respects arouses incompatible processes" (p. 268).

Hebb's explanation of fear helps to explain the traumatic nature of sensory deprivation. Adult humans are well endowed with cell assemblies and phase sequences, which may be triggered by internal stimulation, external stimulation, or a combination of the two. In the sensory deprivation situation, however, no sensory support for any neural activity is available. Thus, various neural circuits are triggered but are not followed by the sensory events that normally accompany them. Under these circumstances, it is not surprising to find the subjects experiencing disorientation and fear.

AROUSAL THEORY

We have seen that when normal humans experience sensory deprivation their cognitive functioning is disrupted, but what about *too much* sensory stimulation? We have all been in situations in which, because of too much noise or commotion, we have not been able to think clearly. This reaction suggests that a level of stimulation that is not too low or too high would result in optimal cognitive functioning. Hebb explored this relationship between level of stimulation and cognitive functioning within the context of **arousal theory.**

Arousal theory involves the functioning of the **reticular activating system (RAS),** an area about the size of a finger that is located in the brain stem just above the spinal cord and just below the thalamus and hypothalamus. The RAS is involved in the processes of sleep, attention, and emotional behavior.

According to Hebb (1955), a neural impulse generated by the stimulation of a sense receptor has two functions. One is referred to as the **cue function of a stimulus.** The sensory stimulus causes an impulse to travel from the sense receptor, up the sensory tract of the spinal cord, to various projection areas, and finally to some area of the cortex. This function of a stimulus allows the organism to gain information about the environment. The second function is the **arousal function of a stimulus.** It has been found that there are collaterals that spill off the sensory tract of the spinal cord into the RAS. As sensory information is on its way to the cortex, it influences the RAS through these collaterals and causes it to increase its activity. This tendency for sensory impulses to increase activity in the RAS is referred to as the arousal function of a stimulus.

The amount of activity in the RAS is used as an index of arousal; the greater the amount of RAS activity, the higher the level of arousal. The **electroencephalogram (EEG)** is generally accepted as a measure of arousal and is therefore thought to reflect RAS activity. A very slow EEG pattern indicates deep sleep. It also indicates a period of relative inactivity in the RAS. The EEG pattern of a very relaxed but awake person is characterized by rhythmic waves of about eight to ten cycles per second, and the excited person shows very fast brain wave activity, or relatively high arousal.

It is generally believed that the RAS stimulates the cortex and thus creates a background of electrical activity without which the cue function of an incoming sensory impulse would be lost. For a number of years, it was believed that the arousal function of a stimulus caused the RAS to bombard the entire cortex with nonspecific electrical activity. Now, however, it is believed that certain stimuli stimulate certain parts of the RAS to stimulate certain parts of the cortex. A visual stimulus, for instance, may cause the RAS to increase the electrical activity only in the occipital lobe of the brain. In general, what seems to occur is that the RAS prepares higher centers of the brain to receive and act on information from the environment.

Hebb (1955) theorized about the relationship between arousal level and performance. He felt that for the cue function of a stimulus to have its full effect, there must be an **optimal level of arousal** provided by the RAS. When arousal level is too low, such as when the organism is asleep, sensory information transmitted to the brain cannot be utilized. Likewise, when arousal is too high, too much information is being analyzed by the cortex, and often conflicting responses or irrelevant behavior results. Thus a level of arousal that is neither too high nor too low is necessary for optimal cortical functioning and therefore optimal per-

FIGURE 15–4   The relationship suggested by Hebb between arousal level and performance. (From *Textbook of Psychology*, 4th ed., p. 237, by D.O. Hebb & D.C. Donderi, 1987, Philadelphia: W.B. Saunders. Copyright © 1958, 1966, 1972 by W.B. Saunders Company. Reprinted by permission of Holt, Rinehart & Winston.)

formance. The proposed relationship between arousal level and performance is shown in Figure 15–4.

Hebb speculated that different tasks have different levels of arousal associated with their optimal performance. For example, a simple, well-practiced habit may be performed optimally across a wide range of arousal levels, whereas a highly skilled task may be performed optimally only within a minimal range of arousal levels. Gross behavioral skills may be performed best under extremely high arousal. The proposed relationship between optimal performance on various tasks and arousal level is seen in Figure 15–5.

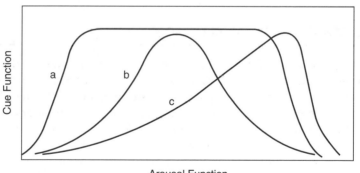

FIGURE 15–5   The relationship suggested by Hebb between arousal level and performance on three different kinds of tasks. Task a is a well-practiced habit such as giving one's name. Such a task is performed optimally over a wide range of arousal levels. Task b is a complex skill such as typing. Such a task is performed optimally only when arousal is neither too high nor too low. Task c is the kind of task that is relatively uncomplicated but requires the expenditure of a great deal of energy, such as weight-lifting or running a race. Such a task is performed optimally when arousal level is high. (From *Textbook of Psychology*, 4th ed., p. 237, by D.O. Hebb & D.C. Donderi, 1987, Philadelphia: W.B. Saunders. Copyright © 1958, 1966, 1972 by W.B. Saunders Company. Reprinted by permission of Holt, Rinehart & Winston.)

Relationship between Arousal Theory and Reinforcement Theory

According to Hebb, if the arousal level is too high for the organism to attend to existing conditions optimally, it will operate on the environment in such a way as to reduce the arousal level. On the one hand, for example, if students are trying to study while people are talking and the television is on, they may have to tell the people to keep quiet and turn off the television, or they will simply have to find an environment more compatible with studying. On the other hand, if it is too quiet and there is not enough sensory input to maintain an optimal level of arousal, the students may turn on the radio, talk out loud, or perform some kind of motor task such as fidgeting or rubbing their feet together. Generally speaking, when the arousal level is too high, decreasing it is reinforcing, and when the arousal level is too low, increasing it is reinforcing. Unlike Hull's theory, which equates drive reduction with reinforcement, Hebb's theory equates reinforcement with either an increase or decrease in drive, depending on the circumstances. According to Hebb (1955), seeking excitement is a significant motive in human behavior:

> When you stop to think of it, it is nothing short of extraordinary what trouble people will go to in order to get into more trouble at the bridge table, or on the golf course; and the fascination of the murder story, or thriller, and the newspaper accounts of real-life adventure or tragedy, is no less extraordinary. This taste for excitement *must* not be forgotten when we are dealing with human motivation. It appears that, up to a certain point, threat and puzzle have positive motivating value, beyond that point negative value. (p. 250)

LONG-TERM AND SHORT-TERM MEMORY

Although G. E. Müller and A. Pilzecker originally suggested as early as 1900 that there are two distinct kinds of memory, the idea has just recently received wide attention. As we saw in the last chapter, it is now generally believed that there are two kinds of memory: **long-term memory** and **short-term memory.** (Short-term memory is also called either *immediate memory* or *primary memory;* long-term memory is also called *secondary memory*.) Like sensory memory, short-term memory is triggered by sensory stimulation, but unlike sensory memory, short-term memory continues for some time after stimulation has ceased. Exactly how long the activity continues is not known, but it seems that the information stored in short-term memory is available for less than a minute. For example, Peterson and Peterson (1959) read their subjects a consonant trigram (e.g., *QHJ*) and then instructed them to start counting backward immediately by 3s or 4s from a 3-digit number they were given. Different subjects had their counting interrupted at different times and were asked to repeat the consonant trigram that was read to them. The recall intervals were 3, 6, 9, 12, 15, and 18 seconds. It was found that the best retention was at a recall interval of 3 seconds, next 6 seconds, and so on. The worst recall occurred after 18 seconds. Thus, short-term memory seems to decay as a function of time, but its decay is much faster than long-term memory.

It is generally believed that sensory experience sets up neural activity that outlasts the stimulation that caused it. Hebb (1949) referred to this as **reverberating neural activity.** It appears that as long as the reverberating neural activity continues after an experience, the memory of that experience can be retrieved.

It is obvious that we retain some information much longer than a few seconds, so there must be some relationship between short-term memory and long-term memory. It is believed that somehow, during the neural activity following an experience, long-term memories consolidate, or become fixed. The short-term memory, which involves continuous neural activity, somehow causes a structural change in the nervous system, which corresponds to the long-term or secondary memory. The contention that short-term memory is somehow translated into long-term memory is referred to as **consolidation theory,** of which Hebb was a major proponent.

Since long-term memory is thought to depend on short-term memory, it follows that anything that disrupts the former should also disrupt the latter. Based on this contention, Duncan (1949) trained rats to jump a barrier to avoid an electric shock. If they jumped from one side of an experimental chamber to the other side within 10 seconds after they were placed in the apparatus, they could avoid being shocked. If they did not cross over to the "safe" side, they were shocked until they did. The animals were given one learning trial per day. Following each trial, each animal was given an **electroconvulsive shock** (ECS) through two electrodes clipped to its ears. The ECS causes convulsions much like those of an epileptic seizure. Depending on what group the animal was in, the shock occurred 20 seconds, 40 seconds, 60 seconds, 4 minutes, 15 minutes, 1 hour, 4 hours, or 14 hours after its learning trial. A control group received no ECS after learning. Training continued for 18 days. Figure 15–6 shows the mean number of correct anticipations of the shock for all groups, that is, jumping to the safe side upon being placed in the apparatus.

FIGURE 15–6 The results of Duncan's study show that as the delay between learning experience and an electroconvulsive shock becomes longer, the disruptive effect of the shock on the retention of the learning experience goes down. (From "The Retroactive Effect of Electroshock on Learning," by C.P. Duncan, 1949, *Journal of Comparative and Physiological Psychology, 42,* p. 35. Copyright © 1949 by the American Psychological Association. Reprinted by permission.

It can be seen that the more closely the ECS followed a learning trial, the more it tended to disrupt the memory of the learning experience. For example, animals receiving ECS 20 seconds after a learning trial never learned the avoidance response. When the ECS was administered within an hour of the learning trial, it interfered with memory. After an hour, ECS apparently had no effect on memory. The animals receiving ECS an hour or more after their learning trial performed as well as the control group that received no ECS. The results of Duncan's experiment lends support to consolidation theory and suggests that the consolidation period lasts about an hour. However, the moments immediately following a learning experience seem to be more important for consolidation than those after about the first minute.

Further evidence is provided for consolidation theory by the phenomenon called **retrograde amnesia,** which refers to the loss of memory for those events just prior to a traumatic experience, such as an automobile accident or a combat injury. This memory loss for events prior to a traumatic event may involve hours, days, or even months. Usually the memory of such events will slowly return except for those immediately prior to the traumatic event. It is assumed that the traumatic event had the same effect as Duncan's ECS; that is, it interfered with the reverberating neural activity that is necessary for consolidation to take place, thereby making long-term memory impossible.

Consolidation and the Brain

A number of interrelated brain structures, collectively referred to as the **limbic system,** are believed to be important for the experience of various emotions. One of these limbic structures is the **hippocampus.** Brenda Milner (1965), one of Hebb's students at McGill University, found that patients with a destroyed hippocampus have no trouble recalling events that took place before its destruction, but it is impossible for them to form new long-term memories. Such patients perform well on intelligence tests and do very well on motor skills that were acquired before the damage to their hippocampus. Also, Milner reports no apparent personality change resulting from the brain damage. The remarkable thing about such patients is that they simply cannot retain any new information. As soon as their attention is distracted from an experience, the memory of it is lost. Such individuals look as if their short-term memory is functioning normally but their long-term memory is not. Milner speculates that in the early stages of learning, there is an interplay between the sensory input, the hippocampus, and the cortex. Through this interrelated activity, the information finally comes to be stored in the cortex as long-term memory. The hippocampus is thus believed to be responsible for consolidation.

Our overview of Hebb's theoretical contributions is now complete. It is hoped that the reader has recognized the fact that Hebb opened lines of investigation in psychology that were previously ignored or did not exist. Hebb was one of the first to search for the neurophysiological correlates of psychological phenomena, such as learning. Due to a large extent to Hebb's efforts, neuroscience is very popular today and has expanded into many areas beyond those studied by Hebb and his students. It would not be appropriate in a book such as this to review the many fruitful lines of inquiry currently occurring within the neurophysiological paradigm. What follows, however, represents a sample of such research. The first topic, reinforcement centers in the brain, is indirectly related to Hebb's theory since it grew out of an accidental discovery made in Hebb's laboratory while the reticular activating system was being studied. The next topic, cerebral asymmetry (the left-brain, right-brain issue) is not directly related to Hebb's theory, although one of his students made important research contributions in the area. The final topic, learning at the cellular level, returns us to the fundamental propositions of Hebb's cell assemblies.

FURTHER EXAMPLES OF NEUROPHYSIOLOGICAL RESEARCH ON LEARNING

Reinforcement Centers in the Brain

In the chapter on Pavlov, we noted that his discovery of the conditioned reflex was quite accidental. **Serendipity,** the finding of one thing while looking for another, has led to the discovery of important phenomena whose investigations sometimes resulted in scientific breakthroughs. Another example of serendipity in science is the discovery of **reinforcement centers in the brain** by Olds and Milner (1954). Olds (1955), who was working in Hebb's laboratory at McGill University, described how the discovery was made:

> In the fall of 1953, we were looking for more information about the reticular activating system. We used electrodes permanently implanted in the brain of a healthy behaving rat….Quite by accident, an electrode was implanted in the region of the anterior commissure.
>
> The result was quite amazing. When the animal was stimulated at a specific place in an open field, he sometimes moved away but he returned and sniffed around that area. More stimulations at that place caused him to spend more of his time there.
>
> Later we found that this same animal could be "pulled" to any spot in the maze by giving a small electrical stimulus *after* each response in the right direction. This was akin to playing the "hot" and "cold" game with a child. Each correct response brought electrical pulses which seemed to indicate to the animal that it was on the right track. (pp. 83–84)

James Olds. (Courtesy of James Olds.)

Since this accidental discovery of reinforcement centers in rats, reinforcement centers have been found in cats, dogs, goldfish, monkeys, porpoises, pigeons, and humans. When a human being's reinforcement center is stimulated, the person sometimes reports erotic sensations and thoughts or simply a feeling of pleasure.

Olds and Milner originally felt that the septal region of the brain housed most of the reinforcement centers. Since then, however, such centers have been found scattered throughout the limbic system of the brain. The limbic system, which is involved in motivated and emotional behavior, contains part of the lower cortex, the hippocampus, the amygdala, the septum, and parts of the thalamus and hypothalamus.

These brain areas are called reinforcement centers because when they are stimulated, the animal tends to repeat what it was doing before the stimulation. Therefore, an animal with an electrode implanted in a reinforcement center can be trained to run a maze or to press a bar in a Skinner box simply by stimulating that area of the brain with a mild electrical current when the animal performs the appropriate response.

Reinforcement by direct brain stimulation, however, has been found to have some unusual characteristics and is therefore thought to operate differently from the more traditional reinforcers such as food or water. The unusual characteristics of reinforcement by direct brain stimulation are summarized below:

1. **No deprivation needed before training.** Unlike training involving food or water as a reinforcer, generally no deprivation schedule is needed when direct brain stimulation is used as a reinforcer. The animal does not need to be in a drive state. There are exceptions, however, and occasionally reinforcement centers are found that do seem to be dependent on the drive state of the organism. For example, it has been found that the stimulation of some brain sites is reinforcing only if the animal is hungry; stimulation of other sites is reinforcing only the animal is thirsty, and still others only if it is sexually aroused.

2. **Satiation does not occur.** When food or water is used as a reinforcer, the animal will eventually satiate; that is, its need for food or water will be satisfied and it will stop responding. With direct brain stimulation, however, the animal will go on responding at an extraordinarily high rate (for example, barpressing rates as high as 7,000 per hour have been reported) until it becomes physically exhausted.

3. **Takes priority over other drives.** Animals continue to press a bar for direct brain stimulation even when food is available and they have not eaten for a considerable length of time. Also, animals will often withstand a greater shock to obtain brain stimulation to a reinforcement center than to obtain food even if they have not eaten for 24 hours.

4. **There is rapid extinction.** Although the rate of responding is extremely high as long as the animal is being reinforced by brain stimulation, it stops responding very rapidly when the brain stimulation stops. In other words, rather than the gradual extinction process observed when food or water are the reinforcers, extinction takes place almost immediately when direct brain stimulation reinforcement is terminated. Although extinction is rapid, the response rate recurs at full strength when the animal is again reinforced.

5. **Most schedules of reinforcement do not work.** Since extinction occurs very rapidly when brain stimulation is terminated, any schedule of reinforcement that produces some amount of delay between responding and reinforcement will cause the animal to stop responding. Cats, for example, will stop responding if the delay between a response and a reinforcer is longer than about fifteen seconds. Therefore, only schedules of reinforcement that provide frequent reinforcement can be used with direct brain stimulation.

As yet, these observations about the reinforcing effects of direct brain stimulation have not been explained in a way that is widely accepted by researchers in the field. The situation is complicated further by the fact that **punishment areas** are often found only millimeters away from a reinforcement area. An animal will quickly learn to perform a response that terminates stimulation to such an area or a response that prevents it from occurring. Humans receiving stimulation in a punishment area report feelings of anxiety or panic.

Research on the Split Brain

The **corpus callosum** is a large mass of fibers that connects the two halves of the cortex. For years, the function of the corpus callosum was unknown, but in the early 1960s it was found to be instrumental in transferring information from one side of the cortex to the other. In a series of experiments, Roger Sperry (1913–1994) noted that there were two possible routes for such a transfer—the corpus callosum and the optic chiasm (Sperry, 1961). The optic chiasm is the point in the optic nerve where information coming from one eye is projected to the side of the cortex opposite to that eye. Thus, Sperry taught intact cats to make a visual discrimination with a patch over one eye. Following discrimination training, he tested for transfer by switching the patch from one eye to the other, and he found that the animal was able to perform just as well with either eye. In other words, complete interocular transfer was found.

Now Sperry (1961) began a search for the mechanism by which information was transferred from one side of the brain to the other. His first step was to ablate (cut) the optic chiasm, both before and after training, and again he found complete transfer of training from one eye to the other. Next, he ablated the corpus callosum *after* the discrimination training, and again he found no interference with the transfer of information from one eye to the other. His next step was to ablate *both* the optic chiasm and the corpus callosum *before* training, and he found that such a preparation prevented transfer from one eye to the other. Cutting both the optic chiasm and the corpus callosum created two separate brains, with one eye going to each and with no exchange of information between them. Sperry's split-brain preparation is seen in Figure 15–7.

When the cat's brain was split and the cat was taught to make a visual discrimination with a patch over one eye, it had no recollection of that learning when tested with the other eye. The two halves of the split brain appeared to learn independently. In fact, with a patch over one eye, the animal could be taught to do one thing, such as approach a door with a cross on it, and with a

Roger W. Sperry. (Photo by Ronald Meyer.)

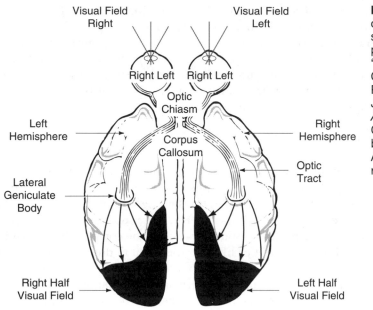

Visual Field Right

Visual Field Left

Right Left   Right Left

Optic Chiasm

Left Hemisphere

Corpus Callosum

Right Hemisphere

Optic Tract

Lateral Geniculate Body

Right Half Visual Field

Left Half Visual Field

patch over the other eye, it could be taught to approach the adjoining door with a circle on it; thus the two brains in the same skull have learned contradictory habits. It is also possible to teach an animal to approach a stimulus (e.g., a circle) with a patch over one eye and to avoid the same stimulus with a patch over the other eye.

For various medical reasons, the **split-brain preparation** has been used on humans. In addition to being effective in treating brain abnormalities, the procedure has been instrumental in providing information about how the left and right hemispheres differ in the way they process information. It is to the differences between left- and right-brain functioning that we turn next.

Left-Brain, Right-Brain Learning and Information Processing

Although there are slight anatomical differences between the right and left hemisphere, these physical differences are not so great as to suggest that the two hemispheres function in dramatically different ways. Furthermore, control over the body's movement and sensation is divided evenly between the two cerebral hemispheres, but in a crossed fashion. That is, the left hemisphere controls the right side of the body and the right hemisphere controls the left side. It is tempting to conclude that because the two hemispheres are similar at the global level, that they also perceive, learn, and process information similarly. But is this the case? The question of whether or not the two hemispheres are functionally symmetrical was not easy to answer.

In 1836, Marc Dax reported that loss of speech resulted from damage to the left cerebral hemisphere but not to the right. Dax's observation was essentially ignored even after Paul Broca, a very prominent physician, made the same observation in 1861. In fact, we still refer to one of the language areas in the left hemisphere as

Broca's area. The finding that, for the majority of people, a speech area exists on the left hemisphere but not on the right provided the first scientific evidence that the two cerebral hemispheres are asymmetrical in function.

It was assumed for many years that the right hemisphere was inferior to the left. The left hemisphere, therefore, was called the dominant or superior hemisphere. Eventually, evidence was provided that necessitated a radical change in this belief. In 1962, a series of reports by such individuals as Mountcastle, Geschwind, Kaplan, Sperry, and Gazzaniga showed that the right hemisphere was not only equal in importance to the left hemisphere but for certain nonverbal functions actually superior. Evidence that the two cerebral hemispheres are asymmetrical in their functioning has been provided by individuals with brain damage; individuals who for medical reasons have had their cortex surgically divided; and with the use of ingenious experimental apparatus, by individuals with normal, intact brains.

For example, it has been found that individuals with damage to their right hemispheres are likely to display difficulties related to attention or perception. They may be disoriented in familiar surroundings and have difficulty recognizing familiar faces and objects. Also, individuals with right-brain damage are more likely than patients with damage to the left hemisphere to display **neglect syndrome,** a disorder characterized by failure to see or attend to the left visual field or even to the left side of the body. Individuals exhibiting neglect syndrome have been known to shave only the right half of their face or eat food only off of the right side of a plate. When patients with right hemisphere damage are asked to reproduce pictures placed in front of them, the results are often like those shown in Figure 15–8. The fact that

Model   Patient's Copy

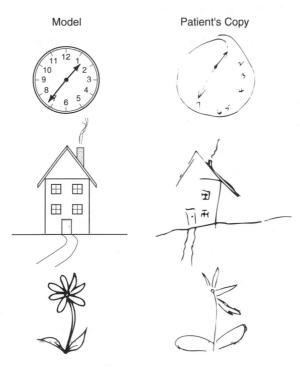

FIGURE 15–8 Attempts of a patient with right-brain damage to copy drawings of various objects. The incomplete copies exemplify the neglect syndrome. (From *Left Brain, Right Brain,* rev. ed., p. 160, by S.P. Springer & G. Deutsch, 1985, San Francisco, W.H. Freeman and Company. Copyright © 1981, 1985. Reprinted with the permission of W.H. Freeman and Company.)

these kinds of difficulties are more likely after damage to the right hemisphere was taken as further evidence that the two cerebral hemispheres function differently.

Interest in how the two cortical hemispheres function has also been stimulated by patients who for medical reasons have had the cortical pathways connecting the two hemispheres severed. Severing the corpus callosum of patients suffering otherwise intractable epilepsy confines abnormal electrical discharge to only one cerebral hemisphere and thereby reduces the frequency and severity of seizures. It is possible, however, to use such patients to study how the cerebral hemispheres function separately. There are now several techniques that can be used to present sensory information to just one hemisphere at a time.

Although results from split-brain subjects are complex, some researchers believed that characteristic right-brain versus left-brain patterns existed in the data. Springer and Deutsch (1985) summarize the popular but premature interpretation of the results: "The left hemisphere has been found to be predominantly involved with analytic processes, especially the production and understanding of language, and it appears to process input in a sequential manner. The right hemisphere appears to be responsible for certain spatial skills and musical abilities and to process information simultaneously and holistically" (pp. 4–5).

Hemispheric Functioning in Normal Brains

On the basis of the study of brain-damaged individuals and those who had their brains surgically split for medical reasons, it was clear that each hemisphere of the brain could perceive, learn, remember, and feel independently of the other hemisphere. The question next became whether or not findings from research on damaged or surgically prepared brains could be generalized to the functioning of normal brains. To answer the question, a number of techniques have been developed that allow hemispheric functioning to be investigated on normal, intact brains. For example, EEG recordings can be taken from each cerebral hemisphere separately. When the brain is resting, it is characterized by a slow EEG pattern called alpha rhythms. When the brain is active, the alpha rhythms are blocked and are replaced by much faster EEG patterns. Using EEG recordings, Ornstein (1978) found that the alpha rhythms of the left hemisphere are blocked when a subject is given problems that require verbal, mathematical, or analytic solutions. The alpha rhythms of the right hemisphere are blocked when the subject is given spatial, perceptual, and other nonverbal problems.

Another method used to determine how the two cerebral hemispheres function in individuals with normal, intact brains is **dichotic listening.** Although dichotic listening was used earlier by Broadbent to study selective attention, it was Doreen Kimura, a student of both Hebb and Brenda Milner, who used it as a safe and reliable method of studying cerebral asymmetry in normal subjects (Kimura, 1961, 1964, 1967). The dichotic listening technique involves sending competing information, such as pairs of syllables or digits, to the left and right ears simultaneously through stereo headphones. For example, the syllable *ba* might be presented to the subject's left ear and the syllable *ga* to the right ear at the same time. In view of the fact that information presented to the left ear is projected mainly onto the right hemisphere

Doreen Kimura. (Courtesy of Doreen Kimura.)

and information presented to the right ear is projected mainly onto the left hemisphere, the question is which of the two simultaneously presented syllables or digits will be reported accurately. Under the circumstances just described, nearly all right-handers and most left-handers accurately report the digits or syllables presented to their right ears more often than those presented to their left ears. Thus, the contention that in most humans, the left hemisphere is responsible for processing verbal information was again confirmed.

Some have argued that instead of concluding from dichotic listening research that the left hemisphere is specialized for speech perception, it is more accurate to conclude that it is specialized for auditory perception in general or for general attention. However, the fact that most normal right-handers perceive melodies (Kimura, 1964) and environmental sounds such as dogs barking and automobile engines (Curry, 1967) better with their left ears (right hemispheres) does not support such an argument.

Speculations

Research into the differences between hemispheres generated a great deal of speculation concerning the role of cerebral asymmetry in everyday life. Springer and Deutsch (1985) describe some of these speculations:

> It has been claimed that these differences clearly show the traditional dualisms of intellect versus intuition, science versus art, and the logical versus the mysterious....It has also been suggested that lawyers and artists use different halves of the brain in their work and that the differences between the halves show up in activities not related to their work. Others have extended this idea further and have claimed that everyone may be classified as a right-hemisphere person or a left-hemisphere person, depending on which hemisphere guides the bulk of an individual's behavior. (p. 6)

Bogen (1977) suggests that the dichotomous ways in which the world or thought processes are often described reflect the two kinds of hemispheric intelligence. According to Bogen, dichotomies such as those listed below are only manifestations of how the left and right brains process information (p. 135):

Left Hemisphere	**Right Hemisphere**
Intellect	Intuition
Convergent	Divergent
Realistic	Impulsive
Intellectual	Sensuous

Discrete	Continuous
Directed	Free
Rational	Intuitive
Historical	Timeless
Analytic	Holistic
Successive	Simultaneous
Objective	Subjective
Atomistic	Gross

The attempt to find dichotomies such as those listed above and then to explain their existence in terms of the ways the cerebral hemispheres process information has been called **dichotomania.** After reviewing the research on laterality, Beaton (1985) concludes that it is inappropriate to describe hemispheric functioning in terms of *any* dichotomies:

> There are certain problems in attempting to encapsulate some "fundamental" hemispheric difference in terms of…dichotomies. In the first place, virtually all investigators are agreed that cerebral asymmetry is not absolute but a matter of degree. It has not been shown, for example, that one hemisphere is totally incapable of carrying out the functions normally ascribed to its partner. Even with regard to language, the area in which left-right asymmetry is most unequivocal, it is evident that the right hemisphere possesses considerable powers of comprehension and can, under certain circumstances, demonstrate some expressive ability.…
>
> Other dichotomies are even less securely founded.…There is, after all, no reason *why* the brain should have evolved so conveniently.…Perhaps then, a single dichotomy of brain function is inherently improbable.…It may, therefore, be profoundly misleading to assume that the relationship between the hemispheres as a whole can be described in terms of any single principle. (pp. 285–288)

Jerre Levy, a longtime researcher of left-brain, right-brain functioning, believes that although it is possible, under special circumstances, to demonstrate that the two hemispheres function differently, it is impossible to separate those functions in a normal, intact brain. In her article "Right Brain, Left Brain: Fact and Fiction," Levy (1985) says,

> The two-brain myth was founded on an erroneous premise: that since each hemisphere was specialized, each must function as an independent brain. But, in fact, just the opposite is true. To the extent that regions are differentiated in the brain, they must integrate their activities. Indeed, it is precisely that integration that gives rise to behavior and mental processes greater than and different from each region's special contribution. Thus, since the central premise of the mythmakers is wrong, so are all the inferences derived from it.…The popular myths are misinterpretations and wishes, not the observations of scientists. Normal people have not half a brain nor two brains but one gloriously differentiated brain, with each hemisphere contributing its specialized abilities.…We have a single brain that generates a single mental self. (pp. 43–44)

Gazzaniga and LeDoux (1978), however, are less generous in their analysis. After an extensive experimentation on split-brain patients, they conclude that the popular, dichotomous conception is an illusion induced primarily by response bias.

That is, the left hemisphere appears to be dominant when patients perform tasks that require speaking or writing. The right hemisphere appears to be dominant when patients are required to respond by drawing, building, touching/feeling, and so on. When response bias is eliminated, so are the differences between hemispheres. These investigators conclude that, although the two hemispheres have different response skills, they perceive, learn, and process in the same manner.

Investigation into the different functional properties of the two hemispheres continues (see Hellige, 1993) although it is no longer guided by earlier speculations about right-brain and left-brain functions. Interestingly, recent work with split-brain patients has provided information about the hemispheres that would not have been predicted from the popular dichotomies of the 1970s and 1980s. For example, Cronin-Golumb (1995) presented "target" pictures of common objects to either the right or left hemispheres of patients. After seeing a target, the patients viewed a set of 20 additional pictures and selected those that were related to the target. When the patients used their right hemispheres for the task, they tended to select related pictures according to a linear ranking system. That is, the first picture selected was more related to the target than the second, the second more than the third, and so on. This type of ordering was not prevalent when patients used the left hemisphere. Recent findings also suggest that the right hemisphere has superior memory for details of visual patterns when compared to the left (Metcalfe, Funnell, & Gazzaniga, 1995) but that the left hemisphere has more sophisticated strategies for searching through a visual display (Kingstone, Enns, Mangun, & Gazzaniga, 1995).

There is no doubt that research on cerebral laterality has led to exciting discoveries and it will continue to do so. However, since such discoveries tend to stimulate the imagination, it is important to concentrate on the actual research data so that the distinction between fact and fantasy will not be blurred.

Real Cells and Real Cell Assemblies

In the years since Hebb first wrote of recruitment, fractionation, cell assemblies, and phase sequences, psychologists have been surprised at the accuracy of his conjectures about the nervous system.

Appreciation of Hebb's speculations depends, in part, on an understanding of learning between two **neurons.** A neuron has a cell body; one or more extended processes called **axons,** which are specialized for carrying electrochemical information away from the cell; and many branching **dendrites,** specialized for receiving electrochemical information from other cells' axons. A simplified schematic pair of brain cells is represented in Figure 15–9.

The mammalian brain cell exists in a watery bath filled with ions of potassium, sodium, calcium, and chloride, as well as ionized protein molecules. We can think of a single brain cell as a fragile and sensitive mediator of a fluctuating electrochemical balance. In the case of a mammalian neuron, the cell is engaged in metabolic processes that function primarily to keep sodium ions outside the cell and to keep potassium ions inside. This particular state of "balanced tension" is called the **resting potential** of the cell. This label is given in reference to the electrical charge difference

FIGURE 15–9 A simplified schematic drawing of two neurons. Cell bodies, dendrites, and axons are indicated.

between the inside and the outside of the cell membrane. In the typical, resting mammalian neuron, the inside of the membrane is negatively charged relative to the outside, and the difference averages approximately 70 millivolts.

If this state of polarization is reduced, the electrical difference between the inside and outside of the cell begins to move toward zero millivolts, and the cell may reach a millivoltage level called the **threshold,** at which level it can no longer maintain ion segregation. At that point, there is a slight reversal of the ionic distribution, primarily involving an exchange of the sodium and potassium ions. This causes the electrical condition of the cell to reverse as well, with the inside becoming positively charged with respect to the outside. The cell then expends energy to reestablish the resting potential. The entire process of ionic reversal and "reloading" is referred to as the **action potential,** an event that actually travels from the cell body down the length of the axon.

The end or terminal of the axon responds to the arrival of an action potential by releasing a chemical **neurotransmitter** such as acetylcholine or dopamine into the extracellular space, or **synapse,** between it and other cells. Surrounding cells respond to released neurotransmitters with chemical reactions that move them toward or away from their own threshold levels.

Brain cells exist in relationships with hundreds and perhaps thousands of other cells. Their individual excitatory and inhibitory activities are the result of continuous summation of chemical information from surrounding cells. We might imagine at the most fundamental level that learning entails a change in the relationship between two cells, and this is the level at which Hebb first focused. Specifically, learning consists of a change in a receiving cell's response to the neurotransmitter released by a sending cell. In a simplified example, we might imagine an unlearned receiving cell that does not generate its own action potentials in response to a neurotransmitter discharge from a sending cell. We infer learning when the receiving cell begins reliably and predictably to generate an action potential in response to the sending cell's activity. Although Hebb suggested that the activity of one cell in contiguity with another might well change the relationship between them, he could only make conjectures about the processes involved. Recent research, however, has revealed mechanisms very much like those that Hebb anticipated.

Learning in *Aplysia*

A major obstacle to understanding the possible mechanisms of learning, recruitment, and fractionation lies in the sheer numbers of neurons involved in even the simplest behaviors in mammals. Eric Kandel and his associates (Castellucci & Kandel, 1974; Dale, Schacher, & Kandel, 1988; Kandel & Schwartz, 1982; Kupfermann, Castellucci, Pinsker, & Kandel, 1970) solved this problem by working with a shell-less sea mollusk called *Aplysia,* which has a relatively simple nervous system and yet displays behaviors similar to cell assembly phenomena. The backside of this marine animal contains three external organs called the gill, the mantle shelf, and the siphon, and all three of these structures are reflexively withdrawn when either the mantel shelf or the siphon are touched.

When one of these reflex-triggering structures is stimulated weakly and repeatedly, the withdrawal response habituates. That is, it slowly disappears. Thus a circuit that was initially activated by an external input is "subtracted" from the larger pattern of neural activity. This process corresponds closely to Hebb's notion of fractionation, but how does this habituation occur?

Kandel's research (Castellucci & Kandel, 1974) has demonstrated that the critical event mediating habituation is a decrease in the release of neurotransmitter(s) from the sensory neuron, which serves to signal the weak stimulation, onto the motor neuron that triggers the reflexive withdrawal of the external organs. Exactly why and how the sensory neuron learns to ignore the weak, repetitive stimulation is not known, but the fact that the response is easily reactivated makes it clear that habituation is more than simple fatigue or depletion of neurotransmitter(s) (Kupfermann et al., 1970).

The reactivation process, called sensitization, occurs when, for example, an electric shock is delivered to the tail (near the organs) of the animal. After the shock,

Eric R. Kandel. (Courtesy of Eric R. Kandel.)

weak stimulation once again produces a withdrawal reflex. Sensitization is a more complex process than habituation. It involves an additional neuron, called an **interneuron,** engaged by, for example, the aversive electric shock. In this case, the additional interneuron stimulates the sensory neuron, causing it to release extra neurotransmitter onto the motor neuron controlling organ withdrawal (Cleary, Hammer, & Byrne, 1989; Dale et al., 1988). Thus, sensitization seems to involve construction of a simple, three-element cell assembly and provides a model for Hebb's notion of recruitment. As the reader might have anticipated, Kandel's studies have further demonstrated that an interneuron-mediated process similar to the one involved in sensitization underlies classical conditioning (Kandel & Schwartz, 1982).

Reverberating Circuits

Kandel's work partly answers questions about how communication patterns between cells change. Additional mechanisms are revealed in the phenomenon called **long-term potentiation (LTP)** (Bliss & Lømo, 1973; Lømo, 1966). This phenomenon involves electrically stimulating part of the hippocampus, a structure already implicated in memory consolidation, with a single, weak electrical pulse. The strength of connections with other parts of the hippocampus are inferred by recording the spread of neuroelectrical activity generated by the initial, weak pulse. More specifically, cells in an area of the hippocampus called the perforant path are stimulated, and the spread of that stimulation is recorded in and near another hippocampal area called the dentate gyrus. If the first weak pulse is followed immediately by a burst of stronger, high-frequency electrical stimulation, the relationship between the perforant path cells and the dentate gyrus cells changes dramatically. Initially, the effect of the weak stimulation is slight, but after the high-frequency stimulation, a weak current applied to the perforant path produces much stronger changes in the activities of cells in and near the dentate gyrus. The stronger stimulation *potentiates* the effects of the initial, weak stimulation, and the effects can last for months (Figure 15–10).

LTP occurs in some areas of the hippocampus as we have described above. In other parts of the hippocampus, LTP will not occur unless the weak stimulation and the stronger, high-frequency stimulation occur simultaneously. Kandel (1991) has suggested that the two different LTP phenomena reflect the neural bases for non-associative learning (habituation and sensitization) on one hand, and for associative learning on the other. Much recent work has been devoted to uncovering the mechanisms of associative LTP. For example, research indicates that the excitatory neurotransmitter glutamate mediates the effect. However, at least two different types of dendritic glutamate receptors are involved (Cotman, Monaghan & Ganong, 1988; Nakanishi, 1992). One of them, called an NMDA glutamate receptor (named after the chemical procedure used to differentiate it from other glutamate receptors), cannot be activated unless other, nearby non-NMDA receptors are also stimulated by glutamate. If both receptor types are stimulated at the same time, NMDA receptors are activated and allow calcium ions to enter dendrite sites. The calcium ions initiate a series of events that increase the sensitivity of surrounding non-NMDA receptors.

It is known that calcium ions must enter the stimulating cell's axon terminal in

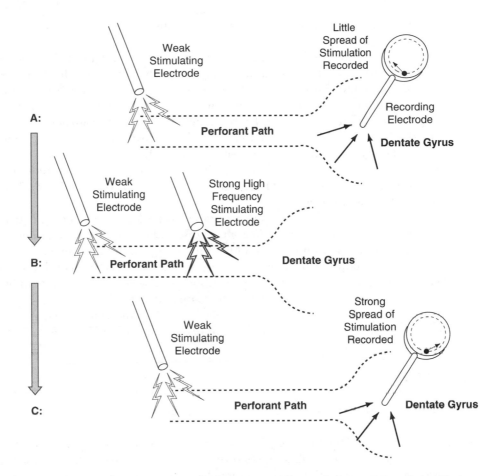

FIGURE 15–10 A) Weak electrical stimulation of the perforant path has little effect on cells in the dentate gyrus. B) Weak stimulation of the perforant path is followed by stronger, high frequency, *potentiating* electrical stimulation. C) Now weak stimulation of the perforant path spreads and readily excites cells in the dentate gyrus.

order for it to release its neurotransmitter into the synaptic space between cells. It is also known that calcium ions enter the dendritic areas of target cells during LTP (Malenka, Kauer, Zucker, & Nicoll, 1988). Lynch and Baudry (1984, 1991) suggest that calcium ions enter the dendrites and activate an enzyme called **calpain**. This enzyme seems to erode a protective protein, called **spectrin,** thus changing the shape of the dendritic receptor site. The calpain-spectrin hypothesis (Lynch & Baudry, 1984, 1991) says that the altered shape of dendrites produces facilitation by affecting either the flow of electrical events in the cell or the sensitivity of receptors (Baudry & Lynch, 1993). A related hypothesis suggests that the calcium ions activate genes that increase long-term responsiveness in non-NMDA receptors (Bading, Ginty, & Greenberg, 1993). An alternative approach states that the calcium ions cause the dendrite to release a chemical, probably nitric oxide, which stimulates nearby axons and causes them to release additional neurotransmitters (Schuman & Madison, 1991).

Interestingly, the hippocampus may produce its own natural form of long-term potentiation—in effect, its own reverbratory activity. When a rat, for example, is in a complex and novel environment and is engaging in exploratory behavior (supposedly learning about the new environment), we can record an internally generated series of pulses (called theta rhythms) that begin near the perforant path and affect cells near the dentate gyrus—the same path studied in the artificially induced phenomenon of LTP (Vanderwolf, Kramis, Gillespie, & Bland, 1975). And as one might guess, artificially produced theta rhythms are as effective as the strong, high-frequency stimulation used in the typical LTP experiment (Diamond, Dunwiddie, & Rose, 1988; Staubli & Lynch, 1987).

We see, then, that there are a number of ways in which simple learning may occur between two neurons or in a small cluster of neurons and a number of ways in which Hebb's cell assemblies could be refined. And although some of Hebb's early speculations about the underlying processes were incorrect, his basic contention that cells develop and operate in aggregates appears to be correct. The human brain is so complex, however, that the actual relationship between the activity of groups of brain cells and complex learning—for example, learning names, languages, and social and cognitive rules—will remain the topic of research for years to come.

THE NEW CONNECTIONISM

Artificial Cells and Artificial Cell Assemblies

One place that Hebb would not have expected his ideas to appear is in the abstract world of computer simulation. However, the newest approach to understanding the ways in which neural systems learn involves no actual neurons at all. Instead, computer models of brain cell activities serve to explore learning, remembering, forgetting, and other brain activity. Two influential investigators in this research area, David Rumelhart and James McClelland, have named their approach parallel distributed processing (PDP) (McClelland & Rumelhart, 1988; Rumelhart & McClelland, 1986) in reference to the assumption that the brain conducts simultaneous or parallel information-processing activities. This field has no agreed-upon name, but it has been called the new connectionism, and the models it uses are called **neural networks** (Bechtel & Abrahamsen, 1991).

The basic task in such computer simulations is first to define a set of computer neurons and their potential interconnections and relationships. Next, a number of simplified assumptions, drawn from our understanding of real neurons, are imposed on these artificial neurons. In addition, simple logical learning rules regulate the changes that occur in individual computer neurons and in their interconnections. Finally, the artificial neural system is "trained" and then observed to determine how it changes as a result of experience.

Input Output

FIGURE 15–11 Two input elements, two output elements, and their possible connections.

A simple example of a neural network, called a pattern associator (Bechtel & Abrahamsen, 1991; Hinton & Anderson, 1981; Rumelhart & McClelland, 1986), may serve to demonstrate the idea, but keep in mind that much more complicated phenomena have been modeled in neural networks.

First, consider the simple set of elements in Figure 15–11. This particular network has only four elements: two input neurons and two output neurons. You may think of these as sensory neurons and motor neurons, respectively. There are also dashed lines representing *possible* neural connections between these elements.

Input from the environment (or a computer programmer) activates the input neurons. The output neurons will become active, depending on (1) the strength of the connections from the input units and (2) the number of input units that are connected with them. This output activation rule reflects the **summation** properties of actual neurons. Summation refers to the observation that a neuron adds the inputs from surrounding cells and that the summed total of inputs determines the cell's level of activity. The rule can be stated as follows:

$$A_o = \sum (w_{oi}) A_i$$

This equation means simply that the output activation (A_o) of a unit is the sum of its input activations (A_i) weighted by their connection strengths (w_{oi}). We can assume, at this point, that nothing has been learned in this hypothetical system—all w_{oi}'s are zero—and that sensory input has no effect on motor output.

Let us say that we want to teach our network to discriminate between pine trees and spruce trees. In effect, we want this system to "say 'pine' " whenever the input is the sight of a pine tree and to "say 'spruce' " whenever it sees a spruce. It is important to remember that in real nervous systems written labels or tags are not attached to sensory input or motor output. In a simplified sense, sensory input representing the sight of a pine tree and the motor output representing the spoken word *pine* are nothing more than patterns of excitation and inhibition in the nervous system. It is in this sense that we will represent "pine" and "spruce" in our hypothetical neural network. We will arbitrarily give "pine" a sensory code of (+1, –1), indicating that the first sensory element has an excitatory activity of +1 and the second sensory element has an inhibitory activity of –1. In contrast, our "spruce tree" will have a sensory code of (–1, +1), indicating an inhibitory activity of –1 and an excitatory activity of +1 in the first and second sensory neurons.

You now know that (+1, –1) is "pine" and (–1, +1) is "spruce," and you can already reliably categorize these two types of trees. The problem, of course, is to teach the computer's neural network to categorize correctly and therefore exhibit discrimination between these two kinds of input. That is, when given (+1, −1) as sensory input, we want the first motor neuron to output +1 and the second to output −1 and to exhibit the opposite pattern for the "spruce" input. To accomplish these effects, we have to train the system. Specifically, we need to develop the connections between the sensory and motor elements so that the desired input-output relationship can occur. Note that the cells themselves do not learn to be excited (+1) or inhibited (−1). It is assumed that like real neurons, the abilities to be excited or inhibited are simple inherent properties of the cells. Learning occurs at the *connections* between cells, and it is both the *kind* and *strength* of the connections that are trained in neural networks.

At this point we must invoke a learning rule—a logical but arbitrary rule that our computer system will follow in order to change the connections between cells. The most simple rule is called the **Hebb rule** (or the Hebbian rule). It is a mathematical statement that attempts to capture Hebb's contention that the connection between two cells that are active simultaneously will be strengthened or made more efficient. The Hebbian rule is written

$$\Delta w_{oi} = \text{lrate } (A_i) \ (A_o)$$

where

Δw is the *change* in the strength or *weight* of a connection between the input and output

lrate is a constant that reflects learning rate

A_i is the activation value level of the input unit

A_o is the activation value level of the output unit

and in our simple example, activation values will be either −1 or +1

The rule indicates that when two units are activated in the same direction (both +1 or both −1), the product of the mutual activity is positive and therefore the connection weight becomes more positive. When they are simultaneously active in different directions (one element +1 and the other −1), the product is negative and the connection weight becomes more negative. It will be easy to see how the connections change in our "pine" versus "spruce" example.

We will start with all weights or connections set at zero (0), and we will set learning rate (lrate) equal to $1/n$, where n is the number of input units. In other words, learning rate in our example is ½. (This is an arbitrary setting that assures one-trial learning and is ideal for our simple example.)

We can begin by training or teaching the network "pine." The computer program sets the activation values of input to +1 and −1 for the first and second input units and sets the activation values of the output cells to the desired values of +1 in the first cell and −1 in the second. The matrix below shows the state of inputs, outputs, and weights (connection strengths) at the beginning of training.

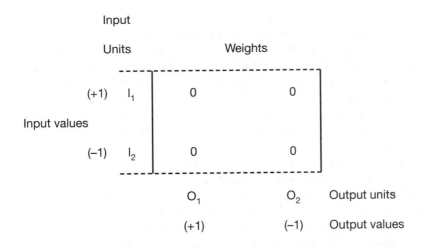

We use the Hebbian rule to change the strengths of the connections from their initial zero values. For example we can change the connection between input unit 1 and output unit 1 by simple substitution in the learning formula:

Δw is the amount of change (from zero) due to activation of the first input and first output neurons.

$$
\begin{aligned}
A_i & = \text{activation of input } 1 = +1 \\
A_o & = \text{activation of output } 1 = +1 \\
\text{lrate} & = \tfrac{1}{2} \\
\text{therefore, } \Delta w & = \tfrac{1}{2}(+1)\,(+1) = \tfrac{1}{2}, \text{ or } .50
\end{aligned}
$$

The other weights will change accordingly, and after training the neural network, weights have the following values:

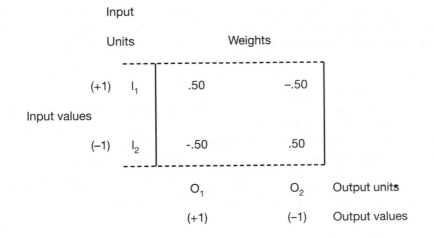

We can test this neural network to see if learning was effective by giving it an input and letting the network generate its own output according to the output activation (summation) rule above. When given the input for "pine," (+1, –1), output cell 1 adds (.50)(+1) + (–.50)(–1) to yield +1; output 2 adds (–.50)(+1) + (.50)(–1) to yield –1; and the network produces the appropriate (+1, –1) response. This result occurs reliably because the weights or connection strengths were created from the "pine" input and output values. What might be surprising is the output that occurs when the trained system is given "spruce" (–1, +1) as its input. Try it and see.

Back-propagation systems. Research in neural networks has reached levels of complexity that go well beyond the scope of this text, and the simple case of "pine" versus "spruce" provides only an introduction to an area that has already shown great promise. Imagine a network with, say, ten inputs and ten outputs plus a number of intermediate units. Our simple explanation and example can provide only a glimpse of the phenomena that might be mimicked by such a network, although the general summation principle remains much the same. The simple Hebbian learning rule, however, is usually replaced in more sophisticated networks by a form of the *delta rule* (McClelland & Rumelhart, 1988; Rummelhart & McClelland, 1986), sometimes called a back propagation rule. The fundamental delta rule is

$$\Delta w_{oi} = \text{lrate}(d_o - A_o)(A_i)$$

Notice that it is similar to the Hebbian rule except that the output activation term is more complex. Here (d_o) refers to the desired output of a unit and (A_o) refers to the actual output. The system is programmed to change connection strengths so that the difference between desired and real output is minimized. It is, in a sense, a self-correcting learning rule that adjusts connection strengths until output matches a target state. If $(d_o - A_o)$ reaches zero, the weights no longer change and learning is complete.

NETtalk (Sejnowski & Rosenberg, 1987) is a back propagation system that has received a great deal of attention among neural network researchers. The system consists of a computer scanning device with seven windows, each of which can scan a single printed letter from the English alphabet. Each scanning window is connected to 29 input units in the network. The output consists of 26 units, each of which represents a distinct phoneme in the English language. Each of the output units, in turn, is programmed through a voice synthesizer to produce its specific phoneme. There are 80 embedded or hidden units between the input units and the output units. Every input unit is connected to every hidden unit, and every hidden unit is connected to each of the outputs. There are therefore $7 \times 29 \times 80 \times 26$ or 18,320 weighted connections in NETtalk. Initially, weights are assigned randomly. And when a printed word is scanned as input, the output is a random garble of sound. A back-propagation rule is used to adjust weights so that the actual output of the system gets closer and closer to the desired output with each word presentation, and eventually NETtalk reads words aloud. Interestingly, after initial training with 1,000 words, NETtalk is able to accurately read words that are not in the training set, although it still makes mistakes common to novice readers. For example, if the word "rough" is in the training set, it will read the new word "tough" correctly, but will misread the new word "dough."

Clark (1990) describes how NETtalk learns to read aloud.

> The network began with a random distribution of hidden unit weights and connections (within chosen parameters), i.e. it had no "idea" of any rules of text-to-phoneme conversion. Its task was to learn, by repeated exposure to training instances, to negotiate its way around this particularly tricky cognitive domain (tricky because of irregularities, subregularities, and context-sensitivity of text→phoneme conversion). And learning proceeded in the standard way, i.e. by a back-propagation learning rule. This works by giving the system an input, checking (this is done automatically by a computerized "supervisor") its output, and telling it what output (i.e. what phonemic code) it should have produced. The learning rule then causes the system to minutely adjust the weights on the hidden units in a way which would tend towards the correct output. This procedure is repeated many thousands of times. Uncannily, the system slowly and audibly learns to pronounce English text, moving from babble to half-recognizable words and on to a highly credible final performance. (p. 299)

It would be incorrect to conclude that research in neural networks is merely "computership," that is, skilled computer programmers making sophisticated computer programs that re-create phenomena we already know and understand. The new connectionism's networks begin with relatively simple assumptions: Hebb's learning rule and Lashley's contention that memory is distributed rather than localized in one or two neurons. From these starting points, neural networks have been constructed to simulate processes as simple as pattern association, demonstrated above, and as complex as language learning or recovery from brain damage. We can expect to be reading more about neural networks for several years to come.

SUMMARY

After a shaky academic start, Hebb entered graduate school at McGill University, where he was trained in the Pavlovian tradition. He became disenchanted with Pavlov when he read about Gestalt psychology and Lashley's work on the brain. At the University of Chicago, while working with Lashley, Hebb was convinced that the brain did not work as a complex switchboard, as the behaviorists and associationists maintained; rather, it worked as an interrelated whole. This Gestalt conception of the brain was further reinforced when Hebb, while working with Wilder Penfield, observed that large areas of the human brain could be removed without any apparent loss in intellectual functioning.

Hebb's major theoretical terms were *cell assembly* and *phase sequence*. A cell assembly is the neural package associated with an environmental object. If this neural package is stimulated in the absence of the object with which it is associated, an idea of the object is experienced. A phase sequence is a series of interrelated cell assemblies. If a series of events typically occurs together in the environment, they become represented on the neural level as a phase sequence. The stimulation of a phase sequence causes a flow of related ideas. For Hebb there were two kinds of learning. First, there is the slow buildup of cell assemblies and phase sequences early in life. Second, there is the more insightful kind of learning that characterizes adult life. Adult learning involves the rearrangement of cell assemblies and phase sequences rather than their development.

Sensory deprivation disrupts normal cognitive functioning because it interferes with the relationship between neural circuits and environmental events. Results of sensory deprivation studies show that organisms need normal stimulation just as they need food, water, and oxygen. Research indicates that animals reared in enriched sensory environments are subsequently better learners than animals reared in relatively simple sensory environments. Hebb's explanation was that animals reared in enriched environments develop more complex neural circuitry, which later can be applied to new learning.

While studying fear, Hebb discovered that chimpanzees were not frightened of either completely familiar or completely unfamiliar objects. What did frighten the chimpanzees was presenting a familiar object in an unfamiliar way. Hebb's explanation was that a familiar object triggered the neural circuits associated with it, but then subsequent events did not support or confirm those neural circuits; thus a conflict occurred, which stimulated fear. This theory could also explain why sensory deprivation is so disabling.

Arousal theory states that an environmental cue has two functions: (1) a cue function, which conveys information about the environment; and (2) an arousal function, which stimulates the reticular activating system (RAS). To allow optimal intellectual functioning, arousal must be neither too high nor too low. If arousal is too low for the optimal performance of a given task, anything that increases it is reinforcing; if arousal is too high for the optimal performance of a certain task, anything that decreases it is reinforcing.

Hebb believed that there were two kinds of memory—short-term memory and long-term memory. Short-term memory lasts less than a minute and is associated with the reverberating neural activity caused by an environmental event. If an experience is repeated often enough, it is stored in long-term memory. The process whereby short-term memory is converted into long-term memory is called consolidation. If a traumatic experience occurs during the consolidation period, short-term memory is prevented from being transferred into long-term memory. Research indicates that the entire consolidation period lasts about an hour. A brain structure that appears vital for consolidation is the hippocampus.

While Olds and Milner were doing research in Hebb's laboratory on the arousal system, they accidentally discovered reinforcement centers in the brain. By stimulating these centers they were able to shape a variety of behavioral patterns. Reinforcement by brain stimulation was found to have several unusual characteristics: (1) No deprivation is needed for it to be effective; (2) the animal does not seem to be able to get enough of it; (3) it takes priority over other drives; (4) behavior maintained by it extinguishes very rapidly; and (5) most schedules of reinforcement do not work with its use.

Sperry found that by ablating both the optic chiasm and the corpus callosum, he could create two independent brains in one skull. Such brains could be taught opposing habits, and one could be active while the other relaxed. Further work on the brain has indicated that although the left and right cerebral hemispheres are alike anatomically, they perform different functions. The left hemisphere is associated with verbal and mathematical skills and the right hemisphere with perceptual, attentional, and artistic skills. It is inappropriate to dichotomize hemispheric functions completely, however, since most human activities and thought processes involve both hemispheres, and at least to some extent, functions performed by one hemisphere can be performed by the other.

Although, with the exception of Hebb's work, research using the neurophysiological paradigm is often diffuse and unrelated, it is beginning to contribute to our further understanding of the learning process. In Chapter 3, it was said that our understanding of the learning process is enhanced when viewed from different angles. The neurophysiological paradigm provides us with one additional viewing angle.

EVALUATION OF HEBB'S THEORY

Contributions

Hebb's most important contribution was his conceptual demonstration that we could study higher cognitive processes using single neurons and synapses as our fundamental tools. In this respect, Hebb differentiated his position from theories relying on abstract S-R bonds. Although contemporary students of psychology or neuroscience may take for granted the fundamental relationship between synaptic activity and all higher order brain phenomena, Hebb was the first researcher to make that connection and to build simple models of how higher processes are constructed from synaptic events.

Hebb's fundamental learning principle required only repetition and contiguity, and it was guided by a reasonable understanding of what neurons actually could do. Although he was willing to modify his basic neurophysiological postulate to include learning via reinforcement, Hebb's theory clearly does not need such a process. The postulate can account for everything from perceptual learning to conditioning via reinforcers to higher emotional and cognitive processes. In this respect, the theory has the same kind of elegance that we saw in Guthrie's theory and is scientifically appealing for its simplicity—not because it relies on biological or physiological mechanisms.

Like Tolman, Hebb saw the distinctions between motivation and learning and the difficulties inherent in separating the two by observing behavior. His development of arousal theory and the concept of optimal arousal did not resolve the problem, but it did provide a new way to conceptualize it. In doing so, Hebb provided resolution to questions about Hull's drive reduction hypothesis, explaining why we sometimes seek drive reduction and at other times seek drive induction. Thus, with his research concerning the nature of arousal, sensory deprivation, reinforcement and fear, Hebb had an important influence on the study of motivation as well as the study of learning.

Criticisms

Hebb certainly was not the first to locate learning in the brain, and in some ways, his ideas concerning formation of associations between areas that are contiguously active are not that much different than Pavlov's. Similarly, he was not the first researcher to use his ideas about brain function to speculate about higher cognitive processes. It might be said that Hebb changed the level of analysis from larger areas of the brain to smaller numbers of neurons but maintained the general principle utilized by Pavlov.

A second criticism concerns Hebb's apparent unwillingness to change aspects of his theory in the light of important findings in the neurosciences. However, it must be noted that Hebb treated his system as a speculative model for a theory rather than as a finished, formal theory. It may well have been the case that Hebb viewed the discoveries of numerous chemical neurotransmitters, physiological bases of reinforcement, and neural structures implicated in consolidation as interesting but irrelevant to his basic model or as transitional phases in the development of brain sciences. On the other hand, there is a single, rather simple issue that should have had major significance for Hebb.

As Quinlan (1991) indicates, Hebb's neurophysiological postulate relied exclusively on the phenomenon of excitation. As our understanding of the nervous system developed, however, it became increasingly clear that the majority of neural communications—and most neurotransmitters—are inhibitory. That is, the most frequent mode of action in the nervous system is that of one cell restricting the firing of a second cell. Certainly this fundamental fact is not a passing phase in the brain sciences, yet Hebb ignored this fact in the neurophysiological postulate. Neural networks must apply a Hebbian rule to change the strength of connections, but these models would not work if they relied strictly on the original learning postulate.

DISCUSSION QUESTIONS

1. Discuss several observations Hebb made during his early years as a psychologist that he later attempted to account for with his neurophysiological theory.
2. Discuss Lashley's concepts of mass action and equipotentiality.
3. Describe the switchboard conception of the brain. What was Hebb's opposition to such a conception and what did he offer as an alternative?

4. Why, according to Hebb, were neurophysiological explanations of learning so unpopular at the time that he accepted his professorship at McGill?
5. Discuss the concepts of cell assembly and phase sequence.
6. What, according to Hebb, is the difference between childhood learning and adult learning?
7. Describe the effects of sensory deprivation and Hebb's explanation of them.
8. How might Hebb explain dreams? For example, why might a backfiring car cause a person to have a crime-related dream?
9. How might Hebb explain the Gestalt principle of closure?
10. Summarize Hebb's research on fear. What did he find and how did he explain what he found?
11. What does Hebb mean by an optimal level of stimulation?
12. Differentiate between the cue function and the arousal function of a stimulus.
13. Why, according to Hebb, do people sometimes go out of their way to seek stimulation?
14. Describe the relationship between arousal theory and reinforcement theory.
15. Differentiate between short-term and long-term memory. In your answer include an explanation of consolidation and those things that interfere with consolidation.
16. Describe the unique characteristics of reinforcement by direct brain stimulation.
17. Summarize Sperry's research on the split brain.
18. Summarize the functions that appear to be associated with the left and right cerebral hemispheres.
19. Describe how Kimura used dichotic listening to study cerebral asymmetry.
20. Why may it be inappropriate to describe hemispheric functioning in terms of dichotomies?

KEY TERMS

action potential   A nerve "impulse" or "spike." During action potential, the conditions of resting potential are reversed and reset. (See also **resting potential** and **neuron**.)

arousal function of a stimulus   That function of a stimulus that increases the activity of the reticular activating system, thereby increasing the electrical activity in certain higher centers of the brain.

arousal theory   The contentions that brain wave activity ranges from very fast to very slow with a rate in between that allows for the optimal performance of certain tasks.

axons   Extended processes of neurons that are specialized for carrying electrochemical signals away from the cell body. (See also **neurons.**)

calpain   An enzyme released when calcium ions enter the dendrite areas of neurons in the hippocampus. (See also **dendrite.**)

cell assembly   The pattern of neural activity that is caused when an environmental object or event is experienced. When the cell assembly is well developed, the person is able to think of the entire event following the stimulation of the assembly, even if the object itself or the event is physically absent.

consolidation theory   The contention that a short-term memory is converted into a long-term memory following a period of consolidation.

corpus callosum   A massive bundle of fibers that connects the two hemispheres of the cortex.

cue function of a stimulus   That function of a stimulus that provides us with information about the environment.

dendrites   Extended processes of neurons that are specialized for receiving electrochemical signals from other neurons. (See also **neurons.**)

dichotic listening   The technique whereby conflicting information is simultaneously presented to the two ears of a subject.

dichotomania   The tendency to explain the functioning of the left and right cerebral hemispheres in terms of two clearly delineated sets of functions.

electroconvulsive shock   A severe shock that causes convulsions, thereby preventing the electrical activity that appears to be necessary for consolidation to take place.

electroencephalogram (EEG)   A recording of the electrical activity in the brain, usually taken by placing electrodes on the scalp of the subject. (Also called electroencephalograph.)

enriched environment   An environment that contains many objects and events, which according to Hebb, stimulates the development of complex neural circuitry.

equipotentiality   The finding that the cortex functions as a whole and that if one part of the cortex is destroyed, any one of a number of cortical areas can take over its function.

fear   According to Hebb, the emotion experienced when there is an incompatibility between ongoing neural activity and the environmental events that accompany it.

Hebb rule   A learning rule in computer simulation referring to Hebb's idea that when two cells are active together, the connection between them is strengthened.

hippocampus   A brain structure within the limbic system thought to be involved in the conversion of short-term memory into long-term memory.

interneuron   A neuron-mediating activity between a sensory neuron and a motor neuron.

limbic system   A number of interrelated brain areas related to emotional experience.

long-term memory   Also called secondary memory; the memory of an experience that lasts for a considerable length of time after the experience. Whereas short-term memory is usually measured by seconds, long-term memory can be measured by years.

long-term potentiation (LTP)   A procedure whereby weak electrical stimulation of part of the hippocampus is made stronger or more effective. It occurs if the weak electrical stimulation is followed by a stronger, repetitive electrical pulse.

mass action   The finding that disruption of learning and memory is a function of the amount of cortical tissue destroyed.

neglect syndrome   The tendency for patients with damage to the right cerebral hemispheres to ignore or neglect the left side of their bodies or perceptual fields.

neural networks   Computer models used to study interrelationships among computer-simulated neurons.

neurons   Brain cells (or nerve cells).

neurotransmitter   A chemical messenger released from the end of an axon. (See also **axon.**)

optimal level of arousal   The level of brain activity that is most conducive to the performance of a certain task.

phase sequence   A sequence of temporarily related cell assemblies. Cell assemblies that consistently follow one another in time form a unit or a phase sequence.

punishment areas   Areas of the brain that when stimulated cause the organism to refrain from whatever behavior preceded their stimulation.

reinforcement centers in the brain   Areas of the brain that when stimulated cause the organism to repeat whatever behavior preceded their stimulation.

resting potential   The "ready" state of a neuron during which sodium ions are outside the cell and potassium ions are inside the cell. The inside of the cell is −70 millivolts in relation to the outside.

reticular activating system (RAS)   A structure located in the brain stem that appears to be responsible for regulating the electrical activity in the higher centers of the brain.

retrograde amnesia   The inability to remember the events that took place just prior to a traumatic experience, such as an automobile accident.

reverberating neural activity   A system of self-perpetuating neural activity that lasts for a few seconds after the source of stimulation has been removed. Reverberating neural activity is thought by some to be the basis of short-term memory.

sensory deprivation   The condition whereby an organism's sensory stimulation is drastically reduced.

serendipity   Finding one thing while looking for something else.

short-term memory   Also called immediate memory and primary memory; the memory of an experience that persists for only a short period of time after the experience.

spectrin   A protein that determines the shape of a dendrite receptor site. (See also **dendrite.**)

split-brain preparation   The arrangement whereby both the optic chiasm and the corpus callosum are severed, thereby causing the two halves of the cortex to function independently.

summation   The activity of single neurons is determined by the added or summed activity of the surrounding cells.

switchboard conception of the brain   The view that the brain acts only as a relay station between sensory events and responses.

synapse   The space between the axon of one neuron and the dendrites or cell body of another neuron. (See also **axon** and **dendrite.**)

threshold   The millivoltage difference between the inside and outside of a neuron at which the cell can no longer keep sodium ions outside the cell.

Chapter 16

IMPLICATIONS FOR EDUCATION

In this chapter we attempt to relate the major theories of learning covered in the preceding chapters to education. We begin by discussing ways to establish objectives and goals in education and then proceed to identify educational practices derived from the theories we have studied. The specification of the relationship between learning and education is easier for some theories than for others. Theorists such as Thorndike, Skinner, Guthrie, and the Gestalt theorists have written extensively about how their views on learning relate to teaching practices. For them, therefore, what follows is mainly a review of the material covered earlier in this text. Theorists like Pavlov and Hull, however, never made an effort to extend their theory to the realm of education. Tolman's theory of learning is especially difficult to relate to education since he postulated six different kinds of learning. In our treatment of his theory below, we emphasize only the kind of learning that he called "cognitive."

After discussing what each of the major theorists says, or seems to say, about education, we will turn to some of the more general differences between cognitive and behavioristic theories as they apply to the classroom.

EDUCATIONAL OBJECTIVES STATED IN BEHAVIORAL TERMS

Clearly, the best teaching technique is the one that allows teachers to meet their course objectives most effectively and efficiently. Any teaching method must be evaluated in terms of course objectives. That is, instructors must be able to determine whether or not, and to what extent, the objectives of their course have been met. In other words, performance on each course objective must be measurable, and unless the objectives manifest themselves in behavior, they cannot be measured. The course objectives should tell the students what the instructor hopes they will learn in the course, and the evaluative devices, such as examinations, should allow both the instructor and the student to determine to what extent the objectives have been met. In *Preparing Instructional Objectives* Mager (1961) puts the matter as follows:

Robert F. Mager. (Courtesy of R.F. Mager.)

Suppose I offered to teach your children to be logical thinkers for $1,000. Now, if I could do it, you would be getting a real bargain. But would you agree to such a bargain unless I told you beforehand more explicitly what I intended to accomplish and how we would measure my success? I hope not. In a sense, a teacher makes a contract with his students. The students agree to pay a certain sum in return for certain skills and knowledge. But most of the time, they are expected to pay for something that is never carefully defined or described. They are asked to buy (with effort) a product that they are not allowed to see and that is only vaguely described. The teacher, who does not describe to the best of his ability how he intends the learner to be different after his instruction, is certainly taking unfair advantage of his students. (p. 16a)

Preparing measurable educational objectives is difficult since educational goals have traditionally been stated in subjective terms. Mager (1972, p. vi) calls these subjective goals "Fuzzies" because "There is no way of telling when you have one." To "unfuzzify" an abstract concept or goal, Mager suggests a **goal analysis**, involving the following steps:

1. Write down the goal.
2. Jot down, in words or phrases, the performances that, if achieved, would cause you to agree the goal is achieved.
3. Sort out the jottings. Delete duplications and unwanted items. Repeat steps one and two for any unwanted abstractions (Fuzzies) considered important.
4. Write a complete statement for each performance, describing the nature, quality, or amount you will consider acceptable.
5. Test the statements with the question. If someone achieved or demonstrated each of these performances, would I be willing to say he has achieved the goal? When you can answer yes, the analysis is finished. (p. 72)

Elsewhere, Mager (1961, p. 11) offers a comparison between some words used in defining educational objectives that are easily translated into behavior and some that are not (that is, Fuzzies):

Words Open to Many Interpretations

To know	To grasp the significance of
To understand	To enjoy
To really understand	To believe
To appreciate	To have faith in
To fully appreciate	

Words Open to Fewer Interpretations

To write	To construct
To recite	To list
To identify	To compare
To differentiate	To contrast
To solve	

It should be noted that what applies to defining course objectives also applies to defining institutional objectives. For example, the extent to which institutional objectives—such as "to realize the interrelatedness of knowledge" or "to appreciate fully the impact of one's values on one's behavior"—have been met would be very difficult to determine.

Once they are clearly stated, measurable course objectives create a situation in which students may meet those objectives in a variety of ways. Some students may wish to take the class as a traditional lecture class. Other students, however, may meet the course objectives by independent reading, related employment or travel, interviewing certain individuals, or writing a research paper. Once course objectives are stated in measurable terms, it is possible to determine the extent to which anyone has met them. It should not matter where or how the necessary information was gathered. If students can demonstrate that they have met the course objectives, they can be given credit in the course.

Although a number of alternative educational formats are currently being explored, the structured course with scheduled lectures and examinations is still very popular among both instructors and students. As popular as the lecture format is, however, in some cases it may not be the most effective teaching technique.

APPLICATION OF SPECIFIC THEORIES OF LEARNING TO THE CLASSROOM

Thorndike

Thorndike would have an orderly classroom with the objectives clearly defined. These educational objectives must be within the learner's response capabilities, and they must be divided into manageable units so that the teacher can apply "a satisfying state of affairs" when the learner makes an appropriate response. Learning proceeds from the simple to the complex.

Motivation is relatively unimportant, except in determining what will constitute a "satisfying state of affairs" for the learner. The learner's behavior is determined primarily by external reinforcers and not by intrinsic motivation. Emphasis is on bringing about correct responses to certain stimuli. Incorrect responses are to be corrected rapidly so that they are not practiced. Therefore, examinations are important: They provide the learner and the teacher with feedback concerning the learning process. If students learn their lesson well, they are to be reinforced quickly. If students have learned something incorrectly, their mistakes must be corrected quickly; thus examinations must be taken regularly.

The learning situation must be made to resemble the real world as much as possible. As we have seen, Thorndike believed that learning will transfer from the classroom to the environment outside only insofar as the two situations are similar. Teaching children to solve difficult problems does not enhance their reasoning capacity. Therefore, teaching Latin, mathematics, or logic is only justified when students will be solving problems involving Latin, mathematics, or logic when they leave school. With his identical elements theory, Thorndike opposed the traditional **formal discipline** or "mental muscle" approach to explaining the transfer of language.

The Thorndikian teacher would use positive control in the classroom, since satisfiers strengthen connections but annoyers do not weaken them. The Thorndikian teacher would also avoid lecturing, preferring to deal with students on a one-to-one basis.

Guthrie

Like Thorndike, Guthrie would begin the educational process by stating objectives, that is, stating what responses are to be made to what stimuli. Then he would have the learning environment arranged so that the desired responses are elicited in the presence of the stimuli to which they are supposed to be attached.

Motivation was even less important for Guthrie than it was for Thorndike. All that is necessary for Guthrie is that the student respond appropriately in the presence of certain stimuli.

Practice is important in that it causes more and more stimuli to elicit desired behavior. Since each experience is unique, one must "relearn" things over and over again. Guthrie would say that learning to add two and two at the blackboard is no guarantee that students will add two and two at their seats. Students must not only learn that two red blocks plus two more equals four red blocks, but they must make new two-plus-two-equals-four associations with apples, dogs, books, and so on.

Although learning constantly takes place, classroom education is an attempt to associate purposefully certain stimuli and responses. Learning, however, can be easily interfered with outside the classroom if new responses are made in the presence of stimuli similar to the ones the student experienced in school. It is also possible that a student will learn to attach responses to the stimuli in the classroom and another set of responses to similar stimuli outside the classroom. For example, seeing an elderly person in school may tend to elicit "respectful" behavior, whereas an elderly person outside of school may elicit "disrespectful" behavior.

Like Thorndike, Guthrie believed that formal education should resemble real-life situations as much as possible. In other words, the Guthrian teacher would have students do in school what they are expected to do when they leave school.

Guthrian teachers may sometimes use a form of punishment in dealing with disruptive behavior, but they would realize that to be effective, punishment must be used as the disruptive behavior is occurring. Furthermore, the punishment must cause behavior that is incompatible with the disruptive behavior. If, for example, students are being too noisy and the punishment (such as yelling at them) causes them to become noisier, the punishment will strengthen the very behavior that the teacher is attempting to eliminate.

Hull

The major differences among Hull, Thorndike, and Guthrie concerns their emphasis on motivation. You will recall that Hull's was a drive reduction, or a drive-stimulus reduction, theory of learning. As for the issues of specifiability of objectives, orderliness of the classrooms, and proceeding from the simple to the complex, Hull would be in agreement with Thorndike and Guthrie. Learning for him, however, must involve a reducible drive. It is hard to imagine how the reduction of a primary drive can play a part in classroom learning; however, some of Hull's followers (e.g., Janet Taylor Spence) have emphasized anxiety as a drive in human learning. From this line of reasoning, it would follow that encouraging some anxiety in students that would subsequently be reduced by success would be a necessary condition for classroom learning. Too little anxiety would result in no learning (because there is no drive to be reduced) and too much anxiety would be disruptive. Therefore, students who are mildly anxious are in the best position to learn and are therefore easiest to teach.

Practice would be carefully distributed so that inhibition would not be built up. The Hullian teacher would intersperse the topics to be taught so that the learner would not build up fatigue that would interfere with learning. Likewise, topics would be arranged so that those that are maximally dissimilar would follow one another. For example, one reasonable sequence of subjects might be math, physical education, English, art, and history.

Miller and Dollard (1941) have summarized Hull's theory as it applies to education:

Drive:	The learner must want something.
Cue:	The learner must attend to something.
Response:	The learner must do something.
Reinforcement:	The learner's response must get him or her something he or she wants.

Spence's revision of Hull's theory suggested that students learn what they do. Thus, Spence was a contiguity theorist, as Guthrie was. For Spence, however, incentives were important since they motivated students to translate what had been learned into behavior. By relating incentives (reinforcers) to performance instead of to learning, Spence's position was close to the positions of Tolman and Bandura.

Skinner

Skinner, of course, had much in common with the theorists mentioned so far. For example, he would insist that the course objectives be completely specified before teaching begins. Further, he would insist that the objectives be defined *behaviorally*. If a unit is designed to teach creativity, he would ask, "What are students *doing* when they are being creative?" If a unit is designed to teach the understanding of history, he would ask, "What are students *doing* when they are understanding history?" If educational objectives cannot be specified behaviorally, instructors have no way of knowing whether or not they have accomplished what they had set out to do. Likewise, if objectives are specified in terms not easily transformed into behavioral terms, it is next to impossible to determine to what extent the course objectives have been met. We will have more to say about behavioral objectives later in this chapter.

The stimuli associated with certain responses were not as important for Skinner as they were for Thorndike, Guthrie, or Hull. Skinner was more interested in starting with the responses as they occur "naturally" or, if they do not occur naturally, *shaping* them into existence. As with most behaviorists, he would start with the simple and proceed to the complex. Complex behavior is thought to consist of simpler forms of behavior. Skinner's approach to presenting material to be learned is best exemplified by programmed learning, which we will discuss in a later section of this chapter.

As with Thorndike, motivation to Skinner was only important in determining what will act as a reinforcer for a given student. Secondary reinforcers are very important, too, since these are normally utilized in the classroom. Examples of secondary reinforcers include verbal praise, positive facial expressions, gold stars, feelings of success, points, grades, and the opportunity to work on what one wants to. Like

Thorndike and Hull, Skinner stressed the use of extrinsic reinforcers in education. In fact, for the Skinnerian teacher, the main function of education is to arrange reinforcement contingencies so that the behavior that has been deemed important is encouraged. Intrinsic reinforcement is thought to be of minimal importance.

It is also important for the Skinnerian teacher to move from a 100 percent reinforcement schedule to a partial reinforcement schedule. During the early stages of training, a correct response is reinforced each time it occurs. Later, however, it is only reinforced periodically, which, of course, makes the response more resistant to extinction.

All the S-R behaviorists would prescribe a learning environment that allows for individual differences in learning rate. They would either want to deal with students individually or provide a group of students with material that allows for individual self-pacing, such as teaching machines or specially constructed workbooks. The behaviorists would tend to avoid the lecture technique since there is no way of knowing when learning is taking place and therefore when to administer reinforcers. We will have more to say about both individualized courses and the lecture technique later in this chapter.

Skinnerian teachers would avoid the use of punishment. They would reinforce appropriate behavior and ignore inappropriate behavior. Since the learning environment would be designed so that students experienced maximal success, they would usually attend to the material to be learned. According to the Skinnerians, behavior problems in school are the result of poor educational planning, such as failing to provide self-pacing, failing to use reinforcers appropriately, offering the material in chunks too large to be easily comprehended, using discipline to control behavior, having rigid plans that all students must follow, or making unreasonable demands on students (such as not moving or not making noise).

In his article "The Shame of American Education," Skinner (1984), insisted that the greater use of programmed instruction, discussed below, would not only facilitate student learning but also increase respect for teachers:

> Success and progress are the very stuff on which programmed instruction feeds. They should also be the stuff that makes teaching worthwhile as a profession. Just as students must not only learn but know that they are learning, so teachers must not only teach but know that they are teaching. Burnout is usually regarded as the result of abusive treatment by students, but it can be as much the result of looking back upon a day in the classroom and wondering what one has accomplished. Along with a sense of satisfaction goes a place in the community. One proposed remedy for American education is to give teachers greater respect, but that is putting it the wrong way around. Let them teach twice as much in the same time and with the same effort, and they will be held in greater respect. (p. 952)

Gestalt Theory

The Gestalt-oriented teacher would stress meaningfulness and understanding. Parts must always be related to a whole so that they have meaning to the student. Historical names or dates will have little meaning unless they are related to current events or to something personally important to the student. An understanding of history is the important thing, and it is gained by studying individual events. But the under-standing of history is always greater than the sum of individual events.

As we have seen, the Gestaltists view unsolved problems as creating ambiguity or an organizational disbalance in the student's mind, a condition that is undesir-able. In fact, ambiguity is looked on as a negative state that persists until a problem is solved. Students confronted with a problem will either seek new information or rearrange old information until they gain insight into the solution. The solution is as satisfying to the problem solver as a hamburger is to a hungry person. In a sense, the reduction of ambiguity can be seen as the Gestalt equivalent to the behaviorist's notion of reinforcement. However, the reduction of ambiguity can be thought of as an intrinsic reinforcer, whereas the behaviorists usually stress external, or extrinsic, reinforcers.

Jerome Bruner (1966), while discussing curiosity as an innate human motive, comes close to what the Gestaltists refer to as a need to reduce ambiguity. Bruner says:

> Curiosity is almost a prototype of the intrinsic motive. Our attention is attracted to some-thing that is unclear, unfinished, or uncertain. We sustain our attention until the matter on hand becomes clear, finished, or certain. The achievement of clarity or merely the search for it is what satisfies. We would think it preposterous if somebody thought to reward us with praise or profit for having satisfied our curiosity. (p. 114)

John Holt (1967) makes a similar point in his book *How Children Learn*:

> What we want to know, we want to know for a reason. The reason is that there is a hole, a gap, an empty space in our understanding of things, our mental model of the world. We feel that gap like a hole in a tooth and want to fill it up. It makes us ask How? When? Why? While the gap is there, we are in tension, in suspense. Listen to the anxiety in a per-son's voice when he says, "This doesn't make sense!" When the gap in our understand-ing is filled, we feel pleasure, satisfaction, relief. Things make sense again—or at any rate, they make more sense than they did. When we learn this way, for these reasons, we learn both rapidly and permanently. The person who really needs to know some-thing, does not need to be told many times, drilled, tested. Once is enough. The new piece of knowledge fits into the gap ready for it, like a missing piece in a jigsaw puzzle. Once in place, it is held in, it can't fall out. (pp. 187–188)

Bruner and Holt share the Gestalt notion that learning is personally satisfying and that it need not be prodded by external reinforcement. Holt concludes his book with the following statement:

> Birds fly, fish swim; man thinks and learns. Therefore, we do not need to "motivate" children into learning, by wheedling, bribing, or bullying. We do not need to keep pick-ing away at their minds to make sure they are learning. What we need to do, is bring as much of the world as we can into the school and the classroom; give children as much help and guidance as they need and ask for; listen respectfully when they feel like talk-ing; and then get out of the way. We can trust them to do the rest. (p. 189)

The Gestalt-oriented classroom would be characterized by a give-and-take rela-tionship between students and teacher. The teacher would help students see rela-tionships and organize their experiences into meaningful patterns. Planning a Gestalt learning experience includes starting with something familiar and basing each step in the education process on those already taken. All aspects of the course are divided into meaningful units, and the units themselves must relate to an overall concept or experience. The Gestalt-oriented teacher might use the lecture technique but would insist that it allow for student-teacher interactions. Above all, rote memorization of facts or rules would be avoided. It is only when students grasp the principles involved in a learning experience that they truly understand them. When what is learned is understood instead of memorized, it can easily be applied to new situations and it is retained for a very long time.

Piaget

According to Piaget, educational experiences must be built around the learner's cognitive structure. Children of the same age and from the same culture tend to have similar cognitive structures, but it is entirely possible for them to have different cognitive structures and therefore require different kinds of learning material. On the one hand, educational material that cannot be assimilated into a child's cognitive structure cannot have any meaning to the child. If, on the other hand, the material can be completely assimilated, no learning will take place. For learning to occur, the material needs to be partially known and partially unknown. The part that is known will be assimilated, and the part that is unknown will necessitate a slight modification in the child's cognitive structure. Such modification is referred to as accommodation, which can be roughly equated with learning.

   Thus, for Piaget, optimal education involves mildly challenging experiences for the learner so that the dual processes of assimilation and accommodation can provide for intellectual growth. To create that kind of experience, the teacher must know the level of functioning of each student's cognitive structure. We find, then, that both Piaget (a representative of the cognitive paradigm) and most of the behaviorists have reached the same conclusion about education; namely, that it must be *individualized*. Piaget reached this conclusion by realizing that the ability to assimilate varies from child to child and that educational material must be tailored to each child's cognitive structure. The behaviorists reached the conclusion through their recognition that reinforcement must be contingent on appropriate behavior, and the proper dispensing of reinforcers requires a one-to-one relationship between the student and the teacher or between the student and programmed educational material.

Tolman

In many respects, Tolman and the Gestaltists agree about educational practices: Both would emphasize the importance of thinking and understanding. For Tolman, it would be important to have the student test hypotheses in a problem situation. On this matter, Tolman is in close agreement with Harlow's error factor theory, which states that learning is not so much a matter of building up correct responses or strategies as it is a matter of eliminating incorrect responses or strategies. Both Tolman and the Gestalt theorist would encourage small groups for classroom discussions. The important thing is for students to have the opportunity, individually or as part of a group, to test the adequacy of their ideas. Hypotheses or strategies effective in solving a problem are those that are maintained by the student. The teacher, then, acts as a consultant to assist students in clarifying and then confirming or disconfirming hypotheses.

Like the Gestalt theorist, Tolman would also suggest that the student be exposed to a topic from different viewpoints. This process would allow the student to develop a cognitive map, which could be utilized to answer questions about that particular topic and related topics.

Finally, like the Gestalt theorists, Tolman would say that extrinsic reinforcement is unnecessary for learning to take place. Learning, according to Tolman, occurs constantly. Students, like everyone else, are attempting to develop expectancies or beliefs that reliably conform to reality. The Tolmanian teacher aids students in formulating the testing hypotheses and provides confirming experiences when hypotheses are accurate. In this way students develop complex cognitive maps that guide their activities.

Popper

In Chapter 2 we encountered Karl Popper's influential views of science. In their book *Learning from Error: Karl Popper's Psychology of Learning*, Berkson and Wettersten (1984), have attempted to distill Popper's views of the learning process from his writings on the philosophy of science. We include Popper's views on learning here because they seem especially applicable to education.

Like Tolman, Harlow, and the Gestalt theorists, Popper saw learning as problem solving. As was mentioned in Chapter 2, he sees science as a means of effectively solving problems. For Popper, a problem exists when an observation is contrary to what was expected. This discrepancy between observation and expectancy stimulates efforts to correct expectancies so that they are compatible with the previously surprising observation. The newly formulated expectancies remain intact until observations are made that are incompatible with them, at which point they are revised again. This process of adjusting and readjusting one's expectations so that they agree with observation is an unending process. However, it is a process that, one hopes, makes expectancies and reality increasingly compatible. According to Popper, this process of adjusting one's expectations so that they agree with actual experience is motivated by an innate **cognitive hunger,** which refers to the fact that "we have been born with the task of developing a realistic set of expectations about the world" (Berkson & Wettersten, 1984, p. 16).

According to Popper, both scientific knowledge and personal knowledge grow in the same way and for the same reason. First, as we have seen, there is a problem (a discrepancy between what is observed and what is expected). Next, possible solutions to the problem are conjectured, and if possible, the proposed solutions are refuted. Solutions that survive serious attempts at *refutation* are retained until they, too, are contradicted by observation, at which point the process starts over. In the process of problem solving, Popper believed that conjectures should be bold and creative and attempts at refutation severe. Berkson and Wettersten (1984) summarize Popper's beliefs concerning how both scientific and personal knowledge grows and improves:

"Because we do in fact learn by conjectures and refutations in an effort to solve problems, the best way to make progress in the growth of knowledge is to focus on and articulate problems, to conjecture solutions boldly and imaginatively, and to assess the proposed solutions critically" (p. 27).

The implications of Popper's theory of learning for education seem clear. A problem is presented to the class, and students propose solutions to the problem. Each proposed solution is critically analyzed and those found ineffective are rejected. The process continues until the best possible solution is found. Problems could be scientific, sociological, ethical, philosophical, or even personal. The classroom atmosphere should be informal and relaxed enough to encourage bold conjecture, but at the same time, the participants should be encouraged to offer objective criticism when it is called for. "What is wrong with that proposed solution?" would be a recurring question. With appropriate adjustments for age levels, there is no reason why this classroom procedure could not be used from primary to graduate school. It is hoped that students involved in such exercises would be better able to articulate problems, be more creative in seeking solutions to problems, and be better able to distinguish between effective and ineffective solutions to problems.

Pavlov

Pavlovian principles are difficult to apply to classroom education, although they are no doubt operating all the time. In general, we can say that every time a neutral event is paired with a meaningful event, classical conditioning occurs; obviously, pairings of that kind take place all the time. When a cologne that was consistently worn by a favorite teacher is smelled later in life, it will tend to elicit favorable memories of school; learning math in a rigid authoritarian atmosphere may create a negative attitude toward math; being made to write something over and over again as a disciplinary action may create a negative attitude toward writing; having difficult subjects in the morning may create at least a mild dislike for mornings; and a likable, knowledgeable teacher may inspire certain students to consider a teaching career. The feelings of anxiety associated with failure in school may create an aversion to problem-solving situations outside of school. You will remember that the Garcia effect showed that strong aversions to a situation can develop if a negative experience is associated with that situation. Thus, animals that eat a certain food and become ill develop a strong aversion to that food. It is possible that if classroom experiences are negative enough, students may develop lifelong aversions to education. In addition, students with this negative attitude toward education may be the ones who attack either teachers or school property in order to vent their frustrations.

Although the influence of classical conditioning in the classroom is strong, it is usually incidental. The principles of classical conditioning, however, can be purposively utilized in an educational program, as they were in the case of Albert (see Chapter 7). When Pavlovian techniques are used to modify behavior, the situation appears to resemble brainwashing more than education. To find examples of Pavlovian principles used to modify attitudes, one needs only to observe television commercials carefully. The advertiser's procedure involves pairing a neutral object (the product) with something someone likes (e.g., wealth, health, youth, sex, or prestige). Gradually, the product will cause viewers to have the same feeling that they used to get only from the object or event it was paired with. Next, it is assumed that the viewer will feel successful because of smoking Brand X cigarettes, be sexier because of driving a certain kind of car, or be more youthful because of using a certain hair preparation.

Again, these "incidental" aspects of education are no doubt occurring all the time that a child is in school. The modification of attitudes and emotions involved in learning based on classical conditioning must be taken into consideration in designing any truly effective educational program.

Bandura

Bandura's theory has many implications for education. You may recall that Bandura believes that anything that can be learned by direct experience can also be learned from observation. Bandura also believes that models are most effective if they are seen as having respect, competence, high status, or power. Thus, in most cases, teachers can be highly influential models. Through careful planning of what is presented, teachers can teach not only routine information and skills but also problem-solving strategies, moral codes, performance standards, general rules and principles, and creativity. Teachers can model conduct, which is then internalized by students and thus becomes the standard for self-evaluation. For example, internalized standards become the basis for self-criticism or self-praise. When students act in accordance with their own standards, the experience is reinforcing. When the actions of students fall short of their standards, the experience is punishing. Thus, for Bandura, as for the Gestalt theorists and Tolman, intrinsic reinforcement is far more important than extrinsic reinforcement. In fact, says Bandura, extrinsic reinforcement can actually reduce a student's motivation to learn. Reaching a personal goal is also reinforcing, and thus teachers should help students formulate goals that are neither too easy nor too difficult to achieve. This formulation, of course, needs to be done individually for each student.

To say that students learn what they observe is an oversimplification since observational learning is governed by four variables that must be taken into consideration by the teacher. *Attentional processes* will determine what is observed by the student, and such processes will vary as a function of both maturation and the student's previous learning experiences. Even if something is attended to and learned, it must be retained if it is to be of any value; thus *retention processes* are important. According to Bandura, retention is largely determined by one's verbal ability. A teacher must, therefore, take the verbal ability of the students into consideration when planning a modeling experience. Even if something is attended to and retained, the student may not have the motor skills necessary to reproduce a skill after it has been learned. Thus, a teacher must be aware of a student's *behavioral production processes*. Lastly, even if students attend to and retain what has been observed and are capable of behaviorally producing their observations, they must have an incentive for doing so. Thus the teacher must be aware of *motivational processes*. At this point extrinsic reinforcement may be useful. For example, students may be willing to demonstrate what they have learned if they are offered points, stars, grades, or the admiration of the teacher. Note, however, that extrinsic reinforcement is being used to influence *performance* rather than learning.

We see then that observational learning has many educational implications, but to use it effectively in the classroom the teacher must take into consideration the attentional, retentional, motor, and motivational processes of each student. With these things in mind, films, television, lectures, slides, tapes, demonstrations, and displays can all be used to model effectively a wide variety of educational experiences.

Norman

In Chapter 15, we noted that Norman feels that most complex learning occurs by analogy. That is, new material is learned by relating it to material already known. Effective teaching, then, requires the teacher to know something about the student's cognitive structure or, using Norman's iceberg analogy, the submerged portion of the student's iceberg. Understanding the nature of a student's cognitive structure is not an easy matter, but Norman suggests that one important source for such understanding is the number of questions a student asks. Miyake and Norman (1979) tested the hypothesis that frequency of question asking in class is a function of the amount of knowledge that a student possesses as well as task complexity. To test their hypothesis, Miyake and Norman taught a class on computer programming. Half of the students were given pretraining on the material (trained) and half were not (novices). Also, half the students used a difficult training manual and half used an easy training manual. Thus, the four following groups participated in the experiment:

Pretraining   —   easy material
No pretraining   —   easy material
Pretraining   —   difficult material
No pretraining   —   difficult material

It was found that for easy material, students with no pretraining asked more questions than students with pretraining, and that for difficult material the students with pretraining asked more questions than students with no pretraining. Thus, the hypothesis was supported. The results were interpreted as indicating that for difficult material, untrained students did not know enough to formulate meaningful questions; that is, they did not have available an appropriate cognitive structure. Trained students did have such a structure and, therefore, were able to ask questions that allowed refining and expansion of their cognitive structure. With easy material, untrained students could use previous knowledge to at least partially understand the material and, therefore, formulate questions. The trained students knew the easy material so well that there was no need to ask questions. Thus, according to Miyake and Norman (1979), both knowing too little and knowing too much inhibits question asking. The highest frequency of question asking occurs when there is a reasonable match between a student's cognitive structure and the material being presented. On this matter, Norman and Piaget are in close agreement.

Hebb

For Hebb, there were two kinds of learning. The first involves the gradual buildup of cell assemblies and phase sequences during infancy and early childhood. This early learning results in the objects and events in the environment having neurological representation. When this neural development has taken place, the child can *think* of an object or event, or a series of objects and events, when it is not physically present. In a sense, copies of those environmental objects now exist in the child's nervous system. During this early learning it would be important for the child to experience an enriched environment, which consists of a wide variety of sights, sounds, textures, shapes, objects, and so on. The more complex the environment, the more there is to be represented on the neurological level. The more that is represented on the neural level, the more the child can think about. Thus, the Hebbian teacher dealing with young children would create an educational environment with great variety. According to Hebb, during early learning certain associationistic principles may be operating. Those that seem most important for the development of cell assemblies and phase sequences are the principles of contiguity and frequency. For example, if a series of environmental events occurs often enough, it becomes represented neurologically as a phase sequence. Reinforcement appears to have nothing to do with it.

The second kind of learning, according to Hebb, is explained more by Gestalt principles than by associationistic ones. Once cell assemblies and phase sequences have been developed early in life, subsequent learning typically involves their rearrangement. In other words, once the building blocks have been established, they can be rearranged in almost an infinite number of configurations. Later learning then is perceptual, rapid, and insightful. The job of the teacher dealing with older children is to help them see what they have already learned in new, creative ways.

Hebb also said that the physical characteristics of the learning environment are very important. For any given task and for any given student there is an optimal level of arousal that will allow for most efficient learning. Since arousal level is controlled primarily by external stimulation, the level of stimulation in the learning environment will determine, to a large extent, how much learning takes place. If there is there too much stimulation (e.g., commotion in the classroom), learning will be difficult. Likewise, if there is not enough stimulation (e.g., a deadly quiet classroom), learning will also be difficult. What is needed is an optimal level of stimulation for both the task and the student at hand.

Left-Brain, Right-Brain Learning

Some educators, unaware of important progress in the research, were misled by speculations made in the 1970s and 1980s. Many were influenced by Robert Ornstein (1978), for example, who believes that the Western world emphasizes the kind of intelligence associated with the left hemisphere and minimizes the kind associated with the right hemisphere. He says that because of the emphasis in our schools on left-brain functions

> Our intellectual training unduly emphasizes the analytic, with the result that we have learned to look at unconnected fragments instead of an entire solution. Perhaps when the history of the 20th century is written, it will be said that the overriding belief of its dom-

inant cultures was an entity referred to as The Facts. All questions seemed to be resolved by an appeal to them.

As a result of this preoccupation with isolated facts, it is not surprising that we face so many simultaneous problems whose solutions depend upon our ability to grasp the relationship of parts to wholes....

Split- and whole-brain studies have led to a new conception of human knowledge, consciousness, and intelligence. All knowledge cannot be expressed in words, yet our education is based almost exclusively on its written or spoken forms....Our schools offer an education for half our minds, and it is time to reinstate a balance. (pp. 82–83)

Similarly, Bogen (1977) believes that there are two kinds of intelligence based on hemispheric dominance, and students possess them to varying degrees. According to Bogen, frustration occurs when there is a mismatch between what a student is asked to learn and the kind of intelligence that he or she possesses:

When a child's talents lie in visual-spatial relations and he or she is being forced into a curriculum that emphasizes the verbal articulatory modes of solving a conceptual problem, this child will encounter enormous frustration and difficulty which may well result in hostility toward the teacher and, worse, toward the learning process itself. If the teacher were to be made aware that the child is specialized in visual-spatial skills and the same conceptual problem is introduced, both the discouragement and the subsequent hostility might be avoided if the child is allowed to use his special talents. Conversely, the child with high verbal skills may quite frequently be unable to visualize the spatial aspect of an assigned task; in this case also, far better results could be obtained if he is not forced into academic areas for which he is not naturally equipped. (pp. 94–95)

We learned in the last chapter that, except for individuals in whom the corpus callosum is severed, the left and right hemispheres do not learn or behave independently and that their differences are not well described by dichotomies. Thus while it is valid to criticize the content of a curriculum for its exclusive emphasis on the analytical or because it ignores special skills in different individuals, it is invalid to tie these criticisms to differences between the hemispheres. Because the normal brain functions as an interrelated whole, it is impossible to arrange an educational experience exclusively for one hemisphere. Levy (1985) makes this point: "Since the two hemispheres do not function independently, and since each hemisphere contributes its special capacities to all cognitive activities, it is quite impossible to educate one hemisphere at a time in a normal brain. The right hemisphere is educated as much as the left in a literature class, and the left hemisphere is educated as much as the right in music and painting classes." (p. 44)

GENERAL DIFFERENCES BETWEEN COGNITIVE AND BEHAVIORISTIC THEORIES

What Is Learned?

In describing what is learned, behaviorists use terms like S-R associations, habits, and contingencies. Cognitive theorists describe what is learned in terms of information, expectancies, schemata, principles, and insights.

What Is the Function of Reinforcement?

For most behaviorists, reinforcement is a necessary condition for learning. For them, it is reinforcement that causes S-R associations to form, contingencies to be learned, or the rate or probability of responding to change. In contrast, most cognitive theorists believe that learning occurs independently of reinforcement. For them, what reinforcement does is provide the organism with information that can act as an incentive to translate what has already been learned into behavior.

How Are Problems Solved?

Most behaviorists claim a problem is approached in accordance with its similarity to other problems individuals have experienced in the past. If the attempted solutions fail or if learners have never confronted such a problem, they resort to trial-and-error behavior until they hit on a solution. The cognitive theorist maintains that learners "think" about the problem until they gain an insight into its solution. The behaviorist would emphasize *behavioral* trial and error; the cognitivist would emphasize *cognitive,* or vicarious, trial and error, that is, thinking.

What Assumptions Are Made about the Learner?

Certainly what teachers believe to be the nature of the human mind will influence what they believe would be effective teaching practices. We have already seen two examples of this. The behaviorists, who tend to accept Aristotle's and Locke's position that the mind begins as a *tabula rasa* (blank slate), emphasize the importance of sensory experience in formulating the content of the mind. Teachers accepting this position would specify educational objectives in behavioral terms and then define the kinds of experiences that would bring about the desired behavior. Behavioristically oriented teachers would be more educational arrangers than anything else. Their most important task would be to arrange an environment that is responsive to the behaviors deemed important by the school; that is, they must create an environment that allows the student to be reinforced for behaving in accordance with various course objectives.

The cognitive theorists believe that the mind is not a blank slate at birth and that the mind is active, not passive. The mind is capable of weighing alternatives (thinking) and has the built-in need to reduce ambiguity and to make everything as simple as possible. Teachers accepting this Gestalt point of view are not mere arrangers of the learning environment; rather, they are active participants in the learner-teacher relationship. Teachers must help the students to see that facts and ideas are part of a larger concept. That the students are able to recite numerous facts without seeing their interrelationship is meaningless to such teachers. If one took an automobile completely apart and threw all the parts on a pile, it would not be what we ordinarily call an automobile, although all the parts would be there. *How* the parts are arranged is at least as important as *what* the parts are. As we have seen, the Gestalt point of view always emphasizes that the whole is different from the sum of its parts.

The cognitively oriented teacher's job consists of two duties: (1) to induce ambiguity and (2) to help the student clarify the ambiguity. The teacher induces ambiguity by introducing problems and then helps clarify the ambiguity by suggesting strategies for solving the problems. As stated earlier, classroom practices based on Gestalt principles would involve give and take between the teacher and the students. Unlike the behavioristically oriented teachers, Gestalt-oriented teachers would not strongly emphasize working with individual students, and they would be perfectly content to work with small groups. Self-pacing and small-step learning procedures may or may not be important to the Gestalt-oriented teacher; their suitability must be determined for each student. These teachers attempt to determine for each student the best strategy for learning; that is, they must know the conceptual basis from which each student is starting before they can help the student continue toward understanding the concept being taught. This, of course, is another reason why there must be close contact between the student and the teacher.

How Is the Transfer of Training Explained?

The behaviorist tends to accept Thorndike's identical elements theory of transfer: As the number of common elements in two situations goes up, the tendency to make similar responses in both situations goes up. According to the behaviorist, if you want to enhance transfer of training from classroom education to experiences outside the classroom, you are obliged to increase the similarity between the two situations. For example, if one purpose in teaching mathematics is to provide students with the information necessary for filling out tax forms, the behavioristically oriented teacher would have students work on tax forms.

The cognitive theorist would tend to emphasize the transfer of principles. Using the tax form example, the cognitively oriented teacher might claim that the learning of mathematical skills will transfer readily to filling out tax forms and grocery shopping, even if tax forms and shopping had not been experienced in the classroom, because the *principles* involved in both situations are believed to be the same.

The issue of transfer of training, clearly one of the most important problems in education, is still highly controversial. In fact, it appears that the notion of formal discipline, based on faculty psychology, is still alive and well in the American school system. For example, the prominence given to the teaching of mathematics in our schools seems to reflect the belief that studying mathematics creates a stronger "reasoning faculty," especially since most Americans require less than a fifth-grade level of proficiency in mathematics for the needs of their daily lives. For a discussion of the reappearance of formal discipline in American schools see Kolesnik (1958) or Symonds (1960).

PROGRAMMED LEARNING

Programmed learning is a technique that is much more likely to be used by a behavioristically oriented teacher than a cognitively oriented one. Programmed learning incorporates many of the principles of reinforcement theory, although the technique was not invented by a reinforcement theorist. It was originally developed by Sidney L. Pressey (1926, 1927), whose "testing machine" was effective, but it did not become popular. Thus, we have an example of Zeitgeist (spirit of the times). Although Pressey's idea was good, it was not appropriate to the spirit of the time in which he proposed it. It was left to Skinner to rediscover programmed learning and make it popular. Skinner's detailed account of the rationale behind programmed learning can be found in Chapter 5.

Skinner's approach to programming has been called *linear* and involves the following features derived from his theory of learning:

1. *Small steps.* Learners are exposed to small amounts of information and proceed from one **frame,** or one item of information, to the next in an orderly fashion. This is what is meant by a **linear program.**
2. *Overt responding.* **Overt responding** is required so that students' correct responses can be reinforced and their incorrect responses can be corrected.
3. *Immediate feedback.* Immediately after making responses, students are told whether or not they are correct. This **immediate feedback** acts as a reinforcer if the answers are correct and as a corrective measure if the answers are wrong.
4. *Self-pacing.* Students proceed through the program at their own pace.

Figure 16–1 provides an example of a Skinnerian linear program.

There are a number of variations of the linear program. For example, some provide students with the opportunity to skip information that they are already familiar with. This procedure usually involves giving students a pretest on a certain section of the program, and if they perform adequately they are instructed to advance to the next section.

Another kind of programming that allows for even more flexibility is the **branching program.** The branching program is much more complicated than the linear program since it attempts to *diagnose* the student's responses. The branching program usually involves a multiple-choice format. After students have been presented with a certain amount of information, they are given a multiple-choice question. If they answer correctly, they advance to the next body of information. If they answer incorrectly, they are directed to additional information, depending on the mistake that was made. For example, the program may say, "If you picked B as your answer, go back and review the material on page 24; if you picked D as your answer, repeat Section 3; if you chose A, you are correct; please proceed to the next section." Diagrams of various programming techniques are shown in Figure 16–2 (see p. 454).

The generalizations from reinforcement theory on which programmed learning is based can be summarized as follows:

1. Individuals must have feedback in order to learn. That is, they must have the opportunity to determine whether or not their actions or thoughts were correct. Ordinarily, reinforcement acts as feedback in a learning situation.

FIGURE 16–1 (facing page)   An example of a linear program in which all students cover the same information in the same order. (From *A Self-Directing Introduction to Psychological Experimentation,* 2nd Ed., p. 13, by B.R. Hergenhahn, 1974, Monterey, CA: Brooks/Cole.)

Programmed Instruction
Measures of Central Tendency and of Variability

1. A mass of data, by itself, would be of little use to a researcher unless he had certain procedures for describing or analyzing it.

2. Procedures used to analyze data are called *statistics*. One important function of statistics is to provide information concerning a distribution of individual datum, or *scores*.

3. Procedures used to "make sense" out of a large number of scores are called _____.

   statistics

4. The most common questions researchers ask about scores concern *measures of central tendency* and *measures of variability*.

5. Measures of central tendency provide information about the *typical* or *average score*.

6. Measures of variability provide information about how the scores are spread out—that is, how dispersed they are.

7. Measures of central tendency and measures of variability are both procedures used to "make sense" out of a distribution of scores. They are therefore both called _____.

   statistics

8. Measures of central tendency are used to find the _____ score.

   typical/average/ representative

9. In order to find information about the dispersion of scores we use measures of _____.

   variability

10. There is no one measure of central tendency; there are many. Which one is used depends on the situation. Three of the most commonly used are the *mode*, the *mean*, and the *median*.

11. The average score in a distribution is found by using a measure of _____.

    central tendency

12. The mode is merely the score that occurs most frequently in a distribution of scores.

13. The score occurring most frequently in a distribution is called the _____.

    mode

14. What is the mode of this distribution?

    20
    18
    18
    18   _____   *18*
    17
    17
    13
    12

15. Is 18 the *average* score of the above distribution? _____

    yes

16. Is 18 the *typical* score of the above distribution? _____

    yes

17. The *mean*, like the mode, is a measure of _____.

    central tendency

18. The mean is found by first adding up all the scores in the distribution and then dividing the sum by the number of scores in the distribution. This can be summarized as follows:

$$\frac{\Sigma X}{N}$$

    Where: Σ = add everything that follows

    X = a score in the distribution

    N = the total number of scores.

19. The mean is found by first adding up all the _____ in the _____ and then _____ the sum by the _____ of scores in the distribution.

    scores
    distribution
    dividing
    number

FIGURE 16–1

Linear Programming

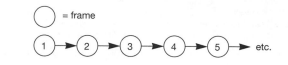

Modified Linear Programs

1. Linear program in which information can be skipped if it is too easy or already known:

2. Conversational chaining, in which the answer to a question asked in a previous frame is answered somewhere in the next frame:

Branching Program

With the branching program, the student's response is used more as a diagnostic tool than a learning device. Typically with this kind of program, students are instructed to move forward if they answer questions correctly. If they answer incorrectly, however, they are instructed to different parts of the program, *depending on what kind of mistakes they make.* Students may, for example, be instructed to repeat an entire section of the program, or they may be directed to other information that attempts to clarify their particular type of misunderstanding. In either case the students are again tested and thereafter proceed through the program in a manner dictated by their performances on the test.

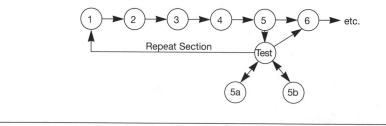

FIGURE 16–2   Diagrams of various programming techniques.

2. The more quickly a reinforcer follows a desired act, the greater is the likelihood that the act will be repeated. Absence or delay of reinforcement following an act reduces the likelihood that the act will be repeated.
3. The more often an act is reinforced, the more likely the act will be repeated.
4. Through the process of differential reinforcement and successive approximation, students' behavior can be shaped toward a desired goal.
5. Students' behavior can be developed into a complex pattern by first shaping the basic elements of the pattern and then combining the elements into a chainlike sequence.

Is Programmed Learning Effective?

Schramm (1964) reviewed 165 studies of programmed learning. Of the 36 studies that compared programmed instruction with the more traditional kinds of instruction, 17 found programmed instruction to be more effective, 18 found both kinds of instruction to be equally effective, and only 1 found traditional techniques to be more effective. Therefore, the answer seems to be that programmed learning *is* effective, at least in the areas where it has been tried.

The question of *why* it is effective is not so easily answered. At present, there is widespread disagreement concerning which aspect of programmed learning results in its effectiveness. For example, the Guthrians maintain that programming is effective because it ensures that an appropriate response terminates each frame. It is this event, and not the reinforcing of overt responses, as the Skinnerians would claim, that makes for effective learning (see, e.g., Lumsdaine, 1964). Controversy also exists over the importance of all other aspects of programmed learning, for instance, the nature and importance of knowledge of results, what constitutes a small step, and the importance of self-pacing. At this time it can be concluded that programmed learning is an effective teaching device, but the essential ingredients that make it effective are still a matter of speculation.

COMPUTER-ASSISTED INSTRUCTION

Programmed instructional material can be presented in book form, by a teaching machine (see Chapter 5), or by a computer. When a computer is used to present programmed or other kinds of instructional material, the process is called **computer-assisted instruction** (**CAI**). We will discuss several advantages CAI has over other ways of presenting instructional material.

Using CAI, student-computer interactions can be personalized by giving each student an identification number which when typed into the computer causes the computer to greet the individual student. For example, the computer can print or vocalize, "Good morning, Linda. You did a fine job yesterday. Let's see how you do today. Are you ready?"

The computer can present complex branching programs that, depending on a student's response, can provide the student with various kinds of corrective information or can send the student on to the next segment of the program. In this regard, some computers are programmed so that they are capable of carrying on a kind of dialogue with the student by providing various kinds of feedback. For example, if a student responds correctly to a question, the computer may print or vocalize, "That's correct. Good job! Please continue." If a student responds incorrectly, the computer may respond, "That is incorrect. Please press A, read the material carefully, and try again. Good luck!"

Not only can the computer be used to present instructional material, it can also evaluate how well that material has been learned. After a segment of a program has been completed, the computer can give an achievement test, grade it, and compare the score with the scores of others taking the program. Thus, the computer provides not only immediate feedback during the learning process, but also immediate results of achievement tests for both the students and the teacher. Depending on how students perform, the teacher can determine how well the instructional material is working and take whatever corrective measures that may be necessary. This step cannot be done as easily when a textbook and lectures are used to present the material and a midterm and final examination are used to evaluate student learning.

By providing immediate feedback, personal attention, exciting visual displays, and a gamelike atmosphere, CAI motivates students to learn in ways that traditional instruction may not. In fact, students are often so motivated by CAI that depriving them of their turn with the computer acts as a punishment, and giving them additional time with the computer acts as a reinforcer (Hess & Tenezakis, 1970).

There is considerable evidence that students learn more from CAI than from traditional instruction, and they do so in a shorter period of time. Linskie (1977), for example, reports that third-grade students learning math through CAI achieved much more than students taking traditional classes, and they did so with much greater enthusiasm:

> The students watched the clock to get down to the computer center on time. Once there, seated before the keyboard, the degree of concentration was almost unbelievable. No matter that the nine other students were typing away and that the nine other computers were typing back: nothing seemed to distract the students. The math period became almost like a daily relay race with students waiting impatiently for their own ten minutes with the machine. And there was no paper work to take home, no dirty smudges to displease the teacher, and no plague of broken pencils...At the end of the year, the third-graders using the computer-assisted instruction showed a gain of just under two years in achievement while the third-graders taught by conventional methods progressed just over one year. When the experiment was tried in other schools, similar results were achieved through grade six. (p. 210)

Although CAI has been widely used to present various kinds of linear and branching programs, it can do much more. Programs have been written that allow the implications of different kinds of political and sociological systems to be studied, simulate a variety of psychological experiments, perform chemistry experiments without the need to handle equipment or chemicals (Bunderson, 1967), and teach problem-solving skills to engineers (Brown & Burton, 1975). A brief review of recent literature found nearly 300 published reports of CAI between 1993 and 1995.

Indeed, CAI is becoming so sophisticated that there are many who believe that it can be used to teach anything that a good teacher is capable of teaching. It is claimed that even such topics as philosophy, religion, art appreciation, and creativity could be taught by CAI if instructional goals could be clearly specified. If we can get teachers to describe clearly what a student is doing when he or she is being creative or appreciating art, say CAI enthusiasts, we can write a program that will teach those behaviors.

Criticisms of Programmed Instruction and CAI   Many feel that these techniques do not exemplify "true" teaching because they minimize the role of the teacher. Critics say that these approaches create an instructional situation that is cold, mechanical, and dehumanizing. That is, the important, spontaneous interactions between teacher and students, and among students themselves, is absent from programmed learning or CAI. Some critics also say that the most important kind of educational material cannot be specified to the point where it can be programmed or arranged in segments. A related criticism concerns the usual demand on the part of those using programmed learning or CAI that course objectives be specified in behavioral terms. Many critics insist that the loftiest and most desirable educational objectives cannot be easily measured and perhaps never fully reached. For example, Meek (1977) maintains that because such courses must have course objectives that are clearly specified and measurable, they generally do not have very important objectives. Meek offers the following suggestions about what the goals of any kind of course should be:

> The primary goals of such courses should involve an attempt to develop the ability of the student to think critically, to sort, to order, to choose among, to evaluate, and to interrelate competing ideals and ideas. The student must learn how to learn, how to evaluate ideas and data, and how to relate information acquired to her or his own values and those that are present in the larger society."…It is basic nonsense to talk about the degree of "mastery" of such goals. (pp. 115–116)

In his now famous article, "Good-Bye Teacher," Fred Keller (1899–1996) described his individualized approach to education. Upon noting the superiority of this technique over the more traditional lecture technique, Keller (1968) concluded the following about the teacher of tomorrow:

> He becomes an educational engineer, a contingency manager, with the responsibility of serving the great majority, rather than the small minority, of young men and women who come to him for schooling in the area of his competence. The teacher of tomorrow will not, I think, continue to be satisfied with a 10 per cent efficiency (at best) which makes him an object of contempt by some, commiseration by others, indifference by many, and love by a few. No longer will he need to hold his position by the exercise of functions that neither transmit culture, dignify his status, nor encourage respect for learning in others. No longer will he need to live, like Ichabod Crane, in a world that increasingly begrudges providing him room and lodging for a doubtful service to its young. A new kind of teacher is in the making. To the old kind, I, for one, will be glad to say, "Good-Bye." (p. 89)

Keller's point, of course, is that instructors will need to become more concerned with how their students learn. The time is near when an instructor no longer will be able merely to dispense information and leave it up to the students to learn it. Tomorrow's instructor, whether cognitively or behavioristically oriented, will need to ponder various classroom formats to discover which one is optimally conducive to learning. The teacher will need to be converted from the traditional college professor to what Carl Rogers calls a "facilitator of learning" or what Keller calls either an "educational engineer" or a "contingency manager."

THE LECTURE AS A TEACHING TECHNIQUE

There are a number of instructors who, for one reason or another, question the effectiveness of the lecture as a teaching technique, and as we have seen, a number of learning theorists also have reservations about lecturing. One concern about lecturing is the fact that it typically moves along at a certain pace although there are vast individual differences among the students in terms of their ability to keep up and understand what is being presented. Another concern with the lecture is over its usefulness in teaching factual information. For example, Bugelski (1979, p. 379) reports a study in which 30 facts were presented to college students in a short lecture. After one presentation of the material the average number of facts remembered was only seven.

Obviously, one alternative to lecturing is simply to have students read the material they are to learn. Printed material can be read at the student's own pace, and if something is missed, the student can go back over the material as many times as necessary. The idea that reading may be a more efficient way of learning than attending a lecture is not new. Samuel Johnson had the following to say in 1766: "People have nowadays…got a strange opinion that everything should be taught by lectures. Now, I cannot see that lectures can do so much good as reading the books from which the lectures are taken" (Boswell, 1952, p. 144). And in 1781, he said, "Lectures were once useful; but now, when all can read, the books are so numerous, lectures are unnecessary. If your attention fails and you miss a part of a lecture, it is lost; you cannot go back as you do upon a book" (p. 471).

Even with the possible shortcomings of the lecture, there appears to be at least three conditions under which its use is clearly justified. First, it may be the best way to disseminate new ideas that are not yet available in print. Second, most of us enjoy listening to a prominent individual present his or her ideas to an audience. For example, the major addresses given by prominent psychologists at conventions are almost always well attended. Third, a good lecturer can instill interest in a topic because of his or her enthusiasm and manner of presentation. Thus, a good lecturer can sometimes motivate students to learn in a way that printed material cannot.

What about the situation in which a great person is not available; lectures are less than exciting; and the information lectured on is readily available in other forms, such as books, articles, handouts, films, tapes, and so on? Under these circumstances, many instructors seek an alternative to lecturing, and of course there are many. Some instructors restrict the size of their classes so that active discussion is possible. Some have students do independent study, which is then discussed either with the instructor alone or with a small group. Others use programmed material extensively.

DISCUSSION QUESTIONS

1. What would be the basic differences between behavioristically oriented teachers and cognitively oriented teachers in their approach to teaching?
2. Why, according to Skinner, do teachers get so little respect and what did Skinner say they could do to get more respect?
3. Summarize Popper's theory of learning and show how it might be applied in the classroom.
4. What, according to Norman, can the frequency with which questions are asked in the classroom tell the teacher about the students' cognitive structures?
5. Discuss what implications the findings from research on hemispheric functioning may have for educational practices.
6. Contrast the behaviorist's view of reinforcement with that of the cognitive theorist.
7. Why, according to Mager, is it important to avoid terms such as "to know," "to understand," "to appreciate," and "to grasp the significance of" while specifying course objectives?
8. Describe how, according to Mager, an abstract concept or goal can be "unfuzzified."
9. What is meant by the statement "Different assumptions about human nature suggest different approaches to education"? Give a few examples of how an assumption about human nature might affect one's approach to teaching.
10. Do you feel that it is important for teachers to be familiar with various theories of learning? Defend your answer.
11. What theory of transfer of training do you feel public school curriculum is based on? Do you see any remnants of formal discipline in American education? Explain.
12. Describe the advantages and disadvantages of programmed learning.
13. Discuss the advantages of CAI over other methods of presenting educational material. Also, describe any disadvantages you feel CAI has.
14. Discuss the pros and cons of lecturing as a teaching technique.
15. React to the statement "Either students meet the objectives of a course or they do not. If they do, they should be given credit for taking the course. If they do not, no credit should be given. In other words, students are either given credit or not, with no shades in between."

KEY TERMS

behaviorally defined objectives   Course, or institutional, objectives that are defined in terms of the behavior that is exhibited when a student meets a specified objective.

branching program   A type of programmed learning that directs learners to different parts of the program, depending on their performance at any particular point of the program. For example, if they make a serious mistake, they may be directed to repeat a previous section of the program.

cognitive hunger   Popper's term for the innate desire to revise expectancies continuously so that they are increasingly accurate in reflecting reality.

computer-assisted instruction (CAI)   The utilization of computers to present and evaluate a wide variety of educational materials.

formal discipline (also called mental discipline)   See Key Terms for Chapter 3.

frame   A term used in programmed learning to describe the small amount of information presented to the learner. In a linear program, the learner proceeds through the program frame by frame until a body of information is mastered.

goal analysis   A procedure that converts a subjective goal into examples of the kinds of behavior that will be engaged in when the goal is reached.

immediate feedback (also called immediate knowledge of results)   The arrangement whereby learners are informed about the accuracy of their answers immediately following a learning or testing experience.

linear program   A type of program that requires each student to go through the same sequence of information in the same order.

overt responding   A response that can be observed by others, as opposed to a covert response, which is not publicly observable.

programmed learning   See Key Terms for Chapter 5.

self-pacing   A procedure that allows students to determine their own pace(s) for studying and testing.

Chapter 17

A FINAL WORD

In Chapter 1, an effort was made to define learning and to differentiate it from other processes such as habituation, sensitization, and instinct. In Chapter 2, the characteristics of science were discussed as they apply to the study of learning. Chapter 3 outlined the historical antecedents of learning theory. Subsequent chapters provided detailed accounts of the major theories that grew out of this rich philosophical heritage. Each of the major theories was listed under one of four paradigms, depending on which historical theme it followed. The theories that were strongly influenced by Darwin were listed under the functionalistic paradigm. Those theories following in the tradition of Aristotle and Locke were listed under the associationistic paradigm. The theories following in the tradition of Plato, Descartes, Kant, and the faculty psychologists were listed under the cognitive paradigm. Hebb's theory was offered as an example of the neurophysiological paradigm, which also has its historical roots in the work of Descartes.

In this final chapter, we will discuss what the trends seem to be within current learning theory. Our discussion of current trends in no way implies that the information presented in the preceding chapters is obsolete. Almost everything occurring in learning theory today is, in some way, an extension of one of the major theories of learning presented in this book. To understand such an extension it is necessary to understand the theory from which it is derived.

Thus, we have explored learning theory's past and present. In this chapter, we will attempt to indicate where learning theory seems to be heading and ponder a few questions that it will need to address in the future.

CURRENT TRENDS IN LEARNING THEORY

At least four major trends can be seen in today's approach to the study of learning. First, today's learning theory is more humble in scope. Instead of attempting to explain all aspects of learning, today's theorist is content to investigate some aspect of the learning process. The theories of Estes in Chapter 9 offer examples of the reduced domain of contemporary learning theories.

Second, there is the increased emphasis on neurophysiological techniques. As we saw in Chapter 15, neurophysiological explanations of learning have come from a position of obscurity during the peak of the behavioristic movement to one of the most popular approaches to the study of learning today, as seen by the enthusiasm for neural networks and the new connectionism.

Third, cognitive processes such as concept formation, risk taking, and problem solving are again a respectable and popular topic of study. Cognitive processes, because of their apparent close relationship to introspection, were largely ignored during the dominance of behaviorism. It should be clear that in turning again to cognitive processes, psychology is broadening its base, but it is not becoming unscientific. Behaviorism was an extreme reaction to the method of introspection and was an attempt to make psychology a science by giving it a reliable, observable subject matter—behavior. There are those who maintain that behaviorism threw out the baby with the bathwater by defining behavior in such a way as to exclude "higher mental processes," such as concept formation and problem solving or thinking in general. Currently, these areas are of vital interest to psychologists and they are being explored scientifically. As with any other scientific research, the ultimate authority in research on cognitive processes is empirical observation. Theories are devised, hypotheses are generated, experiments are run, and as the result of their outcome, theories are strengthened or weakened. The method is the same as that of the traditional behaviorist; what has changed is the behavior that is being studied. Saltz (1971) says,

> After many years of very self-conscious empiricism, the psychology of human learning has begun to show signs of a vigorous interest in new (and often dramatic!) theoretical approaches. We find the postulations of multiple storage systems for memory; the distinction between learning systems and retrieval systems; the attempt to analyze "what is learned" into a complex system of interacting variables.
>
> Further, there is evidence to suggest that psychologists in the area of human learning may have lost some of their fear of studying complex processes. There has developed a lively new interest in such issues as the nature of concept acquisition; the role of strategies in learning; and the more general question of the nature and function of variables like intention, meaning, and imagery. In short, there is a new interest in the role of the *cognitive*, information-processing variables in human learning. (p. vii)

The trend toward cognitive theory by no means indicates that behaviorism is dead. Behaviorism remains a powerful force in psychology. Skinner (1974) said that true behaviorism has never really been tried. If it had, he maintained, it would be possible to solve many human problems. Skinner pleaded for the development of a technology of human behavior based on behavioristic notions. He claimed that older strategies for solving major human problems based on mentalistic or cognitive theories of behavior have been totally ineffective, and unless a more effective means of dealing with these problems is found, they will persist:

> I contend that behavioral science has not made a greater contribution just because it is not very behavioristic. It has recently been pointed out that an International Congress on Peace was composed of statesmen, political scientists, historians, economists, physicists, biologists—and not a single behaviorist in the strict sense. Evidently behaviorism was regarded as useless. But we must ask what the conference achieved. It was composed of specialists from many different fields, who probably spoke the commonsense lingua franca of the layman, with its heavy load of references to inner causation. What might the conference have achieved if it could have abandoned this false scent? The currency of mentalism in discussions of human affairs may explain why conferences on peace are held with such monotonous regularity year after year. (p. 250)

Skinner (1974) never waivered in his attack on cognitive psychology. At best, he said, cognitive psychology is simply old wine in new bottles: "Cognitive psychology is certainly in the ascendant. The word *cognitive* is sprinkled through the psychological literature like salt—and, like salt, not so much for any flavor of its own but to bring out the flavor of other things, things which a quarter of a century ago would have been called by other names" (p. 949).

At worst, cognitive psychology makes flagrant mistakes that retard our understanding of human behavior. Skinner (1987) listed the many mistakes he felt cognitive psychology was making in the form of accusations:

I *accuse* cognitive scientists of misusing the metaphor of storage. The brain is not an encyclopedia, library, or museum. People are changed by their experiences; they do not store copies of them as representations or rules.

I *accuse* cognitive scientists of speculating about internal processes which they have no appropriate means of observing. Cognitive science is premature neurology.

I *accuse* cognitive scientists of emasculating laboratory research by substituting descriptions of settings for the settings themselves and reports of intentions and expectations for action.

I *accuse* cognitive scientists of reviving a theory in which feelings and state of mind observed through introspection are taken as the causes of behavior rather than as collateral effects of the causes.

I *accuse* cognitive scientists, as I would accuse psychoanalysts, of claiming to explore the depths of human behavior, of inventing explanatory systems that are admired for a profundity more properly called inaccessibility.

I *accuse* cognitive scientists of speculation characteristic of metaphysics, literature, and daily intercourse, speculation perhaps suitable enough in such arenas but inimical to science.

Let us bring behaviorism back from the Devil's Island to which it was transported for a crime it never committed, and let psychology become once again a behavioral science. (p. 111)

Presently it appears that Skinner's brand of behaviorism is losing ground to cognitive psychology, but the battle is far from over.

Fourth, there is increased concern with the application of learning principles to the solution of practical problems. Recently, there have been many attempts to show how learning principles can be used to improve teaching and child-rearing. Learning is currently being emphasized in the explanation of personality development. Some of the more effective psychotherapeutic techniques of today are based on learning principles. Learning principles are being used as a basis for redesigning mental and penal institutions. Learning principles are currently being investigated in their relationship to warfare, international relations, legal and judicial procedures, and public health. Learning is being explored as a means of modifying national attitudes toward pollution and population control. And related to the last point, learning is being studied as a means of instituting cultural change in general. Also, as we saw in Chapter 14, Norman is calling for the development of a field called cognitive engineering, which would wed technology with the principles of cognitive science. Such a marriage, Norman believes, would reduce errors that result from human-machine interactions and also would increase productivity. No doubt the next decade will see an ever-growing concern with the application of learning principles to the solution of many human problems.

SOME UNANSWERED QUESTIONS ABOUT LEARNING

How Does Learning Vary as a Function of Maturation?

Many investigators (e.g., Piaget and Hebb) have found that the learning that occurs at one maturational stage is not the same as that which occurs at another maturational stage. Instead of thinking of learning as a unitary process that either occurs or not, we need to explore further how the learning process may change as a function of maturation. Indeed, such information will be vital in education and child-rearing.

Does Learning Depend on Reinforcement?

Many learning theorists would say that learning does depend on reinforcement, but their opinions would vary about the nature of reinforcement. Thorndike's concept of reinforcement was "a satisfying state of affairs." Pavlov equated reinforcement with an unconditioned stimulus. For Guthrie, it was anything that causes an abrupt change in stimulating conditions. For Skinner, it was anything that increases the rate of responding. For Hull, it is anything that causes drive stimulus reduction. For Tolman, it was the confirmation of an expectancy. The Gestaltists likened reinforcement to the reduction of ambiguity. For Bandura, intrinsic reinforcement is the feeling one has when one's performance matches or exceeds one's internalized standards or when a personal goal is attained. Also for Bandura, as for Tolman, Norman, and Spence, extrinsic reinforcers can be used to cause an organism to convert what had previously been learned into behavior. Thus for Bandura, Norman, Spence, and Tolman, extrinsic reinforcers influence performance, not learning. Although these definitions of reinforcement, in some cases, are substantially different, they all point out that some of our innumerable daily experiences "stick" and others do not. The process that causes some experiences to be retained can be loosely referred to as reinforcement. What, if anything, all these versions of reinforcement have in common has not yet been determined.

How Does Learning Vary as a Function of Species?

Bitterman (1960) observed that some species of animals cannot learn at all what others can learn with ease. Later, as we saw in Chapter 7, Seligman (1970) also found that whereas some species are biologically prepared to learn certain associations, other species are contraprepared to learn them. Observations such as these raise questions concerning the extent to which we can generalize what we learn about learning from one animal species to another. What, for example, can studying the learning process in the rat tell us about the learning process in humans? The problem of the generalizability of research findings in learning is currently receiving wide attention.

Can Some Associations Be Learned More Easily Than Others?

Not only does preparedness apply to differential learning among species, it also applies to differential learning within a particular species. Thus the preparedness continuum is both an inter- and an intraspecies variable. As evidence for the latter, Seligman (1970) offered the work of Garcia and his colleagues, who found within a species (e.g., coyote) that taste aversions are formed rapidly (sometimes in just one trial) and last for a very long period of time. Furthermore, Garcia and his colleagues found that other associations that were less natural were difficult to form, suggesting that those associations that are directly related to an organism's survival are easiest for the organism to form. Thus, we have another example of how an organism's genetic endowment interacts with the learning process. Which associations are easiest to learn for various species and why some are easier to learn than others are questions that are currently receiving considerable attention.

How Does Learned Behavior Interact with Instinctive Behavior?

We noted in Chapter 5 that the Brelands (1961) observed that animals that were conditioned to perform various tricks, such as placing coins in a bank, would eventually revert to behaviors that they would normally engage in under the circumstances. For example, raccoons that were reinforced with food for dropping coins in a bank eventually refused to give up the coins. Instead they would hold the coins and rub them together. In other words, they treated the coins as if they were food. This phenomenon was referred to as instinctual drift because it seemed that the organism's learned behavior gradually gave way to its instinctive behavior. Such observations have led many psychologists to conclude that an organism's innate response tendencies may place limits on the extent to which its behavior can be modified through learning. The extent of these limits and whether such limits exist on the human level remain unanswered questions.

How Does Learning Vary as a Function of Personality Characteristics?

After operationally defining such traits as introversion or extroversion by using existing paper-and-pencil tests, is it possible that learning ability may be found to differ as a function of such traits? Research has shown, for example, that high-anxious subjects are conditioned more rapidly than low-anxious subjects (Taylor, 1951). In Taylor's research, high- and low-anxious subjects were distinguished by using the Taylor Manifest Anxiety Scale. How many other personality traits can be operationally defined and found to interact with learning rate? The answer to this question will be especially important in education. Since personality is currently thought of as the product of early learning, the question here is really how learning early in life affects later learning, or how the development of a cluster of strong habits influences the development of subsequent habits.

To What Extent Is Learning a Function of the Total Environment?

How does what children learn in school relate to what they learn from their parents, from television, from books, from toys and games, or from their peers? What happens when teachers encourage behavior that is not supported by anyone else in the children's lives? What happens if parents are encouraging certain behavior patterns in their children, but their peer groups encourage other, and perhaps incompatible, forms of behavior? Of concern here is how the many learning experiences a person has in a short period of time are related to one another.

How Do All of the Preceding Questions Interact with Type of Learning?

The term *interaction* is one of the most important terms in science. In general, two variables are said to interact when the effect of one variable is different at different levels of the second variable. Aspirin, for example, has different effects on people, depending on whether or not they consumed alcohol before taking it. Aspirin and alcohol, then, are said to interact. Lack of sleep may have no effect on weight lifting, but it may have a deleterious effect on typewriting. In this case, the effects of sleep loss on performance are said to interact with task complexity. That is, at one level of task complexity—weight lifting—loss of sleep has little or no effect, whereas at another—typing—it has a considerable effect.

Assuming that there is more than one kind of learning, it is possible that motivation (e.g., drive) may be important for one kind of learning but not for another. Drive may be important for instrumental conditioning but not for what Tolman called sign learning. It may be that the laws of classical and instrumental conditioning are the same for all species of animals, but other forms of learning are found only in animals high on the phylogenetic scale. It could be that some learning occurs in an all-or-none fashion, whereas other kinds of learning may be incremental. It may be that personality type also interacts with type of learning. For example, there may be a difference in learning rate between high- and low-anxious subjects in a classical conditioning situation but not in a problem-solving situation. A crisscross interaction is even possible in some cases. For example, high- and low-anxious subjects may perform in an opposite manner when the type of learning required of them is changed. This theoretical possibility is shown in Figure 17–1.

Obviously, it is possible that mediational processes are very important for concept formation and problem solving but may not be at all important for classical or operant conditioning. Thus, Thorndike's contention that learning is direct and inde-

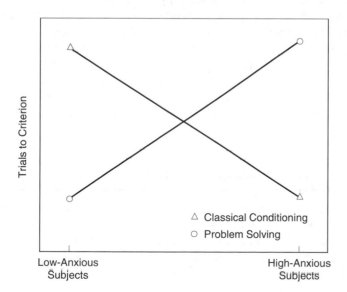

FIGURE 17–1 A theoretical interaction showing how anxiety level has a different effect on learning rate, depending on what kind of learning is involved. In this case, low-anxious subjects learn to solve a problem much faster than high-anxious subjects. When classical conditioning is examined, however, it is seen that low-anxious subjects take much longer to condition than high-anxious subjects.

pendent of mediational processes would be true of only some kinds of learning. Likewise, the Gestalt contention that learning involves the conscious reduction of ambiguity would also be only partially true. Whether or not "thinking" is important may depend entirely on what kind of learning one is talking about.

Also, it could turn out that everyone's notion of reinforcement is correct. Classical conditioning could, indeed, depend on the presentation of an unconditioned stimulus. Instrumental conditioning may depend on drive stimulus reduction, as described by Hull, or on a "satisfying state of affairs," as described by Thorndike. Other kinds of learning may be more conveniently explained by using the concept of reinforcement suggested by Guthrie, Skinner, Premack, Tolman, or the Gestaltists. The belief that there are a number of different kinds of learning, rather than one or two, makes all these positions plausible. This, of course, is the approach that Tolman (1949) was suggesting in his article "There Is More Than One Kind of Learning" and more recently, Gagné (1970).

As we have seen, learned behavior appears to interact with instinctive behavior. It is possible that when certain lower animals are in certain situations in which instinctive behavior is appropriate, learned behavior cannot compete. This may be true for only certain organisms and certain situations. Furthermore, it may not be at all true at the human level. Also, we have seen that for certain organisms, learning principles can be used to form some associations readily, but other associations are formed with great difficulty. Thus, we see that genetic endowment, the nature of the learning task, and learning principles all seem to interact in a complex way.

It seems that as more is known about any area, it is easier to make finer distinctions within it. As more is known about the area of learning, it becomes more differentiated. The area of learning has become very heterogeneous, compared to the rather undifferentiated field it was not too many years ago. Like most subjects that we come to know more about, learning has become more complicated instead of less complicated. As it stands today, the field of learning can justify a number of different approaches to its study and a variety of explanations of its facts. As each of the new subdivisions of learning is studied more extensively, we will see more spinoffs from the general field of learning into separate autonomous fields, such as the neurophysiology of learning, cognitive learning, and mathematical models of learning. As these areas themselves become more differentiated, we will begin to see spinoffs from them, for example, Markov models of learning, learning and the single cell, and the effects of early experience on learning. And on it goes. One can see this process of differentiation in the evolution of any science.

NO FINAL ANSWERS ABOUT THE LEARNING PROCESS

There are no final answers concerning the nature of the learning process in this book. But that fact should not bother the student since in science there are never any final answers. In science, knowledge evolves and evolution depends on variety. Clearly, most of what is now known about learning came out of the great debates among learning theorists that took place in the 1930s and 1940s. Healthy criticism and defense of one's position seem to provide an atmosphere conducive to the growth of a young science. Fortunately, such an atmosphere still exists in psychology, but the debate among theorists is not as intense as it once was.

Where does this leave the student who is interested in learning about learning? Students have a smorgasbord of approaches to the study of learning before them. They can either choose the one that best satisfies their appetite and concentrate exclusively on it or sample from all of them. While building a house, sometimes a hammer is the most effective tool, sometimes a screwdriver, and at still other times a saw. The student who decides to sample from the smorgasbord is like the house builder who selects different tools as different problems emerge. A third approach may result if a student cannot develop an appetite for any of the theories developed thus far. Such a student may someday develop his or her own theory. After all, this is what Thorndike, Pavlov, Skinner, Hull, Guthrie, Piaget, Tolman, Bandura, Norman, Hebb, and the Gestalt psychologists did. At this stage of knowledge concerning the nature of learning, all three approaches are necessary.

In the determination of humans' behavior, there is no process more important than learning, and if that be so, one of the most worthwhile enterprises a person could engage in is to help unravel the mysteries of that process.

DISCUSSION QUESTIONS

1. Define the term *interaction*. Give a few examples of interactions not described in this chapter.
2. Discuss four major trends in learning theory today.
3. Summarize Skinner's opposition to cognitive psychology.
4. What is meant by the statement "The field of learning is becoming increasingly differentiated"?
5. List and briefly discuss the unanswered questions about learning.
6. Why, in your opinion, are there no final answers in science? Relate your answers to the study of the learning process.
7. In outline form, respond to the question "What is the nature of the learning process?"
8. Write what you feel is an acceptable definition of learning.

REFERENCES

ADER, R. (1974) Letter to the editor. *Psychosomatic Medicine, 36,* 183–184.

ADER, R. & COHEN, N. (1975). Behaviorally conditioned immunosuppression. *Psychosomatic Medicine, 35,* 333–340.

ADER, R. & COHEN, N. (1993) Immunomodulation by conditioning: Recent developments. *International Journal of Neuroscience, 71,* 231–249.

ALLPORT, G. W. (1961). *Pattern and growth in personality.* New York: Holt, Rinehart & Winston.

AMSEL, A. (1958). The role of frustrative nonreward in noncontinuous reward situations. *Psychological Bulletin, 55,* 102–119.

AMSEL, A. (1962). Frustrative nonreward in partial reinforcement and discrimination learning: Some recent history and a theoretical extension. *Psychological Review, 69,* 306–328.

AMSEL, A., & ROUSSEL, J. (1952). Motivational properties of frustration: I. Effect on a running response of the addition of frustration to the motivational complex. *Journal of Experimental Psychology, 43,* 363–368.

ANDERSON, B. F. (1971). *The psychology experiment.* Belmont, CA: Brooks/Cole.

ANDRESEN, G.V., BIRCH, L.L. & JOHNSON, P.A. (1990) The scapegoat effect on food aversions after chemotherapy. *Cancer, 66,* 1649–1653.

ANDRYKOWSKI, M.A, & REDD, W.H. (1987). Longitudinal analysis of the development of anticipatory nausea. *Journal of Consulting and Clinical Psychology, 55,* 36–41.

ANDRYKOWSKI, M.A., REDD, W.H., & HATFIELD,A. (1985). The development of anticipatory nausea: A prospective analysis. *Journal of Consulting and Clinical Psychology, 53,* 447–454.

ANOKLIN, P. K. (1968). Ivan P. Pavlov and psychology. In B. B. Wolman (Ed.), *Historical roots of contemporary psychology* (pp. 131–159). New York: Harper & Row.

ASHBY, W. R. (1952). *Design for a brain.* New York: Wiley.

ATHEY, I. J., & RUBADEAU, D. O. (EDS.). (1970). *Educational implications of Piaget's theory.* Waltham, MA: Ginn-Blaisdell.

ATKINSON, R.C., & ESTES, W.K. (1963). Stimulus sampling theory. In R.D. Luce, R.R. Bush, & E. Galanter (Eds.), *Handbook of Mathematical Psychology, 2,* (pp. 121–268). New York: Wiley.

BABKIN, B. P. (1949). *Pavlov: A biography.* Chicago: University of Chicago Press.

BADING, H. GINTY, D.D., & GREENBERG, M.E. (1993). Regulation of gene expression in hippocampal neurons by distinct calcium signaling pathways. *Science, 260,* 181–186.

BAILLARGEON, R. (1987). Object permanence in 3 ½ and 4 ½ month-old infants. *Developmental Psychology, 23,* 655–664.

BAILLARGEON, R. (1992). The object concept revisited. In *Visual perception and cognition in infancy: Carnegie-Mellon Symposium on Cognition, 23.* Hillsdale, NJ: Erlbaum.

BAKER, A. G., & MACKINTOSH, N. J. (1977). Excitatory and inhibitory conditioning following uncorrelated presentations of CS and US. *Animal Learning and Behavior, 5,* 315–319.

BANDURA, A. (1965). Influence of a model's reinforcement contingencies on the acquisition of imitative responses. *Journal of Personality and Social Psychology, 11,* 589–595.

BANDURA, A. (1973). *Aggression: A social learning analysis.* Englewood Cliffs, NJ: Prentice Hall.

BANDURA, A. (1977). *Social learning theory.* Englewood Cliffs, NJ: Prentice Hall.

BANDURA, A. (1980a). The self and mechanisms of agency. In J. Suls (Ed.), *Social psychological perspectives on the self.* Hillsdale, NJ: Erlbaum.

BANDURA, A. (1980b). Self-referent thought: The development of self-efficacy. In J. Flavell & L. D. Ross (Eds.), *Cognitive social development: Frontiers and possible futures.* New York: Cambridge University Press.

BANDURA, A. (1983). Temporal dynamics and decomposition of reciprocal determinism: A reply to Phillips and Orton. *Psychological Review, 90,* 166–170.

BANDURA, A. (1986). *Social foundations of thought and action: A social cognitive theory.* Englewood Cliffs, NJ: Prentice Hall.

BANDURA, A., BLANCHARD, E. B., & RITTER, B. J. (1969). Relative efficacy of modeling therapeutic changes for inducing behavioral, attitudinal and affective changes. *Journal of Personality and Social Psychology, 13,* 173–199.

BANDURA, A., GRUSEC, J. E., & MENLOVE, F. L. (1967). Vicarious extinction of avoidance behavior. *Journal of Personality and Social Behavior, 5,* 16–23.

BANDURA, A., & KUPERS, C. J. (1964). The transmission of patterns of self-reinforcement through modeling. *Journal of Abnormal and Social Psychology, 69,* 1–9.

BANDURA, A., & MENLOVE, F. L. (1968). Factors determining vicarious extinction of avoidance behavior through symbolic modeling. *Journal of Personality and Social Psychology, 8,* 99–108.

BAUDRY, M., & LYNCH, G. (1993). Long-term potentiation: Biochemical mechanisms. In M.Baudry, R.F. Thompson, & J.L. Davis (Eds.) *Synaptic Plasticity* (pp. 87– 115). Cambridge, MA: MIT Press.

BEACH, F. A. (1987). Donald Olding Hebb (1904–1985). *American Psychologist, 42,* 186–187.

BEANBLOSSON, R.E. & LEHRER, K. (1983). *Thomas Reid's inquiry and essays.* Indianapolis, IN: Hackett.

BEARD, R. M. (1969). *An outline of Piaget's developmental psychology for students and teachers.* New York: Mentor.

BEATON, A. (1985). *Left side, right side: A review of laterality research.* New Haven, CT: Yale University Press.

BECHTEL, W., & ABRAHAMSEN, A. (1991). *Connectionism and the mind.* Cambridge, MA: Basil Blackwell.

BENNETT, E. L., DIAMOND, M. C., KRECH, D., & ROSENZWEIG, M. R. (1964). Chemical and anatomical plasticity of brain. *Science, 146,* 610–619.

BERKSON, W., & WETTERSTEN, J, (1984). *Learning from error: Karl Popper's psychology of learning.* LaSalle, IL: Open Court.

BERNSTEIN, I.L. (1978). Learned taste aversions in children receiving chemotherapy. *Science, 200,* 1302–1303.

BEST, M. R. & GEMBERLING, G. A. (1977). Role of short-term processes in the conditioned stimulus preexposure effect and the delay of reinforcement gradient in long-delay taste-aversion learning. *Journal of Experimental Psychology: Animal Behavior Processes, 3,* 253–263.

BIJOU, S. W., & BAER, D. M. (1961). *Child development, Vol. 1. A systematic and empirical theory.* Englewood Cliffs, NJ: Prentice Hall.

BIJOU, S. W., & BAER, D. M. (1965). *Child development, Vol. 2. The universal stage of infancy.* Englewood Cliffs, NJ: Prentice Hall.

BITTERMAN, M. E. (1960). Toward a comparative psychology of learning. *American Psychologist, 15,* 704–712.

BLANCHARD, E.B., KIM, M., HERMANN, C., & STEFFEK, B.D. (1994). The role of perception of success in the thermal biofeedback treatment of vascular headache. *Headache Quarterly, 5,* 231–236.

BLISS, T. V. P., & LØMO, T. (1973). Long lasting potentiation of synaptic transmission in the dentate area of the anaesthetized rabbit following stimulation of the perforant path. *Journal of Physiology, 232,* 331–356.

BOGEN, J. E. (1977). In M. C. Wittrock (Ed.), *The human brain.* Englewood Cliffs, NJ: Prentice Hall.

BOLLES, R. C. (1970). Species-specific defense reactions and avoidance learning. *Psychological Review, 77,* 32–48.

BOLLES, R. C. (1972). Reinforcement, expectancy, and learning. *Psychological Review, 79,* 394–409.

BOLLES, R. C. (1975). *Theory of motivation* (2nd ed.). New York: Harper & Row.

BOLLES, R. C. (1979). *Learning theory* (2nd ed.). New York: Holt, Rinehart & Winston.

BOSWELL, J. (1952). *Life of Samual Johnson LL.D.* Chicago: Encyclopedia Britannica.

BOUTON, M.E. (1984). Differential control by contact in the inflation and reinstatement paradigms. *Journal of Experimental Psychology: Animal Behavior Processes, 10,* 56–74.

BOUTON, M.E. (1988). Context and ambiguity in the extinction of emotional learning: Implications for exposure therapy. *Behaviour Research and Therapy, 26,* 137–149.

BOUTON, M.E. (1991). Context and retrieval in extinction and in other examples of interference in simple associative learning. In L Dachowski & C.F.Flaherty(Eds.), *Current topics in animal learning: Brain emotion and cognition* (pp. 25–53). Hillsdale, NJ: Erlbaum.

BOUTON, M.E. (1993). Context, time, and memory retrieval in the interference paradigms of Pavlovian learning. *Psychological Bulletin, 114,* 80–99.

BOUTON, M.E. (1994). Context, ambiguity and classical conditioning. *Current Directions in Psychological Science,3,* 49–52.

BOUTON, M.E. & BOLLES, R.C. (1979a). Contextual control of the extinction of conditioned fear. *Learning and Motivation, 10,* 445–466.

BOUTON, M.E. & BOLLES, R.C. (1979b). Role of conditioned contextual stimuli in reinstatement of extinguished fear. *Journal of Experimental Psychology: Animal Behavior Processes, 5,* 368–378.

BOUTON, M.E. & KING, D.A. (1983). Contextual control of the extinction of conditioned fear:Tests for the associative value of the context. *Journal of Experimental Psychology: Animal Behavior Processes, 9,* 248–265.

BOUTON, M.E. & KING, D.A. (1986). Effect of context on performance to conditioned stimuli with mixed histories of reinforcement and nonreinforcement. *Journal of Experimental Psychology: Animal Behavior Processes, 12,* 4–15.

BOUTON, M.E. & PECK, C.A. (1989). Context effects on conditioning, extinction, and reinstatement in an appetitive conditioning preparation. *Animal Learning & Behavior, 17,* 188–198.

BOWER, G. H. (1962). The influence of graded reductions in reward and prior frustrating events upon the magnitude of the frustration effect. *Journal of Comparative and Physiological Psychology, 55,* 582–587.

BOWER, G.H. (1994). A turning point in mathematical learning theory. *Psychological Review, 101,* 290–300.

BOWER, G. H., & HILGARD, E. R. (1981). *Theories of learning* (5th ed.). Englewood Cliffs, NJ: Prentice Hall.

BOWERS, T.G.R. (1989). *The rational infant: Learning in infancy.* New York: Freeman.

BREGMAN, E. O. (1934). An attempt to modify the emotional attitudes of infants by the conditioned response technique. *Journal of Genetic Psychology, 45,* 169–198.

BRELAND, K. & BRELAND, M. (1961). The misbehavior of organisms. *American Psychologist, 16,* 681–684.

BROOKS, D.C. & BOUTON, M.E. (1993). A retrieval cue for extinction attenuates spontaneous recovery. *Journal of Experimental Psychology: Animal Behavior Processes, 19,* 77–89.

BROWN, J. S., & BURTON, R. (1975). Multiple representations of knowledge for tutorial reasoning. In D. G. Bobrow & A. Collins (Eds.), *Representation and understanding: Studies in cognitive science.* New York: Academic Press.

BROWN, P. L., & JENKINS, H. M. (1968). Auto-shaping of the pigeon's key-peck. *Journal of the Experimental Analysis of Behavior, 11,* 1–8.

BROWN, R. (1965). *Social psychology.* New York: Free Press.

BRUNER, J. S. (1966). *Toward a theory of instruction.* Cambridge, MA: Harvard University Press.

BUGELSKI, B. R. (1979). *Principles of learning and memory.* New York: Praeger.

BUNDERSON, V. (1967). The role of computer-assisted instruction in university education. *Progress Report to the Coordination Board of the Texas College and University System.* Austin: University of Texas Press.

CARLSON, J. G. (1980). Guthrie's theory of learning. In G. M. Gazda & R. J. Corsini (Eds.), *Theories of learning: A comparative approach.* Itasca, IL: Peacock.

CASTELLUCCI, V. F., & KANDEL, E. R. (1974). A quantal analysis of the synaptic depression surrounding habituation of the gill withdrawal reflex in *Aplysia. Proceedings of the national academy of sciences, U.S.A., 71,* 5004–5008.

CHANCE, P. (1984, September). The revolutionary gentleman. *Psychology Today,* pp. 44–48.

CHOMSKY, N. (1959). [Review of *Verbal Behavior* by B. F. Skinner]. *Language, 35,* 26–58.

CLARK, A. (1990). Connectionism, competence, and explanation. In M.A. Boden (Ed.), *The Philosophy of Artificial Intelligence,* (pp. 281–308). New York: Oxford University Press.

CLEARY, L. J., HAMMER, M., & BYRNE, J. H. (1989). Insights into the cellular mechanisms of short-term sensitization in *Aplysia.* In T. J. Carew & D. B. Kelley (Eds.), *Perspectives in neural systems and behavior.* New York: Alan R. Liss.

COTMAN, C.W., MONAGHAN, D.T., & GANONG, A.H. (1988). Excitatory amino acid neurotransmission: NMDA receptors and Hebb-type synaptic transmission. *Annual Reviews of Neuroscience, 11,* 61–80.

CRAIGHEAD, W. E., KAZDIN, A. E., & MAHONEY, M. J. (1976). *Behavior modification: Principles, issues, and applications.* Boston: Houghton Mifflin.

CRESPI, L. (1942). Quantitative variation of incentive and performance in the white rat. *American Journal of Psychology, 55,* 467–517.

CRESPI, L. (1944). Amount of reinforcement and level of performance. *Psychological Review, 51,* 341–357.

CRONIN-GOLOMB, A. (1995). Semantic networks in the divided cerebral hemispheres. *Psychological Science, 6,* 212–218.

CURRY, F. K. W. (1967). A comparison of left-handed and right-handed subjects on verbal and non-verbal dichotic listening tasks. *Cortex, 3,* 343–352.

DALE, N., SCHACHER, S., & KANDEL, E. R. (1988). Long term facilitation in *Aplysia* involves increase in transmitter release. *Science, 239,* 282–285.

DALY, H. B. (1969). Learning of a hurdle-jump response to escape cues paired with reduced reward or frustrative nonreward. *Journal of Experimental Psychology, 79,* 146–157.

DARWIN, C. (1872). *The expression of emotions in man and animals.* London: John Murray.

DAVISON, M., & MCCARTHY, D. (1988). *The matching law: A research review.* Englewood Cliffs, NJ: Prentice Hall.

DEESE, J. (1951). Extinction of a discrimination without performance of the choice response. *Journal of Comparative and Physiological Psychology, 44,* 362–366.

DEUTSCH, J. A. (1954). A machine with insight. *Quarterly Journal of Experimental Psychology, 6,* 6–11.

DEWEY, J. (1896). The reflex arc concept in psychology. *Psychological Review, 3,* 357–370.

DIAMOND, D. M., DUNWIDDIE, T. V., & ROSE, G. M. (1988). Characteristics of hippocampal primed burst potentiation *in vitro* and in the awake rat. *Journal of Neuroscience, 8,* 4079–4088.

DICARA, L. V. (1970). Learning in the autonomic nervous system. *Scientific American, 222,* 30–39.

DOLLARD, J. C., & MILLER, N. E. (1950). *Personality and psychotherapy.* New York: McGraw-Hill.

DUNCAN, C. P. (1949). The retroactive effect of electroshock on learning. *Journal of Comparative and Physiological Psychology, 42,* 34–44.

EBBINGHAUS, H. (1913 [1885]). *On memory* (H. A. Ruger & C. Bossinger, Trans.). New York: Teachers College Press.

EGAN, K. (1983).*Education and psychology: Plato, Piaget, and scientific psychology.* New York: Teachers College Press.

EGGER, M. D., & MILLER, N. E. (1962). Secondary reinforcement in rats as a function of information value and reliability of the stimulus. *Journal of Experimental Psychology, 64,* 97–104.

EGGER, M. D., & MILLER, N. E. (1963). When is a reward reinforcing? An experimental study of the information hypothesis. *Journal of Comparative and Physiological Psychology, 56,* 132–137.

EISENBERG,D.M., DELBANCO, T.L., BERKEY, C.S., KAPTCHUK, T.J., KUPELNICK, B., KUHL, J., & CHALMERS, T.C. (1993). Cognitive behavioral techniques for hypertension: Are they effective? *Annals of Internal Medicine, 118,* 964–972.

EISENBERG, D.M., KESSLER, R.C., FOSTER, C., & NORLOCK, F.E. (1993). Unconventional medicine in the United States: Prevalence, costs, and patterns of use. *New England Journal of Medicine, 328,* 246–252.

ESTES, W. K. (1944). An experimental study of punishment. *Psychological Monographs, 57* (Whole No. 263).

ESTES, W. K. (1950). Toward a statistical theory of learning. *Psychological Review, 57,* 94–107.

ESTES, W. K. (1954). Kurt Lewin. In Estes et al (Eds.), *Modern Learning Theory,* (pp. 317–344). New York: Appleton-Century-Crofts.

ESTES, W. K. (1960). Learning theory and the new "mental chemistry." *Psychological Review, 67,* 207–223.

ESTES, W. K. (1964a). All-or-none processes in learning and retention. *American Psychologist, 19,* 16–25.

ESTES, W. K. (1964b). Probability learning. In A. W. Melton (Ed.), *Categories of human learning.* New York: Academic Press.

ESTES, W. K. (1969a). New perspectives on some old issues in association theory. In N. J. MacKintosh & W. K. Honig (Eds.), *Fundamental issues in association learning.* Halifax, Nova Scotia: Dalhousie University Press.

ESTES, W. K. (1969b). Reinforcement in human learning. In J. Tapp (Ed.), *Reinforcement and behavior.* New York: Academic Press.

ESTES, W. K. (1971). Reward in human learning: Theoretical issues and strategic choice points. In R. Glaser (Ed.), *The nature of reinforcement.* New York: Academic Press.

ESTES, W. K. (1972). An associative basis for coding and organization in memory. In A. W. Melton & E. Martin (Eds.), *Coding processes in human memory.* New York: Halstead.

ESTES, W. K. (1973). Memory and conditioning. In F. J. McGuigan & D. B. Lumsden (Eds.), *Contemporary approaches to conditioning and learning.* Washington, DC: Winston & Sons.

ESTES, W. K. (1976). The cognitive side of probability matching. *Psychological Review, 83,* 37–64.

ESTES, W. K. (1978). On the organization and core concepts of learning theory and cognitive psychology. In W. K. Estes (Ed.), *Handbook of learning and cognitive processes* (Vol. 6). Hillsdale, NJ: Erlbaum.

ESTES, W.K. (1994). *Classification and cognition.* New York: Oxford University Press.

ESTES, W. K., HOPKINS, B. L., & CROTHERS, E. J. (1960). All-or-none and conservation effects in the learning and retention of paired associates. *Journal of Experimental Psychology, 60,* 329–339.

ESTES, W. K., KOCH, S., MACCORQUONDALE, K., MEEHL, P.E., MUELLER, C.G., SCHOENFELD, W.N., & VERPLANCK, W.S. (1954). *Modern learning theory: A critical analysis of five examples.* New York, NY: Appleton-Century-Crofts.

ESTES, W. K., & SKINNER, B. F. (1941). Some quantitative properties of anxiety. *Journal of Experimental Psychology, 29,* 390–400.

ESTES, W. K., & STRAUGHAN, J. H. (1954). Analysis of a verbal conditioning situation in terms of statistical learning theory. *Journal of Experimental Psychology, 47,* 225–234.

FENWICK, S., MIKULKA, P. J., & KLEIN, S. B. (1975). The effect of different levels of preexposure to sucrose on acquisition and extinction of conditioned aversion. *Behavioral Biology, 14,* 231–235.

FERSTER, C. B., & SKINNER, B. F. (1957). *Schedules of reinforcement.* Englewood Cliffs, NJ: Prentice Hall.

FESTINGER, L. (1957). *A theory of cognitive dissonance.* Stanford, CA: Stanford University Press.

FLANAGAN, O. (1991). *The science of the mind* (2nd ed.). Cambridge, MA: MIT Press.

FLAVELL, J. H. (1963). *The developmental psychology of Jean Piaget.* New York: Van Nostrand Reinhold.

FOWLER, H., & MILLER, N. E. (1963). Facilitation and inhibition of runway performance by hind- and forepaw shock of various intensities. *Journal of Comparative and Physiological Psychology, 56,* 801–805.

FURTH, H. G. (1969). *Piaget and knowledge: Theoretical foundations.* Englewood Cliffs, NJ: Prentice Hall.

FURTH, H. G. (1970). *Piaget for teachers.* Englewood Cliffs, NJ: Prentice Hall.

GAGNÉ, R. M. (1970). *The conditions of learning* (2nd ed.). New York: Holt, Rinehart & Winston.

GARCIA, J. (1981). Tilting at the paper mills of academe. *American Psychologist, 36,* 149–158.

GARCIA, J., ERVIN, F.R., & KOELLING, R.A. (1966). Learning with prolonged delay of reinforcement. *Psychonomic Science, 5,* 121–122.

GARCIA, J., & KOELLING, R. A. (1966). Relation of cue to consequence in avoidance learning. *Psychonomic Science, 4,* 123–124.

GARCIA, J., MCGOWAN, B., ERVIN, F.R., & KOELLING, R.A. (1968). Cues: Their relative effectiveness as a function of the reinforcer. *Science, 160,* 794–795.

GAZZANIGA, M. S. & LEDOUX, J. E (1978). *The Integrated Mind.* New York: Plenum Press.

GINSBURG, H., & OPPER, S. (1979). *Piaget's theory of intellectual development* (2nd ed.). Englewood Cliffs, NJ: Prentice Hall.

GOLDSCHMID, M. L., & BENTLER, P. M. (1968). *Conservation concept diagnostic kit: Manual and keys.* San Diego, CA: Educational and Industrial Testing Service.

GUSTAVSON, G. R., GARCIA, J., HANKINS, W. G., & RUSINIAK, K. W. (1974). Coyote predation control by aversive conditioning. *Science, 1843,* 581–583.

GUTHRIE, E. R. (1935). *The psychology of learning.* New York: Harper & Row.

GUTHRIE, E. R. (1938). *The psychology of human conflict.* New York: Harper & Row.

GUTHRIE, E. R. (1940). Association and the law of effect. *Psychological Review, 47,* 127–148.

GUTHRIE, E. R. (1942). Conditioning: A theory of learning in terms of stimulus, response, and association. In N. B. Henry (Ed.), *The forty-first yearbook of the national society for the study of education: Pt. II. The psychology of learning.* Chicago: University of Chicago Press.

GUTHRIE, E. R. (1952). *The psychology of learning* (rev. ed.). New York: Harper & Row.

GUTHRIE, E. R. (1959). Association by contiguity. In S. Koch (Ed.), *Psychology: A study of a science* (Vol. 2). New York: McGraw-Hill.

GUTHRIE, E. R., & HORTON, G. P. (1946). *Cats in a puzzle box.* New York: Rinehart.

GUTHRIE, E. R., & POWERS, F. F. (1950). *Educational psychology.* New York: Ronald Press.

HARLOW, H. F. (1949). The formation of learning sets. *Psychological Review, 56,* 51–65.

HARLOW, H. F. (1950). Analysis of discrimination learning by monkeys. *Journal of Experimental Psychology, 40,* 26–39.

HARLOW, H. F. (1959). Learning set and error factor theory. In S. Koch (Ed.), *Psychology: A study of a science* (Vol. 2). New York: McGraw-Hill.

HARRIS, B. (1979). Whatever happened to little Albert? *American Psychologist, 34,* 151–160.

HEBB, D. O. (1946). On the nature of fear. *Psychological Review, 53,* 259–276.

HEBB, D. O. (1949). *The organization of behavior.* New York: Wiley.

HEBB, D. O. (1955). Drives and the C.N.S. (Conceptual nervous system). *Psychological Review, 62,* 243–254.

HEBB, D. O. (1959). A neuropsychological theory. In S. Koch (Ed.), *Psychology: A study of a science* (Vol. 1). New York: McGraw-Hill.

HEBB, D. O. (1972). *Textbook of psychology* (3rd ed.). Philadelphia: W. B. Saunders.

HEBB, D. O. (1980). [Autobiography]. In G. Lindzey (Ed.), *A history of psychology in autobiography* (Vol. VII). San Francisco: Freeman.

HEBB, D. O., & DONDERI, D. C. (1987). *Textbook of psychology* (4th ed.) Hillsdale, NJ: Erlbaum.

HECHT, H. & PROFFITT, D. R. (1995). The price of expertise: Effects of experience on the water-level task. *Psychological Science, 6,* 90–95.

HELLIGE, J. B. (1993). *Hemispheric aymmetry: What's right and what's left.* Cambridge, MA: Harvard University Press.

HENLE, M. (1986). *1879 and all that: Essays in the history of psychology.* New York: Columbia University Press.

HERGENHAHN, B. R. (1972). *Shaping your child's personality.* Englewood Cliffs, NJ: Prentice Hall.

HERGENHAHN, B. R. (1974). *A self-directing introduction to psychological experimentation* (2nd ed.). Monterey, CA: Brooks/Cole.

HERGENHAHN, B. R. (1997). *An introduction to the history of psychology.* (3rd ed.) Belmont, CA: Wadsworth.

HERMANN, C., KIM, M., & BLANCHARD, E.B. (1995). Behavioral and prophylactic pharmacological intervention studies of pediatric migraine: An exploratory meta-analysis. *Pain, 60,* 239–255.

HERON, W. (1957, January). The pathology of boredom. *Scientific American,* pp. 52–56.

HERRNSTEIN, R. J. (1961). Relative and absolute strength of response as a function of frequency of reinforcement. *Journal of the Experimental Analysis of Behavior, 4,* 267–272.

HERRNSTEIN, R. J. (1970). On the law of effect. *Journal of the Experimental Analysis of Behavior, 13,* 243–266.

HERRNSTEIN, R. J. (1974). Formal properties of the matching law. *Journal of the Experimental Analysis of Behavior, 21,* 159–164.

HERRNSTEIN, R. J. (1990). Rational choice theory: Necessary but not sufficient. *American Psychologist, 45,* 356–367.

HERRNSTEIN, R. J. (1991). Reply to Binmore and Staddon. *American Psychologist, 46,* 799–801.

HESS, E. H. (1958). "Imprinting" in animals. *Scientific American, 198,* 81–90.

HESS, R. D., & TENEZAKIS, M. D. (1970). *The computer as a socializing agent: Some socio-affective outcomes of CAI.* Stanford, CA: Stanford Center for Research and Development in Teaching.

HEYES, C. M. & DAWSON, G. R. (1990). A demonstration of observational learning using a bidirectional control. *Quarterly Journal of Experimental Psychology, 42B,* 59–71.

HEYES, C. M., DAWSON, G. R., & NOKES, T. (1992) Imitation in rats: Initial responding and transfer evidence. *Quarterly Journal of Experimental Psychology, 45B,* 229–240.

HEYES, C. M., JALDOW, E., & DAWSON, G. R. (1993). Observational extinction: Observation of nonreinforced responding reduces resistance to extinction in rats. *Animal Learning and Behavior, 21,* 221–225.

HILGARD, E. R., & BOWER, G. H. (1975). *Theories of learning* (4th ed.). Englewood Cliffs, NJ: Prentice Hall.

HILGARD, E. R., & MARQUIS, D. G. (1940). *Conditioning and learning.* Englewood Cliffs, NJ: Prentice Hall.

HILL, W. F. (1990). *Learning: A survey of psychological interpretations* (5th ed.). New York: Harper & Row.

HINDE, R. A., & TINBERGEN, N. (1958). The comparative study of species-specific behavior. In A. Roe & G. G. Simpson (Eds), *Behavior and evolution.* New Haven, CT: Yale University Press.

HINTON, G. E. & ANDERSON, J. A. (EDS.). (1981). *Parallel models of associative memory.* Hillsdale, NJ: Erlbaum.

HOBBES, T. (1962 [1651]). *Leviathan.* New York: Macmillan.

HOFFMAN, H. S. (1962). The analogue lab: A new kind of teaching device. *American Psychologist, 17,* 684–694.

HOLLAND, J. G. & SKINNER, B. F. (1961). *The analysis of behavior: A program for self-instruction.* New York: McGraw-Hill.

HOLLAND, P. C. (1977). Conditioned stimulus as a determinant of the form for the Pavlovian conditioned response. *Journal of Experimental Psychology: Animal Processes, 3,* 77–104.

HOLLIS, K. (1982). Pavlovian conditioning of signal-centered action patterns and autonomic behavior: A biological analysis of function. In J. S. Tosenblatt, R. A. Hinde, C. Beer, & M. Busnel (Eds.), *Advances in the study of behavior* (Vol. 12). New York: Academic Press.

HOLT, J. (1967). *How children learn.* New York: Pitman.

HOMME, L., CSANYI, A. P., GONZALES, M. A., & RECHS, J. R. (1970). *How to use contingency contracting in the classroom.* Champaign, IL: Research Press.

HOMME, L. E., DE BACA, P., DIVINE, J. F., STEINHORST, R., & RICKERT, E. J. (1963). Use of the Premack principle in controlling the behavior of school children. *Journal of the Experimental Analysis of Behavior, 6,* 544.

HULL, C. L. (1928). *Aptitude testing.* Yonkers-on-Hudson, NY: World Book.

HULL, C. L. (1933a). Differential habituation to internal stimuli in the albino rat. *Journal of Comparative Psychology, 16,* 255–273.

HULL. C. L. (1933b). *Hypnosis and suggestibility: An experimental approach.* New York: Naiburg.

HULL, C. L. (1943). *Principles of behavior.* Englewood Cliffs, NJ: Prentice Hall.

HULL, C. L. (1952). *A behavior system: An introduction to behavior theory concerning the individual organism.* New Haven CT: Yale University Press.

HULSE, S. H. (1958). Amount and percentage of reinforcement and duration of goal confinement in conditioning and extinction. *Journal of Experimental Psychology, 56,* 48–57.

HULSE, S. H., EGETH, H., & DEESE, J. (1980). *The psychology of learning* (5th ed.). New York: McGraw-Hill.

HUMPHREYS, L. G. (1939a). Acquisition and extinction of verbal expectations in a situation analogous to conditioning. *Journal of Experimental Psychology, 25,* 294–301.

HUMPHREYS, L. G. (1939b). The effect of random alternation of reinforcement on the acquisition and extinction of conditioned eyelid reactions. *Journal of Experimental Psychology, 25,* 141–158.

INHELDER, B., & PIAGET, J. (1958). *The growth of logical thinking from childhood to adolescence* (A. Parson & S. Milgram, Trans.). New York: Basic Books.

JACOBSEN, P. B., BOVBJERG, D. H., SCHWARTZ, M. D., ANDRYKOWSKI, M. A., FUTTERMAN, A. D., GILEWSKI, T., NORTON, L., & REDD, W. H. (1993). Formation of food aversions in cancer patients receiving repeated infusions of chemotherapy. *Behavior Research and Therapy, 31,* 739–748.

JAMES, W. (1890). *The principles of psychology* (2 vols.). New York: Henry Holt.

JAMES, W. (1892). *Psychology: Briefer course.* New York: Henry Holt.

JENKINS, H. M., & MOORE, B. R. (1973). The form of the autoshaped response with food or water reinforcers. *Journal of the Experimental Analysis of Behavior, 20,* 163–181.

JONAS, G. (1973). *Visceral learning: Toward a science of self-control.* New York: Viking Press.

JONCICH, G. (1968). *The sane positivist: A biography of Edward L. Thorndike.* Middletown, CT: Wesleyan University Press.

JONES, M. C. (1924). A laboratory study of fear: The case of Peter. *Pedagogical Seminary, 31,* 308–315.

JONES, M. C. (1974). Albert, Peter, and John B. Watson. *American Psychologist, 29,* 581–583.

KAGAN, J. (1980, September). Jean Piaget's contributions. *Phi Delta Kappan,* pp. 245–246.

KALICHMAN, S.C. (1988). Individual differences in water-level performance. *Developmental Review, 8,* 273–295.

KAMIN, L. J. (1969). Predictability, surprise, attention, and conditioning. In B. A. Campbell & R. M. Church (Eds.), *Punishment and aversive behavior.* Englewood Cliffs, NJ: Prentice Hall.

KANDEL, E. (1991). Cellular mechanisms of learning and the biological basis of individuality. In E. R. Kandel, J. H. Schwartz & T. M. Jessell (Eds.), *Principles of Neural Science (3/e),* 839–852. New York: Elsevier.

KANDEL, E. R. & SCHWARTZ, J. H. (1982). Molecular biology of learning: Modulation of transmitter release. *Science, 218,* 433–443.

KAUFMAN, A., BARON, A., & KOPP, R. E. (1966). Some effects of instructions on human operant behavior. *Psychonomic Monograph Supplements, 1,* 243–250.

KELLER, F. S. (1968). Good-bye teacher. *Journal of Applied Behavior Analysis, 1,* 69–89.

KELLER, F. S., & SCHOENFELD, W. N. (1950). *Principles of psychology.* New York: Appleton-Century-Crofts.

KIMBLE, G. A. (1961). *Hilgard and Marquis' conditioning and learning* (2nd ed.). Englewood Cliffs, NJ: Prentice Hall.

KIMBLE, G. A., & GARMEZY, N. (1968). *Principles of general psychology* (3rd ed.). New York: Ronald Press.

KIMBLE, G. A. (1993). A modest proposal for a minor revolution in the language of psychology. *Psychological Science, 4,* 253–255.

KIMMEL, H. D. (1974). Instrumental conditioning of autonomically mediated responses in human beings. *American Psychologist, 29,* 325–335.

KIMURA, D. (1961). Cerebral dominance and the perception of verbal stimuli. *Canadian Journal of Psychology, 15,* 166–171.

KIMURA, D. (1964). Left-right differences in the perception of melodies. *Quarterly Journal of Experimental Psychology, 16,* 355–358.

KIMURA, D. (1967). Functional asymmetry of the brain in dichotic listening. *Cortex, 3,* 163–178.

KINGSTONE, A., ENNS, J. T., MANGUN, G. R., & GAZZANIGA, M. S. (1995). Guided search is a left-hemisphere process in split-brain patients. *Psychological Science, 6,* 118–121.

KOCH, S. (1954). Clark L. Hull. In Estes et al (Eds.), *Modern Learning Theory,* (pp. 1–176). New York: Appleton-Century-Crofts.

KOFFKA, K. (1963 [1935]). *Principles of Gestalt psychology.* New York: Harcourt, Brace, and World.

KÖHLER, W. (1925). *The mentality of apes.* London: Routledge & Kegan Paul.

KÖHLER, W. (1929). *Gestalt psychology.* New York: Liveright.

KÖHLER, W. (1947). *Gestalt psychology: An introduction to new concepts in modern psychology* (rev. ed.). New York: Liveright.

KOLESNIK, W. B. (1958). *Mental discipline in modern education.* Madison: University of Wisconsin Press.

KUHN, T. S. (1973). *The structure of scientific revolutions* (3rd ed.). Chicago: University of Chicago Press.

KULIK, J. A., KULIK, CHEN-LIN, & CARMICHAEL, K. (1974). The Keller plan in science teaching. *Science, 183,* 379–383.

KUPFERMANN, I., CASTELLUCCI, V., PINSKER, H., & KANDEL, E. (1970). Neuronal correlates of habituation and dishabituation of the gill withdrawal reflex in *Aplysia. Science, 167,* 1743–1745.

LABBE, E. E. (1995). Treatment of childhood migraine with autogenic training and skin temperature biofeedback: A component analysis. *Headache, 35,* 10–13.

LACHMAN, R., LACHMAN, J. L., & BUTTERFIELD, E. C. (1979). *Cognitive psychology and information processing.* Hillsdale, NJ: Erlbaum.

LASHLEY, K. S. (1929). *Brain mechanisms and intelligence.* Chicago: University of Chicago Press.

LEAHEY, T. H. (1980). *A history of psychology.* Englewood Cliffs, NJ: Prentice Hall.

LEEPER, R. (1935). The role of motivation in learning: A study of the phenomenon of differential motivational control of the utilization of habits. *Journal of Genetic Psychology, 46,* 3–40.

LEFRANÇOIS, G. R. (1968). A treatment for the acceleration of conservation of substance. *Canadian Journal of Psychology, 22,* 277–284.

LEHMAN, D. R., LEMPERT, R. O., & NISBETT, R. E. (1988). The effects of graduate training on reasoning: Formal discipline and thinking about everyday-life events. *American Psychologist, 43,* 431–442.

LEVY, J. (1985, May). Right brain, left brain: Fact and fiction. *Psychology Today,* pp. 38–39, 42–44.

LINDSAY, P. H., & NORMAN, D. A. (1977). *Human information processing: An introduction to psychology* (2nd ed.). New York: Academic Press.

LINSKIE, R. (1977). *The learning process: Theory and practice.* New York: D. Van Nostrand.

LOFTUS, G. R., & LOFTUS, E. F. (1976). *Human memory: The processing of information.* Hillsdale, NJ: Erlbaum.

LØMO, T. (1966). Frequency potentiation of excitatory synaptic activity in the dentate area of the hippocampal formation. *Acta physiologica Scandinavica, 68,* 128.

LORENZ, K. (1952). *King Solomon's ring.* New York: Crowell.

LORENZ, K. (1965). *Evolution and modification of behavior.* Chicago: University of Chicago Press.

LORENZ, K. (1970). *Studies in animal and human behavior* (Vol. 1). Cambridge, MA: Harvard University Press.

LUMSDAINE, A. A. (1964). Educational technology, programmed learning, and instructional sciences. In E. R. Hilgard (Ed.), *Theories of learning and instruction*. Chicago: University of Chicago Press.

LUNDIN, R. W. (1974). *Personality: A behavioral analysis* (2nd ed.). New York: Macmillan.

LYNCH, G., & BAUDRY, M. (1984). The biochemistry of memory: A new and specific hypothesis. *Science, 224*, 1057–1063.

LYNCH, G. & BAUDRY, M. (1991). Reevaluating the constraints on hypothesis regarding LTP expression. *Hippocampus, 1*, 9–14.

MacCORQUODALE, K., & MEEHL, P. E. (1953). Preliminary suggestions as to a formalization of expectancy theory. *Psychological Review, 60*, 55–63.

MACKINTOSH, N. J. (1975). A theory of attention: Variations in the associability of stimuli with reinforcement. *Psychological Review, 82*, 276–298.

MAGER, R. F. (1961). *Preparing instructional objectives*. Palo Alto, CA: Fearon.

MAGER, R. F. (1972). *Goal analysis*. Belmont, CA: Fearon.

MAIER, S. F., SELIGMAN, M. E. P., & SOLOMON, R. L. (1969). Pavlovian fear conditioning and learning helplessness: Effects on escape and avoidance behavior of (a) the CS-US contingency, and (b) the independence of the US and voluntary responding. In B. A. Campbell & R. M. Church (Eds.), *Punishment and Aversive Behavior*. New York: Appleton-Century-Crofts.

MALENKA, R. C., KAUER, J. A., ZUCKER R. S., & NICOLL, R. A. (1988). Postsynaptic calcium is sufficient for potentiation of hippocampal synaptic transmission. *Science, 242*, 81–83.

MALONE, J. C. (1991). *Theories of Learning: A Historical Approach*. Belmont, CA: Wadsworth.

MARKOVIC, B. M., DIMITRIJEVIC, M., & JANKOVIC, B. D. (1993). Immunomodulation by conditioning: Recent developments. *International Journal of Neuroscience, 71*, 231–249.

MARX, M. H., & CRONAN-HILLIX, W. A. (1987). *Systems and theories in psychology* (4th ed.). New York: McGraw-Hill.

McCLELLAND, J. L. & RUMELHART, D. E. (1988). *Explorations in parallel distributed processing: A handbook of models, programs and exercises*. Cambridge, MA: MIT Press/Bradford Books.

MEDIN, D. L. & SHAFFER, M. M. (1978). Context theory of classification learning. *Psychological Review, 85*, 207–238.

MEEHL, P. E. (1950). On the circularity of the law of effect, *Psychological Bulletin, 47*, 52–75.

MEEK, R. L. (1977). The traditional in non-traditional learning methods. *Journal of Personalized Instruction, 2*, 114–119.

MELZACK, R., & THOMPSON, W. R. (1956). Effects of early experience on social behavior. *Canadian Journal of Psychology, 10*, 82–90.

METALINKOV, S. (1934). Role du système nerveux et des facteurs biologiques et psychiques dans l'immunitié. [The role of the nervous system and of biological and psychic factors in immunity.] Paris: Masson.

METALINKOV, S. & CHORINE, V. (1926). Rôle des réflexes conditionnels dans l'immunitié. [The role of conditional reflexes in immunity.] *Annales de l'Institut Pasteur, 40*, 893–900.

METCALFE, J., FUNNELL, M., & GAZZANIGA, M. S. (1995). Right-hemisphere memory superiority: Studies of a split-brain patient. *Psychological Science, 6*, 157–164.

MILLER, G. A. (1965). Some preliminaries to psycholinguistics. *American Psychologist, 20*, 15–20.

MILLER, N. E. (1969). Learning of visceral and glandular responses. *Science, 163*, 434–445.

MILLER, N. E. (1983). Behavioral medicine: Symbiosis between laboratory and clinic. In M. R. Rosenzweig & L. W. Porter (Eds.), *Annual Review of Psychology, 34*, 1–31.

MILLER, N. E. (1984). *Bridges between laboratory and clinic*. New York: Praeger.

MILLER, N. E., & CARMONA, A. (1967). Modification of a visceral response, salivation in thirsty dogs, by instrumental training with water reward. *Journal of Comparative and Physiological Psychology, 63*, 1–6.

MILLER, N. E., & DOLLARD, J. C. (1941). *Social learning and imitation.* New Haven, CT: Yale University Press.

MILNER, B. (1965). Memory disturbance after bilateral hippocampal lesions. In P. Milner & S. Glickman (Eds.). *Cognitive processes and the brain.* Princeton, NJ: Van Nostrand.

MIYAKE, N., & NORMAN, D. A. (1979). To ask a question, one must know enough to know what is not known. *Journal of Verbal Learning and Verbal Behavior, 18,* 357–364.

MOLTZ, H. (1957). Latent extinction and the fractional anticipatory response mechanism. *Psychological Review, 64,* 229–241.

MORGAN, C. L. (1891). *An introduction to comparative psychology.* London: W. Scott.

MOUNT, G. R., PAYTON, T., ELLIS, J., & BARNES, P. (1976). A multimodal behavioral approach to the treatment of alcoholism. *Behavioral Engineering, 33,* 61–66.

MOWRER, O. H. (1956). Two-factor learning theory reconsidered, with special reference to secondary reinforcement and the concept of habit. *Psychological Review, 63,* 114–128.

MOWRER, O. H. (1960). *Learning theory and behavior.* New York: Wiley.

MUELLER, C. G. & SCHOENFELD, W. N. (1954). Edwin R. Guthrie. In Estes et al (Eds.), *Modern Learning Theory* , (pp. 345–379). New York: Appleton-Century-Crofts.

MÜLLER, G. E., & PILZECKER, A. (1900). *Experimentelle Beiträge Zur Lehre Vom Gedachtniss.* Leipzig.

MUNN, N. L., FERNALD, D. L., JR., & FERNALD, P. S. (1972). *Introduction to psychology.* Boston: Houghton Mifflin.

MURDOCK, B. B., JR. (1961). The retention of individual items. *Journal of Experimental Psychology, 62,* 618–625.

NAKANISHI, S. (1992). Molecular diversity of glutamate receptors and implications for brain function. *Science, 258,* 597–603.

NEWELL, A. (1970). Remarks on the relationship between artificial intelligence and cognitive psychology. In R. Banerji & M. D. Mesarovic (Eds.), *Theoretical approaches to non-numerical problem solving.* New York: Springer-Verlag.

NICOL, C. J. & POPE, S. J. Food deprivation during observation reduces social learning in hens. *Animal Behaviour, 45,* 193–196.

NORMAN, D. A. (1980a). Twelve issues for cognitive science. *Cognitive Science, 4,* 1–32.

NORMAN, D. A. (1980b). What goes on in the mind of the learner? *New Directions for Teaching and Learning, 2,* 37–49.

NORMAN, D. A. (1981). A psychologist views human processing: Human error and other phenomena suggest processing mechanisms. *Proceedings of the International Joint Conference on Artificial Intelligence.* Vancouver, British Columbia.

NORMAN, D. A. (1982). *Learning and memory.* New York: Freeman.

NORMAN, D. A. (1988). *The psychology of everyday things.* New York: Basic Books.

OBRIST, P. A., SUTTERER, J. R., & HOWARD, J. L. (1972). Preparatory cardiac changes: A psychobiological approach. In A. H. Black & W. F. Prokasy (Eds.), *Classical conditioning II.* Englewood Cliffs, NJ: Prentice Hall.

OLDS, J. (1955). Physiological mechanisms of reward. In M. R. Jones (Ed.), *Nebraska Symposium on motivation.* Lincoln: University of Nebraska Press.

OLDS, J., & MILNER, P. (1954). Positive reinforcement produced by electrical stimulation of septal area and other regions of rat brain. *Journal of Comparative and Physiological Psychology, 47,* 419–427.

OLTON, D. S. (1992). Tolman's cognitive analyses: Predecessors of current approaches in psychology. *Journal of Experimental Psychology, General, 121,* 427–428.

ORNSTEIN, R. E. (1978). The split and whole brain. *Human Nature, 1,* 76–83.

PAVLOV, I. P. (1927). *Conditioned reflexes.* London: Oxford University Press.

PAVLOV, I. P. (1928). *Lectures on conditioned reflexes.* New York: Liveright.

PAVLOV, I. P. (1941). *Conditioned reflexes and psychiatry.* New York: International.

PAVLOV, I. P. (1955). *Selected works.* Moscow: Foreign Languages Publishing House.

PETERSON, L. R., & PETERSON, M. J. (1959). Short term retention of individual verbal items. *Journal of Experimental Psychology, 58,* 193–198.

PHILLIPS, D. C. & ORTON, R. (1983). The new causal principle of cognitive learning theory: Perspectives on Bandura's "reciprocal determinism." *Psychological Review, 90,* 158–165.

PHILLIPS, J. L., JR. (1975). *The origins of intellect: Piaget's theory* (2nd ed.). San Francisco: Freeman.

PHILLIPS, J. L., JR. (1981). *Piaget's theory: A primer.* San Francisco: Freeman.

PIAGET, J. (1966). *Psychology of intelligence.* Totowa, NJ: Littlefield, Adams.

PIAGET, J. (1970a). *Genetic epistemology* (E. Duckworth, Trans.). New York: Columbia University Press.

PIAGET, J. (1970b). Piaget's theory. In P. H. Mussen (Ed.), *Carmichael's manual of child psychology* (Vol. 1). New York: Wiley.

PIAGET, J., & INHELDER, B. (1969). *The psychology of the child* (H. Weaver, Trans.). New York: Basic Books.

POPPER, K. (1963). *Conjectures and refutations.* New York: Basic Books.

PREMACK, D. (1959). Toward empirical behavior laws: Vol. I. Positive reinforcement. *Psychological Review, 66,* 219–233.

PREMACK, D. (1962). Reversibility of the reinforcement relation. *Science, 136,* 255–257.

PRESSEY, S. L. (1926). A simple apparatus which gives tests and scores—and teaches. *School and Society, 23,* 373–376.

PRESSEY, S. L. (1927). A machine for automatic teaching of drill material. *School and Society, 25,* 549–552.

QUINLAN, P. T. (1991). *Connectionism and psychology: A psychological perspective on new connectionist research.* Chicago: The University of Chicago Press.

RACHLIN, H. (1976). *Behavior and learning.* San Francisco: Freeman.

RACHLIN, H. (1991). *Introduction to modern behaviorism* (3rd ed.). San Francisco: Freeman.

RACHLIN, H., & GREEN, L. (1972). Commitment, choice and self-control. *Journal of the Experimental Analysis of Behavior, 17,* 15–22.

RAZRAN, G. (1961). The observable unconscious and the inferable conscious in current Soviet psychophysiology. *Psychological Review, 68,* 81–147.

RAZRAN, G. (1965). Russian physiologists' psychology and American experimental psychology. *Psychological Bulletin, 63,* 42–64.

REISS, B. F. (1946). Genetic changes in semantic conditioning. *Journal of Experimental Psychology, 36,* 143–152.

RESCORLA, R. A. (1966). Predictability and number of pairings in Pavlovian fear conditioning. *Psychonomic Science, 4,* 383–384.

RESCORLA, R. A. (1967). Pavlovian conditioning and its proper control procedures. *Psychological Review, 74,* 72–80.

RESCORLA, R. A. (1988). Pavlovian conditioning: It's not what you think. *American Psychologist, 43,* 151–160.

RESCORLA, R. A. & HETH, C.D. (1975). Reinstatement of fear to an extinguished conditioned stimulus. *Journal of Experimental Psychology: Animal Behavior Processes, 1,* 88–96.

RESCORLA, R. A., & WAGNER, A. R. (1972). A theory of Pavlovian conditioning: Variations in the effectiveness of reinforcement and non-reinforcement. In A. H. Black & W. F. Prokasy (Eds.). *Classical conditioning II.* Englewood Cliffs, NJ: Prentice Hall.

RIESEN, A. H. (1947). The development of visual perception in man and chimpanzee. *Science, 106,* 107–108.

RIMM, D. C. & MASTERS, J. C. (1979). *Behavior therapy.* New York: Academic Press.

ROBERTS, A. H. (1994). "The powerful placebo" revisited: Implications for headache treatment and management. *Headache Quarterly, 5* , 209–213.

ROBINSON, D. N. (1986). *An intellectual history of psychology.* (Paperback text edition). University of Wisconsin Press.

ROBINSON, D. N. (1981). *An intellectual history of psychology* (rev. ed.). New York: Macmillan.

ROMANES, G. J. (1882/1897). *Animal intelligence.* London: Kegan Paul, Trench.

ROMANES, G. J. (1884). *Mental evolution in animals.* New York: Appleton-Century-Crofts.

ROMANES, G. J. (1885). *Mental evolution in man.* London: Kegan Paul.

RUJA, H. (1956). Productive psychologists. *American Psycholgist, 11,* 148–149.

RUMELHART, D. E., & McCLELLAND, J. L., and the PDP RESEARCH GROUP. (1986). *Parallel distributed processing* (Vols. 1 and 2). Cambridge, MA: MIT Press/Bradford Books.

RUMELHART, D. E., & NORMAN, D. A. (1981). Analogical processes in learning. In J. R. Anderson (Ed.), *Cognitive skills and their acquisition.* Hillsdale, NJ: Erlbaum.

RYAN, B. A. (1974). *PSI: Keller's personalized system of instruction: An appraisal.* Washington, DC: American Psychological Association.

SALTZ, E. (1971). *The cognitive bases of human learning.* Homewood, IL: Dorsey Press.

SARGENT, S. S., & STAFFORD, K. R. (1965). *Basic teachings of the great psychologists.* Garden City, NY: Doubleday.

SARTAIN, Q. A., NORTH, J. A., STRANGE, R. J., & CHAPMAN, M. H. (1973). *Psychology: Understanding human behavior* (4th ed.). New York: McGraw Hill.

SCHRAMM, W. (1964). *The research on programmed instruction: An annotated bibliography.* Washington, DC: U.S. Office of Education (OE–34034).

SCHUMAN, E. M. & MADISON, D. V. (1991). A requirement for the intercellular messenger nitric oxide in long-term potentiation. *Science, 254,* 1503–1506.

SCHWARTZ, B. (1989). *Psychology of learning and behavior* (3rd ed.). New York: Norton.

SCHWARTZ, B. & ROBBINS, S. J. (1995). *Psychology of learning and behavior* (4th ed.). New York: Norton.

SEARS, R. R. (1944). Experimental analysis of psychoanalytic phenomena. In J. McV. Hunt (Ed.), *Personality and the behavior disorders.* New York: Ronald Press.

SEARS, R. R., MACCOBY, E. E., & LEVIN, H. (1957). *Patterns of child rearing.* New York: Harper & Row.

SEARS, R. R., WHITING, J. W. M., NOWLIS, V., & SEARS, P. S. (1953). Some child-rearing antecedents of aggression and dependency in young children. *Genetic Psychology Monographs, 47,* 135–236.

SEJNOWSKI, T. J. & ROSENBERG, C. R. (1987). Parallel networks that learn to pronounce English text. *Complex Systems, 1,* 145–168.

SELIGMAN, M. E. P. (1969). Control group and conditioning: A comment on operationism. *Psychological Review, 76,* 484–491.

SELIGMAN, M. E. P. (1970). On the generality of the laws of learning. *Psychological Review, 77,* 406–418.

SELIGMAN, M. E. P. (1972). Phobias and preparedness. In M. E. P. Seligman & J. L. Hager (Eds.), *Biological boundaries of learning.* New York: Appleton-Century-Crofts.

SELIGMAN, M. E. P. (1975). *Helplessness.* San Francisco: Freeman.

SELIGMAN, M. E. P., & HAGER, J. L. (EDS.). (1972). *Biological boundaries of learning.* New York: Appleton-Century-Crofts.

SELIGMAN, M. E. P., & MAIER, S. F. (1967). Failure to escape traumatic shock. *Journal of Experimental Psychology, 74,* 1–9.

SENDEN, VON, M. V. (1932). *Raum-und gestaltauffassung bei operierten blindgeborenen vor und nach der operation.* Leipzig: Barth.

SEWARD, J. P., & LEVY, N. J. (1949). Sign learning as a factor in extinction. *Journal of Experimental Psychology, 39,* 660–668.

SHANNON, C. E., & WEAVER, W. (1949). *The mathematical theory of communication.* Urbana: University of Illinois Press.

SHAPIRO, D., TURKSY, B., GERSON, E., & STERN, M. (1969). Effects of feedback and reinforcement on the control of human systolic blood pressure. *Science, 163,* 588–589.

SHARPLESS, S., & JASPER, H. (1956). Habituation of the arousal reaction. *Brain, 79,* 655–680.

SHEFFIELD, F. D., & ROBY, T. B. (1950). Reward value of a non-nutritive sweet taste. *Journal of Comparative and Physiological Psychology, 43,* 471–481.

SHELLICK, S. & FITZSIMMONS, G. (1989). Biofeedback: An exercise in self-efficacy. *Medical Psychotherapy: An International Journal, 2,* 115–124.

SHEPARD, R. N. (1992). The advent and continuing influence of mathematical learning theory: Comment on Estes and Burke. *Journal of Experimental Psychology, General, 121,* 419–421.

SIEGEL, S. (1979). The role of conditioning in drug tolerance and addiction. In J. D. Keehn (Ed.), *Psychopathology in animals: Research and clinical implications.* New York: Academic Press.

SKINNER, B. F. (1938). *The behavior of organisms: An experimental analysis.* Englewood Cliffs, NJ: Prentice Hall.

SKINNER, B. F. (1948). *Walden Two.* New York: Macmillan.

SKINNER, B. F. (1950). Are theories of learning necessary? *Psychological Review, 57,* 193–216.

SKINNER, B. F. (1951). How to teach animals. *Scientific American, 185,* 26–29.

SKINNER, B. F. (1953). *Science and human behavior.* New York: Macmillan.

SKINNER, B. F. (1954). The science of learning and the art of teaching. *Harvard Educational Review, 24,* 86–97.

SKINNER, B. F. (1956). A case history in scientific method. *American Psychologist, 11,* 221–233.

SKINNER, B. F. (1957). *Verbal behavior.* Englewood Cliffs, NJ: Prentice Hall.

SKINNER, B. F. (1958). Teaching machines. *Science, 128,* 969–977.

SKINNER, B. F. (1960). Pigeons in a pelican. *American Psychologist, 15,* 28–37.

SKINNER, B. F. (1967). In E. G. Boring & G. Lindzey (Eds.), *A history of psychology in autobiography.* New York: Naiburg.

SKINNER, B. F. (1971). *Beyond freedom and dignity.* New York: Knopf.

SKINNER, B. F. (1974). *About behaviorism.* New York: Knopf.

SKINNER, B. F. (1984). The shame of American education. *American Psychologist, 39,* 947–954.

SKINNER, B. F. (1986). What is wrong with daily life in the Western world? *American Psychologist, 41,* 568–574.

SKINNER, B. F. (1987). *Upon further reflection.* Englewood Cliffs, NJ: Prentice Hall.

SMEDSLUND, J. (1961). The acquisition of conservation of substance and weight in children: I. Introduction. *Scandinavian Journal of Psychology, 2,* 11–20.

SPENCE, K. W. (1936). The nature of discrimination in animals. *Psychological Review, 43,* 427–449.

SPENCE, K. W. (1937). The differential response in animals to stimuli varying within a single dimension. *Psychological Review, 44,* 430–444.

SPENCE, K. W. (1942). The basis of solution by chimpanzees of the intermediate size problem. *Journal of Experimental Psychology, 31,* 257–271.

SPENCE, K. W. (1952). Clark Leonard Hull: 1884–1952. *American Journal of Psychology, 65,* 639–646.

SPENCE, K. W. (1956). *Behavior theory and conditioning.* New Haven, CT: Yale University Press.

SPENCE, K. W. (1960). *Behavior theory and learning: Selected papers.* Englewood Cliffs, NJ: Prentice Hall.

SPENCE, K. W., & LIPPITT, R. (1940). "Latent" learning of a simple maze problem with relevant needs satiated. *Psychological Bulletin, 37,* 429.

SPERRY, R. W. (1961). Cerebral organization and behavior. *Science, 133,* 1749–1757.

SPERRY, R. W. (1964). The great cerebral commissure. *Scientific American, 210,* 42–52.

SPRINGER, S. P., & DEUTSCH, G. (1985). *Left brain, right brain* (rev. ed.). San Francisco: Freeman.

SPURZHEIM, G. (1834). *Phrenology, or the doctrine of mental phenomena.* Boston: Marsh, Capen, & Lyon.

STADDON, J. E. R. (1991). Selective choice: A commentary on Herrnstein (1990). *American Psychologist, 46,* 793–797.

STADDON, J. (1995). On responsibility and punishment. *Atlantic Monthly, February,* 88–94.

STAUBLI, U., & LYNCH, G. (1987). Stable hippocampal long-term potentiation elicited by "theta" pattern stimulation. *Brain Research, 444,* 153–158.

STEVENS, S. S. (1951). Psychology and the science of science. In M. H. Marx, *Psychological theory: Contemporary readings.* New York: Macmillan.

SYMONDS, P. M. (1960). What education has to learn from psychology: VII. Transfer and formal discipline. *Teachers College Record, 61,* 30–45.

TAYLOR, J. A. (1951). The relationship of anxiety to the conditioned eyelid response. *Journal of Experimental Psychology, 41,* 81–92.

TERRACE, H. S. (1963). Errorless transfer of a discrimination across two continua. *Journal of the Experimental Analysis of Behavior, 6,* 223–232.

THORNDIKE, E. L. (1898). Animal intelligence: An experimental study of the associative processes in animals. *Psychological Review* [Monograph Suppl., 2, No. 8].

THORNDIKE, E. L. (1901). The mental life of the monkeys. *Psychological Review Monograph, 3*(15).

THORNDIKE, E. L. (1905). *The elements of psychology* (2nd ed.). New York: Seiler.

THORNDIKE, E. L. (1906). *The principles of teaching: Based on psychology.* New York: Seiler.

THORNDIKE, E. L. (1911). *Animal intelligence.* New York: Macmillan.

THORNDIKE, E. L. (1912). *Education, a first book.* New York: Macmillan.

THORNDIKE, E. L. (1913a). *Educational psychology: Vol. 1. The psychology of learning.* New York: Teachers College Press.

THORNDIKE, E. L. (1913b). *Educational psychology: Vol. 2. The original nature of man.* New York: Teachers College Press.

THORNDIKE, E. L. (1922). *The psychology of arithmetic.* New York: Crowell-Collier and Macmillan.

THORNDIKE, E. L. (1924). Mental discipline in high school studies. *Journal of Educational Psychology, 15,* 1–22, 83–98.

THORNDIKE, E. L. (1932). *The fundamentals of learning.* New York: Teachers College Press.

THORNDIKE, E. L. (1940). *Human nature and the social order.* New York: Macmillan.

THORNDIKE, E. L. (1949). *Selected writings from a connectionist's psychology.* New York: Appleton-Century-Crofts.

THORNDIKE, E. L., & WOODWORTH, R. S. (1901). The influence of improvement in one mental function upon the efficiency of other functions. *Psychological Review, 8,* 247–261, 384–395, 553–564.

THORPE, W. H. (1963). *Learning and instinct in animals* (2nd ed.). Cambridge, MA: Harvard University Press.

TIMBERLAKE, W. (1980). A molar equilibrium theory of learned performance. In G. H. Bower (Ed.), *The psychology of learning and motivation* (Vol. 14, pp. 1–58). San Diego, CA: Academic Press.

TIMBERLAKE, W. & ALLISON, J. (1974). Response deprivation: An empirical approach to instrumental performance. *Psychological Review, 81,* 146–164.

TIMBERLAKE, W. & FARMER-DOUGAN, V.A. (1991). Reinforcement in applied settings: Figuring out ahead of time what will work. *Psychological Bulletin, 110,* 379–391.

TOLMAN, E. C. (1932). *Purposive behavior in animals and men.* New York: Naiburg.

TOLMAN, E. C. (1938). The determiners of behavior at a choice point. *Psychological Review, 45,* 1–41.

TOLMAN, E. C. (1942). *Drives toward war.* New York: Appleton-Century-Crofts.

TOLMAN, E. C. (1945). A stimulus-expectancy need-cathexis psychology. *Science, 101,* 160–166.

TOLMAN, E. C. (1949). There is more than one kind of learning. *Psychological Review, 56,* 144–155.

TOLMAN, E. C. (1959). Principles of purposive behavior. In S. Koch (Ed.), *Psychology: A study of a science* (Vol. 2). New York: McGraw-Hill.

TOLMAN, E. C., & HONZIK, C. H. (1930). Introduction and removal of reward, and maze performance in rats. *University of California Publications in Psychology, 4,* 257–275.

TOLMAN, E. C., RITCHIE, B. F., & KALISH, D. (1946a), Studies in spatial learning. I. Orientation and the short-cut. *Journal of Experimental Psychology, 36,* 13–24.

TOLMAN, E. C., RITCHIE, B. F., & KALISH, D. (1946b). Studies in spatial learning. II. Place learning versus response learning. *Journal of Experimental Psychology, 36,* 221–229.

UNDERWOOD, B. J., & KEPPEL, G. (1962). One-trial learning? *Journal of Verbal Learning and Verbal Behavior, 1,* 1–13.

VANDERWOLF, C. H., KRAMIS, R., GILLESPIE, L. A., & BLAND, B. G. (1975). Hippocampal rhythmical slow activity and neocortical low voltage fast activity: Relations to behavior. In R. L. Isaacson & K. H. Pribram (Eds.), *The hippocampus. Vol. 2. Neurophysiology and behavior.* New York: Plenum Press.

VERPLANCK, W.S. (1954). Burrhus F. Skinner. In Estes et al (Eds.), *Modern Learning Theory,* (pp. 267–316). New York: Appleton-Century-Crofts.

VOEKS, V. W. (1950). Formalization and clarification of a theory of learning. *Journal of Psychology, 30,* 341–363.

WAGNER, A. R. (1961). Effects of amount and percentage of reinforcement and number of acquisition trials on conditioning and extinction. *Journal of Experimental Psychology, 32,* 234–242.

WAGNER, A. R. (1963). Conditioned frustration as a learned drive. *Journal of Experimental Psychology, 64,* 142–148.

WAGNER, A. R. (1969). Stimulus selection and a "modified continuity theory." In G. H. Bower & J. T. Spence (Eds.), *The psychology of learning and motivation* (Vol. 3). New York: Academic Press.

WAGNER, A. R. (1971). Elementary associations. In H. H. Kendler & J. T. Spence (Eds.), *Essays in neobehaviorism: A memorial volume to Kenneth W. Spence.* Englewood Cliffs, NJ: Prentice Hall.

WAGNER, A. R. (1978). Expectancies and the priming of STM. In S. H. Hulse, H. Fowler, & W. K. Honig (Eds.), *Cognitive processes in animal behavior.* Hillsdale, NJ: Erlbaum.

WAGNER, A. R., & RESCORLA, R. A. (1972). Inhibition in Pavlovian conditioning: Application of a theory. In R. A. Boakes & M. S. Halliday (Eds.), *Inhibition and learning.* New York: Academic Press.

WALKER, E. L. (1969). Reinforcement-"the one ring." In J. T. Tapp (Ed.) *Reinforcement and Behavior. New York: Academic Press.*

WALTER, W. G. (1953). *The living brain.* New York: Norton.

WALTERS, G. C., & GRUSEC, J. E. (1977). *Punishment.* San Francisco: Freeman.

WATSON, J. B. (1908). Imitation in monkeys. *Psychological Bulletin, 5,* 169–178.

WATSON, J. B. (1913). Psychology as the behaviorist views it. *Psychological Review, 20,* 158–177.

WATSON, J. B. (1925). *Behaviorism.* New York: Norton.

WATSON, J. B. (1926). Experimental studies on the growth of the emotions. In C. Murchison (Ed.), *Psychologies of 1925.* Worcester, MA: Clark University Press.

WATSON, J. B. (1936). John B. Watson. In C. Murchison (Ed.), *History of psychology in autobiography* (Vol. 3). Worcester, MA: Clark University Press.

WATSON, J. B., & McDOUGALL, W. (1929). *The battle of behaviorism.* New York: Norton.

WATSON, J. B., & RAYNER, R. (1920). Conditioned emotional reactions. *Journal of Experimental Psychology, 3,* 1–14.

WATSON, R. I. (1978). *The great psychologists* (4th Ed). Philadelphia: Lippincott.

WEIMER, W. B. (1973). Psycholinguistics and Plato's paradoxes of the Meno. *American Psychologist, 28,* 15–33.

WERTHEIMER, M. (1912). Experimentelle studienüber das sehen von bewegung. *Zeitschrift Für Psychologie, 61,* 161–265.

WERTHEIMER, M. (1959 [1945]). *Productive thinking,* enlarged ed. by Max Wertheimer, edited by Michael Wertheimer. New York: Harper & Row.

WERTHEIMER, MICHAEL. (1980). Gestalt theory of learning. In G. M. Gazda & R. J. Corsini (Eds.), *Theories of learning: A comparative approach.* Ithasca, IL: Peacock.

WIENER, N. (1948). *Cybernetics.* New York: Wiley.

WILCOXON, H. C., DRAGOIN, W. B., & KRAL, P. A. (1971). Illness-induced aversions in rat and quail: Relative salience of visual and gustatory cues. *Science, 171,* 826–828.

WILLIAMS, D. R., & WILLIAMS, H. (1969). Auto-maintenance in the pigeon: Sustained pecking despite contingent non-reinforcement. *Journal of the Experimental Analysis of Behavior, 12,* 511–520.

WINDHOLZ, G. (1992). Pavlov's conceptualization of learning. *American Journal of Psychology, 102,* 459–469.

WOLPE, J. (1958). *Psychotherapy by reciprocal inhibition.* Stanford, CA: Stanford University Press.

WOODWORTH, R. S. (1938). *Experimental psychology.* New York: Henry Holt.

ZEAMAN, D. (1949). Response latency as a function of the amount of reinforcement. *Journal of Experimental Psychology, 39,* 466–483.

ZENER, K. (1937). The significance of behavior accompanying conditioned salivary secretion for theories of the conditioned response. *American Journal of Psychology, 50,* 384–403.

ZIRKLE, G.A. (1946). Success and failure in serial learning: I. The Thorndike effect. *Journal of Experimental Psychology, 36,* 230–236.

ZUBEK, J. P. (1969), *Sensory deprivation: Fifteen years of research.* New York: Appleton-Century-Crofts.

NAME INDEX

SUBJECT INDEX